Ethernet and Token Ring Optimization

Daniel J. Nassar

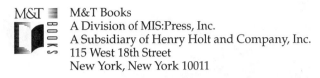
M&T Books
A Division of MIS:Press, Inc.
A Subsidiary of Henry Holt and Company, Inc.
115 West 18th Street
New York, New York 10011

Copyright © 1996 by M&T Books

Printed in the United States of America

All rights reserved. No part of this book may be reproduced or transmitted in any form or by any means, electronic or mechanical, including photocopying, recording, or by any information storage and retrieval system, without prior written permission from the Publisher. Contact the Publisher for information on foreign rights.

Limits of Liability and Disclaimer of Warranty
The Author and Publisher of this book have used their best efforts in preparing the book and the programs contained in it. These efforts include the development, research, and testing of the theories and programs to determine their effectiveness.

The Author and Publisher make no warranty of any kind, expressed or implied, with regard to these programs or the documentation contained in this book. The Author and Publisher shall not be liable in any event for incidental or consequential damages in connection with, or arising out of, the furnishing, performance, or use of these programs.

All products, names and services are trademarks or registered trademarks of their respective companies.

Library of Congress Cataloging-in-Publication Data

ISBN 1-55851-464-3

98 99 97 96   4 3 2 1

Associate Publisher: Paul Farrell
Managing Editor: Cary Sullivan
Acquiring Editor: Jono Hardjowirogo
Copy Editors: Peter Bochner
Production Editor: Anthony Washington

About the Author

Daniel J. Nassar is president of LAN Scope Incorporated, a Philadelphia area based national LAN consulting firm that specializes in emergency network troubleshooting, network optimization, and baseline health studies, and associated training through structured analysis courses

Dan is experienced in an extensive range of computer system areas. He is proficient in LAN layout and design and strong in all phases of LAN problem analysis and performance tuning, especially in the Token Ring and Ethernet environments. Dan also is skilled in all phases of computer system maintenance and diagnostics.

Dan also is the author of the bestselling book *Token Ring Troubleshooting*; he can be reached for questions concerning this book at:

LAN Scope Inc.
(610) 359-3573
(610) 446-3831

Acknowledgments

Vince Sondej gave the manuscript its initial audience and introduced the project to Ray Capece at *LAN Times*, who took the venture forward. Ray put the project into the very capable hands of Camille Craze, who has spent many long hours managing the complete project. She steered this book from inception to reality. Tim Barnard from *LAN Times* did most of the internal figure graphics. Tim took my hand-scratched circle concepts and transformed them into graphical Token Rings.

At M&T: Books, a special thanks to Jono Hardjowirogo, Acquisitions Director, who saw the potential of this project from the beginning. Shari Chappell, Copy Edit Manager, and Anthony Washington, Production Editor, brilliantly saw the project through production — My gratitude for their efforts.

A number of individuals from certain network product vendors must also be acknowledged for their efforts and contributions, including graphics and equipment. In some sort of order, they are Ben Merritt, Bob Berger, Charlie Schachter, Kent Sterling, Alex Cannara, and Teri Fitzmaurice from Network General; Steve Genova from Novell; Gina Kilker from Microtest; Axel Tillmann from Azure Technologies; Phil Kim from Dolphin; Robin Greisdoff from Spider Systems; Wendy Truax and Ellen Recko from Pro Tools; Dave Shute and Bill Cohn from FTP; Barry Trent, Loren Moriearty from Triticom; Larry Hart, Carole McCarthy, Dave Ushler, and Steve Screncsi from Digilog; Christine Seale from Bytex; James Wainwright from Antel; Frank Actis and Chris Miranda from Hewlett-Packard; and Jack Armstrong and Linda Ubertini from AlCorp.

I also want to thank a special friend, Dave Middlecamp. My writing skills would never have matured without his infamous red pen.

Thanks to Janice Pellegrini for her excellent services in transcribing my many hours of long and confusing tapes for this manuscript. Another thank you is owed to the complete past and present staff of LAN Scope, especially — Tom Kern, Janice, Jean, Chris Murray, and Ed Morris for the patience they showed with my stress level during the project's active writing phase.

Finally, I owe an overall and special thanks to my family my mother Jean, my brother David, my best friend and wife Kathy, and my two wonderful sons, Danny and Mikey for showing their love by supporting me through the many long hours and late evenings when I had to be isolated inside my office.

Table of Contents

INTRODUCTION ....**xxv**

CHAPTER 1: What Is Network Optimization? **1**
   Understanding when to Perform a Network Optimization Project 3
   New Network Implementations 5
   Reactive Problem Analysis 6
   Wide Area Network (WAN) and Internetwork Analysis 7
   Network Modification Analysis 8

CHAPTER 2: Introduction to Topologies **9**
   Understanding the History of Token Ring and Ethernet 10
      Understanding 802.3/Ethernet 11
      Understanding Token Ring 12
   Understanding the OSI Model for LAN Communication 15
      OSI and the Token Ring Network 17
      OSI and the Ethernet Network 17

ETHERNET AND TOKEN RING OPTIMIZATION

CHAPTER 3: Network Optimization Theory 19
Deciding about Exact Goals of Network Optimization 19
    Measuring Response Time 20
    Measuring Network Application Efficiency 21
    Maximizing Hardware and Software Technologies 23
    Sizing a Network Communication Link 25
    Verifying a Network's True Interoperability 26
    Ensuring Technology Peak Performance 28
Understanding Categories of Measurement for Network Optimization ..29
    Network Baselining and Workload Characterization Measurement 30
    Bandwidth Utilization 31
    Node-by-Node Utilization 31
    Protocol Breakdown 32
    Error Types and Levels 32
    Physical Layer Packet Statistics and Operations 33
    Upper Layer Protocol Packets Statistics and Operations 34
Block and Packet Size Examination 35
Network Timing 37
File Throughput Measurements 39
Network Transfer Integrity 41
Network Error Measurement 42
Workstation and File Server Memory Configuration 43
Application Tuning 45
Network Packet Compatibility 46
Workstation and File Server Configuration 47
Product Integration Measurement 48

CHAPTER 4: Optimization and Troubleshooting Tools 49
Protocol Analysis and Performance Tuning Methodology 50
    Protocol Analysis Methodology 50
    Performance Tuning Methodology 51

Table of Contents

Operating a Protocol Analyzer 53
    Basic Components of a Protocol Analyzer 54
    Basic Operational Modes of a Protocol Analyzer 55
Understanding Protocol Analyzers and Network Monitoring Tools 56
    Network General Sniffer Analyzer 57
    Network Strategies Inc. Auto-Baseliner 66
    IBM Network Manager with Trace and Performance 67
    Telecommunications Techniques Corp.
        FireBerd and LANHAWK Analyzers 69
    Wandel & Goltermann's DominoLAN
        Internetwork and WAN Analyzers 72
    Azure Technologies LANPharaoh Scope 75
    FTP Software's LANWatch Network Analyzer 77
    Triticom's LANdecoder and LANVision Monitors 79
    Network Communications Corp. (NCC) LAN Network Probe 83
    Novell LANalyzer for Windows 2.X Software Analyzer 88
    Dolphin Networks ESP Family of Protocol Analyzers 90
    Digilog LANVista 91
    Hewlett-Packard Network Advisor 95
Understanding Time Domain Reflectometer (TDR) Theory 98
    Using a Time Domain Reflectometer 99
Examining Cable-Testing Equipment 100
    Microtest Ring Scanner, MT350 Scanner,
        PentaScanner, and Pair Scanner 100
    Bytex RingOut Cable Tester 105
    The Fluke 670 and 672 LANMeters 108
    Scope Communication, Inc.'s Frame Scope 803 Network
        Analyzer and Wire Scope 100/155 Cable Testers 109
    IBM Cable Tester (IBM P/N 4760500) 113
    Antel Optronics AOC10 OTDR 113

ETHERNET AND TOKEN RING OPTIMIZATION

CHAPTER 5: Optimization Techniques 117

Understanding Broadcast Levels Examination 118
Technique Specifics 119
Understanding Duplicate Addresses 121
    Technique Specifics 122
Understanding Response Time 123
    Technique Specifics 124
Understanding Network Retransmissions 126
    Technique Specifics 127
Understanding Request-to-Reply Overlaps 128
    Technique Specifics 130
Understanding Network Throughput 131
    Technique Specifics 132
Understanding Network Overloads 133
    Technique Specifics 134
Understanding Internetwork Route Identification 136
    Technique Specifics 136
Understanding Application Characterization 139
    Technique Specifics 139

CHAPTER 6: Analysis for Major Operating System Protocols 141

Analyzing the Protocol Palette 142
    Network Connections 143
    Logon Sequences 144
    Network Keep-Alive Connection Transmissions 144
    Broadcasts 145
    Network Error Messages 145
    File Search Methodology 146
    Internetwork Addressing 146
    Routing Methodologies 147
    Specific Packet Identification Problems 147

Table of Contents

Analyzing the Protocol Layers 148
Understanding Methodology of Multiprotocol Analysis 151
    Addresses for the Network 152
    File Specifics 153
    Time Frames 153
    Frame Length 153
    Routing Information 153
    Broadcast Information 154
    Specific Protocol Information 154
Examining the Protocols 156
    Encapsulation and Connection Protocols (LLC and SNAP) 157
    Novell 159
    SNA 175
    DEC 185
    TCP/IP—Transmission Control Protocol/Internet Protocol 189
    Internet Protocol (IP) 195
    Items to Analyze in the TCP/IP Protocol Suite 205
    TCP/IP Protocol Types 210
    AppleTalk 214
    The Banyan VINES Protocol Suite 218

CHAPTER 7: Optimization for Specific Routing Protocols .225

Exploring Routing Technology and Analysis Points 226
Understanding Routing Protocols 228
    Routing Information Protocol (RIP) 230
    Open Shortest Path First (OSPF) 231
    Interior Gateway Protocol (IGP) and Exterior Gateway Protocol (EGP) 232
    Border Gateway Protocol (BGP) 232
    OSI-ES to IS and IS to IS and IDRP Routing Protocols 233
    Cisco's Interior Gateway Routing Protocol (IGRP) 233
    Novell Routing Information Protocols and Analysis Tips 234

VINES Routing Information Protocols and Analysis Tips 235
TCP/IP Routing Information Protocols and Analysis Tips 236
AppleTalk Routing Information Protocols and Analysis Tips 238
DEC Routing Information Protocols and Analysis Tips 239
Quick Notes on Routing SNA 240

CHAPTER 8: Documenting the Network 243
Understanding Network Layout Documents 244
    Building Blueprints 244
Network File Server and Ring Station Documentation 246
    Network Maintenance and Service Logs 247
    Network Vendor and Personal Resource Tables 249
Exploring Network Documentation Software Tools 251
Examining Token Ring–Specific Documentation 252
    MAU Rack Layouts 252
    Patch Panel Layouts 253
    IBM Token Ring Planning Forms 254
Exploring Ethernet-Specific Documentation 258

CHAPTER 9: Planning a Network Optimization Project ..261
Examining Specific Methods for a Network Optimization Project Plan ..262
A Scenario of Planning a Network Optimization Project 263

CHAPTER 10: Case Studies 267
Case Study #1: The Central Bank of the South 268
Case Study #2: CitiSteel USA 272
Case Study #3: John Steel Ltd. 279
Case Study #4: SFP 283
Case Study #5: Gray Chemical Co. 289
Case Study #6: State Auto Credit Corporation 295
Case Study #7: The Delaware Group 305
Case Study #8: The Soda Company 309

Summary 313

CHAPTER 11: Architecture 315

Exploring Token Ring Design and Layout 315
    Terminology 316
    MAUs 316
Understanding How the Token Ring Network Works 320
    Downstream and Upstream 321
    NAUNs 321
    Addressing Schemes 322
    4Mbps Versus 16Mbps and Early Token Release 323
Token Ring Technology Advances 324
    Understanding Token Ring Switching 325
    Understanding Dedicated Token Ring 325
    High-Speed Upgrade Options from Token Ring 328
    Differential Manchester Encoding 331
    Frame Types 332
Controlling the Ring Environment 333
    Management Roles of the Ring 333
    Standby Monitors (SMs) 334
    Active Monitor (AM) 334
    Configuration Report Server (CRS) 337
    Ring Parameter Server (RPS) 337
    Ring Error Monitor (REM) 338
    LAN Bridge Server (LBS) 338
    LAN Reporting Mechanism (LRM) 339
LAN Manager and SNA Relationship 339
IBM Network Management Direction 342
Understanding Token Ring Communication 342
    Phase 0: Lobe Media Check/Physical Insertion 343
    Phase 1: Monitor Check 343

ETHERNET AND TOKEN RING OPTIMIZATION

    Phase 2: Duplicate Address Verification 344

    Phase 3: Neighbor Notification 344

    Phase 4: Request Initialization 345

    Token Claiming 346

    Priority Access 348

    Neighbor Notification 348

    Normal Repeat Mod 349

    Ring Purge 350

    Beaconing 350

    Fault Domain 351

    Soft Error Counting 353

    Hard Error Counting 354

    Finite State Machines 354

    Token Ring Protocol Timers 354

  Examining 802.5 IEEE Standard Frame Format 358

    Token Frame 358

    Data Frame 360

    Abort Sequence Frame 365

    DLC.LAN and DLC.MGR 365

    MAC Frame Types 366

CHAPTER 12: Devices and Specifications 369

  Examining Cables 369

    Cable Lengths 371

    Cabling Connectors 373

    Multistation Access Units and Wiring Hub Technology 375

  Understanding Bridges 379

  Examining Repeaters 385

  Understanding NICs 387

CHAPTER 13: Token Ring Fault Isolation 389

- Troubleshooting Fault Domains and Lobe Areas 389
  - Troubleshooting a Fault Domain 390
  - Troubleshooting Lobe Areas 390
- Understanding Cable Problems 392
  - Cable Failure Types and Causes 392
- Troubleshooting Cable Failures 394
  - Troubleshooting Lobe Cables 394
  - Troubleshooting Main Ring Path Cables 395
- Understanding MAU and Wiring Hub Problems 396
  - MAU and Wiring Hub Failure Symptoms, Causes,
    and Troubleshooting 396
- Exploring NIC Problems 398
  - NIC Failure Symptoms and Causes 399
  - Troubleshooting NICs 401
- Ring Station Problems 402
  - Ring Station Failure Symptoms and Causes 403
  - Troubleshooting Ring Stations 403
- Examining File Server Problems 405
  - File Server Failure Symptoms, Causes, and Troubleshooting Hints ...406
- Exploring Token Ring Network Peripheral Problems 408
  - Network Peripheral Operations 408
  - Network Peripheral Failure Symptoms, Causes, and Troubleshooting 408
- Exploring Bridge, Router, Repeater, and Gateway Problems 409
  - Bridge Failure Symptoms, Causes, and Troubleshooting 410
  - Router Failure Symptoms, Causes, and Troubleshooting 413
  - Repeater Failure Symptoms, Causes, and Troubleshooting 414
  - Gateway Failure Symptoms, Causes, and Troubleshooting 415
- Understanding Protocol Analysis 416
- Examining and Troubleshooting Low-Level 802.5 Communications 417
  - 802.5 Frame Communication 417
  - Error Recording 419

Soft Error Breakdown 420
Hard Error Breakdown 424
Token Ring Rotation Time 426
Examining and Troubleshooting High-Layer Communication Problems .426
   Performance Testing 428

CHAPTER 14: Token Ring Troubleshooting Flow Guides ...431

14.1 Network Problem Entry Flow Guide 432
   Main Network Failure Symptoms 432
14.2 Fault Domain and Lobe Area Problem Flow Guides 434
   14.2.1 Failure Symptom Is Located to a Fault Domain 434
   14.2.2 Failure Symptom Is Located to a Specific Lobe Area 435
14.3 Cable Problem Flow Guides 436
   14.3.1 A Lobe Cable Appears to Be Causing a Failure
          Symptom in a Lobe Path 436
   14.3.2 The Main Ring Path Calling Appears to be
          Causing a Problem with a Group of Ring Stations
          or the Complete Token 437
14.4 Multistation Access Unit (MAU) and Wiring Hub
     Problem Flow Guides 438
   14.4.1 A Specific MAU or Hub Port Appears to be
          Encountering a Failure 439
   14.4.2 A Suspected Bad MAU or Wiring Appears
          to be Causing Failure Symptoms with Multiple Token Ring ...440
14.5 NIC Problem Flow Guides 441
   14.5.1 Error Indication Occurs in a Protocol Analysis Session ...441
   14.5.2 Vectoring from Lobe Area, Ring Station, Network
          File Server, MAU/Wiring Hub, Cable, or Network
          Peripheral Flow Guide 442
14.6 Ring Station Problem Flow Guides 444
   14.6.1 All the Ring Stations Have the Symptom 444
   14.6.2 A Group of Ring Stations Has the Symptom 445

14.6.3 One Ring Station Has the Symptom 446
14.7 Bridge Problem Flow Guides 448
  14.7.1 No Data Traffic Can Get from One Side of the Bridge to the Other, or Data is Intermittently Getting Corrupted when Passing through the Bridge 448
  14.7.2 Only Partial Data Traffic Can Pass Across the Bridge 449
  14.7.3 An Overlooked Bandwidth Condition is Present on a Certain Ring 450
14.8 Router Problem Flow Guides 451
  14.8.1 Particular Protocol are Not Being Passed through Another Ring .452
  14.8.2 No Data Traffic Can Get from One Side of the Router to the Other, or Data is Intermittently Getting Corrupted when Passed through the Router 453
  14.8.3 Only Partial Data Traffic Can Pass across the Router 454
  14.8.4 An Overloaded Bandwidth Condition is Present on a Certain Ring 455
14.9 Repeater Problem Flow Guide 456
  14.9.1 No Data Traffic Can Get from One Side of the Repeater to the Other, or a Hard Error Such as a Beaconing is Present on the Ring 457
14.10 Network Peripheral Problem Flow Guides 459
  14.10.1 Error Indication Occurs in a Protocol Analysis Session 460
  14.10.2 A Failure Symptom Appears to be Directly Related to a Problem with a Specific Network Peripheral 461
14.11 Modem Problem Flow Guides 463
  14.11.1 You Have a Problem Accessing or Using a Modem Connected to the Ring as a Shared Modem 464
  14.11.2 You Have a Problem Accessing or Using a Modem Connected to a Specific Ring Station or File Server as an Unshared Modem 465
  14.11.3 You Have a Problem Accessing or Using a Modem Connected to a Ring from a Remote Location 466
14.12 Printer Problem Flow Guides 466

ETHERNET AND TOKEN RING OPTIMIZATION

14.12.1 You Have a Problem Accessing or Using a Printer
Connected to the Ring as a Shared Printer 467

14.12.2 You Have a Problem Accessing or Using a Printer Connected
to a Specific Ring Station or File Server as an Unshared Printer 468

14.13 Gateway Problem Flow Guides 469

14.13.1 The Entire Network Has a Problem Accessing or Using a
Host Gateway Connected to a Local Ring 470

14.13.2 One Ring Station or a Group of Ring Stations Has a Problem
Accessing or Using a Host Gateway Connected to a Local Ring 471

14.13.3 You Have a Problem Accessing or Using a Host Gateway from a
Non-Local Ring Bridged, Routed, or Connected through a Remote
Connection 472

14.13.4 The Gateway Sessions Appear to be Running Slowly or
Unresponsively 473

14.13.5 LAN-to-Host Sessions are Intermittently Locking
Up or Freezing 474

14.14 File Server Problem Flow Guides 475

14.14.1 There is a Problem with a Ring Station, a Group of Ring Stations,
the Entire Network, or a Network Peripheral Accessing or Using a
Particular Application/Group of Applications, or Certain
Directories/Files on the Network File Server 476

14.14.2 A Particular NOS Feature or Set of NOS Features on the
Network File Server is Not Working 478

14.14.3 There Is a Problem Accessing or Using an Extra Network Server
Other than the Main Network File Server (for Example, Database, Fax,
Communication, or Print Server) 479

14.14.4 There Appears to be a Problem with Abnormal Network
Bandwidth between a Particular Ring Station/Group of Ring Stations,
or a Network Peripheral, and the Network File Server 481

14.15 Protocol Analysis Flow Guides 482

14.15.1 Perform a Protocol Analysis Session to Examine the Low-Layer
802.5 Frame Communication Processes 483

14.15.2 Encountering Specific Soft or Hard Errors on the Network, or the
Whole Network is Freezing or Hanging 485

14.15.3 Perform a Protocol Analysis Session to Examine the High-Layer Network Frame Communication Processes 488

14.15.4 The Network is Experiencing One or More of the Following Failure Symptoms: The Whole Network is Operating Slowly; a Specific Network Application is Operating Slowly; or Logon Failures are Occurring 490

CHAPTER 15: Architecture 493

Understanding Design and Layout 494
    Thin Ethernet 10BASE2 495
    Thick Ethernet 10BASE5 498
    Twisted Pair Ethernet 10BASE-T 500
    CSMA/CD 503
    CSMA/CD Detailed Operation Transmission Access Approach 505
    CSMA/CD Receiving Approach 506
    Addressing of the Ethernet Environment 508

Understanding Data Transmission Methodology for Ethernet 508

Understanding Physical and Higher Layer Management of the Ethernet Environment 509

Understanding Ethernet Frame Types 511
    Ethernet II 511
    RAW 802.3 Ethernet 512
    IEEE Standard 802.3 Ethernet 513

Defining Protocols Used in Ethernet Frame Transfer 514
    Logical Link Control 514
    Subnetwork Address Protocol 516

CHAPTER 16: Devices and Specifications 519

Exploring Ethernet Cabling and Layout Specifications 520
    Thick Ethernet—10BASE5 520
    Thin Ethernet—10BASE2 521
    Twisted-Pair Ethernet—10BASE-T 521

Fiber Optic Ethernet—10BASE-F 522
Ethernet Cabling Connectors 522
Wiring Hubs for the Ethernet Environment 523
Ethernet Technology Advances 527
    Understanding Ethernet Switching 527
    Understanding 100Mbps Ethernet Transmission 530
Using Network Interface Cards 533
Ethernet Bridges 534
Understanding Ethernet Routers 536
Understanding Ethernet Repeaters 539

CHAPTER 17: Ethernet Fault Isolation 541

Troubleshooting Ethernet Cabling Environments 542
    TDR Testing Methodologies for Ethernet 543
    Troubleshooting Ethernet Transceivers or MAUs 547
    Troubleshooting Thick and Thin Ethernet Repeaters 548
    Troubleshooting 10BASE-T Wiring Hubs and Repeaters 548
    Troubleshooting Ethernet NICs 550
    Troubleshooting Ethernet Workstations and File Servers 552
    Troubleshooting Ethernet Bridges and Routers 553
    Ethernet Network Peripheral Problems 556
    Exploring Gateway Failure Symptoms, Causes, and Troubleshooting .556
Examining Protocol Analysis for Ethernet 557
    Error Detection in the Ethernet Physical Layer Environment ...559
The Advantages and Disadvantages of Ethernet 565
    Advantages of Ethernet 565
    Disadvantages of Ethernet 565
    Ways to Make Ethernet Perform 565

CHAPTER 18: Ethernet Troubleshooting Flow Guides 569

Network Problem Entry Flow Guide 570

Table of Contents

18.1 Main Ethernet Network Failure Symptom Flow Guide .... .570
18.2 Ethernet Segment Area Problem Flow Guides .... .572
    18.2.1 Failure Symptom Is Experienced on Multiple Ethernet Segments 573
    18.2.2 Failure Symptom Is Located on a Specific Ethernet Segment ...574
18.3 Ethernet Cabling Problem Flow Guides .... .575
    18.3.1 A Complete Ethernet Segment Cabling Run Is in Question .... .575
    18.3.2 A Specific Ethernet Drop Cable Is in Question .... .576
18.4 Ethernet Multiport Repeater and Wiring Hub Problem Flow Guides .576
    18.4.1 A Specific Repeater or Hub Port Is Encountering a Failure ..... .577
    18.4.2 A Suspected Bad Repeater or Wiring Hub Module Is Causing Failure Symptoms with Multiple Users or the Complete Ethernet Internetwork .... .578
18.5 Ethernet Station Node Problem Flow Guides .... .579
    18.5.1 All the Ethernet Station Nodes Are Experiencing the Symptom .579
    18.5.2 A Group of Ethernet Station Nodes Is Experiencing the Symptom .... .580
    18.5.3 One Ethernet Station Node Is Experiencing the Symptom ..... .581
18.6 Ethernet NIC Problem Flow Guides .... .583
    18.6.1 Error Indication in a Protocol Analysis Session .... .583
    18.6.2 Vectoring from Segment Area, Ethernet Station Node, Network File Server, MAU/Transceiver, Repeater/Wiring Hub, Cable, or Network Peripheral Flow Guide .... .584
18.7 Ethernet Bridge Problem Flow Guides .... .586
    18.7.1 No Data Traffic Can Get from One Side of the Bridge to the Other, or Data Is Intermittently Getting Corrupted when Passing Through the Bridge .... .587
    18.7.2 Only Partial Data Traffic Can Pass Across the Bridge .... .588
    18.7.3 An Overloaded Bandwidth Condition Is Present on a Certain Segment .... .589
18.8 Ethernet Router Problem Flow Guides .... .590
    18.8.1 Particular Protocols Are Not Being Passed Through to Another Segment .... .591

ETHERNET AND TOKEN RING OPTIMIZATION

18.8.2 No Data Traffic Can Pass from One Side of the Router to the Other, or Data Is Intermittently Getting Corrupted When Passed Through the Router 592

18.8.3 Only Partial Data Traffic Can Pass Across the Router 592

18.8.4 An Overloaded Bandwidth Condition Is Present on a Certain Segment 594

18.9 Basic Thick and Thin Repeater Problem Flow Guide 595

18.9.1 No Data Traffic Can Pass from One Side of the Repeater to the Other 596

18.10 Ethernet Network Peripheral Problem Flow Guides 598

18.10.1 Error Indication in a Protocol Analysis Session 599

18.10.2 A Failure Symptom Appears to be Directly Related to a Problem with a Specific Network Peripheral 600

18.11 Modem Problem Flow Guides 602

18.11.1 You Cannot Access or Use a Modem Connected to an Ethernet Segment as a Shared Modem 603

18.11.2 You Cannot Access or Use a Modem Connected to a Specific Ethernet Station Node or File Server as an Unshared Modem 604

18.11.3 You Cannot Access or Use a Modem Connected to an Ethernet Segment from a Remote Location. 604

18.12 Printer Problem Flow Guides 605

18.12.1 You Cannot Access or Use a Printer Connected to the Segment as a Shared Printer 606

18.12.2 You Cannot Access or Use a Printer Connected to a Specific Ethernet Station Node or File Server as an Unshared Printer. 607

18.13 Gateway Problem Flow Guides 608

18.13.1 The Complete Network Has Trouble Accessing or Using a Host Gateway Connected to a Local Segment. 609

18.13.2 One Ethernet Station Node or a Group of Ethernet Station Nodes Has Trouble Accessing or Using a Host Gateway Connected to a Local Segment 610

18.13.3 You Have Trouble Accessing or Using a Host Gateway from a Non-local Segment Bridged, Routed, or Connected Through a Remote Connection 611

18.13.4 The Gateway Sessions Are Running Slowly or
Are Unresponsive 612

18.13.5 LAN-to-Host Sessions Are Intermittently Locking
Up or Freezing 613

18.14 File Server Problem Flow Guides 614

18.14.1 There Is a Problem with an Ethernet Station Node, a Group of
Ethernet Station Nodes, the Complete Network, or a Network
Peripheral Accessing or Using a Particular Application/Group of
Applications, or Certain Directories/Files on the Network
File Server 615

18.14.2 A Particular NOS Feature or Set of NOS Features on the
Network File Server Is Not Working 616

18.14.3 You Have Trouble Accessing or Using an Extra Network Server
Other Than the Main Network File Server (For Example,
Database, Fax, Communication, or Print Server) 617

18.14.4 There Appears to Be a Problem with Abnormal Network
Bandwidth Between a Particular Ethernet Station Node/Group of
Ethernet Segments or Network Peripheral and the Network
File Server 619

18.15 Protocol Analysis Flow Guides 621

18.15.1 Performing a Protocol Analysis Session to Examine the
Low-Layer Ethernet Frame Communication Processes 622

18.15.2 You Encounter a Specific Error on the Network, or the
Whole Network Is Freezing or Hanging 623

18.15.3 Perform a Protocol Analysis Session to Examine the
High-Layer Network Frame Communication Processes. 625

18.15.4 The Network Is Experiencing One or More of the
Following Failure Symptoms: The Whole Network Is
Operating Slowly; a Specific Network Application Is
Operating Slowly; or Logon Failures Are Occurring 627

APPENDIX A: 631
APPENDIX B: 651
INDEX 653

INTRODUCTION

As LANs grow and organizations become dependent on LAN services, high costs can become associated with poor network performance and reliability. Most organizations regret cost-cutting on LAN cabling systems and diagnostic tools after a failure results in a major service interruption. Organizations have come to realize that it pays to install a robust, high-performance network. They also realize that they should purchase diagnostic and management tools and have available trained personnel who are familiar with their operation before a major failure occurs.

Two network physical layer (cabling) standards are most common in local area networks: Ethernet (TYPE II, RAW, IEEE 802.3) and Token Ring (IEEE 802.5). The purpose of this book is not to persuade you that one of these standards is "best." Both work; both have adherents; and both are likely to be around for years in the future. Your organization will have its own reasons for selecting one of these or another standard.

After you choose your physical layer standard, you face the challenge of ensuring that it performs well and reliably. That's where this book comes in. *Ethernet and Token Ring Optimization* is a thorough, practical guide that explains the Ethernet and Token Ring networks and the technologies needed to safeguard your network investment. This book also brings you into the internals of major protocols such as NetWare and TCP/IP. Specific network analysis techniques are discussed for multi-protocol environments.

How Does This Book Differ from Other Network Books ?

Books about network technology have traditionally fallen into the following two categories:

- General theoretical introductions that do not give readers enough information to undertake genuine troubleshooting
- Technical books for engineers and highly technical readers

Ethernet and Token Ring Optimization strikes a middle ground between these extremes. You are introduced to the real, "under the hood" LAN technologies, but always accessibly and in the context of your networking activities. The details that network designers must understand are necessary for network managers. In this book, the focus is on network managers and analysis consultants.

The Token Ring and Ethernet sections give you something you find in no other book: troubleshooting flow guides. These guides walk you through the problem solving sequences required for Token Ring and Ethernet analysis troubleshooting. These guides are the results of extensive testing and research by the author to determine the most common causes of network failures and the strategies for correcting them.

Who Should Read This Book ?

Anyone who requires more knowledge of the details of network troubleshooting and optimization will find this book highly valuable. If you are a network administrator, you will need to repair a broken network or correct a serious performance problem at some time. Arm yourself with this book now so that you can prepare for that day. Do not be concerned that the material is too difficult for you. The troubleshooting flow guides take over when your knowledge fails.

If you are a professional network installer or technician, you will find this book indispensable. The protocol analysis chapters and troubleshooting flow guides will accelerate your problem solving.

In short, *Ethernet and Token Ring Optimization* is indispensable for anyone whose profession includes the management of Token Ring, Ethernet and multi-protocol networks.

How This Book Is Organized

Part 1 describes the various technologies you must contend with when performing network optimization. First, you are introduced to the Ethernet and Token Ring topologies. Then you examine the theory and practice of network optimization in various network environments including Novell, SNA, DECnet, TCP/IP, Banyan, and Apple. Part 1 ends with ten case studies in which the information from the preceding chapters is put into actual practice.

Part 2 is an in-depth discussion of Token Ring LANs. You learn in detail how Token Ring works and the hardware components of a Token Ring network. You then examine specific troubleshooting procedures for Token Ring. The section ends with a set of flow guides that guide you through all the decisions needed to isolate and solve a Token Ring network problem.

Part 3 repeats the approach of Part 2, this time applied to the Ethernet environment. Together, these two parts prepare you to face the majority of problems you are likely to encounter on your network.

CHAPTER 1

What Is Network Optimization?

What has happened to your simple network? Do you struggle daily to make your network perform like it still has youth, stability, and endurance? Do users call with complaints, such as "The network is running slow;" "I've been waiting ten minutes for my document to print;" or "Our file server just went down?" Is this the same network that used to have one file server, 25 workstations, and only one network protocol?

What you have now is an internetwork. Your network runs TCP/IP, SNA, NetWare, and NetBEUI protocols. Your simple network has grown and now comprises five separate token rings with over 400 workstations and 30 file servers.

The easy days are over. A network that used to be easy to manage now requires a complicated, intricate set of steps involving calculated technical moves to manage.

Techniques are available to help you get a handle on your network to understand how it is running and performing, and how it is utilizing the innovative technologies you implemented yesterday. You can also use certain

2 ETHERNET AND TOKEN RING OPTIMIZATION

techniques based on calculated measurements to implement changes so that your network will run and perform better. This is known as *network optimization*.

Network optimization is the process of measuring to a defined level a network's workload characteristics and then making modifications to the network's layout, design, and configuration to improve its overall performance.

Most often, network optimization involves using a protocol analyzer to evaluate the operation of the complete network, including all its hardware and software components. After evaluating the operational state of the network, the next step is to tune all the components. The goal is to make the network components work together so that your internetwork can perform the mission-critical operations for which it was intended at a higher performance level.

Protocol analyzers enable you to optimize and view data on your network to help you understand how that data is performing. Protocol analyzers are mostly independent of protocols, the network operating system you are running, or the type of applications on your network. Protocol analyzers need to be configured, and you need a certain skill set to use them effectively; nonetheless, these tools are extremely valuable.

Chapter 4, "Optimization and Troubleshooting Tools," discusses in detail the internal operations and workings of a protocol analyzer. It also reviews some well-known, field-applied protocol analyzers on the market today.

It is important to understand that a protocol analyzer enables you to examine the protocols on a network. The protocols are the actual transmission vehicles used to get data from one point to another within the internetwork, regardless of the entity doing the transmitting on the network. The only way to actually view and troubleshoot any problems in the protocols themselves is with a protocol analyzer.

Some tools available today enable you to view just the statistics from the protocols and how they affect the network. These tools could be appropriately labeled monitoring tools, but they are not true protocol analyzers. A protocol analyzer is more in-depth than a monitoring tool, and enables you to view the internals of the protocol and its operations.

Understanding when to Perform a Network Optimization Project

Good network optimization requires an understanding of when to use a protocol analyzer or network monitoring tool to obtain the statistics for the particular phase of network optimization that applies at a given time. Some problems identified while troubleshooting a large internetwork immediately trigger the need for a protocol analyzer or a network monitoring tool. (Later in this book, a detailed discussion illustrates the differences between an internal operation of network monitoring tools and protocol analyzers.)

Before you go any farther, the following terms should be defined:

- *Topology* is the physical and logical layout of a network. Most types of networks have a characteristic topology.
- *Network protocol* is an orderly, predefined method by which devices on a LAN communicate with each other.
- *Network architecture* is the design that integrates the network topology with the network protocols. The network architecture describes the physical components of the network, including the wiring and any electronic devices.

When a network is newly installed or implemented at a single or multilocation site, it is important to evaluate the overall health of the network. But when a network has grown over a period of time and has undergone modifications, this network is considered a mature, technically migrated network, and will most likely exhibit a range of behaviors that require a network monitoring tool or a protocol analyzer. Usually these networks are prime candidates for network optimization to attain their best possible performance.

When networks are not performing well and are having problems that require troubleshooting, a better approach might be to attempt the optimization of their performance and operation, rather than just troubleshooting to resolve the current problem. In other words, a company might need to take a fresh look at its approach to network problems: instead of simply isolating the problem, it might be better to examine the entire network using a protocol analyzer or monitoring tool to optimize the network's performance.

4 ETHERNET AND TOKEN RING OPTIMIZATION

A focal point of network optimization today is that many networks now are connected to other networks through wide area network (WAN) connections. A variety of wide area connection methodologies and approaches are being used, from direct connect circuits to frame relay implementations. All these types of configurations need to be optimized. A protocol analyzer enables an analyst to perform communication link sizing and optimization of throughput from link to link.

For networks currently in place that have undergone extensive technical migration over a period of time, the focus should be to examine the network from its baseline. Chapters 3 and 5 discuss network baselining: what it is, and how to use it as a study methodology for networks with problems.

Networks that have undergone extensive technical migrations may have a range of technology components implemented throughout their infrastructure. For example, networks may have multiple file servers in place; multiple applications placed at different points; a range of different user groups using services from multiple points; a group of network communication connections, including incoming and outgoing lines for a variety of reasons; and an extensive range of general network usage hardware and software points that are utilized throughout the infrastructure.

A network that has undergone extensive migration usually is a network that has frequent changes made. In today's networking environment, the staff who maintains this type of network often does not have time to measure the effects of each change; the tools, however, are available to do so. There are ways to measure these changes relatively quickly, and to gain an understanding of how the network performs from phase to phase and change to change.

Each network operates in a characteristic manner. As new hardware and software technologies are implemented upon the network, certain operational statistics can show how the network has changed in response to that particular modification. A protocol analyzer can be used to examine the network after any major modification has been implemented on any network design. After the changes are implemented, the protocol analyzer can be used to examine the traffic flow and a range of statistics on the network. This enables the network manager or analyst to look at the efficiency and performance of the network, and how the change actually affected its performance.

Through proper documentation and organization skill sets, the analyst or network manager can measure the change with a protocol analyzer or network monitoring tool, and then document that change. This enables the network management team to take a close look at whether a particular modification was warranted and if the change actually improved the operation the way it was intended.

The goal here is to start utilizing an analyzer to optimize the network's performance as changes occur. The products should be picked not only for their functionality, but also for their utility in optimization. The future holds many new requirements for networks; the network bandwidth, along with all the hardware and technology investments, can only provide so much capacity. The tools available today enable an analyst to make maximum use of each network and optimize it, in the face of daily changes.

New Network Implementations

The installation of a new network usually involves a variety of personnel and a group of products to be implemented, all in a fairly short period of time. Usually the approach is to have some sort of project plan, implement the products, and turn the network live into a production phase. A range of tests can be run with a protocol analyzer or network monitoring tool to ensure that the network is performing at its optimum level from the day it is turned back to production mode. This book discusses various baselining and testing statistics that can be examined with network monitoring tools and protocol analyzers to verify the health of a newly installed network.

The key is to make sure that a network operates at its optimum level on its original production installation date. Because a new network installation can involve new protocols, new applications, new workstation and file server shells, and new network operating systems, it is critical to use a protocol analyzer to focus on the performance of the applied protocols immediately upon the network's initial implementation.

In addition, many shell and file-server configuration parameters need to be set upon the initial installation of a new network that will affect network communication processes. A protocol analyzer enables the user to examine the network performance upon installation, and to make changes to configurations on both workstations and file servers to implement the best network communication performance possible.

ETHERNET AND TOKEN RING OPTIMIZATION

Industry-standard throughput considerations exist for how fast network data is transferred across networks and how the network performs. This book discusses in detail those throughput levels and standards. A modern protocol analyzer is equipped for network analysis in all the main network performance areas.

Reactive Problem Analysis

Internetwork support means daily troubleshooting of a range of issues and problems. A large number of complaints about internetworks today concern performance: the network runs slow, the network file server hangs, service is interrupted during certain file server operations, and so on. Clearly, a high number of these connection problems are related to network communication failures due to hardware or software configuration and layout problems. A protocol analyzer specifically allows for examining the network communication that occurs between workstations and file servers in all key internetwork points of communication.

A protocol analyzer can be used to examine from beginning to end a conversation that may occur between a workstation and a file server. The specific time of a conversation indicates whether the conversation occurs in what is considered a normal range. Later in this book, those standards and ranges are discussed, along with how to examine those timing intervals. The point is that a protocol analyzer can be used to examine the communication on networks that are having problems, and you can troubleshoot many network failures and performance problems from the network communication point of view. Many times, a simple configuration parameter or a small modification to the hardware or software layout is all it takes to make the network perform at its optimum level.

This book discusses several techniques that focus on the performance and timing operation for network communications. Be aware that when certain types of failures occur (for example, a file server cannot be located or a certain operation is aborted), a protocol analyzer can be used to examine the timing between the particular processes of the workstation and file server, and may clearly identify the source of the problem for the network timing problem that is occurring.

Some statistics obtained from network monitoring tools and protocol analyzers can identify whether other contributing factors are on the network, such as a high traffic level, might cause a symptom to occur. Chapters 3 and 5 discuss all the techniques and operations for optimizing a network for its best communication timing to eliminate impediments to network performance.

Wide Area Network (WAN) and Internetwork Analysis

In today's corporate environment many networks are being connected to other networks to create a WAN configuration. This happens frequently in larger corporations, but many small companies also are finding the need to interconnect to remote sites for network communications.

An *internetwork* is a group of networks that connect together across common or multiple topologies to communicate with common or multiple protocols to achieve full interoperability. The term *open networking* also is used sometimes . *WAN* is a network or internetwork configured over different geographical locations. Note that the focal point of networks is to have communication between a range of different entities without limitations and with the most productive computing possible. Protocol analyzers enable the user to examine communication between multiple networks to determine the effectiveness of operation along with the measure of true interoperability across multiple communication links.

When multiple networks communicate, extensive routes usually are traveled between the various network points by the different processes involved. Point-to-point timing issues are therefore critical. A protocol analyzer or network monitoring tool, if properly implemented, enables an analyst to examine transaction times between different network points within an internetwork.

Communication links are required from point to point within the networks, and these need to be configured for optimum communication. If communication links are not properly configured, bottlenecks can occur and limit point-to-point data speed. The communication links chosen need to be sized to handle the applied/proper data flow for the different network concerns. A protocol analyzer enables the user to examine the overall communication link sizing between different points, and examine whether the throughput actually is performing at its optimum level. Overall, the user can examine these internetwork layouts from point to point, to verify that the WAN is configured the way it should be and is performing at an optimum level.

A range of devices are involved in a WAN configuration, including bridges, routers, hubs, and communication link configurations. All these devices need to be examined, and protocol analyzers and network monitoring tools are the way to do it.

Network Modification Analysis

After any major network modification, a critical final step is to retest the network with a protocol analyzer to get a benchmark of the network's performance level. Only one change should be made to a network at a time, followed by retesting the network with a protocol analyzer to see the effect on performance.

Testing the network before and after the change enables you to evaluate and document the performance effect of the network modification. For example, if a protocol analyzer captured a particular workstation-to-file-server read at one minute and there now has been a 16-MB upgrade in file server memory, the network read should be remeasured; this is called post analysis. After the analyzer test is complete, the results of the post analysis shows a workstation-to-file-server read of 20 seconds. This is a 40-second increase in performance for the particular task.

Now you have a better understanding of what network optimization is and why it is required to keep an internetwork functioning at its optimum performance level. The next chapter introduces the two main topologies utilized most frequently for internetwork configurations today: Ethernet and Token Ring. Chapter 3 is a discussion of network optimization theory; Chapter 4 focuses on optimization and troubleshooting tools and their applied techniques.

CHAPTER 2

Introduction to Topologies

Although you may be familiar with the basic theory of Token Ring and Ethernet operation, basic theory is insufficient when complex problems develop on your Token Ring or Ethernet network. If you know the basics of Token Ring or Ethernet, you may want to skip to Chapter 3, "Network Optimization Theory," which contains a nitty-gritty discussion of the inner theory of network optimization of a Token Ring or Ethernet network. If, however, your familiarity with Token Ring or Ethernet stops with the name Token Ring or Ethernet or with the pieces plugged together to create a Token Ring or Ethernet network, you may want to stick around.

This chapter describes the two most often used network topologies, Token Ring and Ethernet. This discussion includes some analogies to help you sort out the Token Ring and Ethernet terminology that awaits you in subsequent chapters.

Understanding the History of Token Ring and Ethernet

Of the dozens of types of network wiring systems, two standards dominate in LANs: 802.3 (popularly, but inaccurately, called Ethernet) and 802.5 (Token Ring). The numbers 802.3 and 802.5 tag both these systems and their associated standards, which have been established by committees of the Institute of Electrical and Electronics Engineers (IEEE).

These network types are popular because they are open standards, not systems under the control of a particular equipment manufacturer.

Currently the most popular network standard, 802.3 was derived from a networking system developed jointly by Xerox and Digital Equipment Corporation (DEC). The original system was called Ethernet, and that name has been commonly applied to the 802.3 standard as well, despite some differences. Over the years, new versions of 802.3 have been standardized to reduce the cost of installation and improve manageability. At least three reasons explain the popularity of Ethernet:

- Ethernet has been standardized longer than Token Ring.
- Ethernet offers high performance at low cost.
- Ethernet has become an integral component of many vendors' computer network architectures.

Token Ring, developed by IBM and Texas Instruments, was defined as the IEEE standard 802.5 in 1985. Ethernet was developed by the Xerox Corporation in 1975 and was supported by a multitude of vendors, including DEC and AT&T.

IBM probably developed Token Ring, at least in part, so that it would have a unique networking system that could be clearly differentiated from the 802.3/Ethernet network standards. In addition to marketing considerations, however, several engineering goals motivated the development of Token Ring. To understand some of these goals, you need background in the theoretical workings of 802.3 and 802.5.

Networks function in one of two modes: baseband or broadband. In a *baseband* network, all the transmission capacity of the network media is used by one signal. *Broadband* networks enable a single medium to carry several signals, the way a single television cable carries a large number of television channels into your home.

Token Ring and Ethernet are both baseband networks. The Ethernet topology was originally available in the broadband spectrum with the 10Broad36 design, but today it is mainly seen in only the baseband mode. Baseband networks are restricted to transmitting one message at a time through the network cabling medium.

Token Ring and Ethernet differ in at least two significant respects:

- The method they use to ensure that only one message at a time is transmitted and that each message is transmitted correctly
- The cabling arrangement that carries their electrical signals

By understanding these differences, you can understand the reasons for the complicated cabling and signaling designs that engineers developed for Token Ring.

Understanding 802.3/Ethernet

The technical term to describe the control mechanism of this standard is impressive: *Carrier Sense Multiple Access with Collision Detection* (CSMA/CD). This is easy to understand in the context of a simple analogy.

CSMA is like a telephone party line with everyone listening in. Multiple Access simply means that each person on the party line can originate a conversation at any time. Carrier Sense means that a speaker is expected to listen for silence on the line before beginning to speak. (The *carrier* is a signal that indicates that the line is idle.)

Collision Detection comes in when, despite efforts to start talking on a quiet line, two conversations begin at once and interfere with each other. The rules of CD instruct all parties to stop talking, clear the line, and wait a random period of time. Then new attempts can be made to initiate messages. Collisions are a fact of life in CSMA/CD networks.

Under the 802.3 standard, conversations are transmitted through the wire at 10Mbps (10 mega, or million, bits per second). Because the average message is only about a thousand bytes long, collisions are fairly unlikely unless a very high number of messages need to be transmitted by a large number of stations.

Theoretically, if enough transmitters attempt to send many messages on a CSMA/CD network, the percentage of collisions can become so high that most of the network's available capacity is lost to collision detection and recovery. In practice, however, high data rates are required for this to take place. Nevertheless, there is a random aspect to CSMA/CD, and any given station may need to make several attempts to transmit a message. This characteristic results in some criticism of CSMA/CD networks in situations when messages must be reliably transmitted at specific times.

A potential criticism of 802.3/Ethernet, therefore, is that network traffic is managed statistically. Network managers cannot ensure that critical messages will not encounter delays.

A second criticism of 802.3/Ethernet comes from its cabling system. Technically, Ethernet is a bus topology, meaning that its physical arrangement (*topology*) puts every network station in a position to transmit through a common wire to every other network station. In fact, every message transmitted on the network is received at every node simultaneously; it is simply ignored by everyone except the intended recipient.

The 802.3/Ethernet cabling system is typically a long coaxial cable that loops past each workstation, connecting to the network port of the workstation through a tap connector. Although coaxial cable is an excellent medium for transmitting data at high data rates with high performance at reasonable cost, it is difficult to isolate the cause of some problems. A crimp or break in the cable at one location, for example, can disable the entire network because interfering signals may be reflected back into the cable.

The second criticism of 802.3/Ethernet is that it can be difficult to isolate a problem to a particular location on the network. The recently popular 10BASE-T wiring standard for 802.3 networks was designed to make it easier to isolate problems, but vestiges of the problem remain.

Understanding Token Ring

Token Ring was developed to address the criticisms of 802.3/Ethernet technology. The Token Ring design guarantees each station on the network an opportunity to transmit at regular intervals. In addition, the cabling design for Token Ring makes it easy to isolate most problems to a particular part of the network or a *fault domain*.

The control method for Token Ring is called *Token Access*. The telephone analogy used to describe an Ethernet system does not work well for Token Access. Token Ring is more effectively described in terms of a somewhat artificial parlor game.

In the game, the participants are seated in a ring. Each participant is eager to send written messages to other players. They each write down their message and pass the message to their neighbor on the left. Players receive messages from their neighbor on the right.

If everyone were writing and transmitting messages at once, however, a player might be too busy writing and sending messages to pass other messages around the ring. Therefore, a control mechanism is required. The players pass a marble (a token) around the ring. Only the person currently holding the marble can write a message and pass it to the left. The message is passed hand-to-hand around the ring until it reaches the intended recipient who reads it, marks it as received, and then sends it on its way until it returns to the original sender. The originator notes that the message was read and releases the marble to the ring so that other players can have turns to transmitting.

Because only the person holding the token can transmit, collisions cannot occur. But many other problems must be anticipated in the Token Access method.

Suppose the marble token is dropped and lost. How can the players be assured that they need not remain silent forever? One player on the ring, AM, monitors the token status by maintaining a master clock. Numerous timers monitor events on the ring and determine when the AM should generate a new token. One, called T(ANY TOKEN), indicates if a token has passed through the AM within a specific period of time.

Suppose a player wants to enter or leave the game and does so exactly when and at the spot a message is passing. During the shuffling of chairs to make room, the message may be lost or damaged. How do the players reestablish the ring and smooth transfer of messages? Token Ring defines a ring insertion process that ensures an orderly reconfiguration of the ring.

Suppose a player falls asleep and the token comes to rest in his or her lap. How can the other players detect this failure and resume normal operation? The players are blindfolded; Token Access is complicated, and the required analogies can get fairly strained.) After losing contact with a neighbor for a certain period of time, a player can send out a distress signal, called a *beacon*, that initiates an attempt to recover proper ring functionality.

ETHERNET AND TOKEN RING OPTIMIZATION

Suppose a message is smudged while being handed around. How can the sender and receiver know that the message was garbled? Each message contains an error-checking component (called a cyclic redundancy check) that enables the recipients to determine whether the message is damaged.

These potential problems required the designers of Token Ring to put in numerous complicated safeguards to cover the many possible error conditions. The mechanisms of Token Ring are more complicated than of CSMA/CD.

The token-passing mechanism ensures that each station on the ring has an opportunity to transmit at regular intervals. If a station holds the token, it has exclusive access to the network. This is a significant advantage of using Token Ring under heavy network traffic conditions. A system with Token Access is regarded as *deterministic*, whereas a system with CSMA/CD is *probabilistic*. The complexity of Token Access control is, therefore, necessary if precise transmission control is required.

The design of Token Ring also makes it far easier to isolate the causes of a network failure. In the parlor game, players expect all messages to arrive from the player to the right (in Token Ring, that player is the nearest active upstream neighbor, the *NAUN*). If neither a token nor a message arrives within a reasonable period of time, the player can raise an alarm. The game moderator, knowing the order of the players in the ring, can start addressing the problem by checking on the NAUN of the complaining player. In fact, for any given player, the likely cause of failure can be isolated to the player and to the NAUN. This unique feature is the inherent troubleshooting of a fault domain for Token Ring. The second advantage of Token Ring is that you can usually isolate problems to fault domains.

A third advantage of Token Ring is that the network components are designed with a high level of diagnostic capability. Components can perform self-checks and checks on the cables to which they are attached; a component can automatically remove itself from the network if an error is found. Further, components can exchange management data with monitor stations; the monitors can often determine the health of a network component and take corrective action.

The reliability of deterministic control and the ease of troubleshooting fault domains have made Token Ring the fastest growing type of network. Although 802.3/Ethernet remains popular, Token Ring is increasingly being chosen for more mission-critical networks. Later in this book, the Ethernet and Token Ring topologies and their respective applied troubleshooting methods are discussed at length. Next is a detailed discussion of the OSI model and how it relates to the Token Ring and Ethernet topologies.

Understanding the OSI Model for LAN Communication

The *Open Systems Interconnection* (*OSI*) model for LANs was defined by the *International Organization for Standardization* (*ISO*). The model was originally developed as a platform on which network vendors could standardize uniform protocol communication on networks. The IEEE uses the OSI model when developing its own LAN standards.

The model is a hierarchical structure that defines and relates seven layers of communication protocols. The seven layers operate interactively with each other to provide a method for end-to-end communication between source and destination roles and functions. The bottom three layers are intended for transmission and routing definition. The top three layers are intended for communication for user and host applications. The middle layer acts as an interface between the top and bottom layers (see Figure 2.1).

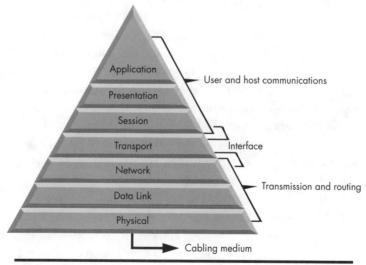

Figure 2.1 The International Organization for Standardization's seven-layer OSI model for LAN communication protocols.

The OSI Seven-Layer Design

Each of the seven layers of the OSI model depends on the others for key elements of its operation. The layers are as follows:

- **Physical Layer**. The *Physical* layer is responsible for actually transmitting the bitstream on the medium. This layer is concerned with the actual coding of the data signal and how it is composed with relation to the following hardware elements: current, voltage, connectors, interface layouts, and the network card.
- **Data Link Layer**. This layer is responsible for communicating with the actual bitstream at the Physical layer. The *Data Link* layer is where the bitstream is assembled and disassembled into data frames. This layer decodes all the necessary flags and error-checking data to provide accurate data transmission. This is also the layer where the addressing of the data frame occurs.
- **Network Layer**. The *Network* layer is where a virtual data path is defined between two network nodes. The data frames are actually assembled into packets at this layer. Addressing and routing for the packet are assigned at this layer.
- **Transport Layer**. The *Transport* layer handles communications between the Network layer and the Session layer. However the Transport layer is mainly defined to handle host-to-host communications. This layer takes packets at the Network layer and assembles and disassembles them into larger transmission segments for communication to the higher layers.
- **Session Layer**. The *Session* layer is responsible for establishing and terminating host-to-host communications. This layer provides timing and control for communicating between hosts within the model. Overall host session management takes place at this layer.
- **Presentation Layer**. The *Presentation* layer takes the actual data transmitted between two nodes and encodes and decodes it into the proper syntax for presentation to the Application layer. Actual code conversion and compression occurs at this layer.
- **Application Layer**. The *Application* layer communicates with the end user. At this layer, you find end-user applications such as electronic mail, file transfer, and networking programs.

OSI and the Token Ring Network

Every LAN topology relates to the OSI model a little differently. To clarify the differences between these various topologies, the Token Ring version is referred to in this book as the Token Ring Protocol model.

Overall, the Token Ring Protocol model relates closely to the OSI model. Figure 2.2 shows an example of how a specific group of protocols overlays the Token Ring Protocol model.

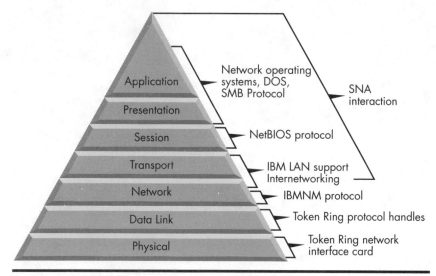

Figure 2.2 The individual pieces of the Token Ring Protocol model relate quite closely to the seven layers of the OSI model for LANs.

OSI and the Ethernet Network

The Ethernet topology relates to the OSI model in a similar way as Token Ring topology does. A direct correlation is at the Physical and Data Link layers, and depending on the protocol environment, there is a specific layer overlay against the OSI model.

The next chapter discusses the overall internal theory and details of network optimization.

CHAPTER 3

Network Optimization Theory

Chapter 2 discussed some of the key reasons for performing a network optimization project. Generally, there are particular reasons behind an effort to optimize a network's performance or operation, and focusing on these reasons enables you to plan the proper phases for the project. The phases for performing an optimization project are discussed later in this book. This chapter discusses the goals of a network optimization project and some of the specific categories of measurement for performing an optimization project on a network.

Deciding about Exact Goals of Network Optimization

Pinpoint several goals for your network optimization project. Possible goals might be to improve the users' desktop response time, improve application efficiency, maximize hardware and software platforms, maximize communication links, examine interoperability between internetwork points, or optimize your network so that the hardware and software technologies provide their best possible performance.

Measuring Response Time

Improving response time usually becomes necessary when network or internetwork users globally have complaints about performance at the workstation desktop level. Users may complain that an application or network function is too slow, has significantly slowed down recently, or has been slow since the initial installation date. Performance problems at the user desktop level can be related to configuration and operation of the workstation, the file server, or any of the involved internetwork communication components and factors. Performance problems also can be related to an application or network operating system configuration.

No calculated way exists to work on a problem of this type; just start on one end and work to the other, using a protocol analyzer or network monitoring tool to examine the response time between the workstation and the file server for the particular operations concerned. (Response time is the time required for a specific network entity to respond to a request from a specific network operation from other network entities.) For example, if a user who normally requests a certain file from an application with a set of keystrokes and receives it in two seconds suddenly complains that it is taking 15 seconds, it is possible that the response time has changed by 13 seconds. This event needs to be verified and trapped to the specific timing intervals involved, and the actual response time needs to be calculated exactly.

Several available protocol analyzers can examine and time-stamp this type of event. By examining the response time, it can be possible to isolate where the 13-second slowdown occurs. If, for example, the total time for the transfer is 15 seconds, and 13 of those seconds are actually spent within the file server, you can document that the delay is in the file server. Perhaps the configuration of the file server was changed, or perhaps other failures occurred and need to be identified.

A protocol analyzer is the only tool that allows capturing the complete event and examining where on the network the performance bottleneck actually is located. Figure 3.1 displays a protocol analyzer positioned to measure response time between a workstation and a file server.

Chapter 3: Network Optimization Theory

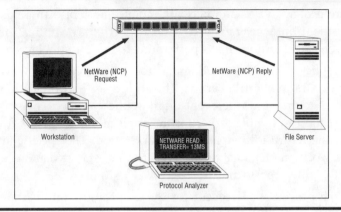

Figure 3.1 A protocol analyzer can measure response time between a workstation and a file server.

After the problem is located, the analyst may be able to examine the configuration or the respective device, perhaps to improve and optimize the performance of the particular application event. Response time can be examined not only for problem events, but also for network optimization of newly installed networks, or for networks newly connected to other networks, as in WAN.

Properly measuring response time is a skill that must be acquired. When the technique is mastered, you can use it to examine performance problems or operation verification between a wide range of specific network communication points. Chapter 5 describes in detail the exact steps for examining response time and specific network throughput.

Measuring Network Application Efficiency

Optimizing application efficiency is a goal to be established when a particular application is having problems on the network. The usual symptom is a user or group of users complaining about a particular application's performance. There are fairly easy ways to benchmark the application's performance with respect to its standard configuration as it is documented, and how it is actually operating on a particular network.

Some protocol analyzers and network monitoring tools can be used to trap certain application access events. After a particular application event is captured, you can determine if it is performing to its optimum level.

For all applications, some application processing occurs in the workstation, and some occurs in the file server. Through examination with a protocol analyzer of a complete traffic event of an application access, an analyst can watch the request to the file server for the application, the access from the file server, and the return to the particular workstation. The specific interprocess times at the workstation and at the file server can be stamped and benchmarked for their actual interprocess time.

File search processes also occur for the application, and certain hand-off techniques are available for reading and writing files across the network involved. A protocol analyzer helps to pinpoint whether the application is working the way it was originally intended by the designer or manufacturer. The efficiency of the application can only be measured against its original specifications from the designer or manufacturer; if a particular application is performing at its optimum level, that specifically needs to be verified.

Additionally, some applications may not work well on certain internetwork configurations. The network operation staff may have a perception of how an application will work, but the analyst must capture some events of the application's actual operation on the network to verify its overall integrity. It is possible that a certain application can contribute to bandwidth peaks on a network. Figure 3.2 depicts a protocol analyzer measuring an application load on a network.

At times, applications may perform general file searches inefficiently. These are easily picked up by examining the network for multiple file searches during searches for an application. Application-tuning approaches can be used to examine ways to reconfigure an application so that it performs at its peak.

Chapter 3: Network Optimization Theory

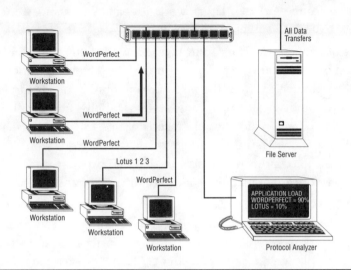

Figure 3.2 A protocol analyzer can measure application load on a network.

Maximizing Hardware and Software Technologies

The many products that make up a complete network are costly: PCs, printers, modems, all the major platforms within the network, and so on. Most hardware and software platforms have what is called a maximum specification for their possible utilization. Some hardware and software platforms are not being used to even half their actual capacity for performance. Most have a set of configuration parameters that sometimes can be changed to allow them to work better on a standard networking platform. But the only way to actually verify whether they are performing well on the network is to capture events and transmissions from the particular devices.

At times, a workstation may transmit on the network with a certain type of block size. A protocol analyzer can capture that transmission and enable you to identify if that block size is the optimum on a specific network for that particular workstation or file server. It may be possible to reconfigure that particular device to work at a larger block size, allowing its network interface card buffers to be used at their most peak level.

A range of network transfers occur between workstations and file servers in which memory utilization can be optimized by changing block size and configuration parameters from the network communication standpoint. Many devices and many types of operating systems, shells, and applications are available; all require specific research. A book of this scope cannot detail all the configuration parameters in the industry. For example, a 4Mbps Token Ring network has a maximum frame size in the 4KB range. Certain file server configurations for certain platforms allow a frame size transmission in the 4KB range; others do not.

Selecting the correct hardware and software configuration parameters to meet the network requirements raises network transfer rates to their optimum level. An example would be to take an OS/2 LAN Server file server and to maximize the frame size for the best rate in transferring data in and out of the network interface card and cache memory. The overall goal is to have the best possible throughput in a conversation between the applied workstations and file servers. Network throughput theory is discussed later in this book, but it is basically the amount of data transmitted in a specific time period. The goal is always to transmit with true integrity the most data in the least amount of time. This uses the network configuration at its optimum level.

The overall point is to make sure that the workstations, file servers, and all the network devices are utilizing their memory and platforms as effectively as possible. Some of this can be easily changed by configuration after you understand what the network traffic requirements are and what the network data transfer rates are actually like, through utilizing a protocol analyzer. Figure 3.3 displays the theory of maximizing the hardware and software platforms in a workstation and file server platform.

Chapter 3: Network Optimization Theory

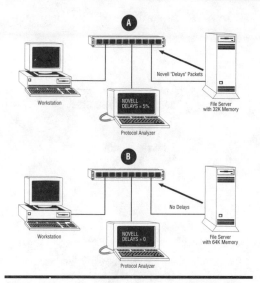

Figure 3.3 Maximizing platform performance.

Sizing a Network Communication Link

A goal of network optimization is to properly size all the communication links in a network. For instance, in WANs, it may be necessary to evaluate the size of a certain WAN point to WAN point link. But even with small networks, some communication links from building to building may not be maximized to their optimum level.

There are a variety of optimization techniques (discussed later in this book) that enable you to examine the communication upon a WAN or LAN. Basically, communication link sizing involves looking at the capacity of the communication link with a protocol analyzer, then utilizing the protocol analyzer to calculate how much of the communication link actually is being used.

For example, if a 56Kbps link connects two WAN points, you can use a protocol analyzer to examine how much of that 56Kbps link is being used. If the analyzer captures a set of transmission events for one second on the 56Kbps link, and analysis finds that only 32Kbps is actually being transmitted in one second across the link, a total of approximately 24Kbps of actual data space for timing can be implemented upon the communication link to maximize its capacity. Figure 3.4 depicts an example of this approach for maximizing a communication link.

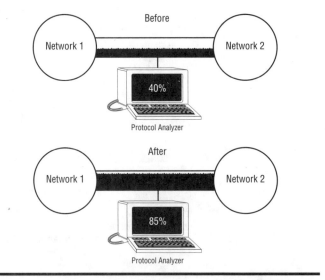

Figure 3.4 Maximizing performance of a communication link.

Note that the goal is not always to completely maximize the capacity of a communication link—that in itself can cause a performance problem—but to actually use as much of the capacity as possible without taking a performance hit. In this example, it is reasonable to say that at least 10–15KB of space is available on this particular 56KB link. Optimization of this network link would involve utilizing as much as possible of that available capacity.

Verifying a Network's True Interoperability

Network optimization includes verifying the interoperability of all networking devices in a network's infrastructure. With the rate of advancement of the technology, more products need to work together within a network. These products include workstations, file servers, network applications, and operating systems, plus all the internal components of those devices. The challenge is to optimize their interoperability while maintaining their individual operational integrity.

A main struggle in internetwork operations today is to allow different operating systems at the file server level to integrate with other operating system platforms. For example, it is still a battle to achieve the pure integration of the TCP/IP-UNIX and Novell environments. Both Novell and all the different UNIX manufacturers advertise their products as having easy integration, but actually implementing the products is another story. When interoperability becomes a concern, a protocol analyzer or network monitoring tool can be an analyst's best friend.

Network optimization is a key phrase here. Connecting two entities is one issue, but actually making them perform effectively together is another. A protocol analyzer can be used to view the conversations between the Novell and UNIX environments and the respective communication can then be examined from a workstation to a file server across two different networking platforms. A protocol analyzer captures particular errors occurring regularly, allowing for diagnosis.

Sometimes it can be easy to pick up an incompatible operation version of a software operating system or a particular network interface card driver. For example, if a particular error is picked up and is found to be an incompatible version, it might be possible to upgrade the version or change and reconfigure the software to alleviate the particular network error. This may in turn result in better performance between the two platforms at the user's desktop level.

Chapters 3 and 5 discuss techniques having to do with timing, block size, and frame compatibility that help make products, platforms, and software operations interoperable. Figure 3.5 shows the concept of network component interoperability.

28 ETHERNET AND TOKEN RING OPTIMIZATION

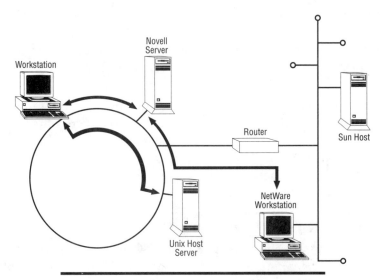

Figure 3.5 Network component interoperability.

Ensuring Technology Peak Performance

In a perfect world, every network's hardware and software products would operate at their optimum level. Every product has specifications for its operation, and any network team should try to make sure that these tools are operating at their peak. A protocol analyzer helps to do this. For example, if a certain bridge is supposed to forward packets at 50Kbps, a protocol analyzer can be used to measure the product's performance upon installation. If it is only forwarding 30Kbps, perhaps the product needs to be reconfigured.

Configuration changes should be made according to instructions for a particular product. A protocol analyzer also enables the user to verify if configuration changes have an effect on a particular product and the network. Figure 3.6 shows a protocol analyzer being used to verify a new bridge's frame forwarding rate.

This section discussed the initial goals of network optimization, and why an analyst wants to focus on network performance from an optimization standpoint. The actual technique for meeting these goals is discussed in Chapter 5. The next section discusses categories of measurement that have significance for a network optimization analyst.

Chapter 3: Network Optimization Theory 29

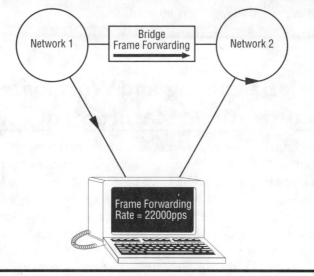

Figure 3.6 A protocol analyzer verifying a new bridge's frame forwarding rate.

Understanding Categories of Measurement for Network Optimization

Network optimization generally includes measurement of the following:

- Network baselining and workload characterization
- Block and packet size examination
- Network timing
- File throughput measurement
- Network transfer integrity
- Network error measurement
- Workstation and file server memory configuration
- Application tuning
- Network packet compatibility

- Workstation and file server configuration
- Product integration measurement

Network Baselining and Workload Characterization Measurement

Network baselining is the actual recording and measurement of a network's state of operation over a specified period of time. Every network has a mode of operation that can be considered its static baseline. At times, due to some of the application usage and network operational changes that can occur in a network, the static baseline may change for a particular area of measurement. There is always a need for the average statistical set of characterizations per network for a baseline. If varying traffic levels are on a network, the baseline always shows those traffic levels clearly, through its statistical values. This is known as applying a workload to a network.

When more than the normal workload is applied to a particular network, its static baseline changes, especially after failures and abnormal network events. An unusual change to the static baseline can be clearly measured by examining the statistics from a baseline.

Whether a network baseline is at its static or its changed state, measuring the network statistics is called measuring the *workload characterizations* of the network. Specifically, a workload characterization is the particular portion of the character of a network in relation to its statistical points when a certain workload is applied.

Think of when you go a doctor for an annual physical. If the doctor examines all your vital signs—heart rate, blood pressure, temperature, and so on—these statistics encompass your health baseline.

A key to network optimization is to always analyze a network in relation to a previous baseline. To baseline a network is to examine the current state of operations, which must be done by examining the network's workload characterizations.

The following categories are the main workload characterizations that should be measured in any network baseline study:

- Bandwidth utilization

- Node-by-node bandwidth utilization
- Protocol breakdown
- Error types and levels
- Physical layer packet statistics and operations
- Upper layer protocol packet statistics and operations

Bandwidth Utilization

The *composite bandwidth utilization* of a network is the percentage of the total capacity available for data transmission on the network that is actually being used. For example, on a 4Mbps Token Ring network, four million bits of data are allowed on the network cabling medium in one second. The total capacity of that particular network is four million bits per second. If a protocol analyzer finds two million bits on the wire in one second, the effective overall bandwidth utilization is 50%.

Most protocol analyzers and network monitoring tools can be used to measure this statistic. Depending on the workload applied to a particular network or its state of operation at the time of measurement, the bandwidth utilization can change. At times of certain network failures or during high stress workload periods on a network, the utilization factor must be measured immediately to see what the actual bandwidth level is on the network involved; this is critical for network optimization. For any type of network optimization project, an analyst must know what the bandwidth utilization is.

Node-by-Node Utilization

Node-by-node utilization is a key measurement for an internetwork, as it involves breaking down the overall bandwidth utilization between the active nodes on the network. For example, if 20 nodes are on a 4Mbps network and the overall bandwidth utilization is 50%, how much is each of the 20 nodes using out of the 50% utilized overall?

If a node was found to be using over 60% of the available bandwidth, the node should be investigated. If this node is a file server, such behavior is normal. But if the node is a workstation, further investigation is needed. Perhaps the workstation was running a back-up process, or perhaps an abnormal condition exists, such as a hardware or software failure.

ETHERNET AND TOKEN RING OPTIMIZATION

Protocol Breakdown

Protocol statistics gathered through baselining are a key workload characterization. Most networks today probably have more than one protocol operating. (As mentioned earlier, network protocols are the set of orderly predefined methods by which devices on LANs communicate with each other.)

A group of defined methods of communication exists for each protocol that may be on the particular network you are attempting to optimize. This workload characterization measurement breaks down by percentage the actual amount of protocols on the network being analyzed. For example, a network protocol breakdown might show these figures: 55% NetWare, 35% SNA, and 10% TCP/IP. These protocols would then be defined and organized in relation to their actual percentage on the network.

This measurement is important from an optimization standpoint because as networks change over a period of time, it is important to keep track of the protocol levels across the respective network. Certain protocols may be found through this measurement that do not need to be applied to the particular network because they are non-required broadcasts from another network. Network optimization techniques such as filtering with a protocol analyzer, might determine the actual location of these protocols and aid in efforts to eliminate them from a network where they are not required.

Protocol breakdowns need to be performed in every baseline study and used in network optimization projects.

Error Types and Levels

Capturing and recording errors that may be present on a network are important for network optimization. Most protocol analyzers and network monitoring tools can capture and decode Token Ring and Ethernet errors.

The following is a list of Token Ring and Ethernet errors that can be recorded. The actual counts and location of certain errors can indicate possible marginal hardware failures. In some cases these errors can point out certain application problems with the higher-layer data on a LAN.

Token Ring Soft Errors:

- Internal Error
- Burst Error

- Line Error
- Abort Delimiter Transmitted Error
- AC Error
- Lost Packet Error
- Receiver Congestion Error
- Packet Copied Error
- Frequency Error
- Token Error

Token Ring Hard Error:
- Beacon

Ethernet:

- Local Collision Error
- Remote Collision Error
- CRC Error
- Illegal Packet Length Error
- Short Packet

Physical Layer Packet Statistics and Operations

The physical layer typically is considered to include the cabling or other media as well as the rules that govern how traffic is managed on the transmission medium. The low-level physical layer of any topology needs to be examined for proper communication exchange and general health.

The MAC (media access control) sublayer defines the rules that govern how nodes access the network to transmit data. Token Ring has 25 MAC packet types, which handle the actual Token Ring medium access control communication; you should focus on these when examining the low-level packet communication processes. There is a normal state of low-level MAC packet communications for proper and fluent communication exchange between network entities. Network communication fluency is a normal communication exchange flow between two network entities. Any deviances from a normal state of low-level packet communication process can indicate an intermittent network component failure.

Although Ethernet does not have 25 MAC packets, it has a normal state of low-level packet communications required for proper and fluent communication exchange. The difference is that the basic 802.3 or standard Ethernet packets that are captured represent one of the error types mentioned earlier. The Ethernet topology does not have as much overhead traffic at the MAC layer as Token Ring. High traffic levels recorded at the physical Ethernet layer may indicate a possible failure on the network.

Upper Layer Protocol Packets Statistics and Operations

After the physical packet communication processes are examined for proper and fluent communication, the next main workload characterization to be measured is the high layer protocol communication that occurs concurrently between general network workstations and the network file servers.

The application and network operating system communication process between workstations should be examined in detail. All applications and network operating systems communication uses a predefined protocol for exchanging information. An analyst should look closely at all protocol communications at the higher layer for any deviation from the normal process. Specific tests should be performed for all the major protocols within the specific network environment. All the applied high layer protocols need to be examined for high level of health. Figure 3.7 displays a set of graphs that depict the findings of a network baseline.

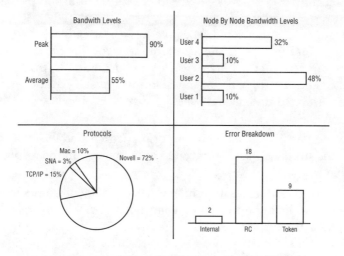

Figure 3.7 The results of a network baseline.

Block and Packet Size Examination

Block size is a feature of the various packet types that a protocol uses for transmission on the network. The block size relates to the amount of data that an application or process puts in a packet for transmission. A *packet* is the actual capsule containing data for transmission. Packets are the vehicles that carry data from active node to active node on a network. The term packet also is used in this context, especially in some high-layer protocols such High Level Data Link Control (HDLC). The terms packet and frame are somewhat interchangeable throughout the networking industry. Depending on the form of analysis and the type of internetwork protocol, application, and topology involved, either term can be used. This book uses the term packet more frequently.

With a protocol analyzer, you can capture upon transmission and reception the packets that are emitted from different devices on an internetwork. For example, if a protocol analyzer is used to examine the conversations from a workstation to a file server, all the packets generated between the two devices could be captured and examined for the block size of the data within the packet.

The packet composite includes a physical header to transmit the packet from one device to another across the network. Internally within the packet is an area where the actual data is retained. The data has a certain block size, depending on the protocol and the application configurations for that network. Block sizes can be considered inefficient or efficient, depending on the network infrastructure and the type of transmission involved. It requires the analyst's time and expertise to understand whether a packet's block size is efficient or inefficient, but the block size itself can be examined quite easily.

Most protocol analyzers allow for capturing packets and examining them for block size. It is simply a matter of turning on a function in the display mode of the particular analyzer.

Today's networks often are frightfully inefficient when it comes to block size, simply because so many applications (and operating systems) were built for much smaller and simpler networks. Today, however, you commonly find networks with nodes for as many as 2,000 to 5,000 users.

Some transmission media and their applied capability also limit the maximum block size that can be used. For example, if the Novell protocol is used on a Token Ring network that has a 16Mbps transmission speed, the maximum packet size for the Token Ring platform is as high as the 18KB range. The internal packet block size transmission for some Novell protocols today, even in the 3.x release, is still as low as 100B per packet. This is extremely inefficient for, say, a 100KB file requiring transmission. Other limitations also are due to the fact that certain bridges and routers only support particular transmission throughput capability for certain packet sizes.

The trick, then, is to understand whether the network being examined can pass, through its bridges, router, cabling medium, and applied topology, a larger packet size than the application or network operating system is actually utilizing for block size implementation. When the maximum packet size of transmission capability is defined, the actual application or network operating system can be configured to pass a larger internal block size.

Larger packet sizes should be considered the most efficient mode if the network infrastructure can support them. For example, if a file of 100KB has to be transferred and only a 100-byte packet size can be used, 1,000 packets will need to be transferred between the workstation and the file server to complete the file transfer. If the packet size is in the 1KB range, however, only 100 packets are required to complete the file transfer. A protocol analyzer can be used to examine this overall transfer and capture the complete event.

Note that changes may be required for the overall network infrastructure, including the cabling medium, bridge and router capacities, and configuration,

Chapter 3: Network Optimization Theory

to allow for a larger packet size. For example, if through examining the network configuration you find that a particular bridge link can only pass a 2KB packet size but the rest of the bridge and router packet sizes can go as high as 10KB, the transmission channel is still limited to a 2KB throughput because of the one bridge channel with the lower packet size setting of 2KB. Figure 3.8 displays this event.

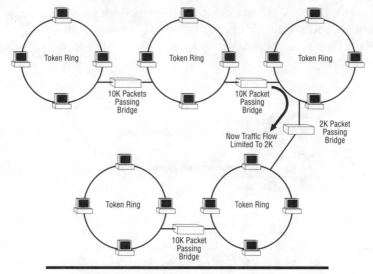

Figure 3.8 A bridge misconfigured for small packets.

When the 2KB packet size is brought up to the 10KB packet size through configuration or modification of the network interface card (NIC) type, the network applications can pass all the packet sizes in the 10KB range. This allows reconfiguring the operating system or applications to pass larger packet sizes to produce higher efficiency across the whole network.

Network Timing

Network timing needs to be performed throughout a network optimization project. Network timing may be a focal point for examining response time or complete file throughput, or interprocessing time for the workstations or file servers.

ETHERNET AND TOKEN RING OPTIMIZATION

Specifically, a protocol analyzer can be used to capture the log-on sequence and application access event of any file server and workstation operation. Standard times are established for a file to be returned from a file server to a workstation, and for a file server or workstation to handle a particular event.

After capturing all data transactions from the network side with a protocol analyzer, network optimization can be performed by examining the timing spent upon the network and also within the file servers and workstations for a particular application or network operating system process. This is a clear measurement, and a valuable one for examining problems on a network. Figure 3.9 displays how a protocol analyzer can be used for capturing a workstation and file server timing event.

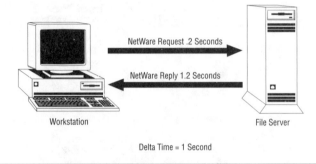

Figure 3.9 A protocol analyzer capturing a workstation and file server timing event.

Remember three time factors when performing network optimization:

- Absolute time of the packet transmission
- Delta time or Interpacket between two consecutive packets
- Relative time between two select packets

Absolute time is the actual time stamped on a particular packet transmission across the network. A protocol analyzer can capture a specific set of events that may involve multiple packet transmissions between a workstation and a file server. For example, if 100 packets are involved, each packet has an absolute time it was generated on the network from the workstation or file server. That actual generation time can be stamped with most protocol analyzers; the analyst can then examine the packet in detail.

Delta time is the amount of time between two consecutive packets on a network. This is a key measurement for examining workstation requests and replies for any type of protocol. For example, if a workstation on a Banyan network requests a file from a Banyan server, and the next packet on the network happens to be the response from the file server, you easily can examine the amount of time from the request packet to the response from the file server. This results in an understanding of that real transfer time and timing effectiveness on the network.

Relative time is the amount of time between two specific network events. Consider a data transmission event with over 100 packets involved. If packet 1 is a request from a workstation, and packet 18 is the response from the file server, the amount of time between packet 1 and packet 18 is the relative time between those specific network events. Another example is a workstation requesting a file to be printed, generated in packet 4. If packet 28 is the packet initiating the send of the file to the printer from a printer server, then packet 28 can be measured as how it is relative in time to the actual workstation request (packet 4). The relative time can be easily calculated between the workstation request for printing and the print server generation of the print request to the printer.

There are also other areas where network timing is used for network optimization projects. This book presents many examples concerning network timing.

File Throughput Measurements

The file throughput analysis function is a category of measurement for any network optimization project, because all network communication is based on file transfers. Basically, networks are in place for file access across a particular cabling medium. Every network transmission is based on file access across the networks, just as in a personal computer.

With a personal computer, you can read, write, save, and delete disk files; only so many things can be done with a disk drive. Network communication is actually disk drive access across a particular cabling medium. Yes, at times a network is used for broadcasts or connection set-up queries, and other defined issues, but the main reason for networks is file access.

Network transmissions take some amount of time, and only a certain amount of data can be passed in that specific time. The amount of data passed in a block of time is called the actual effective network throughput for a certain file transfer event across a network.

Given that definition, file throughput also can be measured with a protocol analyzer. Most protocol analyzers and some network monitoring tools can be used to capture a file access event from a workstation to a file server, and to actually examine the total amount of data passed across the network for the file transfer. The file transfer is measured for the total amount of time for the complete transfer over the given cabling medium between a workstation and the file server, giving the effective file transfer throughput. Figure 3.10 depicts a protocol analyzer being used to measure effective file throughput.

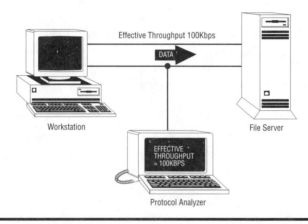

Figure 3.10 A protocol analyzer measuring effective file throughput.

The process can be examined by capturing a workstation file request through a file open and file close across a network. This complete event takes a certain amount of time and a certain number of cumulative bytes are transmitted in that time. Most analyzers capture the absolute starting time and cumulative bytes to the end of the final transmission to provide the overall effective file transfer throughput. This particular technique is detailed in Chapter 5.

Network Transfer Integrity

Measuring network transfer integrity also is known as *examining packet fluency*. This is the actual fluency of network packet communication on a given network. All packets have certain requests and response codes considered normal for the type of network communication.

Chapter 3: Network Optimization Theory

For example, a file should be opened, read, and then closed. Protocol analyzers capture any errors or problems that occur during a network file transmission if normal packets are not generated on the network from the workstations and file servers. Errors or abnormal packets are non-fluent conditions. Examples include a file not found; a bindery error; a file cannot be opened; or security not proper for access.

Every protocol has its own packet communication types for problems in file access, but through analyzing a network conversation at the higher protocol layer, an analyst can see files opened and closed in a normal manner, or can capture errors and general packet communication problems.

The overall focus on this category of measurement is network transfer integrity, to make sure that all files are opened and closed without error in any particular process.

This measurement technique requires a focused view on the higher layer protocol being examined. At times this involves a detailed approach and actually analyzing the particular protocol for free-of-error conditions on file access open and close conditions.

For example, if a Novell workstation requests a file, the file server should be able to open and send down the file within multiple packets (as required for the particular network). Eventually, the workstation requests a close of the file, and the file server should be able to close that file. That is considered a normal event. If a workstation requests the file from the Novell file server and the file server returns a File Not Found completion code, this indicates that a problem may exist with the file search path (see Fig. 3.11).

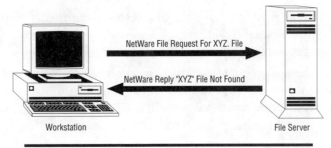

Figure 3.11 A File Not Found condition in NetWare.

There are many possible reasons for this sort of event, but what is clear is that the network transfer integrity is not proper, and the protocol analyzer shows this. To optimize a network, you must examine the network transfer integrity.

Again, this technique involves examining upper layer fluency on the network. This approach can be performed through using proper protocol analysis techniques along with network optimization techniques. Note the additional detail in Chapters 4 and 5 leading to an overall technical approach for examining network transfer integrity.

Network Error Measurement

In optimizing a network, keep an eye open for network errors at the physical or upper protocol layers. For example, if the analyst is involved in a NetWare optimization project but the network has Banyan protocols on it, the Banyan layers require a watchful eye, too. Any type of error on networks in any of the protocols in the physical layer or upper layers of the network involved can affect the overall operations of a particular network.

In the physical layer, every topology on a particular network has its own set of errors. This book discusses both Ethernet and Token Ring. However, if a WAN topology is involved, or another LAN topology such as ARCnet, you need to be familiar with the physical layer errors that may occur for that particular topology. Your protocol analyzer should be able to pick up the physical layer errors for the topology involved, along with any upper protocol errors that may occur.

The upper layer protocols should always be examined for any packet communication problems. Some of these errors and upper protocol layer packet communication problems are discussed in the Chapter 6.

Again, both the upper and lower layer protocols need to be free of errors for proper communication across internetworks, and a protocol analyzer can capture these events if the analyst is in tune with all error detection techniques. Figure 3.12 displays this concept.

Chapter 3: Network Optimization Theory

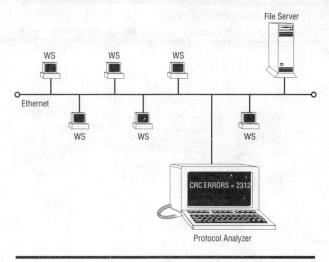

Figure 3.12 Analyzing upper and lower layer protocols.

Workstation and File Server Memory Configuration

Examining the memory configuration on both the workstations and the file servers in a network is a key measurement for any network optimization project. The proper amount of memory is required in both the NICs and the workstations' and file servers' core processing centers to allow for fluent network transfer.

The memory levels affect the actual effective timing and speed of the network transfers. If the memory levels are proper, all the network entities work more in concert to provide network fluency. The workstation, file server, and associated NIC memory levels can be examined through understanding the applications and configurations of the hardware and software platforms involved.

For network optimization, the key is to use a protocol analyzer to examine network transfers for minimal interprocessing timing in workstations and file servers. Interprocessing time is the time spent inside a device such as a workstation or file server to process a packet event. When interprocessing times are high in the workstation or the file server, the trigger point should be to examine the memory configuration of the device. For example, if a workstation-to-file server operation involves a total of 150 millisecond time transfer, and the interprocessing time in the workstation is over 100 milliseconds but the rest of the time transfer is split between the file server and the network, it should be clear that the predominant amount of time is spent in the workstation (see Figure 3.13).

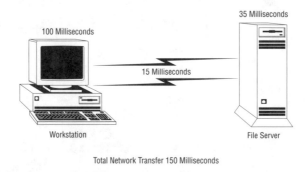

Figure 3.13 Most of the processing delay takes place in the workstation.

It is possible that the workstation platform memory or processing power may be inadequate for resources for this network transfer. In this situation, one factor to examine is memory configuration. This category of network optimization can be especially useful for identifying bottlenecks in certain platforms throughout a network.

Application Tuning

If an application does not seem to be performing at its best, first check all the documentation available to make sure that the workstation and the file servers are set up correctly to work with the application.

Next, examining some of the application parameters and total configuration possibilities may show that the block size for network transfer of the application can be affected by some internal configuration for the application. Through examination of the block size parameters of a particular application in relation to what is actually used to transfer on the network, it may be possible to modify the size of an application transfer packet size to allow the application to respond in a better manner.

It also may be possible to increase or decrease the communication timing values on a particular application to increase the throughput from the user desktop level to the file server for the particular application. Some applications have what is called an interpacket handling time that is considered minimum in the configuration. It may be possible to minimize or decrease this value to allow

Chapter 3: Network Optimization Theory

the application to work on a network that can handle faster transfer capabilities than those for which it was originally designed. It usually is easy to research applications and the most recent network modifications to their communication parameters, even though they have been on the network for quite some time. Figure 3.14 depicts an application tuning example.

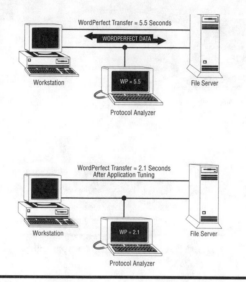

Figure 3.14 An example of application tuning.

Network Packet Compatibility

Especially in the Ethernet environment, but even in other topology environments, multiple packet types can be generated on the network. The packet is actually defined by the NIC and its hardware and software configuration within a particular device. For example, in a file server, not just the NIC but even the file server parameters can actually form the final packet type to be generated on the network.

A protocol analyzer enables an analyst to capture packets from workstations and file servers throughout an internetwork layout to examine the packet types for possible incompatibilities. Certain protocol analyzers (such as Network General's Sniffer) have internal expert systems that pick up packet incompatibilities from most major protocols. The internals of the actual packet can be displayed on the screen of a protocol analyzer and can be decoded for the actual packet type.

Packet capability is a key issue in network optimization, as packet incompatibilities can cause network non-fluent conditions, such as retransmissions. Chapter 5 discusses network retransmissions in detail. Figure 3.15 displays a packet incompatibility.

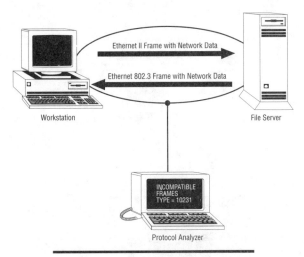

Figure 3.15 A packet incompatibility.

Workstation and File Server Configuration

The file server and workstation configurations are measurement factors in network optimization projects. Both the file server and workstation platforms are factors in examining the network communication capabilities. By using a protocol analyzer, an analyst can examine communication between workstations and file servers and pinpoint any delays in particular workstations or file server communication on a network.

An example is a network with a total of 200 nodes isolated as workstations with four file servers. If one particular file server is operating too slowly from a network standpoint and a group of 60 workstations are also having performance problems, those devices can be examined for their internal configuration that would work best on the network. Certain shell and file server parameters can be modified to allow a particular file server or workstation to work at a more optimal level. Even if a particular file server has a lower memory level than other file servers, it may be possible to reconfigure its parameters to work better with its internal memory in the NIC. The capability to perform this type of optimization varies depending on the type of operating system and hardware platforms deployed on the respective networks. However, through examining all the communication parameters, it may be possible to make modifications enabling the network hardware and software operations of the file server to perform better. Figure 3.16 illustrates this concept.

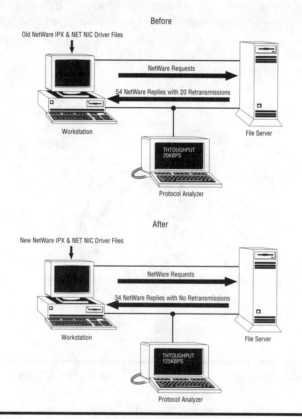

Figure 3.16 Adjusting communication parameters to improve server performance.

Product Integration Measurement

A final category of measurement for network optimization is product integration. New products are constantly being implemented in networks today, including software applications, NICs, print servers, modems, and file servers.

48 ETHERNET AND TOKEN RING OPTIMIZATION

When these products are implemented, the overall workload characterizations of the network change and the baseline is affected. Through proper network optimization approaches, such as baselining and general workload characterization measurements, the effects of the changes can be captured fairly easily and displayed on the particular protocol analyzer.

When a new product is implemented on a network, an analyst should examine the network immediately for any changes, including bad ones. For example, if a new file server version is implemented on one server and three other servers have the standard version, the network should be re-analyzed upon implementation of the new version on the one file server. Figure 3.17 illustrates this concept.

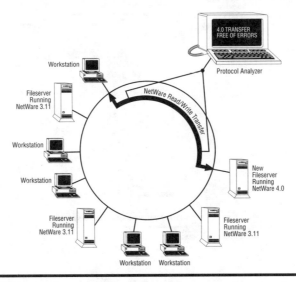

Figure 3.17 Re-analyze your network when new products are implemented.

All these measurement categories, including network timing, memory configuration, application tuning, and file server and workstation platforms, work together as the factors for network optimization. Network transfer integrity can be examined with a protocol analyzer and problem areas can be clearly identified in the block and packet sizes, memory configuration, application tuning, or file server and workstation platforms that can be remedied to improve network performance

Now that the main goals and theory of network optimization have been presented, you can understand how the tools work that allow for measuring the categories of analysis. The next chapter focuses on the internal theory and product palettes of protocol analyzers and network monitoring tools.

CHAPTER 4

Optimization and Troubleshooting Tools

This chapter covers some LAN test equipment and explains how you use the equipment to optimize or troubleshoot a LAN. Most of this chapter refers to the Token Ring or Ethernet topologies due to their large installation base. This chapter begins with an overview of protocol analysis and performance tuning methodology, then turns to the basic use of a protocol analyzer and Token Ring and Ethernet cable testers. Next, you learn some of the industry-standard Token Ring and Ethernet protocol analysis and cable testing devices. Many manufacturers have designed superb test instruments for the Token Ring and Ethernet environment. Because these instruments are too numerous to be detailed in this book, this chapter discusses only the most commonly used testing devices.

Protocol Analysis and Performance Tuning Methodology

To use these test tools efficiently, you must develop skills in protocol analysis and performance tuning. *Protocol analysis* is the process of capturing, viewing, and analyzing how a communication protocol is operating in a particular network architecture. *Performance tuning* is using the statistics gathered in a protocol analysis session and making modifications to the software or hardware components of a LAN to improve the network's operational performance.

Before you can tune your Token Ring or Ethernet LAN, you must initiate a protocol analysis session. Then you can study your LAN statistics and decide what action to take.

Protocol analysis and performance tuning both are arts. The art of protocol analysis is an expression of a troubleshooter's initial approach to capturing the right protocol data, followed by the logical process of deciphering the protocol being viewed. The art of performance tuning is the process of closely focusing on detailed data to reshape a LAN for optimal performance.

To develop your engineering abilities in protocol analysis and performance tuning, you should take a methodical approach to learning both. The proper way to do this is to have a defined methodology; the next sections introduce the methodology used for both these approaches.

Protocol Analysis Methodology

The following six steps should be used in a protocol analysis session. Consider these steps to be an actual methodology.

1. Capture. Start capturing data for all layers of your Token Ring or Ethernet protocol model.
2. View. Examine the data at each layer, starting with the MAC layer and working up to the Application layer.
3. Analyze. Observe and scrutinize the data at each layer for the proper fluent communication processes.
4. Check errors. View and note any soft errors transmitted to the REM functional address.

5. Benchmark performance. Monitor the network bandwidth utilization at an overall baseline view and at individual workstation levels.

6. Focus. Further analyze any potential problems by focusing on the particular component through filtering, triggers, time setting marks, and other categorizing techniques.

Chapter 6 discusses each of these steps in further detail.

As Figure 4.1 shows, when you start a protocol analysis session at step 1 of the methodology, your scope of vision is wide and your detail of focus on the LAN is narrow. By step 6, your scope of vision is narrow because your detail of focus on the LAN is wide.

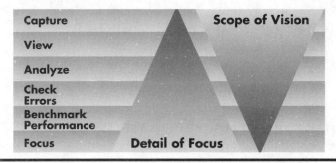

Figure 4.1 During a Token Ring or Ethernet protocol analysis session (from "Capture" to "Focus"), your detail of focus expands while your scope of vision narrows.

This approach increases your scope of vision on your LAN's overall technicalities. You now should be able to get an initial feeling for the health of your Token Ring or Ethernet network, and if any problems do exist, you can focus more directly on those problems.

Performance Tuning Methodology

Performance tuning is an art; it can be developed, but it requires extensive experience in LAN design. After you gather your conclusions from a protocol analysis, you must take the necessary actions to increase the performance of the LAN. This action requires an understanding of both the network software and hardware intricacies and their synergies.

ETHERNET AND TOKEN RING OPTIMIZATION

The details of the following steps are not covered because the scope of this book is not LAN design. Nevertheless, you can develop dexterity for performance tuning by following a defined methodology. Use the following eight basic steps for performance tuning:

1. Review. Study all gathered statistics for layer communication from the protocol analysis session.
2. Target. Pinpoint specific trends in network bandwidth utilization.
3. Isolate. Segregate any captured errors to specific network components.
4. Allocate. Designate resources to test any problem areas for a closer benchmark.
5. Define. Specify any network improvements needed in the software and hardware components. Look at all alternatives. Assess all LAN environmental impacts.
6. Implement. Implement the changes to a network component one at a time. For network integrity, it is extremely important to make changes one at a time, and then retest.
7. Retest. Next, rerun a protocol analysis session focused on that particular component. If no improvements in the test results occur, you may need to redefine and re-implement the changes.
8. Document. Record all your findings. Sometimes you should publish the results to let other technical people and management understand the scope of what has occurred and its impact on the LAN.

Figure 4.2 depicts the relational flow of LAN performance tuning methodology.

Chapter 4: Optimization and Troubleshooting Tools 53

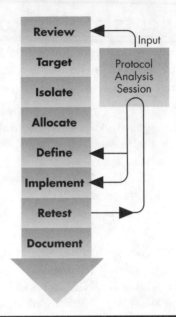

Figure 4.2 Proceeding through the eight steps of the Token Ring or Ethernet LAN performance tuning methodology.

Operating a Protocol Analyzer

To use a protocol analyzer effectively, you must have a good overall perception of the following combination of domains:

- Knowledge of the involved LAN architecture
- Consciousness of a protocol analysis methodology
- Understanding of the basic operational modes of the particular protocol analyzer used

You already have some understanding of the Token Ring and Ethernet LAN architectures and applied protocol analysis methodology. The Token Ring and Ethernet in-depth sections later in this book present more comprehensive discussions on the topologies. The next section of this chapter overviews the basic components of a generic protocol analyzer and its operational modes.

Basic Components of a Protocol Analyzer

A protocol analyzer is a hardware/software device that can peek into the cabling medium of your LAN. The protocol analyzer physically connects to a network and captures data traveling on the network cabling medium for the purpose of decoding the specific data for analysis.

Most protocol analyzers consist of a PC configured with the specific LAN topology NIC and network analysis software loaded onto the disk drive in the PC. The protocol analyzer is then connected to the LAN by means of the NIC, just like a regular network node. The difference between the protocol analyzer node and a regular node is that the analyzer copies all the packets that pass through its NIC. A regular node copies only those packets addressed to its own specific network address.

Most Token Ring and Ethernet protocol analyzers operate within this mode. The Token Ring NICs used for analyzer applications usually have a special chipset modification that allows the NIC to be indiscriminate as to packet addressing. These types of Token Ring NICs are nicknamed promiscuous mode NICs.

The network analysis software loaded onto the disk drive is built according to a layered model. This model is composed of a base operating code that handles the actual control and decoding of the particular data captured. Above the base operating code is the topology-specific code that enables the protocol analyzer to interrelate with the particular topology. The next layer above the topology code is the layer that deciphers the protocols being analyzed. Figure 4.3 shows a representation of this model.

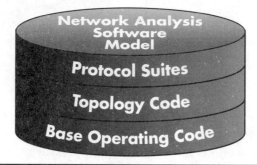

Figure 4.3 Protocol Analyzer network analysis software consists of layers that allow control and decoding of topology and protocol-suite data.

Chapter 4: Optimization and Troubleshooting Tools

Basic Operational Modes of a Protocol Analyzer

The main operational modes of a protocol analyzer are capturing, decoding, and displaying network protocol data. Three techniques built into the protocol analyzer allow the standard operating mode parameters—triggering, filtering, and display options—to be modified.

The triggering and filter techniques enable you to select which part of the network data you want to capture or display and when to capture or display. With filtering, captured data can be displayed and a particular packet can be filtered to display only certain data on the protocol analyzer. Capturing a packet from a PC LAN transmission is a good example. Suppose that you just want to see the SMB protocol. You can filter out the MAC, DLC, and NetBIOS protocols. The only protocol left to view and analyze is SMB.

Triggering enables you to capture and display only if certain events occur. If, for example, you set the protocol analyzer to trigger on an SMB read file command, the analyzer should start capturing or displaying network data only after an SMB read event occurs.

The display options usually allow for displaying data in numerical and graphical formats. Most protocol analyzers allow for certain time-relationship options. Most of the display options correlate with a protocol analyzer's capabilities to print and access disks so that almost anything you can display to the analyzer screen you can print and log to disk.

In summary, the guide for using a protocol analyzer is to follow the methodology capture; view, analyze, and check errors; benchmark performance; and then focus on a puzzling area by using the filtering, triggering, and display techniques.

Figure 4.4 depicts the relational flow of the way you can use a protocol analyzer's operational features and techniques.

Remember to take the time to thoroughly learn the features and capabilities of a protocol analyzer. If you have a strong understanding of a protocol analyzer's operation, you can analyze your data in a more timely and effective manner.

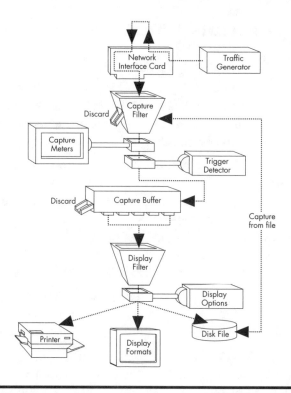

Figure 4.4 The operational features of protocol analyzers provide the tools for protocol analysis and the subsequent performance tuning session.

Understanding Protocol Analyzers and Network Monitoring Tools

The Token Ring and Ethernet environments are supported by a wide assortment of protocol analyzers, with new technology emerging daily. Many protocol analyzers parallel each other's operational modes and features, but new ones are being designed with more innovative features. As the different types of protocol analyzers are introduced, concentrate on their respective features for monitoring and analyzing the Token Ring or Ethernet topology.

The following section is an overview of some of the industry-standard Token Ring and Ethernet protocol analyzers and their specifications.

Network General Sniffer Analyzer

Founded in 1986, Network General is currently the industry leader in producing high-performance protocol analyzers, and has developed products that span today's complex environment of multiple networking topologies and protocols.

The Sniffer Analyzer product family has a full menu of protocol analyzer configurations, including both stand-alone analyzers and complex Distributed Sniffer configurations. The stand-alone product is offered in three versions: a preconfigured PC analyzer packaged in either a Compaq or Toshiba portable, a PCMCIA version for most compatible laptops, and an NIC/software package so that you can configure the Sniffer Analyzer in your own PC (see Figure 4.5).

Figure 4.5 The stand-alone Sniffer Analyzer family comes preconfigured in a variety of portable PCs, including the new laptop PCMCIA version.

The Distributed Sniffer System (DSS) is a new Network General product that supports the same analysis functions as the stand-alone product; its main focus, however, is to monitor from a central point LANs dispersed across intricate geographical layouts. The DSS product line is discussed in detail later in this section.

ETHERNET AND TOKEN RING OPTIMIZATION

The Sniffer Analyzer products are designed across a full range of topologies, including Token Ring (4Mbps and 16Mbps), IBM PC Network, Ethernet, ARCnet, StarLAN, LocalTalk, FDDI, and WAN Synchronous Links.

The Sniffer supports the following protocol suites: IBM general suites, IBM SNA, NetBIOS, OS/2 IBMNM, SMB, Novell 2X, 3X, and 4X plus NDS decodes, XNS:MSNET, TCP/IP, DECnet, Banyan VINES, AppleTalk, XNS, SUN:NFS, ISO, PPP, SNMP V1 and 2, LAPD, Frame Relay, FDDI and FDDI SMT, DLSw, X Windows, X.25, SDLC, and HDLC.

The Sniffer Analyzer implements the basic modes of operation and added features through a creative menu system. Figure 4.6 shows the main menu. From this menu, you can vector to submenus to further configure the features for a specific analysis session.

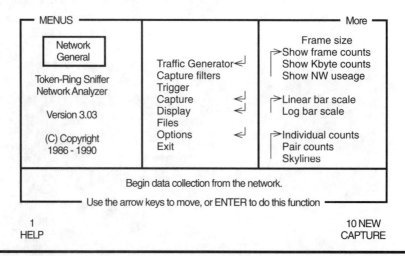

Figure 4.6 The main menu of the Sniffer Analyzer provides access to the operational modes for a Token Ring or Ethernet protocol analysis session.

The Sniffer Analyzer enables you to filter network data when capturing and displaying by protocol, data pattern matches, addresses, and time relationships. You can trigger when capturing and displaying by external and internal pattern matching.

The Display features display data in both numerical and graphical formats. You can set up multiple viewing windows to view the summary of packets, packet detail, and hex representation on the same screen. A display option

Chapter 4: Optimization and Troubleshooting Tools

presents network bandwidth utilization by packet. All statistics can be viewed in multiple time relationships. The Sniffer Analyzer also is capable of symbolic naming of specific addresses, which is helpful when viewing traces of data for easy identification of nodes.

The main menu options also include a traffic-generation feature and a cable tester. The traffic-generation feature enables you to load the network with traffic to check its flexibility of load. The cable tester operates as a time domain reflectometer (TDR). TDRs are discussed later in this chapter.

The Sniffer Analyzer offers excellent report-generating features. Almost all the statistics you can view can be printed in various formats and fed into most major PC applications for management reports.

A strength of the Sniffer Analyzer is its Advanced Monitoring for Token Ring and Ethernet, which was originally developed as the Network General Watchdog product, but now comes bundled with the basic analyzer. It functions as a separate software module from the main Sniffer protocol analyzer software. Its main mission is to monitor and display vital Token Ring or Ethernet network statistics. The main menu is shown in Figure 4.7.

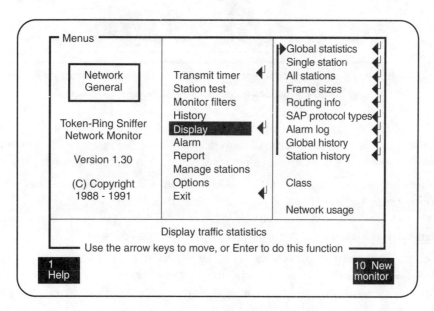

Figure 4.7 The Network General Sniffer includes an Advanced Monitoring for Token Ring and Ethernet feature, which provides vital network statistics.

ETHERNET AND TOKEN RING OPTIMIZATION

The major statistics gathered by Advanced Monitoring for Token Ring and Ethernet are Global Statistics (see Figure 4.8), Station Statistics, Transmit Timing, Error Statistics (including CRC, collisions, TR hard and soft errors), Protocol Statistics, Packet Size Statistics, Traffic History, Routing Information, Report Writer, and Alarms.

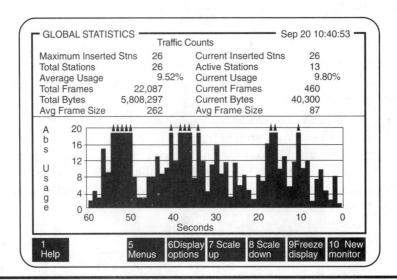

Figure 4.8 The Global Statistics screen of the Sniffer's Advanced Monitoring for Token Ring and Ethernet includes numeric and graphical representations.

Figure 4.9 is a screen shot of the Routing Path—one of the many useful Analyzer Sniffer features. This display shows the location and percentage of packets routed through a multiple-ring environment, in relation to each ring.

Network General recently introduced enhancements to an expert system that offers computer-based assistance during protocol analysis sessions. This advanced expert system automatically locates problems on your network and offers advice on resolving particular network issues or problems.

The expert analysis software can locate internetwork faults, performance slowdowns, protocol errors, and physical layer problems. It is one of the first expert systems in an analyzer product that is accurate on its findings and suggestions. Figure 4.10 displays one of the Expert screens.

Chapter 4: Optimization and Troubleshooting Tools 61

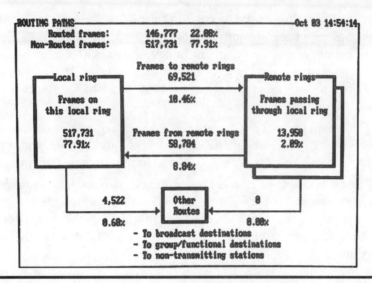

Figure 4.9 The Sniffer's Routing Path screen depicts the location and percentage of packets routed through a multiple-ring environment.

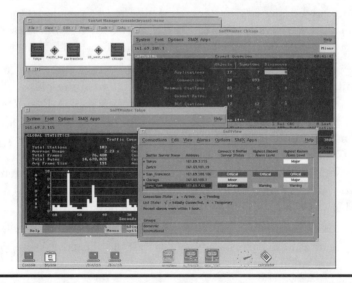

Figure 4.10 The Network General Sniffer displays an expert analysis.

Another notable feature is the Network General Telesniffer. This feature now also functions as a separate software module from the main Sniffer protocol analyzer software. Using a modem link and remote communications software, it provides remote access and control of the Sniffer analyzer. This type of access is also available through other remote control software products, such as Carbon Copy and PC Anywhere.

The DSS is an innovative approach to protocol analysis. Rather than physically connecting a stand-alone unit to a LAN, the DSS integrates protocol analysis devices with a LAN. The DSS is ideal for multiple ring environments.

The DSS method is to implement monitoring devices on individual rings and then have those units capture, analyze, and communicate network data to a master monitoring console. This method provides a web effect, permitting protocol analysis on multiple rings to be monitored dynamically from one central point.

Network General's DSS product line has three main components: SniffMaster Consoles, Sniffer Servers, and DSS application software.

Sniffer Servers are placed on each ring as slaves and continuously monitor the statistics for that ring. They communicate across rings to the SniffMaster Console through bridges and routers. The SniffMaster Console acts as a client to the server and gathers the statistics from the Sniffer Servers. The DSS application software provides all the main Sniffer functions, with the addition of multiple ring statistics.

The Sniffer DSS product can be implemented with the Network General RMON tools that allow for internetwork access via SNMP to RMON MIB agents. The data can be imported into the Sniffer and RMON combination, which works with other SNMP managment systems such as HP Openview. Network General has also developed many strategic relationships with key industry vendors such Bay Networks to offer protocol analysis agents within internetwork devices such as the Bay 5000 hub. The new Bay 5000 now offers integrated Data Collection Engines (DCE)s within hub modules.

Because the actual analysis processing is done at each Sniffer Server, minimal data traffic is transmitted across the LAN to the SniffMaster Console. Figure 4.11 depicts an application for the DSS system.

The Sniffer analyzer's strengths are its full range of support for major multiple topologies and extensive protocol suite support.

Chapter 4: Optimization and Troubleshooting Tools 63

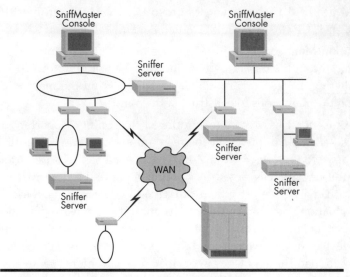

Figure 4.11 The DSS allows monitoring geographically dispersed networks from a central point.

Also, the DSS approach is significant because it creates a new niche in network protocol analysis by allowing protocols on internetworks to be analyzed from a central point.

Network General recently released a group of new product packages that support analysis for most WAN protocols including Packet Relay, HDLC, X.25, and SDLC. Network General also supplies a product that fully analyzes the FDDI topology.

Recently, Network General acquired the Protools company which was based in Beaverton, Oregon. The most significant product in the company acquisition was the ProTolyzer, which is now offered by Network General as Foundation Manager.

Foundation Manager is designed to run under the Microsoft Windows interface. The Foundation Manager Series products are based on the philosophy that a protocol analyzer should provide a proactive approach to LAN management. The tool is a software product that can be configured on certain recommended NICs. Foundation Manager can provide analysis of a complete local network or a combined LAN and WAN connection. Topologies supported include Token Ring (4Mbps and 16Mbps) and Ethernet. Protocol suites supported are IBM LAN Server, Microsoft LAN Manager, NetBIOS, SMB, Novell, 3Com, TCP/IP, AppleTalk, Digital, Banyan VINES, and XNS.

Foundation Manager offers basic modes of operation, capturing, decoding, and display through Icon access in Windows. The product incorporates all of the key filtering, triggering, and display features. From the main window, you can click on the main icons to construct path strands.

Network General has recently introduced the "Sniffer Reporter," a software module that allows a Sniffer user to create numerical and graphical reports on the data captured with the Sniffer Monitor and Analyzer. The Reporter software can interpret data that is saved in Comma-separated value format from the Sniffer analyzer. The Reporter then can save the data in a database format for further evaluation and manipulation. The analyst can now review the data and then plot certain key trends from the Expert system such as the amount of times different devices have a connection break symptom occur on the network. The Reporter can also intercept key workload measurements from the Monitor Global History program and chart key statistics such as utilization, protocol levels, and associated traffic rates. Figures 4.12 (a) and (b) depict some of the key Reporter screens. Aimed at network management concerns on LANs and WANs, the product offers a solution for integrating protocol analysis capabilities directly into overall internetwork operations.

Chapter 4: Optimization and Troubleshooting Tools 65

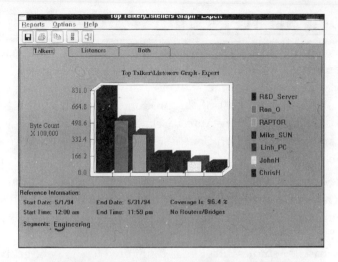

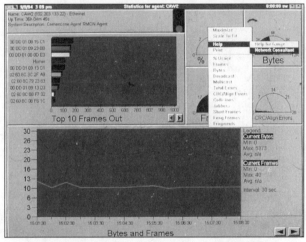

Figure 4.12 The Sniffer Reporter product.

Other key products from Network General include products such as OffNet Sniffer, which allows technical staff to read traces captured with a Sniffer offline on basic PCs. This product will assist technical support departments in multiple review cycles on trace data.

Network Strategies Inc. Auto-Baseliner

Network Strategies is a privately owned company in New York, that offers an excellent product for developing from the Network General Sniffer. As mentioned earlier, Network General offers many unique reporting capabilities along with its products. Most of the products are built within the Sniffer Monitor and Analyzer program. Auto Baseliner is a third-party software option that allows an analyst to import Sniffer standard CSV files for Microsoft Excel chart assembly on an automatic basis.

Network Strategies has developed a set of unique scripts that can be loaded onto the Network General Sniffer which allow for initial data acquisition into unique report styles. Next, the files can be imported into custom Excel macros that allow for viewing and printing a pallete of charts. The charts are all designed for baseline studies. The tool is configured to allow the analyst to pick certain monitoring periods that accommodate network baselining.

Once a certain time period is set up, the analyst can enter names for key addresses required in the report, or use Sniffer's built-in naming system. The product lets the analyst build the reports in a custom manual approach or it can build the reports independently off the Auto Print and Global History functions of the Sniffer Monitor. Once the report files are assembled, the CSV files can be imported into a PC with Microsoft Windows and Excel for Macro charting. Network Strategies offers a range of pre-configured charts including: Average Daily Rates, Error Rate Skyline, Average Daily Utilization Rate, Utilization Skylines, Protocol and Frame Size Distribution, Top Ten Traffic Transmitters, Receivers, and Error station views. The reports can be further customized with naming conventions for the network baselined.

The product is easy to use and makes reporting a snap. To actually locate and resolve a network problem may require in-depth study of trace data by a trained protocol analyst, but this product is excellent for network analysts and managers that require a way to easily report on network statistics gathered with the Network General Sniffer. A key screen from the AutoBaseliner is shown in Figure 4.13.

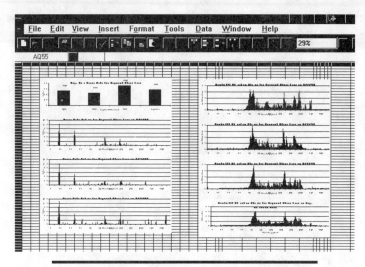

Figure 4.13 A key screen from the AutoBaseliner.

IBM Network Manager with Trace and Performance

IBM's contribution to the LAN analysis arena is really a composite of two IBM programs: LAN Manager or Network Manager and Trace and Performance. These tools are TokenRing specific.

The IBM Network Manager software was originally called IBM LAN Manager. IBM Network Manager enables you to monitor a single or multiple Token Ring network layout. It can gather a variety of network statistics and log them to a disk and a printer. The program has full Token Ring error-logging capabilities.

Trace and Performance includes the software package and an IBM Token Ring Trace and Performance Adapter. The Trace and Performance program consists of two utilities: the Trace facility and the Performance facility.

The Trace facility captures, decodes, and displays network data. The only protocol suites supported fully are IBM protocol suites, such as Token Ring MAC and LLC, NetBIOS, and IBM SNA.

ETHERNET AND TOKEN RING OPTIMIZATION

The Performance facility collects Token Ring statistics on network bandwidth utilization and allows for displaying, printing, or disk logging of the gathered data.

Figure 4.14 depicts the IBM Network Manager's main menu. It has full Token Ring event-logging capabilities. A ring configuration can be captured and viewed. Individual ring station

```
DFIPCP10                    IBM LAN MANAGER
Normal                         MAIN MENU

Select one of these functions:

ID  FUNCTION              DESCRIPTION

 1  EVENT LOG             Generate event log report or erase event log.
 2  SYSTEM DEFINITION     Display/set system options and definitions.
 3  ADAPTER FUNCTIONS     Query and remove adapters.
 4  NETWORK FUNCTIONS     Network status, path test, ring test.
 5  RING CONFIGURATION    Display order of adapters on ring.
 6  SOFT ERROR OPTIONS    Display/set soft error logging and conditions.
 7  BRIDGE FUNCTIONS      Link, unlink, query; set single-route broadcast.

 R  RESET                 Reinitialize system and reopen adapter.
 S  SHUTDOWN              Shutdown the LAN manager.

Type the ID of the function and press Enter ===> [ ]
```

Figure 4.14 The main menu of IBM's Network Manager for monitoring Token Ring networks.

statistics can be gathered down to the NIC microcode level. The program implements full Token Ring hard and soft error monitoring and logging features.

As Chapter 2 discussed, the original IBM LAN Manager program was designed to interact with all ring management servers to collect, analyze, and log statistical data about a complete Token Ring environment. Now the IBM Network Manager actually can query bridges in a multiple ring environment. That is, if a multiple ring environment is configured with multiple IBM Network Managers through bridges, a controlling Network Manager can be configured to gather statistics about the complete Token Ring internetwork.

The Trace and Performance program can display breakdown decodes of network data in total packets, MAC packet format, or LLC format. The program has some limited filtering and triggering features.

The only topology supported by both programs is Token Ring (4Mbps and 16Mbps). Obviously, both of these programs are Token Ring-only solutions but by combining both programs on the same PC, you can assemble a good protocol analyzer for a pure IBM-based Token Ring environment.

Telecommunications Techniques Corp. FireBerd and LANHAWK Analyzers

Telecommunications Techniques Corp. (TTC) was founded in the mid-1970s. The home office is located in Germantown, MD. The original products included data communication test equipment such as BERT testers. In the 1990s, TTC acquired several protocol analyzer products through the acquisition of LPCOM, a Tektronix subsidiary. The main product acquired, the SpiderAnalyzer product line, was reengineered and is now called the NetLens line.

Further development has produced Remote Monitoring (RMON) tools and high-end internetwork analyzers such as the FireBerd series analyzers. The other key developments have been in the FDDI topology with the acquisition of Digital Technology and the introduction of the FDDI LANHAWK.

The FireBerd product family has a full palette of protocol analyzer configurations, including standard stand-alone analyzers and complex multi-network configurations through the RMON NetLens probes.

The Fireberd 300 and 500 are high-end portable protocol analyzers that have the capability for a full window interface. The analyzer systems are based on a portable computer and weigh under 20 lbs. The Fireberd strengths include extensive decodes and built-in horsepower to allow for high-end filtering of data as captured. The system bus is designed for high-speed access at over 155Mbps which allows the individual NICs which are used for the topology to perform a high-end capture technique. The buffering capabilities are enhanced by over 1.5 MB of memory onboard each one of the NICs utilized for capture.

The FireBerd 300 and 500 analyzers are offered in preconfigured PCs that offer specialized processing design. The 500 unit is a multi-port analyzer that can function as the master analyzer in multi-port capturing configuration. The 300 unit offers the same capturing techniques, but is configured in a lower cost configuration, and can be upgraded to the full 500 capability. Both units can support the two main LAN topologies, Ethernet and Token Ring. A full

ETHERNET AND TOKEN RING OPTIMIZATION

connection to internetwork analysis capability can be achieved through the NetLens probes or RMON agent MIB collection schemes.

The protocol suite decode capability is extensive: IBM general suites, IBM SNA, NetBIOS, OS/2 IBMNM, SMB, Novell, XNS:MSNET, TCP/IP and SNMP, DECnet, Banyan VINES, AppleTalk, XNS, SUN:NFS, 3COM, ISO, X Windows, X.25, SDLC, Frame Relay, PPP,SMDS, ISDN, and HDLC.

FireBerd and NetLens analysis tools offer ease of use and excellent reporting features which are assisted through the Microsoft Windows interface. Figure 4.15 shows the TTC FireBerd Analyzer.

Figure 4.15 TTC FireBerd Analyzer.

Some of the strengths and applications for the Fireberd 500 are:

- Internetwork testing and frame relay network analysis
- Dual port anaylsis testing
- Simulation of ISDN primary rates

Chapter 4: Optimization and Troubleshooting Tools 71

The internetwork testing capabilities include the capability for the Fireberd 500 to be directly connected on both sides of a router and a T1 in a concurrent fashion. This allows for two views of data flow on the WAN and LAN side in composite. Basically, this allows the Fireberd 500 to have a two-view-port analysis of LAN and WAN traffic. In this particular application, two analysis test points can be engaged to examine issues such as WAN traffic levels, LAN-to-WAN encapsulation and LAN-to-WAN traffic differences.

The frame relay network analysis strengths include full byte error rate testing (BERT), the capability to fully emulate a management interface and to insure that the proper polling processing. The frame relay decodes are extensive and the capability for a full emulation of frame relay is built within the FireBerd for packet transmission concerns.

Dual port analysis allows multi-port capability, which provides a complete independent analysis of two individual networks. For example, with two WAN modules, one side of the network with a T1 direct circuit can be monitored in conjunction with analysis of a SMDS link. This allows for two WAN circuits to be looked at in a two-viewport view.

Regarding the ISDN primary rate analysis, full capabilities are built in for decoding. Specifically, the Fireberd can be connected to emulate a full D channel link and also provide BERT testing on an NXB channel. This allows for the 500 to perform full ISDN primary rate emulation as either a network termination or terminal equipment connection. When emulating a network termination connection, the Fireberd 500 can check the network by placing a call into a full PBX channel, then analyze whether or not the PBX is performing a correction operation. This tool capability to be put in a multiple test configuration for LAN and WAN studies in a concurrent fashion makes it one of the more stronger internetwork analyzers in the industry.

With the TTC acquisition of the LANHAWK FDDI analyzer product line, the company now offers an excellent set of FDDI tools. The 5750 LANHAWK tool is based on a center tool analyzer and a tower pickup tool design. High-speed multiple processors are utilized to increase performance when supporting a full FDDI bandwidth level. The tools can analyze FDDI line states and capture on four FDDI rings in concurrent mode. Full analysis is available for the FDDI Station Management Layer (SMT) and all required Upper layer Protocols.

Wandel & Goltermann's DominoLAN Internetwork and WAN Analyzers

Wandel & Goltermann is known as a manufacturer of high-end network analyzers. The North Carolina company is best known for the DA30 analyzer. The DA30, which has been utilized for quite some time by development departments and engineering departments, is geared toward engineering and does not offer some of the new user-friendly techniques that some Windows-based analyzers currently offer.

Recently, W&G released the DominoLAN Internetwork and WAN analyzers. These two tools offer a Microsoft Windows-based interface. They have the capability for multi- topology LAN and WAN analysis. The filtering techniques are excellent through most of the protocol suite layers. Auto configuration capabilities are built into the tool, which is lightweight and highly portable. The DominoLAN analyzer tool set is broken into two specific products: the Internetwork DA-320 analyzer and the WAN DA-310 analyzer.

The DominoLAN Internetwork Analyzer offers a complete analysis solution. It weighs less than 3 lbs. and actually sits under a notebook computer. The device then connects to the notebook computer via the parallel port. If daisychain techniques are employed, internetwork analysis on both Token Ring and Ethernet networks can be performed concurrently. The DominoLAN analyzer has the capability to allow any notebook analyzer that runs the Windows interface to be the controlling main unit for the tool. Due to the footprint size of the DA-320, the tool actually can be transported fairly easily with a notebook computer. The Windows interface on the notebook computer has the capability to control the monitoring, capturing and decoding of network traffic. W&G has included a set of applications that run under Windows that allow for high-end monitoring of workload characterizations. Some of the built-in interfaces include full traffic monitoring and network application characterization.

The protocol suite is extensive for the internetwork analyzer. The following protocols are included: 802.3 MAC, 802.5 MAC, LLC, LLC2; TCP/IP; UDP; OSPF, TFTP, SMTP; SNMP, TELNET, FTP, PPP, ARP, IPX, SPX, NCP, ISO, HDLC, SDLC, SMB, SNA, QLLC, NetBios, SUN, DECNET Complete, X.25, Frame

Chapter 4: Optimization and Troubleshooting Tools

Relay, S.75, LAPB, LAPD, CISCO SLE, AppleTalk Complete Suite, VINES, XNS, SMDS.

Of the features that the DominoLAN Internetwork Analyzers offers, the following are key:

- Monitor
- Capture
- Examine
- Transmit

In Monitor mode, the tool can provide a full overview of the internetwork traffic flow, including protocol distribution, frame size utilization charts, error statistics, graphical, and other statistical formats.

In Capture mode, particular icon access via Windows allows for full configuration of active capturing.

Examine mode allows for a detailed view based on how the capture techniques are configured. This mode will allow for summary breakout of frame overviews, combination of protocol fields and viewing formats. The display features are strong with this tool. Time stamp analysis is available for absolute, relative and delta interframe gap timing. The capability to search throughout the trace is built within for character strings, hex strings, patterns of particular data, and protocol types.

The full set of data that is captured with this tool can be imported into a full Common Separated Value CSV format and then imported into multiple spreadsheet charting programs, including Excel and Lotus 1-2-3. The tool has built-in macros that are designed for the key charting programs.

The tool also has the capability through icon access to transmit data onto the network. This can be useful for network ICMP echo ping commands, for frame generation related to traffic loading techniques, and also for replaying certain capture buffers for application characterization.

The filters, which are built-in, are smart for both Token Ring and Ethernet, and the tool includes a strong route discovery feature for Token Ring source routing-based networks.

The DominoWAN Analyzer also provides the same type of footprint. It is a separate tool which again has the same platform as the Domino Internetwork 320. The WAN analyzer is labeled as the DA-310. It also sits under a laptop computer and links to the parallel port. This tool also uses the same type of interface as the 320, including Microsoft Windows as a user interface. The WAN analyzer has the capability to decode most required major protocols and generate network traffic on WAN links. It has the capability to strip off key encapsulation layers that may be involved on the WAN link. Specifically, if there are any concerns relating to transmissions and applied overhead, these data fields can be separated from the trace analysis standpoint. Again, the DominoWAN analyzer has the capability to be controlled through most notebook computers that can run the standard Windows-based interface.

Built-in application software allows for analysis for key WAN circuit techniques. Features include analysis for X.25, frame relay traffic, and full BERT functionalities built within the tool. Key applications involve WAN bandwidth monitoring through the LAN Link monitor tool, which allows LAN utilization to be compared to WAN utilization.

The Internetwork 320 and WAN 310 analyzers can be combined for innovative analysis test points. Specifically, both the LAN and WAN can be monitored together through a combination of these tools. The capability for the LAN Link monitor within the DA-310 to also monitor LAN statistics from the WAN link allows for an excellent comparison. Network performance can also be monitored for new routers and bridges through compliance testing built into the tool.

The network interfaces include RS232/V.24, V.35, RS-449/V.36, RS- 530, and V.11. The Icon access is comparable to the internetwork analyzer's full monitor/capture/examine and transmit capabilities.

One of the strengths of this tool is the frame relay application analysis capability, including the capability to emulate a frame relay network, measure frame relay performance, then perform monitoring and surveillance at the frame relay link. CIR and other key statistics can be picked up and monitored. Full capability for monitoring and surveillance of X.25 networks is also built.

It should also be noted that W&G has also released a small transportable FDDI domino analyzer. Most FDDI tools are large in general form factor and hard to transport on a portable basis. The new W&G DA-330 is a full blown FDDI internetwork analyzer. The tool is fully portable and allows for quick diagnosis of FDDI network health and traffic levels. The tool has the ability to connect with both the Single Attachment Station (SAS) and Dual Attachment Station approach. It can capture all Station Management Layer (SMT) protocol operations and full decodes are available for Beacon and Claim frame types.

The Domino analyzers (Figure 4.16) support the most notebook connections in the industry. Standard, bidirectional and enhanced parallel port communication can be utilized for performance concerns. One of the strengths of the tool is the built-in high-end architecture. Due to the fact that the W&G Domino analyzers are actually separate tools and are not actually loaded on a standard notebook, high-end RISC processors can be built into the design. The built-in RISC processing with high-speed links to processors allows for full frame capture without loss of any packet traffic analysis.

Figure 4.16 The Domino analyzers.

Azure Technologies LANPharaoh Scope

Azure Technologies, founded in 1987, is based in Hopkinton, Massachusetts. This company is dedicated to the LAN and WAN analyzer marketplace. All the Azure NICs are based on RISC technology.

The Azure analyzer product lines are designed to support the Ethernet, Token Ring, Coax, Twinax, and WAN topology layouts. The specific product that Azure offers for the Token Ring and Ethernet marketplace is LANPharaoh. The Azure WAN analyzer product is called WANPharaoh, and supports all major WAN protocols.

ETHERNET AND TOKEN RING OPTIMIZATION

LANPharaoh for Token Ring and Ethernet is a full-blown protocol analyzer. The product comes packaged as a hardware-and-software kit. The Token Ring and Ethernet NIC is based on a full 20 MHz, 10 Mips RISC processor. The board alone has 1MB of on-board RAM to handle a 100% capture of all the data present on a network.

The product offers analysis of all the major Token Ring and Ethernet statistics. LANPharaoh enables you to view all the errors on a Token Ring and Ethernet network, including CRC and TR soft errors against their respective address. The Token Ring and Ethernet errors can be viewed in an effective subcategory screen.

The current protocol suites supported by LANPharoah are as follows:

- BM full suites
- IBM SNA
- SMB
- NetBIOS
- Novell:Full
- TCP:IP
- DECnet
- DOD
- Banyan
- AppleTalk
- XNS

The main menu of the Token Ring LANPharaoh enables you to view a ring as a full ring, a filtered ring, or just bridge traffic. All the LANPharaoh displays are straightforward; the protocol decode menus are easy to use. The LANPharaoh menu interface now works under the Windows environment.

Azure recently added the capability to analyze multiple networks within one single analysis session. This feature, called DuoTrak, enables you to monitor, decode, and analyze data for two Token Ring or Ethernet networks at the same time. This feature is further strengthened with the capability of viewing two sides of a network bridge at the same time. This is a useful testing approach for analyzing the source routing operation in Token Ring bridged environments.

The LANPharaoh scopes appear to be leaders in the marketplace. The use of sophisticated NICs, coupled with excellent filtering and triggering features, allows for a thorough Token Ring and Ethernet analysis session.

FTP Software's LANWatch Network Analyzer

FTP Software Inc., a Massachusetts-based company founded in 1986. is known for developing reliable, sophisticated PC networking software at reasonable prices. The company is dedicated to supporting open architectures for the LAN marketplace. This review concentrates on the company's LAN analyzer, called LANWatch.

LANWatch Network Analyzer is a software-only product that relies on the user having a specific type of hardware. The software package requires a PC with an FTP-supported, topology-specific NIC.

LANWatch Network Analyzer supports the following topologies: Token Ring 4Mbps (FTP is currently working on support for 16Mbps), Proteon's ProNET-10, and Ethernet.

The protocol suites supported are as follows:

- Novell
- TCP/IP
- UDP
- ICMP
- DECnet
- NFS
- Banyan VINES
- XNS
- CHAOSNET
- ISO
- X.25
- SMB
- SNMP
- AppleTalk

ETHERNET AND TOKEN RING OPTIMIZATION

LANWatch Network Analyzer has two basic modes of operation: Real Time Display and Examine. Real Time Display mode captures and displays a chronological list of network packets dynamically as they are captured. Multiple display modes are available for all seven OSI layers.

Examine mode allows the network packets captured during Real Time Display mode to be decoded and examined. Captured data can be displayed in two modes, Short and Long. The Short mode gives an overall list of packets received. The Long mode shows detailed information for a selected packet. Figure 4.17 shows LANWatch's Examine Long mode screen.

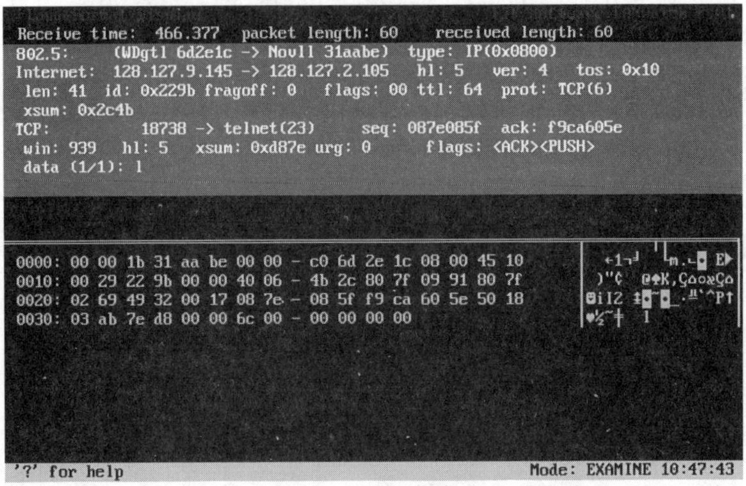

Figure 4.17 LANWatch analyzer includes an Examine Long mode screen, which gives detailed information about an individual captured packet.

LANWatch Network Analyzer has a good set of filtering, triggering, and alarm features that enable you to modify the Real Time Display and Examine modes for optimal viewing and decoding. By keying a question mark (?) at any of the main modes, you can enter the LANWatch Help main menu, which guides you through most of the custom setup features that you will need.

LANWatch has a histogram feature that can capture, display, and record packets captured and general network traffic statistics. The package also includes statistics gathering for most network errors, including Ethernet CRC, collisions, and Token Ring MAC soft errors.

FTP offers a programmer's aid that enables you to develop custom protocol decodes, filters, printing routines, and report generators. FTP is also working on new developments such as auto-print report generation and network bandwidth monitoring. Currently, the LANWatch Network Analyzer's main focus is to provide capture and decode capabilities for most major protocols and topologies. The complete protocol analysis capabilities of LANWatch and its cost-effectiveness give the LAN analyst a good reason to consider this product.

Triticom's LANdecoder and LANVision Monitors

Founded in 1989, Triticom, a company based in St. Paul, Minnesota, designs and markets high-quality LAN monitoring, management, and modeling products, including LANdecoder/tr, LANdecoder/e, TokenVision, EtherVision, and ArcVision.

LANdecoder products are software-only protocol analyzers that currently supports Token Ring and Ethernet. LANdecoder can be loaded on a variety of PC platforms, including PCMCIA as specified by Triticom. It also requires a high-performance NIC. LANdecoder offers a full seven-layer protocol decode for the Token Ring or Ethernet topology and includes decodes for the following protocols:

- IEEE 802.2
- IEEE 802.3
- IEEE 802.5
- MAC LLC XNS
- PEP TCP/IP
- Full NetBIOS Novell
- Full NetWare Lite

The product offers full trace file conversions to other major protocol analyzer formats, such as the Network General Sniffer. Thus, you can capture a file with LANdecoder and then import the file to a Network General Sniffer for further analysis. This is helpful if you capture a protocol that the LANdecoder cannot fully decode.

LANdecoder includes comprehensive capture filters and triggers. The product supports full symbolic naming for address monitoring. LANdecoder decodes most NIC manufacture codes for easy viewing of the vendor code. Traffic Generation features make the job of loading a Token Ring or Ethernet network during a LANdecoder analysis session more manageable.

LANdecoder is a powerful protocol analyzer for the software category. If configured with a high-performance promiscuous mode NIC, LANdecoder offers excellent performance. The menu system is superb.

LANdecoder includes a full group of monitoring features for major Token Ring and Ethernet statistics. These are the same features that Triticom includes in the LANVision product line, described next.

LANVision Monitor is precisely that: a Token Ring and Ethernet network monitoring tool. Designed specifically for Token Ring and Ethernet topology, LANVision Monitor monitors and displays all major Token Ring and Ethernet environmental statistics.

LANVision also is a software product for which the user must have specific types of PC hardware with a Triticom-supported Token Ring and Ethernet NIC. LANVision runs on most promiscuous Token Ring NICs.

LANVision is a monitoring tool; it does not function as a protocol analyzer, so it does not identify and display high-level protocol suites. Only certain pertinent MAC types are identified.

The LANVision Monitor has a user-friendly menuing system; Figure 4.18 shows its main menu.

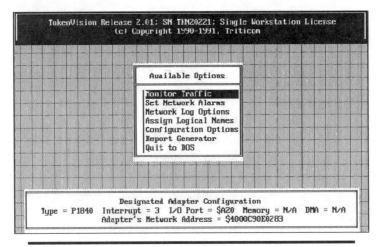

Figure 4.18 The main menu of Triticom's LANVision Monitor.

Chapter 4: Optimization and Troubleshooting Tools

The LANVision Monitor uses one main operational mode, Monitor Traffic mode, the first choice on the main menu. The other menu choices are as follows:

- Set Network Alarms
- Network Log Options
- Assign Logical Names
- Configuration Options
- Report Generator
- Quit to DOS

These choices are for configuring the main operating environment. Monitor Traffic mode is based on four real-time display modes for viewing the traffic being captured, as follows:

- Statistic mode. Shows an extensive view of all Token Ring and Ethernet statistics
- Skyline mode. Displays a skyline graphical view of network bandwidth utilization or packet count statistics
- Station mode. Traces packets sent from individual stations
- MAC mode. Displays an overall information screen about captured MAC packets

After you enter Monitor Traffic Mode, you can vector into any of the Real Time Display Modes for viewing the network traffic.

All the Real Time Display Modes interrelate to show a synergistic and chronological list of network packets dynamically, as they are captured. Multiple display modes are available by packet and individual stations.

Station Mode shows the full variety of station-to-packet statistics, such as total packet count, total kilobytes, average packet size, and number of soft errors. Statistic Mode is a plus in that it displays a total overview of the network and shows important Token Ring and Ethernet statistics, such as source-routing information.

MAC mode is an excellent Token Ring and Ethernet feature that displays critical Token Ring and Ethernet information such as CRC errors, collisions, Active Monitor MAC packets, Ring Recovery packets, and a full detailed Token Ring Soft Error MAC packet report. Figure 4.19 shows the MAC Mode screen.

82 ETHERNET AND TOKEN RING OPTIMIZATION

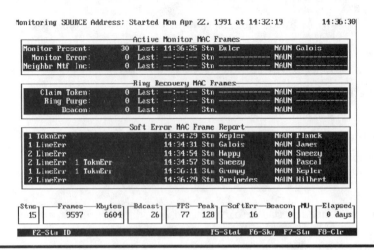

Figure 4.19 LANVision Monitor MAC mode includes information about CRC, collisions, Active Monitor, Ring Recovery, and Soft Error MAC packets.

The Set Network Alarm feature permits the LANVision monitor to dispatch alarms when specific network events happen.

A troubleshooting aid, the Network Log Options feature maintains an event log of major network events such as monitor traffic mode ON and OFF, errors, alarms, and peak network utilization. You can set up this log to be sent dynamically to a disk file or printer. The important part of this feature is that you can set up your network testing environment, and then let the testing statistics be saved automatically.

The Assign Logical Names feature enables you to assign specific Token Ring addresses with symbolic names. The Configuration Options feature is for setting up additional alarm features.

A new feature is the Report Generator, which has report-generating features for the Token Ring and Ethernet environment. Statistics that can be generated include Packet Distribution, Global Network Summaries, Network Utilization, Individual Station Statistics, Station Bandwidth, and Logical Name Assignments. You can print most of the viewable statistics in various formats and feed them into several popular PC report applications.

Triticom has recently introduced a series of new products that enhance the LANdecoder and LANVision product lines. These products include MasteRMON, a full SNMP montoring toolset that is compatable with Microsoft Windows, and the DecodesPLUS product line, which offers add-on decodes for Banyan VINES, DECnet, SMB and NetBIOS protocols the integrate with

Chapter 4: Optimization and Troubleshooting Tools

Novell's NMS and LANalyzer systems. Triticom offers cross-market support with other analyzer manufactures

Triticom's LANdecoder and LANVision products are solid analysis and monitoring tools for the Token Ring and Ethernet topologies. Their key functions are easy to use, and the screen displays are easy to understand.

Network Communications Corp. (NCC) LAN Network Probe

LANalyzer was originally designed by Excelan in 1984. In 1989, Novell acquired Excelan, and in 1990 formed a separate internal division called the LANalyzer Products Division, which developed and marketed network monitoring and management products. Novell licensed the LANalyzer product technology to Network Communications Corp. (NCC) in Bloomington, Minnesota. NCC has renamed the product line LAN Network Probe.

NCC has developed an additional product line that includes remote monitoring through RMON Probes which work with the stand-alone LAN Network Probe . Specifically, the RMON Probes can focus on remote monitoring and management of multiple LANs from a central point.

The LAN Network Probe is a full-blown high-performance protocol analyzer. This product offers full decoding for most major protocol suites and can interface with most topologies.

You can buy LAN Network Probe from NCC in an NIC-and-software kit package and configure it in your own PC. Some resellers offer the LAN Network Probe kit preconfigured in selected portable PCs.

The LAN Network Probe supports the following topologies:

- Token Ring (4Mbps and 16Mbps)
- Ethernet

The protocol suites supported are as follows:

- IBM SNA
- NetBIOS
- SMB
- Novell (including decodes for 2.X, 3.X, and 4.X)

ETHERNET AND TOKEN RING OPTIMIZATION

- TCP/IP
- DECnet
- Banyan VINES
- AppleTalk
- XNS
- SUN:NFS
- ISO
- NCP Burst
- EGP
- NIS
- DNS
- ISIS
- SBP
- AFP2.1
- SNMPv1 and v2

LAN Probe executes all the basic modes of operation, with a user-friendly menu system. From the main menu you can maneuver to other submenus. Figure 4.20 shows the main menu.

Figure 4.20 The main menu of LAN Network Probe provides access to the application suites for analysis of various protocols.

Chapter 4: Optimization and Troubleshooting Tools

The Application menu is the main entry point for setting up the LAN Network Probe capturing mode, concerning all selections for protocol suites, filters, triggers, alarms, and so on. From the Application menu, you can either choose and configure custom applications test suites, or you can pick one of the predefined Token Ring or Ethernet application test suites.

LAN Probe is designed so that you can activate a particular application test suite that has predefined triggers, filters, and other custom setup parameters. An innovative feature in the LAN Network Probe setup parameters allows you to define up to nine custom receive channels. Receive channels are the actual filter channels for what you want to capture during a protocol analysis session. LAN Network Probe also has six custom transmit channels, which enable you to generate six selective traffic patterns onto the network.

The Edit Current Application menu option enables you to dynamically modify the original parameters for the current application test suite. From its submenu, you can specify certain data collection parameters, such as the main statistics disk-logging file and printing options. LAN Network Probe does not offer any custom report-generation features, but statistics files can be imported into various PC applications.

The Run Current Application menu option simply activates the current application test suite selected in the main Application menu. When it is activated, you are sub-vectored to the main network monitoring display modes.

The following four main modes for displaying the network environment can be selected:

- Global Display mode. This mode gives you a detailed screen that displays network utilization statistics in a blended graphical and numerical format. This screen also displays vital Token Ring or Ethernet statistics such as CRC, collisions, Ring Recoveries, and Token Rotation Time (see Figure 4.21).

- Rate Display mode. This mode displays statistical information about the individual packets received through the receive channels.

- Utilization Display mode. This gives a universal depiction of the network bandwidth being used by any active channels.

- Station Display mode. This displays statistics on an individual station's interaction with the active channels being monitored.

86 ETHERNET AND TOKEN RING OPTIMIZATION

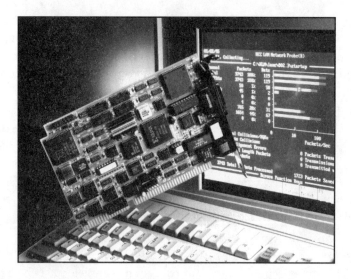

Figure 4.21 LAN Probe Global Display mode depicts overall network statistics in both graphic and numeric formats.

The Display Packet Trace menu enables you to view captured packets in an overall chronological packet list or in detailed packet view. From this mode, you can load previously captured traces from disk or view the current captured trace. You also can save a current trace to disk. The Display Packet Trace mode has individual setup parameters for most decoding needs.

The Test Network Cabling menu option enables you to perform a series of network tests, including a basic cable test, LAN Network Probe connection status, and ring condition status tests to detect failures such as beaconing.

The Utilities menu option activates a submenu that includes the following four LAN Network Probe utilities for performing certain tasks to further customize how you use a particular application test suite:

- Name utility. This enables you to assign names to specific Token Ring or Ethernet addresses.
- Genname utility. This NCC-related feature automatically generates a name file for a set of specific node addresses on a network.
- Stats utility. This enables you to view a previously saved file from an application test in the main display modes.
- Template utility. This enables you to further customize how the main transmit and receive channels are configured.

Chapter 4: Optimization and Troubleshooting Tools

In the Configure LAN Network Probe menu, you can configure the main operating environment for the LAN Network Probe. This feature enables you to configure the network topology type, file buffer options, disk-logging routes, and alarm parameters.

LAN Network Probe has some Token Ring and Ethernet strengths. An automatic mapping feature (MAP) dynamically generates all the Token Ring and Ethernet network nodes in chronological order. NCC includes a special application test suite called ERRMON that is configured for the receive channels to capture a specific Token Ring and Ethernet error. Another application test suite called SEGMENTS dynamically monitors Token Ring and Ethernet bridge traffic.

One of LAN Network Probe's main advantages are the custom application test suites shown is Figure 4.22. NCC includes with LAN Network Probe some excellent predefined application test suites designed specifically for the Token Ring or Ethernet architecture. With some ingenuity, you can even customize special, unique tests for the Token Ring or Ethernet environment. Another point for the LAN Network Probe is its capability to dynamically handle routing of multiple transmit and receive channels.

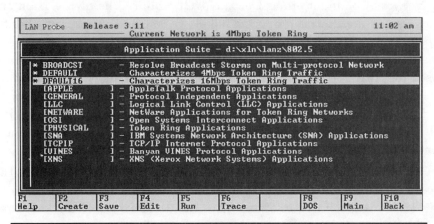

Figure 4.22 The main menu of the LAN Network Probe application test suites provides the capability to predefine specific testing for various Token Ring or Ethernet network problems.

NCC has made the LAN Network Probe extremely cost-effective by including most of the major protocol suites at no additional cost. This product has powerful performance, in combination with excellent statistics-gathering features. The menuing system is well-designed and simple to operate.

For the record, NCC's newest software release for the LAN Network Probe offers Post-Filtering, which enables data capture filters to be set up prior to the analysis. The reporting features incorporate macro creation utilities for Excel and Lotus 1-2-3. Full historical charting can be performed for utilization levels, packet per second rates, error levels, and protocol percentages. The LAN Network Probe is an excellent baselining analyzer. NCC also has added some artificial intelligence to the LAN Network Probe with an Automated Troubleshooting System that assists the user with troubleshooting steps. Te newest release is now available in a palmtop system that packs all the power and features of the larger platform.

Novell LANalyzer for Windows 2.X Software Analyzer

In the mid-1990s, when Novell's hardware LANalyzer platform was acquired by Network Communications Corp., Novell produced its own version of a software LANalyzer. This product, a full-blown software analyzer that has the capability to work on multiple Token Ring and Ethernet NIC platforms, is labeled the LANalyzer for Windows. The LANalyzer is a Microsoft Windows-based tool that allows for monitoring and analyzing network traffic in the Ethernet and Token Ring environments. Traffic can be analyzed on a periodic basis for troubleshooting and baselining concerns. Robust techniques built into this tool allow network baselining to be a snap for most network managers. Some of the screens utilized in this tool are extremely network-friendly.

One of the LANalyzer's strengths is monitoring for network statistics. This type of analysis can be performed in the LANalyzer standard dashboard screen. This screen is illustrated in Figure 4.23. The dashboard screen allows for a graphical view of packet-per-second rate, utilization levels and error-per-second rate views. This screen runs in an gauge type format and lets network managers clearly see problems when they start to occur. For example, if network utilization levels go to a high point on the gauge, this might show concurrently on the packet-per-second rate and error rate gauges.

Chapter 4: Optimization and Troubleshooting Tools

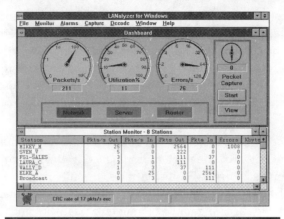

Figure 4.23 LANalyzer standard dashboard screen.

The LANalyzer also includes a Windows screen which provides individual statistics. Called the station monitor, this screen allows an analyst to view key statistics for stations connected to a certain network.

The user's ability to stop the analyzer and review network trace data is made simple through the analyzing network operation features. The decode screen is simple to use. Data can be displayed in the summary window, decode window, or full hexadecimal format. The performance that is achieved through this tool in relation to packet capture really depends on the platform and how the tool is configured. Novell recommends a high-end PC with certain memory configurations, and only authorizes certain types of NICs as being usable to achieve performance. As long as the Novell directions are properly followed, this tool does seem to be fully comparable to most high-end analyzers.

Protocols offered via the LANalyzer for Windows 2.X versions include the full Novell protocol suite 2X, 3X and 4X, Appletalk Protocol Suite, TCP/IP protocol suite and others. LANalyzer decode support is available from third-party manufacturers such as Triticom. Triticom offers a set of extra decodes through the Decodes Plus product which can be used for protocol suites that Novell is not currently offering.

Some of the robust features within the analysis mode allow for full network view on the dashboard, but then a breakout can be performed on a detailed station monitor. Specific stations can be queried for statistics related to their exact traffic flow on a node-by-node configuration. Statistics can be captured and displayed for key views of global traffic such as packets per second, packets average, packets peak, packets total, broadcast rates per second and multicast rates. The LANalyzer also offers a built-in full reporting capability. Real Time statistics can be brought out to the detailed packet windows, and legends can be configured for utilization over time periods. These types of technical screens related to graphical configuration can also be charted in a historical mode to most spreadsheet charting applications. Files that are captured with the LANalzyer for Windows can be imported into a CSV format.

One of this tool's strengths is the capability for the physical layer analysis in both the Ethernet and Token Ring environments. In the Ethernet environment, CRC errors, frame size errors, collision rates, fragmentation errors and jabber errors can be clearly monitored. In the Token Ring environment, the tool can also monitor full, nonisolating and isolating error statistics and capture Beacons upon demand. Decode is again extensive due to the capability to view in a summary, detail and hexadecimal format. The tool's capability to filter on certain stations makes it similar to some hardware analyzers. The tool also provides the ability for real time network view on a high-end graphical interface, packaged along with the capability to trend data in the reporting monitoring mode.

Dolphin Networks ESP Family of Protocol Analyzers

Dolphin Networks was originally called Dolphin Software. The Norcross, Georgia company was acquired by Dynatech Corp in 1991.

Two protocol analyzer product lines are offered by Dolphin Networks: the Dolphin Expert System Protocol (ESP) analyzer, and the Dolphin ESP Plus analyzer.

The Dolphin ESP analyzer is a powerful protocol analyzer that works on Ethernet, ARCnet, and 4/16Mbps Token Ring. The ESP is a hardware-and-software kit that includes an NIC for the specific topology and applied software. The package requires at least a 386 PC with 4MB of memory.

The current protocol suites supported are:

- IBM Suites
- SMB
- NetBIOS

- Novell
- TCP/IP
- Banyan
- AppleTalk
- XNS
- ISO

The main menu of the Dolphin ESP enables you to start a new analysis session through the open menu option. You can capture, analyze, and replay any captured data traces from the same menu. Dolphin ESP's menu system displays a series of main menu alternate function keys from which you can access a group of optional menu windows for configuring and customizing the analysis testing environment.

Dolphin ESP can fully capture 100% of a data trace direct to disk. The ESP offers real-time displays for all the major Token Ring and Ethernet network traffic statistics. The product also includes an Expert Alerts System that enables the user to set thresholds and to be alerted when a set threshold is exceeded.

Dolphin's ESP Plus comes preconfigured on a 486DX/50MHz EISA custom platform PC, and is now offered in a PCMCIA version for laptop users. ESP Plus supports a full seven-layer decode for the Ethernet, ARCnet, Token Ring, and FDDI topologies. The unit can support up to 32MB of RAM and 27GB of disk storage. The ESP Plus product can decode over 140 protocols. The filtering and triggering processes are easy to use and yet are comprehensively detailed.

This powerful tool can monitor two networks simultaneously and store data interactively for quite a long time without missing a packet. ESP Plus is intended for the serious analyst.

Digilog LANVista

CXR/Digilog is a subsidiary of the CXR Corp., which develops communication and test equipment. Digilog was formed in 1969 and specializes in communication test equipment and network management products. Recently, Digilog introduced the LANVista protocol analysis product line.

The LANVista analyzer product family has a full array of protocol analyzer configurations. It includes both standard stand-alone analyzers and distributed systems. The stand-alone product is offered as a board/software package for

ETHERNET AND TOKEN RING OPTIMIZATION

configuring within your own PC, or preconfigured in a Dolch or Compaq portable PC.

Digilog markets the LANVista systems in a 100 and 200 series. The 200 series is the same as the 100 series except that it is designed to support a larger database and distributed systems. With its capability to be upgraded to the series 200, the low-cost 100 series offers a single segment, stand-alone LAN analysis alternative for small and mid-sized network configurations. The 200 series can accomplish advanced precapture filtering and support multiple protocol suites simultaneously.

The distributed LANVista system's core mission is to view monitored data from one central point with LANs dispersed across complex networks. Obviously, another manufacturer has caught on to the need for observing LANs from a central point.

Digilog implements its distributed system through a master/slave design scheme. The slave units are self-contained units with full capture and analysis capabilities. The master unit is a PC with a Master Interface Card (MIC) and software designed to continuously gather and decode statistics from the slaves and then provide a real-time overview of the internetwork environment.

The slave units can communicate with a master unit through two different methods: by the internetwork itself, or by RS232 links. The RS232 links allow for a fault-redundant backup path between the master and slave units in the event of a LAN segment failure.

The LANVista analyzer products are designed for the Token Ring (4Mbps and 16Mbps) and Ethernet topologies. The current protocol suites supported are as follows:

- IBM SNA
- SMB
- NetBIOS
- Novell
- TCP/IP (DOD)
- DECNet
- XNS:MSNET
- Banyan VINES
- AppleTalk

Chapter 4: Optimization and Troubleshooting Tools

- SNMP
- ISO
- 3Com's NBP

The basic modes of operation for the LANVista analyzer are listed on the main menu shown in Figure 4.24. They include the following:

- Configure
- Monitor Segment
- Network Management
- Simulate Traffic
- Test LAN Cable
- Examine Packets
- Run Diagnostics
- Modify Password
- Quit LANVista

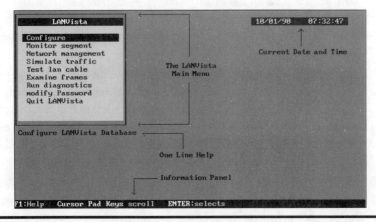

Figure 4.24 The basic protocol-analyzer modes of operation are accessible from the main menu of the LANVista analyzer.

Configure mode enables you to set the analysis operating environment. With this feature, you can set up the network type, the protocols to decode, filtering, the capture buffers, and all the custom configurations for the distributed system, if it is being implemented.

Monitor Segment mode enables you to initiate capturing and decoding of network data for protocol analysis. Also, in this mode, you can configure triggering, alarms, additional filtering, and disk or printer logging routes. Most of the statistics that you can capture can be printed in various forms.

Network Management mode enables you to view statistical information on the performance of the LANs being monitored. Statistics are available for Token Ring or Ethernet functional addresses, individual nodes, bridge utilization, protocols, packets, and network utilization parameters.

Generating traffic onto the LAN for troubleshooting purposes can be done through the Simulate Traffic mode. The Test LAN Cable mode includes some of the basic TDR functions. Examine Packets mode enables you to view captured packets in a packet list format or in detailed packet breakdown (decode) mode. From Examine Packets mode, you can view the protocols at all layers.

With all LANVista configurations, the slaves can be tested with the Run Diagnostic mode. The diagnostics enable you to test and verify the LANVista hardware and software configuration, run internal board diagnostics, and test and verify the communications path to all attached slaves.

LANVista analyzer has excellent security features built into the core operations, including enhanced security features in the LANVista analyzer. Three basic modes are available for entering the main menu: Administrative (Admin), Secure, and User.

Admin mode allows for overall LANVista operations, including the initial designing of the master/slave configurations for a distributed system. Secure mode allows for all operations except setting up master/slave parameters. User mode allows most LANVista operations, but does not allow the user to enter the Examine Packets mode or the Simulate Traffic mode, or to modify any master/slave parameters. Through Modify Password mode, you can update the Administrative and Secure mode passwords.

LANVista analyzer has excellent Token Ring and Ethernet monitoring features. In reference to Token Ring, Digilog has included a Token Ring Statistics (TRSTATS) monitoring screen from which you can view vital Token Ring statistics, such as beacon packets, Ring Purge packets, MAC and non-MAC packet breakdowns, errors, and network utilization bandwidth for local and multiple ring environments. The TRSTATS screen is shown in Figure 4.25.

LANVista screens are fully compatible with Microsoft Windows, an excellent feature for integrating with a distributed system when you need to view multiple networks from a master console.

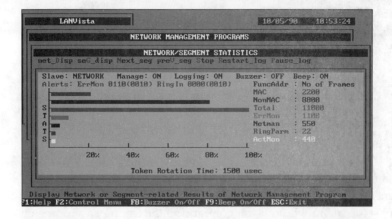

Figure 4.25 The LANVista Token Ring Statistics screen displays vital Token Ring and Ethernet network statistics.

Because of its thorough approach to protocol analysis features and its distributed system capabilities, LANVista is an excellent analysis product for both basic and extensive Token Ring and Ethernet installations. One of its best features is the available security attributes, which can play a major role when you are implementing a distributed system in a multiple network environment.

Hewlett-Packard Network Advisor

Hewlett-Packard has long been a leader in the test equipment arena. It is no surprise that HP has also entered the LAN protocol analyzer market with the recent introduction of its Network Advisor protocol analyzer.

The Network Advisor has a unique feature called the Finder Expert System. This innovative, artificial intelligence system analyzes captured data from a protocol analysis session and gives logical suggestions as to a general analysis of the network communication processes. It also can identify possible causes of failure for any network errors encountered during an analyzer session.

The HP Network Advisor is a self-contained stand-alone unit based on RISC architecture. Currently, the Network Advisor product is designed for the Token Ring (4Mbps and 16Mbps) and Ethernet topologies.

The current protocol suites supported are as follows:

- IBM SNA

ETHERNET AND TOKEN RING OPTIMIZATION

- SMB
- NetBIOS
- Novell
- TCP/IP
- DECnet
- 3Com
- XNS

The main menu of the Network Advisor has graphical displays of a series of main menu control windows from which you access the Control, Config, and Display setup menu windows for configuring the testing environment.

The Network Advisor can display vital Token Ring or Ethernet statistics with unique gauge-type displays that show dynamically occurring network measurements, such as statistics about CRC errors, collisions, ring purges, the claim token process, and both soft and hard errors. Figure 4.26 shows the Token-Ring MAC Protocol screen.

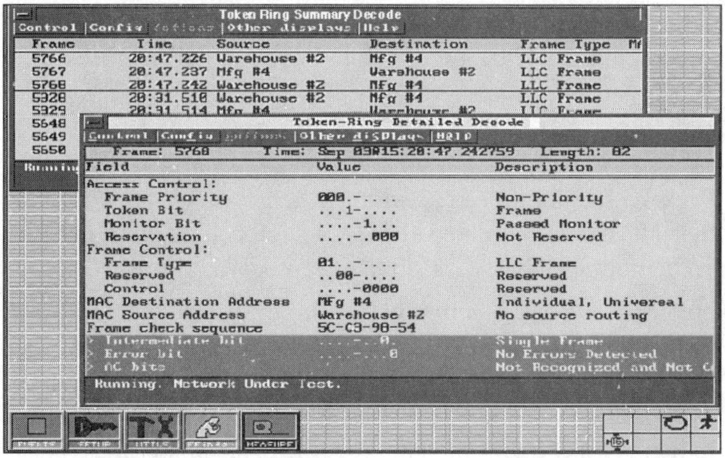

Figure 4.26 Hewlett-Packard's Network Advisor analyzer provides some excellent Token Ring and Ethernet-specific information.

Chapter 4: Optimization and Troubleshooting Tools

You also can plot testing results in graphical algorithmic bar and line charts. Figure 4.27 shows the Token-Ring Detail screen.

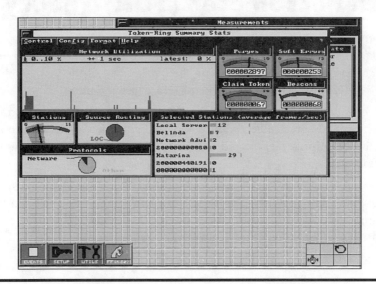

Figure 4.27 The Token Ring and Ethernet Detail screen of the Network Advisor includes graphical depictions of analysis-session statistics.

The Network Advisor's RISC-based hardware architecture allows for high-performance gathering and decoding of network data, with the added touch of being dynamic.

The Finder Expert System gives you the option of focusing on the network symptoms that occur rather than spending time analyzing the data captured during a protocol analysis session. You can still view and decode the captured data from a protocol analysis session, but with the Finder Expert System, you often can locate the cause of a failure more quickly and efficiently.

The overall advantage of this product is that it gives you all the basic protocol analyzer features, along with an expert system to help you decode and make logical analysis assessments and troubleshooting conclusions as to the causes of network failures.

Understanding Time Domain Reflectometer (TDR) Theory

Cable problems cause a very high percentage of failure symptoms in today's networks. Years ago, troubleshooting a possible bad cable was a chore. But today, the variety of test equipment on the market makes the task much easier. The new TDRs that have hit the marketplace are fast and effective.

A Time Domain Reflectometer (TDR) is a device that generates and transmits a specific signal down a cable and monitors the cable for a signal reflection. This process is sometimes nicknamed cable radar because it acts somewhat like normal radar.

The signal sent out by a TDR has a predefined amplitude and time span. The TDR next eavesdrops on the cable to sample and then measure any signal reflection that occurs. If no problems are present with the cable and it is properly terminated, a signal reflection should not occur.

A cable can have a number of different problems as follows:

- Open cables (physically broken)
- Shorted cables (two or more internal conductors crossed)
- Crimped cables
- Bad cable termination (improper or no termination)
- Other miscellaneous problems (cable kinks, bends, and so on)

Depending on the type of problem, a problem-type-specific signal reflection occurs. This unique reflection is sometimes called cable signal fault signature (CSFS). Today, TDRs are designed to capture and interpret most of the different CSFS-type problems that can occur on a cable. Most of the units analyze the polarity and amplitude of the CSFS to determine the probable cable fault type. Some of the units actually tell you the probable fault type and fault distance, to the approximate foot, from the test point.

Optical TDRs are available for testing fiber cable. They operate in the same manner, except that they use a laser for a light source to generate optical pulse signals, and they use an optical receiver. OTDRs contain a microprocessor that converts the received optical signal to a digital signal. The digital signal results are typically decoded by custom data-acquisition software.

Fiber testing employs different terminology for problem causes and measurements. OTDRs measure signal losses as Rayleigh Backscattered Signals. Opens, bends, kinks, and splices are usually measured as Fresnel Reflections or splice losses. OTDRs also measure fiber signal signature spikes as ghosts.

For the Token Ring or Ethernet environment, there are TDRs that also address some of the Token Ring and Ethernet topology error conditions, such as beaconing. TDR manufacturers have been coming out with imaginative gear for testing a ring, including TDRs with actual network bandwidth monitoring features.

Using a Time Domain Reflectometer

Before testing any cable, the first step is to make sure that the suspect section of cable is isolated from the rest of the LAN. Some PCs, hubs, repeaters, and bridges may respond with return signals in response to a TDR signal test. The best way to avoid this is to unplug these devices and test each cable section separately.

It is also important to make sure that the section of cable being tested is properly terminated. Most TDRs come with terminators for the type of cable they can test. A good way to be sure is to use one of the TDR terminators.

When first using a TDR, you should select the switch for the type of cable you are going to test. Next, generate a general signal test. If problems exist, the TDR should tell you. It is that easy.

With a fairly sophisticated TDR, you can receive a full complement of information. If no cable problems are present, you should receive some sort of cable OK message. If problems exist, most TDRs tell you the probable type of cable fault and the distance to the fault.

Some TDRs have separate tests for cable resistance, DB loss (signal loss), continuity (opens and shorts), and cable noise. Other units collate the tests in different ways. It is always best to first generate a general signal test to get a cable quality benchmark, and then perform any specific categorized testing. Some innovative units enable you to save and print the test results—a great feature for documenting your test results.

Some industry-standard cable testing equipment is presented in the next section.

Examining Cable-Testing Equipment

For the Token Ring and Ethernet topology, a good selection of cable-testing equipment is available. LAN cable test gear has been available for many years, but today the LAN marketplace features many new innovative types of instruments.

The following section gives an overview of some of the cable-testing equipment currently standard in the Token Ring and Ethernet industry. Most of the products here have been designed with specific features for testing and monitoring the Token Ring and Ethernet topology cabling medium.

Microtest Ring Scanner, MT350 Scanner, PentaScanner, and Pair Scanner

Microtest has been developing testing gear since 1984. The company has a reputation for excellent products in the LAN test equipment arena.

In 1988, Microtest introduced its Cable Scanner, one of the first cost-effective hand-held cable-testing tools. This section focuses on the newer Ring Scanner because it is designed specifically for Token Ring topology. The Pair Scanner and MT350 Scanner also are discussed because Microtest has included features in both products that enhance the effectiveness of the Ring Scanner to offer extended Token Ring monitoring features.

The MT350 Scanner is part of the MT300 product series of highly intelligent cable-health verification tools. It is Microtest's most advanced scanner. MT350 supports UTP, STP, and all coax cabling systems. It specifically supports Ethernet, 10BASE-T, 4/16 Mbps Token Ring, and ARCnet networks. The new PentaScanner supports advanced monitoring for level 5 UTP-based cable. Figure 4.28 shows the MT350 Scanner.

The internal MT350 FLASH ROM database has an extensive cable type library accessed by the scanner when determining what types of tests to run on a specific cable type. The unit actually determines what tests are to be run and produces the results. The MT350 can store the data in its memory, and then output it to almost any printer. It also has the capability to download the data to Microtest's advanced Cable Management Systems (CMS) database or any other main PC database.

Chapter 4: Optimization and Troubleshooting Tools 101

Figure 4.28 Microtest's MT350 Scanner.

The MT350 is one of the first scanners that fully assists the user by documenting the network through structured network cable management.

Microtest Pair Scanner is a TDR that has leading-edge network-monitoring features. Figure 4.29 shows the Pair Scanner. It includes all the basic functions, TDR signal testing, DB Loss, continuity testing, noise testing, and resistance testing, along with UTP-specific testing.

Figure 4.29 Microtest Pair Scanner is a TDR that checks for cable and termination problems.

The Pair Scanner can test the following cable types:

- Token Ring
- Thick and thin Ethernet
- ARCnet and RX-Net
- PVC
- Full twisted-pair support, including 10BASE-T
- Additional support for testing IBM cable types 1, 2, 3, 6, and 9

Pair Scanner also has a slew of extended features. Microtest includes a set of data communication tests that allows Pair Scanner to function as an RS232 data line monitor. A choice of advanced twisted-pair-specific tests are available, such as Activating a Twisted Pair Hub, Checking for Crosstalk, Office Locator for checking cable drops, Conductor Wiring Checks, and a complete overall Twisted Pair Cable Scan Test.

Pair Scanner interfaces with the Microtest 10BASE-T injector to accomplish some of these tests. Pair Scanner also is fully compatible with the Microtest Cable Tracer II to detect cables that may be hard to locate in walls, floors, and ceilings.

One of Pair Scanner's foremost features is its capability to produce printed reports for all its testing functions. The unit has a Print Data Store Library buffer and can print serially at 300 to 38,400 baud from its data communication printer interface port.

Another feature is the Pair Scanner Management software, which enables the scanner's data communication port to be interfaced to PC COM ports 1 or 2, so the reports can be saved to a text file for future viewing and printing.

The unit can fully interface with an oscilloscope to view all the generated TDR signals and their respective CSFSes. Microtest has also included an alarm mode that monitors the cabling medium and triggers an alarm when certain events occur.

A Network Monitoring Buffer feature allows the Pair Scanner to capture data transmitted on a cabling medium and to display and print the relative network traffic. Interfaced with the Ring Scanner, the Token Ring bandwidth utilization can be measured and also displayed and printed.

Ring Scanner, the newest member of the Microtest scanner family, does not include TDR capabilities, but interacts with the Microtest Pair Scanner and other

Chapter 4: Optimization and Troubleshooting Tools

Microtest scanners for TDR testing and monitoring. It was designed for testing only the Token Ring topology cabling medium. It quickly can test and isolate bad Token Ring cabling sections and defective MAU ports. The unit tests both 4Mbps and 16Mbps rings.

The Ring Scanner functions logically divide into two categories:

- Token Ring cable tests for IBM cable types 1, 2, 3, 6, and 9. This category includes specific testing for general loopback testing and unshorted tests.
- Network tests. This category includes data-rate detection, ring-status indication, fault-simulation capability, and data-traffic monitoring.

The two modes for testing Token Ring cable sections are as follows:

- Mode 1 enables you to test a specific Token Ring cable section, such as a lobe, to determine if the shorting pins in the cable connector are working properly. This test can be performed with the standard IBM data connector and a type-3 RJ45 connector (with RJ45 female coupler).

  If the shorting pins are correctly looping back the internal transmit and receive pairs, the green OK LED illuminates. If any of the four individual conductor LEDs (red, orange, green, black) illuminate red, a problem exists. The Microtest manual can guide you to the exact probable problem and solution.

- Mode 2 is for testing a specific Token Ring cable section with its cable connector shorting pins open. This enables you to detect cable problems that cannot be found when the shorting pins are internally looping back. This test is different because without the cable connector internal pins shorting, data should be able to fully flow in and out of the data connector. By using a special loopback connector and the Activate Cable Test button, you can perform an actual data loop test.

This tool also tests for proper shielding in all cabling types except for type 3. The green OK LED illuminates if no test failures occur. If any problems are detected, a combination of the four individual conductor LEDs illuminate red. Again, the Microtest manual guides you to the probable problem and solution.

A LAMP test mode can verify proper operation of all the Cable Test LEDs. By putting the Ring Scanner in the LAMP test mode and pressing the Activate Cable Test button, you can test all the LEDs.

In the area of network monitoring tests, Ring Scanner includes an automatic Data Rate Detection feature. The ring speed can be dynamically identified as either 4Mbps or 16Mbps.

The Ring Status Indication feature enables you to test the capability of passing data completely around the ring. By using the Activate Ring Test button, you can generate a data pattern onto the ring. If the data makes a complete trip around the ring, the Ring Status LED illuminates green. The LED turns red if it does not receive the transmitted data. This simply is a ring path integrity test and is excellent for verifying MAU port relays.

The Fault Simulation feature enables you to introduce a simulated fault onto your Token Ring network. This type of feature can be a good aid for troubleshooting, in conjunction with other network monitoring tools such as protocol analyzers and LAN management/diagnostic packages.

During this test, the Ring Scanner enters the ring as a node but does not generate any data. This is a simulation of an actual failed ring station. Exercise extreme caution when performing this test because it causes your ring to go through Ring Recovery. Make sure that your ring users are not active and no open files are on the file server. This is a good test to benchmark other testing gear.

A Data Traffic Monitoring function is built into the Ring Scanner. It is a dynamic function that enables you to monitor data traffic on the ring. Every time data travels around the ring, the Ring Scanner Data Traffic LED illuminates.

The Data Traffic Monitoring and the Data Rate Detection features work together to provide the necessary data for the bandwidth utilization testing by means of the Pair Scanner and other Microtest Scanners, as discussed earlier. For this discussion, the Pair Scanner is used as the main example for interfacing the Ring Scanner.

The Ring Scanner interfaces to the Pair Scanner through an RJ45 connector (To Scanner Port). What actually occurs is that the Ring Scanner collects the Token Ring-specific data rate and transmit frequencies and passes them to the Pair Scanner. The Pair Scanner then uses its Network Monitoring Buffer feature to display and print the Token Ring bandwidth utilization. Figure 4.30 shows a sample Network Monitor Report printout from a Ring Scanner/Pair Scanner test.

Chapter 4: Optimization and Troubleshooting Tools

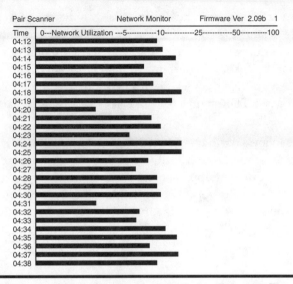

Figure 4.30 Microtest's Pair Scanner processes data from the Ring Scanner for display or printing.

Note that the Ring Scanner monitors only data packets, not tokens. Also note that other Microtest units—the MT300 series scanners, the Cable Scanner, the Next Scanner, and the Quick Scanner—include most of the same Network Monitoring Buffer features to work with Ring Scanner.

Microtest has shown a dedication to the cable-testing environment. Microtest is due to release a TDR called the Next Scanner that will include built-in artificial intelligence for determining which tests should be run and dynamically measuring the specific cable type.

All Microtest's testing instruments are well-documented and easy to use. The Ring Scanner and its interoperability with the other Microtest Scanner's TDR and monitoring capabilities provide a superb testing approach for the Token Ring topology.

Bytex RingOut Cable Tester

Bytex Inc., a Massachusetts-based company, specializes in LAN products. In 1990, Bytex introduced the RingOut Cable Tester, which is designed specifically for Token Ring topology.

Bytex's approach to testing the Token Ring cabling medium is unique. The RingOut Cable Tester does not function as a TDR, but can interface with an oscilloscope to perform signal trace testing. The Bytex philosophy is that you can troubleshoot the Token Ring cabling system more effectively by using Token Ring-specific tests rather than TDRs. It is true that certain Token Ring cable sections may pass a TDR signal test and yet not properly carry Token Ring packets on the medium.

The sell is as follows. With the Token Ring topology, if you only troubleshoot a section of cable at a time, there is really no need to know how far the distance of failure is. This is a different approach, and it is effective if your troubleshooting methods follow along. It works if you test a cable by first unplugging each section, terminating it, and then testing that cable section separately.

RingOut Cable Tester includes the following four main testing modes:

- Cable Test mode
- Ring Test mode
- DC Continuity Test mode
- Signal Degradation Test mode

Figure 4.31 displays the Bytex RingOut Cable Tester.

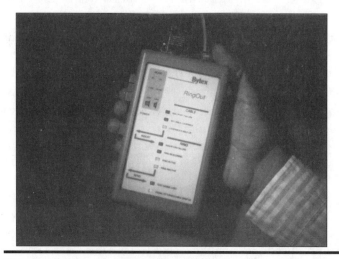

Figure 4.31 RingOut Cable Tester performs Token Ring-specific testing of the cabling medium.

Chapter 4: Optimization and Troubleshooting Tools

Before using any of the main test modes, you must preset the RingOut Tester operation parameters switches. The parameters switch choices are: either STP or UTP cabling; either 4Mbps or 16Mbps; and either Data or Cont modes. (Cont mode is set only for DC Continuity Test mode.)

The Cable Test mode allows an intelligent loopback test. After you set the parameter switches and connect the unit to a cabling medium section or MAU port, all you have to do is turn the unit on, and it initiates a cable loopback test. The RingOut Tester acts intelligently by monitoring the cable for network traffic before activating a cable loopback test.

The unit indicates no cable problems by illuminating the green LOOPBACK/CABLE OK LED. If problems exist, the RingOut Tester either illuminates the red MAU PORT FAILURE LED (indicates bad loopback in MAU port) or the red NO CABLE LOOPBACK LED (indicates bad cable or bad loopback in the shorting pins of the cable connector).

The Ring Test mode includes two subtests: the Insertion Test and the Send Test. To activate an Insertion Test, you need only push an Insert button on the RingOut Tester. During the Insertion Test, the RingOut Tester activates an actual ring insertion by asserting DC phantom voltage to the MAU port. Four possible LED responses may occur from the RingOut Tester as follows:

- The yellow RING INACTIVE LED. This response indicates either no traffic on the ring, a data transmission rate mismatch, or a signal degradation.
- The green RING ACTIVE/DROP OK LED. This response indicates successful insertion to a normally functioning ring.
- The red INSERTION FAILURE LED. This response indicates unsuccessful insertion to the ring.
- The red BEACONING LED. This response indicates presence of a beaconing ring station on the ring.

The RingOut Tester actually can enter a beaconing ring. This feature is helpful when troubleshooting a beaconing ring because you can remove stations until the beaconing LED goes out.

The Send Test mode follows the Insertion Test mode. When the RingOut Tester is inserted, activate the Send Test by pushing the Send button on the tester. The Send Test transmits an actual Token Ring test signal onto the ring, and then waits to receive the signal back. The RingOut Tester provides two possible LED Responses as follows:

- The green SIGNAL RETURNED/DROP OK LED. This indicates successful transmission and receive back status.
- The red TEST SIGNAL LOST LED. This indicates either an MAU port failure or a ring signal degradation.

The Signal Degradation Test mode enables you to perform a more detailed Token Ring signal signature analysis. You can simulate certain tests to receive the data that a normal TDR provides. These tests can be performed by connecting the RingOut Cable Tester to an oscilloscope by means of instructions in the RingOut manual.

The DC Continuity Test identifies specific cable faults such as cable shorts and open cables. To perform the DC Continuity tests, you must use the RingOut Tester in conjunction with the Bytex Continuity Tester. The Bytex RingOut manual guides you through testing a specific Token Ring cable section and helps you isolate the exact problem and solution.

The tests monitor the cable's internal transmit and receive pairs and illuminate four LEDs with different result combinations. Four individual conductor LEDs (red, orange, green, and black) on the Continuity Tester represent the test results.

The overall strength of the Bytex RingOut Tester is that it can generate, capture, and decipher actual Token Ring data patterns. When it enters a ring, it does so transparently, without affecting the ring state. Its capability to enter and test a beaconing ring also gives the troubleshooter a conclusive edge.

The RingOut Tester has a well-documented manual. Bytex has put much careful Token Ring thought and performance into the hand-held RingOut Tester.

The Fluke 670 and 672 LANMeters

This network tool resides in both the Protocol Analyzer and TDR category. In fact, it is the first tool of its kind. The John Fluke Manufacturing company is known for its accurate industry testing equipment. Now Fluke has developed a new innovative tool that can monitor all the major Token Ring network statistics and also can comprehensively test a Token Ring cabling layout. The product is the Fluke 670 LANMeter, and it is exactly that—a meter for your Token Ring LAN (see Figure 4.32). Note also that Fluke recently introduced a meter for Ethernet, called the 672 LANMeter.

Chapter 4: Optimization and Troubleshooting Tools

Figure 4.32 The Fluke 670 LANMeter is designed for the Token Ring.

The 670 is a hand-held instrument, but still offers accurate measurements for most of the important physical-layer Token Ring statistics. Some key statistics included are Token Ring soft errors, beaconing data, network utilization, Token Rotation Time, broadcast levels, and node-by-node utilization factors.

A global naming feature is supported for Token Ring addresses. One feature is a 4Mbps or 16Mbps auto speed detection. This is useful when troubleshooting in a multiple ring environment. The 670 supports simultaneous measurements, which, for example, enable you to measure the Token Ring network utilization while keeping an eye on the Token Ring soft error counts. Another plus is that the 670 can monitor any new stations that leave or enter the ring.

The 670 also includes a full-blown TDR that gives a comprehensive view of the cabling layout integrity and also can test MAU ports for accurate operation. This tool is excellent for field troubleshooting and network installation projects. Overall, the 670 is a network monitor for your Token Ring network that offers true portability and precision. The tools can be combined in a new platform called the "675".

Scope Communication, Inc.'s Frame Scope 803 Network Analyzer and Wire Scope 100/155 Cable Testers

Scope Communications Inc. based in Massachusetts, currently offers excellent products in the LAN frame analysis area and also in the general wire testing

110   ETHERNET AND TOKEN RING OPTIMIZATION

arena. In reference to the frame analysis area, the product that is most well known is the Frame Scope 802 Network Analyzer. The Wire Scope 100 and 155 analyzers are high-end TDRs utilized for configuration testing in LAN based wiring schemes.

The Frame Scope 802 Analyzer is a small tool that can be used by field engineers and technical support groups for testing frame integrity on LAN based networks. The Frame Scope 802 has the capability through excellent graphical interfaces to monitor frame traffic on LAN. The tool is built to monitor both Token Ring and Ethernet environments in a held-held configuration. A key feature included in the Frame Scope is the capability for monitoring different types of frames and associated levels on a LAN. Frame Scope has the capability to monitor and display network utilization levels, error rates, physical error rates for both Token Ring and Ethernet, including collision levels, non-isolating and isolating errors. The tool also has internal frame techniques that will allow individual stations to be monitored for their packet-per-second rate, utilization levels and contribution to the node-by-node configuration on a LAN.

Unique built-in testing techniques include the Echo Requests and Reply tests, which is basically a built-in ICMP Ping that can be utilized in a hand-held test mode. Novell Echo testing allows for testing Novell end nodes for availability through the Novell protocol suite. There are loop back tests built in for the MAC protocol and also physical error tests that allow for testing the internal physical error integrity of both Token Ring and Ethernet.

Certain wiring tests can be performed for both the Token Ring and Ethernet physical layer including the signal strength, jitter test and lobe test configurations.

Some of the statistics built into the tool are extensive. It should be noted that this tool is not a full-blown protocol analyzer and will not allow full review of packet traffic. However, the critical frame statistics can be displayed. Some of the frame display strengths include the capability to monitor an individual station for its packet traffic, its count of errors, and its ability to go into the individual errors and see the actual type and count. The capability to see this for the complete network and go to an individual station view is one of the key product's strengths.

Performance plotting can also be accomplished with the tool, where a station can be compared to the complete graphical snapshot of the whole network.

The capability to generate traffic on the network is a higher end protocol analysis feature. This feature allows for a capability to configure a frame size

Chapter 4: Optimization and Troubleshooting Tools

and then attempt to adjust the frame-per-second rate for how high the traffic load should be sent on to the network. Any of the statistics that are picked up with a Frame Scope analyzer can be printed or brought into certain applications for either charting or review for data.

Scope Communications offers its own graphical interface, which is labeled as the Scope Data product. This product allows for any of the information picked up in the Frame Scope or Wire Scope tools to be brought into a Windows interface application, which then can be charted and reviewed for certain statistics. These types of features allow this tool to be utilized in the field as a first-level testing tool before a full-blown protocol analyzer is required. The Frame Scope 802 analyzer is shown in Figure 4.33.

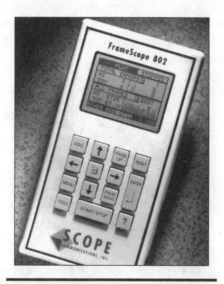

Figure 4.33 Frame Scope 802 analyzer.

The Wire Scope 100 was the first TDR from Scope Communications. Shown in Figure 4.34, it has the full capability for category 5 cable testing and allows for automatic testing of pair combinations and individual category testing. This high-end user-friendly tool allows for a database to be configured on certain wire testing configurations. It has built-in auto testing that allows the type of cabling to be detected and then to be quickly checked for general integrity. If there are problems with the cable, further detail testing can be performed where network certification can be engaged. The tool has the capability to check the type of cabling, perform a quick loop back test for cable continuity, and then identify any problems with wiring, shorts or opens. The actual distance to the problem can be located and pointed out clearly on the Wire Scope screen. It will even identify wiring problems and give a clear representation on the hand-held screen of possible misconfigurations between certain pins and recommend the re-wiring scheme that should be utilized.

The results of all these tests can then be plotted and brought into the Scope Data application. Network certification is a snap, due to the fact that when new cables are installed, the tool will allow for auto testing, quick charting of key issues related to cable performance such as continuity, DB loss, crosstalk and attenuation measurements. The capability to provide the wire map breakout to show miswiring is a very strong feature. This is called the Wire Map Application. Again, this will allow the Wire Scope to identify whether or not pairs of wires are properly wired, and it shows the user a graphical breakout of how the miswiring may be set up.

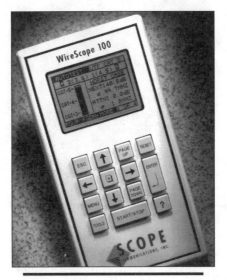

Figure 4.34 The Wire Scope 100.

Regarding cable length testing, full capability is built in for the length of the cable to be tested and calculated, and then the results can be brought to a database for either charting or printing for result review. This tool is a high-end hand-held scope analyzer that allows for these types of testing.

The Wire Scope 155 analyzer is the first tool offered in the industry that has a full 155 MHz capability for ATM cabling verifiaction analysis. The tool is compliant with most ATM and ISO testing standards. It has the capability to be utilized in ATM wiring environments for full digital spectrum analysis. The 155 unit employs Near End Crosstalk (NEXT) testing and can store up to 500 cable reports for full review in a PC charting format. This type of tool will be strong in combinations of category 5 testing environments and will involve requirements for testing ATM environments. The Wire Tester 155 analyzer has the capability to also work with multiple probe connections and different block wiring schemes. This tool also includes a remote attachment tester, the DualRemote 155 unit, which allows for end-to-end testing for unique mesurements like NEXT at two remote ends with Autotest. The 155 unit has test features are built within that include with full explanations of possible problems. Basically, the tool has a high-end expert system designed that allows for NEXT, attenuation monitoring, ambient noise protection and wire map identification for miswiring schemes. This is a strong hand-held TDR.

IBM Cable Tester (IBM P/N 4760500)

IBM introduced the IBM Cable Tester years ago when Token Ring was first conceived. It was the first cable tester specifically designed for the Token Ring LAN arena. It has most of the features included in basic Token Ring loopback and DC continuity tests. It is a hand-held unit that includes data wrap connectors for specific cable-section testing.

The unit also includes four LEDs (red, orange, green, and black) to monitor the four individual conductors. It can test the Token Ring cable's internal transmit and receive pairs, and illuminate the LEDs to signify different test conclusions.

The unit is still a good test instrument for basic Token Ring cable medium testing.

Antel Optronics AOC10 OTDR

Antel Optronics, founded in 1985, is a Canadian company that specializes in the design and manufacture of fiber optic instruments and optelectronic semiconductor components. In 1990, this company introduced a product called the AOC10 OTDR, which is a portable PC-based optical time domain reflectometer.

ETHERNET AND TOKEN RING OPTIMIZATION

The AOC10 OTDR is offered in both a stand-alone board-and-software package and a preconfigured PC portable configuration. The stand-alone product is offered as a fiber NIC-and-software package. The PC OTDR is packaged by preconfiguring the fiber NIC/software in a portable PC. Figure 4.35 displays both configurations.

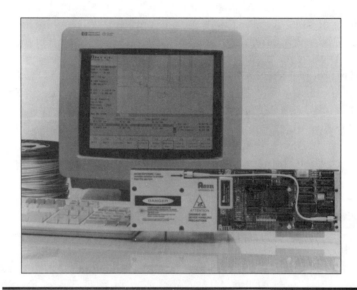

Figure 4.35 Antel Optonics' AOC10 is an optical TDR that includes both software and hardware components.

The AOC10 OTDR NIC is the heart of the unit. It has a highly advanced on-board laser light source, receiver, and processor. It works interactively with the Antel data-acquisition software to provide the full OTDR package.

The NIC can be switched between single and multimode fiber. It also can be dynamically switched between 850/1300 NM and 1310/1550 NM fiber wavelengths.

The AOC10 OTDR includes the following five main test display modes:

- Parameter Display mode. Displays all fiber and OTDR parameters
- Distance Bar Graph mode. Gives full graphical display of OTDR signal distance ranges

Chapter 4: Optimization and Troubleshooting Tools

- Measurement Display mode. Gives marked display of absolute and relative OTDR signal position
- Splice Loss mode. Displays a measurement of splice loss in least-squares approximation and two-point methods
- Dual Waveforms mode. Displays two real-time or stored-waveform OTDR signal traces

The menuing system offers a full set of function keys for displaying and testing, along with custom setup modes for the OTDR environmental parameter settings. A Comment Pad feature enables you to keep real-time notes on testing results.

Because of its PC-based operation, the Antel AOC10 can forward testing data to disk files or printers.

The AOC10 OTDR is designed specifically for testing a fiber cabling medium and is not restricted to the Token Ring topology. The overall strengths of the portable Antel AOC10 are its full range of fiber testing features, along with its innovative data-testing software, which offers a user-friendly menuing system.

CHAPTER 5

Optimization Techniques

This book has already covered the theory behind network optimization, including the goals and categories of measurement for performing certain phases of a network optimization project. The following techniques can be used throughout the project to optimize your network precisely.

The following techniques employ various measurements of workload characterizations for average networks. But they are not general, and they may require extensive practice to master. These are techniques for real-world conditions on most major networks. They require specific analysis processes and calculations and can make an optimization project successful. These techniques also can be used to troubleshoot problems and keep a network running at its optimum level.

This section covers major areas for analysis. It includes the overall examination and measurement of the key areas, including broadcast levels, network retransmissions, network bandwidth overload conditions, application read efficiency analysis, and general network throughput calculations.

Some optimization techniques presented in this section involve both the physical and upper protocol layers, and ways to measure their operation. The techniques follow a specific pattern to ensure coverage of the whole network.

Each technique requires a methodical and analytical approach and a knowledge of the protocol analyzer being employed. After you master the protocol analyzer you are using, focus on the steps presented in this section and on understanding the applied measurement category for producing a truly optimized network.

Successful network optimization requires good documentation of the software and hardware components involved. The techniques here can be applied to any network, as long as all the documentation for the particular network is available for review.

It also should be mentioned that these are proactive steps that can be engaged on any network, even when it is running in normal mode. These techniques also can be used for troubleshooting a network.

The first technique to consider is broadcast level examination.

Understanding Broadcast Levels Examination

Networks always have a *broadcast level*. A broadcast level consists of the packets of a certain protocol type used for connection verification or general communication between nodes. Network or internetwork nodes use packet broadcasts to say hello and verify certain means of communication between their respective entities. Broadcasts are also important as the means by which certain devices on the network become aware of other devices, such as routers and certain file servers for naming conventions.

Certain levels of broadcasts are normal, but because limited bandwidth is available on any network, broadcasts should be kept to a minimum. Although broadcast packets are necessary to keep a network in operation, some network broadcasts can cause problems, especially if they filter over from other networks, but are not required on the network where they are captured.

Protocol analysis allows measuring in detail the broadcast level on a network. In general, the broadcasts on any network should be under 8% to 10%

at most. If broadcasts average over 10% and as high as 20% to 25% they potentially can cause communication problems. This is sometimes called a broadcast storm. At times, however, a particular broadcast level is necessary, such as when users are logging on or off a network. At those times, very high broadcast levels may be observed on the network.

At other times, a certain device may have a problem that causes it to generate high broadcast levels. This definitely can be termed a broadcast storm. This most often occurs when certain types of routers or file servers are installed that fail to receive an expected type of response from another device. They sometimes actually cause a broadcast level that hinders communication throughout the network.

The real danger, though, appears when networks are bridged to other networks experiencing high broadcast levels. Because they are bridged to other networks, their particular broadcast levels can filter across the bridge and affect other networks. This is a common internetworking problem.

Note that the only way to properly examine a network's broadcast level is proactively, using a protocol analyzer or appropriate network management tool. The following section breaks down the actual technique of examining broadcast levels on a network.

Technique Specifics

- A protocol analyzer should be used to examine the overall broadcast rate on a network. Whatever protocol analyzer is used, the technique is to examine what part of the overall traffic is related to general broadcast breakdowns.
- Use the protocol analyzer to capture all the traffic and then filter out the broadcast type packets. Most protocol analyzers can do this.
- After the broadcast traffic levels are broken out, go through the broadcast traffic and relate the broadcast packets to specific addresses. Then see what broadcasts are not needed for specific processes on the specific network.

For example, a protocol analyzer records a high broadcast level of 18% of overall traffic. The analyst filters out the 18% level and finds it to be mainly

ETHERNET AND TOKEN RING OPTIMIZATION

related to a particular NIC MAC address (10005Ab6f542). Next, the analyst discovers that the address is looking to participate in a network management operation with an IBM LAN Manager. After investigation, the analyst discovers that no IBM LAN Manager function is present on the network. The analyst disables the net management function on the station called the configuration report server. The network is again analyzed, and the broadcast level is found to be reduced to 6% of overall traffic.

- Most networks have more broadcast traffic than required. Filter through data to examine what broadcast traffic is not needed and identify specific addresses related to the unnecessary broadcasts. Consider putting filters on the bridges or routers, or on whatever processes generate the broadcasts.
- Check to see if the broadcast levels on the network are lower.

Figure 5.1 shows the Network General Sniffer Expert system displaying a high broadcast level.

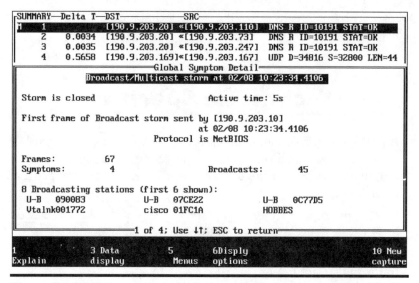

Figure 5.1 A high broadcast level displayed by the Network General Sniffer.

Understanding Duplicate Addresses

The problem with duplicate addresses appears across a range of topologies and protocol environments. Duplicate addresses can cause major problems, especially in a multiple network environment.

A duplicate address condition exists when two devices have the same physical or upper protocol layer addresses. Any attempt at communication on the network by these devices causes direct conflict.

The general topology of certain networks prevents duplicate addresses at the physical layer. For example, if a device on a Token Ring network attempts to log on with a duplicate address, the topology itself prevents the address from connecting to the network.

The problem occurs when duplicate addresses are in use by the upper layer protocols. For example, if the physical layer allows an address on a network, but the upper protocol layer (for example, Novell IPX) is in direct conflict with another node attaching to the network with a duplicated IPX address level, it causes a general internetworking traffic flow problem. Since both the network and transport layers and even upper protocol layers have specific addressing conventions, you need to be aware of all addresses within particular nodes on the network.

A protocol analyzer can be used to capture a packet from any device on the network and examine all the key addressing points throughout the packet. For example, in a standard Novell packet is the data link control layer, which has the physical MAC address that can be decoded. At the Internetwork Packet Exchange (IPX) layer is a source node, a source network, and source process addressing convention for the Novell layers. The higher layers may have even other addressing schemes, having to do with particular applications. All this information can be decoded through protocol analysis, and need not be a major problem in today's networking.

A multiple network environment can have big problems if two physical layer addresses are duplicated and are logged on across multiple networks. This is a potential problem in gateway access and file server access, and can occur if two nodes are accessing the same internetwork device, but are actually connected to different source networks in a multiple network environment. Catching this duplicate address takes extensive protocol analysis.

The following section describes steps and approaches to prevent duplicate addresses from disrupting a network's operation.

Technique Specifics

- Most protocol analyzers today allow for trapping duplicate addresses throughout a network, in both the physical layer and the upper protocol layer.
- Duplicate addresses might be at the physical layer, network layer, or application layerfor example, at the IPX layer in the NetWare protocol suite, the IP layer in the TCP/IP protocol suite, or in DRP layers of the DEC protocol suite.
- A protocol analyzer should be set to filter the network addressing fields of the specific protocol being examined for duplicate addresses.

For example, in a Novell network, users intermittently cannot get to certain Novell servers. An analyst addresses the NetWare protocol suite by setting a filter on a Novell network designation in the IPX header. The trace is started with an IPX filter, and the analyst captures a duplicate Novell network number designation. The analyst identifies the duplicate net address and renames the network address for IPX. The network is reanalyzed, and the duplicate addresses are gone.

- Duplicate addresses are a specific problem on very busy networks, and this allows for eliminating network irregularities that have to do with possible duplicate address conflicts.

Figure 5.2 shows the Network General Sniffer Expert system displaying a duplicate address problem.

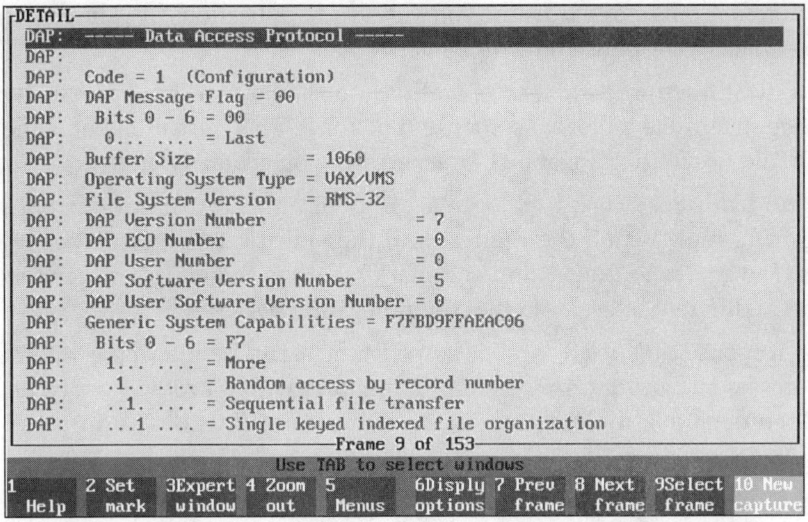

```
┌DETAIL─────────────────────────────────────────────────────────────────┐
│ DAP: ───── Data Access Protocol ─────                                 │
│ DAP:                                                                  │
│ DAP:   Code = 1  (Configuration)                                      │
│ DAP:   DAP Message Flag = 00                                          │
│ DAP:    Bits 0 - 6 = 00                                               │
│ DAP:    0... .... = Last                                              │
│ DAP:   Buffer Size          = 1060                                    │
│ DAP:   Operating System Type = VAX/VMS                                │
│ DAP:   File System Version  = RMS-32                                  │
│ DAP:   DAP Version Number        = 7                                  │
│ DAP:   DAP ECO Number            = 0                                  │
│ DAP:   DAP User Number           = 0                                  │
│ DAP:   DAP Software Version Number = 5                                │
│ DAP:   DAP User Software Version Number = 0                           │
│ DAP:   Generic System Capabilities = F7FBD9FFAEAC06                   │
│ DAP:    Bits 0 - 6 = F7                                               │
│ DAP:    1... .... = More                                              │
│ DAP:    .1.. .... = Random access by record number                    │
│ DAP:    ..1. .... = Sequential file transfer                          │
│ DAP:    ...1 .... = Single keyed indexed file organization            │
│─────────────────────────Frame 9 of 153────────────────────────────────│
│                    Use TAB to select windows                          │
│1      2 Set   3Expert 4 Zoom 5        6Disply 7 Prev 8 Next 9Select 10 New│
│ Help   mark   window   out   Menus    options  frame  frame  frame  capture│
└───────────────────────────────────────────────────────────────────────┘
```

Figure 5.2 Network General Sniffer displaying a duplicate address.

Understanding Response Time

Response time is the effective amount of time for a node to respond to another node after a particular request for data.

Through general analysis techniques and calculated measurements, it is easy to determine normal and abnormal response times on a particular network. Industry benchmarks are available from manufacturers that present normal response times for a particular network operation. Industry consensus is that a response should be obtained within 100 milliseconds for any particular node transmission in response to any request. Across a WAN, response times should be a minimum of 200-250 milliseconds for any response to any type of node request.

These are standard industry benchmarks; the network or internetwork being analyzed has its own normal baseline operation for response timing. As mentioned earlier, a normal operational mode always exists on a network, which is considered its static baseline. Because all networks and internetworks have different mixes of hardware, software, and applications, it is impossible to specify a normal response time for all networks.

You must learn in detail the operations on the network you are analyzing, and then determine a normal response time for it. This measurement is the one you should use for optimization of the network you are analyzing.

To find this response time, use a protocol analyzer or proper network monitoring tool. Watch the request and the specific response between two nodes. The goal is to time-stamp and mark what the timing is between the two devices at different intervals in the communication session.

The response time itself can be trapped very easily by filtering certain types of addresses and using certain timing techniques with a protocol analyzer. You can document this information and perform modifications to improve the overall response time.

The following section describes measuring response time on a network.

Technique Specifics

- Remember that most LAN and WAN configurations should have at least a minimum standard response time for responses between host or servers and particular clients.
- Specifically, the response time can be monitored from the file server as related to specific workstation requests.
- Most workstations on LANs should generally receive a response within 100 milliseconds from the file server.
- Monitor the file server response time for a minimum response within 100 milliseconds.
- You can easily capture the standard response time from a particular server by filtering the file server's address or the particular workstation involved in the transfer.
- The first step is to filter the device, and then to examine the data from the protocol analyzer using the absolute and relative time fields in the display mode of the analyzer. The analyzer displays the actual response time that it takes for a reply to a request between the particular file server and workstation.
- Monitor the file server response time for a response within 100 milliseconds at a minimum.

Chapter 5: Optimization Techniques

For example, a network user is complaining of slow response time when using Microsoft Excel. The analyst sets up a protocol analyzer to filter the user's NIC MAC address. Next, the analyst examines the data trace from the protocol analyzer using the absolute and relative time fields in the display mode of the analyzer.

The analyst notices on the analyzer that the total time spent from the Excel file open request packet until the file server responds with an acknowledgment to search for the file is 235 milliseconds. This figure is attained by marking the actual relative time between the first workstation request packet and the first response packet from the file server to the specific workstation request.

After further analysis of the delay issue, it is found that the delay is actually located in the file server, which takes about 153 milliseconds to process the command. An audit of the file server reveals that the server is misconfigured for the required memory resources. After the addition of more memory, the network transfer is re-analyzed. The new relative time displays a total of 83 milliseconds for the response time for the file server and workstation request-to-reply sequence.

Figure 5.3 shows the Network General Sniffer Expert system displaying a response from a file server to a workstation.

```
┌DETAIL─────────────────────────────────────────────┐
 SMB:  ──────── SMB Transaction Command ────────
 SMB:
 SMB:  Function = 25 (Transaction)
 SMB:  Tree id       (TID) = 0000
 SMB:  Process id    (PID) = 0000
 SMB:  Word count = 17
 SMB:  Transaction name = "\MAILSLOT\LANMAN"
 SMB:  Total size of mail data = 18
 SMB:  Additional information = 0000
 SMB:       .... .... .... ..0. = Response expected
 SMB:       .... .... .... ...0 = Do not disconnect TID
 SMB:  Time to wait for completion: 1000 msec
 SMB:  Op code = 1 (Write mail slot)
 SMB:  Priority of transaction = 0
 SMB:  Class = 2 (Unreliable)
 SMB:  Command = 1 (Announcement)
 SMB:  Services = 13
 SMB:       .... ...1. = Server
 SMB:       .... ...1  = Work station
 SMB:  Major version number = 2
         ────────Frame 557 of 20571────────
              Use TAB to select window
 1         2 Set    3Expert 4 Zoom  5         6Disply 7 Prev  8 Next  9Select 10 New
  Help      mark    window    out   Menus     options frame   frame   frame   capture
```

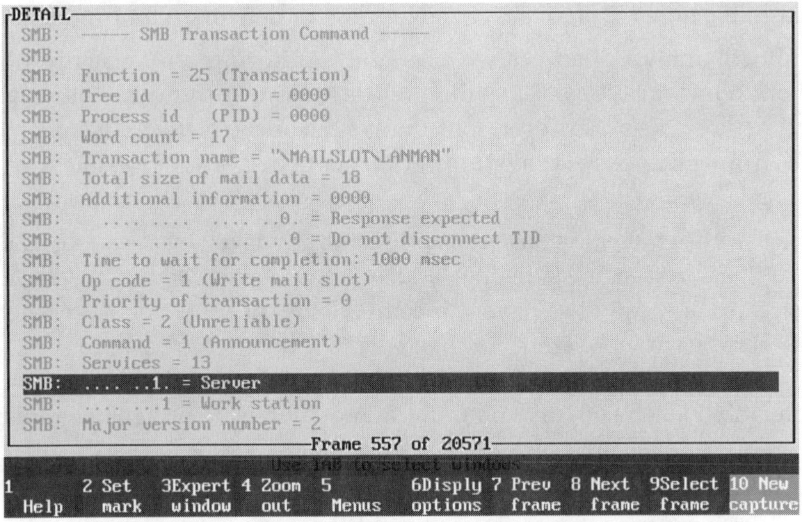

Figure 5.3 Network General Sniffer displaying a response from a file server to a workstation.

Understanding Network Retransmissions

A high number of network retransmissions can be a major problem for overall network operations. Some network devices expect responses to data transmissions within a certain amount of time; if that time elapses without a response, they may retransmit the data. This is known as *network retransmission*.

Sometimes applications retransmit data due to communication problems on the network. Some applications are designed to continue requesting data if they do not receive a proper response from the destination node. Another major reason for network retransmissions is when a node's NIC network driver version is incompatible with its destination node's NIC network driver.

All these problems can cause a high traffic level from the physical to network layers across the network, eventually causing a general disruption in overall communication and the network's operation. If this situation is occurring at the application level, the particular application may eventually time out at the desktop for the user and could possibly cause a network failure at the file server level.

The complexity of communications in today's networking environment increases the urgency of proactive monitoring for network retransmissions.

Protocol analyzers and other network monitoring tools usually pick up network retransmissions. Depending on the analyzer, this can require specific decoding of packets. However, some tools such as the Network General Sniffer have high-end expert systems that capture and present network retransmissions.

If network retransmissions are captured at any level, even as few as one or two network retransmissions per address, the particular address should be investigated at the physical layer for compatibility of packet types and network driver versions. If those areas are covered and found not to be a problem, all the applications at the OSI layer should be examined for any type of incompatibilities in network communication parameters or general application timing.

Some applications and certain types of software modules for destination nodes allow configuration modifications to prevent network retransmissions. The overall goal of network retransmission analysis is to eliminate the retransmissions altogether. Most networks have some network retransmissions present, and an analyst can prevent the network retransmission levels with the proper use of a protocol analyzer and applied troubleshooting skills.

The following is a general breakdown of how to monitor network retransmissions.

Technique Specifics

- Network retransmissions occur when a workstation or file server needs to retransmit data for a particular process. Many times a workstation requests a retransmission because it has not received all the data in the standard time window, or it has not received the data with true integrity. A high bandwidth level also can cause network retransmissions.
- If network retransmissions occur too frequently, it is very possible that physical layer error conditions exist, or that some of the upper protocol layers are having problems receiving or transmitting data.
- Network retransmissions can be most easily captured by filtering on the type of workstation that appears to have performance problems.
- By trapping the specific address of the workstation, it is possible to capture all the data and examine for retransmission packets.
- The retransmission may be noted in higher protocol layer fields throughout the packets. After the network retransmissions are captured, determine when it is occurring.
- Next, look at the time when this is occurring in relation to the addresses, internal packet notes on operating systems versions, file access information, and network bandwidth levels.
- Through examining the complete packet internals, it is possible to identify an incompatibility, bottleneck, or other network occurrence causing the retransmission.

For example, a group of workstations appears to have a performance problem when working with a mail application. The analyst chooses one specific workstation that is having the problem and notes its specific NIC MAC address. Next, the analyst sets up a protocol analyzer to filter the address and requests the user to start a mail open search process. The analyst captures the mail search event and identifies that the workstation repeatedly sends packet requests for file searches that are retransmissions almost 25 times before the file server finds and opens the file. Further analysis of the data shows that the workstation continues to change the search path attributes in the file request open packets 22 times before the file is actually found and opened by the file server. The analyst's search discovers that the path statements in the workstation's AUTOEXEC.BAT file are incorrect. Corrections are made to the AUTOEXEC.BAT file, and the search transfer is reanalyzed. The total search requests drops to three packet retransmissions.

Figure 5.4 shows the Network General Sniffer Expert system displaying a network transmission event.

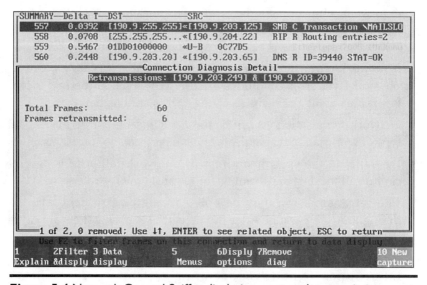

Figure 5.4 Network General Sniffer displaying a network transmission event.

Understanding Request-to-Reply Overlaps

Protocol analysis allows for some very detailed review of data on a network. All the upper layer protocols use specialized approaches for reading data across a network. Remember that all network access is based on standard disk drive access across the network. Read and write packet types exist, and the protocols involved deal in requests and replies of data from one node to another. This usually occurs in a workstation and file server environment, with a workstation requesting data from a file server, and the file server replying. A normal mode of operation and standard fluency always exists, as mentioned in the network optimization theory section of this book.

High-end expert systems can analyze a network's fluency, but doing so without an expert system requires a good technique, careful analysis, and a clear understanding of what network fluency is for the network at normal level.

Keep in mind that a workstation should be able to request data and receive a proper reply back from a file server. Through measuring request-to-reply efficiencies, an analyst can understand key factors in the overall health of the particular protocol. On a standard file request (for example, if a workstation requests a file from a particular file server), a certain number of records always are involved in the file read from the file server's disk drive. For example, if file records 0 to 1,000 are requested, a file server may need to send the particular file in subsections to the workstation to transfer all the data.

The scenario might go as follows. The workstation requests records 0 to 1,000. The file server may reply by sending records 0 to 400. Then the workstation acknowledges receiving the request, and the file server replies with records 400 to 1,000. If for some reason the file server were to reply with an overlap of records, for example 200 to 1,000, that would be a clear overlap of records 200 to 400. This is a *request-to-reply overlap*.

This is a clear inefficiency in network communications, but one that occurs frequently on today's networks. The only way to troubleshoot this type of problem is to use an advanced protocol analysis technique of monitoring the request to replies internally within the packet subsets. All transmissions across the network for requests and replies include individual record subset markings in the internals of the packet. The analyst must look at the file record transmission from a file server to workstation response packet and decode the file records sent from the file server in response to the workstation's request. This requires advanced analysis skills and judgment.

The following is a description of how to evaluate requests-to-reply efficiency, and to identify any overlap conditions.

Technique Specifics

- Request-to-reply overlaps occur when a workstation requests a file from a particular server or host, and, in the course of several response transmissions, the server sends information that has already been sent in a previous transmission. This constitutes inefficient file transfer.
- If this situation continues to occur, the only thing that can be focused on is the actual application involved in the transmission.
- Request-to-reply overlaps can be most easily captured by filtering the particular address that seems to be performing poorly. If the slow performance continues, it is important to examine that particular address by looking at all the data.

For example, a user complains about a spreadsheet application taking three minutes to be loaded from a file server to a workstation. An analyst sets up an analysis session with a filter on the protocol analyzer for the user's workstation NIC MAC address. The analyst examines the data trace from the protocol analyzer for all the spreadsheet's file requests to the file server. Examining the file pointer data numerics, the analyst discovers that the file server continues to resend the same data. Looking at the file pointers clearly shows request-to-reply overlaps.

This information was found in the detail of the packet and showed duplicate areas of the file being transmitted twice or more back to the workstation from the file server. Through research, the analyst found that the application loaded on the server is an old version. The most current version is loaded, and the transfer is reanalyzed. With the new version of the application, the spreadsheet load to the workstation transfer takes only 43 seconds.

This technique is effective for troubleshooting performance issues and identifying possible inefficient applications.

Figure 5.5 shows the Network General Sniffer Expert system displaying a request-to-replay overlap condition event.

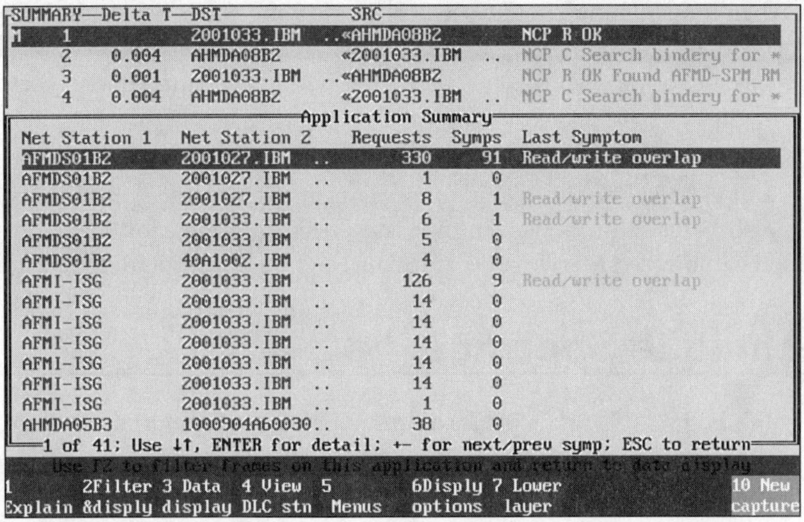

Figure 5.5 Network General Sniffer displaying a request-to-replay overlap condition event.

Understanding Network Throughput

The network analyst's goal should always be to provide the highest throughput of data in the least amount of time across LAN and WAN links. Measuring and calculating effective throughput is a specific skill that can be developed and fine-tuned through the use of a protocol analyzer.

Finding effective throughput is simply a matter of measuring the actual data transmitted from one specific node to another in a specific amount of time. The process includes capturing a set amount of data within a specific time period from one node to another with a protocol analyzer. It is easy to use a protocol analyzer to benchmark the absolute time of transmission from one node to another and to mark the transaction for a period of one second.

Throughput is usually measured in the one-second time-packet. A standard on a LAN is for the effective throughput from one node to another to be transmitted at least over the 200KB per second range. For a WAN transmission route, data transmission should occur at least in the 50KB per second range. A protocol analyzer can study this type of event and easily categorize if a particular network transmission is operating within a normal time-packet range for throughput.

The following breakdown shows how to measure effective throughput on LANs and WANs. Use this technique whenever performance problems appear. It can also be used on networks that have been migrated for some time and need to be optimized for overall performance across the particular spectrum.

Technique Specifics

- For both LANs and WANs, examine network throughput by looking at the number of bytes transferred in a standard amount of time—for example, one second—between two devices on the network.

For example, filter a workstation as it communicates with a file server; watch the amount of time that it takes, and the number of cumulative bytes transferred within a one-second time-packet. To calculate cumulative bytes, simply add up all the bytes in each individual packet for all the packets in one second. This gives the throughput in kilobytes per second from the workstation to the file server.

- Make sure to filter the specific addresses and zero out the time packets in the trace in such a way as to look at throughput from the beginning of one second to the ending of another second. Then again add up all the bytes that are accumulated in each packet through that one-second transfer. This enables you to calculate the effective throughput on the network.
- On LANs, a minimum of 200KB per second is considered standard for a normal transfer.
- On WANs, a minimum of 50KB per second is considered standard.
- This technique is excellent for examining overall throughput issues on the network and related to time response issues at the user's desktop.
- This technique enables you to examine the overall traffic routes throughout a network to identify any bottlenecks or areas of concern.

For example, a clothing store chain has a main office in New York City and a small design center in a New Jersey suburb. A wide area link dedicated circuit at 128KB between the two office locations connects two Ethernet networks. The clerks in the New Jersey design center are complaining about poor performance when requesting product information from a New York file server. The analyst uses multiple analyzers to capture the total data transferred in one second between the two sites.

The analysis session indicates that the total effective throughput is 3KB per second. Further research of the captured data shows that the files are very large and are saturating the available 128KB circuit between the two locations. The circuit is upgraded to 512KB, and the WAN link transfer throughput is reanalyzed. The new effective throughput is found to be 88KB per second.

Understanding Network Overloads

Optimizing includes checking for bandwidth utilization overload. Bandwidth levels can be monitored at average and peak utilization levels. An average utilization is the amount of utilization on a network over a specified standard period of time. A peak utilization is the highest peak of utilization reached during a specified time.

Through analysis on networks, it is important to understand the difference between the two bandwidth levels. Both the Token Ring and Ethernet environments have figures for average and peak levels. Through multiple analysis studies and specified techniques, you can measure what is considered a normal and a peak level for a particular network. This measurement factor can vary somewhat across different networks due to general environmental differences, such as the type of applications and the number of technology components and users.

On a Token Ring network, an average bandwidth level of 40% is considered the highest average that would normally be reached, and a peak utilization of no more than 65% should be reached at any time. On an Ethernet network, 30% is considered to be the maximum normal level for overall average utilization, and 55% is considered to be the maximum peak utilization level. These are considered standard benchmarks in the industry for Token Ring and Ethernet.

Through analysis of a network, the analyst learns to understand the specific network and can decide what the average and peak utilization factors are for that network over an extended period of time. This requires not only a highly skilled analyst, but also one with a specific understanding of the network operations being analyzed.

The following section describes the proper approach for baselining the average and peak utilization on any network. This is a general approach that may need to be modified, depending upon the network and analyzer being used.

Technique Specifics

- A high number of network failures today are due to peak bandwidth overloaded network conditions.
- The bandwidth on a network easily can be examined with any protocol analyzer. The key is to understand when an actual network overload will occur. A network overload occurs when the bandwidth exceeds a safe operational condition for a network due to its topology, applications, and user profiles.
- Recognizing a network overload on a specific network requires knowing the normal bandwidth on a general baseline. For example, say a network normally runs at an average 20% level and peaks at a 50% level on the normal baseline. If the network has problems, and it is found that the threshold is now a 40% average and a 60% peak, the network is considered to be in a network overload condition.
- To measure average and peak utilization, a protocol analyzer can be easily installed. It should be set to measure utilization for a least one hour. The measurements for average and peak utilization should be monitored very carefully and then documented.
- Certain industry standards exist for most LAN environments.
- On a Token Ring network, the bandwidth level should not exceed an average of 40% and a peak of 65%.
- On an Ethernet environment, the average bandwidth level should not exceed 30%, and the peak should be no more than 55%.
- These are considered standard ratios for network overload thresholds throughout the industry, but the figures can vary depending on the overall configuration of a specific network.

Chapter 5: Optimization Techniques

For example, an investment office in Chicago has a 4Mbps Token Ring network. Every morning at stock market opening time, the stock brokers have problems with their workstations rebooting as they attempt to log on to the LAN file server. An analyst connects a protocol analyzer to the network and finds that the bandwidth levels at 9 AM are reaching five-second peaks of 90 % of the 4Mbps available bandwidth.

The cause of this behavior is that certain ring stations have to re-attempt ring insertion because of the bandwidth saturation. Through data analysis, the analyst finds that the logon sequence block sizes for the stock market application are in the approximate 2KB packet transmission block size. The analyst works with the application developers to recommend reducing the block transmission packet sizes at logon to 200 bytes maximum.

The new application patch is designed and loaded, and the network is reanalyzed. Now the bandwidth levels only reach 45% at logon market time. The modification also showed a clear business benefit to the investment firm, because at the brokers' desktop level there were no more interruptions at market open time.

Figure 5.6 shows the Network General Sniffer Expert system displaying a network bandwidth overload condition.

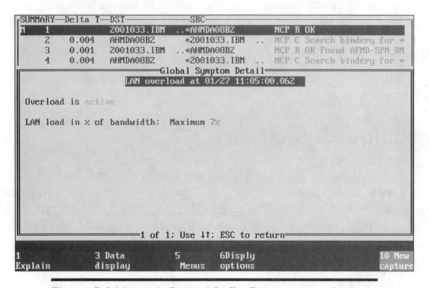

Figure 5.6 Network General Sniffer Expert system displaying a network bandwidth overload condition.

Understanding Internetwork Route Identification

Internetworking route identification is the study of what routes are taken when data travels from one network to another. Although some advanced protocol analyzers can trap this type of statistic easily, this specific study requires an analyst experienced in internetworking.

The protocol analyzer monitors a specific conversation between two nodes on multiple networks. Normally, when a conversation occurs between two nodes on different networks, as the data travels from network to network, certain routing information is contained in the different protocol layers of the packets transmitted between the two nodes.

At times, depending upon network traffic levels and certain problems with bottlenecks in either Ethernet or Token Ring networks, it is possible that excessive routes can be taken. A protocol analyzer can be used to easily decode the traffic routes taken between the two nodes.

This book cannot cover all the concepts of internetworking routing analysis, but after reading all the protocol sections later in this book, the analyst can understand more clearly the importance of internetworking route analysis. The goal is to examine the internals of a network packet for routing identification information to see what actual route has been taken from a source node to a destination node in a multiple network environment.

The following section describes the proper approach for examining an internetwork route.

Technique Specifics

- This technique allows for analyzing when those excessive routes occur and actually benchmarking and carefully studying the overall internetwork route methodology. This helps the analyst improve and optimize the actual route throughout the network layout. This requires an analyst very experienced in multiple protocols.

- A protocol analyzer must be attached to the network. The idea is to monitor a transmission of multiple network routed frames from one specific point between the two networks.
- Next, the analyst needs to decode all the routing information for the packets involved. This is different for each protocol. The routing fields usually show the networks and bridges/routers that the transmission traveled through.

For example, a Dallas oil firm has a Token Ring internetwork including a central backbone and eight subuser rings with multiple distributed file servers located on different rings. There were specific issues with certain workstation logons across the internetwork intermittently taking as long as 30 seconds. The analyst connects a protocol analyzer to the backbone ring and monitors network transfers.

It is found that at times certain route connections between rings are congested with traffic levels from high user count traffic levels on the subrings. Some transmissions from network 1 to network 5, which should be a straight pass through along three bridges, actually travel through six bridges on an excessive route through the ring 8 and 9 networks.

The MIS department attempts to achieve better balance by placing users more equally across rings 1, 2, 3, 4, and 5. The analyst reanalyzes the transfers and finds that the majority of transfers are decreased to nine seconds.

The following are two trace examples from a Network General Sniffer of possible internetworking routing examination through packet decoding. One example (Figure 5.7) presents a source routing identification analysis of the routing information fields within a Token Ring transmission across multiple networks. The second example (Figure 5.8) includes the routing identification between two Novell networks by examining the IPX header within the Novell protocol. These examples clearly show ways to examine internetwork routes through protocol analysis.

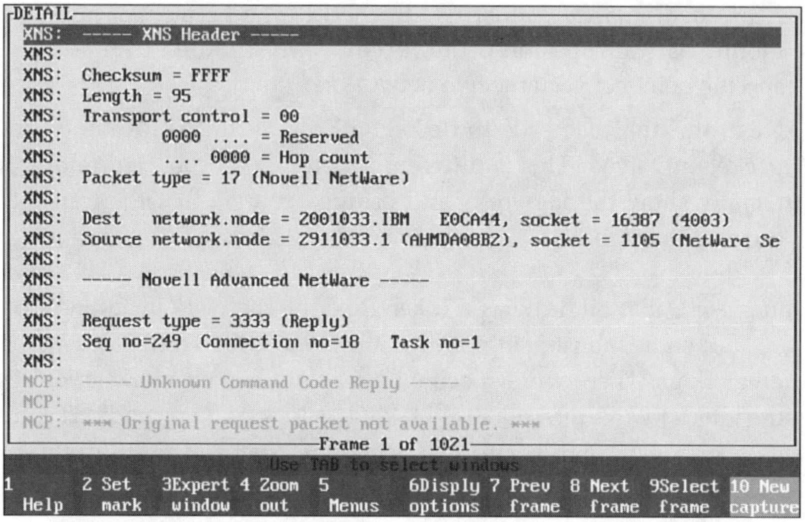

ETHERNET AND TOKEN RING OPTIMIZATION

```
┌DETAIL─────────────────────────────────────────────────────────────
│XNS: ─────── XNS Header ───────
│XNS:
│XNS: Checksum = FFFF
│XNS: Length = 95
│XNS: Transport control = 00
│XNS:         0000 .... = Reserved
│XNS:         .... 0000 = Hop count
│XNS: Packet type = 17 (Novell NetWare)
│XNS:
│XNS: Dest   network.node = 2001033.IBM    E0CA44, socket = 16387 (4003)
│XNS: Source network.node = 2911033.1 (AHMDA08B2), socket = 1105 (NetWare Se
│XNS:
│XNS: ─────── Novell Advanced NetWare ───────
│XNS:
│XNS: Request type = 3333 (Reply)
│XNS: Seq no=249  Connection no=18   Task no=1
│XNS:
│NCP: ─────── Unknown Command Code Reply ───────
│NCP:
│NCP: *** Original request packet not available. ***
│                        ─── Frame 1 of 1021 ───
│                        Use TAB to select windows
│1      2 Set    3Expert 4 Zoom  5        6Disply 7 Prev  8 Next  9Select 10 New
│ Help    mark    window   out    Menus    options  frame   frame   frame  capture
```

Figure 5.7 Routing identification between two Novell networks.

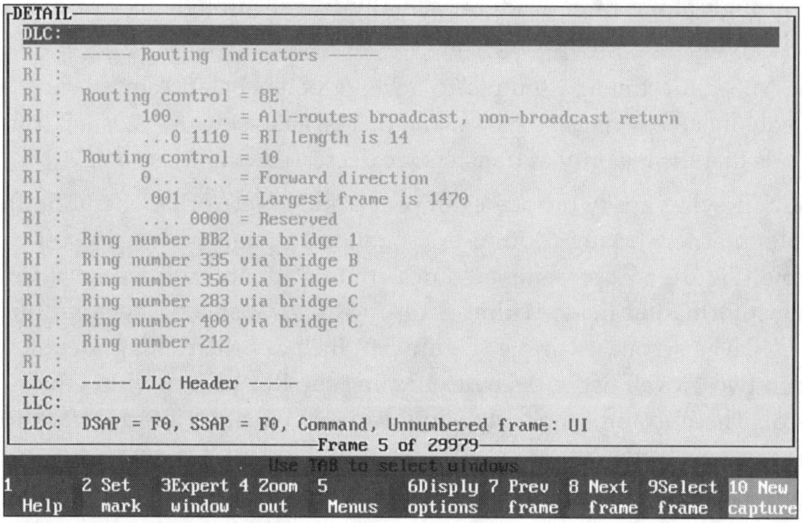

```
┌DETAIL─────────────────────────────────────────────────────────────
│DLC:
│RI : ─────── Routing Indicators ───────
│RI :
│RI : Routing control = 8E
│RI :      100. .... = All-routes broadcast, non-broadcast return
│RI :      ...0 1110 = RI length is 14
│RI : Routing control = 10
│RI :      0... .... = Forward direction
│RI :      .001 .... = Largest frame is 1470
│RI :      .... 0000 = Reserved
│RI : Ring number BB2 via bridge 1
│RI : Ring number 335 via bridge B
│RI : Ring number 356 via bridge C
│RI : Ring number 283 via bridge C
│RI : Ring number 400 via bridge C
│RI : Ring number 212
│RI :
│LLC: ─────── LLC Header ───────
│LLC:
│LLC: DSAP = F0, SSAP = F0, Command, Unnumbered frame: UI
│                        ─── Frame 5 of 29979 ───
│                        Use TAB to select windows
│1      2 Set    3Expert 4 Zoom  5        6Disply 7 Prev  8 Next  9Select 10 New
│ Help    mark    window   out    Menus    options  frame   frame   frame  capture
```

Figure 5.8 A source routing identification analysis across multiple networks.

Remember that many more types of routing information fields and decodes exist that may need to be analyzed, and this requires extensive experience in those particular protocols.

Understanding Application Characterization

In today's internetworks daily troubleshooting becomes more complex. A new factor is the rightsizing of single point of entry applications onto LANs and the implementation of new client-server applications. As these migrations occur, the applications must be monitored for how they will affect current LAN traffic levels and for how they will be effected by the LAN.

The process of properly monitoring a new application can be done through several techniques. There are various third party applications that offer metering and characterization approaches, but the most exact way to monitor an application is through protocol analysis.

When a new application is about to be deployed on an internetwork, it should be captured and analyzed with a protocol analyzer. This should first be done in a pure test LAN environment if possible. The application can be launched on a specific workstation. The protocol analyzer can be configured to filter and capture the workstations transmission to a specific server. Next, the trace file can be decoded to measure packet sizes, time for key events such as logon, file access, and close operations. The following subsection details the technique specific approach that can be used.

Technique Specifics

- List the event steps of operation that the application will perform on the network, such as logon, open file, modify, print, logoff.
- Identify a workstation to run the application.
- Configure a physical address station filter for the workstation.
- Utilize the example chart in Figure 5.9 to note the key frame sequences. Tell the user start the application sequencing.
- Keep the analyzer in a mode where the amount of packets in the buffer can be monitored.
- When the logon is completed note this in the column for frame count.
- Next perform the same step for the other event steps.
- When the test is completed, save the trace file.

ETHERNET AND TOKEN RING OPTIMIZATION

- Last, enter the data review mode in the trace analyzer and examine utilization levels, time sequences, data integrity.

Application Load Factor Analysis Table

Customer _____
Network analyzed upon _____
Application name _____
Trace file _____

Frame number	Event	Relative time between farme numbers	Peak network utilization reached between consecutive frame markings

Figure 5.9 Application load factor analysis table.

CHAPTER 6

Analysis for Major Operating System Protocols

Today, the actual data traffic upon networks and internetworks is composed of multiple protocols. A key focus of network optimization is to understand and decode most of the major protocols. These protocols should work with each other in full concert for communication from end node to end node, in an environment of multiple protocols that may not share the same rules, commands, or even language. As an analogy, think of the United States, where people of different races and creeds attempt to live together in synergy, but where the different backgrounds of people can lead to problems and misunderstandings. The same is true for the networking environment: When certain protocols do operate properly, they probably do not work in concert with other protocols on the same network.

The goal of networking is to have an open computing environment in which different types of networking applications, hardware, and software can achieve the synergy required for the end goal of computing: to get information from one place to another in an organized and fluent fashion. When all protocols work at their optimum level, are configured properly, and work with each other from node to node they way they should, achieving this end goal is more likely.

If a problem exists involving one protocol, it may cause performance problems across a network. These problems can range from general performance problems to network timeout values that prevent stations from working properly with each other. Errors can occur due to incompatibilities between two nodes in the revision of a protocol or subset of a protocol loaded on a specific networking device.

At times, networks may experience high traffic levels or general network overloads due to protocol communication problems on specific networks. If a protocol has an error, it can cause a broadcast level of high traffic due to its general protocol communication. Incompatibilities in the revision of the protocols or the proper configuration of a protocol may cause high network retransmission rates; this is evident when network drivers across a network are of different versions, or when network operating systems are incompatible.

By using a protocol analyzer and deciphering what is; called a trace, an analyst can obtain information on the internals of how a protocol operates on a specific network. A *trace* is a data record made by a protocol analyzer that can be reviewed to decode a specific protocol. Analysts familiar with the details of the protocols involved can use a protocol analyzer to obtain a trace when a network has a problem, and to review that trace in detail to isolate the specific cause of a problem.

Analyzing the Protocol Palette

The complexities of today's networks and internetworks have given rise to a complex range of issues to consider when optimizing or troubleshooting. An analyst has to focus on many components when analyzing a network, such as hardware and software platforms and even the actual cabling.

At times, applications may need to be decoded for their overall performance and operation on a particular network. It is important to understand the network drivers involved from node to node across a workstation when analyzing specific protocols.

All these subcomponents on the complete network must work together, and these devices can communicate only by properly employing protocols. Certain hardware and software platforms sometimes have specific protocols that must be used for them to communicate across the particular network. These protocols

Chapter 6: Analysis for Major Operating System Protocols

may depend on the quality of the network infrastructure, including the cabling and the hardware and software platforms they are communicating upon. In some instances, applications may require multiple protocols to provide a surface across a network. At times, the network drivers are the actual handlers of the packets that include the protocols that have to get from one node on a network to another.

In a network optimization project, the operations that need to be analyzed include the specific phases of communication which, when combined, result in the overall network goal of effective communication. An analyst needs to troubleshoot and optimize the following phases of communication by using a protocol analyzer:

- Network connections
- Logon sequence
- Connection keep-alive transmissions
- Broadcasts
- Network error messages
- File search methodology
- Internetwork addressing
- Routing methodologies
- Specific packet identification problems

The following sections describe each of these operations and its importance for network optimization.

Network Connections

From a protocol analysis standpoint, it is important to be able to analyze a proper network connection. A *network connection* is the actual network connection sequence, involving an initiation from one device for a connection, the final establishment of a true connection, and then some sort of transmission. At some point after this set of events, a device requests a termination of connection, and the connection finally disconnects.

There is always a fluent manner by which a network connection should be established on a network, and most protocol analyzers can capture this event clearly. Specific protocols have different rules for network connections, and the protocol being analyzed must be understood as far as its general initiation and connection setup and disconnect parameters. A protocol analyzer can examine most network connection operations.

Logon Sequences

A protocol analyzer can be used to examine most logon sequences within any protocol across any network. Every protocol has a particular sequence where a workstation requests to be connected to a particular file server and its network operating system and applications. The logon sequence can involve ten to hundreds of frames, and is usually complex. Negotiations occur between the workstation and the file server for packet size and password issues that need to be examined.

At times, logon sequences may be inefficient. An inefficient logon sequence can cause a very high bandwidth level, particularly in the morning and afternoon hours when large groups of people are logging on. The examination of the logon sequence requires a focused approach and a solid understanding of the protocol, but remember that the logon sequence needs to be examined as a network operation. Network optimization requires that network logon sequences work properly.

Network Keep-Alive Connection Transmissions

Every protocol has some sort of communication between workstations and file servers to keep the specific connection in a constant status when no data is to be transmitted. The DECnet protocol may use a Hello timer, and the Novell protocol may use a Watch Dog parameter. Each protocol has its own keep-alive connection type of transmission.

A protocol analyzer can usually pick up this type of transmission, which at times may even be considered a polling event, depending on the protocol. This can be examined by watching specific devices when they actually transmit a poll or a response to a poll from a particular file server or host. Polling is common in the SNA environment.

The main thing to remember is that connection keep-alive transmissions may occur between nodes and workstations. If at times some nodes on a network do

Chapter 6: Analysis for Major Operating System Protocols

not comply with the proper reply to a poll or keep-alive connection request, a device may be dropped off the network without a logical connection.

Particular protocols have certain times when the actual polling or request connection transmissions may occur. Analysts must understand these parameters and make sure that the devices on a network are tuned for the overall operation involved.

Broadcasts

As mentioned in Chapter 5, certain broadcast levels should be present on a network, usually an eight to ten percent maximum level. Broadcasts occur on a network for a variety of reasons, for example, to establish a certain type of connection or to identify an operation. They also occur to establish a certain route on a particular network. Sometimes broadcasts occur to update certain types of naming cables or general network addressing cables across a specific network.

All protocols have their forms of broadcast. The main point is that broadcasts need to be examined as a general network operation. They must be performed on a timely basis as required for a particular network. It is also important to verify whether the broadcasts even are required for a certain network's operations. If a broadcast is not required on a network, it can filter across the multiple network environment and cause problems in communication at the higher layers.

Network Error Messages

Network error messages are most easily identified by a particular sequence of different types of packets. For example, in the NetWare protocol suite, some analyzers easily pick up an NCP error, which is defined as a particular packet that cannot return a certain type of file.

Network error messages vary from protocol to protocol, so an analyst must understand the network error messages for the protocol being analyzed. The goal is to analyze the particular protocol for any errors. If the errors are at a high level, the analyst must troubleshoot the type of addresses involved to find out what type of devices and what type of problem is actually occurring.

File Search Methodology

File search methodology is a network operation that should be analyzed on any network. The most important function of a network is to access files across a network.

Each protocol on a network defines a search approach that is used to access files. The analyst must learn the file search methodology for all the protocols to be analyzed, and must understand how they are utilized on the network. In a NetWare environment, the approach is as follows:

A workstation requests a NetWare file from a file server. The file server opens the file; the file is accessed by the workstation; and a transfer occurs between the workstation and the file server. At some point, the file is closed by a request from the workstation, and the file server responds with the proper close. The file will have then been opened, accessed, and closed properly.

At times, problems may exist with the internals of a file search operation due to incorrect file attributes in a certain protocol. For example, a file is not searched upon properly from a workstation to a file server or a file is not even located in the requested directory. This varies from protocol to protocol, but the key is fluency. The analyst should look for a fluent open, access, and close operation on file access across the network.

Internetwork Addressing

Protocols usually have internal addressing parameters different from the physical layer addresses at the network interface card level. For example, in the NetWare protocol suite is an IPX layer that has a source network, a source node, and a source process or socket to which communication goes. These are effectively three layers of addresses that are going to need communications of the respective fields from node to node.

An analyst needs to understand the protocol involved, and then be able to decode the internals of the protocol fields involved. Acquiring the skills and an understanding of each internal protocol is in itself quite a task. Once these skills are mastered, it may be possible to identify addressing problems at the higher protocol layers for any protocol being troubleshot. At times, file servers may not be able to locate certain workstations or processes across the network due to internetwork addressing problems at the higher layers. This will be on a protocol-by-protocol basis, but an experienced analyst should be able to identify this type of issue quickly.

Chapter 6: Analysis for Major Operating System Protocols

Routing Methodologies

Routing methodologies allow a workstation to communicate with another workstation in a multiple network environment; or a workstation may need to communicate with a file server, or with a specific type of networking device. Generally, routing occurs between networks, and within the protocol being analyzed is a routing protocol layer that contains the internals of the route taken from device to device in each respective packet of communication on the network.

For example, in an IBM Token Ring environment, it is quite common to analyze the routing information field within a Token Ring frame to find the networks passed through and the particular bridges or routers along the network transmission from node to node. Within the DEC environment, it is common to analyze the DEC protocol for the same type of information, but in this case the analyst watches the hop count and cost of transmission from one network to another. The analyst needs to understand the internal routing protocols of the particular network, and how the hop from network to network occurs in the protocol and topology involved.

Specific Packet Identification Problems

Every protocol has certain types of packets considered problems on a particular network. These are packets usually transmitted from one of the nodes utilizing a particular protocol that may have a problem on the network. These types of packets, when picked up by a protocol analyzer, can be decoded by the analyst to identify the packet type. After the packet type is identified as an actual problem, it is easy to identify from the internals of the packet a specific address that may have a problem.

Again, every protocol has different types of packets that may present a problem. These problem packet types are described briefly in the respective protocol sections of this book. An analyst needs to be able to decode these types of packets, and to understand what they mean and from where they can be generated. For example, in the NetWare environment, if a delay packet is transmitted that is also internally marked as a request-being-processed packet, this packet may identify a busy file server.

Analyzing the Protocol Layers

In network optimization, analyzing the protocol layers means specifically looking at how the layers are defined in the overall protocol suites and the methodology of analyzing any particular network or internetwork.

In a multiprotocol network, it is important to understand the protocol communication occurring between the protocols and also the different protocols that may be key for the overall operation of a particular network. This can be based on understanding all the individual protocols and their communications within their own protocol suite.

A protocol suite is the subset of internal protocols contained within a protocol. For example, the NetWare protocol suite has approximately seven protocols actually utilized; each is considered an individual protocol within the NetWare protocol suite.

Each protocol of a composite protocol has a purpose. A standard organization of communication exists on a LAN or WAN for protocols to communicate internally. Standards in the industry, such as the Open Systems Interconnection (OSI) model, are defined by a certain organization on which most hardware and software platforms are based.

Within a particular protocol, such as Novell, the individual protocols rely upon each other to establish connections and effect a final data transaction across the Novell environment. The protocols work hand in hand on certain types of transactions, and rely upon each other to complete a transaction of data.

It is necessary to define the term layer. A *layer* is a subsection of an overall network communication session. Specific protocols are responsible for operations within certain layers of a transaction. Multiple layers are utilized by each protocol, and certain protocols may have more layers than others.

Most of these layers actually conform or work fairly closely with the OSI model discussed in Chapter 2. Note that some protocols do have layers that correspond to the OSI model. The discussions of specific protocols in this chapter attempt to correlate their layers with the OSI model. This is helpful from an analyst's standpoint, because a protocol analyzer normally breaks out a particular packet and shows the internal layers of communication being transmitted from one node to another.

When looking at an overall communication session, remember that certain layers on certain nodes communicate with each other across the network communication session. This may involve a packet transmission, for example,

Chapter 6: Analysis for Major Operating System Protocols

from node 1 to node B. When this communication occurs, a network layer internal setting may communicate with the network on another station's internal setting. Figure 6.1 displays a communication session between two OSI nodes on a network. This example shows how the network layer of one node is communicating with the network layer of another node.

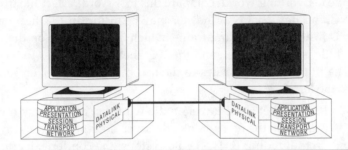

Figure 6.1 A communication session between two OSI nodes on a network.

You will encounter another term in connection with protocol analysis: encapsulation. *Encapsulation* is the enveloping of protocols within other protocols to allow transmission across a network. Enveloping of protocols is critical because certain protocols may require a vehicle of transmission from one network node to another.

Figure 6.2 shows how the NetWare Core Protocol (NCP) is enveloped within the IPX protocol, which is in turn enveloped within a Token Ring physical frame header. The Token Ring frame is carrying the NetWare protocol suite IPX, which in turn is carrying piggyback the NCP protocol from node A to node B across the network.

Figure 6.2 The NetWare Core Protocol is enveloped within the IPX protocol, which is enveloped within a Token Ring physical frame header.

By way of analogy, consider the act of mailing a letter. Suppose that the letter must get from Building A to Building B across the city of Chicago. The letter is put in an envelope and placed on a desk. A courier arrives at the 20th floor of Building A and walks into the office to pick up the letter. The courier places the envelope in a briefcase and proceeds down the elevator to the bottom floor of

Building A. The courier walks out the front door and hails a taxi cab. The taxi cab travels to a river, waits for a ferry, and is actually transported within the ferry across the river. The letter is now inside an envelope inside the courier's briefcase. The briefcase is inside a taxi cab, and the taxi cab is now inside a ferry traveling across a river.

Back in the networking world, compare this to a WordPerfect file that may be inside an NCP header. That NCP header may be inside an IPX header, and the IPX header is inside a Token Ring frame, which is not yet out on the wire. The WordPerfect file is like the letter, and the NCP header correlates to the courier's briefcase. The IPX header correlates to the taxi cab, and the Token Ring packet correlates to the ferry.

The Token Ring packet must travel on the wire, just as the ferry travels on a river. The ferry lands on the other side of the river, and the taxi cab drives out of the ferry and on to Building B. The taxi cab stops; the courier exits the taxi cab and takes the elevator up to the 30th floor. At that point, the courier exits the elevator into the proper office, opens the briefcase, and takes out the envelope. The secretary then opens the envelope to receive the letter.

This analogy hints at what occurs on a network, where many large transactions may occur just to get a simple piece of data from one node to another. This concept is shown in Figure 6.3.

The preceding example shows how important proper communication is in all the protocol layers on a network. The protocol analyst is responsible for capturing a full packet of information. Just like a single envelope on a ferry on a river, a large set of protocols is within the particular packet, but only a small amount of data is actually being transmitted. The protocol analyst is responsible for decoding all the protocols in the packet, making sure that the communication is proper.

If the door of the taxi cab did not open, if the elevator did not work, or if the ferry could not travel across the river, the packet with the letter would never reach the source destination, Building B. The equivalent scenario holds in network communications: if any problem occurs with one protocol working with another protocol in a particular network communication session, it is possible that the WordPerfect data will never arrive at node 2 from node 1.

As a protocol analyst, you must understand all the details of the individual protocols being analyzed to effectively examine all these different network communication hand-off sessions. This comes with time.

Chapter 6: Analysis for Major Operating System Protocols

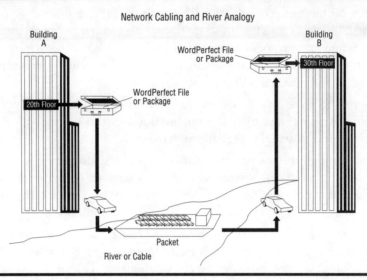

Figure 6.3 On a network, many transactions occur to move a single piece of data from node to node.

Understanding Methodology of Multiprotocol Analysis

Many protocols exist in the internetworking environment, and within those protocols are multiple layers of functional protocol operations. All the complexities of the protocols in the internal layers can mean a large group of issues and questions resulting from a general analysis of the protocols. Today's protocol analyzers are advanced, which enables an analyst to more easily decode the respective protocols. Nonetheless, it is still a complex task.

The most efficient way to analyze a multiprotocol environment is to page through the trace. This is tedious and requires much patience on the part of the analyst. Paging through the trace means actually stepping through each particular packet in a full captured data gathering with a protocol analyzer from a network. The protocol analyzer is usually attached to the network, and the capture or initial start of the protocol analysis section is engaged. At some point the protocol analyst stops the analyzer, and the data trace can be displayed on the screen on the protocol analyzer. The analyst at that point can actually step through all the packets within the data trace. This technique should generally be applied when the protocol analyst is involved in a complex multiprotocol environment. This procedure is much the same as when a scientist pages through a book to research information.

It is great to have a protocol analyzer, such as the Network Expert Sniffer, that alerts the user of a particular problem. But sometimes even with the Expert Sniffer, you need to actually page through the trace.

Paging through the trace is an excellent technique for getting involved with the internals of protocols themselves, and it also usually alerts the analyst of problems that may be hiding within the internals of the packets. This technique requires an advanced skill set, much patience, and dedication.

It is important to analyze all the internals of each packet and to look for any problems in the packet format, or a possible error message within the packet. Every topology or protocol can have problems specific to that protocol or topology. Although all packets—whether Ethernet, Token Ring, NetWare, or Banyan—have common areas, they may have different formats, depending on the topology and the protocol. The following areas should be examined, in the particular packet format, for general analysis:

- Addresses for the network
- Source and destination addresses
- File specifics
- User nodes
- Time frames
- Frame length
- Routing information
- Broadcast information
- Specific protocol information

Addresses for the Network

Any type of packet has a physical address category, and even a higher-layer protocol address breakdown. In the physical layer area, there usually is a data

Chapter 6: Analysis for Major Operating System Protocols

link control (DLC) or medium access control (MAC) address that has the specific identification of the NICs communicating across the particular communication session. Usually higher-layer protocol information is in the source and destination address area, which may include node addresses, network addresses, and specific process addresses identified with the protocol involved. These need to be decoded on all networks.

File Specifics

File specifics refers to a specific type of request, reply, and access mode for a particular file. All protocols have a certain file request mode for a workstation to use to search a file server for a particular file. In a certain access mode, the file server searches its drives for the file, and then provides acknowledgment to the workstation. At that point, a transfer may occur where the workstation receives the file from the file server. Later, a close takes place where either the workstation or the file server initiates the final close of the file. This normal sequence can be discovered within internal packets.

Time Frames

The time frame is the actual time that a frame is generated from a node. It usually is marked within all internal packets on any type of topology or protocol. This should be analyzed and noted in any analysis session.

Frame Length

There are usually legal and illegal frame sizes for any topology or protocol. Frame sizes are usually identified within the particular frame, often with a size for the complete frame and a size for the internals of the protocols enveloped within the frame. The frame length and particular packet section length should always be noted in an analysis session.

Routing Information

A packet always includes a routing information breakdown if it is sent from one network to another across a multiple network environment. The packet usually contains the networks and the bridges where routers pass through.

Broadcast Information

A packet may contain internal broadcast information when a particular node is broadcasting either to obtain a connection or to continue a conversation with another node in a broadcast fashion. Broadcast information should always be noted; broadcasts are quite common on Token Ring networks in the mode of either single or multiple broadcast information. This should also be noted through all analysis sessions. Broadcast storms occur when a station transmits while trying unsuccessfully to receive a response. This can be very easily identified in the broadcast information from an analysis session.

Specific Protocol Information

During a protocol analysis session, be on the lookout for odd or abnormal information from a particular protocol. When paging through the trace, the analyst should always note specific protocol information that seems important.

Always note any particular issues or problems in a high level trace; also note anything that seems to stand out in paging through the trace. Be patient, take notes, and carefully document any information in a trace. When looking at the complete problem or the optimization of a particular network, it helps to refer back to particular addresses or nodes in protocols found through a trace.

Some of the techniques mentioned in the network optimization tools section of this book, such as filtering and triggering, are important in an analysis session. Filtering data is important because specific workstations or specific protocols may need to be examined in detail. Most protocol analyzers allow for filtering on protocols or address-level information to enable an analyst to look at the specifics and focus on the actual problem being troubleshot or that is of concern for network optimization.

Filtering also allows listening in on specific conversations between workstations and certain file servers, or between file servers. This allows for examination of specific conversations so as to focus on a certain problem or issue.

Remember that certain protocols always require certain responses in reference to certain requests. Problems can occur when the requests are not followed by the expected response, such as if a workstation requests a file, and a file server does not respond with the file. In paging through a trace, the analyst should always focus on file access to make sure that the proper responses are provided during file access. It is also important to watch for proper responses between any respective nodes in a file server during network communication,

Chapter 6: Analysis for Major Operating System Protocols

especially for bridge and router communication between devices on an internetwork.

In connection environments, watch for a proper initiation of a connection, for the connection to actually occur in communication to flow through properly, and then for a proper disconnect of that particular connection. An analyst should always make sure that abrupt or early disconnects do not occur from respective devices during communication sessions. This is a key analysis approach in the SNA environment.

Also watch for any errors that may occur in a routing information environment. In an internetwork, nodes on different networks are trying to communicate with each other. At times, certain connections may be established, but communication may eventually fail due to a throughput problem or a communication or configuration problem in a bridge or router.

Watch all the routing information transmitted to set up the connection and to keep a connection established. Certain file servers and workstations update each other frequently on their location on an internetwork, and this requires a certain approach, such as routing information protocols.

Later, in the routing protocol section, a discussion is presented on routing information protocols and troubleshooting a routing environment. The focus here, however, is from a general analysis standpoint, paging through traces to note any information that seems important to the troubleshooting or optimization session. Figure 6.4 shows a detailed internal view of a data trace that identifies key areas requiring analysis.

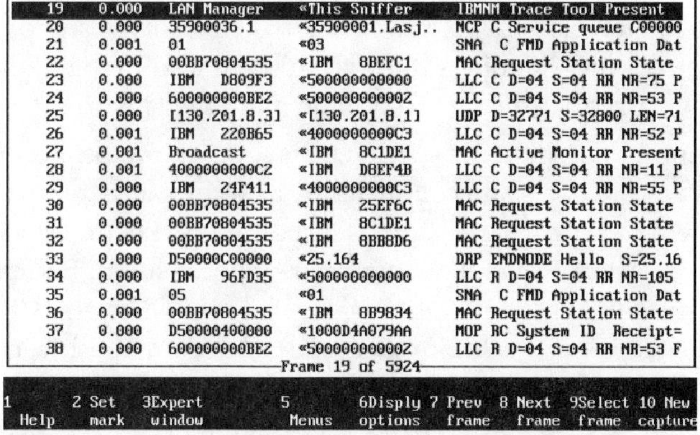

```
SUMMARY—Delta T—DST         SRC
   19   0.000  LAN Manager      «This Sniffer    IBMNM Trace Tool Present
   20   0.000  35900036.1       «35900001.Lasj.. NCP C Service queue C00000
   21   0.001  01               «03              SNA  C FMD Application Dat
   22   0.000  00BB70804535     «IBM    8BEFC1   MAC Request Station State
   23   0.000  IBM    D809F3    «500000000000    LLC C D=04 S=04 RR NR=75 P
   24   0.000  600000000BE2     «500000000002    LLC C D=04 S=04 RR NR=53 P
   25   0.000  [130.201.8.3]    «[130.201.8.1]   UDP D=32771 S=32800 LEN=71
   26   0.001  IBM    220B65    «4000000000C3    LLC C D=04 S=04 RR NR=52 P
   27   0.001  Broadcast        «IBM    8C1DE1   MAC Active Monitor Present
   28   0.001  4000000000C2     «IBM    D8EF4B   LLC C D=04 S=04 RR NR=11 P
   29   0.000  IBM    24F411    «4000000000C3    LLC C D=04 S=04 RR NR=55 P
   30   0.000  00BB70804535     «IBM    25EF6C   MAC Request Station State
   31   0.000  00BB70804535     «IBM    8C1DE1   MAC Request Station State
   32   0.000  00BB70804535     «IBM    8BBBD6   MAC Request Station State
   33   0.000  D50000C00000     «25.164          DRP ENDNODE Hello  S=25.16
   34   0.000  IBM    96FD35    «500000000000    LLC R D=04 S=04 RR NR=105
   35   0.001  05               «01              SNA  C FMD Application Dat
   36   0.000  00BB70804535     «IBM    8B9834   MAC Request Station State
   37   0.000  D50000400000     «1000D4A079AA    MOP RC System ID  Receipt=
   38   0.000  600000000BE2     «500000000002    LLC R D=04 S=04 RR NR=53 F
                                Frame 19 of 5924
1      2 Set    3Expert      5         6Display 7 Prev  8 Next  9Select 10 New
 Help  mark    window        Menus      options  frame  frame   frame   capture
```

Figure 6.4 An internal view of a data trace identifying key areas.

ETHERNET AND TOKEN RING OPTIMIZATION

Examining the Protocols

The following section describes the major protocols seen most often in today's internetworking environment. Earlier sections of this book have presented in-depth discussions of protocol analysis and network optimization. The goal of network optimization is to analyze the protocols at the most discrete level for complete fluency between their particular layers. As noted earlier, it is important that each protocol works properly with other protocols for a communication session to occur properly.

Within the layers of any particular protocol is discrete information that contains the internals of how a communication session is working for general connection setup or file access. An analyst must monitor the internals of the frame for any types of errors or file transfer problems that may be present. There always will be messages present that may show problems with a file open, a general transmission session, or a close of a file. It is imperative that the analyst be focused on all the fields and take proper notes.

Along with node-to-node connection, it is also important to watch for setup of a connection, proper communication of a session, and setup disconnection. Every protocol has its own layers and its own field for these processes. The following sections outline the specifics of most of the major protocols used in an internetwork environment. Each respective layer within the protocol is mentioned as an internal protocol and the respective field breakdowns are presented. The analyst who uses this book must study the fields in this section, refer back to the technical approaches mentioned earlier, and finally take a careful approach (and a notebook) to a protocol analysis session.

It takes time to develop the technical expertise to analyze any protocol, and a particular protocol may require extensive study. It also may require taking the time to sit down and analyze the protocol on multiple networks.

The following section includes specific hints for each protocol layer. At the end of the next section are notes and comments on areas or packet types that may be a problem in the protocols. This section describes the packet descriptions as far as the internal protocols for the following major protocol suites: Encapsulation and Connection Protocols (LLC and SNAP), Novell, SNA, DECnet, TCP/IP, Banyan, and Apple. These are the major protocols used in the internetworking environment, but other protocols may be encountered. These sections present extensive discussions on both the Novell and TCP/IP protocols. Those also can be troubleshot using the theories presented in this book.

Encapsulation and Connection Protocols (LLC and SNAP)

The following protocols are used frequently in network transfer for encapsulating key upper layer protocols (ULPs). The 802.2 LLC standard is considered a separate protocol, but is used in Ethernet and Token Ring networks to encapsulate data and provide connection maintenance. The Sub Network Access Protocol (SNAP) is used quite often to encapsulate carry across certain topologies. These two protocols are described in the next section.

Logical Link Control (LLC)

The logical link control (LLC) protocol is considered a standard by the IEEE, and is labeled the 802.2 standard. It is a communication and carrying protocol which can provide reliable transmission of information across a LAN. The way data is routed across a network with LLC is somewhat defined by the MAC layer of the particular topology. Specifically, the LLC protocol can be used to envelope data and provide flow control in the transfer of data. Node and internal processes that use the LLC protocol for data transfer are defined as source and destination Service Access Points (SAPs). Both the source and destination address will normally be specified in the 802.2 LLC protocol. Each process between a destination and source node address may have a unique SAP. These would be labeled Source Service Access Point (SSAP) and Destination Service Access Point (DSAP). That SAP address can be up to 8 bytes in length.

There are three different types of communication that can occur in an LLC environment; a control field will identify what the type of the communication is being utilized for the LLC protocol.

This LLC protocol would normally be carried by a physical frame as a Protocol Data Unit (PDU). The PDU will hold the data which is communicated from node to node. The PDU data may include other multiple ULP protocol layers to carry the actual application data that is most related to the complete packet.

The LLC Protocol has three type fields:

- Type 1—Unacknowledged Connectionless Service
  The sending and receiving stations (SSAP and DSAP) send their data from point to point. Broadcasts are supported by this type, but there is no acknowledgement required, and no connection is maintained.

- Type 2—Logical Connection

    The SSAP and DSAP would maintain a connection, and full flow control acknowledgement and error control will take place between their connection.

- Type 3—Acknowledgement When Required—No Connection

    The SSAP and DSAP would acknowledge each transfer if required but no actual connection maintenance takes place.

An LLC session involves the establishment of a virtual connection between two network nodes. The connection can be maintained or not maintained. It is common to see LLC utilized to set up a session and then maintain a poll between a network PC and a network host, such as in SNA environments.

The SSAP and DSAP will have preassigned codes and may indicate the subprotocol for the rest of the packet.

The LLC protocol control field may also have information relating to whether the LLC frame is Informational (I), Supervisory (S), or Unnumbered (U).

If LLC is labeled Informational (I), there is going to be data inside the PDU, and there may be a sequence number and sequence assigned to the communication. If LLC is labeled Supervisory (S), it will assume that the node-to-node communication will have some sort of command or response involved. There are certain types of sub-actions within supervisory that can be labeled, such as receive ready, receive not ready, and reject. This activity represents the flow control strength of LLC. If LLC is labeled as Unnumbered (U), the LLC packet is usually involved in a mode of connection control. The following modes may occur: Asynchronous Balance Mode (ABM); Disconnect Mode (DISC); Disconnected Mode (DM); Unnumbered Acknowledgement (UA); Frame Reject (FRMR); Exchange Information (XID); Testing (TEST); and Unnumbered Information.

Subnetwork Access Protocol (SNAP)

SNAP is an encapsulation protocol that was originally used when Ethernet frames had to be carried across a Token Ring environment. In today's networks, SNAP is seen as a universal protocol for carrying other key ULPs in multiprotocol internetworks. The SNAP protocol works well in environments that incorporate complex protocol stacks. SNAP is also seen commonly as encapsulated within 802.2 LLC PDUs as a more defined identifier.

The SNAP header will include other data internally, such as other ULPs or raw data. The breakout for the SNAP header is as follows:

Protocol ID—3 Bytes
This field identifies the next ULP encapsulated.

Ethertype ID—2 Bytes
This field identifies the Ethertype.

Data—Variable
This is the field that will include the next ULP and actual data.

Novell

The Novell protocol suite is probably the most well known, given that Novell has the largest hold on network software operations throughout the internetworking environment. The Novell protocols have been a strong presence since the mid-1980s. You will encounter Novell's protocols frequently in most protocol analysis sessions. When approaching any type of large internetwork, the Novell protocol suites usually are part of the overall protocol mix. Generally, the Novell protocols are quite easy and organized as far as analysis is concerned. Their methodologies for addressing and network file access are among the most uniform and strong in the industry.

Generally, Novell uses the Xerox networking system protocols as the model for its internal protocol suite. Different versions of the Novell protocol architecture exist. Most internetworks include the following: a network layer protocol labeled Internetwork Packet Exchange (IPX); and a transport layer protocol the Sequence Packet Exchange (SPX). The main application protocol in the Novell protocol suite is the NetWare Core Protocol (NCP). A more efficient version of the NetWare Core Protocol, labeled NetWare Burst Mode Protocol, is discussed later.

The NetWare protocol suite has its own routing protocol, the Routing Information Protocol (RIP), and a server communication protocol called Service Advertising Protocol (SAP). The main connection keep-alive protocol is the Watch Dog protocol. The Novell protocol layers are related to the OSI packet format shown in Figure 6.5.

ETHERNET AND TOKEN RING OPTIMIZATION

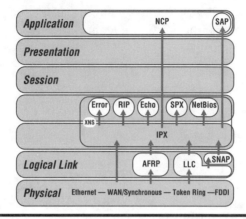

Figure 6.5 The Novell protocol layers compared to the OSI model.

Novell Protocol Types

The following sections briefly describe each of the main layers of the Novell protocol suite. Due to the wide implementation of the Novell protocol types, an in-depth field description is included for the key protocol layers IPX, SPX, and NCP.

Internetwork Packet Exchange (IPX)

The IPX protocol generally is a nonconnection protocol designed for network layer communications on Novell networks. The protocol is not a connection-oriented protocol because it does not guarantee delivery across the network. It does allow for the communication between two nodes, but does not guarantee that particular connection.

IPX is an organized protocol for setting up and breaking down connections, and its goal is to ensure that proper setup and transfer sessions occur across the Novell network. The IPX protocol does not support any particular broadcast methodology across the network, but is used for setting up general connections.

The breakdown of the IPX packet format includes a checksum and a length reading with a transport control field, which is actually a hop count. There is a packet type designation for what protocols can be layered on top of the IPX format, and then a detailed breakdown of the destination network, node, and socket or internal process of the particular Novell session. Then there is a simple noting of the source network address, node address, and the source socket or process ID.

Chapter 6: Analysis for Major Operating System Protocols

Probably the most important information in analysis of IPX is the addressing fields, and then the transport control field, which actually identifies the number of networks passed through. This is the routing information obtained within the IPX format.

The following is a breakout of the IPX fields.

- IPX Protocol Field Specifics:
- Checksum
- Length
- Transport Control
- Packet Type
- Destination Network Address
- Destination Node Address
- Destination Socket
- Source Node Address
- Source Socket

Checksum—2 Bytes
The Checksum field in the IPX header is a math algorithm used for a Cyclic Redundancy Check (CRC).

Length—2 Bytes
The Length field presents the length of the IPX packet.

Transport Control—1 Byte
The Transport Control field represents the number of routes an IPX packet has passed through on a network transmission. This is also called the Novell Hop Count field.

Packet Type—1 Byte
This field indicates the ULP in the IPX packet.

NCP packet = 17

SPX packet = 5

IPX packet = 5

Other packet types possible are reserved

Source or Destination Network—4 Bytes

This field represents the source or destination network for the IPX packet.

Source or Destination Node—6 Bytes

This field represents the node (workstation) within the source or destination network for the IPX packet.

Source or Destination Socket—2 Bytes

This 2-byte field represents the host process within the source or destination node that for the IPX packet.

Example Socket Types:

0451H—NCP

0452H—SAP

0453H—RIP

0455—NetBIOS

0456H—Diagnostic Packet

0457H—Serialization Packet

4000 to 6000H—Custom reserved sockets

Sequence Packet Exchange (SPX)

The Sequence Packet Exchange is a protocol used at the transport layer. Unlike the IPX packet format, SPX establishes a formal connection between communicating nodes and is called a connection-oriented protocol. The connected nodes use the SPX protocols to guarantee a complete successful message delivery. Unlike IPX, SPX enables nodes to detect errors and retransmit packets in the event of non-delivery.

Chapter 6: Analysis for Major Operating System Protocols

The SPX packets have fields that carry information to allow nodes to confirm the completion of network transfers. The SPX protocol is usually implemented for print servers, remote console servers, and gateways on Novell networks. These are the types of devices that usually require a guaranteed connection.

The SPX frame format includes a connection control field and a data stream type that actually sets up the overall connection. Then there is a source address and destination address setup. An internal sequence number and acknowledgment number field communication also occurs, which allows for checking back and forth that the sequence and the acknowledgments are proper for a guaranteed connection.

The following is a breakout of the SPX fields.

SPX Protocol Field Specifics:

Connection Control

Datastream Type

Source ID

Destination ID

Sequence Number

Acknowledgment Number

Allocation Field

Connection Control—1 Byte

The Connection Control field is used to note the phase of the bi-direction connection between the NetWare nodes.

Types:

Attention

System Type

Acknowledgment Requested

End

Datastream Type—1 Byte
This field contains the type of data that is going to be contained within the SPX header of information. It usually contains end-of-message indication.

Source and Destination ID—2 Bytes
This field notes the virtual process identification for the source or destination node in the SPX packet.

Sequence Number— 2 Bytes
This field notes the number of data packets transferred. This field will be incremented throughout the SPX transfer.

Acknowledgment Number—2 Bytes
This field notes the update for acknowledgement to sequence numbers in the bi-directional data flow between the source and destination IDs throughout the SPX transfer.

Allocation Number—2 Bytes
This field notes the number of receive buffers in available count in the destination and source IDs. This field is used for flow control.

Data—Variable
This field will include the key data for SPX operations such as application data. Data is usually carried by NCP.

NetWare Core Protocol (NCP)
The NetWare Core Protocol is the main application protocol used for file access across Novell networks, and is also the main communication language used in Novell internetworks. Every time a workstation or file server intends to communicate with another, it usually uses NCP. This is the protocol that has the internal file request and reply formats for file access across a Novell network. The NCP includes a request frame format and a reply format. The request format includes a general request type, a sequence type, and a specific task number. There also is an internal function of the particular request and possible subfunctions, and then the particular data.

Chapter 6: Analysis for Major Operating System Protocols

The reply format includes the same types of fields, but also a completion code, which is important for analysis. Reply and request codes are key fields used by the internal functions being accessed. Analysis of completion codes is critical for discovering whether the proper completion occurred on the request-to-reply sequence.

NCP Protocol Field Specifics —NCP will use a NCP Request packet type for workstation requests and a NCP Reply type for Novell server replies.

NCP Request Frame Format:

Request Type

Sequence Number

Connection Number Low

Task Number

Connection Number High

Function

Subfunction

Subfunction Structure

Data

Request Type—2 Bytes
This field notes the NCP client request type.

Type 1111—Create A Service Connection

Type 2222—NetWare Service Request

Type 7777—Burst Mode Transfer

Type 5555—Connection Destroy

Sequence Number—1 Byte
This field notes the number of transfers between a workstation and a file server in sequence of transfer.

Connection Number Low—1 Byte
This field notes the server connection number.

Task Number—1 Byte
This field indicates the task number assigned to the particular workstation's operation.

Connection Number High—1 Byte
This field can be used along with Connection Low to reference the connection for the workstation.

Function—1 Byte
The field notes the exact NCP attached function direction, such as a file read or file write.

Sub-Function—1 Byte
This field would note any extension to main function and is optional.

Sub-Function Structure Length—2 Bytes
This field notes the length of any data attached.

Data—Variable
This field would carry any specific data for transfer in the NCP Request header. Data could include how to search for certain files, such as file offsets and pointers.

NCP Reply Frame Format

Reply/Response Type

Sequence Number

Connection Number Low

Task Number

Connection Number High

Completion Code

Connection Status

Data

Chapter 6: Analysis for Major Operating System Protocols

NCP Reply Type—2 Bytes
This field indicates the Novell server valid NCP reply type back to a workstation.

Type 3333—Service Reply To Request

Type 7777—Burst Mode Reply

Type 9999—Request Being Processed(Server Busy)

Sequence Number—1 Byte
This field notes the number of transfers between a workstation and a file server in sequence of transfer.

Connection Number Low—1 Byte
This field notes the server connection number.

Task Number—1 Byte
This field indicates the task number assigned to the particular workstation's operation.

Connection Number High—1 Byte
This field can be used along with Connection Low to reference the connection for the workstation.

Completion Code—1 Byte
This field notes the server's completion indication on the requested NCP operation.

Connection Status—1 Byte
This field indicates whether or not there is still a valid connection.

Data—Variable
This field will include the key data for NCP operations such as application data.

ETHERNET AND TOKEN RING OPTIMIZATION

NCP Packet Burst Mode

The NCP protocol layer has a more advanced derivative called Burst Mode. Burst Mode was designed by Novell to allow the NCP packet process to provide a more fluent flow of data between a workstation and a file server.

Burst Mode allows a workstation to request a file from a file server such that the file server can send the file back to the workstation in a burst type of transaction. Normally in NCP, a file is requested from a workstation, and the file server replies with a single packet. Then the workstation requests again, and the file server again replies. In Burst Mode, the workstation requests the file once, and the file server provides multiple packets without multiple requests. This is accomplished by employing multiple fields inside the Burst Mode frame format for NCP. These multiple fields require even further decodes by a protocol analyst.

Generally, packets that cross bridges and routers in NetWare networks are limited in size to 576 bytes, which allows only 512 bytes for data. A Large Internet Packet (LIP) option is available for use with Ethernet, Token Ring, and other networks that support larger packet sizes. Workstations configured for LIP interrogate the network to determine the largest packet size supported by the routers on the path that the packets follow. This enables the workstation to specify the most efficient packet size that matches network restrictions.

The Burst Mode frame format includes the normal request and reply sequences inside an NCP header, but there are additional internal frame packet fields such as delay times, sequence numbers, burst length, burst offset, fragments, and file handle breakdowns. This information enables communication between the workstation and the file server to be checked on a constant basis and actually enables more data to flow on a Novell network.

Service Advertising Protocol (SAP)

Service Advertising Protocol is an application layer protocol. NetWare servers use it to broadcast their availability over a Novell network. This type of transmission normally occurs about every 60 seconds. In a large internetwork, all servers must know where other servers are located, so that nodes on one server can locate other servers on the internetwork. This also is important for routing information, as internal routers and bridges have to update their information on Novell servers.

The SAP protocol relies on an IPX header and includes a packet type, an internal server type, and a server name for the server being transmitted. It also includes an associated network and node address and a process address, as well as the number of networks involved in the transmission of the particular SAP packet.

The SAP packet breakdown includes two different types of formats: a request frame format and a response frame format. At times, certain devices on a Novell network may request information on particular services, and may use a request format to engage a possible SAP response frame format transmission from respective servers. This is a good way to actually find which servers are on a network.

It should be mentioned that Novell's new NetWare Link State Protocol (NLSP) is a full link state protocol that is less network intensive in operations and more dynamic. The NLSP protocol combines the functions of Novell SAP and RIP. NLSP is discussed in the next chapter and will be replacing SAP and RIP for Novell service advertising and routing update functions.

Novell Routing Information Protocol (RIP)

The Novell protocol suite includes its own routing information protocol, which is the key information handler for Novell internetwork routing information between servers and routers. Approximately every 60 seconds, Novell routers generate a Novell RIP packet to update servers and routers of their location on the internetwork. The routing information protocol at times may be throttled back through certain Novell NetWare Loadable Modules that may reduce the amount of traffic devoted to routing information protocols.

The routing information protocol is important to the analyst because it can be captured and decoded for the particular type of routers on a Novell internetwork, and also the respective location, length, and actual delay as far as the time to transmit between different network points.

The Novell routing information frame format includes the operation of the particular RIP packet, the network address that the router may be on, and the respective hops away, which is the number of networks away that the router is from where the packet was actually captured. It also includes a Ticks field, which is the time delay (in 1/18 of a second) of where the actual router is in respect to where the packet was captured during the analysis session.

Items To Analyze in the Novell Protocol Suite

The following is a list of hints and analysis items to look for during a protocol session on a Novell network:

- **IPX**. The addressing fields are very important, given that the Novell network has a source and destination network address; a source and destination node address, which is the specific node communicating on the network; and a particular process being used in the IPX packet. These fields all are noted within the IPX header, and they should be analyzed and noted.

  If a problem exists in internetwork addressing on a Novell network, there may be a duplicate address. Note the source node addresses to make sure that they are different and are on the proper networks as to where they should be logically located from the analyst's point of view. The transport control field is very important because it is actually the hop count in the Novell internetworking environment. Take note of the hop count, including the number of hops for a particular frame. The hop count should be on the low end, as this allows for more efficient communication.

- **SPX**. In the SPX fields of the Novell protocol suite, analyze the sequence and acknowledge numbers to look for a proper identification between the two respective nodes. The source and destination ID addresses also are important, as mentioned in the IPX header, to make sure that the addressing is proper between the two SPX nodes. The sequence numbers, acknowledgment numbers, and actual connection control all centers on the evaluation of whether the communication session at the SPX layer occurs in a fluent manner.

  In paging through the trace, make sure that the connection is set up properly and that the proper sequence numbers are following through in an organized manner. There should also be a proper acknowledgment number provided through the transaction of the actual file transfer on the Novell network.

- **NCP**. With the NCP protocol suite, the analyst should closely examine the request and reply types between NCP transmission sessions. Make sure that a proper reply occurs for each request.

  Also note that the function and subfunction codes and the data fields of the NCP header will obtain the exact file information being accessed across the Novell network. This is where the analyst can actually get an idea of what is going on in the communication session. Any information considered important, including possibly the task numbers for the communication session, should be noted specifically through an analysis session. Again, keep a close eye on the internals of the data areas inside

Chapter 6: Analysis for Major Operating System Protocols

the NCP frame areas to make sure that the communication is proper.

- **SAP**. The SAP protocol is used to keep Novell communication between servers updated as far as their location on a Novell internetwork. An analyst who captures an SAP packet should take a very close look to make sure that all the servers are present on the proper network, and all the names apply as perceived by the network management group. Note the server names, their network and node addresses, and make sure that the intermediate network counts appear to be proper from where the analyst is analyzing the network.

- **RIP**. The routing information protocol packets are important because most of the routers on a Novell network generate this packet every 60 seconds. An analyst should be able to capture these packets and get a good idea of the internetworking environment by looking at the routers, their addresses, and their hops away count. The hops away count and Ticks field give an idea of a router's position as far as its performance and communication throughout a Novell internetwork. Depending on where the analyzer is positioned, the analyst may be able to get a clear understanding of how the routers are placed and whether they are placed properly.

Certain key packet types should be monitored through a network optimization or troubleshooting session on a Novell network. Some analyzers may pick up these types of packets and alert the analyst of the packet being present immediately. Other protocol analyzers may not, requiring the analyst to page through the trace frame by frame, analyzing the data captured for having these types of packets present.

A Novell network has three types of packet categories that are considered problem packets: a Novell delay packet or request being processed packet; a Novell file failure packet; and a bindery error packet. The following sections describe these packet types and their problematic effects on the network.

Delay Packet

This packet type indicates that a file server on a Novell network is busy and cannot immediately process a request. Generally, a Novell file server transmits a Novell delay packet onto a network when a problem exists internally with its processing, or due to the fact that it cannot handle the amount of I/O communication being directed to its particular NIC or NICs.

ETHERNET AND TOKEN RING OPTIMIZATION

A Novell delay packet is sometimes labeled a request-being-processed packet, which is the actual NCP identification for this condition. Novell delay packet or NCP busy are two other aliases used for a request-being-processed packet. Internally, the Novell delay packet does not tell the analyst exactly what is wrong, but when the Novell delay packet ratio is over the 2%-3% three percent range of traffic being directed in and out of the Novell file server, that file server needs to be evaluated for its overall resource capabilities. It may be possible that the network design is improper and the file server is just overloaded with the traffic. Figure 6.6 shows the Network General Sniffer displaying an NCP busy (delay) packet.

```
 SUMMARY—Delta T—DST———       SRC———
  22    0.000  2001027.IBM  ..«AHMDA05B3       NCP R OK 79 bytes read
  23    0.002  AHMDA05B3    «2001027.IBM   ..  NCP C F=7DDC Close file
  24    0.001  2001027.IBM  ..«AHMDA05B3       NCP R OK
  25    0.004  AHMDA05B3    «2001027.IBM   ..  NCP C Open file ..../DOSAP
  26    0.001  2001027.IBM  ..«AHMDA05B3       NCP R F=6893 OK Opened
  27    0.004  AHMDA05B3    «2001027.IBM   ..  NCP C F=6893 Read 14 at 0
  28    0.000  2001027.IBM  ..«AHMDA05B3       NCP R OK 14 bytes read
  29    0.003  AHMDA05B3    «2001027.IBM   ..  NCP C F=6893 Read 42 at 83
  30    0.001  2001027.IBM  ..«AHMDA05B3       NCP R OK 42 bytes read
  31    0.002  AHMDA05B3    «2001027.IBM   ..  NCP C F=6893 Close file
  32    0.001  2001027.IBM  ..«AHMDA05B3       NCP BUSY
  33    0.003  AHMDA05B3    «2001027.IBM   ..  NCP C Dir search *.PN3
  34    0.001  2001027.IBM  ..«AHMDA05B3       NCP R OK File=HPDJPORT.PN3
  35    0.003  AHMDA05B3    «2001027.IBM   ..  NCP C Open file ..../DOSAP
  36    0.001  2001027.IBM  ..«AHMDA05B3       NCP R F=72DC OK Opened
  37    0.002  AHMDA05B3    «2001027.IBM   ..  NCP C F=72DC Read 14 at 0
  38    0.000  2001027.IBM  ..«AHMDA05B3       NCP R OK 14 bytes read
  39    0.003  AHMDA05B3    «2001027.IBM   ..  NCP C F=72DC Read 14 at 69
  40    0.000  2001027.IBM  ..«AHMDA05B3       NCP R OK 14 bytes read
  41    0.003  AHMDA05B3    «2001027.IBM   ..  NCP C F=72DC Read 79 at 27
                                Frame 32 of 21682
 1       2 Set   3Expert                   5         6Disply 7 Prev  8 Next  9Select 10 New
 Help    mark    window                    Menus     options  frame  frame   frame   capture
```

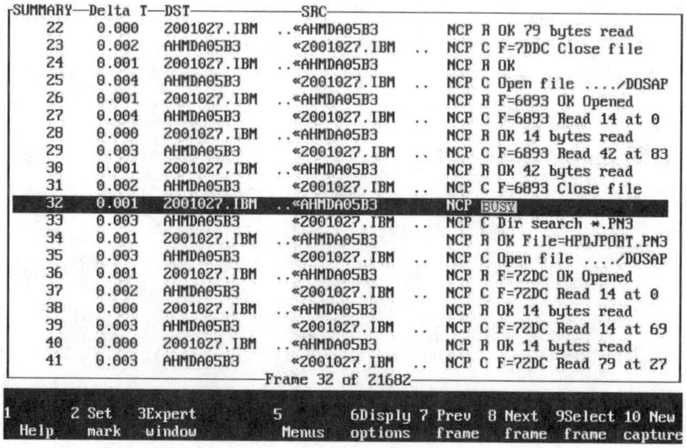

Figure 6.6 The Network General Sniffer displaying an NCP Busy (delay) packet.

File Failure Packet

This packet type indicates that the Novell file server cannot locate a particular file request from a workstation. This may be due to incorrect setups for a search path or a search mode direction from a workstation itself. The file server may not have the file; or the file is in an incorrect directory structure format for normal file access.

When file access failure packets are recorded at more than the 5% of overall traffic within a particular data trace in a NetWare environment, the analyst should examine the file search methodology and file structure on both the workstations and file servers. Figure 6.7 shows the Network General Sniffer displaying an NCP File Failure Packet.

Chapter 6: Analysis for Major Operating System Protocols 173

```
SUMMARY─Delta T─DST──────────SRC─────────
  1141   0.001   2001029.Madge..<AHMDA05B3    NCP R File not found
  1142   0.003   AHMDA05B3      <2001029.Madge..  NCP C Dir search *.*
  1143   0.000   2001029.Madge..<AHMDA05B3    NCP R File not found
  1144   0.003   AHMDA05B3      <2001029.Madge..  NCP C Dir search *.*
  1145   0.000   2001029.Madge..<AHMDA05B3    NCP R File not found
  1146   0.002   AHMDA05B3      <2001029.Madge..  NCP C Dir search *.*
  1147   0.000   2001029.Madge..<AHMDA05B3    NCP R File not found
  1148   0.002   AHMDA05B3      <2001029.Madge..  NCP C Dir search *.*
  1149   0.001   2001029.Madge..<AHMDA05B3    NCP R File not found
  1150   0.002   AHMDA05B3      <2001029.Madge..  NCP C Dir search *.*
  1151   0.000   2001029.Madge..<AHMDA05B3    NCP R File not found
  1152   0.002   AHMDA05B3      <2001029.Madge..  NCP C Dir search *.*
  1153   0.000   2001029.Madge..<AHMDA05B3    NCP R File not found
  1154   0.002   AHMDA05B3      <2001029.Madge..  NCP C Dir search *.*
  1155   0.000   2001029.Madge..<AHMDA05B3    NCP R File not found
  1156   0.003   AHMDA05B3      <2001029.Madge..  NCP C Dir search *.*
  1157   0.000   2001029.Madge..<AHMDA05B3    NCP R File not found
  1158   0.002   AHMDA05B3      <2001029.Madge..  NCP C Dir search *.*
  1159   0.000   2001029.Madge..<AHMDA05B3    NCP R File not found
  1160   0.002   AHMDA05B3      <2001029.Madge..  NCP C Dir search *.*
─────────────────────Frame 1160 of 21682─────────────────────
1      2 Set   3Expert    5        6Disply 7 Prev  8 Next  9Select 10 New
Help   mark   window     Menus    options  frame   frame   frame   capture
```

Figure 6.7 The Network General Sniffer displaying an NCP File Failure Packet.

Bindery Error Packet

Bindery errors indicate a possible problem within the Novell bindery. The Novell bindery is the inherent database of the Novell file server for all user and node access to the file structure within the file server. The bindery is periodically updated within the Novell file server, and it is possible that when a request is made of a Novell file server, a bindery error can occur. If this happens, it is possible the bindery has been corrupted, and the data chaining within the file server drive is not proper.

If bindery errors constitute over 1% of overall traffic, the bindery may need to be repaired. Depending on the Novell operating system release, this might not be possible, and certain other optimization techniques may need to be provided, such as a backup and restore, or even a reload of the operating system. If bindery errors occur at a high level, it is a good idea for the analyst to work with associates who have a high level of Novell expertise on server structure for this particular issue. From an analyst's standpoint, a packet level of bindery errors captured over 1% indicates a possible problem in the file server's operation or respective drive. Figure 6.8 shows the Network General Sniffer displaying an NCP Bindery Error Packet.

Figure 6.9 shows a set of general traces from a Network General Sniffer that display the SPX and SAP formats from a Novell internetwork.

174 ETHERNET AND TOKEN RING OPTIMIZATION

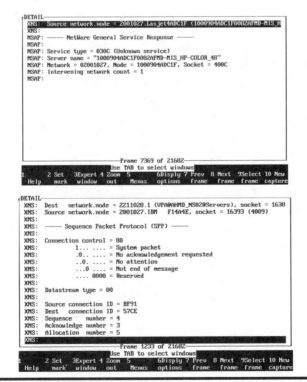

Figure 6.8 Network General Sniffer displaying an NCP Bindery Error Packet.

Figure 6.9 A set of traces from a Network General Sniffer displaying SPX and SAP formats from a Novell internetwork.

Chapter 6: Analysis for Major Operating System Protocols

SNA

SNA stands for System Networking Architecture and is the actual infrastructure for network data communications in the IBM networking environment. SNA was originally developed for the host environment but is now accessed frequently in LAN and WAN environments. SNA was developed for the corporate network environment and is now intercepted quite frequently in Token Ring protocol analysis sessions. There are general issues with its capability to be routed across most LANs, but recent developments include routers and bridges that more easily handle communication of the SNA protocol suite.

A set of operations that normally occurs in the SNA packet headers is of interest for analysis. The majority of the protocol analyzers today can capture most of these operations.

SNA Protocol Suite Internal Layers

The SNA architecture includes a set of approximately seven layers, including transaction services, presentation services, data flow control, transmission control, path control, data link control, and the physical heading. The description includes the SNA layers as they relate to the OSI model.

- **SNA Data Link and Physical Layer.** The SNA physical and data link control layers are related closely to the OSI layers. These layers are responsible for the physical connection and packet breakdown at the medium access control layer. The data link layer in SNA is still responsible for reliable transfer from node to node in a networking environment.

- **SNA Path Control Layer.** The SNA path layer relates directly to the OSI model network layer. It provides almost the same functions, and also involves what would be handled in the transport control layer in the OSI model. Its primary responsibility is to establish connections from node to node and provide routing functions from node to node. An actual route that is considered virtual is set up between the two nodes and communication occurs between the two SNA nodes. The actual routing control between the two particular nodes is accomplished through the SNA transmission control layer.

- **Transmission Control Layer.** In relation to the OSI model, the SNA transmission control layer works at the transport layer for communications in the same way that the session does at OSI. This layer provides flow control between the two particular nodes after a session is actually established. It also accomplishes any encryption or decryption required. The transmission control layer works with the request and response headers in the SNA packet format.

- **SNA Data Flow Layer.** The data flow layer actually works at the session layer. Its function is to establish integrity in the conversation between two ending nodes. The data flow layer organizes the requests and responses in the communication to make sure that all the request and response units are properly chained together. Communication occurs in portions of the overall request and response unit, and the data flow layer is responsible for combining and breaking up the request and response units in an organized fashion.

- **SNA Presentation Services and Transaction Services.** The SNA presentation and transaction services relate to the OSI model, specifically at the application presentation higher layer points. Generally, the presentation and transaction services provide the overall communication from node to node for specific applications at the user level, such as program-to-program communication. This is usually the area where E-mail and higher communications such as database interrelation occurs.

These layers can be easily related to the OSI packet format as shown in Figure 6.10.

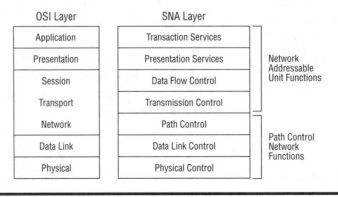

Figure 6.10 The SNA layers easily relate to the OSI packet format.

Chapter 6: Analysis for Major Operating System Protocols 177

An SNA packet on a LAN is assembled as follows: a data link control layer is present as the outside header of the respective frame, especially in the Token Ring environment. Next is a routing information field. The next pad includes the logical link control header, which includes whether a request or response is identified in the class of surface, and whether it is connection oriented.

Within the SNA frame portion itself, an SNA transmission header is present and includes the format identification, the proper header flags, the destination and origin address for SNA, and the sequence number of the communication. Then the request or response header follows all the bytes for the communication. Then the function management data is present, which includes the internal pointers for the function, to perform specific networking services such as initiating or setting up a disconnect of a particular session. If a data flow control is set up for a request or response unit, or a session layer control, those provide specific functions for communications internal to the data flow or session control information. If a network control receiver request or response unit is identified, this carries any overall network management or testing mechanisms for the SNA network management functions.

The SNA environment includes logical units (LUs), physical units (PUs), and system services control points (SSCPs). *Logical units* are logical end-to-end connection identification points on an SNA network. A *physical unit* is a hardware or software device to which communication can be specifically directed. An *SSCP* is the main control mechanism for the entire network, and is implemented by software running in the host system.

The SNA packet format starts with a request to response unit, including the notation of the SNA processes. The response units can be divided into four categories: data flow control, function management, session control, and network control. Specific data usually also is noted in the SNA packet fields.

Overall, the SNA packet includes a transmission header, a request-to-response notation, and then the actual function management header. There is the specific notation on whether the frame is a data control flow control packet, network control packet, or session control. The connection control field is very important in analysis. Figure 6.11 shows an SNA packet format.

Sometimes a NetBIOS datagram may be used as the connection setup protocol for SNA sessions. If this occurs, the packet incorporates the topology header such as Token Ring physical headers and data link layer breakdowns, and then the NetBIOS frame format, which includes a header length field, a data link field, a command subset for NetBIOS, and the appropriate data. There also is a sender's and receiver's name, and a field for the data for NetBIOS.

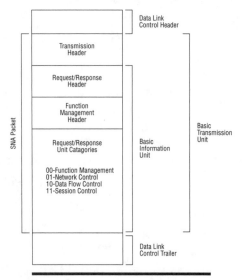

Figure 6.11 SNA packet format.

The following section describes NetBIOS theory as it relates to SNA.

NetBIOS Theory

NetBIOS is a connection-oriented communication protocol jointly developed by Sytek Inc. and IBM for operation on IBM's PC Broadband LAN.

Originally, the NetBIOS code was provided in ROM on the NIC itself. Today, on 4Mbps and 16Mbps Token Ring networks, the NetBIOS is loaded with the Token Ring device drivers by means of the IBM LAN Support Program disk. NetBIOS became popular very quickly, and many PC and host applications were developed based on its protocol and rely on it.

NetBIOS operates at the session layer within the OSI network protocol model. It communicates by establishing a logical connection between two NetBIOS-defined names. NetBIOS sets up a logical channel for higher-level protocols to use for communication. The actual NetBIOS information is encapsulated within the information section of an LLC data frame (see Figure 6.12).

Chapter 6: Analysis for Major Operating System Protocols

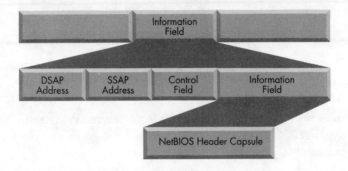

Figure 6.12 The NetBIOS information is contained in the information field of an LLC data frame.

Another important protocol is the server message block (SMB) protocol. Many IBM-oriented LAN operating systems (such as IBM PCLAN and IBM LAN Server) use SMB to communicate at the application layer of the OSI network protocol model. SMB relies on the NetBIOS protocol for communication on the ring.

You often will encounter NetBIOS when monitoring and troubleshooting the SNA and Token Ring network environments. An in-depth discussion of NetBIOS and SMB is beyond the scope of this book.

NetBIOS is used quite frequently in IBM LAN Manager and MicroSoft LAN Manager environments. It is common to see it in both SNA and AS400 host environment communications related to LANs.

There are four main types of NetBIOS communications that take place on a network, including:

- Name Service
- Session Service
- Datagram Service
- Miscellaneous Functions

The Name Service function allows an end node to refer to an application by a name on an internetwork. The name will usually consist of approximately 16 characters. This may be unique to the application or used by a group of applications. The application registers a name on a particular resource or server, and then an end node accesses that name.

ETHERNET AND TOKEN RING OPTIMIZATION

There are three key processes to access the Name Service:

- Add Name
- Add Group Name
- Delete Name

The Session Service is the service that allows for reliable exchange of data between two NetBIOS applications. Each data message may be up to 131,000 bytes approximately in length.

- The Session Service processes are the following:
- Call
- Listen
- Hang Up
- Send
- Receive
- Session Status

The Datagram Service allows for a transfer of information in an unreliable fashion. This is somewhat similar to UDP communications. It should be noted that the Datagram Service is unreliable, nonsequenced and does not maintain a connection in data transfer.

The Datagram Service processes are:

- Send Datagram
- Send Broadcast Datagram
- Receive Datagram
- Receive Broadcast Datagram

Miscellaneous functions related to this NetBIOS protocol are:

- Reset
- Cancel
- Adaptor Status
- Unlink
- Remote Program
- Load

Chapter 6: Analysis for Major Operating System Protocols

NetBIOS includes the capability to perform broadcast, point-to-point, or mixed mode communications. Usually the configuration is such that one device provides the service of the NetBIOS name service, and also has the capability to provide datagram distribution node information.

NetBIOS communicates by means of the following commands that can be intercepted with a protocol analyzer:

SESSION_INITIALIZE	Sets up a session
SESSION_CONFIRM	Notifies receipt of SESSION_INITIALIZE
SESSION_ALIVE	Checks if session is active
SESSION_END	Terminates the session
DATAGRAM	A datagram transmitted by an application
DATAGRAM_BROADCAST	A broadcast datagram
DATA_ACK	Data-only acknowledgment
DATA_FIRST_MIDDLE	Data is first or middle in frame
DATA_ONLY_LAST	Data is last in frame
NAME_QUERY	Requests a name on the network
NAME_RECOGNIZED	Recognizes a name
NAME_IN_CONFLICT	Detects a duplicate name
ADD_NAME_QUERY	Checks for a duplicate name
ADD_GROUP_NAME_QUERY	Checks for a duplicate group name
ADD_NAME_RESPONSE	Detects a duplicate name after query
STATUS_QUERY	Requests status of a remote name
STATUS_RESPONSE	Reply to STATUS_QUERY
TERMINATE_TRACE	Terminates trace on local/remote names
RECEIVE_CONTINUE	Waiting for outstanding receive
RECEIVE_OUTSTANDING	Retransmit last data

SNA Protocol Types

Many protocols are part of the IBM or SNA protocol suite. They are independent protocols and are seen quite frequently in the SNA environment. These independent protocols within the suite are mentioned briefly, but discrete packet field breakdowns are not given for the particular protocols.

182 ETHERNET AND TOKEN RING OPTIMIZATION

The following set of protocols are most often seen in an SNA environment:

- Systems Networking Architecture (SNA). IBM Data Communication Protocol.
- Server Message Block (SMB). Application layer protocol for LAN server environment used for file access.
- Remote Program Load (RPL). Diskless workstation protocol for IBM Token Ring PROMS.
- Network Basic I/O System (NetBIOS). Connection setup protocol for named station addresses.
- IBM Network Management Protocol (IBMNM). Used for functional address communication at Token Ring physical layer.
- Bridge Protocol Data Unit (BPDU). Used for STA communication for bridges.
- Logical Link Control (LLC). Internal connection setup for higher layer protocols.

Figure 6.13 shows the SNA protocol suite as related to the OSI model.

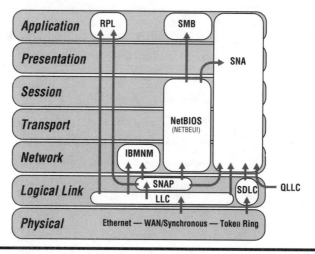

Figure 6.13 SNA protocol suite as related to the OSI model.

The preceding protocols are the predominant protocols in an SNA environment, and individually there are fields that need to be analyzed for each protocol. This book cannot possibly go into all the decode and responsibilities of each field,

Chapter 6: Analysis for Major Operating System Protocols

but the reference sections for SNA and IBM Token Ring in this book are a good place to research the particulars of the Systems Networking Architecture protocol environment and most of the applied protocols.

Items To Analyze in the SNA Protocol Suite

When analyzing an SNA network, look closely at all the routing information in a data trace above the SNA information. For example, if the SNA information is enveloped within a Token Ring frame, there will be MAC layer and routing information headers that are important for the SNA packet transmission. There usually is a connection layer protocol such as NetBIOS that should be analyzed in detail. The analyst should always look closely for a healthy physical layer when examining the SNA environment.

There is always a certain type of process for the connection of an SNA session, usually a link control query setup, which is actually considered the setup process step for the normal connection on an SNA environment. Some sort of communication then occurs back and forth, and finally the SNA session is disconnected through a proper request for disconnect. The analyst should look for standard communication to involve the SNA exchange IDs such as active physical and logical unit setups.

Two particular frame types indicate problems within the SNA environment and the LAN. Now and then an analyst may pick up a receiver-not-ready frame. A receiver not ready frame, when captured at high levels, may indicate a communication bottleneck within an SNA channel connected to a particular network.

It is also possible that a high number of segment continue packets could be picked up on a network. Segment continue packets at a level more than 50% of the overall SNA frames indicate that most of the communication is not occurring in a fluent manner because 50 percent of traffic flow is continued. If these frames are picked up, the SNA channel configurations connected to the network should be troubleshot.

Remember that NetBIOS is a connection-oriented protocol that is going to set up some sort of communication session for other protocols to rely upon. Look for a standard handshaking fluency at the NetBIOS protocol node level.

When decoding and examining the NetBIOS protocol, look closely at the packet types within the NetBIOS environment. Keep in mind that NetBIOS is a connection-layer protocol used to set up communication between two nodes for a complete SNA session.

ETHERNET AND TOKEN RING OPTIMIZATION

Just as in SNA, certain NetBIOS frames are important to watch for, which may indicate session connection problems, such as Name In Conflict (NIC) or No Receive (NR) frames.

NIC indicates NetBIOS naming and addressing problems. NR frame types indicate connection setup problems.

It is important to determine that connections are set up, data is communicated, and the connection is properly broken. This indicates the fluency of the SNA and NetBIOS transactions. Figure 6.14 shows a set of trace displays from the Network General Sniffer that shows some of the key SNA packet types captured through a protocol analysis session.

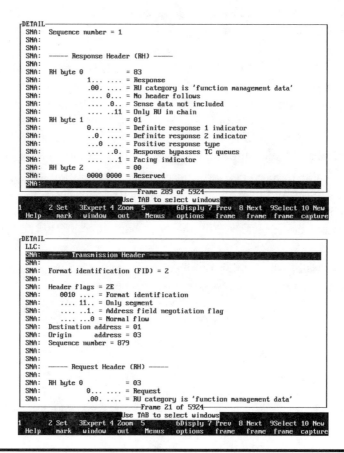

Figure 6.14 Trace displays from the Network General Sniffer showing key SNA packet types captured through protocol analysis.

DEC

The DEC protocol suite centers on the DECnet protocols developed in the 1970s by Digital Equipment Corp. for communication across LANs and WANs. DEC was responsible early in the game for a large number of minicomputers.

In 1976, DEC introduced the original DECnet Phase I protocol, based on PDP 11 transmission. In 1978, DECnet Phase II was introduced, which added host support for the DECnet and VAX environments. DECnet Phase III was introduced in 1980, adding approaches for internetwork routing and network management. The DECnet Phase IV protocol suite was introduced in 1982 and included support for the Ethernet and WAN environments, including X.25 and SNA. In 1991, DEC introduced DECnet Phase V, based heavily on the OSI multiprotocol-protocol stack environment.

The DECnet architecture begins with physical and data link layers, followed by a routing layer. Above the routing layer is an end-to-end communication layer, which is underneath a session control layer. A network application layer follows, beneath a network management layer. Finally, the user and DECnet phase layers are above all these layers. The communication corresponds and interoperates with the OSI model. Figure 6.15 shows how the DECnet protocol suite relates to the OSI protocols.

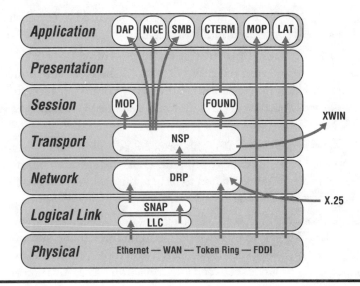

Figure 6.15 The DECnet protocol suite compared to the OSI model.

ETHERNET AND TOKEN RING OPTIMIZATION

DECnet Protocol Types

Analysis in the DECnet environment is quite involved, and one of the key areas to analyze is the routing information between the DECnet nodes. A range of protocols in the DECnet protocol suite need to be analyzed, and multiple fields within those particular protocols. The following is a description of the major protocols in the DECnet computing environment.

- Network Information and Control Exchange (NICE). This is a command/reply protocol that provides network management information on a LAN.

- Server Message Block (SMB). This is an application layer protocol for LAN Server Environment. Its protocol function can be used for remote file access just like DAP.

- Command Terminal (CTERM). This protocol is used for communicating with certain intelligent terminals found in the DEC environment. It correlates with the use of the Foundation Services protocol.

- Foundation Services (FOUND). This protocol is used when working with basic terminal-handling services on a LAN. It is used to initiate and disconnect logical connections between certain workstations and applications. It correlates with the use of the CTERM protocol.

- Session Control Protocol (SCP). This protocol is used to establish an initial virtual connection with the NSP protocol.

- Network Services Protocol (NSP). This protocol ensures a reliable message transmission over an SCP-established virtual connection. Its internal function is to establish and destroy communication links and to provide error and flow control. It is also responsible for the breakdown of messages.

- Data Access Protocol (DAP). This protocol provides operations for remote file access in the DEC environment. DAP provides a command/reply protocol to allow a workstation to initiate the creation of new files on a file server. Then files can be opened, read, written to, and closed.

- DECnet Routing Protocol (DRP). This is the DEC environment's routing protocol. Its focus is to initiate and maintain the router communication on a DEC internetwork. It is responsible for routing packets from source nodes through routers, between DEC areas, and to destination end nodes.

- Maintenance Operations Protocol (MOP). This protocol is used for most network maintenance services in DEC environments. It is seen quite

Chapter 6: Analysis for Major Operating System Protocols

frequently in diskless workstation environments for downloading, remote loads, and problem diagnosis.

- Local Area Transport Protocol (LAT). This is a key DEC protocol designed for terminal (keyboard and screen) traffic to and from end source/destination nodes and timesharing hosts. The LAT protocol is an interface protocol for the DECnet environment to communicate with the general LAN domain.
- Logical Link Control (LLC) (IEEE 802.2). This protocol involves connection control for multiplexing to other enveloped protocols. It is seen frequently in Token Ring analysis sessions.
- SubNetwork Access Protocol (SNAP). This is an enveloping protocol for multiple layer protocols. SNAP specifies that DSAP and SSAP addresses must be in hex designation. It usually carries other major protocols within its fields.

The DECnet protocol suite itself has multiple packet-field formats for its protocols.

Items To Analyze in the DECnet Protocol Suite

The following items are important to analyze in the DECnet protocol suite:

- Physical Integrity. Physical layer health helps ensure normal internetwork communication between the DECnet routing layers on a DECnet network. The physical integrity—the general health of the physical layer on the topology carrying the DEC protocols—is important. The analyst should make sure that the physical layer is healthy.
- LAT Errors. The LAT protocol may include some general error information that certain protocol analyzers can pick up. These types of errors usually are clearly noted in the LAT section. Watch closely for LAT errors in any of the higher layer traces by paging through the trace. Any addresses that may be sources of error messages should also be carefully noted when analyzing the DEC protocol suite.
- Hello Timer Values. In the DECnet protocol suite, DECnet nodes at times may notify each other of their location and keep each other updated through the Hello Timer fields in the DECnet protocols. Most protocol analyzers pick up errors in the Hello Timer Values (specifically, the

Network General Sniffer Expert system has a good approach for this analysis). But Hello Timer information also can be analyzed by paging through the trace. If the Hello Timer Values are not proper, certain devices may not be updated and DECnet routing errors may occur.

- DECnet Routing Protocol. The DECnet Routing Protocol is extensive and includes information such as the hop counts and costs to networks. In an internetworking environment, it is important to examine the DECnet routing protocol for possible errors such as high hop counts or high costs. For performance problems in the DEC environment in a LAN or WAN, an analyst should capture the DECnet routing protocol (DRP packet types) and decode the packet fields to specifically examine whether any high hop counts or high costs levels exist for the DECnet routing protocol.

- Proper Connection Establishment. An analyst should always keep an eye on the overall connection integrity in a DECnet environment. It is important, as in any protocol, that a DEC connection is set up properly, that communication occurs, and that the session breakdown occurs in a fluent manner.

If a high number of diagnostic packets are captured on the network, it is possible that an internal problem exists on the DECnet network. Diagnostic packets should be examined carefully for internal addresses, and then those devices or any components surrounding those devices should be examined for configuration and operation.

The preceding tips for the DECnet environment will prove helpful to an analyst. However, to understand and decode the DECnet protocol suite requires an extensive study of the DEC protocol, and certain references listed in other sections in this book will further your research on the DECnet protocols.

Figure 6.16 displays a set of Network General Sniffer traces, which shows some key packet types recorded in a DEC analysis session.

Chapter 6: Analysis for Major Operating System Protocols

```
┌DETAIL─────────────────────────────────────────────────────────┐
│DRP:   Source Area         = 00                                │
│DRP:   Source Sub-area     = 00                                │
│DRP:   Source ID           = 7.52                              │
│DRP:   Next Level 2 Router = 00                                │
│DRP:   Visit Count         = 0                                 │
│DRP:   Service Class       = 00                                │
│DRP:   Protocol Type       = 00                                │
│DRP:                                                           │
│NSP:   ----- Network Services Protocol -----                   │
│NSP:                                                           │
│NSP:   Message Identifier = 2B                                 │
│NSP:           0... .... = Non-extensible field                │
│NSP:           .010 .... = Connect Confirm Message             │
│NSP:           .... 10.. = Control Message                     │
│NSP:           .... ..00 = always zero                         │
│NSP:   Type     = 2  (Control Message)                         │
│NSP:   Sub-type = 2  (Connect Confirm Message)                 │
│NSP:   Logical Link Destination = 3129                         │
│NSP:   Logical Link Source      = 5139                         │
│NSP:   Requested Services = 01                                 │
│                     ─Frame 5 of 153─                          │
│                Use TAB to select windows                      │
│1      2 Set   3Expert 4 Zoom  5        6Disply 7 Prev 8 Next 9Select 10 New │
│ Help     mark    window   out    Menus    options   frame   frame   frame  capture │
└───────────────────────────────────────────────────────────────┘

┌DETAIL─────────────────────────────────────────────────────────┐
│DRP:   ----- DECNET Routing Protocol -----                     │
│DRP:                                                           │
│DRP:   Data Length = 55                                        │
│DRP:   Control Packet Format = 0B                              │
│DRP:           0... .... = no padding                          │
│DRP:           .000 .... = reserved                            │
│DRP:           .... 101. = Ethernet Router Hello Message       │
│DRP:           .... ...1 = Control Packet Format               │
│DRP:   Control Packet Type = 05                                │
│DRP:   Version Number = 02                                     │
│DRP:   ECO Number     = 00                                     │
│DRP:   User ECO Number = 00                                    │
│DRP:   ID of Transmitting Node = 40.3, HOBBES                  │
│DRP:       Information = 01                                    │
│DRP:           0... .... = reserved                            │
│DRP:           .0.. .... = not blocking request                │
│DRP:           ..0. .... = multicast traffic accepted          │
│DRP:           ...0 .... = verification ok                     │
│DRP:           .... 0... = do not reject                       │
│DRP:           .... .0.. = no verification required            │
│                     ─Frame 91 of 1069─                        │
│                Use TAB to select windows                      │
│1      2 Set   3Expert 4 Zoom  5        6Disply 7 Prev 8 Next 9Select 10 New │
│ Help     mark    window   out    Menus    options   frame   frame   frame  capture │
└───────────────────────────────────────────────────────────────┘
```

Figure 6.16 Network General Sniffer traces showing significant DEC packet types.

TCP/IP—Transmission Control Protocol/Internet Protocol

TCP/IP is an internetwork protocol architecture that allows different computer hosts such as minicomputers and file servers to interact across a global infrastructure. The TCP/IP acronym is used quite frequently to reference a large set of protocols that are actually part of a suite that make up the full TCP/IP protocol group. It should be stated, however, that TCP stands for Transmission Control Protocol and is found encapsulated within another protocol, the

Internet Protocol, which is a common protocol stack configuration. So it is common in the industry that when different entities refer to TCP/IP, they are actually referring to the complete protocol suite.

TCP/IP was originally engineered to accommodate the Internet. The Internet is a world-wide infrastructure that connects key corporate and government agencies through computer to computer communication that crosses corporate and national boundaries.

History of TCP/IP

TCP/IP was originally conceived in 1969 by a direct effort of the U.S. Defense Department. An organization was developed, called the U.S. Defense Advanced Research Project Agency (DARPA). The DARPA developed a large network concept that became a reality, labeled the Advanced Research Project Agency Network (ARPANET). The original direction of ARPANET was to test and configure a new communication scheme based on packet switching technology. The evolution of the actual ARPANET network started through significant testing which occurred in 1969 at four key areas within the internetworking infrastructure. The following locations were utilized for testing:

- University of Utah
- University of California-Santa Barbara (UCSB)
- Stanford Research Institute (SRI)
- University of California-Los Angeles (UCLA)

The original host configuration at these locations was Honeywell-based. The testing went well in 1969 and eventually a proposal was brought forward to the National Science Foundation (NSF) to allow for a more combined effort in the production of the Computer Science Network (CSNET) in the early 1980s.

The progression continued into 1984, when DARPA dictated a split of the ARPANET network into two configurations: MILNET for military traffic, and ARPANET for non-military traffic.

In the early 1990s, the U.S. Department of Defense realized that new technologies were advancing at such a fast rate that the original ARPANET configuration was disassembled.

The original ARPANET concept however, did live on through a network labeled the NSFNET. The NSFNET was brought forward by the Office of

Chapter 6: Analysis for Major Operating System Protocols

Advanced Science and Computing (OASC) to further develop the overall configuration. It should be noted that the initial platforms for the TCP standard was actually developed in 1973 by DARPA. This was early in the ARPANET development and DARPA intended for the internetwork architecture of all of the ARPANET networks to utilize protocol communication based on the TCP/IP protocol suite. The focus was to look at all the main devices across the internetwork as hosts and gateways. Hosts would provide key file services to any specific end nodes as required, and any important interconnection between networks would be provided by gateways. Today, these gateways are essentially routers. The term gateway applies most strongly to the TCP/IP environment.

In 1973, when the standard was developed for TCP/IP, there were four specific protocol layers that were considered as standard. These do relate somewhat to the OSI mode but not directly, due to the fact that there are only four layers instead of seven. The four layers included:

- the Network Interface layer
- the Internet layer
- the Host to Host layer
- the Application layer or Processing Application layer.

The Network Interface layer is the layer that encompasses the physical data link area and includes all of the key devices of the physical layer, including cable medium, NIC physical layer, NIC connectors, and key NIC firmware-related protocols.

The next key protocol layer in the TCP/IP model is the Internet Protocol (IP) Layer. The IP protocol is responsible for encapsulation of data and other Upper Layer Protocols (ULP). The IP layer provides unreliable data transfer through internetwork routing and the main unit of measure for data. Packets of information on the Internet are referred to as Datagrams.

The Host to Host layer is the layer that is reserved for final delivery and servicing to the key ULP operations that may be present in each host across the Internet. There are two specific communication protocols in the Host to Host layer which will be discussed in this book; Transmission Control Protocol (TCP) and User Datagram Protocol (UDP).

The highest layer in the TCP/IP protocol model is the Process and Application layer. This is where the actual application layer protocols would reside, for example, File Transfer protocols (FTP), Telnet, Simple Mail Transfer Protocol (SMTP), Trivial File Transfer Protocol (TFTP), SMNP and others.

The overall growth of the Internet is occurring at a rapid pace. End users are starting to use the Internet on a daily basis, and this is becoming a strategic point also for corporations and government, as far as performing global business operations. The activity and growth of the Internet is monitored by the Internet Activities Board (IAB), and all users who wish to register on the Internet must go through a process with the Internet Registry (IR) Board to assure proper configuration. Any development or troubleshooting involving the core Internet is usually performed by the Internet Research Task Force (IRTF). The IRTF researches all of the key new technologies involved with the Internet configurations.

TCP/IP Protocol Suite Internal Layers

When performing protocol analysis in a TCP/IP environment, the following sections can be utilized as a reference. The TCP/IP protocol suite pallete is immense and this book cannot cover all the protocol types, but we have included the key layer protocol discussions: Address Resolution Protocol(ARP), Internet Protocol (IP), Internet Control Message Protocol (ICMP), User Datagram Protocol (UDP), and Transmission Control Protocol (TCP). For more detailed information on the full TCP/IP protocol suite decodes and applied theory, review the TCP/IP manuscripts in the reference section of this book.

Address Resolution Protocol (ARP)

The Address Resolution Protocol (ARP) is used when a node on a TCP/IP-based network is about to transmit a packet to another node, but requires the destination node's physical address. Addressing is discussed in the section below on the Internet Protocol (IP). In the case of ARP operation, the source node will usually have the destination node's IP address and will send an ARP Request packet to the intended destination node with the destination IP address in the packet. The destination node will then know it is a potential target of the source node and will send back an ARP reply packet, including its physical hardware address. This packet will be received by the original source node, and the transmission will take place.

Reverse Address Resolution Protocol (RARP)—The same process can be utilized in a reverse scenario. A source node requiring either its own IP address

Chapter 6: Analysis for Major Operating System Protocols

other key IP addresses can send a RARP request packet including known physical addresses to key hosts that may act as ARP/RARP servers. When the RARP packet is received by a host, the host can respond with the target IP address. This is used quite often in diskless workstation and remote communication server operations.

Proxy ARP—Proxy ARP is a type of ARP addressing method utilized by an IP gateway or router. This process allows the router to provide the actual hardware address of a destination node on the other side of the router to a source node performing an ARP request with an IP destination address that is not in the same logical network.

Internet Addressing—The Internet addressing scheme specifies that all hosts must have a software address, termed an IP address. A host's IP address will identify the network and sub-network to which it is attached. Routers will send data from a source IP address to a specific destination IP address.

The Internet address is a logical 32-bit address which is assigned to each IP node. The Internet address is required to get the IP Datagram through the Internet from the originating host to the correct destination host. In the Internet addressing scheme, the host address consists of four bytes that will contain both a network and a node address.

For example, if a node is utilizing the IP addressing scheme, it may have a designation of 71.21.53.1.; the address is usually represented in a dotted decimal notation. The Internet addressing scheme includes three classes of addresses.

Class A Network Address—This is the top level in the Internet addressing scheme. There are a total of 128 class A networks. Each of the 128 hosts can address up to approximately 16 million nodes. In a class A network, the first byte is the network address, and the last three bytes are the node or host address. The first bit must be set to zero, making the first byte in the range of 0 to 127. As displayed above, 73.34.103.4 is a class A address.

Class A addresses are designed for very large networks. They are identified through the first 8 bytes; 0 through 7. These bytes identify the network. Again, the first byte 0 is reserved. Bytes 1-7 actually identify the network. The remaining 24 bits identify the host. There are only 128 Class A addresses available; 0 and 127 are reserved.

Class B Network Address—The class B address is in the second level in the IP addressing scheme. The first byte must be in the 128 to 191 area. The first two bytes are used for the network ID, and the last two bytes are for the node or host. An example of a class B address is 134.64.23.5.

Class B addresses are more common. The first two bytes have a binary value of 10 which is standard. The next 14 bytes identify the network. The next remaining 16 bytes in the total 32 byte address configuration identify the host. There are a total of 16,384 Class B addresses possible, but the addresses for 0 and 16383 are reserved.

Class C Network Address—The class C address is the lowest level in the scheme. The first byte will always be in the 193 to 255 area. The network is assigned in the first three bytes and the node or host by only the last byte. An example of a class C address would be 209.43.12.4.

Class C addresses are generally used for smaller networks. They begin with a binary 110. The next 21 bytes identify the network, and the remaining 8 bytes identify the host. A total of 2,097,152 Class C addresses are possible.

Class D Network Address—Class D addresses begin with a binary 1110 and are intended for multi-casting.

Class E Network Address—Class E addresses begin with a binary 1111 and are reserved for future use.

Figure 6.17 shows an example of the Internet A, B, and C class addresses.

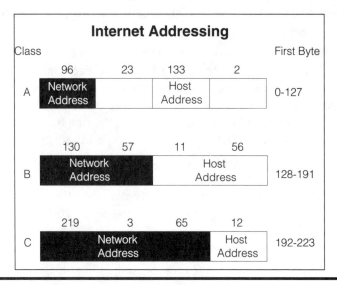

Figure 6.17 An example of the Internet A, B, and C class addresses.

Chapter 6: Analysis for Major Operating System Protocols

Internet Protocol (IP)

The Internet Protocol provides a basic unit of transfer. It is considered a network layer protocol when comparing the OSI model. The IP protocol is considered the main level of the IP datagram. It provides a unit of measure and allows for the routing of data. The IP protocol includes key guidelines for unreliable data transfer that provides the best possible transmission. As an analyst, the key is to be able to capture and decode the IP protocol transmissions across the network. There are certain fields in the IP layer that will reveal important information, such as the source and destination IP addresses for a datagram, the type of IP service requested, and the time which an IP packet can live on a network. The following is a breakout of the IP layer specific fields.

Internet Protocol (IP) Field Specifics

Version

Header Length

Service Type

Total Length

Identification

Flags

Fragment Offset

Time to Live

Protocol

Header Checksum

Source IP Address

Destination IP Address

IP Options

Data (Padding May Be Included)

Version Field—4 Bits
Indicates the current version of IP utilized. Most IP software will check this field to ensure version.

Header Length Field—4 Bits
Indicates the length of IP Header. This field is measured in 32-Bit Words.

Service Type Field—8 Bits Total
Indicates how the IP packet should be processed by an intended destination host. This field is divided into five individual internal fields:

1. Precedence—3 Bits—Priority Levels

—0 (Low/Normal)

   to

- 7(Critical/Network Control)

2. D—1 Bit—Request Low Delay
3. T—1 Bit—Request High Throughput
4. R—1 Bit—Request High Reliability

---

* Bits 6 & 7 Not Used

Total Length Field—16 Bits
This field identifies the total length of the current IP packet. The length includes the IP header and data field. The maximum size of an full IP datagram is approximately 65,535 bytes.

Identification Field- 16 Bits
This field is used for fragmentation control. Each network topology may limit the size of a Maximum Transmission Unit (MTU). The IP software may then have to fragment packets. When fragmentation occurs, packets must be divided and reassembled when transmitted. It is considered standard for IP gateways and routers to handle packets of at least of 576 bytes. This field identifies the unique datagram when fragmentation occurs.

Flags Field—3 Bits
Assists with controlling the fragmentation process. The first bit is a "do not fragment" identifier. If on, it indicates the IP datagram should not be fragmented. The second bit is a "more fragments" identifier. When off, this indicates IP packet holds last fragment of a total IP transmission.

Fragment Offset Field—13 Bits
This field is used when fragmentation occurs. The destination node requires this field for reassembly because packets may not flow in order. This field identifies the current offset point for data that is internal in the current packet as related to the total datagram. The value will be zero to highest offset.

Time to Live (TTL)—8 Bits
This field is critical for analysis concerns and identifies how long in time a IP packet can exist on a network. Time is measured in seconds. Usually the IP Software will put an internal starting value in this field. Any IP based host or gateway that processes the packet on an internetwork transfer must decrease the TTL value by at least one second. All hosts and gateways must also decrease the TTL of the IP packet by the actual second count for internal processing time when routing. If the field is ever found to drop to zero by an IP gateway or host, the device must discard the packet. This prevents packet constant network loops.

Protocol Field—8 Bits
This field indicates the next higher layer protocol that is encapsulated in the IP data field.

Header Checksum Field—16 Bits
This field uses a basic math algorithm to perform a check on IP datagram header, not the data field. It is intended for other higher protocols to provide additional integrity checks on the actual data.

Source and Destination IP Address Field—32 Bits each
This field includes the actual IP address of related end nodes in an IP packet transmission.

IP Options Field—8 Bits to variable length
This is an optional field that is not required. The field is used frequently for testing and debugging. It will contain a : CODE : OPTION CLASS : OPTION NUMBER. Again, this field is used frequently for special processing. Examples include specific source routing and timestamping.

Data Field—Variable length
This is the field that includes the actual data. The padding of zero bits may be used to ensure that the IP datagram reaches at least a 32-bit word.

Internet Control Message Protocol (ICMP)

The ICMP protocol allows for dynamic identification and examining of problems on IP based networks. There may be certain situations where packets are not deliverable due to packet format, or they may have not arrived at a destination station or are attempting to be sent through an incorrect route. It is also possible that propagation delays may be present on a network and the timing of an IP packet transfer may be affected. There are also occurrences when addressing may be incorrect for certain address masking; this may need to be identified. The ICMP protocol was designed to allow these issues to be quickly communicated upon occurrence back to a source node.

This particular protocol has certain key messages, such as the Echo Request/Reply, Destination Unreachable, Source Quench, and Redirect types that will allow for identifying problems on a LAN or WAN. Certain other ICMP packet types such as Time Exceeded and Address Mask Request/Reply packets are also utilized for general troubleshooting.

The following is a breakout of the key message types utilized in ICMP packet transmissions.

Message Types:

Troubleshooting Types

    Type (8) Echo requests and Type (0) Echo Replies

    (PINGS)

    Type (3) Destination Unreachable

    Type (4) Source Quench

    Type (5) Redirect

    Type (11) Time Exceeded (Packet Dropped)

Control Types

    Type (13) Timestamp Request and Type (14) Reply

    Type (15) Information Request and Type (16) Reply

    Type (17) Address Mask Request and Type (18) Reply

    Type (12) Parameter Problem

Chapter 6: Analysis for Major Operating System Protocols

The following subsection presents the field descriptions for the ICMP protocol.

Internet Control Message Protocol (ICMP) Protocol Field Specifics

- Type Field
- Code Field
- Checksum Field
- Datagram Address Field
- ICMP Data

Type Field—8 Bits
This field indicates the ICMP message type.

Code Field—8 Bits
This field provides extended information about the ICMP Type field. The indication of the code will further define the message type. An example: For a message type of destination unreachable, the code will indicate whether the host, network or a specific protocol is unreachable.

Code Identifiers:

(0) — Network Unreachable

(1) — Host Unreachable

(2) — Protocol Unreachable

(3) — Port Unreachable

(4) — Fragmentation Required

(5) — Source Route Failed

(6) — Destination Network Unknown

(7) — Destination Host Unknown

(8) — Source Host Identified

(9) — Prohibited Communicated To Destination Network

(10) — Prohibited Communicated To Destination Host

(11) — Type of Service Cannot Be Used For Network

(12) — Type of Service Cannot Be Used For Host

Checksum Field- 16 Bits
This field provides the checksum for ICMP packet.

Datagram Address and ICMP Fields—Variable
This field contains the specific address of the first 64 bits of original packet involved in ICMP issue. It also contains specific ICMP data.

User Datagram Protocol (UDP)

The UDP is considered a transport layer protocol. The main function of UDP is to provide an unreliable connection between IP-based nodes. UDP is engaged when an IP-host has multiple processes (PORTS) which need to be assigned to end nodes for application access. The UDP protocol will usually rely upon the IP datagram for network transport. UDP does not maintain a connection or provide true reliable data transmission. The UDP protocol is mainly used by Process/Application type protocols for port assignment. It can be utilized to directly carry data to a host protocol port. Again, it is considered an unreliable transfer protocol and does not guarantee transfer integrity. It is more common to see UDP utilized for the TFTP, SNMP, and the Sun NFS protocols.

The following subsection presents the UDP field specifics.

UDP Protocol Field Specifics

- UDP Source Port
- UDP Destination Port
- Message Length
- Checksum
- Data

UDP Source Port—16 Bits
This field contains the source port identifier in the host.

UDP Destination Port—16 Bits
This field contains the destination port identifier in the host.

Chapter 6: Analysis for Major Operating System Protocols

Message Length Field-16 Bits
This field identifies the total UDP header and data field length.

Checksum Field—16 Bits
This field provides a checksum for UDP header and data. This field is optional due to possible overhead concerns, but is recommended because the IP datagram does not check data.

Data Field—Variable
This field contains UDP data.

Transmission Control Protocol (TCP)

TCP is a communication protocol utilized at the transport layer. It guarantees a connection and provides true reliability. TCP is a robust protocol that can maintain a connection between end nodes. TCP will be used to assign the port for host to workstation transmissions. TCP is a full duplex protocol that utilizes an approach of dividing a total TCP data stream into portions called segments. The TCP segments rely upon the IP datagram for transmission. The TCP connection is maintained through sequence and acknowledgment numbers. The flow control of segments is performed through a sliding window. The sliding window process allows the network to be maximized. A source node will send certain segments of a data stream inside a defined window and then wait for acknowledgments. When a portion of the window transmission is responded to through acknowledgments, more segments are sent. This keeps the window sliding as long as the packet transmissions are responded to by receiver. The receiver can also throttle the transmission rate by indicating available window space. If the advertised window size ever drops to zero, the data stream can be stopped and associated applications may timeout or hang. The TCP protocol is used normally with the following key Process/Application protocols: FTP, Telnet, and SMTP Protocol.

The following subsection gives a through description of TCP operations.

Detailed Operation of TCP

TCP/IP protocol communication is utilized in a data transfer of a data stream. The stream is broken into a sequence of bytes (segments) and the stream originates from an upper layer protocol application. TCP is a transport layer host-to-host session-related protocol and handles the following main functions:

- Complex data and reliable data transfer
- Complex data flow processing

The following is a breakout of these key functions.

Complex And Reliable Data Transfer — TCP receives and transmits information related to a segment of TCP information. The segment may be broken into a series of bytes and may be sent from one host to another in a TCP communication session. Data has the capability to flow in a bi- directional configuration which allows for a full duplex operation on LANs utilizing TCP. Each TCP end node will require data delivery to occur in a normal and fluent fashion. If data has to be sent immediately to a host and it must be sent in a rapid fashion, one TCP module may request the other module to perform a push operation.

The reliability of the TCP/IP protocol stack is insured by a Positive Acknowledgement and Retransmission protocol operation (PAR). This means that data that is sent from one end to the other must be acknowledged as received correctly, or it must be retransmitted. Specifically, each TCP end node generates an acknowledgement when data is understood back to the other TCP end node. If a TCP end node does not receive an acknowledgement for data that was sent, it will normally retransmit that data. This allows for the PAR protocol to take effect.

It should be noted that when there are delays on the internetwork, the Round Trip Time (RTT) between the passing of information between TCP end nodes may be affected, and it may be very possible that propagation delays are present on the network. When propagation delays are present, the TCP protocol has internal operations built in to adjust the RTT timing for the TCP tolerance level related to when acknowledgements are received before the retransmission actually occurs.

Complex Data Flow Processing — The actual data flow control across a TCP/IP-based network is maintained by the monitoring of the Window field that is sent from each TCP end node to the other TCP end node. The Window field is a field where each TCP end node will advertise its availability in bytes for data on the next transfer. Specifically, each end node will say, "This is how much data space I have available for the next data transmission that you're

Chapter 6: Analysis for Major Operating System Protocols

going to send me that is part of the stream." The Window size parameter is originally configured on the set-up of the TCP end node, and may require optimization on an internetwork. If the TCP/IP window size ever drops to a value of zero and gets exceeded, it is possible time-outs may occur on a internetwork.

Overall TCP Sequence of Operation — TCP operation includes the following states in a TCP Protocol operation: Listen, Synchronize Sent, Synchronized Received, Established, Finished Wait 1, Finish Wait 2, Close Wait, Closing, Last Acknowledgement Time Wait, and Close.

The following subsection presents the field descriptions for the TCP protocol.

TCP Protocol Field Specifics

- Source Port
- Destination Port
- Sequence Number
- Acknowledgement Number
- Header Length
- Code Bits
- Window Size
- Checksum
- Urgent Pointer
- Options
- Data (May include padding)

Source and Destination Port Fields—16 Bits Each

This field identifies the TCP Port numbers assigned to end nodes in a TCP session. This field may identify application programs at end nodes. A TCP port in a network host can be shared by multiple end nodes.

Sequence Number Field—32 Bits

This field will indicate the source position of the data stream. An initial sequence number will indicate the start of a TCP session.

Acknowledgment Number—32 Bits
This field will show the number of the byte the sender expects to receive back next.

Header Length—4 Bits
This field indicates the length of the TCP header.

Code Bits Field—6 Bits
This field will indicate how the TCP packet should be handled by the destination host. The following code bits apply:

- URG = Urgent
- ACK = Acknowledge field should be examined
- PSH = Push data buffers to full
- RST = TCP connection should be reset
- SYN = Sequence numbers should be reset
- FIN = data stream is at end

Window Size Field—16 Bits
A TCP end node will use this field to notify the other end node of available window buffer size for the next TCP transmission.

Checksum Field—16 Bits
This field is used for a math algorithm that will calculate the value of both the header and data fields to ensure reliability.

Urgent Pointer Field—16 Bits
This field shows where any urgent data ends.

Option and Data Fields—Variable
This field will house the actual data. This options field may indicate upper layer protocols and include padding. The Maximum Segment Size (MSS) may also be indicated.

Chapter 6: Analysis for Major Operating System Protocols

Items to Analyze in the TCP/IP Protocol Suite

The performance analysis and baselining steps discussed in this book are relevant to insuring the TCP/IP Physical layer, Internet layer, and the Host to Host layer operations. Performance analysis will be required to insure that the overall physical/Network environment, the Internet layer communications and the TCP and UDP protocols can operate as normal. In this book, we have discussed Physical/Network layer analysis, the following is a review of how these techniques apply to TCP/IP.

Physical/Network Layer Analysis

We have already discussed how to examine the physical or Network layer (TCP/IP model) health and operation on LANs. To refresh this area of analysis, it should be noted that the physical area is the first area that has to be examined for proper health and operation. On a Token Ring network, there should be a low level of non-isolating and isolating errors, and no hard errors present to show a stable physical layer. Also, the ring purge rate should be fairly low, under 50 ring purges per hour. In an Ethernet-based network, a low level of CRC collision rates, shorts, long frames should be present. Basically, the Ethernet physical layer should be solid. As long as the Ethernet physical layer is solid, then the next layer up can be troubleshot correctly.

The ARP protocol will require that IP hosts and gateways maintaining ARP tables are always refreshed in a standard fashion. The refreshing or aging of these tables must be done on a consistent basis. When there are incorrect refreshment periods or timing between the updates of these tables, it is possible an incorrect address would be provided on a return of a request to a specific device during ARP process. By examining and utilizing a protocol analyzer, it is possible to see the differences between ARP requests and ARP replies by examining the delta time with a protocol analyzer.

Internet Protocol (IP) Analysis

When analyzing the Internet layer in the TCP/IP environment, the address fields have to be verified, and the type of service field should be checked. The Time To Live (TTL) field is key to internetwork analysis; values have to be checked for a high level because IP-based gateways/routers and hosts utilizing routing can discard a packet when the IP Time To Live (TTL) field drops to a zero level. When a packet is received at the TTL level of 1 at a specific gateway, that packet will be discarded. At that point, the gateway must return an ICMP TTL Exceeded message to the original IP source station letting it know that its transmitted packet was discarded. A protocol analyst can capture ICMP TTL Exceeded packets to identify propagation delays related to the internetwork. The maximum IP Time To Live (TTL) value is 255 seconds, but the standard default configuration is 64 seconds.

Internet Control Message Protocol (ICMP) Analysis

A key way to use the ICMP protocol for troubleshooting on IP-based networks is the ICMP Echo Request/Reply, nicknamed an ICMP Ping. The Ping can be used to isolate different problems throughout a LAN. One end node can be used to ping another end node on an IP-based network, and the node that initiates the ping request or Echo Request will wait for another end node to reply. If the destination node replies, it will send back to the source node an Echo Reply, which will indicate that the node is available and active. Depending on the relative time that it takes for a node to reply to the original request, this will also allow the analyst to identify possible propagation delays in an internetwork. When new devices are installed in a LAN that are utilizing TCP/IP, this particular approach can be used to test the availability of those devices, but also the distance away and propagation delays related to the network for the device placement. This is used frequently through installation and implementation phases on TCP/IP-based networks. It is also utilized when certain devices are not available for certain end users as a troubleshooting approach.

Another ICMP message type that is seen frequently in analysis is Fragmentation Required. This ICMP packet type will indicate whether or not fragmentation is allowed across certain gateways and network routes on an IP-based network. IP datagrams are usually fragmented into smaller portions for transmission across LANs. This may be due to limitations in the MTU size setting for a LAN. If a certain gateway encounters a frame that's not fragmented properly, it has the ability through the ICMP Protocol to send back an ICMP Fragmentation Required type packet to the original source node. This will tell the host when it receives the ICMP packet to fragment properly. When ICMP protocol analysis techniques are used on a network, this will identify incompatibilities in MTU size settings for packet size configuration between different key devices on a network. This could be used specifically for identifying configuration problems on NICs, routers or hosts.

Incorrect IP address masks can also be identified with the ICMP protocol. A protocol analyzer or a ICMP monitoring test system can perform an ICMP Address Mask Request packet transmission. This will allow the current address masking to be returned from a respective gateway or host in an IP-based network. Once the Address Mask Request is performed, the Address Mask Reply can be examined for whether or not the proper configuration is present. This helps to identify subnet mask misconfigurations.

Also, it should be noted that ICMP messages can be utilized as far as examination when there may be incorrect routes being provided by certain end nodes or hosts in an internetwork. There are occurrences when a packet may be sent across an internetwork in an IP-based configuration and a certain ,gateway/router receives the packet, then realizes that there is a more efficient route through another gateway or another series of gateways related to a specific source and destination host. That gateway or router then has the ability to send back a packet which is labeled as an ICMP Redirect. ICMP Redirect packets may be captured by a protocol analyst to identify these kinds of anomalies. This may allow the analyst to locate end nodes or hosts that are sending packets in an incorrect fashion across an internetwork. Misdirected datagrams may cause confused routing tables and cause more router anomalies to propagate throughout an internetwork. Certain confused router configurations can then cause extensive problems and eventually cause an internetwork-wide outage.

There are other conditions in an IP-based internetwork where certain overloaded hosts can be isolated through protocol analysis techniques. Specifically, certain hosts may get overloaded on a LAN and then generate an ICMP Source Quench message. A Source Quench ICMP packet is basically saying that the host is busy. In a Unix host environment that is TCP/IP-based, when a particular upper layer protocol or application becomes extremely busy, they may utilize the ICMP protocol suite to send out an ICMP Source Quench message to the source destination station that is currently wishing to communicate with the host. Once the ICMP message is received by the source device, it will then throttle back its transfer to the host. An analyst can capture the ICMP Source Quench packets and, if they seem to be fairly frequent from one particular host, that device may be extremely busy and under-resourced. The device can then be examined through checking its configuration for application configuration, memory caching, general NIC, and CPU configuration.

Host to Host Layer Analysis

It is important that the TCP and UDP protocols are able to establish and complete their session capability. The TCP protocol is normally utilized to transfer information between two specific port processes at the Process/Application layer. The same holds true for the UDP protocol suite. The difference is that TCP maintains a connection and provides reliable stream transfer, whereas UDP is unreliable but still provides Host to Host session capability between specific ports for the Process/Application layer operations.

Both of these Host to Host layer protocols clearly require a solid physical/Network and Internet layer operation. If there is any instability in those areas, there may be certain occurrences such as:

- A high number of TCP session resets
- Retransmitted acknowledgements from key hosts
- TCP window size exceeded concerns
- Addressing conflicts

Some of the specifics are described as follows:

The main addressing schemes in the TCP/IP environment encompass the Physical NIC hardware address, the Internet address, and the UDP or TCP Port address.

The Physical address is unique to each NIC in an end node on each network. The Internet address defines the network-to-network address for each end node. The UDP and TCP port addresses define the process running in each host. Host Port addresses are assigned by Internet administrators and are normally used for communication for specific processes or applications. Both the UDP or TCP Host to Host layer protocols support Port addressing for Internet hosts. Examples of host to host processes could include ports labeled for BootP, TFTP, or FTP protocols.

UDP Analysis Hints

In the UDP protocol, connection maintenance is not an issue, because this is an unreliable transfer protocol. It is important that the correct port numbers are assigned and are utilized on configuration. By using a protocol analyzer, it may be possible to see incorrect port configurations on the UDP protocol environment. By focusing on a UDP session set-up, sometimes a response will not be provided that is correct from a host to an end node and a UDP session transfer will never take place. Specifically, UDP may not allow the upper layer application layer protocol such as Trivial File Transfer Protocol to continue on with its operation until the UDP port set-up configuration is at least established. A connection is not maintained, but again the correct port assignment must be utilized. For example, if the incorrect port number is used, the TFTP session will not be able to take place and utilize the UDP layer for encapsulation.

TCP Analysis Hints

TCP resets may occur frequently if there are extensive propagation delays on a network. It is also possible when upper layer process or applications fail that one TCP module may send out a reset through the flag section of the TCP header to indicate that the connection should be reset. When a host or a file server fails, it may initiate a reset in the TCP module down to the destination station or source session that currently has an active connection. This session then will have to reset its own process to re-establish connections with the host. This is very common in a lot of upper protocol time-out situations. An example would be if there was a FTP session across a large internetwork and the two internetworks were separated through a LAN router. If all of a sudden one end node was attempting to communicate with another end node and did not receive a response, it is very possible that the other end node may have a particular problem. At that point, the one end node that is waiting for the response may eventually time out and send a TCP reset to the original host. At that point the host may have already rebooted and will acknowledge the situation and restart the particular FTP session.

Another condition that may occur is excessively repeated host acknowledgement concerns. There may be conditions where there is a high retransmission rate on a LAN. This is due to the PAR protocol operation. Specifically, if two TCP end nodes are having a conversation and one end node is not receiving a response, it will continue to send the same sequence number to the other TCP end node. If the acknowledgement sequence numbers are not changing and the other end node is not responding, the retransmission level may be extremely high. It may eventually recover or a time-out may occur in a reset manner, just as was expected. The message here is to watch both the retransmission rate levels on TCP-based networks before time-outs occur and loss of session availability takes place.

Another problem in the TCP environments is Window Size Exceeded concerns. As noted earlier in the TCP overview, the Window size availability is critical and must be configured on initial set-up. It is always possible that when a TCP end node is configured, it may not have the proper window size for a particular session. Normally, hosts have a larger window size than end nodes, because they are processing multiple protocol ports in their multiplex operation. TCP window size may need to be adjusted from time to time. Once it drops to a low level, packets may be discarded. If that occurs, one end node may need to send a TCP reset to reactivate a TCP session.

Process/Application Layer and Upper Layer Protocols Analysis

When moving up into the Process/Application layers for the TCP/IP environment, the protocol operation becomes somewhat unique as to the upper layer application protocols. Once the Physical/Network layer is insured, the Internet layer or internetwork is insured; all of the IP addressing routing is proper through the internetwork, and the TCP and UDP host to host layer communication protocols are providing port availability and connection maintenance as required, it will be up to the Process and Application layer to insure final transfer protocol operation.

Once the process and application connection layer is the main focus, the analyst should be someone intimate to the actual type of protocol that is being used at the Process/Application layer. Specifically, knowledge of the Process/Application layer protocol, the correct fields and network operation needs to be understood. This book will not cover in detail the fields for any of these type protocols, but will discuss general protocol operation. Some host processes operate directly with IP, UDP and TCP, as discussed earlier, but certain application protocols may need to be examined to resolve network issues. This book does not review process and application layer protocols in detail. For more information on Application and Process layer protocols, please use the TCP/IP reference in the reference section of this book.

TCP/IP Protocol Types

The number of protocols employed in the TCP/IP suite is extensive, and mastering the internals of all the TCP/IP protocols in the suite can be quite a

Chapter 6: Analysis for Major Operating System Protocols

challenge. If you will be working in the TCP/IP environment, you may want to begin your research with the TCP/IP references listed in the back of this book.

The following is a list of the main subset of protocols that may be found in a TCP/IP environment during a protocol analysis session:

- Network Basic I/O System (NetBIOS). Connection setup protocol for named station addresses.
- File Transfer Protocol (FTP). TCP/IP protocol for guaranteed reliable file transfers.
- Trivial File Transfer Protocol (TFTP). A TCP/IP protocol for exchange of files between TCP/IP network nodes.
- Telnet. A protocol used for transmitting character-oriented terminal and keyboard screen data between networking nodes.
- Simple Mail Transfer Protocol (SMTP). A guaranteed mail transfer protocol for TCP/IP nodes.
- Remote UNIX (RUNIX). A remote UNIX host communication protocol.
- Domain Name Service (DNS). A database query protocol for network addresses in a TCP/IP environment.
- Internet Protocol (IP). Used for end-to-end communication, forwarding, and control.
- Transmission Control Protocol (TCP). A connection protocol for reliable end-to-end communication over IP datagrams.
- User Datagram Protocol (UDP). Used for transmitting data over IP.
- Routing Information Protocol (RIP). Used to exchange routing information among IP related routers, gateways, and end systems.
- Gateway-to-Gateway Protocol (GGP). Used to exchange routing information between IP gateways.
- Internet Control Message Protocol (ICMP). Used for monitoring and testing IP datagram communications.
- Address Resolution Protocol (ARP). Used to identify a DLC physical address from an IP address.
- Reverse ARP (RARP). Used in reverse to identify the IP address from the DLC physical layer address.
- Subnetwork Access Protocol (SNAP). Used as a conversion protocol carrying vehicle; an envelope protocol.

- Server Message Block (SMB). Application layer protocol for LAN Server environment.
- Logical Link Control (LLC). Internal connection setup for higher layer protocols.
- Common Management over TCP/IP (CMOT). A TCP/IP related informational management protocol.

Figure 6.18 shows the TCP/IP protocol suite as related to the OSI model.

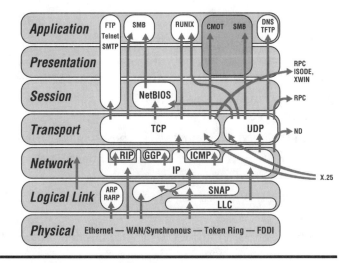

Figure 6.18 TCP/IP protocol suite as related to the OSI model.

The TCP/IP environment is very complex. To become a master in protocol analysis of this environment involves extensive research in the Request for Comment papers (RFC) noted in Appendix B.

Figure 6.19 shows a set of traces from the Network General Sniffer that depicts how some of the key TCP/IP packet types are captured through a protocol analysis session. Note the internal fields and the layers within the TCP/IP packets.

Chapter 6: Analysis for Major Operating System Protocols 213

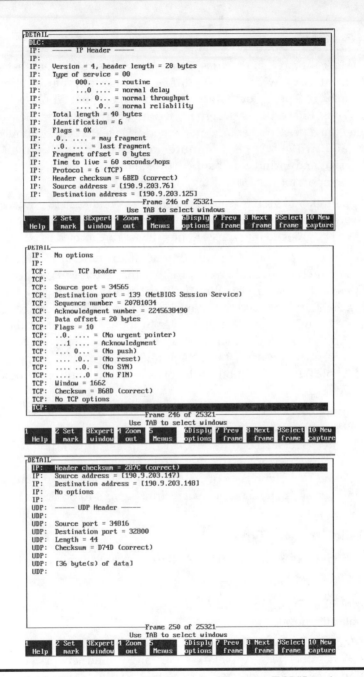

Figure 6.19 Network General Sniffer traces depicting TCP/IP packet types.

AppleTalk

The AppleTalk protocol suite varies in its format due to the fact that there are two implementations, which include different groups of protocols, Phase I and Phase II. In 1985, Apple Computer delivered the original AppleTalk protocol, Phase I. When Phase I was designed, it was configured for the Macintosh environment in a peer-to-peer local node mode. Development continued on this protocol, and in 1989 Apple Computer released Phase II, which is more comprehensive and includes full support for internetworking up to 255 zones along with support for the Token Ring topology.

The AppleTalk addressing scheme encompasses nodes, networks, zones, and ports. A workstation corresponds to a node. The next category is a single network. Networks can be grouped into zones. Router devices are termed as ports.

The AppleTalk protocols relate somewhat to the OSI model, but clear differences exist. The physical layers of either the Token Ring, Ethernet, or the LocalTalk environment correlate directly. The AppleTalk, TokenTalk Link Access Protocol, EtherTalk Link Access Protocol, and LocalTalk Link Access Protocol layers relate to the general data link layer in the OSI model. At the network layer, the AppleTalk protocol suite uses Datagram Delivery Protocol. At the transport layer, the Routing Table Maintenance Protocol, AppleTalk Echo Protocol, AppleTalk Transaction Protocol, and Name Binding Protocol most clearly relate.

At the session layer in OSI, the AppleTalk Protocol utilizes the AppleTalk Data Stream Protocol, the Zone Information Protocol, the AppleTalk Session Protocol, and the Printer AcctsProtocol (PAP). At the presentation layer of OSI, the AppleTalk architecture employs the AppleTalk Filing Protocol and the Postscript Protocols. At the application layer of OSI, the AppleTalk architecture contributes to AppleShare File Server and the AppleShare Print Server Protocols.

AppleTalk Protocol Types

More than 15 protocols are within the AppleTalk protocol suite. The following is a list of the main ones:

- AppleTalk Filing Protocol (AFP). A remote file access protocol at the application level.
- Datagram Delivery Protocol (DDP). A network layer protocol used to carry data between Appletalk nodes on an internetwork. Includes key information on network addressing and hop counts.

Chapter 6: Analysis for Major Operating System Protocols

- Printer Access Protocol (PAP). A protocol used to route in stream mode to print devices.
- AppleTalk Session Protocol (ASP). A protocol used for session establishment, connection, and disconnection.
- AppleTalk Data Stream Protocol (ADSP). A connection-oriented sockets communication protocol.
- Zone Information Protocol (ZIP). A protocol used to establish and maintain a name binding to the applied networks in the form of zones; used for routing environments.
- Name Binding Protocol (NBP). A protocol that translates character names within specific zones to any related sockets.
- AppleTalk Transaction Protocol (ATP). A protocol used to transmit between two specific sockets.
- Routing Table Maintenance Protocol (RTMP). A route discovery protocol for bridges and routers.
- AppleTalk Echo Protocol (AEP). A protocol to allow echoing for specific network nodes for node identification and timing.
- Link Access Protocol (LAP). The main logical link for nodes in an AppleTalk configuration.
- Subnetwork Access Protocol (SNAP). Used as a conversion protocol carrying vehicle; an envelope protocol.

Figure 6.20 AppleTalk protocol suite as related to the OSI model.

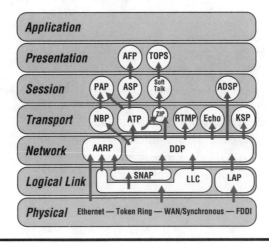

Figure 6.20 AppleTalk protocol suite as related to the OSI model.

Items To Analyze in the AppleTalk Protocol Suite

Due to the complexity of the AppleTalk environment, it takes quite some time to master the AppleTalk protocol suite from a protocol analysis standpoint. However, an analyst should be able to learn more about the AppleTalk environment using the AppleTalk protocol sources in the reference section of this book. This section gives you some tips for analysis of an AppleTalk protocol environment.

Give special attention to analysis of the Zone Information Protocol (ZIP) packets. The Zone Information Protocols are involved in the communication of the internal zones in an AppleTalk internetwork environment. It is possible that within the ZIP packet a problem may be identified. The ZIP protocol is used to translate between the network numbers and zone names in the Apple internetworking environment. The internals of all ZIP packets should be examined for proper addressing between the nodes communicating. For communication problems where certain stations are not connecting or are not able to find their destination or host station, decoding and paging through the trace in the ZIP packet may help to identify an addressing conflict.

Also keep an eye on the Name Binding Protocol packets (NBP). The NBP protocol is used as a name relational transfer across the AppleTalk internetwork. This protocol permits the network stations to refer to different types of services through a process of character names. All services and processes within the AppleTalk environment are named and will have NBP protocol designations.

The NBP packets also can be picked up and decoded to examine the internal addressing information to relate the particular type of information that the packets are associated with to a particular name. When a network user cannot locate a particular service, there may be a conflict in the configuration of a device or an operation. By analyzing the NBP packet, an analyst may be able to identify a misconfiguration on the internetwork.

The Routing Table Maintenance Protocol (RTMP) is a key protocol to examine for problems with routing lengths and wait times in the AppleTalk layers. Routing information is found in the Routing Tuple field. For complaints of poor performance, examine the internals of the Routing Table Maintenance protocol to identify whether the discovery protocol for the bridges and routers is proper. You may capture a wait time that is too high, or a high routing length.

Chapter 6: Analysis for Major Operating System Protocols 217

The hops between nodes should be closely monitored within the AppleTalk Routing protocol for packet communication issues.

The AppleTalk Filing Protocol contains most of the internals for file access on an AppleTalk internetwork. Take a close look at the internals of the file pointers and file access methods in the AppleTalk protocol. This requires paging through the trace; however, through this approach an analyst can identify whether the file access fluency is proper. The same factors apply as in network optimization and analysis theory: a file needs to be opened, accessed, and closed in a fluent manner. Examining the internals of the AppleTalk filing protocol helps to pinpoint whether this type of file access is occurring.

An especially important protocol, the AppleTalk Session Protocol, is used for initiation, connection, transmission, and disconnection. If a node cannot connect to another node in an AppleTalk environment, an attempt may be made to try the connection through the device by filtering on its address and then examining the internal AppleTalk session protocol packets for possible problems with connection.

For additional information on the AppleTalk protocol suite, see the reference sections in the back of this book.

Figure 6.21 presents some of the major trace breakdowns from a Network General Sniffer of key protocols found in the AppleTalk environment.

```
-DETAIL-
DDP:   DDP protocol type = 2 (NBP)
DDP:
NBP:------ NBP header ------
NBP:
NBP:   Control        = 2 (Lookup)
NBP:   Tuple count    = 1
NBP:   Transaction id = 25
NBP:
NBP:   ------ Entity # 1 ------
NBP:
NBP:   Node        = 1293.116, Socket = 254
NBP:   Enumerator  = 0
NBP:   Object      = "="
NBP:   Type        = "AFPServer"
NBP:   Zone        = "Pine"
NBP:
NBP:[Normal end of "NBP header".]
NBP:
------Frame 6 of 253------
 1     2 Set   3Expert 4 Zoom 5        6Disply 7 Prev  8 Next  9Select 10 New
       Help   mark    window  out     Menus    options frame   frame   frame   capture
```

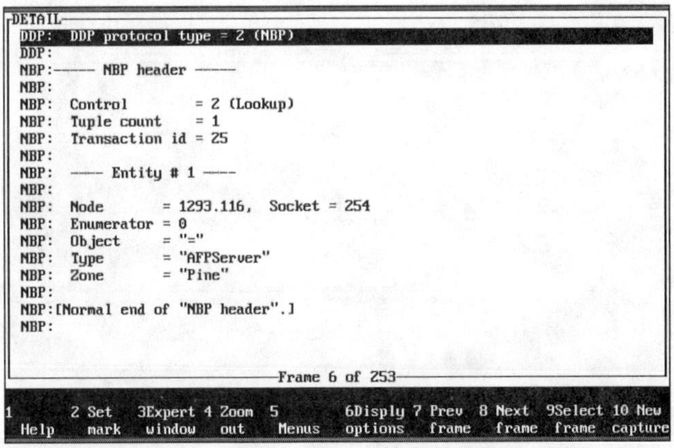

Figure 6.21 Network General Sniffer trace breakdowns of key AppleTalk protocols.

The Banyan VINES Protocol Suite

The Banyan VINES protocol suite was introduced by Banyan Systems, Inc. The VINES (Virtual NEtworking System) network architecture employs protocols drawn from the Xerox XNS suite and TCP/IP. Also included are protocols from the SNA environment.

The VINES architecture relates somewhat to the OSI model. The physical layer in the VINES environment relates closely to the physical layer within the OSI model. The data link layer of the OSI model relates directly to either LocalTalk, EtherTalk, or TokenTalk topologies, similar to the AppleTalk environment. The VINES fragmentation protocol VFRP relates to the data link layer.

The VINES Internet Control Protocol (VICP), Internet Protocol (VIP), Routing Update Table Protocol (RTP), and Address Resolution Protocol (ARP) work at the network layer of OSI. The VIPC works mainly at the transport layer along with the Sequence Packet Protocol (SPP), TCP/IP-related protocols, and AppleTalk-related routing protocols. The Server Message Block (SMB) protocol and some of the higher VINES protocols such as StreetTalk, Mail protocols, and MATCHMAKER protocols relate at the application and presentation layers. Figure 6.22 depicts the VINES protocol model as it relates to the OSI model.

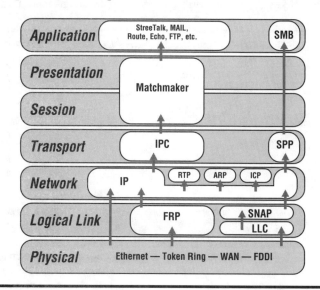

Figure 6.22 The VINES protocol model as it relates to the OSI model.

Chapter 6: Analysis for Major Operating System Protocols

In looking at the OSI layers in relation to the VINES protocols, note that some of the key protocols have specific functions. For example, the VINES Fragmentation Protocol, which works with the data link layer, allows most of the main VINES protocols to communicate with some of the different hardware in the internetworking environment. The VFRP protocol works with the VINES Internet protocol to determine the proper frame size in relation to hardware. At the network layer, the VINES Internet Protocol, VINES Routing Update Protocol and Address Resolution Protocol, and Internet Control Protocols work closely to ensure node-to-node communication.

The VINES Internet protocol works with the VINES Routing Update Protocol for connection between source and destination nodes. The Routing Update Protocol is responsible for updating all the VINES servers and routing nodes with information relating to changing routing information on the network. The VINES Address Resolution Protocol works to assign all the proper addressing schemes at the network layer from node to node. The Internet Control Protocol is important, as it interrelates most of the key information between nodes as far as general integrity of communication between client nodes. This protocol tracks any errors in communication between nodes, and can specifically be analyzed for error data.

At the transport layer, the Sequence Packet Protocol is used to set up a virtual connection between any two specific VINES nodes in an internetwork. The VINES Interprocess Communication Protocol (VIPC) works to handle datagram communication, both for reliable and unreliable formats. If an unreliable datagram communication is considered an issue, internal error information will be marked in the IPC layer.

The higher layer protocols are based on application protocols such as the Remote Procedure Call protocol (Net RPC), and Server Message Block, which is utilized from the SNA protocol suite.

VINES Protocol Types

The VINES suite includes numerous protocols and has much in common with the SNA protocol and TCP/IP environments; some of the protocols correspond directly to the TCP/IP and SNA environment.

The following list describes the protocols in the Banyan VINES protocol suite:

- VINES Interprocess Communication Protocol (VIPC). A transport-level protocol used for providing message services in reliable mode; it supports unreliable datagram service modes.
- Sequenced Packet Protocol (SPP). Transport level protocol used to establish an actual virtual connection operation.
- VINES Routing Update Protocol (VRTP). Protocol utilized in the VINES environment to maintain routing information in an internetwork.
- Address Resolution Protocol (ARP). Utilized for identifying a workstation's DLC addresses from the respective IP address.
- VINES Internet Control Protocol (VICP). Used to broadcast any changes in network topology along with error broadcasts.
- VINES Internet Protocol (VIP). Used for transporting datagrams in the network.
- VINES Fragmentation Protocol (VFRP). Decodes and reassembles network layer packets for transmission to the data link layer, the physical layer, and any higher layers.
- Subnetwork Access Protocol (SNAP). An enveloping protocol.
- MAIL. Used for transmission of messages in the VINES E-mail system.
- Server Message Block (SMB). An application file access layer protocol developed by Microsoft for use with the IBM LAN Server. In the VINES environment, SMB is enveloped in SPP. The Banyan VINES Protocol suite interprets the SMB commands.
- MATCHMAKER. This protocol is utilized by a group of VINES upper layer services and provides program-to-program communication. It also supports remote procedure calls. The MATCHMAKER internal operations include data packet translation for workstations in sender's and receiver's modes. It is possible to see the following protocols transmitted by a MATCHMAKER packet in an analysis session: File, FTP, Server, Echo, Router, Background, Talk, and Network Management.
- Logical Link Control (LLC). Provides essential connection control to other encapsulated protocols.

Items To Analyze in the Banyan Protocol Suite

The first focus in a Banyan VINES analysis session should be the physical layers. As in the DEC protocol suite and the TCP/IP environment, make sure

Chapter 6: Analysis for Major Operating System Protocols

that the physical layers have true integrity. Errors at the physical layer can cause higher layer communication time-out failures in any protocol, but it is especially important in the VINES environment to make sure that the physical layers are healthy.

Examine the server connections and operation of updating some of the server routing update tables and general server addressing environments. By verifying whether the VINES Internet packets communication fields are proper, an analyst can verify the key network health points in a VINES internetwork. The internals of the VINES Internet packets include key addressing information to ensure that the servers are in operation. It is important that all addressing be verified in a VINES environment, because some of the complexities of the addressing in this environment are based on server operation.

The routing update table packets contain information related to server internal addressing, and are used to maintain address information throughout a VINES internetwork. The VINES network communication is based on a WAN scheme whereby servers update other servers in the internetwork regarding the services with which they are associated. The StreetTalk naming system is based on a high integrity information database in each server. It is important that each server update other servers on changes to the addressing environment.

Routing Update Table Protocol packets contain address information regarding network numbers and subnetwork numbers. These packets also are used to maintain some of the key routing information on the efficiency of the routing environment. An analyst can capture Routing Update Table Protocol (VRTP) packets and examine the internal packet fields for normal communication. The internals of the packet also indicate whether routing is occurring normally.

Another area to look at during a VINES analysis session is VRTP updating. In most version setups of VRTP, a transmission should occur every 90 seconds, and a Routing Update Protocol packet should be transmitted from the proper nodes. This is important to ensure that the StreetTalk database and some of the other key addressing databases throughout the VINES environment are operating.

The VINES IP protocol itself includes the transport control field and has metric nodes on the hop counts between two VINES nodes on a large network. These fields should be examined.

The VINES IP header itself includes most of the information for examining and verifying a healthy communication session within a VINES internetwork. When node-to-node communications occur on a VINES network and utilize the

IP protocol, the internals of the packet (which include a transport control field) identify a hop count for the node-to-node transmission.

The internal health of a VINES communication session can be determined with a close look at the IP header. Internal to the IP header is the actual hop count, the protocol type, the network number, and subnet numbers. This information should be noted in any analysis session when troubleshooting communication problems within a VINES internetwork. Take notes on any type of communication session problem occurring by paging through the trace.

Examine the IP header to determine what address communication is occurring. If two nodes are having a communication problem, use the protocol analyzer to filter on those two specific nodes.

Then decode all the IP headers, and record the internal informationsuch as the network number, subnet number, protocol type, and transport control fields. If very high hop counts or incorrect addresses are found, those particular areas of the network should be troubleshot.

The StreetTalk database should update approximately every 10-12 hours. This is important for synchronization in a wide area network environment for the VINES protocol. This integrity can be verified by analyzing with proper filters all packets with StreetTalk data.

Understanding the VINES protocol suite requires extensive study. You can research the VINES protocol in-depth by referencing the VINES texts mentioned in the reference section of this book.

Figure 6.23 presents some of the internal packet types within the VINES protocol suite as captured by the Network General Sniffer.

Chapter 6: Analysis for Major Operating System Protocols

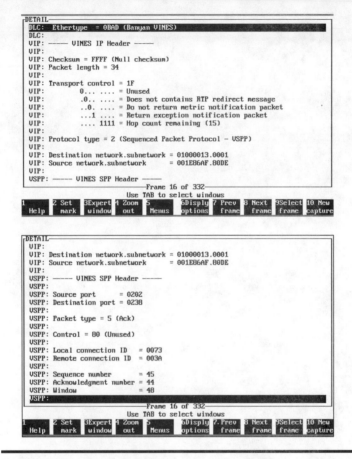

Figure 6.23 Internal packet types within the VINES protocol suite.

CHAPTER 7

Optimization for Specific Routing Protocols

When performing a network optimization project within a large internetwork, the area of internetwork traffic routes requires significant skills and understanding of the routing protocol subset.

Many protocols are involved in different subsets of full protocol suites, and within those protocols are internal routing protocols for almost every subset of the main protocols. For example, the Novell protocol suite has seven main protocols, one of which is used for routing the Routing Information Protocol (RIP). Other major protocol suites are similarly structured. The AppleTalk protocol suite, which has many internal protocols, uses the Routing Table Maintenance Protocol (RTMP) for routing.

This chapter discusses most of the major routing protocols. Before going forward, we will discuss internetwork routing technology.

Exploring Routing Technology and Analysis Points

Routing protocols are used for two main reasons: to determine internetwork routes, and to provide a transfer of information between different networks. The actual determination of internetwork routes is based on a complex set of measurements within the routing protocol. Routers communicate with others utilizing specific algorithms for determining the optimal internetwork routes between multiple networks. They usually maintain a subset of routing tables, to store all the key information to be used in obtaining the correct addressing for different routes between the different routers.

For example, certain routers may have an idea where other routers are located in a large internetwork, which can be as far as five networks away. Certain routers may identify that as five hops away, and store that type of information within a routing table. A workstation on a network connected to that router might request to transfer a packet to the network five routers away. At that point, the router determines whether the hops to that router are too long, and whether a shorter route can be obtained through another internetwork route.

A group of measurements and categories, called *metrics*, is used to determine some of the routing parameters; these usually vary from router type to type. For example, a Cisco router works differently from a Wellfleet router. But all routers normally maintain complex routing tables with all the key information on the other routers on the internetwork. The routers share this information periodically by updating each other through some sort of routing information protocol. The routers communicate with each other and continue to keep the updates current between the different routers. Consequently, when a node on one network wants to transfer information to a node on another network, the complete routing table is current and can obtain the most efficient route.

At times, certain routing algorithms may not be efficient, and this can cause the updates from table to table in routers and file servers not to be performed on a proper time sequence. This can temporarily cause a routing loop, which is not an unusual occurrence on large internetworks that do not support some of the complex routing algorithms that may be required.

Routing algorithms within internal routers can be designed to allow for changes in network size and network delays, including bottlenecks and even

Chapter 7: Optimization for Specific Routing Peotocols

lows or peaks in network bandwidth utilization factors. Some routers have groups of complex routing algorithm configurations, and other basic algorithms are in some standard basic routers. Most routers should be able to maintain either a dynamic or a static routing information table. Dynamic routing is used when routers are updating each other due to general information changes and operation changes on the particular networks involved. Static changes are usually modified by the network design group and can be configured so that the router operates in a standard way in certain areas. Many routers have the capability of supporting static and dynamic routing.

Any protocol should have a centralized algorithm that enables routers to always maintain tables of the precalculated, most efficient routes within standard internetwork layouts. There should also be distributive algorithms so that internetwork routes and time changes on the network can be calculated on a dynamic basis.

Most routers should be able to provide a multipath approach to allow traffic to flow in multiple areas throughout a large internetwork. The term *collapsed backbone* refers to the situation where the external networks throughout an internetwork actually join within the backplane of a large comprehensive router; that router then serves as a complete backbone between the networks. This particular design allows for routing ease and high transfer rates on some of the most complex routing protocols, including the SNA protocol.

Many routers today function efficiently with complex internetworks. These routers can identify performance issues in an internetwork traffic flow and provide reliability when delays and high bandwidth utilization occur. Most routers should be able to calculate whether a packet needs to be communicated in a different route if there is a high communication load factor or cost through a normal route. These routers should be able to make a decision dynamically on whether an alternate route would be more efficient in relation to load or communication cost factors.

At times, routers also may need to adjust their packet size on the network to accommodate communication load factors throughout an internetwork. In today's complex internetworks, router technology needs to take into account bandwidth utilization to allow for this type of transfer.

When performing a network optimization project on a large internetwork, it is important to be able to decode the different routing algorithms present within the internal packets of the routing protocols captured with a protocol analyzer. A protocol analyzer can pick up the routing protocols and allow the analyst to decode the fields for the respective routing protocols. At times, it is an advantage to be able to capture a particular packet between two networks, and display the packet to obtain information on how the packet was transferred from one network to the other. Key information probably will be found in the packet's routing protocol fields that relates to how long the time transfer took between the two networks. Also encoded in the protocol packet is information on the number of delays between the network and the respective hops between the complete internetwork traffic cycle.

For example, Novell RIP packets encode the time required to traverse a network in terms of units called ticks. Data in RIP packets also encode the number of networks passed through on the transfer from network 1 to network 6 in the hops fields in the packet. This type of information is critical during actual troubleshooting of internetwork traffic route issues.

Again, the focus here is that routing protocols provide for a determination of internetwork routes, and the actual transfer of information between those particular networks. An analyst can decode routing information packets to obtain key information about internetwork traffic flow.

With some routing protocol theory taken care of, we can discuss some of the major routing protocols in today's networking environment.

Understanding Routing Protocols

Today, most internetworks are basically connected through routers. If a corporation, government, or any entity employs an internetwork, the routers used will be configured to communicate with an "Interior" gateway protocol. In the Internet this is labeled (IGP). Interior systems are considered independent and self-governing to the particular entity. If two different internetworks need to communicate across their separate environments, an "Exterior" gateway protocol will be used. This is labeled in the Internet as (EGP).

The complexity of routing protocols can be further broken down into two major theories for how routing protocols work. These theories are the Link State Routing Protocols and the Distance Vector Routing Protocols.

The Distance Vector type routing protocols actually divide a network into logical areas and then use a packet research approach for allowing how packets can be transferred between different networks in the shortest path. Distance

Chapter 7: Optimization for Specific Routing Peotocols

Vector is a routing approach that incorporates a method of maintaining the location vector and applied distance to that vector for each network. The routers using Distance Vector algorithms will maintain a routing table that includes the distance and vector to each network in the interior system. The distance vector system usually updates each router in the interior internetwork on standard time intervals such as 30 or 60 seconds. When outages occur, the standard time update approach can cause temporary routing anomalies in internetwork routers. This will eventually recover on the next update. This is called slow convergence. The other disadvantage of Distance Vector tables is that in large internetworks, as the number of routers grows, so does the size of packet transmissions relating to periodic router updates. Basically, Distance Vector routing protocols can become network intensive related to traffic concerns.

Link State Routing Protocols are designed to be more specific as to route forwarding, and can be more easily maintained by a configured approach within the network management team. In LinkBased routing, the internetwork routers employ a scheme of only maintaining a routing table based on the closet attached routers or edge network routers. The Link System is also based on less frequent updates that only check the status of available linked routers and full updates when dynamic changes occur, such as a router going down. This limits the size and amount of routing update traffic.

Two other terms need to be defined: Intra-Domain (within the same area or domain) and Inter-Domain (in different areas or domains).

Following are descriptions of some key routing protocols in the internetworking environment. The routing protocols should not be confused with protocols used to routed data such as Internet Protocol (IP). Router protocols are internetwork protocols used in certain internetworking environments to allow for communication and calculation of routes between respective subnetworks. These protocols include protocols such as the Routing Information Protocol, Open Shortest Path First (OSPF) and proprietary protocols used by certain router manufacturers, such as the Interior Gateway Routing Protocol (IGRP) from Cisco Systems Inc.

Protocols used to transfer data are used in each main network protocol suite in the major computing environments. For example, IP, IPX, and DDP are protocols used for routing data.

The key routing protocols used in internetworking today are as follows:

- Routing Information Protocol (RIP)

- This is the TCP/IP derivative and other such custom versions of RIP in Novell RIP, 3COM RIP, Banyan VRTP, and AppleTalk's RTMP.
- Open Shortest Path First (OSPF)
- Interior Gateway Protocol (IGP)
- Exterior Gateway Protocol (EGP)
- Border Gateway Protocol (BGP)
- OSI-ES to IS and IS to IS and IDRP Routing Protocols
- Cisco's Interior Gateway Routing Protocol (IGRP)

The following is a description of the key routing protocols, along with their use and functions. Some of the major networking protocols described in Chapter 6 use certain derivatives of the key routing protocols. Their routing methodologies are described separately.

Routing Information Protocol (RIP)

The RIP was developed in the Berkeley and Xerox development environment when XNS was developed by Xerox. This protocol has been used in a large subset of high-end computing environments, such as TCP/IP, AppleTalk, Novell, and Banyan. Most of these major computing protocol subsets use a derivative of RIP, but not in its exact form. RIP is normally used in Interior-based routing systems. The RIP protocol is also based on the Distance Vector scheme. The RIP protocol itself is intended to more efficiently route packets in a multiple network environment. It was intended for smaller networks, not the large internetworks that exist today. This is apparent in its design: it has only a 16-hop count limit. Small networks are adequately accommodated under this limitation, but large networks frequently must exceed the 16-hop count limit.

Another concern with RIP is that it uses a simplistic algorithm for metrics and for updating multiple routes. At times, RIP may have problems with incorrect updates in the routing tables for large networks. When resets in routers occur in a RIP environment on large internetworks, incorrect routing tables may be the result. Update mismatches can occur when tables are not updated for 30 or 60 seconds, which is the standard RIP update interval. Newer routing protocols are more robust in complex internetworks, but RIP remains an efficient protocol for most of the more standard size internetworks.

Open Shortest Path First (OSPF)

Open Shortest Path First was developed by the Proteon Corp., along with major educational institutions. This protocol was developed as a linkstate routing protocol, used mainly in Interior-based routing systems, and is extremely dynamic for routing algorithms between large internetworks. The Open Shortest Path First is regarded as one of the best protocols for use in large internetworks.

The Open Shortest Path First routing protocol takes advantage of some of the strengths of the RIP. It conforms to the basic structure within the RIP environment, but it also adds some high-end touches to the protocol algorithm. For example, instead of updating routers throughout an internetwork on the standard every 30 to 60 seconds, the Open Shortest Path First routing protocol updates on-the-fly when there are problems between any routers. This feature eliminates any normal possibility for routing loops; routers can recover quickly and update the internetwork.

Another advantage of Open Shortest Path First is that it allows for multiple path routing dynamics and can route on-the-fly to the most efficient route. This protocol also works with higher-end applications to decide routes on the dynamics of a particular application process. The Open Shortest Path First protocol includes a feature called Type of Service Routing (TOS), where an application can dictate to the IP TOS and allow the internetwork routing protocol (OSPF) to dictate a packet and give it priority on its route and identification path. This capability to work with upper-end applications allows OSPF to dynamically route between destinations in a large internetwork on an application's request. OSPF can also use load balancing techniques to carefully calculate ways to balance traffic over multiple routes on an internetwork. This is an essential capability if low delay factors are to be achieved throughout the internetwork.

Open Shortest Path First is one of the protocols that you are likely to see in a protocol analysis environment.

Keep a close eye on the internal routes and internetwork time delays within routing packets. Always examine the number of network hops taken by an OSPF packet when examining problems in a multiple network environment.

Interior Gateway Protocol (IGP) and Exterior Gateway Protocol (EGP)

In the IP environment, the term *gateway* describes routers. Some routers are used to move packets between networks under the same network management control on the Internet, and are termed core routers or interior routers. The protocol used to route between the interior routers within a specific network management scheme is the Interior Gateway Protocol. Exterior Gateway Routing Protocols are used for routing between the interior routers on one independent internetwork to other exterior routers on another independent internetwork. Normally, in an analysis environment on most internetworks, analysts only work with Exterior Gateway protocols.

The core Internet routers form most of the Internet routing backbone protocol routing updates for the Internet. Other subdomain networks exist that work with the Internet routers at times; Exterior Gateway Protocol is a dynamic protocol that allows for this transfer. It updates based on the number of networks that can be reached, and is also used at a regular interval for updating those routers.

The information within Exterior Gateway Protocol packets varies depending on the subset of the protocol. However, this protocol is considered fairly simple. The concern during analysis is whether routing updates are occurring. There is no key high-end algorithm information contained within Exterior Gateway Protocol, and it is not really considered efficient for large internetworks, where communication needs to occur on a dynamic basis.

Border Gateway Protocol (BGP)

Border Gateway Protocol is a derivative of Exterior Gateway Protocol, and is mainly used on the Internet environment for more comprehensive routing, to allow for detecting any problems with general routing loops throughout the multiple network transfer. The Border Gateway Protocol includes more algorithms internally to allow for detecting routing loops. This protocol actually measures the particular degree of transfer between an internetwork route. That degree of transfer is measured and monitored within the respective fields of the Border Gateway Protocol. This is not normally seen in corporate internetworks, but in the Internet environment, it is probably one of the best of the Exterior

Gateway Protocol types to determine an optimal path. It maintains a peer-to-peer routing table between Border Gateway Protocol routers, and incremental updates are sent out in general, just like an Exterior Gateway Protocol.

An important distinction is that the Border Gateway Protocol can obtain more current information from router to router. Because it can maintain a more dynamic multiple path environment, this protocol only communicates to other routers through the optimal path available for transfer at any give time.

OSI-ES to IS and IS to IS and IDRP Routing Protocols

The International Organization of Standards has developed a group of different routing protocols to communicate across OSI protocol environments. The protocols center on End Systems (ES) and Intermediate Systems (IS). End Systems are devices that do not route; Intermediate Systems are routing devices. These devices can exist in areas called routing domains. It is possible for an ES to route to an IS in the same area through the End System to Intermediate System (ES to IS) version protocol. An IS version can route to another IS device in the same area through the Intermediate System to Intermediate System (IS to IS) version protocol. IS to IS is a derivative of DECnet phase V routing. If an ES or IS device needs to communicate across areas, the Inter Domain Routing Protocol (IDRP) is used. There are level 1 and level 2 routers. Level 1 routers can talk to level 2 routers, and normally, level 2 routers only communicate with other level 2 routers. This provides an organized approach for internetwork routing.

Cisco's Interior Gateway Routing Protocol (IGRP)

IGRP is a proprietary protocol developed by Cisco Systems in the 1980s. A Distance Vector Routing Protocol, it is intended for large internetworking environments. The internal configurations for a router using IGRP can be extensively customized. IGRP has a large group of settings for custom environments. Its metric settings allow for custom multiple path setups with auto switching on-the-fly to other routes when failures in a route occur. A feature called holddown is used to prevent a router from automatically re-establishing routes on a bad link. Routing loops can be prevented by a feature called split horizon, which stops redundant updates on bad routes.

Novell Routing Information Protocols and Analysis Tips

Standard Routing Information Protocol

As discussed earlier, the Novell Routing Information Protocol is a subset of the Novell protocol suite. The Novell RIP is very efficient for keeping routers and file servers updated within the Novell internetworking environment. Normally, the RIP is transmitted within a 60-second time frame and has a field to monitor the hops and ticks away between the routers and their large internetwork.

It is important to keep an eye on the number of hops between networks in the RIP packet, along with the respective tick counts when captured. The focal point should be to capture RIP packets, decode them, and analyze the hops and ticks when troubleshooting between networks.

NetWare Link State Protocol (NLSP)

Novell has recently identified the requirement to reduce the amount of broadcast traffic associated with standard SAP and RIP operations. The standard RIP updates are keyed on 60 second standard intervals. This is due to standard distance vector implementation of Novell's version of RIP. The new NetWare Link State Protocol (NLSP) allows for a link state routing protocol implementation.

NLSP allows for less network overhead traffic and timing by reducing the overall routing update frequency. This in turn reduces the overall amount of processing required for NetWare based servers related to routing operations. The updates are sent in hourly intervals and only during router and server operational changes. The NLSP protocol also addresses internetwork size concerns by allowing routing between 127 hop counts verses the standard RIP limitation of 16 network hop counts. The NLSP processes can also be more easily managed by host management platforms.

VINES Routing Information Protocols and Analysis Tips

The VINES Routing Information Protocol uses a proprietary protocol approach from Xerox Networking Systems protocol. VINES is basically a client/server architecture that mainly uses layer 3 for its routing activities. In the VINES protocol suite, layer 3 includes the VINES Internet Protocol (VIP), which works very closely with its own Address Resolution Protocol (ARP). VINES also uses a version of the main RIP type for its own VINES Routing Update Protocol (VRTP).

The VRTP protocol allows routing between multiple networks in a VINES environment. The VINES internetwork addressing scheme uses a 48-byte address that divides a network ID into 32 bytes and a subnetwork area ID into 16 bytes. The actual addressing scheme is accomplished and maintained in large internetworks by the Banyan servers, which are hardware keyed and work with multiple networks to make sure that each subnetwork is assigned dynamically.

When a new VINES node attempts to attach to a network, it is dynamically assigned a specific network address. Thus there is a minimal chance that a duplicate address will be encountered.

From an analysis standpoint, always keep a close eye on all the VIP and ARP packets captured in an analysis session. Examine the packet for any problems in actual delay between different networks.

The Routing Update Protocol (RTP) is an important protocol between the routers and a VINES environment. The RTP includes the advertisement between the respective routers with a hello packet format. There are different values that various VINES servers update in the different environments; this varies depending on the operating system version of VINES being run. This can vary from a 30- to 90-second version in the most current version of VINES in use today. Certain fields within the VINES Routing Table Protocols need to be monitored, such as cost between the two particular networks.

Focus on the following key protocols when analyzing any internetwork traffic route issues within a VINES environment:

- VINES Internetwork Protocol
- Address Resolution Protocol
- Routing Table Protocol

ETHERNET AND TOKEN RING OPTIMIZATION

Figure 7.1 is a breakout of some key packets involved in routing captured within a VINES environment from a Network General Sniffer.

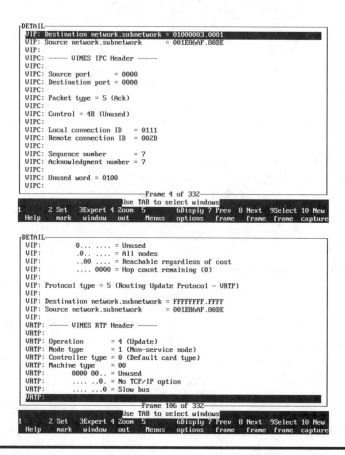

Figure 7.1 A breakout of key routing packets within the VINES environment from Network General Sniffer.

TCP/IP Routing Information Protocols and Analysis Tips

The TCP/IP environment has many complex routing protocols. The IP protocol uses the following protocols to identify addresses within an Internet: Address Resolution Protocol (ARP) and Reverse Address Resolution Protocol (RARP).

Chapter 7: Optimization for Specific Routing Peotocols

The ARP protocol is used to identify any hardware physical addresses that correspond to an Internet address. The RARP can identify whether a specific Internet address is identified with a hardware MAC address.

ARP and RARP packets will be picked up quite frequently in a protocol analysis session. Focus on them and take a close look at whether there are problems with routing between respective networks within an Internet environment. It may be possible that an Internet address cannot be identified, and an ARP is not getting the proper response required to match a physical MAC address to an Internet I.D. Such an occurrence prevents a communication session from even beginning between two networks within the Internet.

The protocol routing reliability can be tracked in the IP environment by analyzing the Internet Control Message Protocol (ICMP). In the protocol session for TCP/IP, the ICMP subprotocol is used to allow for tracking re-routing, node-to-node testing, and failures with an IP networking environment. Again, ICMP allows for testing between respective routing nodes within an IP environment with the ICMP Echo and Reply "ping" type packets. If there are any issues with certain routes within an IP environment, the ICMP redirect packet type allows for identifying whether a more efficient route exists.

Certain packet types indicate problems, such as the ICMP time exceeded message, which may indicate whether a particular packet is about to be discarded from a network. As mentioned earlier, also monitoring the Time-to-Live packet within the IP protocol allows measuring this area.

After the address is identified and assigned, and there are no problems—that is, ICMP does not have any issues—the Routing Information Protocol is used to accomplish the periodic routing updates and transfer of information between routers on an IP network. It may be possible in an IP environment to see multiple routing type protocols, such as Routing Information Protocol, Open Shortest Path First, Interior Gateway protocols, Exterior Gateway Protocols, and Border Gateway protocols. These protocols are considered main subsets used in the IP environment for establishing an internetwork route and transferring information between two specific network nodes within an Internet.

AppleTalk Routing Information Protocols and Analysis Tips

The AppleTalk Routing Protocol is a proprietary protocol from Apple Computer. Apple developed its Routing Table Maintenance Protocol (RTMP) to work mainly within the AppleTalk environment. This protocol also works with other AppleTalk protocols, such as DataGram Delivery Protocol (DDP) to ensure that packets can transfer between AppleTalk networks. The actual delivery of any particular packet between an AppleTalk network is normally accomplished through the DataGram Delivery Protocol. The actual update of routing information between AppleTalk networks is accomplished through the RTMP.

The RTMP works with an AppleTalk network scheme. The most basic network point within an AppleTalk network is the node that connects to a particular network. Those nodes are then part of an individual network, and a network can be a part of a complete AppleTalk zone, which is a logical group of one or more AppleTalk networks.

The addressing applies to zones, networks, and respective nodes. Note that other protocols are used with the RTMP for identifying any particular addresses on an AppleTalk network. For example, the AppleTalk Address Resolution Protocol (AARP) routing protocol is used to map protocols to hardware IDs. The Name Binding Protocol (NBP) is used to identify internetwork addresses to specific network names. The NBP works with the Zone Information Protocol (ZIP) to determine which networks belong to which zones. These are all part of the overall internetworking scheme in an AppleTalk environment.

Keep an eye on the NBP and the ZIP to make sure that the proper addressing identification occurs. The NBP should be monitored to make sure that network names are being properly mapped to addressees. This can be done by actually capturing NBP packets in a routing session and examining the respective data internally in the fields.

When the information is proper between the respective networks, it then is important to monitor the RTMP to make sure that the actual updates between the networks is properly being done in an organized fashion. This can be done by simply examining a Routing Table Maintenance packet.

An analyst must keep an eye on the RTMP to make sure that updates are done in a proper time frame. For example, the RTMP uses various types of internal forms of packets, including a data request, a data response, and a route data request. Data packets actually include the routing update information, and routing tables are normally updated every ten seconds. The request and response packet provides the information for any new AppleTalk nodes to connect to a network. Route data request packets include any nodes that need to update other respective routing tables within the AppleTalk internetwork.

After the establishment of addressing is done by NBP and ZIP, and the RTMP is updating properly, an analyst has to decode the DataGram Delivery Protocol packets for any possible problems and transfer the packets between AppleTalk networks.

DEC Routing Information Protocols and Analysis Tips

The DECnet environment also includes a proprietary routing protocol, mainly developed by Digital Equipment Corp. The routing protocols used in the DEC environment vary from versions of the DECnet environment in Phase 3 to Phase 5. Two key areas in the DECnet environment should be noted when examining routing. The DECnet protocol uses an end node and routing node function within its particular routing protocol. The DEC Routing Protocol (DRP) is the most closely examined internetwork routing protocol. The DEC internetwork routing transfers are based on a decision process of actual costs between the respective networks. A high-end algorithm is used to analyze whether an extensive cost exists between the networks.

Hop counts and actual costs between the networks are maintained. Examining a DRP packet enables you to determine whether the DECnet routing protocol has identified any particular problems between networks. Keep a close watch for any high hop counts or high costs between respective networks on network transfers. When failures occur, the DECnet routing protocol attempts to recalculate routes on a dynamic basis to use the optimum route. This reoptimization may not always occur. Because routing table updates occur on a timed basis and are not always updated if a failure occurs, it is possible that routing loop failures can occur. When routing loops occur, you are likely to observe high hop counts and high costs within the DRP packets.

DECnet routing also is based on level 1 and level 2 routers. A level 1 router communicates within a particular area of the DECnet environment. Level 2 routers actually communicate across respective areas within the DECnet addressing scheme. Level 1 routers can talk to level 2 routers, but normally level 2 routers only communicate with other level 2 routers for a specific area. Normally, only one level 2 router exists per area, but this not a restriction. A level 1 router usually refers a packet to a level 2 router, which then communicates with another level 2 router within a particular network. This is how the internetworking occurs, and the overall technology is called area breakdowns or area partitioning for DEC environments. Figure 7.2 is a breakout of a Network General Sniffer packet of the DEC routing protocol.

```
┌─DETAIL─────────────────────────────────────────────────────┐
│ DLC:  Ethertype  = 6003 (DECNET)                           │
│ DLC:                                                        │
│ DRP: ------ DECNET Routing Protocol ------                 │
│ DRP:                                                        │
│ DRP: Data Length = 41                                      │
│ DRP: Control Packet Format = 0B                            │
│ DRP:          0... .... = no padding                       │
│ DRP:          .000 .... = reserved                         │
│ DRP:          .... 101. = Ethernet Router Hello Message    │
│ DRP:          .... ...1 = Control Packet Format            │
│ DRP: Control Packet Type = 05                              │
│ DRP: Version Number  = 02                                  │
│ DRP: ECO Number      = 00                                  │
│ DRP: User ECO Number = 00                                  │
│ DRP: ID of Transmitting Node = 7.46                        │
│ DRP:    Information = 02                                   │
│ DRP:       0... .... = reserved                            │
│ DRP:       .0.. .... = not blocking request                │
│ DRP:       ..0. .... = multicast traffic accepted          │
│ DRP:       ...0 .... = verification ok                     │
│                    ─Frame 3 of 153──                       │
│                 Use TAB to select windows                   │
│ 1    2 Set    3Expert 4 Zoom 5       6Disply 7 Prev 8 Next 9Select 10 New │
│ Help   mark   window   out    Menus  options  frame frame  frame  capture │
```

Figure 7.2 A packet breakout of a DEC routing protocol from a Network General Sniffer.

Quick Notes on Routing SNA

Routing SNA has been a problem for quite some time on most LANs due to the original design of the protocol. SNA networks require high availability and low response times. Normally, an SNA communication session is established using data link protocols such as Logical Link Control (LLC) to transfer data between specific physical and logical units in an SNA network.

LANs in general do not accommodate a smooth routing protocol for SNA. Instead, SNA is commonly seen on an internetwork enveloped within a TCP/IP packet. Other approaches are being used today for routing SNA, such as gateways with IPX, SPX, or NetBIOS. Multiprotocol routers are used frequently

Chapter 7: Optimization for Specific Routing Peotocols

in a collapsed backbone configuration to allow SNA to route across networks; SNA is actually routed through the internal collapsed backbone.

When examining routing information across a large internetwork, the focus should be on any of the protocols that actually carry the SNA information, such as TCP/IP.

CHAPTER 8

Documenting the Network

When problems occur on a LAN, one of the most important safeguards is proper network documentation. Just as file backups are critical to recovering a blown network operating system, network documentation is the critical archive of your Token Ring or Ethernet LAN layout and design. A LAN installation is not truly complete until the network documentation is complete.

It is impossible to always detect when a failure is going to occur with your LAN, but a proper set of network documentation enables you to isolate a failure more efficiently and quickly. Almost every time you have a problem with your network, you will reference the network documentation.

The Ethernet topology is easy to document due to its bus structure layout. The sophistication of the Token Ring topology complicates the art of documenting its layout and design. So many components are involved, and each must be listed according to its integral configuration within the layout. A methodical approach to documenting the network is a must.

This chapter introduces the documentation most critical to Token Ring and Ethernet LANs. Some of the documentation discussed here is standard, but each type is a component of a proper documentation library.

ETHERNET AND TOKEN RING OPTIMIZATION

Early in my career, I wondered what separated the basic field engineer, which I was, from the technical support specialist. One day, I asked a local technical support representative that question. The answer was: not necessarily remembering every fact or constantly studying, but knowing where to get needed information. The representative told me to look around the office; I did, and all I saw were neatly organized manuals. From that day on, I began to organize my technical documentation. Needless to say, it increased my level of effectiveness when troubleshooting. I was the guy who always had the information needed when a problem occurred.

The point is that after you read this chapter and learn what documentation you need for your network, remember one thing: keeping your documentation neatly organized, in the proper binders, is the key to finding it when you need it.

Understanding Network Layout Documents

Certain documents are critical to implementing a network design. In my career, I have been involved in a slew of installations. Most were a success, but some were stressful experiences. There is nothing like getting halfway through an installation and being unable to continue because you do not know where a particular cable is run, or where a certain workstation needs to reside, or where an MAU or HUB port is supposed to be connected on the wiring panel.

I have learned that certain network layout documents are critical for LAN implementation and need to be at the installation site.

Building Blueprints

When a cabling contractor arrives at a site to design, install, or troubleshoot LAN cabling, the first question the contractor asks is, "Where are the blueprints?" Before a network can be properly designed, you should secure a copy of the building blueprints. They are important initially, at design inception, and are also important to maintaining the site, for the following reasons:

- Depending on the building and where certain stations are to be located, the cabling path and lengths must be properly calculated to stay within network topology specifications.
- After the required lengths are defined to physically lay out the network, another important factor is the cabling type. Depending on the length and layout of the cabling paths, you may need certain cabling types.
- Depending on the physical layout of a network, you might shift your design from standard STP cabling to UTP cabling.
- Another factor of the layout design is the possible need for repeaters to extend the network path or cabling lengths.
- Whenever problems occur, the blueprints are essential during the troubleshooting process for tracking the cabling paths through the building.

Maintaining a copy of the building blueprints allows for a more accurate design and a smoother path for troubleshooting your network.

Figure 8.1 is a sample building blueprint used in a network layout.

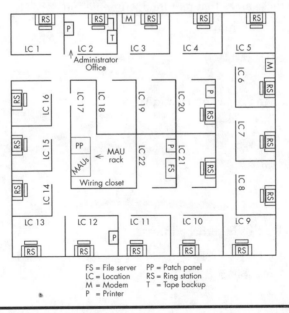

Figure 8.1 A typical building blueprint used for a network layout. Maintaining a set of building blueprints aids both network installation and troubleshooting.

Network File Server and Ring Station Documentation

With any type of LAN topology, documenting the file server and the LAN station configurations is important for future reference. This section overviews the components of both the file server (FS) and workstations (WS) important to document for an Ethernet or Token Ring topology.

The outlined components can be easily documented by building a structured list. Some network operating system (NOS) manufacturers, such as Novell, provide excellent documentation sheets for file server and LAN station configurations. This book calls the list a Station Configuration Sheet. Every file server and workstation should have its own Station Configuration Sheet.

A network environment has four key areas to document for both the FS and the WSes: hardware configuration, software configuration, network architecture management roles, and cable, repeater, and MAU or HUB port and locations. You should enter information in all four areas on the Station Configuration Sheet.

The parts of these areas that require documentation are as follows:

Hardware Configuration:

- CPU type (FS and WS)
- Memory (FS and WS)
- Disk types and capacity (FS and WS)
- All I/O boards (FS and WS)
- NICs (FS and WS)
  - I/O address
  - IRQ
  - DMA
  - Token Ring or Ethernet address
  - cabling connector types
  - 32-, 16-, or 8-bit card
  - Microcode level
  - For Token Ring, primary or secondary level settings

Software Configuration:

- LAN drivers and their configuration (FS and WS)
- Network shell software (WS)
- Network operating system revision, configuration, and drivers (FS)
- CONFIGURE.SYS (FS and WS)
- AUTOEXEC.BAT (FS and WS)
- Bridge configurations (FS and WS)
- Printing configurations (FS and WS)
- Security (FS and WS)
- Users and groups (FS)
- Directory and file structure (FS and WS)
- Server name (FS)
- Particular Protocol Address (FS and WS)

Network Architecture Management Roles:

- Note any Token Ring or Ethernet management roles (such as Active Monitor for Token Ring, or SNMP management consoles on an Ethernet) that are collocated with an FS or WS on the Station Configuration Sheet.

Cable, MAU or HUB Port, and Locations:

- Every Station Configuration Sheet should also contain the station's physical location, MAU or HUB port, and cable that connects to the FS or WS. These notations provide all the proper documentation to map every FS's and WS's actual path to the physical network.

Network Maintenance and Service Logs

When you have a network problem, it is always nice to experience deja vu. Certain failures repeat themselves frequently, and if you have seen that type of problem before, it is an advantage from the troubleshooting angle.

When you encounter a problem that has occurred before, you can rely on your memory to act as a statistical database for information on how you resolved the problem last time. Or you can check the Maintenance and Service Log.

Maintaining a historical log of all problems that occur in your network environment decreases the mean time to repair (MTTR) for your LAN. Most field service outfits track this statistic from their field operations; it is important because, obviously, the goal is to get the customer up and running as quickly as possible.

Keeping a Maintenance and Service Log is simple. First, arrange a binder with the following main network component sections: File Servers, Workstations, Hubs and MAUs, Bridges, Routers, Gateways, Repeaters, Communication Gear, Printers, and so on. Next, separate the sections with labeled inserts.

Now, the most important part: make up a problem entry sheet with the following information:

- Equipment Type
- Serial Number
- Special Notes
- Location
- Network User or Users
- Problem Description or Symptom
- Problem Cause
- Problem Resolution

Next, make multiple copies of the sheets and insert several sheets in each of the main network component sections in the binder. Figure 8.2 shows a sample Maintenance and Service Log problem entry sheet.

Now you have a way to track equipment history, and you have a problem reference guide for your LAN. You can use this method, or you can get more automated by using a statistical database. The point is, by recording in an organized manner the history of all problems that occur on your network, the odds are that you will be more efficient and effective when it comes to troubleshooting.

Chapter 8: Documenting the Network

Problem Entry Sheet

1. Equipment type IBM MOD 55 Ring Station
2. Serial number 9SX52541
3. Special notes Has IBM 4/16 NIC connected by cable-33-to MAU 4/port-28 through PP.16
4. Location #33
5. Network users Tim Ringman
6. Problem symptom Cannot access ring
7. Problem cause Damaged Token Ring driver files
8. Problem resolution Reload new drivers-Tests OK.

a

Problem Entry Sheet

1. Equipment type Bridge-IBM-8209
2. Serial number 89XFQRTS
3. Special notes From ring 3 to ring 4 -(To access FS-WHITEKNIGHT)
4. Location #22
5. Network users All of ring 4 & group WPUSERS on ring 3
6. Problem symptom Intermittent drop in access to file server WHITEKNIGHT
7. Problem cause Bad Token Ring card in slot 2
8. Problem resolution Replace card-Tests OK.

b

Figure 8.2 Sample problem entry sheets in the Maintenance and Service Log.

Network Vendor and Personal Resource Tables

Just as a network has many integral hardware and software components, many people also are associated with its basic existence. These people usually fall into one of three categories: network product vendors, network support personnel, or network users. You should assemble tables for each of the three categories.

For network product vendors, list the following items:

- Company name
- Address
- Phone and fax numbers
- Names of key marketing and service support people
- Logs of all key conversations and meetings

For internal support people, make sure that you have the following information:

- Name
- Location
- Phone, beeper, and fax numbers
- Technical involvement with the LAN
- Logs of all key conversations and meetings

Last, make sure that a composite list of your LAN user base is available, with the following categories:

- Name
- Location
- Phone and fax numbers
- LAN hardware and software resources used

Some of this information is a given. But remember that a documented list of the key people involved with your networking environment might be a lifesaver at a critical time. These people are the society that gives your network its smooth heartbeat.

Exploring Network Documentation Software Tools

This section discusses several software approaches that will make the documentation job a little easier.

Most of the information that you record on File Server/Workstation Configuration Sheets and Network Vendor/Personal Resource Tables can be implemented in a database. You can design a system in many innovative ways to meet your needs.

Another aid to documenting and keeping up with a growing network is a software package that can gather LAN statistics, such as hardware and configurations. Brightwork Development has an excellent package called LAN Automatic Inventory, or LAI. The LAI package dynamically builds and maintains a database of most hardware and software components in a LAN. What is innovative about LAI is that it actually goes onto the LAN and gathers real-time, critical information from the file servers and workstations.

For certain network architectures such as Novell, LAI can gather the NIC addresses and a full array of internal station components such as CPU type, memory, disk drives, and more. The LAI package also scans each workstation for assigned network operating system parameters such as shell type and version. Brightwork's LAI package enables you to perform quickly a thorough hardware and software inventory that could normally take days or weeks.

Brightwork's LAI works in conjunction with some of their other creative products for LAN management, such as NETmanager and NETremote. NETmanager allows for controlling and monitoring multiple LAN stations from a central point. NETremote is a dial-up remote access package that performs much like NETmanager with a diagnostic theme; you can access a LAN remotely, cutting downtime.

Other strong products in the LAN audit category for Token Ring are BindView NCS from the LAN Support Group, Inc., LAN Directory from Frye Computer Systems, Inc., and Network HQ from Magee Enterprises, Inc.

Many products also can be found for CAD design of a network layout. Many graphic programs in the industry assist in laying out a basic network picture.

Other hungry software developers are out there working on packages that do it all for you. Remember, however, that by using the methods outlined in this chapter, you can keep a logical, organized database of all your network components and problems.

Examining Token Ring-Specific Documentation

Next, the main Token Ring network documentation components are discussed. Remember that all the components work together to form a library, which you need for an overall, accurate picture of your Token Ring environment.

Chapter 11 covers Token Ring topology theory in detail. Designing a Token Ring network requires a set of skills gained mainly from years of experience. Maintaining proper network documentation helps you gain these skills.

MAU Rack Layouts

MAUs are the focal points of a Token Ring network, and it is always best to place them physically together in common wiring closets. I have seen sites where the MAUs are placed all over the building, including up in the ceiling and under the floor panels. This is a problem just waiting to happen. If, for example, you encounter a problem that appears to be located in an MAU or the main ring path cabling, your troubleshooting capabilities are affected. If all the MAUs are located in common wiring closets, you can isolate a problem much faster because you can switch MAUs or cabling paths easily.

When you place the MAUs together in a wiring closet, mount them in some sort of rack. The next logical step is to properly number and physically mark each MAU with a small sticker, or any other effective means. Each port should also be numbered and marked.

All lobe cables should run directly from their respective building locations to the common wiring closets. This configuration allows for a physical star layout and provides for a solid, logical design.

Make sure that each lobe cable is properly labeled on both ends. Identify where the cable runs; for example, record that it goes to a particular officeinclude the office number.

Now you have a logical matrix for your wiring and hubbing scheme. As you will see, you can use some standard industry documents for this procedure, or you can create your own. In either case, there is a methodology to this documentation scheme. Understanding this methodology gives you an edge when it comes to troubleshooting problems.

Patch Panel Layouts

Cable patch panels are becoming standard at most large Token Ring installations. A patch panel is a central point at which the lobe cables on the LAN meet before they are attached to MAUs. The patch panel is usually mounted directly in the rack with the MAUs. Most often it is placed on the top part of the rack with the MAUs placed underneath. This setup allows for easier changes of lobe cable location-to-MAU port configurations.

When configuring a wiring closet with a patch panel, follow a certain method. All the lobe and main ring path cables, incoming and outgoing from the wiring closet, should enter and then attach to the rear of the patch panel. Then use patch cables to attach from the front of the patch panel to the respective MAUs.

To document this arrangement properly, all the patch cables from the patch panel to the MAUs should have the same label designation as the lobe cable to which they attach through the patch panel.

I recommend that you document the patch panel layout and its relation to the MAUs and cabling with a diagram table. Figure 8.3 shows how the logical matrix for patch panels, MAUs, and a cabling scheme correlates with a sample diagram table. The diagram can be based on a grid to show how the lobe cable label correlates with its MAU port label.

254 ETHERNET AND TOKEN RING OPTIMIZATION

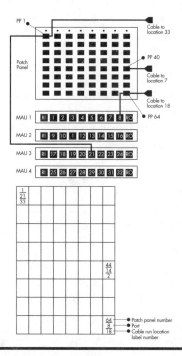

Figure 8.3 A grid-based diagram table and its correlation with the patch panel, MAUs, and cabinets.

IBM Token Ring Planning Forms

IBM has assembled a series of forms for planning and maintaining Token Ring network configurations. They are considered an industry standard for Token Ring documentation. Using the IBM documentation forms is an excellent way to maintain control of your Token Ring network.

IBM has taken into account most of the major areas of the Token Ring topology and has created logical forms to use for documenting those areas. The reference section of this book lists the IBM Token Ring reference guides; throughout most of IBM's documentation (especially the IBM Cabling System Planning and Installation Guide), you will find good descriptions of the purpose of their documentation schemes.

Figures 8.4 through 8.9 show some of the most frequently used IBM Token Ring planning forms. See Appendix B, reference number 3 for more information about these planning forms.

Chapter 8: Documenting the Network 255

Physical Location to Adapter Address Locator Chart

Physical Location	Adapter Address	Device Identification	Ring Number	IBM 8228 Unit No.

Figure 8.4 The IBM Physical Location to Adapter Address Locator chart.

IBM 8228 Cabling Chart

Date _____

Section 1 Identification

Unit Number _____ Building _____ Rack-mounted ☐
Location _____ Wall-mounted ☐ Ring _____

Section 2 Receptacle Connections

Receptacle	1	2	3	4	5	6	7	8
Connect to:								

Device								

Section 3 Ring Connections

A. Connect RI of this 8228 to: _____
B. Connect RO of this 8228 to: _____

Figure 8.5 The IBM Token Ring 8228 Cabling chart.

256 ETHERNET AND TOKEN RING OPTIMIZATION

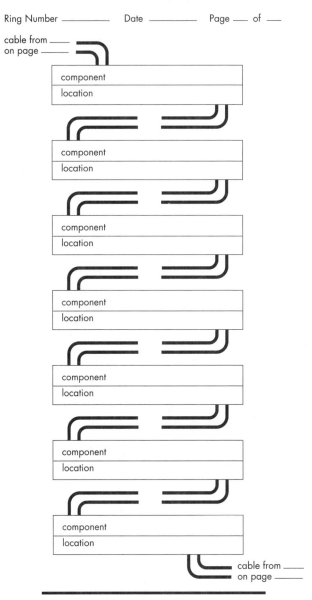

Figure 8.6 The IBM Ring Sequence chart.

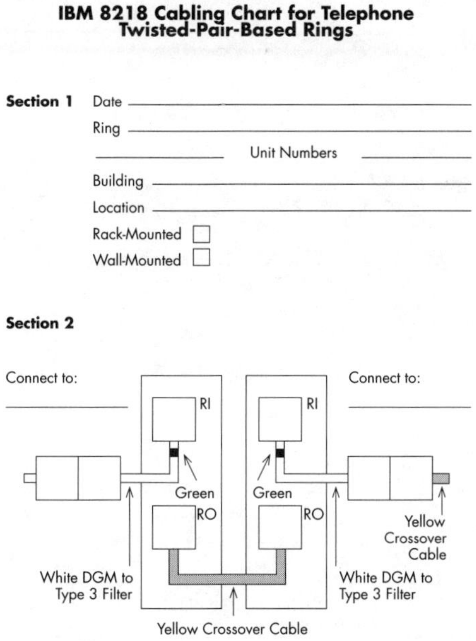

Chapter 8: Documenting the Network   257

Figure 8.7 IBM's 8218 repeater cabling form.

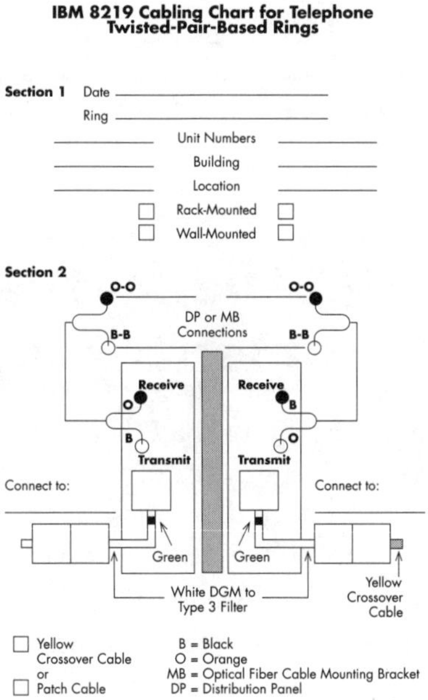

Figure 8.8 The IBM 8219 repeater cabling form.

Bridge Planning Chart

Date _____ Bridge Identification _____

Check one: Load manually ___ Load automatically ___

Section 1 - Bridge Configuration Parameters

Check one: Alter configuration ___ Use defaults ___

Bridge number (Default = 1)	
Ring number connected to primary adapter (Default = 001)	
Ring number connected to alternate adapter (Default = 002)	
Frame forwarding active (Default = Y)	
Bridge performance threshold (Default = 10)	
Restart on error (Default = Y)	
Drive for memory dump no error (Default = 0)	
Drive for error log (Default = 0)	

	Primary Adapter	Alternate Adapter
Hop count limit (Default = 7)		
Single-route broadcast (Default = Y)		
Locally administered address (Defaults = 000000000000)		
Ring parameter server (Default = Y)		
Ring error monitor (Default = Y)		
Configuration report server (Default = Y)		

Shared RAM address (Primary adapter default = 0000)	
(Alternate adapter default = 0000)	

	Old	New
Link password 0 (Default = 00000000)		
Link password 1 (Default = 00000000)		
Link password 2 (Default = 00000000)		
Link password 3 (Default = 00000000)		

Figure 8.9 The IBM Bridge Planning chart.

Exploring Ethernet-Specific Documentation

The network documentation library for the Ethernet topology does not require the same extensive entries and categories of forms as does Token Ring. It is important to make sure that the overall network layout is properly mapped out in drawing form, called a Complete Internetwork Overlay.

For example, if an Ethernet internetwork is composed of a straight ThinNet Bus segment and is connected to a 10BASE-T layout, the complete internetwork should be documented by a drawing that shows a complete overview of the two combined Ethernet environments. The interconnections between the different Ethernet segments should be clearly noted with any applied bridge, router, or repeater addresses and connection port assignments. The segment interconnections should refer to the proper Individual Segment Overlay drawing, which is discussed later. The Complete Internetwork Overlay drawing should show all the separate segments combined in the Ethernet internetwork. The segments should have a proper name or designation that uniquely identifies its location. Figure 8.10 shows an example of a Complete Internetwork Overlay drawing for an Ethernet internetwork.

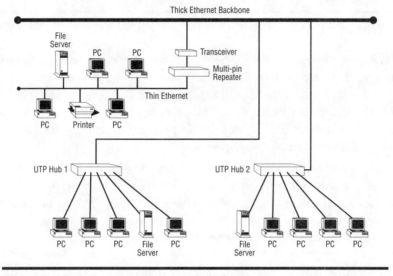

Figure 8.10 A Complete Internetwork Overlay drawing for an Ethernet internetwork.

The next important drawing for an Ethernet environment is an Individual Segment Overlay. Each segment that shows specific nodes and applied transceivers along with all their applied addresses should have an Individual Segment Overlay. These addresses should include an NIC address and any applied subnet address for particular protocols, such as TCP/IP or DECnet. Figure 8.11 shows an example of an Individual Segment Overlay drawing for an Ethernet internetwork.

ETHERNET AND TOKEN RING OPTIMIZATION

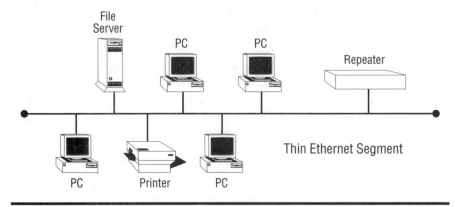

Figure 8.11 An Individual Segment Overlay drawing for an Ethernet internetwork.

If the Ethernet network is a 10BASE-T, the layout should be documented and drawn in a Physical Star Layout Overlay. This drawing depicts the network by showing the central 10BASE-T hubs and how they may connect to other individual segments in the complete Ethernet internetwork. There should be a clear layout of the individual drop runs to the Ethernet network components such as workstations and LAN printers.

It is important in a Physical Star Layout Overlay to also lay out any applied addresses for workstations and other devices. The 10BASE-T environment usually has a network management console setup. This also should be depicted in the overlay drawing. Figure 8.12 shows an example of a Physical Star Layout Overlay drawing for an Ethernet internetwork.

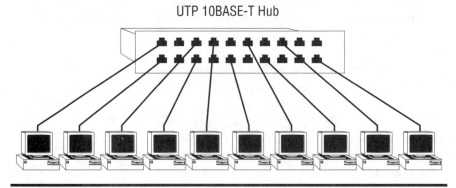

Figure 8.12 A Physical Star Layout Overlay drawing for an Ethernet internetwork.

CHAPTER 9

Planning a Network Optimization Project

This chapter presents a theory of general project management, along with techniques specifically related to network optimization. An actual scenario of project planning is presented to emphasize how important careful project planning can be to effective network troubleshooting.

Today MIS executives, analysts, and network troubleshooters face an increasingly complex set of issues and problems when attempting to perform a network optimization project. High demands are placed upon a company's MIS staff to perform a network optimization project in a careful and concise manner. Actual goals and results are monitored carefully by MIS departmental management. It is important that the analyst performing the network optimization project understand some of the goals and objectives that are of concern to MIS management.

To plan a proper optimization project, specific objectives must be completed throughout the project cycle, and start and end dates must be settled on for each phase of the project. Funding issues may be related to the costs of products or project personnel. You must prepare a complete definition of all required material and personnel resources.

An analyst performing a network optimization project has to track the progress, make comparisons, and possibly quick-change decisions to the specific internal phases throughout a project cycle. The analyst should understand that he or she is required to keep the project within certain defined time-frame and cost guidelines if project goals are to be met.

A project management plan is a model that shows a path to a successful outcome along with the required results of any subtasks that must be achieved on the way to the completed project.

Project management involves the planning, organizing, accurate implementation, and regulation of a company's internal and external resources to accomplish specific goals for an overall project.

Examining Specific Methods for a Network Optimization Project Plan

To perform a network optimization project, assemble a project plan that documents all the steps required to measure, analyze, modify, and optimize the network. Be sure to focus on the initial protocol analysis session and the associated performance tuning steps, and then define a structured time plan.

Give each step an approximate assigned time allocation block and date. Then list the required equipment and personnel for that step and summarize the plan with the expected actions and goals for that step.

You should set goals for each network modification phase. For example, say that the file access failure rate of your sample NetWare file server was recorded at an 8% level; you could set a goal to drop the file access failure rate to 5%. If you record Token Ring receiver congestion errors at 4% of overall traffic, and you would like to see them decrease to 1%, that is a clear measurement goal. Make sure that all your expected goals are documented in the initial project plan. Set initial structured steps, and due to natural dynamics, leave some time for interim changes to the modification schedule. Setting goals enables you to follow all the steps for network changes.

The next area to focus on in project planning is the priority schedule. Which areas are you going to focus on first? You should review the results from your original protocol analysis session and define priorities for your modifications. You need to understand which of the modifications are more critical. To do this, look closely at the error levels and the results from the protocol analysis session. These issues are particular to your own network design and cannot be mentioned in a broad sense across general networks.

You should ensure that network documentation is and remains current. All network areas changed, modified, or even in question should be documented clearly through a structured project plan. After you have defined three or four areas where you want to make changes on the network, make sure that the priority of all modification areas is clearly defined.

Finally, remember each modification that you make should be followed by another protocol analysis session. This is the only way to verify that you have made a change in network performance, and you need to document how the modification affected your network's performance. If you go through your network optimization project with a structured approach, you will benefit by having a clearer picture of the project's effectiveness.

A Scenario of Planning a Network Optimization Project

The following example uses some of the specifics mentioned in the previous sections for planning a network optimization project.

The Edward Fred Morris (EFM) Inc. Manufacturing Supply Company's MIS designers have decided to upgrade a 4Mbps Token Ring backbone ring in their home office building to a 16Mbps backbone ring. The analyst assigned the job must initially understand that the key objective at project completion is to have a 16Mbps backbone ring running in complete health and proper operation, along with providing a higher bandwidth level for all subrings that need to access the complete EFM internetwork.

The first step is to develop an overall plan outline that shows the complete project steps by time frame. The analyst needs to reference the EFM MIS designer's project goals and objectives. This time-frame plan should display individual project steps and their respective time frames. This type of project plan may include the following internal phases:

1. A protocol analysis session must occur on the 4Mbps backbone ring currently in place to verify the general health at the physical and upper protocol layers.

2. If any problems are found on the 4Mbps ring that would still be a potential problem in a 16Mbps ring configuration, a subphase plan must be established for problem resolution. This is necessary to make modifications to fix any immediate issues or problems. Within a subphase of a modification plan, there may be personnel and equipment allocations required to actually implement any specific modifications.

3. A re-analysis testing of any modification made to the current 4Mbps backbone ring must be performed. This involves performing a complete reanalysis on the 4Mbps ring to verify that it is finally healthy and ready for upgrade to 16Mbps.

4. At this point, the upgrade phases of the 16Mbps backbone ring can be scheduled. The plan will include multiple project subphases for the complete 16Mbps upgrade project. These phases include testing equipment allocation, personnel allocation, product configuration, testing, backout/backup plans, and an overall detailed time plan.

5. Next, a complete implementation phase follows the planned time schedule established for the network optimization project. This starts to involve more personnel, testing equipment, and the new products going to be used for completing the actual upgrade of the EFM 4Mbps ring to a 16Mbps. For example, this may require an allocation of multiple technicians, two protocol analyzers, and a set of 16Mbps NIC cards.

6. Immediately after implementation, time should be taken to test any new products such as 16Mbps NIC cards through applied diagnostics for the individual PCs and network devices that received the new 16Mbps NIC cards.

7. After the actual implementation is completed, the analyst schedules a postprotocol analysis session on the 16Mbps backbone ring to fully verify that the complete network is healthy. This requires a complete analysis of

the new 16Mbps backbone ring and other key rings throughout the internetwork. This needs to be done through a protocol analyzer approach. When changes like a 16Mbps upgrade are implemented, it is possible that problems may occur on an internetwork.

For example, if the postimplementation analysis of the new 16Mbps backbone ring identifies high file-read failure rates, the analyst must document this as a problem. Further analysis sessions might show a decreased received congestion rate, but all of a sudden the analyst notices a new high internal soft error rate from two Token Ring NICs. Further analysis traces the problem to a specific problem with the two new 16Mbps Token Ring NICs.

8. Now, the analyst finishes the complete upper- and lower-layer baseline health analysis and determines that these are the only two issues found as possible problems related to the upgrade project. The analyst then identifies and replaces the network interface adapters related to the problem. Then the analyst also may have to determine the Novell file failure rate.

9. Through these steps, note that the analyst must set priorities for the changes that need to be made, taking a close look at which network concerns must be dealt with immediately and which can be postponed. In setting these goals, the analyst must take into account MIS management goals to ensure that the internetwork is operating according to the network optimization project's specifications from the EFM MIS designers.

10. Through all these phases, the analyst must ensure that all the steps are followed and properly documented, so that if any important open issues exist at the end of the project, they can be addressed in the future.

Figure 9.1 presents a flow chart that shows most of the steps in a general network optimization project as related to the specific example discussed.

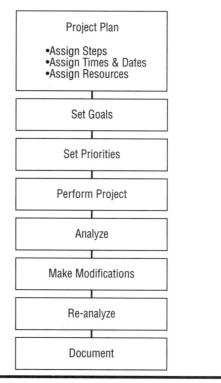

Figure 9.1 Steps in a network optimization project.

CHAPTER 10

Case Studies

This chapter presents a group of eight case studies of authentic network optimization projects performed by my consulting company LAN Scope Inc. The individual case studies present projects on actual institutional and corporate internetworks in place throughout the United States. These case studies discuss some of the different network optimization techniques and troubleshooting procedures for network baselining and protocol analysis presented in this book.

Each case study begins by discussing the particular company's network problem or issue. Next, the overall internetwork layout is presented. Then the focus of each study turns to the actual network optimization and troubleshooting processes used by the LAN Scope analysis team for the specific internetwork.

Some company names mentioned in the case studies are real; others are fictitious. But all the situations in the eight case studies did occur on real-world inter-networks.

Case Study #1: The Central Bank of the South

This case study discusses the troubleshooting of a gateway access network problem at a company. Before we discuss the specific site problem, let's review some basic components of the internetwork troubleshooting arena.

The first occurrence is always a call of panic. When I get one of these calls, my first order of business is to simply ask the following canned series of questions:

1. What is the topology? Topology is defined as the physical and logical layout of a network.

2. Depending on the topology or topologies mix, how many separate segments or rings are actually present in the internetwork?

3. What network operating systems (NOS) are used?

4. What network applications are loaded on the internetwork? From understanding the NOS and application mix on an internetwork, I can put together a list of the network protocols on the internetwork. Network protocols are defined as orderly predefined methods of communication between devices on a network through software and hardware entities.

5. What is the company's main business mission?

6. How many users are on the network?

7. And last, but very important, what is the problem symptom?

When I have answers to these questions, I can assemble a troubleshooting approach. The proper troubleshooting approach includes interpreting the following three factors that surround the network problem:

- Defining the symptom
- Placing the symptom in a specific network area
- Defining the symptom as solid or intermittent

A symptom is the sign of the problem. When I have a feel for the symptom where it is being experienced and whether it can be re-created, I can then decide how to actually troubleshoot the problem.

Today's networking environment uses a complex mix of products and protocols. Because of this, a troubleshooter cannot rely upon the isolation techniques and toolkits of the past. To resolve problems today, you must be aware of the technologies available in the testing market.

The main tool I rely upon is a protocol analyzer. A protocol analyzer is a combined hardware and software device that physically connects to a network and captures data traveling on the network cabling medium, for the purpose of decoding the specific data for analysis.

Now we have a way to properly approach a network problem, including the questions to ask, the proper technical approach, and the toolset. Let's go forward and review the troubleshooting of our first case study.

The call came in as usual. "We've got this problem. We're not sure why, and we've tried everything to resolve it, but the cause is still a mystery...."

LAN Scope was contracted to perform a protocol analysis session. The plan was to arrive on-site, perform a network baseline analysis, and troubleshoot a specific problem via protocol analysis. The problem involved intermittent gateway access problems from multiple points within the internetwork.

The company was the Central Bank of the South in Birmingham, Alabama, a large and prestigious bank in the southern United States. Their internetwork is at the stage of early leading-edge growth. The network is quickly becoming a core component of the bank's business operations. What is unique about this particular network is that the MIS staff has been able to keep the network reliable while tuning it daily for optimum performance and growing it with innovative technologies.

The Central Bank of the South internetwork is composed of multiple 4Mbps Token Ring connected to a 16Mbps backbone ring. Most of the 4Mbps rings are local, and some are connected via 56KB remote lines. The remote links are connected through Microcom and NetWare routing and bridging equipment. There is one ARCnet LAN in Weslayan, Texas. The file server environment is comprised of 11 servers running Novell NetWare 2.15 and 3.11. The complete local network encompasses approximately 600 nodes. The Central Bank of the South WAN is comprised of a five-city location configuration, including Birmingham (home office), Roebuck, and Daniel, all in Alabama; and River Oaks and Weslayan, in Texas. All the sites are connected using Birmingham as the central hub.

ETHERNET AND TOKEN RING OPTIMIZATION

The site uses general LAN applications such as WordPerfect for word processing and WordPerfect Office for an E-mail system environment. The Birmingham home office has a local ring (Ring 3) that contains gateways to an IBM host, AS400 host, and Tandem host, which users access for the Central Bank of the South's main banking applications (see Figure 10.1).

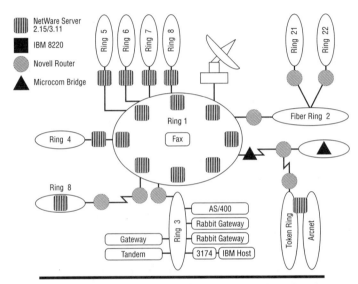

Figure 10.1 Network for Central Bank of the South.

Users at the bank were experiencing intermittent access problems to a Rabbit gateway on the Host Ring 3. The symptom typically appeared when a user attempted to access the gateway. The problem was not found conclusively to be occurring on any particular ring or workstation. Some of the rings were experiencing the problem more frequently, but the symptom was still widespread.

A LANalyzer showed the failure symptom to be directly related to an additional Rabbit gateway installed on the internetwork with a duplicate gateway address.

The bank's Houston, TX, site had added an additional Rabbit gateway with the same address as a gateway at the Birmingham host location without notifying the central MIS control staff. Figure 10.2 shows a LANalyzer trace that depicts the problem.

```
10/31/92                LANalyzer Network Analyzer                    12:46
Press ALT-T to toggle between summary modes                    Trace Summary
                     ─ c:\xln\lanz\802.5\physical\gmac5 ─
   Created On 06/12/92 12:25:08                         Total Packets 95
      Pkt#   Source       Destination     Layer    Highest Layer
         1   ibm793966    RingErrorMon    802.5:   Report Error
         2   ibm793966    RingErrorMon    802.5:   Report Error
         3   RAB6AT1      RAB6AT1         802.5:   sap:SNA Path->SNA Path
         4   ibm793966    RingErrorMon    802.5:   Report Error
         5   ibm793966    RingErrorMon    802.5:   Report Error
         6   ibm793966    RingErrorMon    802.5:   Report Error
         7   ibm793966    RingErrorMon    802.5:   Report Error
         8   ibm793966    RingErrorMon    802.5:   Report Error
         9   ibm793966    RingErrorMon    802.5:   Report Error
        10   ibm793966    RAB6AT1         802.5:   sap:SNA Path->SNA Path
        11   ibm793966    RingErrorMon    802.5:   Report Error
        12   ibmCB3EA     TR_Broadcast    802.5    Ring Purge
        13   RAB6AT1      RingErrorMon    802.5:   Report Monitor Error
        14   ibm39A645    NetworkMgr      802.5:   Report SUA Change
        15   ibmCB3EA     NetworkMgr      802.5:   Report SUA Change
        16   ibm39A645    RingErrorMon    802.5:   Report Error

   F1       F2      F3       F4        F5    F6        F7       F8     F9     F10
   Help     Load    Print    Options         Decode    Compare  Find   GoTo   Back
```

Figure 10.2 A LANalyzer trace depicting a problem.

I recommended that the Texas gateway be changed to a different address. The Central Bank of the South changed the address, and the problem was resolved.

This is a clear example of how a protocol analyzer was the key factor in the actual problem isolation. The problem symptom was very intermittent. When I arrived at the site, the problem was not even occurring. I attached the LANalyzer to the internetwork's backbone ring for general statistical monitoring. All the general statistical components looked healthy. The network bandwidth utilization was OK; the Token Ring health appeared solid; and the overall network communication processes were fluent.

But one day into the troubleshooting process, I was running a LANalyzer application test suite called NONISOER, and I noticed the general amount of low-level Token Ring Frame Copied and Lost Frame Non-Isolating Errors increase (see Figure 10.3). The LANalyzer NONISOER application test suite collects and logs any physical Token Ring Non-Isolating Errors. At roughly the same time, the MIS staff notified me that the gateway access problem was starting to occur.

ETHERNET AND TOKEN RING OPTIMIZATION

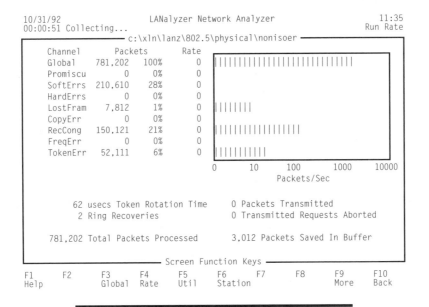

Figure 10.3 The LANalyzer NONISOER test suite.

This is when I stopped the LANalyzer test suite and went into the Trace decode screen. Going through the trace, which was roughly 5,000 frames, I found the problem present in frames 90 to 95. There were clearly gateways on two different rings with the same address. When multiple users attempted gateway access, the problem surfaced. The problem was intermittent because in a routing/bridging environment the path to host is dynamic and can change. So, depending on the location of the workstation attempting gateway access, the problem might appear.

Without a protocol analyzer, I would have not been able to capture and resolve the problem in the one and a half days it took to isolate with the LANalyzer.

Case Study #2: CitiSteel USA

This case study involves an Ethernet network that performed well for the first two years of its original operation, but as more technologies and applications were added, it started to experience performance slowdowns.

Chapter 10: Case Studies

The company is CitiSteel USA, a steel manufacturer located in Claymont, Delaware that processes steel for customers throughout the world. CitiSteel implemented an initial network design in the late 1980s that has recently escalated into a comprehensive Ethernet internetwork being used by all departments in the CitiSteel Corporation.

CitiSteel has a multiprotocol environment with custom applications used by different departments. For example, different applications run on the internetwork for their steel melt shop, the store room, and the rolling mill plants. The CitiSteel applications also are somewhat custom and a variety of programs and database utilities are used. General network applications, such as word processing programs and spreadsheets, also are on the internetwork. CitiSteel uses a variety of network file server approaches, including NetWare software for the core internetwork operations. Developments in the area of the RISC 6000 UNIX and TCP/IP technologies are currently taking place.

CitiSteel has a total of three servers, named Orion, CMSteel, and Pluto. Most applications are equally balanced across the three file servers.

In late 1992, CitiSteel started to experience general performance problems on the corporate Ethernet internetwork. The MIS staff made a proactive decision to have the internetwork thoroughly examined through protocol analysis.

The overall goal of the project was to have a consultant from LAN Scope come on-site to evaluate the overall internetwork design, look at the general network performance, isolate any particular areas of the internetwork that had specific problems, and recommend modifications for improvement of those problems.

In 1992, LAN Scope performed the first analysis for the CitiSteel company to look at its general internetwork health and performance problems. At that time, CitiSteel had an Ethernet environment that was mixed between 10BASE-T twisted pair and a standard Ethernet ThinNet layout. A ThinNet backbone was split between two different segments that connected through the file server Orion. The two backbone segments were called DADA and DEAD. An RS6000 was on the DEAD Ethernet backbone. The DEAD segment also contained three different 10BASE-T hubs, which is where most of the actual users were brought into the internetwork through the backbone.

The users were brought in through the Hewlett-Packard (HP) hubs in a 10BASE-T layout. These HP hubs created three separate Ethernet segments, A, B, and C. The file server CMSteel was also on the DEAD backbone. The DADA backbone was being used to support various MIS connection nodes. Figure 10.4

ETHERNET AND TOKEN RING OPTIMIZATION

shows an example of the CitiSteel internetwork before any performance modifications were made to the network.

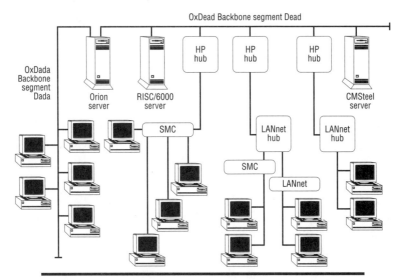

Figure 10.4 The CitiSteel internetwork before modification.

Before performing the first analysis, LAN Scope consulted with the CitiSteel MIS staff to find out what the initial requirements were. The MIS staff explained that they were having intermittent slowdowns on the internetwork and general performance issues. They also explained that a high number of NetWare failures were occurring that they could not attribute to the NetWare protocols or the NetWare software, and they wanted this examined also during the analysis.

After the discussion with the MIS staff and the overview of the site design, LAN Scope began a protocol analysis session on the internetwork. Our first step was to examine the overall physical layer health of the internetwork. We began by running a specific test with the Network General Sniffer in the Sniffer Ethernet Monitor. We examined the overall performance of the two ThinNet backbones and the 10BASE-T segments within the internetwork. Specifically, we were concerned about the average and peak utilization levels.

From examining the internetwork, we could see that the average bandwidth utilization was running anywhere from 10% to 20% of the available 10Mbps on an Ethernet network. We felt that this was a high average utilization level for a 10Mbps network with the current nodes, resources, and applications. We briefly

Chapter 10: Case Studies

looked at the general performance of the different applications on the network and saw instances of two- to four-second delays to service a read request to a file server. This seemed extremely high, and we further examined the general health of the physical Ethernet layer protocols.

When examining the physical layer of the network, we did find a number of different collision rates across the internetwork. Figure 10.5 shows the Sniffer Ethernet Monitor displaying a collision rate. It was specifically noted that an extremely high collision condition was present on one Ethernet 10BASE-T segment. Through further protocol analysis, we identified that the collision rate on this one segment was not due to any specific internetwork layout problem, but more to the fact that there was possibly a bad Ethernet hub within the internetwork design. We recommended that a particular hub be changed, which was done.

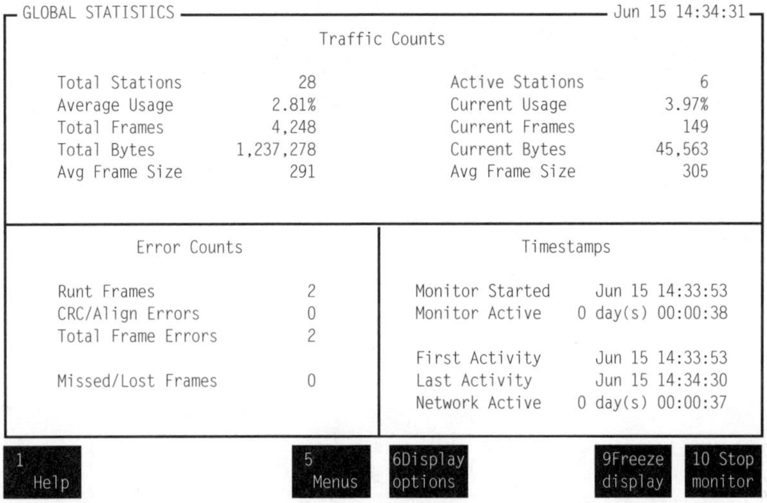

```
┌─ GLOBAL STATISTICS ──────────────────────────── Jun 15 14:34:31 ─┐
│                         Traffic Counts                           │
│                                                                  │
│     Total Stations        28         Active Stations       6     │
│     Average Usage       2.81%        Current Usage      3.97%    │
│     Total Frames        4,248        Current Frames       149    │
│     Total Bytes     1,237,278        Current Bytes     45,563    │
│     Avg Frame Size        291        Avg Frame Size       305    │
│                                                                  │
├──────────────────────────────────┬───────────────────────────────┤
│          Error Counts            │          Timestamps           │
│                                                                  │
│   Runt Frames              2       Monitor Started  Jun 15 14:33:53
│   CRC/Align Errors         0       Monitor Active   0 day(s) 00:00:38
│   Total Frame Errors       2                                     │
│                                    First Activity   Jun 15 14:33:53
│   Missed/Lost Frames       0       Last Activity    Jun 15 14:34:30
│                                    Network Active   0 day(s) 00:00:37
└──────────────────────────────────┴───────────────────────────────┘
  1            5         6 Display              9 Freeze   10 Stop
  Help         Menus       options               display    monitor
```

Figure 10.5 The Sniffer Ethernet Monitor displaying a collision rate.

LAN Scope monitored the segment again and found a significantly decreased collision rate after the hub was changed. Through this protocol analysis troubleshooting exercise, we identified and resolved a specific hardware problem in the internetwork that could have caused an operational outage.

We then approached the upper protocol layer health of the Ethernet internetwork. We started by focusing on the overall frame timing and related utilization levels for the NetWare NCP communication. Through the NCP analysis, we found that the performance between certain NetWare clients and the file servers was still at the two- to four-second range. This indicated that there may be a problem with the Ethernet traffic flow or the NetWare file server operation.

We first examined the NetWare file server. The NetWare Monitor program was checked, and we did not see any problems with the cache buffers, allocation of short-term memory, service processes, disk operations, or the packet receive buffers. (NetWare Monitor is a NetWare Loadable Module [NLM] that gives you valuable information about a NetWare file server's CPU operation, memory utilization, disk operation, and more.)

Our next goal was to examine the NetWare file server network communications. We started a protocol analysis session, focusing on the NetWare upper layer protocol fluency. We had found that the NetWare protocols were responsible for 95% of the traffic on the network. Our analysis of the NetWare protocol suite found that the NCP request-to-responses were operating properly to and from the file server. In other words, there did not appear to be any internal processing errors in the NetWare file servers causing problem-type frame generation onto the network.

When problems exist within a NetWare file server, it is fairly easy to identify the problem by tracking certain NCP problem-type packets. One example of a problem-type NCP packet is the NCP "Request Being Processed" packet. This means that a file server is internally delayed. This type of packet is generated by a NetWare server to signal a delay in processing a request. Frequent appearance of this packet type indicates a need to further examine the server's internal resources and resource configuration. The CitiSteel file servers did not appear to have high levels of NetWare problem type packets.

We next examined overall NetWare frame performance on the ThinNet backbone sections between the different hubs and the file servers, and found that there was a performance issue. The problem was most predominant between the different users coming up through the 10BASE-T segments A, B, and C into the ThinNet backbone to access the different file servers. We used the Sniffer analyzer to determine the timing of file server response packet in response to workstation requests. This was done through trace analysis of the NetWare frame data with timestamps. We clearly saw this delay occurring.

When we examined a workstation-to-file server session communicating across just the backbone, we found that the delay was not present.

We looked at the overall project results up to this point and did not see many problems in the NetWare protocol layers that would indicate any problems in the NetWare file server. We saw acceptable fluency between most of the workstation requests and the file server responses. The only issue was the time delays in the inter-frame timing. Our focus was on the delays in the Ethernet transfer rates across the physical layer of the CitiSteel network. We felt that there was a performance problem for most of the 10BASE-T nodes that had to travel up through the hubs into the ThinNet backbone to access the file servers.

LAN Scope recommended that a high-speed Ethernet switching device would be an excellent cure for the internetwork performance issues. We recommended a Kalpana EtherSwitch because it is a highly intelligent Ethernet hubbing switch that can perform on-the-fly packet routing for Ethernet. The Kalpana device layout and design would actually allow the CitiSteel MIS staff to utilize Ethernet data transactions as they occur in any given time slice. This would allow for high-throughput packet switching in the CitiSteel Ethernet environment. The EtherSwitch would improve overall network throughput and would enable CitiSteel to migrate toward an internetwork design that would improve performance.

CitiSteel evaluated the Kalpana product and decided to implement it in early 1993, along with some other file server changes, application changes, and general layout changes within the internetwork design. CitiSteel implemented the Kalpana EtherSwitch as a new product into its internetwork design and redesigned its complete network based on the Kalpana EtherSwitch capabilities.

CitiSteel connected its MIS department to the K1 section; the users were connected to the K2 section of the Ethernet switch; the K3 section had the CMSteel file server connected to it; and the K4 section had the A, B, and C hubs connected to it for 10BASE-T user segments. The UNIX backbone was segmented over to a K6 section, and the Orion server was now implemented on the K7 section. The K8 section was used for the Pluto server.

With this new layout, many resources were now on their own segment and available to the users at a faster rate due to the capability of the Kalpana EtherSwitch. This device switches a user to a particular segment immediately, rather than going through other traffic routes to get to the particular resource. Figure 10.6 displays the new CitiSteel network layout.

278 ETHERNET AND TOKEN RING OPTIMIZATION

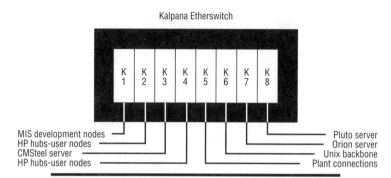

Figure 10.6 The CitiSteel network after modification.

LAN Scope was assigned to do a post-installation check on the CitiSteel network to examine the new network performance with the Kalpana EtherSwitch. When we started the post-modification protocol analysis session, we took the same approach. We examined the physical and upper-layer protocol suites. In examining the inter-network, we saw a decrease in the overall collision rates and a general performance improvement in timing and access between the workstations and file servers. The timing was down to fractions of a second in actual workstation requests-to-responses. This was a tremendous performance improvement that can only be attributed to the Kalpana EtherSwitch. Figure 10.7 displays the timing difference for workstation-to-file servers before and after the Kalpana implementation.

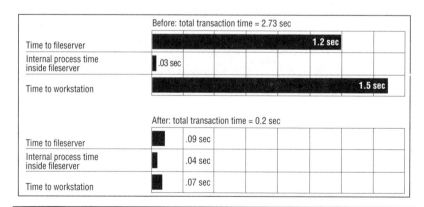

Figure 10.7 The timing difference before and after the Kalpana EtherSwitch implementation.

For the physical-layer health and the upper-layer protocol fluency of this network, we found excellent performance in the CitiSteel internetwork with the Kalpana EtherSwitch implemented.

The CitiSteel MIS staff did an excellent job by evaluating this particular network through protocol analysis and looking at their performance problems carefully in a structured and organized manner. By implementing the Kalpana Switch, they addressed their current issues and also steered their network towards a performance increase for the future. The CitiSteel MIS staff properly ended the project by examining the performance modification change to verify that the Kalpana EtherSwitch actually made some improvements.

This particular network project is an example of how to take a protocol analysis approach to measure your network's performance, implement modifications, and then verify the actual effect of those modifications to your network. Protocol analysis enabled CitiSteel to locate the reason for the performance problem, identify the exact cause, and implement the network change.

Case Study #3: John Steel Ltd.

I received a call from a client, John Steel Ltd., which was having intermittent NetWare File Server Not Found and Abort Retry error messages during general network operations. At first, the problem sounded like a NetWare configuration issue. But, after talking extensively with the client, the problem sounded like it needed further investigation. The client asked if a LAN Scope consultant could come on-site for problem analysis.

I went to the site with a plan to examine the general baseline health of the internetwork. The course of action was to get an overall reading of the network's workload characteristics and then to troubleshoot specific errors related to network performance issues and error recordings.

John Steel Ltd. is one of the largest manufacturers and distributors of handbags in the United States. The home-office internetwork, located in New Jersey, is composed of a main Ethernet backbone LAN ThinNet segment connected to an ARCnet environment. The Ethernet backbone and the ARCnet network are interconnected through internal NetWare file server bridging/routing configurations.

ETHERNET AND TOKEN RING OPTIMIZATION

The home-office ARCnet environment currently has approximately 200 local nodes connected through a series of Thomas Conrad 16-port ARCnet hubs. The Ethernet backbone has a critical business connection via a Retix bridge T1 circuit connection that connects the New Jersey site to a company network in Moorestown, New Jersey, which then connects to the Empire State Building in New York City. The home-office internetwork also employs remote telco network connections to four other John Steel Ltd. regional sites including Dallas; St. Louis; Los Angeles; and Atlanta. Figure 10.8 shows the John Steel Ltd. internetwork.

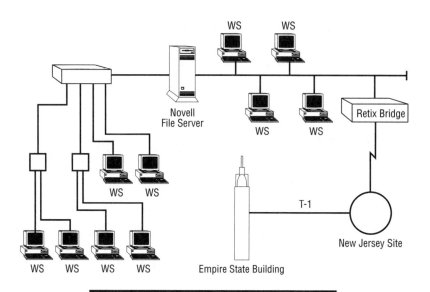

Figure 10.8 The John Steel Ltd. internetwork.

The main LAN operating system environment is Novell NetWare. The operating system environment is comprised of a group of main file servers running Novell NetWare 2.15 and 3.11. The complete local network encompasses approximately 200 NetWare nodes. The business computing environment is based heavily on two custom accounting packages installed on the file servers, MS Accounting and MS Applications. The NetWare LAN users attach via the NetWare file servers to access the MS accounting packages and other general LAN applications such as WordPerfect.

Chapter 10: Case Studies

The John Steel internetwork had all the characteristics of a networking environment sustaining a rapid increase in use and importance. Kathy Walter, Director of Management Information Services, said, "The gradual growth of our network over the past five years has caused us to pause and take a look at the complete internetwork's general performance as it relates to our business requirements. We made a decision to engage protocol analysis services for our current network problems because we needed a calculated technical approach to our issues."

Besides the NetWare error messages, the site was also experiencing general network failures that involved intermittent occurrences of network slowdowns and station disconnects during LAN access. Through multiple protocol analysis sessions via a Sniffer, the actual failure symptoms were found to be mainly associated with one specific issue, a file server disk capacity and layout issue.

The intermittent slowdown symptom was widespread. It occurred at different times of the business day, and its frequency appeared to be related to high usage periods on the LAN. The symptom typically appeared during heavy accounting file access by the users. Some of the network segments were experiencing the problem more frequently, but the symptom was still widespread. The file server disconnects were directly related to the slowdowns.

First, a baseline Ethernet analysis test was performed by running the Baseband Ethernet Default Application Test Suite in the LANalyzer. The Ethernet Default Test Suite characterizes basic Ethernet traffic statistics from an overall viewpoint. An initial trace analysis was taken via the Default Suite.

The testing results showed initial healthy network traffic statistics. Next, I examined the LANalyzer trace decode screen to view the general higher-layer communication processes. The trace decode screen did exhibit a frequent count of NetWare Delay packets. NetWare Delay packets indicate that a NetWare file server is too busy to process an immediate request. At times, this can be a normal situation. But it is not considered healthy if a NetWare Delay packet ratio exceeds 1% of the overall traffic. Levels above 1% of composite traffic can indicate a problem with a file server being excessively busy or overloaded. Just from looking briefly at the trace, in this particular case the ratio seemed quite high.

This occurrence motivated me to run a more defined LANalyzer Test Suite for NetWare traffic called OVERVIEW. The OVERVIEW Test Suite is designed to provide a good measurement of the overall health of higher-layer NetWare-specific traffic on a network. It also has an individual categorical test to break down the actual NetWare Delay packet receive count into its own separate channel.

Running the OVERVIEW Test Suite, I was able to verify that there was a high count level for the Delay packets. Examining the LANalyzer statistical screen made it possible to pinpoint that the Delay packet level was recording at 4% of overall traffic, well above normal range. Figure 10.9 shows the LANalyzer depicting the Delay packet ratio.

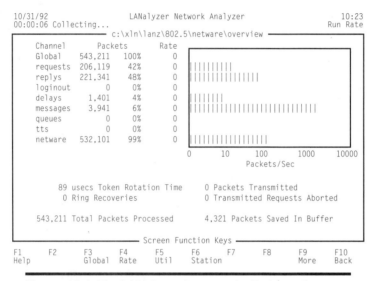

Figure 10.9 The LANalyzer depicting the Delay packet ratio.

The next step was to examine the NetWare file servers for reasons that might support the generation of the NetWare Delay packets. I checked the general operating parameters and the associated logged activity. After analyzing the file server statistics along with the LANalyzer results, it was apparent that the disk access thrashing ratio was intermittently reaching high levels.

The file servers were tight on overall disk capacity for the application design. When excessive disk thrashing occurred, the file servers became too busy to service network requests. This was verified by the LANalyzer, which clearly displayed a high NetWare Delay packet transmission ratio.

In John Steel's case, the disk thrashing level could only be resolved by implementing a larger disk capacity configuration in the file servers. From analysis and general review of the file server statistics, LAN scope recommended that the overall disk capacity be increased to 2-3 GB. The client also was advised that the actual NetWare parameter configurations for disk capacity layout would need special attention when the new disk capacity was implemented.

The recommendation was followed, and the John Steel site is now free from the intermittent failure symptoms. The NetWare file servers are now answering network disk requests faster and at a higher frequency. The complete network is seeing an improvement in general performance.

By using Sniffer and LANalyzer statistics coupled with the NetWare file server statistics, I was able to verify the problem in a technically accurate and decisive manner. John Steel now plans to implement periodic protocol analysis sessions to maintain continued clear operation of its internetwork environment.

Case Study #4: SFP

This case study deals with the measuring of performance on a test model network for a network design. It is always nice to be ahead of the game when troubleshooting a network problem. In other words, when possible, always try to implement preventive measures against long-term network failures. The sophisticated way to do this is to regularly perform a baseline protocol analysis on the network to check the state of the network's health.

First, let's recap some terms and thoughts. When troubleshooting a network via protocol analysis, the proper approach is to first establish a baseline of the network. A baseline protocol analysis session is performed to obtain the statistical measurements of a network when it is operating under normal conditions.

The diagnostic methodology is that if you have the measurement of how a certain network performs when it is operating normally, when a failure occurs you can quickly monitor the network via a protocol analyzer and then look for any deviation from the original measurements. A measurement deviation usually points to specific problem causes.

A baseline protocol analysis must fully capture network data during peak and off peak network usage periods. You cannot perform protocol analysis on a network in a quick or rushed fashion. The proper method is to use a full capture approach and to run a protocol analysis session for at least a complete business day. This full capture approach gives you a palette of the events occurring on your network. In a multiple network environment, each network should get the full capture approach.

284 ETHERNET AND TOKEN RING OPTIMIZATION

A financial company, Systematic Form Processing (SFP), had LAN preventive measures in mind when they contacted my company to perform a baseline protocol analysis session on an SFP internetwork at a location in Newark, New Jersey.

SFP had designed a network layout for its employer services field locations. The same network was closely simulated by SFP personnel at the Newark location. Figure 10.10 shows the actual internetwork layout. The network is composed of a 16Mbps backbone with a mission-critical multiple file server configuration attached. The 16Mbps ring was designed to house the main NetWare 3.11 file server, a GammaFax fax server, an SNA RJE print server, two SNA gateways, an HP laser printer, and an IBM 3174 mainframe connection. The 16Mbps network was connected through an IBM bridge to a 4Mbps ring. The 4Mbps ring contained all the actual user stations for SFP applications.

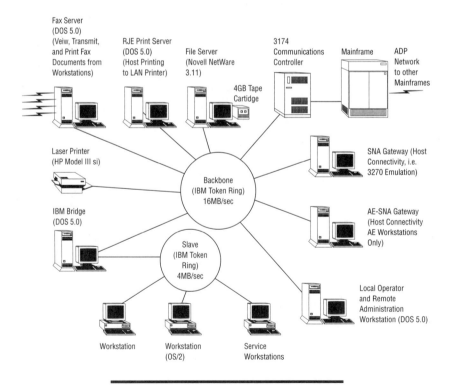

Figure 10.10 The SFP internetwork layout.

SFP designers decided to implement a stress testing phase for the network before the actual field implementation. The stress test was scheduled to investigate how the network design would actually perform in the SFP field locations.

LAN Scope arrived on-site to perform the network baseline analysis. The main goal was to benchmark how the internetwork would perform under the scheduled stress test.

SFP had assembled a comprehensive project plan to examine the network's performance and operational capabilities at four specific intervals of user levels. Application tests were performed on the network at levels of 10, 20, 30, and 40 users. SFP personnel directed the users to run certain applications at specific testing times. During this period, LAN Scope monitored the internetwork via a Sniffer and LANalyzer to capture the statistical measurements from the internetwork. The statistics were measured in synchronization with the SFP stress test intervals of 10, 20, 30, and 40 users.

LAN Scope's methodology was to assemble the testing results for the specific intervals and then examine them for network performance and characterization. The key statistical factors being considered in this stress test were network utilization and error counts. *Error counts* are the error level for the specific topology. In Token Ring there are ten soft error types being monitored. Certain error types and their counts may point to specific network problems.

Network bandwidth utilization is the amount of data-carrying capacity available on a network. By monitoring bandwidth utilization, you can watch how a network design is actually handling changes in network operations. When different events occur on a network, certain amounts of the available network utilization are used or consumed. This is a fluctuating factor. At times, network operation can cause an abnormal bandwidth utilization situation.

Abnormally high network bandwidth utilization can cause considerable performance degradation on a Token Ring network. The performance degradation may present itself in the form of several different failure symptoms: a specific network application operating slowly; the whole network operating slowly; logon failures; or soft or hard error conditions.

The first SFP test subset involved bringing ten users live on the internetwork and initiating an SFP application test script. When users began to logon to the file server, the LANalyzer showed the peak utilization on the 4Mbps ring reach a level of 70% (see Figure 10.11). The 16Mbps network only reached an 18% peak utilization level during the logon interval. The 70% level that occurred on

ETHERNET AND TOKEN RING OPTIMIZATION

4Mbps ring triggered a concern as to how high the peak utilization could conceivably reach in the field with 40 plus users logging on concurrently. When the ten users were actually logged on to the LAN and using the applications in the test script, the overall utilization dropped to a nominal 2% to 5%.

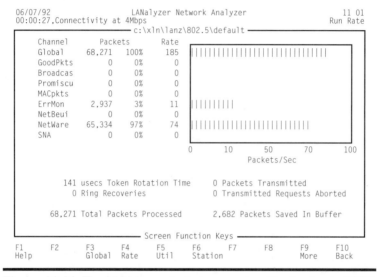

Figure 10.11 The LANalyzer displaying a peak utilization level of 70%.

Testing continued throughout the day in a step-by-step fashion of adding ten users to the base population until a maximum of 40 users was reached. As every group of ten users was added to the base, the LANalyzer exhibited an aggregate growth in utilization. The statistical measurements showed a growth of 2% to 3% increase in baseline utilization per ten users. This benchmark of bandwidth utilization increase proved to be consistent throughout the testing period. The additional peak traffic issue at file server logon also proved to be consistent with a 2% to 3% increase in peak levels. Figure 10.12 shows the logon peaks at various user intervals.

In the afternoon, SFP personnel initiated a group of concurrent 40-user application tests that pushed the overall peak utilization to high levels of 98% at logon/logoff periods. Also, when the SFP application test scripts were unloaded and the final logoffs were initiated, the overall peak utilization also hit high levels of 95% positive.

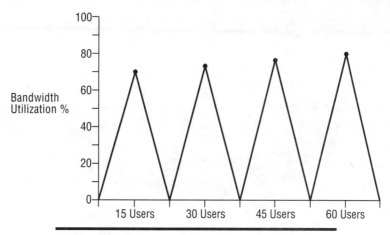

Figure 10.12 Logon peaks at various user intervals.

The baseline study was a lifesaver in this case, again because the protocol analyzers captured these utilization level indications in a testing environment versus it occurring in the field offices unexpectedly. It is possible that high user-logon access could occur in the field, which is dangerous to normal LAN operations. With the baseline study results, SFP could now make a decision on how to address this in the field offices.

Another important test during a baseline protocol analysis session examines the actual protocol breakdown. A protocol breakdown is the distribution of different protocols on a network.

The LANalyzer was examined for protocol statistics. The test displayed a clear domination of the NetWare Core Protocol (NCP) and Internetwork Packet Exchange (IPX) protocol suites over the IBM Systems Networking Architecture (SNA) suite, which was present at minor levels. This breakdown is displayed in Figure 10.13.

The TR Token Rotation Time (TRT) also displayed good levels of 41 to 65 micro-seconds. Normal Token Ring TRT should between 25 and 150 microseconds. TRT is the time it takes for a token to circle the ring once. TRT timing is a good indication of how fast Token Ring frames are being processed.

ETHERNET AND TOKEN RING OPTIMIZATION

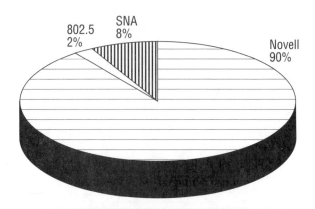

Figure 10.13 LANalyzer displaying NetWare protocol packets on an SNA Network.

The LANalyzer error recording tests exhibited nominal error indications except for the peak logon and logoff periods. During this time frame, multiple devices did exhibit Token Ring Receive Congestion (RC) errors, indicating that those devices were busy attempting to process a flood of data. This was considered normal for the utilization levels reached during the stress test intervals.

Generally, the internetwork displayed proper and fluent communication processes at the low-level 802.5 layer and the higher protocol layers. We saw no evidence of abnormal file access.

From monitoring the internetwork's performance with a LANalyzer during the stress test, LAN Scope recommended that SFP should address the logon/logoff peak utilization issues prior to the LANs being cut live in the field because this had the potential of causing a network failure. Novell NetWare is tolerant of this problem, but failures can occur. It should also be noted that the Token Ring RC error count levels could have increased if there were high traffic levels on a network.

For SFP, performing a baseline protocol analysis session turned out to be a real benefit. It allowed SFP to review how its network design would perform before rolling it out to the field. And after reviewing the statistics gathered during the baseline study, they are now able to carefully benchmark how many users should be logging in or off the file servers concurrently.

Case Study #5: Gray Chemical Co.

I received a call from a client who was in the process of upgrading a Token Ring backbone network from 4Mbps to 16Mbps. The client, Gray Chemical Company, one of the world's largest chemical research and development companies, was looking for a way to verify that its internetwork was operating at an optimum level after the important upgrade was actually implemented.

Network support personnel are starting to realize that it is critical to have a health reading on their network. This becomes particularly important when making modifications to a network. Any time a network modification or change is implemented on a network, it is becoming standard procedure to examine the baseline of the network through protocol analysis. Let's review the following process, which is a form of network performance Tuning and guarantees a careful network modification:

1. Run a thorough protocol analysis session prior to any network modifications to verify the baseline health and operational status of the network.
2. Implement the modification through methodical networking design steps.
3. Re-run a protocol analysis session and compare the measurement statistics against the results captured prior to the network modification.

By following this procedure, you can implement the network modification and then use protocol analysis to capture any operational deviations from the norm. This verifies how the network actually is operating after a modification.

Performance tuning involves using the statistics gathered in a protocol analysis session and making any necessary modifications to either the software or hard-ware design components of a LAN for the purpose of improving its operational performance.

In this case study, Gray had performance tuning in mind when it called for LAN Scope's protocol analysis services. After talking with the client and specifically discussing the backbone upgrade, we agreed that LAN Scope would come on-site and perform a Network Baseline Health Study immediately after the 16Mbps upgrade. Normally, I like to examine the network statistics both prior to and after any network modifications. But in this case, the client had a short timeframe, and the MIS staff had briefly examined the major network statistics on the 4Mbps backbone configuration recently through a site protocol analyzer.

ETHERNET AND TOKEN RING OPTIMIZATION

I went to the site with a plan of inspecting the general baseline health of the internetwork, to get an overall reading of the network's workload characteristics and, if necessary, troubleshoot any specific problems related to network operations and performance.

The baseline study did locate an area of potential concern in Gray's Channelview, Texas location with respect to a group of NetWare file servers and their layout within the internetwork. The problem centered around the number of NetWare hops occurring during LAN traffic. At times, data packets from certain source stations would take 12 to 15 hops to reach destination stations.

The site of our LAN Baseline Study was the company headquarters in Newtown Square, Pennsylvania. The heart of the Gray Chemical internetwork is based in a main corporate office building there. The complete Gray internetwork, including the WAN, encompasses an impressive 65-ring configuration. The Newtown Square location itself houses approximately 30 local rings that tie together the Gray corporate headquarters. A group of Ethernet segments in the internetwork are connected via IBM 8209 bridges.

The internetwork WAN includes eight main remote locations including Los Angeles; Bayport, Dallas, Channelview, and Houston, in Texas; Hinsdale, Illinois; South Charleston, West Virginia; and Beaver Valley, Pennsylvania. Most of the remote locations are tied together by dedicated 256KB circuits via IBM remote 2.2 bridges. A Cisco router also is in place via Channelview, Texas. Figure 10.14 shows the Gray internetwork.

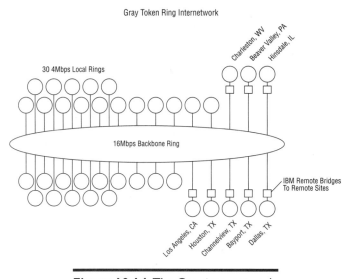

Figure 10.14 The Gray internetwork.

Chapter 10: Case Studies

The LAN operating system environment is based on varieties of NetWare. The main version in place is NetWare 3.11. The Gray computing environment is heavily based on extensive resource sharing and host connectivity. The internetwork layout includes:

- More than 5,000 nodes total in the complete internetwork
- 1,500 local nodes in home-office location
- 65 total rings in the WAN
- 30 local rings in home-office location
- 4 Ethernet segments
- IBM 8228 MSAUs as the hubs for interconnecting network nodes
- IBM PS/2 PCs as the main PC platform choice
- Apple Macintoshes present on the Ethernet segments
- 68 NetWare 3.11 file servers
- 3,174 controllers connecting internetwork to IBM host environment
- 28 IBM 2.2 bridgeslocal/remote location Token Ring connections
- Two IBM 8209 bridgesEthernet-to-Token Ring connections
- One Cisco Systems MGS Routerremote routing in Channelview, TX

The Gray internetwork is currently undergoing several growth migration stages such as bridging to routing and an intelligent hub implementation. Network management, planning, and implementation also is becoming a strategic factor for the MIS staff.

When I arrived at the site, I connected a LANalyzer to the 16Mbps backbone. I started a LANalyzer application test suite called DEFAULT. The 16Mbps DEFAULT test suite collects major statistics to monitor the health of a 16Mbps Token Ring network. The results include bandwidth utilization measurements, Token Rotation Time, error levels, protocol breakdowns, and other critical statistics.

The DEFAULT test suite displayed a normal reading on the bandwidth utilization levels for a 16Mbps network. The traffic only reached a 26% peak utilization level and was generally recording an average utilization of 9%. (Figure 10.15 displays the network utilization.) The average Token Ring frame sizes were in the 300-byte range, which is considered normal. The TR Token Rotation Time (TRT) on the backbone ring displayed consistently steady levels of 36 to 37 microseconds. Normal Token Ring TRT should be between 25 and

150 microseconds. TRT timing is a good indication of how fast Token Ring frames are being processed. The backbone TRT was extremely solid, which indicates a healthy network platform on the backbone.

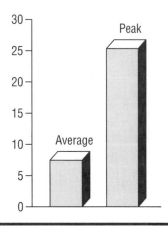

Figure 10.15 Network utilization at Gray Chemical.

The error recording tests exhibited nominal error indications except for the peak traffic periods between remote circuits to the Gray home-office site. During the monitoring time frame, the local/remote IBM bridge connection to Channelview, Texas did exhibit some significant levels of Token Ring Receive Congestion (RC) errors on the LANalyzer. The LANalyzer indicated that those devices were busy attempting to process a flood of data. This is considered normal for the IBM bridges with the peak traffic levels reached during the testing intervals. Specifically, the IBM bridge stats showed a communication overrun situation, which verified the RC errors recorded on the analyzers.

The next sub-test centered on gaining an accurate view of the protocol breakdowns on the backbone. I recorded the protocol categories through the LANalyzer PROTOCOL application test suite. The PROTOCOL test suite characterizes all network protocols on a given network and their percentage levels. The PROTOCOL test suite for the backbone displayed a clear domination of the Systems Networking Architecture (SNA) and the NetWare Core Protocol (NCP)/Internetwork Packet Exchange (IPX) packets. Apple and Internet Protocol (IP) packets were present at minor levels, but they were not significant in distribution levels for the particular testing period. Figure 10.16 shows the Gray protocol breakdown.

Chapter 10: Case Studies

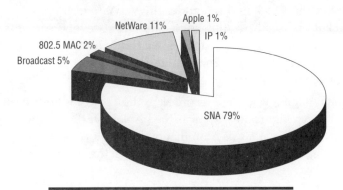

Figure 10.16 The Gray protocol breakdown.

Generally, the DEFAULT and PROTOCOL test suites showed that the internetwork displayed proper and fluent communication processes at the low-level 802.5 layer and the higher protocol layers. There were no issues concerning abnormal file access.

SNA-specific tests were performed via a LANalyzer application test suite called SNA OVERVIEW. The SNA OVERVIEW test suite measures the SNA traffic for overall fluency and health for general SNA frame communications. All the main SNA command parameters were examined and appeared to be fluent. The SNA requests and responses were carefully viewed and frame transmission were free of any file response problems. The SNA routing traffic also was examined through a LANalyzer test suite called SRCROUTE, which showed a good distribution for the hop levels across source routing channels.

Next, the goal was to focus on NetWare-specific traffic tests to check the NetWare Core Protocol (NCP) and Internetwork Packet Exchange (IPX) layer's health. The tests used here were the LANalyzer NetWare-specific tests called NetWare OVERVIEW and HOPCOUNT.

The NetWare OVERVIEW application test suite monitors the general NetWare file server-to-workstation packet traffic for general health. The NetWare OVERVIEW test results in this case exhibited good frame fluency at the NCP and IPX layers.

The HOPCOUNT application test suite examines NetWare packets for the number of actual routing hops. The test records all hop levels from every packet captured and places them in four categories: 1 to 3 hops, 4 to 7 hops, 8 to 12 hops, and 12 to 15 hops. Normally, the majority of NetWare hop-count levels

294 ETHERNET AND TOKEN RING OPTIMIZATION

should stay in the 0 to 7 hop categories. In NetWare terms, a hop occurs each time a packet crosses a router. High hop-count levels can cause network performance to deteriorate due to excessive traffic routing and potential traffic loops. The Gray HOPCOUNT analysis testing did show high hop-count levels for a portion of the NetWare traffic.

Abnormally high levels were recorded in the 12- to 15- hop-count categories on the LANalyzer. Figure 10.17 depicts the LANalyzer displaying the Gray hop-count levels. Through analysis examination, the high levels were tracked to the company's Channelview, Texas network. The actual transmission was via a Cisco Router.

The higher level of hop counts was caused by an inefficient network design in Channelview. Some NetWare file servers in the Gray internetwork were actually seeing redundant traffic. They could have been placed in a more efficient position physically in the network to properly balance the NetWare traffic. If the network configuration was not corrected, the performance of internetwork communication would be seriously degraded. Figure 10.18 displays the hop-count breakdown on the Gray internetwork.

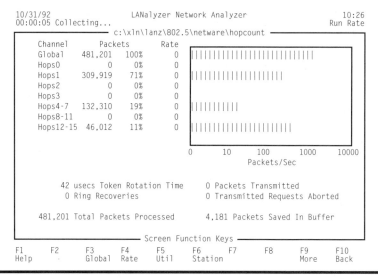

Figure 10.17 LANalyzer displaying the Gray internetwork's hop-count levels.

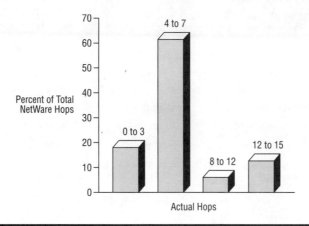

Figure 10.18 The hop-count breakdown on the Gray internetwork.

LAN Scope's recommendation was to redesign the network using a protocol analysis approach. It appeared as though a large portion of the NetWare frames on the Gray internetwork was taking inefficient routes. By decoding frame transmissions and possibly repositioning file servers, efficiency of some of these routes might be improved. The result is less cross-network traffic and better internetwork performance.

The recommendation was followed, and the Gray internetwork is now experiencing better performance. The Network Baseline Study approach definitely helped Gray methodically implement the new network modification and ensure that the 16Mbps upgrade benefits in utilization would be realized by continued performance of the complete internetwork.

Gray is planning to implement continued protocol analysis to keep a focused representation of the internetwork operations through its future growth.

Case Study #6: State Auto Credit Corporation

This case study covers a recent network optimization project for the State Auto Credit Corporation (SACC). SACC had a Token Ring internetwork with five main rings that had over 350 nodes. The LAN environment included seven NetWare file servers. The internetwork user base was starting to grow and utilize host access at a fairly high rate in the SNA environment via two NetWare SNA gateways.

SACC provides credit services to a large group of small auto dealers throughout the State of New York. The company grew from five to over 500 employees in just two years. Over 300 of these employees are using internetwork services for referencing credit checking processes, word processing, and accounting.

What had basically started out as one Token Ring network progressively grew, as users were added onto the network, to the current five Token Ring internetwork. Day by day, more technologies were introduced into the SACC LAN environment, such as new LAN printers, LAN modems, and innovative network applications. Eventually, this network turned into the complex internetwork that SACC has in place today. The MIS support staff at SACC has done well dealing with the daily support and maintenance issues. The internetwork itself has been handling the workload applied through it, and has provided the user base with all the services for which it was intended.

But six months into the second year of its growth stage, the SACC internetwork started to slow down. Users complained, almost daily, about internetwork operations and reliability.

My company was retained by SACC to manage and perform a complete SACC network optimization project. Through protocol analysis, the SACC performance problems were found to be related to a group of network configuration and layout issues. We recommended that SACC implement a sixth ring onto the network as a network backbone and takeced the two NetWare SNA Gateways and place them at different points on the internetwork.

We also located an imbalance in the individual ring user levels and recommended a new ring balance for the user counts throughout the internetwork layout. When the project was over, the Token Ring internetwork was experiencing less cross-traffic and overall increases in general performance. Protocol analysis provided the venue to measure the SACC internetwork's current performance levels and enabled us to tune the network.

The internetwork at SACC has turned out to be the core business engine of the overall business operation. The SACC MIS management group relayed to our consulting group the criticality of this internetwork performing at its best. Any interruption in service to SACC could mean close to $100,000 a day in losses. SACC MIS management calculated that they were currently experiencing intermittent outages of close to an hour per day due to general performance slowdowns.

Prior to our network optimization project, the SACC internetwork was composed of five 4Mbps Token Ring networks, designated as networks one through five. Network one had 122 nodes on it; network two had 91 nodes; network three was composed of 63 nodes; network four was composed of 38 nodes; and network five had a total of 46 nodes.

Six NetWare file servers on the internetwork were running NetWare 3.11, and one was running NetWare 2.15. The company also had recently implemented two NetWare SNA gateways connected to the one and two networks. The gateways were then connected directly into an IBM communication controller connection. Again, a group of new technologies throughout the Token Ring internetwork also were recently implemented, such as the HPIIISI LAN printers along with some Microtest LAN modems.

The individual Token Ring networks were connected through internal NetWare routing via the 3.11 file servers. There was also an additional group of remote communication links coming in through direct PC connections, but at this point no direct communications server configurations were on the internetwork. Several remote sites in New York state also access the SACC internetwork through dial-up connections on an as-needed basis.

The first step was to develop the SACC project plan, which was extensive. We very carefully reviewed the current SACC internetwork layout and design plans. Next, we examined all SACC site records and statistics. We also had an extensive conference with the SACC support personnel to get a briefing on the overall history of the internetwork growth and performance.

It is essential to understand the network you are working on, to become educated on all the business and technical areas that surround the network. Our project plan was structured to perform an overall protocol analysis on the five Token Ring networks. After the detailed protocol analysis sessions, we would implement any network changes, and perform a post-analysis session for every one of the network modifications implemented. Our last step was to review the performance changes to see if they were effective.

We had a total of five Token Ring 4Mbps networks to view. We started by analyzing network one for a full business day, network two for a full business day, and so on, through network five. We were therefore able to capture data events for the networks throughout the full business day cycle. By examining a network for a full business day, you can capture all the peak and off-peak periods of traffic on the internetwork. This enables you to understand how the internetwork is being used in the current business climate.

Each network was monitored for general workload characteristics. A group of analyses was performed on each network at various intervals of the testing period, and specialized tests were used from a Sniffer analyzer and a LANalyzer. From the LANalyzer, we used Application Test Suites to perform a set of protocol analysis tests. During the testing period, we used the analyzers to capture the workload characteristics from the internetwork. The workload characteristics were measured in synchronization with the normal SACC business day.

On every ring, the first test was performed by utilizing a LANalyzer special application test suite for the 4Mbps rings, called Default, and involved looking at the overall Token Ring network utilization and statistics within the individual ring station addresses utilization consumption.

We were looking for any average or peak utilization issues on each of the networks. Generally, on a 4Mbps network, a rule of thumb is that a healthy average utilization level is under 60% of overall utilization, and peaks should not exceed 90%. The network analysis showed that networks four and five both had acceptable traffic levels of approximately 18% on an average, and display peaks of approximately 35%.

But network one and network two, which have 122 and 91 nodes respectively, had peak bandwidth utilization of almost 85% and average utilization levels of around 65% . Network three displayed an average utilization level of 28% , and a peak level of 44%. The utilization levels on rings one and two showed an immediate cause for concern. Figure 10.19 shows the LANalyzer displaying the Default test screen, which depicts a group of workload characteristics from the SACC internetwork.

The next subset of tests on each network centered on gaining an accurate view of the protocol breakdown. The protocol statistic tests were performed using a LANalyzer application test suite called Protocol. Overall, the protocol breakdowns on the Token Ring network at the SACC locations showed the dominance of the NetWare Core Protocol (NCP)/Internetwork Packet Exchange (IPX) and the SNA protocol suites. The SNA levels were due specifically to the fact that NetWare gateways were present on the one and two rings.

A group of Token Ring physical layer tests was performed with the LANalyzer and the Network General Sniffer and produced a range of 802.5 statistics. The average Token Ring frame sizes were in the 200- to 300-byte range across all the rings, which is considered normal.

Chapter 10: Case Studies

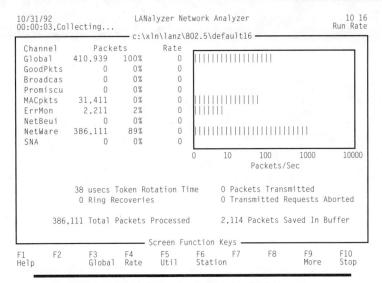

Figure 10.19 LANalyzer displaying the Default test screen.

The Token Ring Token Rotation Time (TRT) on the rings in the internetwork consistently displayed levels of between 30 and 150 microseconds. The normal TRT levels should be between 25 and 150 microseconds. Rings one and two did display intermittently high Token Ring rotation levels, due to the ring traffic levels. Also, rings one and two were receiving the complete internetwork's SNA pass-through traffic because of the gateway placement. As traffic levels increase and internetwork changes occur on a network, the TRT level is an important measure of Token Ring network performance.

The protocol analyzer error logs were examined for Token Ring soft-error levels for each network. Certain soft errors and their corresponding count level can indicate issues and problems within Token Ring nodes.

The analyzer error recording tests across the Token Ring internetwork at the SACC site showed nominal error conditions. But certain Token Ring addresses did exhibit abnormal error levels. On average, the only Token Ring error level high in portions of the SACC internetwork was the Receiver Congestion (RC) error, a Token Ring soft error that indicates a reporting device is attempting to process a flood of data. This is considered normal at times. With the layout of the current SACC internetwork, it is normal for the NetWare file server internal Token Ring cards configured as routers to exhibit Token Ring receiver congestion errors.

The SACC file server cards had the burden of processing LAN data intended for the file servers plus the responsibility of routing internetwork traffic. This is not necessarily healthy for the physical layer of Token Ring. The traffic levels reached on rings one and two at SACC during the normal testing interval cause the NetWare file server Token Ring cards to exhibit the Token Ring receiver congestion. This is basically a Token Ring communication overrun situation, which was verified with the RC errors that displayed on the analyzers.

Except for the traffic levels and associated RC errors, the internetwork itself displayed proper and fluent communication processes at the low level 802.5 layer and the higher protocol layers. The utilization levels issues present on rings one and two did cause issues in file access and performance.

A group of LANalyzer NetWare-specific tests was performed on every Token Ring network. Overall the NetWare subset of tests showed acceptable fluency at the NCP and IPX layers. Networks one and two did exhibit intermittently high NetWare Delay packet ratios. A high NetWare Delay packet rate indicates that a NetWare file server is too busy to process an immediate request. At times, this can be normal.

In rings one and two, the file server Delay packet levels were recorded at levels above 5% of overall traffic, which is above normal; Delay packets should not exceed 1% of the overall traffic. This was clearly related to the file server traffic processing loads due to the utilization levels.

The file servers across the SACC internetwork also displayed high NetWare File Failure access packet ratios from the NetWare file servers. The NetWare file failures also can be related to the internetwork traffic levels.

Each network was subjected to a series of tests in the LANalyzer test suite, called SNA Overview. These tests examined the general fluency of SNA requests and responses. SNA communication appeared to be fluent, and the frame transmissions did not indicate any major file response problems.

By examining the data gathered with the NetWare and SNA tests, we were able to view the overall network routing capability, routing length, and directional traffic flows for the general traffic.

The routing traffic tests did display inefficiencies in the overall routing of traffic. Many routed packets on both networks four and five appeared to be taking excessive routes. The routing traffic ratios were examined thoroughly on every ring with the Sniffer. A Sniffer Routing Information Screen is displayed in Figure 10.20.

Chapter 10: Case Studies

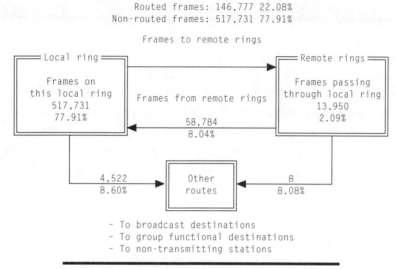

Figure 10.20 A Sniffer Routing Information screen.

Excessive routing was found to be related to the internetwork layout and the SNA gateway placement. All gateway traffic for rings three, four, and five had to flow through rings one and two for gateway access.

For all the tests performed with the Sniffer and the LANalyzer, the goal was to examine general performance on each network by viewing the bandwidth utilization levels, TRT levels, and error statistics for overall network traffic. The process was to examine the Token Ring physical layer on each network through these statistics and then to verify the higher protocol layers. Because SACC's internetwork is based primarily on NetWare, our goal was also to examine each particular network's NetWare operation with regard to NetWare protocol packets.

From the beginning, we noticed an imbalance in the node count across the five Token Ring networks. For example, network one had a total of 122 nodes present; network five only had 46. We felt that this internetwork required some Token Ring balancing with regard to the number of nodes on each network.

In looking at the NetWare higher-layer communications, we noticed that most of the NetWare file servers on this internetwork were performing well but were heavily burdened with routing requests in addition to providing file services.

ETHERNET AND TOKEN RING OPTIMIZATION

The hop counts observed on all the file servers were frequently over four. The hop count is displayed in Figure 10.21 on the LANalyzer. It became clear that much of the traffic from ring one to ring five, for example, had to go through four hops to actually get to the desired destination. This hop count became a major focus of our analysis. We were certain that we could improve routing efficiency by relocating the servers.

We concluded that implementing a backbone ring into the SACC design could decrease the overall number of hops between the respective networks.

The protocol analysis results produced a range of statistics that showed high utilization on rings one and two. Utilization was less a problem on rings three, four, and five, but routing problems remained in evidence as indicated by high hop counts

We identified three specific goals for the network modification stage of the project:

1. To balance the number of nodes across the individual Token Ring
2. To implement a backbone ring that would decrease the number of hops from ring to ring

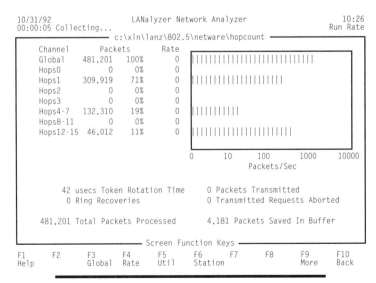

Figure 10.21 LANalyzer displaying the hop count.

3. To place the NetWare SNA gateways on the new Token Ring backbone

To balance the nodes on the Token Ring internetwork, we examined the amount of traffic flowing between rings along with the individual ring node counts. We were able to determine which nodes were most frequently connecting to servers on rings other than their host rings. The goal was to attempt to arrange users on the rings that supported the file server they most frequently used.

We adjusted the node counts on the various rings as follows. Node counts on two rings were reduced: Ring 1 nodes decreased to 75, and Ring 2 nodes decreased to 62. Node counts on the remaining rings increased: Ring 3 nodes increased to 68, Ring 4 to 71, and Ring 5 to 84.

The post-modification protocol analysis tests displayed a clear reduction in utilization levels on the one and two networks. The average utilization level on Ring 1 dropped to 37% and the peaks were limited to 54%. The utilization levels on Ring 2 also showed a significant drop to a 43% average with peaks of 67%. The utilization levels on Rings 3, 4, and 5 did not show any large increase. The NetWare file servers showed a marked reduction in Delay and File Failure rates. Overall, the modification step was extremely successful. We next implemented the new backbone ring at 4Mbps.

The post-protocol analysis tests for the backbone modification also included an analysis re-check on each of the five main rings and a full analysis session on the new backbone. The testing showed a decrease in the internetwork hop-count levels. The result was less internetwork packet cross-traffic. The user base commented on improved access time. These findings verified the success of this optimization phase.

The third modification was to move the NetWare SNA Gateways to the backbone ring. The post-protocol analysis testing showed the success of this phase, with a lower average hop count for the SNA frame types. Figure 10.22 shows the SACC internetwork layout before and after our network modification steps.

ETHERNET AND TOKEN RING OPTIMIZATION

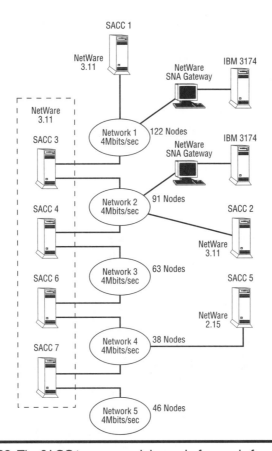

Figure 10.22 The SACC internetwork layout before and after modification.

The overall optimization project at SACC turned out successfully. This was not an extensive project with many intricate steps. It mainly involved the steps of balancing the Token Ring and implementing a backbone that had been needed for quite some time at SACC. Implementing the backbone provided for an overall balance by decreasing the cross-network traffic between the five subsets of rings. The implementation of the backbone also provided a clear route from all rings for the SNA gateways traffic to the SNA gateways on the backbone ring.

By adhering to a structured project plan and employing appropriate protocol analyzer techniques, we were able to verify our initial hunches of the problems involved, and the changes required. Then we were able to verify the health of the internetwork after the modifications.

Case Study #7: The Delaware Group

The Delaware Group contracted LAN Scope to investigate a problem that had been occurring on its internetwork for quite some time. It was decided that a LAN Scope technician would go on-site and perform a brief network baseline analysis. The main network failure symptom was that multiple users on the Delaware Group's internetwork were experiencing intermittent occurrences of Re-transmission Lost errors during LAN-to-DEC host access.

The Delaware Group is a specialized investment firm. The company is growing, as is its internetwork. The internetwork is the heartbeat of the company's business engine. The MIS support staff is busy adding and supporting many new networking products.

But even in the midst of all the day-to-day support tasks, they have been able to keep a proactive stance on maintaining the computing environment. Dan Hartnett, Vice President of Technical Services, said "Demand for network services is increasing much more rapidly than anticipated. The resulting complexity creates an environment where advanced diagnostic capability is an absolute necessity."

The Delaware Group's internetwork in Philadelphia is composed of multiple Ethernet LAN segments connected through a variety of equipment, including products such as SynOptics, Blackbox, David Systems, DEC Delni, and HP bridges. The company has two major locations in the city of Philadelphia, which are connected via a T1 circuit.

The Delaware Group's main LAN operating system environment includes three file servers running a mix of Novell NetWare 2.15 and 3.11. There also is a Lotus One server that handles database transactions.

The complete local network has approximately 90 nodes. The business computing environment is based heavily on a DEC VAX. The NetWare LAN users access the DEC VAX environment via a DEC Delni to DEC 550 Server connection. The Philadelphia site also includes a remote connection to a Massachusetts site for additional VAX access (see Figure 10.23).

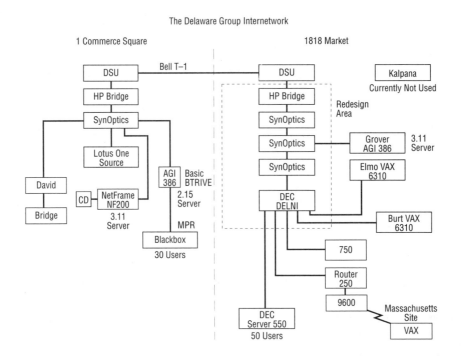

Figure 10.23 Network for the Delaware Group.

Users throughout the internetwork were experiencing intermittent Re-Transmission Lost errors during DEC VAX sessions connected via the LAN. The problem would occur at different times of the business day, and its frequency appeared related to high usage periods on the LAN. The symptom typically appeared when a user was involved in DEC VAX file access. The problem was particularly frequent during actual VAX file transfers. Some Ethernet segments experienced the problem more frequently, but the symptom was widespread.

Through the use of a Sniffer and LANalyzer, the Re-Transmission Lost error symptom was shown to be directly related to an incorrect configuration setting on a DEC Delni unit that interfaces the DEC VAX environment to the LAN domain. The MIS staff reconfigured the parameter, and the problem symptom was resolved.

This is another clear case of how a protocol analyzer was instrumental in isolating a misleading problem. The network users were experiencing an intermittent symptom that was pointing to DEC file access problems. The

Chapter 10: Case Studies

SynOptics concentrator collision LEDs were intermittently flashing, but would not stay on solidly. I connected protocol analyzers to an Ethernet segment near the SynOptics concentrator to obtain an overview of the network health. All the general statistical components looked normal. The network average utilization was only about 25% of maximum, and all frame processes were communicating in a proper fashion.

But an hour into the session, the LANalyzer started to log excessive Local Collision error rates. Collisions are a normal occurrence in the Ethernet topology if they accumulate at normal levels; Ethernet's collision rate should not exceed more than 1% of the overall traffic. In this case, the collision rate was exceeding 3% of the overall traffic.

At this point, I started a specialized test on the LANalyzer application test suite called TRACKCOL, which logs and pinpoints specific collision errors on an Ethernet segment. Within minutes, the TRACKCOL test had recorded excessive local collision errors (see Figure 10.24). The local collision frames showed that the collisions were related to the SynOptics concentrator and the DEC Delni unit Ethernet addresses.

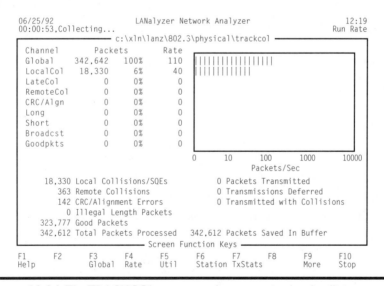

Figure 10.24 The TRACKCOL test recording excessive local collision errors.

This led me to look closely at the hardware. When examining the DEC Delni unit directly, I noticed a configuration parameter for SQE heartbeat. The Delni unit connects directly to a Synoptics LattisNet 10BASE-T Workgroup

ETHERNET AND TOKEN RING OPTIMIZATION

Concentrator via an Ethernet AUI connection. The Synoptics LattisNet documentation states that any device connected to its AUI port must have the Ethernet V2.0 Signal Quality Error Test (SQE) feature disabled. The SQE test, sometimes referred to as "Heartbeat," is an actual signal transmission test used to confirm collision detect circuitry in Ethernet transceivers. To interconnect certain 802.3 Ethernet devices, the SQE feature must be disabled. This is especially true with some repeaters and hubs.

The DEC Delni switch was in the position that enables SQE. This was causing a direct transmission of the SQE signal into the Synoptics concentrator. The SynOptics Concentrator was intermittently displaying an illuminated collision LED on its front panel. The SQE signal was inducing excessive collisions into the LAN internetwork. The collisions would become more extreme with higher traffic levels. High collision rates actually cause excessive amounts of Ethernet packets to be returned to the originating station and then retransmitted. This event eventually causes the Re-Transmission Lost errors.

The SQE parameter was reconfigured, and I started another LANalyzer analysis session. The results of the second session showed a significant drop in the local collision rate to normal levels. Figure 10.25 presents a graph that displays the collision count before and after the Delni SQE parameter was reconfigured.

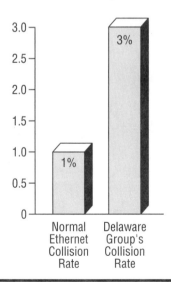

Figure 10.25 Collision count before and after reconfiguring the Delni SQE parameter.

After studying analyzer statistics, including the site problem history, general LAN statistics, and the physical rack containing the SynOptic, DEC Delni unit, and the DEC Server 550, the symptom cause became clear. Without the protocol analyzers and a proper approach, this problem might have caused chaos for some time.

Case Study #8: The Soda Company

One of the major challenges for LAN design teams is the task of converting an expanding and intricate source-routing Token Ring internetwork into a tightly defined, smoothly operating machine. At one time, a simple source-routing bridge adequately supported the traffic needs between multiple Token Ring networks. However, today the traffic requirements in many networks are so complex that new technologies such as specialized bridges and routers are being evaluated as alternatives to source-routing bridging.

This study is an overview of source-routing issues and an analysis of the internetwork source-routing traffic at The Soda Company of North America. This project was implemented by the company to allow its IS Technology Planning staff to maintain a proactive stance in relation to understanding the internetwork traffic statistics.

LAN Scope was contracted to work with The Soda Company on a Token Ring internetwork located in Orlando and Tampa, Florida. LAN Scope would perform an on-site baseline protocol analysis study to get the overall workload characteristics and traffic route identification across the company's Token Ring internetwork. Through the analysis study, we verified that the Token Ring internetwork was healthy, and we identified some specific issues related to source routing traffic.

The networks for this particular case study were approximately 12 Token Ring networks located in the Orlando and Tampa locations. The IS staff was focused on understanding all the internetwork traffic characteristics. They are currently evaluating several technology changes such as a possible move to a router environment. The IS staff realized that the data from this study would allow them to accurately and carefully calculate any future modifications to the layout and design of the Token Ring internetwork.

ETHERNET AND TOKEN RING OPTIMIZATION

The Soda Company internetwork is composed of a total of 11 main Token Ring networks. The user rings are segmented throughout the different floors of corporate headquarters in Tampa. There are two main backbones, C and D, that serve as redundant backbones to all the main floor sub-rings and an IBM host environment. All the floor sub-rings are connected to the backbones in a redundant fashion through IBM source-routing bridges. The floor rings on floors 4 and 6 actually are separated through individual IBM source-routing bridges due to excessive traffic load considerations. Figure 10.26 shows an overview of Token Ring internetwork.

Some of the floor rings have only one source-routing route to the backbone environment, such as the 7th and the 3rd floors. The two bridge paths on floors 4, 5, 6, 8, and 9 are basically there as redundant routes to the backbone rings. The backbone rings are connected to a Cisco router and a dual redundant IBM TIC environment. The internetwork also has some WAN communication links and other resource sharing in place for various host environments. Ring 9 in the Tampa location is connected through a Cisco routing environment back to the Orlando location.

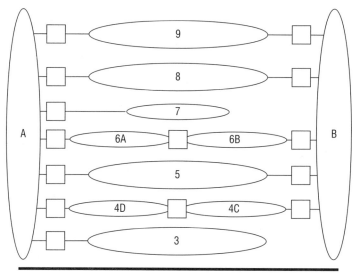

Figure 10.26 The Soda Company Token Ring internetwork.

Using a Sniffer, we started the baseline protocol analysis study by examining the Token Ring 802.5 physical layer health of every specific ring in the Token

Ring internetwork. We further examined every ring for fluent upper-layer communications by looking at the protocol breakdown on every ring.

Our first step was to understand the source-routing traffic distribution across the Token Ring internetwork. We utilized the Sniffer to view the source-routing path identifications. This is displayed on the Sniffer Token Ring Monitor shown in Figure 10.27.

By examining the physical layer Token Ring frames and decoding the frame transmissions, we were able to examine the Routing Information (RI) fields within the Token Ring frames. We used the Token Ring Analyzer from the Sniffer to look at the RI fields of specific frames.

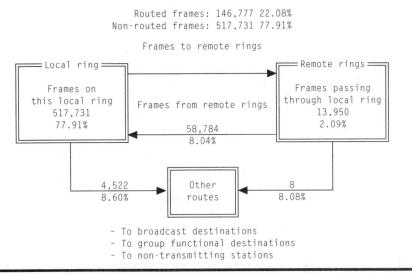

Figure 10.27 The Sniffer displaying source routing paths across the internetwork.

Through examining the source-routing frame details, we found that a good amount of The Soda Company cross-ring traffic (in other words, from ring-to-ring) was taking excessive and redundant routes to get from a source to a destination ring. From viewing the network physical diagram, it was clear that there could be some redundant routes from ring-to-ring in certain situations. Some of this is normal in a Token Ring network that has grown to this range, due to the characteristics of IBM source-routing bridges. Redundant routes from IBM bridges to each ring are often planned to safeguard against times when there is a problem with one particular bridge. However, a problem occurs when excessive routes are taken due to congestion levels at certain bridges.

ETHERNET AND TOKEN RING OPTIMIZATION

For example, if bridge F from Ring 6A to Ring 6F is highly congested, a traffic frame would flow through the 8 or 9 rings to actually get to 6F, when normally it would be able to go the bridge F route. The route through rings 8 or 9 is considered excessive.

Another example is illustrated by the yellow traffic flow diagram in Figure 10.28. A high RC error count is occurring with internetwork bridge C. For traffic to get from Ring 4D to 4C traffic, it had to flow through one backbone Ring 6D, then had to route through either networks 8 or 9 to get onto backbone Ring 6C, and then into Ring 4C its final locationinstead of taking the simple route through bridge C.

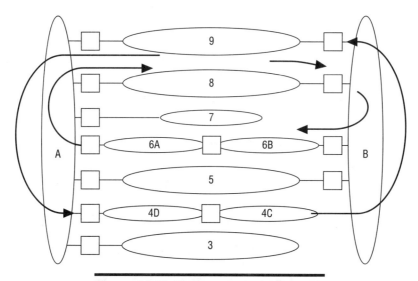

Figure 10.28 Traffic at the Soda Company.

In other words, if some of the IBM bridges in this environment are congested when handling their normal traffic flow, they are not going to be effective in passing a normal frame to other rings, such as 4D to 4C.

This congestion is only part of the problem. The other part was found through identifying some of the source-routing parameters in specific bridges. We were able to locate some bridge parameters also possibly causing a frame to not be forwarded to the destination ring via the closest route.

A specific problem was found in a bridge that had the Single Route Broadcast parameter turned off. This parameter setting was causing a source routing frame to be turned back so that it had to take an alternate route. An example is displayed in the green traffic flow diagram in Figure 10.28. The source-routing bridge 4 is identified as having Single Route Broadcast turned off, but it is the closest route for a frame from backbone Ring 6D to Ring 9. The frame was turned back and had to pass through bridge 8, through Ring 8, up through bridge 5, onto backbone 6C, and finally onto bridge 3 to reach its location ring 9! Under normal circumstances, virtually any frame on backbone 6D intended for Ring 9 should be able to travel through bridge 4.

The most significant issue we identified was source-routing bridge congestion, which can cause an excessive alternate route to be determined. Another issue is that general bridge parameter problems in some of the source-routing bridges might make it unable to forward a frame when required.

We identified a set of options for The Soda Company that may be used in the future to improve overall performance and assist with the current technology migration. The recommendations included a group of general plans for configuration of the overall bridges, along with network layout and configuration plans that included specific recommendations for a routing implementation.

This case study shows how using a proactive protocol analysis approach to examine a source-routing environment can lead to improvements in the overall traffic and directional flow of a Token Ring internetwork.

Summary

These case studies illustrate the basic methodology for conducting an internetwork troubleshooting session. To perform a protocol analysis session, you must have experience in the following areas:

- The involved network topology
- General procedures for using a protocol analyzer
- Detailed experience with the particular analyzer being used

Protocol analysis is the process of capturing, viewing, and analyzing a communication protocol's operation in a particular network architecture.

ETHERNET AND TOKEN RING OPTIMIZATION

The methodology that I use in the field when troubleshooting problems via protocol analysis techniques follows a set of six logical steps:

1. Capture
2. View
3. Analyze
4. Check errors
5. Benchmark performance
6. Focus

While remaining conscious of this prescribed methodology, you need to remember to monitor the main six workload characteristics as they relate to the network workload. The six statistics are as follows:

1. Overall network utilization
2. Node-by-node utilization
3. Protocol statistics
4. Error statistics
5. Low-level layer frame statistics
6. High-level layer frame communications statistics

These characteristics give you a brief view of the network's health. Normally, these statistics would be examined for more significant period of time, preferably at least a full, normal working day.

CHAPTER 11

Architecture

Token Ring's design is one of the most complex in the LAN arena. This chapter explores the Token Ring design and layout and describes how the main functions work. The management roles of the network and the Token Ring communication processes are explained in detail. Finally, Token Ring frame types are examined to provide you with an overall understanding of the architecture.

Exploring Token Ring Design and Layout

The Token Ring architecture was developed by IBM to meet the need for a robust, high-performance network not subject to the probabilistic performance characteristics of Ethernet. IBM submitted Token Ring to the IEEE as a proposed standard, and 4 megabit-per-second (Mbps) Token Ring was established as IEEE standard 802.5. Since the initial standardization of the 4Mbps Token Ring architecture, performance has been pushed to 16Mbps and beyond. This section examines the 802.5 Token Ring architecture in detail.

Terminology

Most of the devices connected to the network are PCs or workstations. A PC serves as a file server, which is where the network operating system resides. Peripherals such as printers and modems are connected to either the workstations or the file server.

The file server and workstations talk to each other through network interface cards (NICs). Every device connected to the network must have an NIC installed. The NICs connect to the multistation access units (MAUs), which serve as the network wiring hubs.

Every device connected to the network has an NIC installed. The NIC has a nine-pin port that connects to a cable connected to a MAU port. It is possible to have a twisted-pair port if the NIC is made for unshielded twisted pair (UTP) cabling medium. The NIC is primarily responsible for handling all the network communication that takes place between a network device and the rest of the network. (UTP cabling is discussed in Chapter 12.)

The NIC actually contains the Token Ring chipset, which contains routines called the Agent. The Agent interprets and routes all the data frames transferred between the device and the network.

The Agent works with the Network Basic Input/Output System (NetBIOS), loaded with the Token Ring device drivers through the IBM LAN Support Program disk. The NetBIOS handles Session-layer protocol communication, allowing the operating system on the PC to talk to the network protocols that the NIC receives from other devices on the network.

MAUs

This discussion uses the IBM 8228 MAU (see Figure 11.1). Each MAU has eight available ports for network devices. The network devices are connected to the MAU ports by means of cables called lobe cables. Each port on the MAU has an internal relay that opens when the network device cabled to it attempts to access the network. The NIC sends a DC current to open the relay. If the device is not using the network, the relay remains closed.

Figure 11.1 The eight available ports and Ring In and Ring Out ports of an MAU.

To expand the network, a port is located at each end of the MAU for cabling it to another MAU. On the left side of the MAU is a port called Ring In (RI); on the right side of the MAU is a port called Ring Out (RO).

Expanding the network from, for example, 8 to 16 devices entails connecting the RO port of the existing MAU to the RI port of the new MAU.

The unused RI and RO ports on the MAUs have self-shorting data connectors that automatically loop the cabling back to form an electrical ring. All the ports on the MAU have this self-shorting feature: When no device is connected to the port, it self-shorts to close the ring. This makes it easy to add and remove network devices from the MAU.

The cabling path that connects the MAUs and goes through the MAUs is called the main ring path. This path is different from the lobe cable, which connects the MAU ports to the network devices.

The MAU configuration makes the Token Ring network easy to expand; all you have to do is run all the network lobe cables to one area. Any time you need to add devices, simply connect a new MAU to the existing chain of MAUs.

When you run a large group of cables to one area, the cables are usually connected to a patch panel (see Figure 11.2). A patch panel allows the flexibility of easily moving lobe cables from one MAU to another MAU. The area in which the patch panel is located is called a *wiring closet*.

ETHERNET AND TOKEN RING OPTIMIZATION

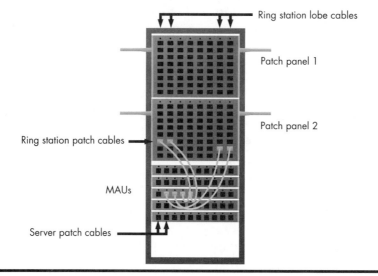

Figure 11.2 A patch panel allows connecting many lobe cables from the network ring stations in a single location. These patch panels are in a wiring closet, which includes the MAUs.

Some Token Ring network installations are so large that they require multiple wiring closets. In the case of long-distance cable runs between wiring closets, devices called repeaters may be needed to compensate for the distance.

Some Token Ring networks are connected to other LANs, requiring the use of a bridge or router. Bridges and routers are hardware and software devices that connect individual networks.

Figure 11.3 shows the actual cabling. The cable used is four-wire, which consists of two shielded twisted pairs. One pair is the main ring path, and the second pair is a secondary or backup path.

If you find a bad cable between two MAUs, remove the cable and the respective RI and RO ports will automatically self-short. Data will automatically flow on the backup path.

The self-shorting feature makes the Token Ring topology fault-tolerant. The backup path allows for the quick, continued operation of the ring if there is just a bad cable on the main cabling backbone. It also is a great aid for troubleshooting ring problems.

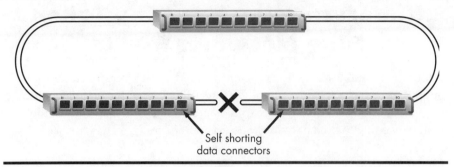

Figure 11.3 Token Ring cabling is four-wire, consisting of two shielded twisted pairs. The RI and RO ports are automatically self-shorting.

Figure 11.4 shows how the Token Ring network layout is a physical star but an electrical ring. This layout allows for great flexibility when designing and laying out the network.

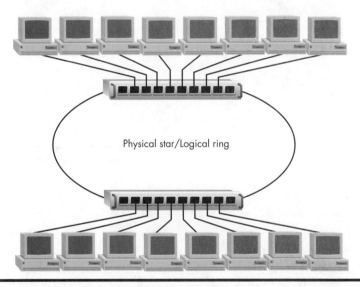

Figure 11.4 The Token Ring topology allows the network to form a physical star but an electrical ring, providing great flexibility for network design and layout.

The physical star/logical ring concept is the most sophisticated LAN topology on the market.

ETHERNET AND TOKEN RING OPTIMIZATION

Understanding How the Token Ring Network Works

Stations (PCs) gain access to the cabling medium through a token passed around the ring. The token is actually a three-byte frame that circulates through the ring, remaining in an idle state until a station needs to transmit on the ring. A station needing to transmit data waits to grab the token (see Figure 11.5).

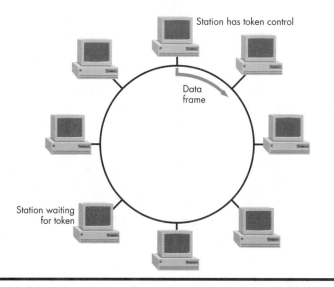

Figure 11.5 A station that needs to transmit data waits to grab the token.

Every station on the ring has the opportunity to grab the token, but can do so only when the token is not in use by another station.

Before the station retransmits the token, it appends an information frame to the token frame. When this occurs, the token becomes either a medium access control (MAC) or a logical link control (LLC) frame. Part of the information is the destination address or addresses for the information being sent.

After the destination station(s) receives the data, the token returns to the originating source station. If the source station is finished transmitting, it resets the token frame by removing any additional information appended to the packet (a process called *stripping*) and passing the token back onto the ring.

Downstream and Upstream

The two logical directions of travel on the ring are upstream and downstream. The direction of travel for data on the ring is always downstream.

A token is always transmitted to the next station in a downstream direction. A station that transmits the token is called the nearest active upstream neighbor (NAUN) with respect to the next active downstream station to which it transmits a token (see Figure 11.6).

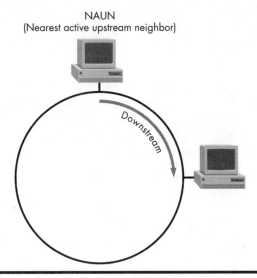

Figure 11.6 A station that transmits the token is called the NAUN of the station that receives the token.

NAUNs

The concept of the NAUN is important in the Token Ring environment because it is a direct reference point for controlling communications and addressing stations on the ring. One of the NAUN's most important roles is in the Neighbor Notification process. The Neighbor Notification process allows a ring station (RS) to learn its NAUN's address, and then to let its respective nearest active downstream neighbor know its address. See the "Neighbor Notification" section later in this chapter for more details.

ETHERNET AND TOKEN RING OPTIMIZATION

A NAUN can also isolate a ring failure to a fault area called the fault domain. When a failure occurs on the ring, the Token Ring architecture inherently locates the problem to the fault domain. The NAUN is used in Token Ring processes to locate the fault domain.

Addressing Schemes

Token Ring architecture dictates that each station on the ring be uniquely identified by a separate defined address. The three different address types are individual, group, and functional:

- **Individual addressing.** Each station is addressed uniquely across the ring.
- **Group addressing.** One or more stations are addressed. Stations defined as part of a common group address can be addressed by a broadcast to their group address. Broadcasting is a method by which a station on the ring communicates with one or more stations through a common address that the destination stations share.
- **Functional addressing.** Stations need to communicate with a station that provides common functions. Some functional addresses are predefined by the Token Ring architecture, and some are reserved for definition by the user as needed. The predefined functional addresses are as follows:

Configuration Report Server	C00000000010
Ring Error Monitor	C00000000008
Ring Parameter Server	C00000000002
Active Monitor	C00000000001
Bridge	C00000000100
LAN Manager	C00000002000

User-defined functional addresses can be assigned to C00000080000 through C00040000000.

Addresses can be defined by two different methods: universal administration and local administration. Universal administration means that stations on the ring are assigned unique individual addresses by the IEEE. In local administration, the stations on the ring are assigned unique individual addresses by a group or person other than the IEEE.

4Mbps Versus 16Mbps and Early Token Release

The main difference between 4Mbps and 16Mbps Token Ring is bandwidth. However, there are other differences as well. For example, 16Mbps Token Ring supports larger frames than does 4Mbps Token Ring. The 4Mbps Token Ring frames are about 4,500 bytes; 16Mbps Token Ring frames are four times that size, or 18,000 bytes. This increase in bandwidth allows for higher throughput of data.

Using 16Mbps Token Ring frames makes good sense for today's complicated environments, with applications such as database client/servers that need a larger network bandwidth.

Another noticeable difference in the 16Mbps speed is the introduction of early token release (ETR) into the Token Ring architecture. ETR allows two frames to travel on the ring at the same time. At 4Mbps, only one frame travels on the ring at any given time (see Figure 11.7).

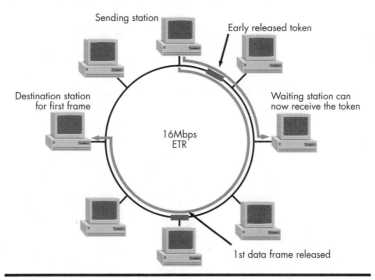

Figure 11.7 For 16Mbps Token Ring networks, ETR allows two data frames to travel on the ring at the same time.

ETR allows two frames on the ring because, at 16Mbps, data frames spend less time on the ring and more open bandwidth is available. The Token Ring architecture transmits idle characters, called *null characters*, to fill the open bandwidth. This is still a waste of bandwidth, but with 16Mbps/ETR, the sending station releases the token immediately after it sends the data frame. This differs from 4Mbps, which holds the token until it receives the old data frame back from the receiving station. A station waiting to transmit data can do so faster.

Currently, 16Mbps networks are most often used for backbone situations within large Token Ring topology environments.

Token Ring Technology Advances

In the early 1990s, Token Ring switching became a reality through technology advances by several manufacturers, including IBM and Bytex. Token Ring switching provides a cost-effective, high-performance capability for Token Ring networks that need an increase in bandwidth and associated performance. Bandwidth-intensive applications are now being deployed on Token Ring networks, and required increases in bandwidth are going to become a critical issue in the near future.

Token Ring switching products are currently expensive. They are also complex to implement and manage, compared to Ethernet switches. They are just starting to become a viable option for internetworks. The complexity is due to the fact that the Token Ring MAC protocol is deterministic and fault redundant. These capabilities have strengths for network operation but require a careful switching design.

The Token Ring switching products that are available today were developed through a migration of dedicated Token Ring switching. The dedicated Token Ring switching platform allows for the capacity of a Token Ring network to be increased by allowing a particular ring station to have a dedicated port to single Token Ring available for its own connectivity and configuration. The capacity of the single ring can then be increased even twofold by implementing full duplex adapters and full duplex port capabilities at the switched port level.

Currently, the ability to implement a dedicated Token Ring port along with a half duplex adapter is probably the most standard implemented configuration within Token Ring switching. However, full duplex Token Ring is available up to 32Mbps and is considered an industry standard.

In reviewing general Token Ring configurations that are in the field today, stations have to gain access to the Token Ring by grabbing the available Token, appending a data frame, and then transmitting it onto the respective 4- or 16Mbps Token Ring. Occasionally, there may be a condition where a Token Ring station requires a high-speed urgent access to the network. In this particular case, the Token has the capability at the physical layer to utilize the Access Control field in the Token to set the reservation and priority bits to transmit out with priority onto the ring. The Token would be grabbed, reservation bits would be flagged in the access control field, and then the particular Token would become a priority Token for a particular high-end station, such as a key imaging application server in a critical environment. However, most NOS and application suppliers do not usually modify the flags the access control field and utilize the priority. This is normally handled at the application layers. But the capability has been there since 1985, when Token Ring became a standard.

Understanding Token Ring Switching

One way to implement high-speed access on a Token Ring environment is to use Token Ring switching modules within the central hub of a Token Ring installation. Switching modules allow for creating internal Token Rings within the intelligent hubs. As an example, if a 16Mbps Token Ring network had an active 40 station count, each particular station would have an approximate divided portion of the 16Mbps Token Ring to allow for up to 0.4Mbps per station. But if a Token Ring switch was designed that could internally create four separate rings from the one 16Mbps ring, this would theoretically allow each station to have approximately 1.6Mbps of available bandwidth. This would increase bandwidth by four times. The switch essentially allows for creating more logical rings, dividing stations across internal rings, and managing bandwidth allocation.

Understanding Dedicated Token Ring

Dedicated Token Ring (DTR) allows for a separate Token Ring network to be created for one ring station. This is accomplished through implementing a unique direct connection between a ring station and a Token Ring switched port. The lobe cabling is basically used as a separate Token Ring between the ring station and the port on the switch. This way a particular station can have either its own 4Mbps or 16Mbps Token Ring instead of just having a portion of a complete ring. Essentially, this allows for an individual ring to be created for just one ring station and single port configuration.

In a standard Token Ring switched port configuration, stations and ports operate in half duplex operations. If a device becomes a critical device, such as a key server, it can now utilize a new full duplex capable adapter. The full duplex adapter utilizes all four wires in the Token Ring lobe cable and also operates at 32Mbps. This is dependent on the port of the Token Ring switch, which must be able to be configured to accommodate the 32Mbps speed.

Certain adapters in the industry, such as the IBM LAN streamers, have the capability to incorporate a full duplex operation on a dedicated Token Ring switched port.

This DTR design allows for immediate access to the Token instead of contending with all the other stations on a standard ring. This technology can be further advanced by incorporating network resource reservation. This feature allows a Token Ring switch to perform bandwidth management through monitoring and allocating bandwidth to specific ports as required. This will become critical when multimedia applications become more heavily deployed. Certain stations will be able to have DTR port assignments and access higher levels of bandwidth if required.

This technology advance was pioneered in late 1993 when IBM introduced the standard. Throughout 1993 and 1994, this finally became an 802.5 revision standard and now is considered a viable capability for Token Ring networks. Due to cost upgrades from half-duplex to full-duplex operation, many network operation managers have not chosen to make the switch from 16Mbps to 32Mbps full duplex at this time. Instead, basic Token Ring switching is becoming a viable option and is being implemented in internetworks. This allows for at least half-duplex Token Ring switching on port-to-port capabilities.

Other technology advances are starting to surface, such as ATM integration into Token Ring switches. Vendors such as Centillion now offer the capability for an ATM core LAN backbone to be implemented within the backplane of the switch. This allows the switch to have a high-speed backplane of over 5GB per second, which in turn allows for high-speed access and ATM technology essentially to be in place in the switch. The ATM technology offers direct cell switching between different Token Ring DTR ports that are available to the attached ring stations. Most Token Ring switches offer support for high-speed bridging protocols and loop prevention protocols such as Spanning Tree, Transparent, and even the standard IBM source routing and source routing transparent protocols.

New network management schemes are allowing the ports on a Token Ring switch to be managed through SNMP-based management systems, such as HP OpenView, IBM Network LAN Manager, and IBM Netview. This allows for virtual LAN configuration between the switched ports, so that when a particular internal Token Ring switch that is virtually configured becomes overloaded, certain DTR ports from that ring can be automatically assigned to other virtual internal switch Token Rings. This allows for a virtual departmental ring configuration where groups of 4Mbps and 16Mbps rings can be connected through DTR ports directly to a switch. When certain rings attached to the switch experience overload conditions, the switch can reduce and balance the load.

Some of the Token Ring switches have high-speed backplanes and processing engines that operate with the RISC processor configurations with actual speeds over 100 MIPS. Internal packet engines are designed within the Token Ring switch so that each DTR port is considered almost a direct connection to the ATM core backplane. This allows for extreme high-speed access.

Some of the new switch virtual configurations allow routing to occur at the DTR-port-to-DTR-port level. Specifically, protocols, physical addresses, and specific patterns of data can be filtered. This allows for high-speed configurations to occur along complex filtering. Essentially, these switches are actually incorporating routing. For example, this technology allows a switch to monitor a frame all the way down to the source routing information contained in the Routing Information Field (RIF), store the information in RIF allocated buffers, examine for NetBIOS broadcast levels, and even learn NetBIOS broadcast names and store the names throughout the particular switch. Depending on the configuration setup, this could reduce NetBIOS broadcast levels in Token Ring environments where NetBIOS broadcast levels are high.

The new switches offer the capability for a true collapsed backbone environment. This will allow the creation of multiple server rings that can be balanced at the switch. With the high-speed switch capability available in the backbone ATM core technology, a switch can allow for server backbone rings to be brought into a true collapsed fashion.

Due to advances in Token Ring switching and DTR, providing certain sites with their own straight DTR port may eliminate the need to upgrade 4Mbps adapters.

Essentially, 4Mbps rings can now be broken into much smaller rings when they are overloaded through a connection directly to a switch. The high cost of these products must be considered when migrating. The capability to jump directly to well over 100Mbps in the standard Token Ring protocol is somewhat of a limitation. However, Token Ring switching technology is available, working, and includes the required management schemes. Technology is available today that is not part of the Token Ring standard, yet provides high-speed access at 100Mbps. The two technologies that offer the easiest integration with Token Ring are 100Mbps VG AnyLAN and Fiber Distributed Data Interface (FDDI).

High-Speed Upgrade Options from Token Ring

One upgrade choice, 100 VG AnyLAN, is offered as a migration path from standard 16Mbps Token Ring. The 100 VG 802.12 standard allows for 100Mbps data transfer to occur over voice grade type cable. This supports frame type connections to not just Token Ring environments but also Ethernet environments. Specifically, 100Mbps VG AnyLAN supports frame type forwarding for both 802.3 and 802.5 packet standards. The technology scheme of 100Mbps VG AnyLAN is to implement a centralized high-speed topology that can interface to both Token Ring and Ethernet. This creates strong integration and upgrade migration possibilities for Token Ring.

The Demand Priority Access (DPA) scheme allows for a ring station or an Ethernet station to initiate a data transfer request to a VG AnyLAN hub. The hub then acknowledges the data transfer and allows the transmission to occur. In this deterministic protocol approach, the hub determines if the Token Ring or Ethernet station can enter the 100Mbps VG AnyLAN environment. There are four pairs of wires being utilized for both the transmit and receive data capability. Each pair of wiring in the 100 VG AnyLAN configuration allows for up to 25Mbps of data transmission to occur. With all four wires utilized, this results in a 100Mbps configuration.

One of the biggest advantages of 100Mbps VG AnyLAN is that there are two levels of priorities available. Normal priority is brought forward in a queuing approach when high-priority requests occur from an AnyLAN connected station. Normally all station requests are forwarded to the AnyLAN hub in a nondirect fashion. High priority can also be engaged for stations that need immediate access to the AnyLAN hub. The hub will give a station high priority only if the configuration is set. The AnyLAN hub also can allow for network delays to be detected and intercepted immediately. For example, if a delay of more than 300 milliseconds is encountered from an AnyLAN attached station, the DPA scheme will automatically forward the frame. This allows for minimum propagation delay in the internetwork.

Design of the VG network calls for a main centralized hub in the configuration. Normally, key internetwork devices such as servers and routers may be attached to the centralized hub. The main centralized hub is intended to dictate to the lower-level hubs. A tiered hub approach, built into the overall network design, allows for the centrally controlled hub to converse with the lower-level hubs and dictate when data transmission takes place. The central controller hub monitors and dictates the data access method of DPA.

For example, if an AnyLAN station is requesting data that is connected to a lower-level hub, the transmission will eventually reach the central controller hub. The central controller hub will assign whether or not the station transmission can be brought forward for an immediate server request. If it is a high-priority transmission request, the hub may allow it to take precedence. The main central controlling hub can instruct the lower-level hub to allow the request of service immediately or it can demand that the transmission be brought forward in the next queue.

The type of cabling that is supported in 100 VG AnyLAN is Category 3, 4, or 5 UTP cable, and Category Type 1 STP-based cable. Data rates of 100Mbps are somewhat sensitive on Category 3 UTP cable, even though they are supported. Crosstalk may occur and other performance problems are possible. 100Mbps VG Any LAN does allow for connections between Ethernet and Token Ring environments, and essentially becomes a centralized cloud type network. It is not recommended to exceed approximately 250 addresses on the centralized hub configuration. Basically, the centralized hub will not allow more than 250 addresses to transverse the addressing scheme. Most advances in the 100Mbps VG AnyLAN configurations have come from IBM and HP development teams. With the capability of two priority schemes, a controlling hub, a tiered hub configuration, and the ability to interface in both Token Ring and Ethernet environments, 100 VG AnyLAN becomes a viable high-speed internetworking topology.

Another high-speed LAN topology that offers a viable integration upgrade from Token Ring is FDDI. FDDI has been around for years, but it has been quite costly. Due to the difference of frame types involved and the complexity of the physical layer management scheme, it has been somewhat of a dark world to most network managers. But FDDI is becoming more cost-effective. In an Ethernet environment, it would make sense to migrate from a 10BASE-T environment to a true 100 BASE-T environment. In a true Token Ring environment that requires fault redundancy and a high-speed technology, FDDI may be the answer.

FDDI offers a true token passing scheme with deterministic protocol, such as standard 4Mbps and 16Mbps Token Ring. If a network manager were considering an upgrade to 32Mbps DTR full duplex Token Ring, an evaluation of 100Mbps FDDI might be warranted. FDDI can also be integrated in a true environment with Ethernet compatibility, but it is seen as a more logical upgrade for Token Ring.

Although this book does not cover the full FDDI configurations, here is a basic explanation of FDDI operation. When a station wishes to enter the ring, it will test its linking configuration just like the ring insertion process in the standard 4- to 16Mbps Token Ring. It will then have to receive a Token, and once it has the Token it can transmit on the network. In FDDI network operation, a station has the ability to transmit more than one frame across the ring. This allows for an advantage over the standard 1- or 2-frame transmission that is available in 4Mbps and 16Mbps configurations.

Bandwidth allocation management is another advantage of FDDI. Bandwidth allocation is possible due to the fact that there are two types of bandwidth allocation types: Synchronous Bandwidth Allocation (SBA) and Asynchronous Service Bandwidth Allocation.

Synchronous bandwidth allocation allows for managers to assign a fixed amount of bandwidth to a specific FDDI station that may be critical, such as a server or a router. Stations that have SBA can take priority on an FDDI network. If a station is a dedicated asynchronous service station, it will wait to receive the Token before it can transmit and does not have priority over an SBA station.

Again, in an FDDI network, there is still a Token being passed around the ring, and each station maintains a Token Ring Rotation Time for the ring and an internal TRT timer that is constantly counting and waiting to receive the Token. When the station receives a Token, it will compare the Token received time for the ring to its internal Token Ring Rotation Timer, which is built into the NIC card. If the actual TRT is less than the Token Ring Rotation Timer, it can grab the Token and then send data. But if its own Token Ring Rotation Timer exceeds the Token Transmit Time received, it has to wait before it can grab the Token and transmit. This would only be true to stations that are running asynchronous mode. Stations that have SBA take priority in this case.

FDDI design allows for Single Attached Stations (SAS) and Dual Attached Station (DAS) configurations. It also allows for dual fiber configurations across the complete ring. Overall, FDDI is a viable option because it offers fault-tolerant capability built into the configuration of standard single attached rings or dual attached backbone ring configurations.

Another feature similar to Token Ring is the physical layer management scheme. Just as Token Ring has a MAC layer protocol to allow for fault redundancy in the NIC operation, FDDI also has a viable MAC layer protocol type configuration that utilizes a protocol labeled Station Management (SMT). This allows the protocols at the physical layer to constantly monitor the integrity of NICs in FDDI. These features allow for frame information to be checked out step by step, but does create an overhead operation. FDDI should be checked out as a viable option for high-speed network configurations related to 4 and 16Mbps Token Ring.

Differential Manchester Encoding

Data transmission on the ring medium is performed using a symbol format called Differential Manchester Encoding (see Figure 11.8). Occurring at the physical layer, the code is produced by synchronizing a half-bit clock signal against a bit slot. A standard digital zero and one pulse form can be represented.

ETHERNET AND TOKEN RING OPTIMIZATION

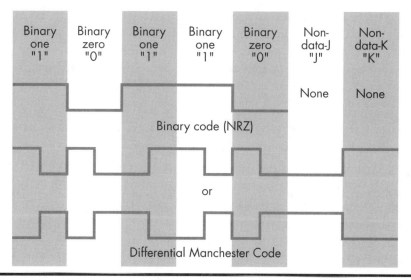

Figure 11.8 The symbol coding for data transmission on a Token Ring network is according to Differential Manchester Encoding.

A zero (0) is represented when a positive or negative transition is at the beginning of a bit slot; a one (1) is represented when no transition at all is at the beginning of a bit slot. A transition will always be at the middle of a bit slot because of the half-bit clock. The resulting symbol is a blended code that provides a unique framing method critical to the starting and ending delimiter frame sequence timing.

Frame Types

Token Ring architecture has three different frame types:

- **Token frame.** A three-byte frame that circulates the ring as a control signal.
- **Data frame.** This frame carries either MAC information or LLC information. MAC information is used to manage the flow of traffic on the ring. LLC information is the user data information to be transmitted on the ring.
- **Abort sequence frame.** This is used to clear the ring when a frame has a problem. The station that currently has control of the token (the

originating station) transmits an abort sequence frame if it detects a problem with the current data frame.

Controlling the Ring Environment

This section discusses the 802.5 IEEE Standard Frame Format frame types in detail.

Management Roles of the Ring

The physical layer of Token Ring is managed through a group of functional roles that are part of the Token Ring architecture. Every station on the ring includes an NIC that contains an Agent. The Agent communicates with certain Token Ring management stations on the ring through MAC frame transmissions. The management station roles are predefined by the Token Ring architecture.

The roles played by these stations are important when it comes to maintaining ring communication integrity. These roles include local ring management roles and ring management server roles. Local ring management roles synchronize communications on a local ring. The ring management server roles interact with the LAN Manager/IBM SNA environment. The ring management roles use the IBM Network Management (IBMNM) protocol to communicate with each other. Some of the management roles do not restrict the stations to only the management role assigned. These stations also can function as general ring stations. The individual role descriptions described in the following sections specify for which management roles this is true.

The ring management roles are:

- Standby monitor (SM)
- Active monitor (AM)
- Configuration report server (CRS)
- Ring parameter server (RPS)
- Ring error monitor (REM)
- LAN bridge server (LBS)
- LAN reporting mechanism (LRM)

Standby Monitors (SMs)

SMs are not solely defined by management functions;t rather they are all general RSs on the ring. SMs do act in local management roles at times because they are responsible for detecting failures that may occur with the active monitor. If the SMs do not detect an Active Monitor Present (AMP) MAC frame on the ring, they go into contention for the active monitor (AM) role. See the Token Claiming section later in this chapter for more information about SMs going into contention to win the AM role.

The Agent on the NIC of every RS is involved in MAC conversations with key management stations, such as the AM, CRS, RPS, REM, LBS, and LRM. SMs communicate with the management stations when they need to engage in ring-control conversations. The management stations themselves also may initiate the conversation, to access certain information from an SM about the station itself or to inquire about the current frame it is controlling. SMs may also request certain important ring parameters from one of the management stations, as discussed later in this chapter.

Active Monitor (AM)

The AM is the main communication manager on the ring. It is responsible for maintaining key transfer of data and control information balanced between all the stations on the ring. Token Ring architecture looks to the AM continually for stabilization reference points to maintain ring integrity (see Figure 11.9).

The AM has seven main responsibilities:

1. Maintaining the master clock
2. Initiating Neighbor Notification
3. Monitoring Neighbor Notification
4. Maintaining proper ring delay
5. Monitoring token and frame transmission
6. Detecting lost tokens and frames
7. Purging the ring

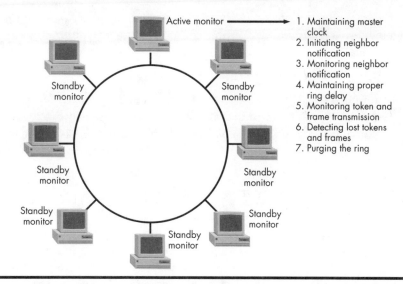

Figure 11.9 One station on the ring serves as the AM; other active stations on the ring serve as SMs.

Maintaining the Master Clock

The AM is responsible for maintaining the ring's master clock, which controls timing on the Token Ring network by making sure that all station clocks are synchronized. The master clock references Token Ring protocol timers inherent to the Token Ring architecture.

Initiating Neighbor Notification

The AM regularly transmits an AMP MAC frame. The frame is transmitted minimally every seven seconds by T(Neighbor_Notification), one of the Token Ring protocol timers built into the Token Ring architecture. The AM is responsible for broadcasting this frame to every station on the ring. The transmission of this frame starts the Neighbor Notification process.

Monitoring Neighbor Notification

The AM maintains a constant status of the Neighbor Notification process as it occurs on the ring. It uses the Token Ring protocol timers to monitor the process. If any interruptions occur during the process, the AM takes appropriate management steps through MAC frame communication to stabilize the ring.

Maintaining Proper Ring Delay

The AM injects a 24-bit delay pattern into the ring. This ensures that a token sent from an originating station is completely transmitted to the destination station before returning to the originating station. Without the 24-bit delay, ring overlap could occur. The 24-bit delay sent by the AM ensures proper ring delay.

Monitoring Token and Frame Transmission

The AM interrogates the monitor bit in the Access Control field of every token and frame it intercepts. The AM uses the monitor bit as a reference point to check for completed frame transmission between stations on the ring. The AM checks if the bit has been reset by the last transmission on the ring. If the status is not correct, the AM purges the ring, as discussed later in this section.

Detecting Lost Tokens and Frames

The Token Ring architecture dictates that it should not take any longer than 10 milliseconds for a frame to circle the ring. The AM references a Token Ring protocol timer called T(Any_Token) for the 10-millisecond interval. The AM checks to make sure that it detects a starting delimiter from a frame or token within that timer period. If it does not see a frame and the timer expires, the AM purges the ring.

Purging the Ring

The AM broadcasts a Ring Purge frame when it has to clear the ring to originate a new token. This occurs when the AM detects a disruption on the ring in the active timing between stations or the improper execution of a Token Ring process. When the AM generates the frame, it resets all the RSs to Normal Repeat mode and resets all Token Ring protocol timers. This restarts the Neighbor Notification process.

Only one station on the ring plays the role of AM at any given time. The role is assigned dynamically according to Token Ring actions on the ring. Any RS on the ring can be assigned the role. The active RS with the current highest active address on the ring that wins a process called Token Claiming becomes the AM.

Configuration Report Server (CRS)

The configuration report server is a ring management server role played by one RS in a multiple-ring environment in which ring management is to be accomplished from a central point. The central point is the Token Ring LAN Manager console. (LAN Manager is discussed later in this section.) Every ring in a multiple-ring environment has one CRS present. The CRS can also act as a general RS.

The main responsibility of the CRS is to collect important statistical information from the ring and forward that information to the LAN Manager console. The information includes individual RS statistics such as NAUN changes and New Monitor MAC frame transmissions.

The CRS also can change and set individual RS parameters on a ring as requested by the LAN Manager console. The LAN Manager console, for example, can request that the CRS remove an RS from the ring.

Ring Parameter Server (RPS)

The RPS plays both local management and ring management server roles. Every ring usually has one RS that acts as an RPS. This role is also critical in a multiple-ring environment because the RPS communicates certain local-ring information to the Token Ring LAN Manager console. The RPS also can act as a general RS.

The RPS provides three main services:

- The RPS is responsible for sending ring initialization parameters to all new RSs attaching to the ring. This information includes the logical ring number, the RPS version level, and the soft-error timer value.
- The RPS monitors the RSs by requesting their ring station address, ring station microcode level, and NAUN's address. The RPS uses this information to monitor all RSs to ensure that their attachment status is consistent with normal ring operational parameters.
- The RPS communicates regularly with the LAN Manager console to forward all the current RS status information that it collects.

Ring Error Monitor (REM)

No troubleshooting role is more important than that of the REM. The REM's sole purpose is gathering ring errors as a reference for troubleshooting ring problems. The REM can play both local management and ring management server roles. The REM usually does not act as a general RS; it is dedicated to the process of gathering error statistics.

The REM performs three main functions:

- The REM collects soft and hard errors from all stations that generate errors on the ring. Each RS's Agent must transmit any errors to the functional address of the REM.
- The REM analyzes the soft errors it receives and decides if Token Ring thresholds are exceeded. If the REM determines that they have been, it attempts to isolate the error to a fault domain.
- The REM is responsible for forwarding all errors it receives to the LAN Manager functional address.

The REM is the role that most Token Ring protocol analyzers assume when they are used on the ring for troubleshooting.

LAN Bridge Server (LBS)

The LBS monitors important statistical information about data routed between two or more rings connected by a bridge. The LBS is a ring management server role.

The LBS communicates the statistics it gathers to the Token Ring LAN Manager console. The LBS also can act as a general RS.

Most multiple-ring environments use the LBS function to keep the LAN Manager updated about dynamic changes that occur on the routing channels between RSs on different rings. The LBS also monitors the actual performance of a bridge on the ring by counting the number of frames actually transmitted through the bridge and by detecting any lost or discarded frames that travel through the bridge.

LAN Reporting Mechanism (LRM)

The LRM is a ring management server function responsible for maintaining communication between a LAN Manager console and any remote management servers. Even though the LRM is defined as a ring management server itself, the LRM is usually collocated within each of the other ring management servers (see Figure 11.10).

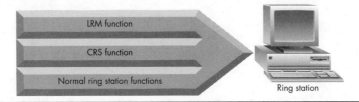

Figure 11.10 A station can play other roles besides that of LAN reporting mechanism.

LAN Manager and SNA Relationship

It should now be apparent that the main purpose of the Token Ring management components is to provide a centralized point from which to manage a complete Token Ring environment.

The central point is a function called the LAN Manager. The LAN Manager interacts with all the ring management servers described previously to collect, analyze, and log statistical data about the whole Token Ring environment. In a multiple-ring configuration, the ring management servers communicate through the LRM to constantly update the LAN Manager with vital ring statistics. The LAN Manager can take necessary management actions based on the information it receives from the other management servers. The LAN Manager function usually resides within a dedicated console, but the function can be collocated within other ring management servers. IBM has a product called LAN Manager that provides a ring with both the REM and LAN Manager functional addressees. Some third-party companies have developed products that use the LAN Manager functional address so that their products can collect and manipulate the data addressed to a LAN Manager console.

ETHERNET AND TOKEN RING OPTIMIZATION

The LAN Manager function also illustrates that IBM has created a function that blends directly into its SNA. SNA is IBM's ultimate design scheme for how IBM hardware and software should communicate over a data communications network. SNA was originally conceived for IBM's mainframe arena, but with the birth of LANs it has become the key access method for LAN-to-IBM host communications.

An SNA network has certain defined communication points. The main three are:

- Systems services control points (SSCPs)
- Physical units (PUs)
- Logical units (LUs)

An SNA network uses these points to establish communication throughout the mix of software and hardware entities within a computing environment (see Figure 11.11).

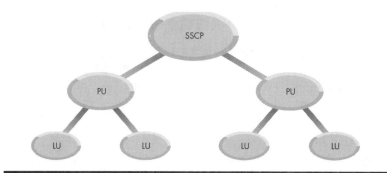

Figure 11.11 The three main communication points in an SNA network.

The SSCP, the main control point in an SNA network, controls communication to a PU, which in turn can communicate with LUs. Through updates in the SNA structure, two LUs can now communicate with each other through multiple SSCPs. This is called a LU-LU session, which allows two remote PCs on remotely different LANs to communicate with each other directly through the SNA architecture (see Figure 11.12).

This book does not cover SNA. To get a full understanding of the SNA architecture and concepts, refer to the SNA source listed in Appendix B.

The Token Ring architecture allows the LAN Manager to communicate with the SNA environment through an SSCP. This makes the Token Ring architecture the most comfortable way to interface with an IBM-host environment.

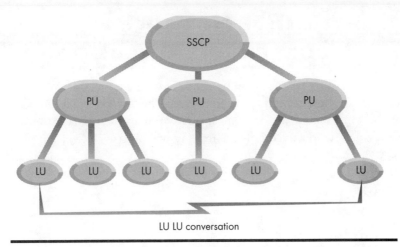

Figure 11.12 LU-to-LU sessions allow remote PCs on different LANs to communicate with each other by means of the SNA architecture.

Figure 11.13 shows an overall view of how the Token Ring management roles and the LAN management roles interact.

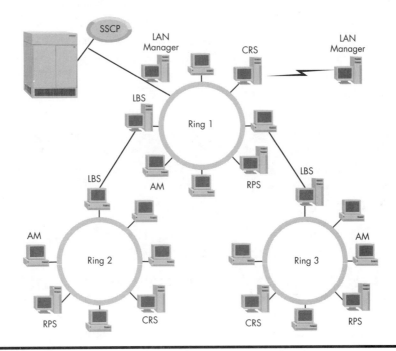

Figure 11.13 Interaction of Token Ring and LAN management roles: LAN manager, SSCP, AM, CRS, RPS, and LBS.

IBM Network Management Direction

IBM has a clear direction for a network management scheme to address the internetworking concerns for Token Ring in the 1990s. Through a group of new IBM network management platforms, it is now possible to manage multivendor, multiprotocol networks in complete harmony with a base Token Ring platform.

IBM's new introductions include three key network management elements:

- Netview 6000
- LAN Netview
- LAN Network Manager

IBM Netview 6000 is a network management system based on an SNMP that runs on an IBM RS6000 workstation. Basically, this version of Netview 6000 works with Transmission Control Protocol/Internet Protocol (TCP/IP) based environments and interrelates with Token Ring and SNA-based internetworks.

LAN Netview works with an open platform approach to support multiple versions of DOS, OS/2, LAN Server, and Windows software products. The combination of these IBM network management platforms has the capability of tying together many third-party software products into an overall management platform for Token Ring.

The last piece of the puzzle is IBM LAN Network Manager, which can monitor the entire physical layer of a Token Ring network.

Working together, these products offer the capability to view a Token Ring network's overall health and performance from almost any viewpoint, including SNA workstations, SNMP workstations, and general Token Ring network management products.

Understanding Token Ring Communication

Every station must go through a Ring Insertion process to attach itself to a Token Ring network. This process usually begins when activated by the station user either by turning on a station or by activating a network start program. (Ring Recovery also can start the process, as discussed later in this section.) A station is not considered an active SM until it completes a five-phase Ring Insertion process.

Phase 0: Lobe Media Check/Physical Insertion

The lobe media check test occurs when the NIC transmits the Lobe Test MAC frame to the MAU port, which tests the loop bit error rate between the NIC and the MAU port. If the frame is received back okay, the NIC sends the station attach signal (phantom DC current) through the station lobe cable to activate the MAU port to which it is going to attach. When this occurs, the station physically connects to the ring through the MAU port (see Figure 11.14).

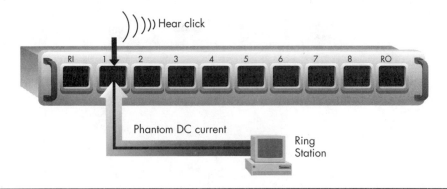

Figure 11.14 A ring station physically attaches to the MAU during Phase 0 of the ring insertion process.

During Phase 0, you can hear the MAU port click. The click is the sound of a relay opening in the port hardware.

Phase 1: Monitor Check

A station that has just connected to the ring next starts its T(ATTACH) Token Ring protocol timer. While this timer is running, the station looks to see if an AM is on the ring. The station waits to see if it receives one of three MAC frames: Active Monitor Present, Standby Monitor Present, or Ring Purge.

If the station detects one of the three MAC frames before the timer expires, it assumes an AM is present on the ring, and moves on to Phase 2. If the station does not detect one of the three frames, it initiates the Token Claiming process.

Phase 2: Duplicate Address Verification

The main purpose of this phase is to ensure that no other station on the ring has the same address as the station trying to attach. The station generates a Duplicate Address Test MAC frame onto the ring. The MAC frame is addressed to the station that transmits it, so the same station should receive the frame back; if it does, no other station on the ring has the same address. It also tests the capability of the station to receive frames. If the station does not receive the frame back, it removes itself from the ring and restarts the Ring Insertion process (see Figure 11.15).

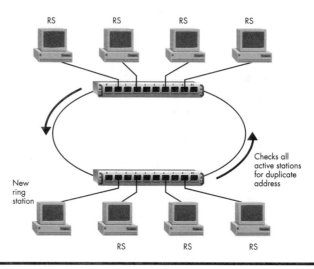

Figure 11.15 Duplicate address verification occurs during Phase 2 of the ring insertion process. If a new station receives its Duplicate Address Test frame back, it knows no other station on the ring has its address.

Phase 3: Neighbor Notification

During this phase, the station participates in the Neighbor Notification process for the first time. The station learns the address of its NAUN and notifies its nearest active downstream neighbor of its own address. If any interruption occurs during this process (such as beaconing), the station removes itself from the ring and restarts the Ring Insertion process (see Figure 11.16).

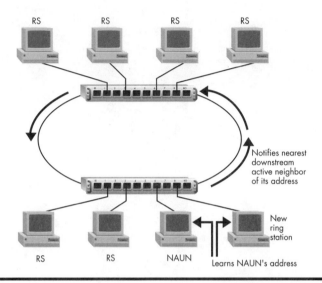

Figure 11.16 A new ring station participates in Neighbor Notification for the first time, learning the address of the NAUN and notifying its nearest active downstream neighbor of its address.

Phase 4: Request Initialization

Every RS has its own preconfigured default operational parameters for the local ring number and soft error report timer values. The Request Initialization phase allows an RPS if present on the ring to check the integrity of every new station attempting Ring Insertion.

During this phase, the new station generates a Request Initialization MAC frame on the ring addressed to the RPS. This frame lets the RPS know that a station has attached to the ring and is ready to accept any special operational parameters that the RPS has available for the ring. The RPS then sends an Initialize Ring Station MAC frame, which sets the new station for the correct ring number and soft error report timer values. If the RPS does have any special parameters, it transmits them to the new station.

If the RPS sees any problem with the information included in the Request Initialization MAC frame or if too many stations are on the ring, it notifies a

ETHERNET AND TOKEN RING OPTIMIZATION

LAN Manager console. The LAN Manager console then notifies the CRS to transmit a Remove Ring Station MAC frame to the new RS, which causes the RS to be removed from the ring.

When all five phases are complete, the new station becomes a physically and logically attached RS (see Figure 11.17).

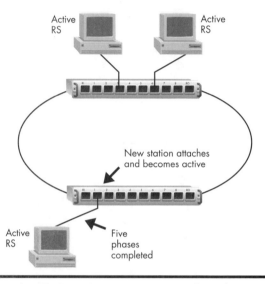

Figure 11.17 When the ring insertion process is complete, the new station becomes a physically and logically attached ring station active on the network.

Token Claiming

Only one RS on the ring is designated as the AM. Token Claiming is the process during which SMs go into contention to win the AM role. Token Claiming occurs on the ring when one of three conditions arises:

- A new station attaches to the ring but does not detect an AM on the ring. This can occur if the new station does not receive an AMP MAC frame on the ring during the Ring Insertion process.
- The AM cannot detect any frames on the ring and its T(Receive_Notification) Token Ring protocol timer expires.
- An SM detects the absence of an AM or cannot detect any frames on the ring, and its T(Good_Token) or T(Receive_Notification) protocol timers expire.

Not all stations participate in the Token Claiming process because the default mode is for a station not to participate. Stations operate under one of two main modes during this process: Claim Token Transmit mode or Claim Token Repeat mode.

All stations participating in the Token Claiming process go into contention to win the AM role. The station with the highest Token Ring address wins the process. When one of the three previously described conditions occurs, the process is initiated by either an SM or the AM.

The stations that participate are in Claim Token Transmit mode. Stations that do not participate are in Claim Token Repeat mode. The station that first initiates the process enters the Claim Token Transmit mode by generating a Claim Token MAC frame addressed to itself onto the ring. Each station that receives the frame enters the Claim Token Repeat mode.

Every station in the Claim Token Repeat mode compares its address to the address in the Claim Token MAC frame it receives. If its address is higher, it also becomes a participant in the Token Claiming process by generating its own Claim Token MAC frame. This process continues around the ring until a Token Claiming participant receives its own Claim Token MAC frame back three times. When this occurs, that station assumes that it has the highest address, and it wins the AM role (see Figure 11.18).

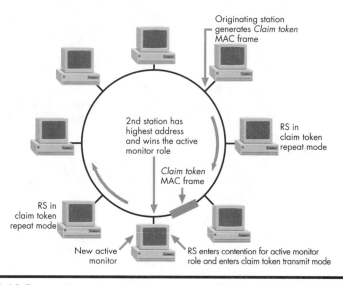

Figure 11.18 During the token claiming process, all the participating ring stations on the network vie for the active monitor role. The station with the highest address assumes the AM role.

Priority Access

Priority Access is the qualifying method by which all RSs attain a certain priority for their turn to gain control of the token. Only one station at a time can have control of the token. The token frame and MAC/LLC frames contain a field called the Access Control field. The Access Control field is a one-byte field that controls how a station actually references a frame or token for access to the ring.

In the Access Control field, the first three bits are the priority bits, which indicate the current priority of a certain token or frame. The last three bits of the Access Control field are the reservation bits, which an RS uses to request a certain priority to gain access to the ring. The priority bits and reservation bits range from 111 (the highest priority) to 000 (the lowest priority). All RSs can request and raise the priority level of the ring. RSs use the Access Control fields to look at both the priority of a given frame or token and to reserve the use of a frame or token for a certain priority.

The Access Control field also contains a bit called the monitor bit, which continuously circles the ring to prevent a frame or token from controlling the ring. The monitor bit can be set to either a 0 or a 1 state. When any RS transmits a frame or token onto the ring, it sets the monitor bit to the 0 state. One of the checks that occurs when an AM interrogates a frame or token is to check the state of the monitor bit. The AM sets this bit to the 1 state if it is in a 0 state.

If the bit is received at the AM in a 1 state, the AM assumes that the frame or token has circled the ring at least once without being received back at its originating station. The AM resets the bit to a 0 state and generates the Ring Purge process to establish ring recovery. This helps to ensure priority fairness on the ring.

The priority access method is a truly fair system. The mechanism ensures that all stations have an equal chance to access the ring. This aim of equality is enforced in that a station that raises the priority level of the ring has to return the priority level back to its original state.

Neighbor Notification

Neighbor Notification is a logical consecutive process by which every RS is informed of its NAUN's address.

Every MAC/LLC frame has in its structure a Frame Status (FS) field—a one-byte field that reflects the current status of the respective frame. Within the FS field are two important bits: the addressed recognized bits (A bits) and the frame copied bits (C bits). The Neighbor Notification process then does the following:

1. Looks at the A bits to verify if the frame is currently recognized by the last station source address (SA) included in the frame
2. Looks at the C bits to see if the SA copied the frame successfully

The AM initiates the Neighbor Notification process, and the following events occur:

1. The AM initiates the process by generating an AMP MAC frame onto the ring. When it starts the process, it sets an internal flag signaling that the process is starting. The frame is broadcast on the ring to all stations. The A and C bits can be set to one of two logical states, 0 and 1. When the AM generates the frame, the A and C bits in the FS field are set to a 0 state.
2. The first active SM that receives the AMP MAC frame resets the A and C bits to the 1 state. Next, the SM copies the frame into its buffer. It stores the Upstream Neighbors Address (UNA) from the SA field of the AMP frame. It then starts its T(Notification_Response) timer. When the timer expires, the SM transmits a Standby Monitor Present (SMP) MAC frame back on the ring in an all-stations broadcast. The A and C bits in the SMP frame are reset to the 0 state.
3. The next active SM on the ring that receives the SMP frame repeats the preceding process.
4. This process continues around the ring until the AM copies the last SMP frame and then sets its internal flag.

This completes the Neighbor Notification process.

Normal Repeat Mod

Every RS has a state called Normal Repeat mode. When in this state, the RS can interrogate all the tokens and frames it receives and can properly copy and repeat them.

Ring Purge

The Ring Purge process is the attempted resetting of the ring to Normal Repeat mode. The AM initiates the Ring Purge process for four possible reasons:

1. When the AM detects an error condition on the ring, such as a lost token or frames, a disruption on the ring in the active timing between stations, or the improper execution of a Token Ring process
2. When the AM detects the M bit set to the 1 state in the Access Control field of a token or frame
3. To set the ring back to Normal Repeat mode
4. When the AM sees the T(Any_Token) timer expire

After the AM generates the frame, it waits to receive the frame back. If the AM receives the frame back, it assumes that the ring is stabilized and resets all Token Ring protocol timers. Next, the AM initiates the Neighbor Notification process to restart and put the ring back into Normal Repeat mode. If for some reason the AM does not receive the frame back, it enters Claim Token Transmit mode.

Beaconing

Beaconing is the Token Ring process that occurs when an RS generates a warning signal onto the ring after it sees a hard error occur with itself or with its NAUN. This warning signal is the Beacon MAC frame and has three important fields: the Beacon Generating Station Address, the NAUN, and the Beacon type. The Beacon type can help isolate the location of the hard error problem.

The Agent on every NIC can detect soft and hard errors on the ring. When an RS detects a hard error (such as a cable fault or an improper bitstream transmission), that respective station transmits the Beacon MAC frame onto the ring. The frame is addressed to all stations.

Note that if an REM is present on the ring, it is the key responder to this frame. The REM generates an Alert warning to the LAN Manager and records the error in a statistical log.

The station that transmits the Beacon MAC frame is not necessarily the faulty station. The main suspect is usually the NAUN of the station that generates the frame because every RS is in a listen/receive mode at Normal Repeat mode. But it is also possible that the failure area is either the beaconing station, the NAUN, or even the medium (cable) between the two stations. This logical area is defined by the Token Ring architecture as the fault domain (see Figure 11.19).

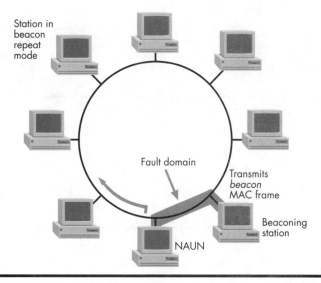

Figure 11.19 A fault domain is the logical area of a hard error fault in the Token Ring network.

Fault Domain

The fault domain is the logical area of a hard-error fault as determined by the Token Ring architecture. The architecture uses the beaconing process to isolate a failure to a fault domain.

The logical area includes three subcomponents:

1. The RS transmitting the Beacon MAC frame
2. The beaconing station's NAUN
3. The connection medium (cable) between the beaconing station and its respective NAUN

The fault-domain concept is a key factor in pinpointing the true location of the cause of failure. To locate the exact true point of failure within the fault domain, the Token Ring architecture uses the statistics it intercepts from the beaconing process to enter a testing phase called attempted auto-recovery, or auto-reconfiguration.

During attempted auto-recovery:

- An RS encounters a hard error and transmits a Beacon MAC frame to an all-stations' broadcast. The frame identifies the address of the beaconing station's NAUN.
- Every RS on the ring enters the Beacon Repeat mode, which means each RS copies and repeats the frame around the ring.
- The Token Ring architecture locates the fault domain.
- After the beaconing station's NAUN copies the Beacon MAC frame eight times, it removes itself from the ring and goes through a series of self-tests. These tests include the Lobe Media and Duplicate Address tests used in the Ring Insertion process.
- If the NAUN station fails any of the self-tests, it removes itself from the ring. The beaconing station then receives the Beacon MAC frame back, and it retransmits a token frame back onto the ring. At this point, the ring will have auto-recovered.
- However, if the NAUN station passes all the self-tests, it reinserts itself back onto the ring without going through the full Ring Insertion process. Then the beaconing station assumes that its NAUN test has passed, and it takes itself off the ring and goes through the same series of self-tests.
- If a beaconing station fails any of the self tests, it removes itself from the ring. The AM initiates a ring recovery by issuing a Ring Purge and restarts the Token Claiming process.
- If the beaconing station does not fail any of the self-tests, it also reinserts itself back onto the ring without going through the full Ring Insertion process. If this occurs, and a beaconing condition still exists, the problem requires manual troubleshooting. The ring cannot auto-recover, and all Token Ring operations are impaired. At this point, it is highly probable that the problem is with the cabling medium.

To summarize, the concepts of beaconing and fault domains allow for a hard error to be automatically located and eliminated with minimal effect on normal ring operations. These functions add to the fault-tolerance claims of the Token

Ring architecture.

Soft Error Counting

Soft errors are less serious errors that can occur on the ring. Classified as intermittent, these errors do not necessarily indicate the presence of a serious failure on the ring. When the ring encounters soft errors, the normal mode of operation is only temporarily disrupted.

When a soft error occurs, the Token Ring architecture attempts to go through a recovery process to log the soft error and stabilize the ring. Every RS maintains a group of counters to gauge the level of soft errors that it encounters.

The following steps occur after a soft error:

1. If an RS encounters a soft error, the RS's internal counter increments its soft error counter and starts a Token Ring protocol timer T(Soft_Error_Report).

2. When the timer expires, the RS generates onto the ring a Report Soft Error MAC frame addressed to the REM functional address.

3. After the RS transmits the Report_Soft_Error MAC frame, it resets its soft error counter and enters the normal mode of operation.

The Report Soft Error MAC frame includes the number of soft errors that occur, the RS transmitting station, its NAUN, and the classification type of the soft error.

Some errors that occur cause ring performance degradation, which can be measured by the number of ring recoveries that occur. Ring recovery is the process of the ring resetting itself back into a normal mode of operation. Ring recoveries are one of the statistics that can be recorded through protocol analysis. Ring reconfiguration is the logical process that occurs during Neighbor Notification when certain active RSs enter or leave the ring.

One last note on soft error counting: If the transmitting RS T(Soft_Error_Report) timer expires and does not transmit a Report Soft Error MAC frame, the AM detects the condition and transmits the Report Soft Error MAC frame onto the ring, addressed to the REM.

Hard Error Counting

Hard errors are more serious errors that can occur on the ring. A hard error is an actual solid failure. When an RS detects a hard error, it enters the beaconing/fault domain processes to attempt Ring Recovery.

The Ring Recovery process for hard errors is different from its soft error equivalent. When an RS encounters a soft error, the Ring Recovery process is usually successful in restoring the ring to normal operation. But with hard errors, the actual locating and resolving of hard failures may require that an RS be removed or that the cabling medium be repaired.

When hard errors occur, the REM works in conjunction with the LAN Manager console to provide an overall error-management strategy. This strategy effectively provides alert notification and statistical logging of errors that occur on the ring.

Finite State Machines

The Token Ring architecture defines the different modes of relationship between the Token Ring processes as finite state machines. As the Token Ring protocols interrelate on the ring, they are constantly changing states, meaning that the ring itself is always undergoing transitions in its actual mode of operation.

This is analogous to the human brain as it constantly enters different states of thought that cause us to take certain actions. The Token Ring architecture also undergoes constant changes in state, causing certain events on the ring that affect the status of the ring. This process is extremely dynamic.

Many finite state machines are on the ring. This presentation does not cover all the different states; for further information, see reference 1 in Appendix B.

Token Ring Protocol Timers

The Token Ring architecture includes a set of clock utilities called the *Token Ring protocol timers*, which are used to synchronize the protocols that interrelate on the ring. The architecture also uses the timers to reference proper communication and enters certain finite states depending on the protocol-related action.

Timer characteristics break down into four categories:

- The activation point of the timer

- The action of the timer
- The condition that cancels the timer
- The timing value or duration of the timer

The following sections detail each timer's specific role in the Token Ring architecture.

T(Attach)

The T(Attach) timer sets how long a station can stay in the Ring Insertion process. It is activated when a station enters Phase 1 (Monitor Check) of the Ring Insertion process. T(Attach) times out after an 18-second period if the Ring Insertion process encounters any problems and is not completed. The timer can be canceled earlier if the process is completed before the 18-second period.

T(Claim_Token)

The T(Claim_Token) timer sets the length of time that an RS can wait for an AM to win the Token Claiming process while in Claim Token Repeat mode or Claim Token Transmit mode. The timer starts when an RS enters either of the two modes. The timer can time out after one second if an AM is not selected. If the Token Claiming process is completed, this timer can be canceled.

T(Any_Token)

The T(Any_Token) timer sets the amount of time an AM can wait before it detects a starting delimiter sequence from a token or frame. The timer starts when the AM transmits its first token. The timer times out after 10 milliseconds if it does not detect a starting delimiter.

T(Physical_Trailer)

The T(Physical_Trailer) timer helps to detect improperly transmitted frames. The timer starts when a station transmits a frame. When the station receives the frame back, it attempts to strip the frame's ending delimiter. If the frame is not returned or is not properly copied in 4.1 seconds, the timer times out and increments a lost-frame counter.

The next attempts to enter Normal Repeat mode. A soft error may be counted, and the ring can possibly be purged by the AM.

T(Good_Token)

The T(Good_Token) timer helps monitor the ring for problems related to failure of the AM function. It starts at the beginning of the SM function and is reactivated when it detects a proper token/frame sequence on the ring. The timer detects loss of the AM and frame or bitstreaming, which is the unintentional continuous transmission of data. The timer times out in 2.6 seconds if it detects a failure, and the RS enters the Claim Token Transmit mode.

T(Response)

The T(Response) timer monitors the length of time an RS must wait before receiving a proper response to a transmitted frame. The timer starts when an RS transmits a frame that requires a response. The timer times out in 2.5 seconds if the RS does not see the response frame return, but it stops if the response frame is returned and properly copied. If the timer does time out, the station usually reattempts transmission.

T(Soft_Error_Report)

The T(Soft_Error_Report) timer is used to balance the length of time during which an RS can transmit a Report Soft Error MAC Frame. This balance allows the soft error counter to accrue multiple error counts without constantly transmitting the errors and congesting the ring. The timer starts when a ring station soft error counter is incremented. It times out in two seconds and generates a Report Soft Error MAC Frame.

T(Transmit_Pacing)

The T(Transmit_Pacing) timer helps monitor how long an RS must wait before transmitting Beacon and Claim Token MAC frames. The timer starts when an RS transmits a Beacon or Claim Token MAC frame. The timer times out in 20 milliseconds if the RS improperly transmits one of the frames. When the timer times out, the RS attempts to retransmit the appropriate frame.

T(Beacon_Transmit)

The T(Beacon_Transmit) timer helps to monitor the length of time an RS can transmit Beacon MAC frames before it removes itself from the ring to run a self-test. The timer starts when an RS transmits a Beacon MAC frame. If the RS detects Ring Recovery, the timer stops. If it does not detect recovery after 16 seconds, the timer expires and the RS removes itself and runs the self-tests.

T(Escape)

The T(Escape) timer is used to monitor how long an RS can stay in Beacon Repeat mode before it enters Claim Token Transmit mode. The timer starts when an RS receives a Beacon MAC frame. Every RS can stay in the Beacon Repeat mode for 200 milliseconds without copying another Beacon MAC frame. If it does not within 200 milliseconds, the timer expires, and the RS also enters Claim Token Transmit mode.

T(Ring_Purge)

The T(Ring_Purge) timer monitors the length of time the AM can stay in the Ring Purge process before it stops and enters Claim Token Transmit mode. The timer length is one second, starting at the beginning of the ring-purge process. When it times out, the AM enters Claim Token Transmit mode.

T(Neighbor_Notification)

The T(Neighbor_Notification) timer monitors the Neighbor Notification process. The timer starts when the AM transmits an AMP MAC frame. The timer runs for seven seconds. If it does not copy an SMP MAC frame in that time, the AM retransmits an AMP MAC frame and attempts to restart the Neighbor Notification process.

T(Notification_Response)

The T(Notification_Response) timer balances the delay between the time in which an RS receives either an SMP or an AMP MAC frame and attempts to transmit another SMP MAC frame back out onto the ring.

The timer starts when an RS receives an AMP or an SMP MAC frame. The timer runs for 20 milliseconds before transmitting an SMP MAC frame.

T(Receive_Notification)

SMs use the T(Receive_Notification) timer to verify that the Neighbor Notification process occurs in a timely manner on the ring. The timer starts at the beginning of the SM function. Its duration is 15 seconds, during which it expects to receive an AMP MAC frame. If T(Receive_Notification) times out, the SM enters Claim Token Transmit mode.

Examining 802.5 IEEE Standard Frame Format

As mentioned, the three different frame types are the token, the data, and the abort sequence. The following sections describe the three frame types at the sequence field level.

Token Frame

The token frame is a three-byte frame. It is the actual control signal for the ring. Figure 11.20 shows its format.

Token Frame

Starting Delimiter	Access Control	Ending Delimiter
SD	AC	ED
0 7	0 7	0 7

Figure 11.20 The format of the three-byte token frame.

Field 1—Starting Delimiter Field

The Starting Delimiter field signals the start of a token frame, a data frame, and the abort sequence. The field is one byte and is formatted as shown in Figure 11.21.

SD

Bit 0							Bit 7
J	K	0	J	K	0	0	0

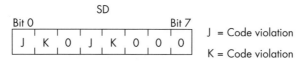

Figure 11.21 The starting delimiter field.

Bits 0 to 7 are always represented exactly as shown in Figure 11.21. The J and K bits are code violation symbols. They represent intentional improper transitions against the clock signal in the Differential Manchester Code. This combination is derived to uniquely exhibit the frame sequence as delimiter.

Field 2—Access Control Field

The Access Control field is a status byte that shows the current access level of a frame or token. The field is one byte and is formatted as shown in Figure 11.22.

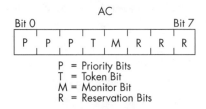

Figure 11.22 The one-byte-long access control field of the token frame.

Bits 1, 2, and 3 are the priority bits. They indicate the current priority of the token or frame. Priority bits range from 111 (the highest priority) to 000 (the lowest).

The fourth bit is the token bit, which distinguishes the frame as either a token frame or a data frame. If the bit is set to 1, the frame is a data frame; if the bit is a 0, it is a token frame.

The fifth bit is the monitor bit. The AM monitors this bit to prevent a frame or token from continuously circling the ring. The monitor bit can be set to either a 0 or 1 state. The AM always checks the status of this bit to ensure that it is in a 0 state.

Bits 6, 7, and 8 are reservation bits. An RS sets these bits to request a required priority for gaining access to the ring. Reservation bits range from 111 (highest priority) to 000 (the lowest).

Field 3—Ending Delimiter Field

The Ending Delimiter field signals the end of a token frame, a data frame, and the abort sequence. The field is one byte and is formatted as shown in Figure 11.23.

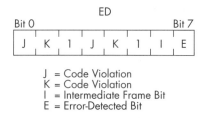

Figure 11.23 The one-byte ending delimiter field of a token frame.

Bits 0 to 5 are always represented exactly as shown in the figure. They represent intentional violations in the Differential Manchester Code, just as with the starting delimiter.

Bit 6 is the intermediate bit, and it signals that a frame is either the first frame or an intermediate frame of a multiple-frame transmission. The bit state may be either 0 or 1, depending on the frame transmission state.

Bit 7 is the error-detected bit; it flags a frame that contains possible errors in the frame-check sequence. The status should be 0 at normal state.

Data Frame

The data frame is a variable-length frame because it contains either ring control or data information. The frame includes ten mainframe sequences.

The frame carries a designation as either a MAC frame or an LLC frame. There are 25 MAC frame types, discussed later in this section. The LLC frames carry the protocol data unit (PDU), which envelopes the actual high-level user-data information transmitted on the ring. The PDU is detailed later in this section.

A data frame has multiple-frame sequences, including addressing, control, and data information (see Figure 11.24).

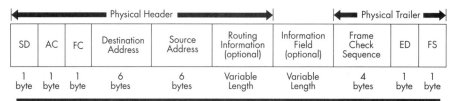

Figure 11.24 The data frame is a variable-length frame designated MAC or LLC.

Field 1

This first byte is a standard Starting Delimiter, as already discussed in the token frame description.

Field 2

The second byte is a standard Access Control field as discussed in the token frame description.

Field 3

The third byte is the Frame Control field, which defines whether a frame is an MAC or an LLC data frame. The field is one byte and is formatted as shown in Figure 11.25.

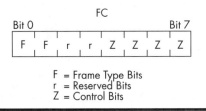

Figure 11.25 The one-byte frame control field designates a data frame as MAC or LLC.

Bits 0 and 1 designate the frame type. The breakdown is Status (00) = MAC frame; Status (01) = LLC frame; Status (10) and (11) = undefined frames.

Bits 2 and 3 are reserved for future IBM designations. Bits 4 to 7 are called control bits. If the frame is designated as an LLC frame, the bits are also reserved for future IBM designations.

If the frame is an MAC frame, the control bits designate how the frame is supposed to be copied into the destination station's input buffers. Each station has normal input buffers and express buffers. If the bits' value equals zero (0000), they are copied into the normal buffer. If the bits have a higher value, the frame is tagged as an express buffer frame, copied into the express buffer, and processed at the MAC layer immediately. A frame is usually only tagged express if the destination address's normal buffers are full.

Field 4

The next six bytes are the identifiers of the Destination Address. This is the address or addresses of the RS or group of stations that are supposed to receive the frame. The destination address identifier always occupies six bytes and is formatted as shown in Figure 11.26.

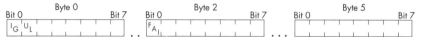

- Bit 0 of byte 0 (the I/G bit) indicates whether the destination address is an individual address (B '0') or group address (B '1').

- Bit 1 of byte 0 (the U/L bit) indicates whether the address is universally administered (B '0') or locally administered (B '1').

- Bit 0 of byte 2 (the functional address indicator) indicates whether a locally administered group address is a functional address (B '0') or a group address (B '1').

Figure 11.26 A data-frame destination address identifier.

Field 5

The next six bytes identify the Source Address. This is the address of the RS that generated the frame (also called the originating station). The source address identifier always occupies six bytes and is formatted as shown in Figure 11.27.

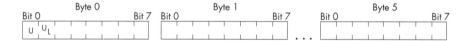

Figure 11.27 The six-byte source address identifier of a data frame.

Field 6

This field is called the Routing Information field and contains routing information if the frame is addressed to an RS on a ring other than the source ring in a multiple-ring environment. A bridge or router interrogates this field. The field has a variable length from two to 18 bytes and is formatted as shown in Figure 11.28.

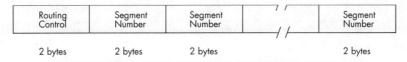

Figure 11.28 The routing information field of a data frame.

Field 7

This field is the Information field that carries MAC or LLC information. If the frame is designated as an MAC frame, this field starts with a two-byte sequence called a *length identifier* (LI). The LI marks the length of the information field.

The next two bytes are the major vector ID (MVID). The MVID indicates the main function and class of the MAC-frame information that follows next.

The next sequence is a variable-length sequence called the MAC subvector, which is the MAC control information data and is formatted as shown in Figure 11.29.

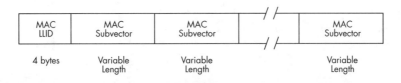

Figure 11.29 The format of the variable-length MAC subvector of a data frame's field 7.

If the frame is an LLC frame, this field is called an LLC PDU because it carries data and the necessary protocol information to exchange the data.

The LLC PDU is broken down as follows: The first sequence is a one-byte sequence called the destination service access point (DSAP), which labels the service access point for the following data.

The next byte is the source service access point (SSAP), which identifies the service access point that originated the data. The DSAP and SSAP are used locally by the path control layer in the Token Ring network protocol model. They are mainly referenced for addressing in an SNA environment.

The next field is called the Control field and is either one or two bytes long. It designates the type of data as being normal user data, supervisory, or unnumbered. The supervisory destination means that the data is control data for exchanging PDUs. The unnumbered destination means that the data is in unsequenced format.

The next field is a variable-length field containing the actual data information and is formatted as shown in Figure 11.30.

Figure 11.30 The variable-length information field contains the actual data.

Field 8

This field is called the Frame Check Sequence and is a 32-bit cyclic redundancy check (CRC). The CRC is an error-checking method that involves a calculation of the bit transmission at the sending and receiving ends of each RS. The CRC can detect errors in transmission by bit-calculation errors. The field is four bytes long and is formatted as shown in Figure 11.31.

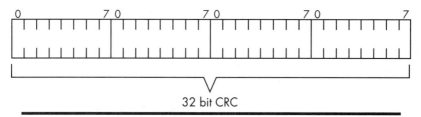

Figure 11.31 Field 8, the frame check sequence, contains a 32-bit CRC.

Field 9

This one-byte sequence is a standard Ending Delimiter, as discussed earlier in the token frame description.

Field 10

This field is called the Frame Status field and is a one-byte field that contains the current status of the data frame. It is formatted as shown in Figure 11.32.

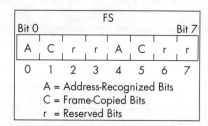

Figure 11.32 The format of field 10 of the frame status field.

Bits 0 and 4 are the address-recognized bits (A bits) used by the Neighbor Notification process to verify if the frame is currently recognized by the last station source address (SA).

Bits 1 and 5 are the frame-copied bits (C bits). The Neighbor Notification process looks at the C bits to see if the SA copied the frame successfully.

Bits 2, 3, 6, and 7 are reserved for future IBM designations.

Abort Sequence Frame

The Abort Sequence frame is a two-byte frame used to clear the ring when there is a problem with a frame. It is composed of a standard starting and ending delimiter. Figure 11.33 shows its format.

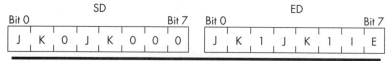

Figure 11.33 The format of the two-byte-long abort sequence frame.

DLC.LAN and DLC.MGR

The data link layer of Token Ring is called the DLC.LAN. The DLC.LAN is the layer that encodes, decodes, and routes MAC and LLC information.

The DLC.LAN encompasses a manager function called the DLC.MGR. The DLC.MGR is responsible for managing the control of information between both the LLC and the MAC layers at the data link level. This important manager also is used as a routing manager between the data link and other layers of the Token Ring network protocol model. Both the physical layer and the upper layers interact with the DLC.MGR for routing management. The SNA structure protocol model also interacts heavily with the DLC.MGR. Figure 11.34 depicts where the DLC.MGR resides.

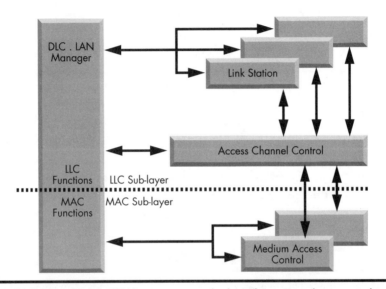

Figure 11.34 The DLC.LAN Manager controls the information that passes between the LLC and the MAC layers at the data link layer. It also acts as a routing manager between the data link and the OSI layers.

MAC Frame Types

The 25 MAC frames are the communication-protocol tools for the Token Ring architecture. They interact with all the Token Ring processes that occur on the medium. The 25 MAC frame types are:

1. Standby Monitor Present. This frame is mainly used during the Neighbor Notification process. An RS generates it to notify the Nearest Active Downstream Neighbor of its address.

2. Active Monitor Present. This frame notifies all SMs that an AM is functioning properly on the ring. The AM typically generates this frame to initiate the Neighbor Notification process.

3. Ring Station Initialization. An RS transmits this frame to the RPS to announce that it is a new RS and is ready to receive any special ring parameters.

4. Initialize Ring Station. This frame is generated by the RPS to respond to an RS's Ring Station Initialization MAC frame. The frame will set any special ring parameters.

5. Lobe Test. An RS generates this frame to test for a bit-error rate with its loopback path to the MAU port. The frame is generated before the actual attachment to the ring or during the beaconing process.

6. Duplicate Address Test. An RS generates this frame to ensure that no other stations on the ring have the same address. The frame is addressed to itself and also is generated before the actual attachment to the ring or during the beaconing process.

7. An RS generates this frame when it detects a hard error on the ring. It is important in identifying the fault domain, as discussed earlier.

8. Claim Token. An RS that wants to contend for the AM role generates this frame. It is used during the Token Claiming process.

9. Ring Purge. The AM transmits this frame to all RSs to clear the ring and set it back to Normal Repeat mode. It is generated in the event of an error. This frame is also used at the end of the Token Claiming process.

10. Report Neighbor Notification Incomplete. An RS transmits this frame during the Neighbor Notification process if it does not receive notification from its NAUN before its T(Neighbor_Notification) timer expires. The frame is transmitted to the REM functional address.

11. Transmit Forward. The LAN Manager console or the CRS transmits this frame to an RS to initiate testing of the communication path on the ring.

12. Report Transmit Forward. An RS transmits this frame to the LAN Manager console or the CRS to respond to a Transmit Forward MAC frame, confirming that the communication path is okay.

13. Report Active Monitor Error. The AM generates this frame when it detects an error with its process. This frame is transmitted frequently during the Token Claiming process and is transmitted to the REM functional address.

14. Report Soft Error. An RS generates this frame when its T(Soft_Error_Report) timer has expired, and the RS has accumulated errors in its counter. The frame is transmitted to the REM functional address.

15. Change Parameters. The CRS transmits this frame to an RS that needs special operating parameters to be set.

16. Remove Ring Station. The CRS transmits this frame to an RS that must be removed from the ring.

17. Request Ring Station State. The CRS transmits this frame to an RS to request the operational status of the NIC in that RS.

18. Report Ring Station State. An RS transmits this frame to the CRS to properly respond to a Request Ring Station State MAC frame.

19. Request Ring Station Attachments. The CRS transmits this frame to an RS to interrogate the RS for the Token Ring functions that it has operational.

20. Report Ring Station Attachments. An RS transmits this frame to the CRS to properly respond to a Request Ring Station Attachments MAC frame.

21. Request Ring Station Address. The CRS transmits this frame to an RS to request address information.

22. Report Ring Station Address. An RS transmits this frame to the CRS to properly respond to a Request Ring Station Address MAC frame.

23. Report NAUN Change. An RS transmits this frame to the CRS to announce that it has received a change in its internally stored NAUN address. This usually occurs when an RS receives a new NAUN during the Neighbor Notification process.

24. Report New Active Monitor. An RS transmits this frame to the CRS to notify the CRS that it has become the new AM.

25. Response. An RS transmits this frame to another RS to announce the receipt of a Response MAC frame from an originating station. It is also used to communicate syntax errors in received frames from a respective station.

CHAPTER 12

Devices and Specifications

When troubleshooting LAN problems, you need a good understanding of the devices on the LAN, their specifications, and how they are designed to meet those specifications. You need a solid understanding of the technical guidelines for the particular topology being used. This is critical for isolating a specific area of the network as the point of failure. One of the trigger points will be whether particular hardware or software entities are operating within their standard specifications.

This chapter provides an overview of some industry-standard Token Ring devices and their specifications, and of various Token Ring products widely used in the industry. Many manufacturers have excellent products for the Token Ring environment; all cannot be detailed here. This chapter presents some of the most commonly used products in the LAN marketplace.

Examining Cables

The Token Ring standard has seven recognized cabling types, often referred to as the IBM cabling system. Many vendors manufacture cabling for the Token

Ring community, and most try to comply with the IBM cabling design specifications. All seven cabling types have design specifications, along with length guidelines for use and installation. The seven IBM cabling types are listed here by their design and use specification. Figure 12.1 shows each cable type. Later, this chapter discusses the way in which the lengths relate to installation.

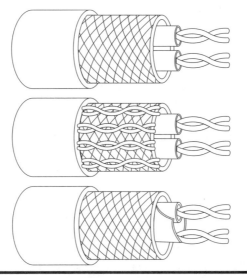

Figure 12.1. The IBM cabling types: (a) shielded twisted pair, (b) unshielded twisted pair, and (c) fiber optic.

- **Type 1.** Type 1 cable consists of two twisted pairs of wire enclosed by a common shield. The conductors consist of data-grade 22 AWG (American Wire Gauge) solid wire. Type 1 is the most widely used Token Ring cable type and is considered the most reliable. However, because of the high cost of Type 1 cable, most new Token Ring networks are being wired with unshielded twisted-pair wire such as IBM type 3 cable. Type 1 is not very susceptible to interference from electrical and high frequencies and remains the preferred copper cable in electrically noisy environments. This cabling type supports both 4Mbps and 16Mbps transmissions.
- **Type 2.** Type 2 cable is similar to the Type 1 specification. It also has two wire-shielded twisted pairs, but adds four twisted pairs of unshielded 22 AWG telephone grade wire. Type 2 cable is used frequently for cutting the

expense of running extra cable in areas that need both voice and Token Ring connections.

- **Type 3.** Type 3 cable is unshielded twisted pair. It is telephone-grade wire: 22 or 24 AWG. The number of pairs is usually two, but varies depending on the manufacturer. Given that this cable type is unshielded and is not considered data grade, Type 3 is more susceptible to crosstalk and electrical interference from power cables, radio frequencies, and HVAC. With the introduction of new hubbing technologies, however, twisted pair is fast becoming the new standard for LAN cabling.

  Type 3 cable's strong points are that it is easy to install and many buildings are already cabled with (unused) telephone wire.

- **Type 5.** Type 5 has two solid fiber conductors. It is data grade: 100/140 micron fiber cable. Because Type 5 cable offers extremely high-quality transmission over increased distances, it is a good choice for a variety of installations. Fiber cabling is expensive and today is still mainly used in main ring path and backbone cabling applications. (Backbone cabling is a common cabling path that connects primary LANs.)

  Type 5 cabling is insusceptible to virtually all interference. It is used frequently in repeater configurations at both 4Mbps and 16Mbps transmission.

- **Type 6.** Type 6 cable has two twisted-wire pairs enclosed in a common shield. It is data-grade stranded wire: 26 AWG. Due to distance limitations, Type 6 is only used for patch and jumper cable applications. (Adapter cables are used between a ring station (RS) and a wall plate. Adapter cables are usually used at a patch panel.)

- **Type 8.** Type 8 cable has two wires with plastic ramp insulation. It is data-grade solid wire: 26 AWG. With its parallel design, Type 8 is used for under-carpet installations.

- **Type 9.** Type 9 cable has two wire-shielded twisted pairs. It is data-grade solid or stranded wire: 22 AWG. Its lower cost makes Type 9 an alternative to Type 1 when distance requirements are not as critical.

Cable Lengths

The two types of ring-wiring schemes are the main ring path and the lobe. For designing a Token Ring network layout, the distance can be critical to proper functioning of the network. The cables listed in the preceding section have distance specifications that must be used as guidelines for designing the actual lengths of a LAN layout.

The main ring path length varies depending on the number of wiring closets, MAUs, and repeaters in the configuration. These factors determine an adjusted ring length (ARL).

This book does not cover ARL calculations (see references 3, 6, and 7 in Appendix B). The rough mean distance for the main ring path is approximately 1,200 feet for one wiring closet and one or two MAUs. This calculation changes depending on the number and types of hardware technologies used in the layout. Later, this chapter discusses new hubbing technologies and how they allow standard distances to be exceeded.

The lobe distance also varies depending on the technology used, but each cable type has defined specifications for lobe installation length. With new technologies, these specifications are being exceeded. The following standard lobe lengths are listed by cabling type.

- **Type 1.** Maximum lobe length is 330 feet (100 meters). This cabling type supports up to 260 nodes.

- **Type 2.** Maximum lobe length is 330 feet (100 meters) for the 22 AWG pairs and approximately 220 feet (66 meters) for the 26 AWG pairs. The 26 AWG cable limits the Type 2 distance and node capacity to about two-thirds that of Type 1 cabling.

- **Type 3.** Maximum lobe length is 150 feet (45 meters). This cabling type supports up to 72 nodes. Type 3 cabling requires Type 3 media filters at the termination point to convert to the standard IBM data connector and to filter any interference encountered on the medium. Type 3 cabling usually uses a standard RJ11 or RJ•5 phone plug for termination.

- **Type 5.** Type 5 cable is typically used for the main ring path and for backbones. If fiber is used in the main ring path, the rough mean distance increases from 1,200 feet to approximately 2.5 miles. Currently, there are no defined hard lobe lengths for Type 5 cabling.

- **Type 6.** The 26 AWG cable aspect of Type 6 limits its distance and node capacity to about two-thirds that of Type 1 cabling. Maximum lobe length is approximately 220 feet (66 meters).

- **Type 8.** Maximum lobe length is approximately 165 feet (50 meters). The Type 8 design limits its distance and node capacity to about one-half that of Type 1 cabling.
- **Type 9.** Type 9 is also 26 AWG cable and, thus, is limited to about two-thirds of Type 1 cabling's distance and node capacity. The maximum lobe length for Type 9 is approximately 220 feet (66 meters).

Cabling Connectors

The Token Ring network cabling scheme uses two main types of connectors: the IBM data connector and the male/female DB9 connector.

The IBM data connector is a self-shorting connector, which means that when disconnected it self-shorts and loops the internal twisted pairs. This self-shorting feature is important for fault redundancy. Chapter 11 discusses fault redundancy in the section on design and layout.

The data connector is made to connect with another identical data connector (see Figure 12.2). Most Type 6 patch cables use this connector on at least one end to terminate. This allows Type 6 patch cables to connect to patch panels, wall faceplates, and MAUs, all of which use this connector as a standard internal connector.

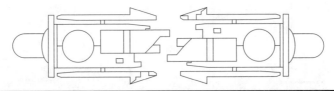

Figure 12.2 The IBM data connector connects to another identical data connector.

The male DB9 connector is usually used on the other end of Type 6 patch cables to connect to a Token Ring NIC. Figure 12.3 shows the pin layout of the male DB9 connector as it relates to the patch cable, with the associated Token Ring conductor color codes and polarities. The NIC uses the female DB9 connector for its own external port.

Figure 12.3 A DB9 male connector, at the end of a type 6 patch cable, attaches to a Token Ring NIC.

Because of improvements in the Type 3 unshielded twisted pair (UTP) wiring, many Token Ring NICs and MAUs today use RJ45 phone-type connectors for termination. Figure 12.4 shows how the standard Token Ring connectors mate to create an RS-to-MAU link.

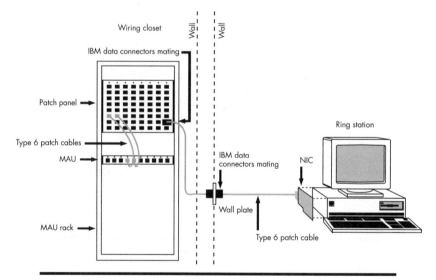

Figure 12.4 The cable (type 6 in this example) and data connectors work together to connect a ring station to the MAU.

Multistation Access Units and Wiring Hub Technology

Chapter 11 discussed the standard IBM 8228 MAU. When the 8228 MAU was introduced, it was considered state-of-the-art. Today, however, the selection of wiring hubs offers many more choices for configuring a Token Ring LAN. A wide selection of new Token Ring hubbing technology is available, and this new technology can have a significant effect on how a Token Ring LAN operates and performs.

Many hubs in the LAN marketplace still parallel the original 8228 design, but many hubs also are being designed with intelligence built in. Hubs are available with LED diagnostic ports and diagnostic software to test the hub independent of the NOS.

Most popular new hub product lines consist of intelligent hubs that support UTP cabling, such as those of SynOptics and Cabletron. UTP cabling systems are cost-effective and easy to maintain. In some cases, they support increased cabling distances. Some of them can mix topologies for internetworking. A large segment of the LAN marketplace is quickly shifting over to UTP.

The IBM 8228 MAU has an excellent track record for reliability. It uses passive ports, and the MAU itself does not use an external power source. The ports have a relay, which is actuated by the phantom DC current from the NIC. These ports may need to be charged at installation or at certain intervals to open their relays. A charger usually shipped with the 8228 is used for this purpose (see Figure 12.5).

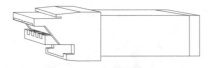

Figure 12.5 Having no external power source, the IBM 8228 MAU requires a charger.

Before troubleshooting a suspected bad port, the port should always be charged by inserting the charger into the port. The 8228 does not require a power supply and is both rugged and dependable. It therefore remains a popular choice for use in small networks where the need for simplicity outweighs management concerns. In larger networks, however, the 8228 has been overshadowed by newer active MAUs. Although active MAUs require power supplies and are more complex than the 8228, active MAUs can support management functions that make it possible to monitor and manage all the MAUs on a network from a central management console.

IBM has explored many technology directions, including design of a hub platform that could be more easily managed. The 8230 Controlled Access Unit (CAU) was IBM's first step in this direction. This intelligent concentrator is configured as an attachment center for lobe attachment modules (LAMs) that allow 20 RS connections. Using a maximum of four daisy-chained LAMs, the 8230 unit can handle up to 80 RS connections. LAMs can come configured with either IBM data connector ports or with type 3 RJ45 phone plugs so that UTP cabling can be connected directly to the ports on the LAM.

The CAU unit allows LAMs to be switched between 4Mbps and 16Mbps (see Figure 12.6). The 8230 also can be configured with optical fiber converter modules for implementing a fiber backbone. The unit also has bidirectional internal repeaters and often allows for increased lobe lengths over the 8228 MAU.

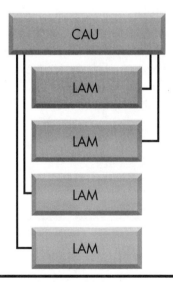

Figure 12.6 An IBM 8230 CAU serves as an attachment center for LAMs.

Next, IBM released its 8000 series wiring hubs, which are based on a more centralized design. The hubs include modules that can be added to a hub cage to increase port availability. The hubs still include standard ring-in and ring-out ports. The internal design is more sophisticated and fully supports UTP and STP wirings, SNMP management, and IBM network management schemes. The modules also include more active monitoring features such as LEDs.

Recently, to develop more integrated products for Token Ring wiring hubs, IBM has explored partnering relationships with key vendors in the internetwork hub market, such as Bay Networks, Cabletron, and Chipcom.

The new IBM network management platformsmentioned in Chapter 11 have features capable of interfacing with the 8000 series platform, resulting in a more intelligent and cohesive Token Ring hub management platform.

Significant developments made by key network vendors in the hub market include: Proteon Series 70 Wiring Centers, Bay Network/SynOptics 5000 and LattisNet Hubs, and Cabletron MMAC Token Ring Wiring Hubs. Figures 12.7, 12.8, and 12.9 show examples of these technologies.

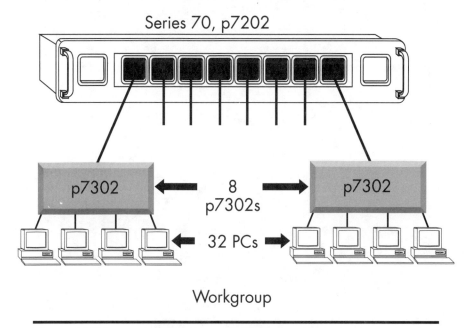

Figure 12.7 Proteon's p7302 Series 70 Workgroup Wire Centers with power provided by a p7202 Intelligent Wire Center.

ETHERNET AND TOKEN RING OPTIMIZATION

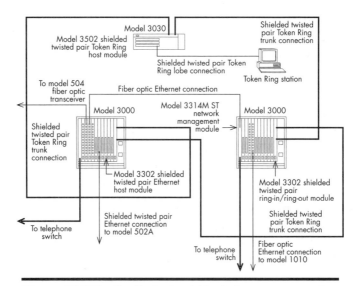

Figure 12.8 The SynOptics LattisNet hubs support a variety of Token Ring topologies and cabling types.

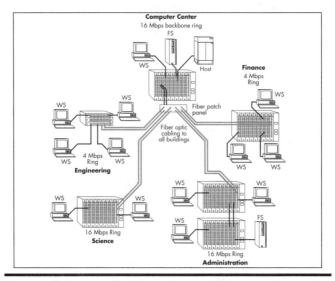

Figure 12.9 Cabletron's Token Ring hubs can be configured to run at both 4Mbps and 16Mbps.

Understanding Bridges

A bridge is a device that connects a LAN to another LAN at the data link level of OSI. Bridges are mainly used to segment traffic when the need is to have the internetwork still look like one large network, so the individual LANs seem transparent to the user. Typically, in the Token Ring environment, bridging is done for ring load balancing and to segment 4Mbps and 16Mbps rings.

Because bridges communicate at the data link level, they are protocol-independent. This means they can forward frames that contain high-level protocols such as SMB and SNA.

Some bridges are labeled MAC-layer bridges, meaning that they communicate at the MAC level; in this case, both LANs must be similar. For example, if a Token Ring LAN is bridged to another Token Ring, it can communicate fully on a MAC-layer bridge. But if a Token Ring LAN is bridged to an Ethernet LAN, the LANs are dissimilar and cannot communicate at the MAC layer. In this case, an LLC-layer bridge is used.

Several bridging techniques are employed in LANs. The Token Ring topology relies heavily on a bridging methodology called source routing (SR).

IBM developed SR to allow Token Ring frames to cross a multiple-ring environment. SR differs considerably from the bridging technique used most by Ethernet, transparent bridging (TB), which depends on a bridge being intelligent. TB expects a bridge to decide which frames are to be forwarded and where frames are to be forwarded, and to build tables for routing.

Some bridge manufacturers and organizations are working to develop a standard that combines the two techniques to form a new standard called source routing/transparent bridging. Some bridges today, in fact, employ this technique for internetworking.

The SR method requires the RS that originates a frame to determine the actual route the frames take through a multi-ring network. SR uses the Routing Information (RI) field in the data frame to accomplish the task. The originating RS sets certain bits within the RI field and transmits a query frame onto the ring to locate the most efficient path to the destination station. After the destination station receives the frame, it copies it and transmits the frame back to the source station.

On the return trip, routing information is appended to the RI field of the reply frame. By the time the reply frame reaches the originating station, the RI field contains a complete record of every ring through which the frame was routed. When the originating station receives the frame back, it interrogates the RI field for the newly established route to the destination station. Now the originating station has a selected route for transmission, and it builds an internal routing table for its destinations.

In large ring configurations, there may be many routes from an originating ring to a destination ring. You need a method to select the best possible path for transmission.

Token Ring's most commonly used method is the spanning tree algorithm (STA), which has two impacts on bridging. First, it ensures that the best possible path is being used; second, it inherently stops looping, which is when a frame arrives on a ring from two different paths.

The STA method determines the best possible path by first selecting the highest priority bridge within the WAN as a root bridge. Next, every other bridge identifies the port logically the closest to the root bridge as a root port. The selection process follows as the individual LANs next pick the closest bridge to the root bridge as their designated bridge.

When the election of the main bridge components is complete, the main logical route, or tree-branching scheme, is considered defined. The algorithm looks for redundant paths (multiple paths to one ring), and it locks the root ports on those designated bridges. This establishes a nonlooping multiple ring path.

Source-routing bridges use two routing methods to forward frames: a single-route broadcast and an all-routes broadcast. A single-route broadcast sends a query frame so that it passes through every individual ring only once. An originating station employing the single-route broadcast method uses the STA method to communicate with all other bridges on the internetwork.

An all-routes broadcast sends the query frame on all possible paths and then determines the best path. Whereas a single-route broadcast actually reduces the amount of overhead traffic on the ring, an all-routes broadcast increases the amount of overhead traffic on the ring. The only real advantage of an all-routes broadcast is that it dynamically balances the traffic among all bridges.

Source-routing bridges have an inherent feature called the hop count limit (HCL). The HCL's purpose is to stop frames from continuously circling a Token

Ring internetwork. The HCL limits the number of bridges a frame may travel, or "hop," through. IBM source-routing bridges allow frames up to seven hops. Some other manufacturers have designed bridges that can increase the hop limit to more than seven.

Bridges in a multiple-ring configuration work together by communicating through a message protocol called Hello Bridge Protocol Data Units (BPDU). The frame transmission has its own format based on an LLC Type-1 connection. This book does not discuss BPDU frames; for further information see Appendix B.

For Token Ring, the source-routing method works with the STA method to allow stations to determine the best possible method for transmission over a multiple Token Ring configuration.

Some bridges (nicknamed kit bridges) are composed of a software/hardware kit that must be configured in a workstation or a file server. A kit bridge configured in a file server is called an internal bridge by some NOS and bridge suppliers. A kit bridge configured in a workstation is called an external bridge.

There are a group of products that offer excellent technology in the Token Ring bridge arena. IBM pioneered the Token Ring bridging area and released a standard industry product, the IBM source routing bridge program. Other vendors have also released strong products for bridging Token Ring networks.

Not all vendor bridging products talk to Token Ring through straight SR method technology; some use the TB method and communicate to source routing.

Some significant bridge products are:

- The IBM Token Ring Bridge Program v2.2X
- IBM 8209 Bridge
- 8000 Series Token Ring Bridges
- Andrew Bridgeport Source-Routing Token Ring Bridges
- Netronix TokenMaster Bridges

Figures 12.10, 12.11, 12.12, and 12.13 show examples of these technologies.

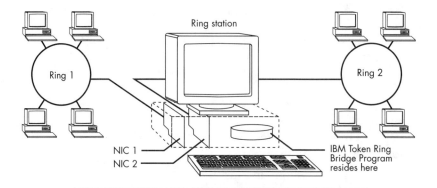

Figure 12.10 The IBM Token Ring Bridge Program v2.2 configuration includes a dedicated PC.

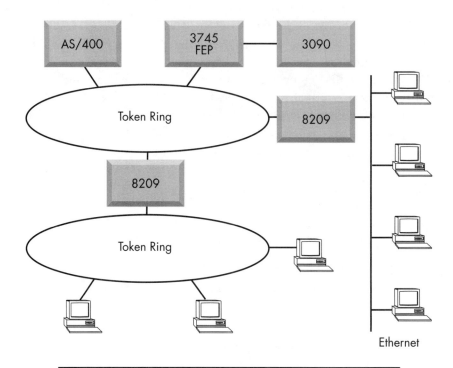

Figure 12.11 The IBM 8209 Token Ring bridge can be configured for either two Token Ring networks or an Ethernet LAN.

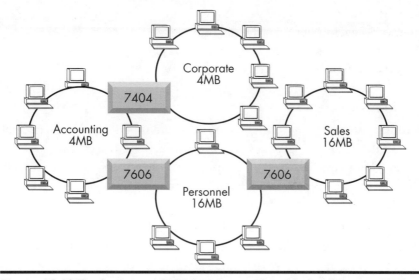

Figure 12.12 The Bridgeport 7606 bridge is configurable for 4Mbps or 16Mbps operation; the 7404 provides 4Mbps connections for 4Mbps and 16Mbps networks.

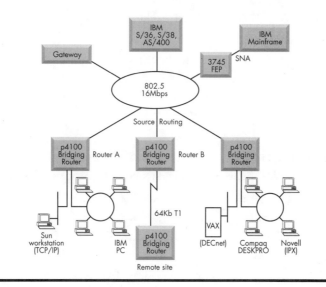

Figure 12.13 Netronix TokenMaster 100 bridges can support both 4Mbps and 4/16Mbps Token Ring networks.

A router differs from a bridge in that it connects a LAN to another LAN at the OSI network level rather than the data link level. Routers are used to connect LANs that need to share the same protocols. They are protocol-dependent devices that must understand the protocol they are forwarding. They are most commonly used in larger internetworks where a need exists to logically separate LANs.

A router still segments traffic, but at the same time it can be selective as to which protocols are being passed through to the next LAN. This can be very important; for a large internetwork running multiple protocols, a router allows boundaries to be defined and allows for administrative control over which protocols are running on each LAN.

Most Token Ring routers support SR and the STA. A router is highly intelligent and maintains internal routing tables that contain the protocols it can pass through, along with statistical data about other routers in the internetwork.

Some routers do allow logical loops so that redundant paths are available on the internetwork. This is not a problem because they can selectively filter by protocol, which means that unwanted packets do not have to arrive on certain networks.

Installation of a router is usually more complex than that of a bridge because setting up the protocol configurations requires a good understanding of the protocols being used. Some routers are slower on packet throughput because they are doing more processing at the protocol level than bridges do.

Today, another router category exists. Brouters. are hybrids between a bridge and a router. They combine the data Link layer and the network layer forwarding capabilities. Brouters can be selective of protocols or not. A brouter is sometimes called a bridging router.

Some of the key routing platforms that support routing in the Token Ring environment are Proteon 4000 series Bridging Routers; Proteon CNX Series RISC Bridging Routers; and Cisco Systems 7000 and MGS Series Routers. Figures 12.14 and 12.15 show examples of these platforms.

Chapter 12: Devices and Specifications   385

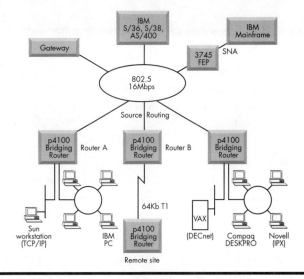

Figure 12.14 Proteon's p4100+ Bridging Routers can work with multiple media types and multiple protocols.

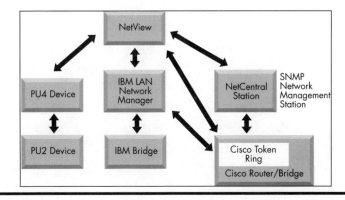

Figure 12.15 With full IBM SNA routing communication capabilities, Cisco routers can interface with both IBM LAN Manager and NetView.

Examining Repeaters

A repeater operates at the physical layer, the lowest layer of OSI. Repeaters electrically extend the physical lengths of a LAN cabling segment. They take the signal from one cabling segment, regenerate it, and then pass it on to another cabling segment. The repeater actually boosts the strength of the signal.

Because repeaters just regenerate a signal, they are protocol-dependent devices. A repeater is limited to passing the same protocols that are present, and it must be connected to the same type of topology. Repeaters do not perform the high-level processing of bridges and routers. Thus repeaters usually have the highest throughput capability.

With Token Ring, repeaters are mainly used to regenerate the signal on the main ring path, but in some cases, a repeater is installed to extend a lobe for a critical RS. You often see repeaters in large buildings where standard cable lengths do not allow a ring to function as a stand-alone without regeneration.

Repeaters were originally available for only standard STP, but today they can accommodate the new fiber and UTP backbone configurations.

There are many products available for repeating in the Token Ring topology. Well-known products include IBM 8218, 8219, 8220, and 8000 Series Repeaters, and the Andrew 8200 Series Repeaters.

Figures 12.16 and 12.17 show examples of these platforms.

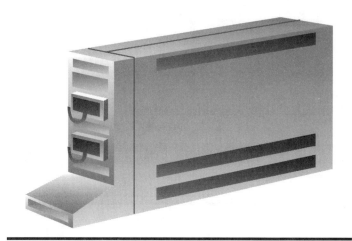

Figure 12.16 The IBM 8218, 8219, and 8220 Token Ring Network Repeaters include models for both copper and fiber optic media.

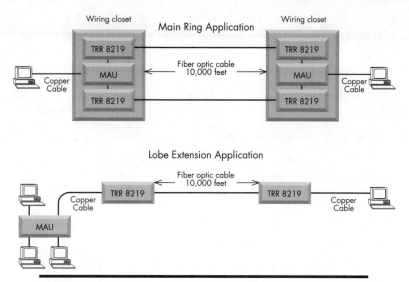

Figure 12.17 The Andrew TRR 8219 fiber optic repeaters can extend main ring and lobe paths up to 10,000 feet.

Understanding NICs

Recent significant technologies include 32-bit EISA boards running at 16Mbps along with EISA and PCI CPU Bus compatible NICs with internal RISC processing that provide 32Mbps full duplex. Improvements in UTP hubbing technology have brought a wealth of new designs for Token Ring UTP NICs.

Vendors for Token Ring NICs have been busy working on new Token Ring drivers for their cards to enhance performance. Some of the drivers enable 16Mbps NICs to take maximum advantage of the new, full 18,000-byte frame size.

Most Token Ring NICs also are available with remote program load (RPL) capability, which allows a diskless RS to attach to a server through a PROM on the Token Ring NIC. The PROM contains the firmware code to go out on the ring, access the file server, and download the necessary shell code from an NOS.

Some significant driver developments are allowing the CPU bus to take full advantage of the NIC processing speed. The packet per second (PPS) rate of the

NICs is starting to increase in new cards. The higher PPS rates on Token Ring NICs will start to allow for maximizing traffic flow by allowing larger packet sizes between stations to be used without high increases in network utilization. This is critical for deterministic networks such as Token Ring. Madge Networks has been a strong player in the area of fast drivers for Token Ring NICs.

This is a list of some of the most popular Token Ring NICs available today:

- IBM Standard 4Mbps and 4/16Mbps Token Ring NICs
- IBM LANStreamer Token Ring NICs, including 32Mbps /DTR and bandwidth allocation technology
- IBM Token Ring Network PS/2 Adapters
- IBM Token Ring Network 16/4 Adapters
- Proteon ProNET 4/16Mbps UTP/STP Token Ring NICs
- Madge Networks Smart Ringnode NICs with FastMAC microcode

CHAPTER 13

Token Ring Fault Isolation

This chapter introduces essential troubleshooting techniques for when you encounter problems in a Token Ring network. Every logical component of a Token Ring network has distinct failure symptoms, causes, and appropriate troubleshooting methods. This chapter presents a detailed discussion of the methods of fault isolation for each network component.

Each of the following sections builds on the preceding section. Read and study the sections in this chapter consecutively.

Troubleshooting Fault Domains and Lobe Areas

Sometimes a network symptom leads you directly to a specific network component; other times network symptoms lead you to specific network areas, such as a fault domain or a lobe area. The first step in troubleshooting a fault domain is to isolate the failure to a specific lobe area. Next, you must isolate the failure to a specific network component within that lobe area.

Troubleshooting a Fault Domain

If a ring station (RS) beacons, and both the station and its NAUN pass all the self-tests performed during the beaconing process, both will reinsert back onto the ring. When this occurs, a solid beaconing condition exists on the ring, and you need to troubleshoot the problem manually.

One of the best ways to start troubleshooting a fault domain is by examining the Beacon MAC frame through a protocol analysis session. The Beacon Type field in the Beacon MAC frame helps to isolate the exact location of failure within a fault domain. Beacon types are discussed in detail later in this chapter.

If the addresses in the Beacon MAC frame stay consistent on multiple captures, the problem can easily be isolated to one single fault domain. When the addresses are constantly changing, it is very possible that the Main Ring Path (MRP) has a serious fault in the wiring or hub/MAU path.

The next step is to isolate one of the two lobe areas as the source of failure. The easiest way to accomplish this is to remove one lobe area from the fault domain by actually removing one of the lobe cables from the MAU or wiring hub. Next, retest the ring.

If the failure symptom is gone, you have isolated the problem to the removed lobe area. If the problem still is present, reconnect the first suspect lobe area, disconnect the second lobe area, and retest. The problem should not be present, and the failure now is located to a specific lobe area.

Troubleshooting Lobe Areas

Sometimes network symptoms point to a specific lobe area. This may be because you have already troubleshot an assigned fault domain and isolated the failure to one of the lobe areas.

If the problem is isolated to a lobe area, the following components are possible failure causes:

- The RS NIC
- The RS
- The lobe cable
- The MAU or wiring hub

Chapter 13: Token Ring Fault Isolation 391

In some cases a network file server problem can cause an RS to continuously insert and deinsert itself into the ring.

To isolate the specific network failure component within a lobe area, use the following process:

1. Disconnect the lobe cable from its respective MAU port or wiring hub port and connect it to another MAU port or wiring hub port. Retest the ring. If the failure is gone, you have isolated the failure to the MAU port or wiring hub port. If the problem is still present, connect the lobe cable back to its original port. (MAU and wiring hub troubleshooting are discussed further in the section on MAU and wiring hub problems later in this chapter.)

2. If possible, attempt to verify the integrity of the lobe cable. Test the lobe cable with a time domain reflectometer (TDR) or a ring cable tester. If any clear cable failures are evident, the lobe cable is most likely your problem. Another good troubleshooting method is to attach the RS to the same MAU or wiring hub port with another lobe cable. Sometimes this can be accomplished by bringing the RS into the wiring closet and attaching it to the MAU or wiring hub port by means of a test patch cable. (Try to have a cable set aside that you know is good.) Next, retest the ring. If the ring tests indicate that the ring is operating properly, the original lobe cable is your problem. If the failure is still occurring, either the RS or the NIC is probably the cause of failure.

3. The cause of the failure now has to be identified as the RS or its respective NIC. The first step is to double-check the RS for proper configuration and good functionality. This is discussed in the section on Ring Station problems later in this chapter. If the RS is properly configured and is functioning properly, the NIC is the next assumed fault.

4. If the NIC is targeted as the cause of failure, the first step is to check all the NIC configuration settings and test the NIC operation. NIC configuration and testing is discussed in the section on NIC problems later in this chapter. If all the NIC configuration settings are correct and the NIC passes diagnostic tests, you can assume that the NIC has an intermittent failure. Swap the NIC with a known good NIC and thoroughly retest the ring.

5. As mentioned earlier, in some instances a network file server problem causes an RS to continuously insert and deinsert itself into the ring. If you

are using relay-based MAUs such as the IBM 8228, you can actually hear the MAU port continually clicking when insertion and deinsertion take place. This indicates some software incompatibility between the RS and the network file server. If you are dealing with an active electronic wiring hub, you do not hear clicking because there are no mechanical relays. Many active MAUs such as the Proteon 7302 have an LED on each port to indicate that a station is inserted. You also can diagnose insertion/deinsertion by means of protocol analysis.

The sections that follow discuss how to troubleshoot each of the individual network components that may fail within an assigned fault domain, lobe area, or the overall Token Ring network. The problem reversal theory introduced earlier is an excellent problem verification method that can be applied to all the troubleshooting steps introduced next. This approach can be used across the fault-isolation spectrum and can provide you with conclusive testing results.

Understanding Cable Problems

The most common failure within a Token Ring network is a cable fault. Cable faults are usually unexpected. The symptom frequently exhibits itself as another network component failure. The symptom may appear as either a soft- or a hard-error condition on the ring. The worst thing about cable problems is that they can cause just one network area component to fail, or they can bring the whole network to its knees. Cable problems can be both solid and intermittent.

Cable Failure Types and Causes

Several distinct problems can occur within a cable. Some TDRs may indicate that a cable is experiencing certain types of signal degradation such as crosstalk or noise.

Noise is any signal that interferes with the intelligibility of the data signal being transmitted. Noise is frequently caused by electrical or magnetic fields that produce electrical currents in a wire. These currents interfere with the desired data signals.

Crosstalk is noise that results when the magnetic fields in a wire generate an electric current in another nearby wire. If the conversation of another party has

Chapter 13: Token Ring Fault Isolation

ever intruded into one of your telephone calls, the interference is most likely the result of crosstalk.

When signal degradation such as crosstalk or noise occurs, the actual cable failure usually fits into one of the following problem categories:

- Open cables
- Shorted cables
- Crossed conductors
- Bad cable termination
- Bad connectors
- Improper cable placement

An open cable results from an actual physical break of a cable conductor. An open cable problem is usually caused when a cable is crimped or bent. This can occur easily when a cable is improperly fed through a building area, such as a wall, a ceiling, or a conduit. Using proper strain reliefs when running a cable can stop a cable from being stretched beyond its intended distance run.

A shorted cable occurs when two or more internal conductors touch. This problem is usually caused when a cable is crimped or bent. If an unintentional crimp or strain is put on a cable that has twisted-pair conductors, it is more probable that a short will occur rather than an open, because the pairs are physically crossed. Because the Token Ring cabling system uses twisted pair, shorts are a common type of cable failure.

Crossed conductors occur when two or more cable conductors are connected to the incorrect connector terminals. This problem can be deceiving because it usually exhibits itself as a failed RS, MAU port, or another network device by attempting ring attachment. This problem can easily occur during installation of the cable connectors.

The best way to avoid crossed conductors is to coordinate a color-coded connector to a corresponding connector terminal. Most cables have internal color coding. Token Ring cabling usually uses a standard red, green, orange, and black color code for its internal conductors.

Bad cable termination is probably the most common type of cable problem in a Token Ring environment. Bad cable termination is the improper connection of the internal Token Ring cabling conductors to a corresponding Token Ring cabling connector. This can be categorized as loose conductors, disconnected conductors, an improper shielding connection, or even crossed conductors. The symptoms of this type of problem can also be deceiving. It is vital to use the proper tools and to follow the recommendations of the connector manufacturer when installing connectors.

Bad connectors are sometimes the culprit of a suspected bad cable. Be aware that sometimes the IBM data connector shorting pins can break and cause cable failure or improper termination symptoms. Improper cable placement can cause interference that can introduce noise into a cable. Cables should not be run or placed next to electrical sources, high-voltage AC, certain lighting, or other possible sources of interference. Huge numbers of network problems can be traced to cables run through elevator shafts or near fluorescent lights.

The following section discusses some ways to effectively troubleshoot cable problems that occur in the Token Ring environment.

Troubleshooting Cable Failures

Troubleshooting the Token Ring cabling system, which physically uses a star-wired network, requires a different approach from troubleshooting other LAN topologies such as Ethernet, which uses a bus configuration. When you suspect a cabling problem in a Token Ring cabling section (such as a lobe path cable), the proper approach is always to remove that particular cabling section from the ring and separately test that section. Because the network is a physical star, this usually does not affect the entire network unless the suspected bad cable section is in the main ring path. When troubleshooting suspected cabling problems in the Token Ring environment, divide the system into two cabling areas: the lobe cables and the main ring path cabling.

Troubleshooting Lobe Cables

Cables account for a high number of lobe path failures. If you suspect a problem in a lobe area, the first component of the lobe path that you should troubleshoot is the lobe cable.

Later, this chapter discusses how analyzing a low-level MAC frame can isolate a Token Ring problem to two lobe areas within a fault domain.

First, remove the lobe cable from the MAU port and the NIC. Next, test the particular lobe cable with either a TDR or a ring cable-specific tester, like the testing instruments discussed in Chapter 4. If the cable section has a problem, these devices should detect the problem and verify the problem type. If the TDR or ring cable tester detects no errors, chances are another network component such as the MAU port, an RS, or an NIC in the suspected bad lobe path is probably at fault.

Troubleshooting Main Ring Path Cables

Sometimes a group of RSs or the whole Token Ring network is experiencing problems, such as the incapability to connect to the ring, a crashing LAN NOS, or a beaconing ring. In these cases, the main ring path may have an internal cable failure. If all the MAUs are neatly organized in MAU racks and wiring closets, troubleshooting the main ring path is relatively easy.

The proper way to approach a suspected main ring path cabling problem is to start with the first MAU and disconnect its RI and RO cables. Next, test the particular MAU by verifying that the RSs connected to it can properly perform ring insertion. If the MAU and NICs used in the network do not have specific MAU connection diagnostics, you probably need to connect the ring file server to the MAU being tested and bring the NOS up so that the RSs can connect. This topic is discussed in more detail later in this chapter.

If the first MAU is operational, connect the second MAU with an RO cable from the first MAU to the second MAU's RI port. Next, test the two new MAU rings as previously described. If the network file server is up and RS shells are running, you should bring the network down before connecting the second MAU.

Continue this troubleshooting method until a problem is encountered. What usually occurs is that a bad cable or MAU is located by adding it to the ring, and a problem arises.

It comes down to a basic elimination process. If your ring is functioning with the first three MAUs, and you add a fourth MAU and the ring does not come up properly, a problem exists in one of three areas:

- the main ring cable connecting the RO and RI ports between MAU 3 and MAU 4
- the fourth MAU

- a network component connected to a MAU

At this point if a problem is located, put aside the suspected network problem area, reconnect the rest of the network, and test the new ring configuration. If problems still exist, start troubleshooting back from the last MAU that tested as functional. The possibility of more than one failure on a network always exists.

If the network comes up, troubleshoot the defined problem area by first testing the main ring cable path section with either a TDR or a ring-specific tester. Then test the MAU and, finally, test any network components connected to the MAU. When troubleshooting cable problems within the Token Ring topology, you may find that you encounter another problem or that the actual failure is due to another Token Ring network component. For example, you may be troubleshooting a suspected bad RS and find out that you actually have a bad cable. By being aware of how you are vectoring when troubleshooting, you can effectively isolate your problem to the correct network component.

Understanding MAU and Wiring Hub Problems

Troubleshooting an MAU or wiring hub problem can be relatively easy if the proper measures are taken, meaning the MAU layout is properly configured in a standard MAU rack/wiring closet and, in the case of wiring hubs, the hub layout is centralized and properly documented. Having all the proper network documentation available is a great aid. All these measures make the troubleshooting task that much easier.

The physical star layout of lobes in a Token Ring network allows port changes to be made quite easily. This is critical to the next section, which presents the causes of certain types of MAU and wiring hub failure, along with some specific troubleshooting methods for MAU and wiring hub failures.

MAU and Wiring Hub Failure Symptoms, Causes, and Troubleshooting

Three types of problem situations in the Token Ring topology can cause MAU or wiring hub failure:

1. MAU- or hub-specific port failures that affect either just one lobe area or a fault domain
2. Complete MAU or hub module faults that cause failure symptoms with just one MAU or hub module
3. Complete MAU or hub module faults that cause either solid or intermittent failure symptoms to multiple MAUs, multiple hub modules, or the complete Token Ring network

In the case of any intermittent problems suspected with MAUs or wiring hubs, always run a protocol analysis session to be thorough and conclusive. Also, note that the failure symptoms in all three of these problem situations may appear as either soft or hard errors on the ring.

Assume the following technical approach when troubleshooting MAU or wiring hub problems:

- MAU- or hub-specific failures affecting one lobe area or fault domain. When a specific port on a MAU or wiring hub has a problem, the troubleshooting step is straightforward. Because of the physical star layout, all you need to do is verify that a port problem exists in the MAU or in a specific wiring hub module.

  This can be done by simply moving the lobe cable from the suspected bad port to another port on the same MAU or wiring hub module. (Make sure that the new port is functioning.) Next, retest the RS on the new port. If everything passes the diagnostic tests, the suspected bad port is at failure.

  To verify your testing results, reverse the troubleshooting procedure by reconnecting the found bad port to a lobe cable to re-create the problem, then put the lobe cable back into the newly tested port. This shows that your testing results are correct. If a failure still exists with the same RS on a new port, troubleshoot the respective lobe area for that RS.

- MAU or hub faults affecting only one MAU or hub. In case of a complete unit failure with a particular MAU or wiring hub module, the troubleshooting steps also are forthright. You should remove the MAU or wiring hub module from the ring configuration, then retest the ring. If no problems are encountered, the MAU or wiring hub module has probably failed. Replace the removed unit with a spare unit, and reconnect all the respective lobe cables.

The next step is to retest the new ring configuration thoroughly. If everything is functioning correctly, the suspected bad MAU or wiring hub module is indeed bad. Again, the testing results can be verified by reversing the troubleshooting procedure by reinserting the found bad MAU or wiring hub module into the ring configuration to re-create the problem.

- MAU or hub faults affecting multiple MAUs or hubs. When you suspect that a MAU or a hub module failure is causing solid fault effects with either multiple MAUs, multiple hub modules, or the complete Token Ring network, the best procedure is to remove the MAU or wiring hub module from the ring configuration and retest the ring. In essence, follow the procedure described in the preceding paragraph.

If the failure is intermittent, try a protocol analysis session. By running a comprehensive analysis session integrated with the manual troubleshooting steps, chances are you can isolate the problem.

Some MAU and wiring hub manufacturers include their own diagnostic tools with their products. Some manufacturers have designed specific diagnostic programs along with special hardware built into the units for testing purposes. Refer to all vendor documentation to see if any specific diagnostic tools are available for the respective MAU or wiring hub.

Exploring NIC Problems

NIC problems can cause the most misleading Token Ring failures. This is because the NIC is responsible for generating and receiving the final data signal transmitted on the ring cabling medium. NICs do not always fail solidly; sometimes an NIC still operates in marginal condition. When this occurs, an NIC can introduce numerous intermittent failures onto the ring.

If you review the Token Ring theory presented in Chapter 2, you will see that the Token Ring topology employs sophisticated communication techniques. These communication techniques rely upon the NIC for accurate data transmission, reception, processing, and timing. If an NIC fails even marginally, any of these important network processes can be impaired.

NIC Failure Symptoms and Causes

Token Ring NIC failure symptoms fall into the following three categories:

- Generate hard errors onto the network
- Generate soft errors onto the network
- Ring insertion failure

If an NIC encounters a solid internal fault or a solid fault in its holding RS, the NIC may generate a hard error such as a Beacon MAC frame onto the ring. Figure 13.1 shows a Network General Sniffer Advanced Token Ring Analyzer depicting a beaconing ring.

```
 SUMMARY Delta
    613   0.019   Broadcast   NwkGnlE004FA   MAC Claim Token
    614   0.020   Broadcast   NwkGnlE004FA   MAC Claim Token
    615   0.019   Broadcast   NwkGnlE004FA   MAC Claim Token
    616   0.019   Broadcast   NwkGnlE004FA   MAC Claim Token
    617   0.019   Broadcast   NwkGnlE004FA   MAC Claim Token
    618   0.020   Broadcast   NwkGnlE004FA   MAC Claim Token
    619   0.009   Broadcast   NwkGnlE002D0   MAC Beacon
    620   0.020   Broadcast   NwkGnlE004FA   MAC Beacon
    621   0.019   Broadcast   NwkGnlE004FA   MAC Beacon
                       Frame 619 of 828
 DETAIL
    MAC:   ---- MAC data ----
    MAC:
    MAC:   MAC Command:
    MAC:   Source: Ring station, Destination: Ring Station
    MAC:   Subvector type: Beacon Type - Streaming signal, Claim Token
    MAC:   Subvector type: Physical Drop Number 00000000
    MAC:   Subvector type: Upstream Neighbor Address NwkGnlE004FA
    MAC:
                       Frame 619 of 828
                   Use TAB to select windows
    1      2     3   4 ZOOM   5       6 DISPLAY   7 PREV    8 NEXT    9    10 NEW
    HELP   MARK      IN       MENUS   OPTIONS     FRAME     FRAME          CAPTURE
```

Figure 13.1 This Sniffer Analyzer trace shows a beaconing Token Ring network.

In this case the particular RS, including the NIC, is the network failure area of an assigned fault domain. If the result of troubleshooting the assigned RS and NIC is that the NIC is at failure, the problem normally is an NIC hardware failure. If the NIC has been operating for a while without failure, usually the problem is hardware; but if it is a new RS installation or the RS has recently been reconfigured, that there may be an improper configuration setting.

ETHERNET AND TOKEN RING OPTIMIZATION

The solid-failure-cause exceptions typically related to improper configuration are ring speed settings and NIC firmware microcode versions.

When an NIC generates a soft error onto the ring, it may be detecting a marginal internal failure. Before an RS actually generates the soft error, it starts an internal NIC timer, T(Soft_Error_Report). The timer runs for two seconds to acquire soft error information.

Various types of soft errors can be accumulated and generated, and the specific type of soft error may point to a potential cause of failure. Figure 13.2 shows a Network General Sniffer Analyzer trace that depicts a Token Ring soft error, Internal Error, which may indicate that one of the NICs within a specific fault domain is in marginal operating condition. A complete soft-error breakdown is detailed later in this chapter. Remember that an NIC that generates certain types of soft errors may cause ring degradation that in turn exhibits intermittent ring failure symptoms.

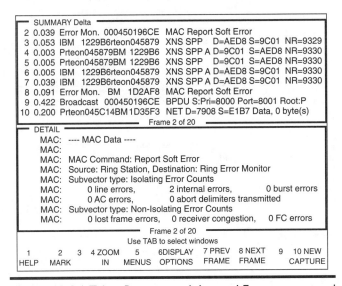

Figure 13.2 A Token Ring network Internal Error, as captured by the Network General Sniffer Analyzer.

Ring insertion failure is the incapability of a particular RS to enter the ring. The network area of failure usually is a specific lobe area. If, after troubleshooting the lobe area, you definitely identify the failure component as a specific NIC, the failure usually is caused by one of the following reasons:

- Actual NIC hardware failure
- Improper NIC configuration with respect to the following settings: I/O address; IRQ; DMA; Token Ring address; slot settings, 32- or 16- or 8-bit card; NIC microcode level; primary or secondary setting; speed settings
- Improper NIC software driver microcode or bad remote program load (RPL) PROM, specifically, the LAN drivers and their configuration or bad firmware in an RPL PROM chip
- Incompatibility with the particular RS, MAU, cable type, or the STP/UTP cabling connector

If any of these problems is present, the NIC rarely completes the ring insertion process.

The following section examines some of the ways to troubleshoot NIC problems that occur in a Token Ring network.

Troubleshooting NICs

When troubleshooting a suspected NIC failure, first categorize the problem as solid or intermittent. Next, research whether the NIC has been functioning properly and the failure is unexpected, or if this is a new or interim RS installation.

Observe the following logical guidelines for troubleshooting an NIC failure:

- If the NIC has been operating for a reasonable period of time and the problem is solid, chances are that the NIC has an internal hardware problem. Some NIC manufacturers include NIC diagnostics; if possible, run the diagnostics to confirm the NIC failure. If no diagnostics are available, swap the NIC and run a protocol analysis session to check the ring integrity.
- If the NIC has been operating fine and the problem is intermittent, run some type of NIC diagnostics. A thorough protocol analysis session is recommended because it may further confirm any intermittent failures by capturing soft errors generated from the NIC address in question. Document all test benchmark results from the protocol analysis session. Try both methods to confirm the NIC failure. If after testing you have no conclusive results, attempt swapping the NIC and rerunning a protocol analysis. Thoroughly check all testing benchmarks. Sometimes by

checking the previous test results against the new tests result, the cause of the failure presents itself.

- If the NIC is part of a new or interim RS installation and the problem is solid or intermittent, chances are that the NIC has a configuration problem. Some NIC diagnostics help to isolate a configuration problem, but most of the time you need to thoroughly check all the configuration settings, as listed in the "MAU and Wiring Hub Failure Symptoms, Causes, and Troubleshooting" section. If, after you've checked and set all possible configurations, an NIC failure still exists, the NIC may have an internal hardware problem and should be swapped. To be conclusive, rerun a thorough protocol analysis on the ring.

Some Token Ring NICs do use an RPL chip to accomplish the task of network software drivers. Because an RPL PROM chip contains the firmware code to go out on the ring and access the file server, this chip sometimes can fail and cause many of the same symptoms listed in this section.

An RPL chip operation can fail for two reasons: because it is bad or because it is the wrong firmware revision needed to work with the current NOS. If you suspect a bad RPL chip, swap the chip and retest the ring.

Ring Station Problems

With the Token Ring topology, the ring station itself can be the source of many problems. If you suspect an RS failure, it is probably because you have already defined it as the specific network component containing the source of failure. This most likely is the case because either the network user has complained of a problem or because the RS is part of a new installation or modification. RS failures usually are not the cause of soft errors being generated; those normally are caused by the NIC.

The next section outlines some of the common failures that occur with RSs on the Token Ring topology.

Ring Station Failure Symptoms and Causes

RS failure symptoms fall into three categories:

- RS failure and ring insertion failures due to hardware configuration or hardware failure
- RS failure and ring insertion failures due to software configuration or corruption
- RS failure and ring insertion failures due to RS-to-NIC incompatibility

Often when an RS fails or it cannot access the ring, it is because the station has recently been worked on. Sometimes a new PC option is added, and the hardware configuration parameters get changed.

Hard failure occurrences do not happen that often. Note that when they do occur, a soft or hard error condition may be present on the ring.

One of the most common failures with RSs is that their particular NIC drivers get placed in the wrong directories. Sometimes a particular path statement gets wiped out by a modification to the AUTOEXEC.BAT file. Another common occurrence is that the CONFIG.SYS is incorrectly configured. For example, a Driver statement may be missing or the Files/Buffer statements are incorrect or get changed. Sometimes actual software corruption occurs, but this happens infrequently. These conditions may generate a soft or hard error onto the ring. RSs and NICs sometimes experience certain incompatibilities that cause RS failures or ring insertion failure. In certain instances this is due to a simple slot or setup configuration issue. At other times a particular PC simply is incompatible with a certain NIC.

The following section offers some logical suggestions for troubleshooting RS problems.

Troubleshooting Ring Stations

Categorize an RS problem as solid or intermittent and also research whether the RS has been operating properly for a while or if it has recently been involved in a new installation or any hardware/software modifications.

As you troubleshoot an RS problem, use the following guidelines:

- When a solid hardware failure occurs, the PC usually indicates some sort of error during its self-test. If you suspect a problem, attempt to run some local PC diagnostics. If a problem occurs, troubleshoot the PC by removing all I/O boards and retesting the RS.

  Next, reverse this process by adding boards back into the PC one at a time and retesting. Sometimes a particular I/O board causes a conflict when attaching to the ring. If a particular board is at fault, it should cause a failure when it is reinserted into the PC.

  If you don't have problems with any of the I/O boards, it is possible the PC has a hardware configuration problem. Check all necessary I/O and PC configurations. Sometimes the PC settings straighten out simply as a result of your going through the configuration process. If none of these methods locates the failure, recheck the NIC as a possible cause of failure.

- Software configuration errors within a PC are one of the most frequent causes of ring insertion failure. All the necessary network files, including Token Ring NIC drivers, network shell drivers, AUTOEXEC.BAT, and CONFIG.SYS, must be in the correct file structure and must be uncorrupted.

- If a software configuration or corruption failure is suspected, check to make sure that all the files are in the correct file structure respective to their directory placement.

  If a file corruption is suspected, attempt to reload and reconfigure the particular file or files. Network documentation and vendor software manuals are an aid in this process. RS software problems can cause a significant number of failures in the Ring Insertion process or in an RS's capability to access the network file server. Figure 13.3 shows a Network General Sniffer Analyzer trace depicting an RS attempting a normal ring insertion process. Keep in mind that a simple incorrect statement in either AUTOEXEC.BAT or CONFIG.SYS can cause network failures.

- Especially with new installations and modifications, you will encounter general RS-to-NIC incompatibilities that may cause RS failure or ring insertion failure. This problem really does fall into the new installation category and sometimes is quite deceiving.

  If this type of problem is suspected, attempt to run all available PC and NIC diagnostics and recheck all relevant documentation. Another good step is to call all the manufacturers involved to see if they have any record

Chapter 13: Token Ring Fault Isolation

of certified testing between the particular PC being used as an RS and the respective NIC.

Many RS failures revolve around the NIC. Keep in mind all the suggestions offered in the NIC and RS sections for a thorough troubleshooting process.

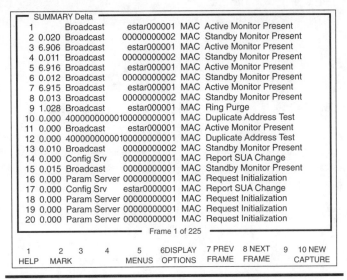

Figure 13.3 This trace shows a Token Ring network ring station attempting insertion into the ring.

Troubleshooting an RS problem by running a thorough protocol analysis session on the ring enables you to capture any network communication problems and any present soft- or hard-error conditions. This information enables you to identify a specific RS failure cause.

To ensure network integrity, after taking any measures during troubleshooting an RS, rerun the protocol analysis session.

Examining File Server Problems

A file server on a Token Ring network falls into the same category as a general RS—a file server basically has the same hardware and software modules as an

RS. Because of this, the failure symptoms of communication processes and soft- or hard-error conditions that may be present on the ring may appear in the same way as they do with an RS. A file server does contain different software and hardware LAN resources than a general RS—the NOS, database, bridging modules, etc. But as far as the Token Ring architecture is concerned, it is just another Token Ring address. Most of the failure causes and troubleshooting guidelines also apply to a file server in a Token Ring network. The next section has some extra notes for differentiating specific file server problems in the Token Ring topology.

File Server Failure Symptoms, Causes, and Troubleshooting Hints

This chapter concentrates specifically on the Token Ring topology, and does not discuss a specific NOS in detail. But whether you have Novell NetWare, IBM LAN Server, Microsoft LAN Manager, Banyan VINES, or any other NOS, the same failure causes and troubleshooting methods apply.

When you encounter a suspected file server problem, employ the following guidelines:

- A file server contains the same important network files as an RS, such as the network shell software, CONFIG.SYS, and AUTOEXEC.BAT, with the addition of an NOS and its specialized configuration and drivers.

  As mentioned earlier in this chapter, a network file server problem can cause an RS to continually insert and deinsert itself from the ring. This is usually due to incompatibility between the NOS revision or configuration and the respective RS network shell software revision or configuration. When this type of problem occurs, focus closely on these possible causes. Your best aid is the network software vendor documentation and the general network documentation.

- File structure configurations are a frequent cause of problems with file servers. A particular RS might be configured to look for certain files within a certain defined directory on the file server, for example, but cannot find them because they are in another directory or are missing. Be methodical about checking for the directory structure as it relates to RS access.

- Security rights are the number one reason for ring insertion failure. If a particular RS inserts itself onto the LAN, attempts to log onto the file

Chapter 13: Token Ring Fault Isolation 407

server, and is denied access, the RS may deinsert itself from the ring. Here, the best suggestion is to check all the user rights. Security access at certain directory levels also can cause certain soft-error messages due to increased traffic on the ring.

- In general, network software file server problems can cause the Token Ring bandwidth to be eaten up with abnormal traffic between a certain RS and the file server. If you suspect this, the situation begs for a protocol analysis session.

With a protocol analyzer, you can capture this type of occurrence and view the high-layer protocol communication between an RS and a network file server. This data enables you to identify and troubleshoot the higher-layer communication processes. You also can identify quickly any abnormal network bandwidth between a particular RS and the file server.

In Figure 13.4, a Sniffer analyzer trace depicts a problem with a communication session between a Banyan file server and an RS. Notice the abnormal amount of redundant communication traffic between the RS and the file server. This topic is covered further in the section on troubleshooting high-layer communication problems later in this chapter.

```
┌─ SUMMARY Delta ──────────────────────────────────────────
2  0.003  IBM         7976DBanyan Ser..  SMB R  OK
3  0.009  Banyan Ser..BM   7976DB  SMB C  F=0167 Read 161 at 66
4  0.003  IBM         7976DBanyan Ser..  SMB R  OK
5  0.008  Banyan Ser..BM   7976DB  SMB C  F=167 Close
6  0.002  IBM         7976DBanyan Ser..  SMB R  Closed
7  0.024  Banyan Ser..BM   7976DB  SMB C  Open \LEGAL\EVELYNP\WP\001
8  0.005  IBM         7976DBanyan Ser..  SMB R  F=0168 Opened
9  0.006  Banyan Ser..BM   7976DB  SMB C  F=0168 Seek to end
10 0.002  IBM         7976DBanyan Ser..  SMB R  Seek to 1387
11 0.010  Banyan Ser..BM   7976DB  SMB C  F=0168 Read 16 at 0
12 0.002  IBM         7976DBanyan Ser..  SMB R  OK
13 0.010  Banyan Ser..BM   7976DB  SMB C  F=0168 Read 16 at 0
14 0.003  IBM         7976DBanyan Ser..  SMB R  OK
15 0.008  Banyan Ser..BM   7976DB  SMB C  F=0168 Read 10 at 16
16 0.003  IBM         7976DBanyan Ser..  SMB R  OK
17 0.011  Banyan Ser..BM   7976DB  SMB C  F=0168 Read 50 at 16
18 0.003  IBM         7976DBanyan Ser..  SMB R  OK
19 0.010  Banyan Ser..BM   7976DB  SMB C  F=0168 Read 50 at 16
20 0.003  IBM         7976DBanyan Ser..  SMB R  OK
21 0.009  Banyan Ser..BM   7976DB  SMB C  F=0168 Read 158 at 66
                    ── Frame 12 of 24 ──

 1      2     3     4     5      6DISPLAY  7 PREV   8 NEXT   9   10 NEW
 HELP   MARK              MENUS  OPTIONS   FRAME    FRAME         CAPTURE
```

Figure 13.4 A Sniffer analyzer trace tracks communication problems between a file server and a network ring station.

Exploring Token Ring Network Peripheral Problems

Peripherals such as printers and modems are incorporated in any standard network; in today's networks, the peripherals are much more sophisticated. All sorts of new products are appearing, such as communication servers (modem pools with specialized network access hardware and software), network printers (printers with their own NIC card so they do not need to attach to an RS or file server), and fax servers (fax machines with internal NIC cards).

In taking this form, these devices are not simple peripherals any more—they are now actual nodes on the Token Ring network. Because they contain their own NICs, they also assume a unique Token Ring address, just like an RS. You can't troubleshoot these devices as simple peripherals anymore; you must view them as Token Ring nodes.

The following section describes network peripheral operations, failure symptoms and causes, and some troubleshooting methods.

Network Peripheral Operations

When a network peripheral such as a printer contains its own Token Ring address, it has to be viewed as a unique Token Ring node, almost as if it were an RS. Some of the network peripherals access the Token Ring network with NIC and hardware/software components; others just use NIC hardware with firmware contained within PROM chips. Both configurations allow the assigned network peripheral to access the ring through standard ring insertion, and they both operate according to the Token Ring architecture operating-mode principles.

Network Peripheral Failure Symptoms, Causes, and Troubleshooting

Network peripheral failure symptoms are different from standard RS failure symptoms because a peripheral actually is a different device. A standard RS, for example, cannot log onto the network file server if it cannot complete ring insertion, whereas a network printer may not be able to print because it cannot access the ring. A network peripheral failure can cause soft- and hard-error conditions to be generated on the ring.

Even though a network peripheral failure symptom is different from that of a standard RS, the causes of the network peripheral failure and RS failure are somewhat analogous. Both a network peripheral and a standard RS contain an NIC, and both access the ring through the 802.5 rules, so they both can be assumed to have some common failure causes. If, for example, a network printer cannot access the ring, the logical network area of fault is isolated to a lobe area containing the following components: a printer, an NIC, a lobe cable, and an MAU or hub port. If an RS cannot access the ring, then the lobe area components are a PC, an NIC, a lobe cable, and MAU or hub ports. The only major difference is that one lobe area contains a printer rather than a PC.

Certain network peripheral failures may be related to either improper internal or external network configurations because they sometimes rely upon and cooperate with other network devices to operate.

With all this in mind, approach troubleshooting a network peripheral with the standard lobe area troubleshooting methods discussed earlier in this chapter. One important difference for troubleshooting a network peripheral is that a protocol analysis session is a key to resolving any problems. Because network peripherals are new entities to the standard Token Ring network configuration, a protocol analysis session is recommended. With a protocol analyzer, you can capture and view any network communication data traffic and soft- or hard-error conditions involving the assigned network peripheral.

Exploring Bridge, Router, Repeater, and Gateway Problems

When you are troubleshooting a Token Ring internetwork, the bridges, routers, and repeaters usually are involved. Because these devices separate the rings or ring route for their respective purposes, the actual troubleshooting of these devices requires a good understanding of their operational theory. For a more thorough understanding of a particular bridge, router, or repeater specification and operations, contact the particular manufacturer.

If a bridge, router, or repeater has a failure or improper configuration, most of the time the problem exhibits a fairly straightforward solid symptom. But there also are failure-cause instances that make the problem symptom intermittent.

Whether the symptom is solid or intermittent, the failure symptom may be present in the form of a soft- or hard-error condition on the ring. This section describes some useful information for the failure symptoms, causes, and troubleshooting suggestions for bridges, routers, and repeaters in the Token Ring environment. The information is generic as to manufacturer type.

Bridge Failure Symptoms, Causes, and Troubleshooting

Because bridges connect rings at the data link level and are mainly used to segment traffic, a failure symptom normally is clear. When a bridge failure occurs, the problem usually is evident. Some of the common bridge failure symptoms are as follows:

- No data traffic at all can get from one side of the bridge to the other.
- Partial traffic cannot pass across the bridge, and the problem is solid.
- Partial traffic cannot pass across the bridge, and the problem is intermittent.
- Overloaded-bandwidth problems exist on a certain ring.

If no traffic can get from one side of the bridge to the other, the cause usually is a hardware configuration or hardware failure. To troubleshoot this type of problem, first double-check the software and hardware configuration of the bridge. Configuration problems are common with new installations, network add-ons, and changes.

If the configuration does appear to be at fault, attempt to run some bridge diagnostics (if they are provided by the bridge manufacturer). The last and most comprehensive way to troubleshoot the problem is to run a protocol analysis session.

If partial traffic cannot pass and the problem is solid, the symptom most probably is related to a bridge table configuration or a source-routing problem with certain RSs. First, thoroughly check the bridge configuration. Next, run a protocol analysis session. Examine the Routing Information field of the frames not being passed through the bridge. A protocol analyzer is the key in this

Chapter 13: Token Ring Fault Isolation

instance. If a particular bridge addressing problem is found in the source-routing field, the originating RS may be at fault.

When partial traffic does not pass though the bridge and the problem is intermittent, the first and foremost step is to take out the protocol analyzer. Do a full capture and again examine all the routing information fields of the frames in question. Often an RS causes an intermittent bridge problem. Sometimes this is due to a bad NIC, but most of the time the particular RS has a software application configuration problem in relation to its source-routing information for the particular bridge.

Figure 13.5 shows a frame sequence captured with a Network General Sniffer Analyzer. The frame sequence depicts a bridge forwarding source-routing information from a source ring to a destination ring.

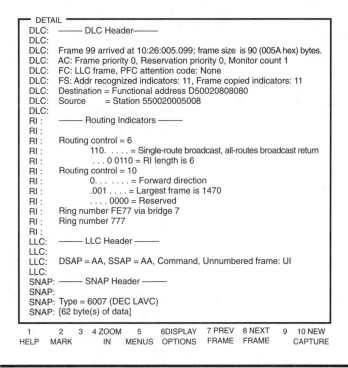

Figure 13.5 This trace depicts a bridge forwarding source-routing information to its destination ring.

ETHERNET AND TOKEN RING OPTIMIZATION

Sometimes an incorrect bridge configuration parameter or source-routing problem with a specific RS causes bandwidth problems in a multiple-ring environment. Certain bridges contain configuration parameters that can control the amount of traffic to be forwarded to another ring. This is an important setting because the bandwidth of the destination ring can be seriously affected if an abnormal amount of traffic is being forwarded.

In a source-routing environment, the problem may not lie with the bridge; it may be due to a particular software application configuration problem relating to source-routing information from a specific RS, but the problem is sometimes hard to identify. If certain rings in a multiple-ring configuration appear to have bandwidth problems, the importance of running a full protocol analysis session on the multiple-ring configuration cannot be stressed enough.

Figure 13.6 shows the routing information screen from a Network General Sniffer Token Ring Advanced Monitor Analyzer, displaying data traffic from one ring to another. This particular screen capture depicts a source-routing overhead problem from one ring to another. The percentage of frames being forwarded is overloading the destination ring with traffic.

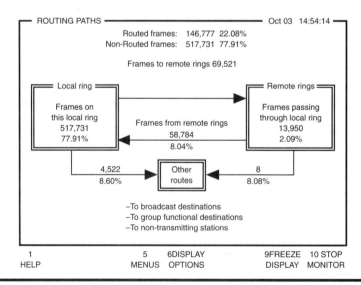

Figure 13.6 Token Ring-specific protocol analysis tools display useful information, such as the source routing overhead problem shown here.

Router Failure Symptoms, Causes, and Troubleshooting

Router failure symptoms can be misleading. Sometimes the problem symptom appears as a particular application, or the NOS does not work on certain rings. Note that the software application and NOS rely on certain LAN communication protocols to communicate across the LAN. If a certain protocol is not being passed through a router, the application or NOS access may work on one ring and not another. Router failure symptoms fall into the following categories:

- They do not allow particular protocols to be passed through to another ring, and the problem is solid.
- They do not allow particular protocols to be passed through to another ring, and the problem is intermittent.
- They do not allow any data traffic to pass through, and the problem is either solid or intermittent.
- Overloaded-bandwidth problems exist on a certain ring.

Because a router is used to segment traffic, many of the troubleshooting points discussed in the preceding section also apply with a router, specifically, partial data transmission and destination ring overhead problems.

Because a router's main purpose is to connect rings that need to differentiate between protocols, they must understand and be configured for the protocol they are forwarding. One of the main points to look for with a suspected router problem is incorrect configurations with the protocol routing table in the particular router. Sometimes these particular configurations are extremely complex and can easily be adversely affected.

Figure 13.7 depicts a routing problem captured by a Sniffer trace. The trace shows a summary view of a TCP/IP DNS packet that could not be forwarded across a router. Further decoding of various frames shows that the problem is there because the router is not configured to forward TCP/IP DNS packets. This is a simple setting, but the problem denied all the users on the source ring access to a remote file server on the destination ring.

```
┌─ SUMMARY Delta ──────────────────────────────────────────────────┐
│  1          Prteon045C14IBM  1D35F3        DSAP=E0, UI frame     │
│  2  0.002  IBM  1D35F3Prteon045C14          DSAP=E0, UI frame     │
│  3  0.184  Broadcast     Prteon046101 DNS C ID=2478 OP=REGISTER NAME=T │
│  4  0.001  IBM           61C09Wellfleet DNS C ID=2478 OP=REGISTER NAME=T │
│  5  0.338  Broadcast         Wellfleet BPDU S:Pri=8000 Port=8001 Root:P │
│  6  0.982  IBM  1229B6Prteon045879          DSAP=E0, UI frame     │
│  7  0.003  Prteon045879IBM  1229B6          DSAP=E0, UI frame     │
│  8  0.005  Prteon045879IBM  1229B6          DSAP=E0, UI frame     │
│  9  0.005  IBM  1229B6Prteon045879          DSAP=E0, UI frame     │
│ 10  0.039  IBM  1229B6Prteon045879          DSAP=E0, UI frame     │
│ 11  0.242  Prteon044525Prteon045C14         DSAP=E0, UI frame     │
│ 12  0.005  Prteon045C14Prteon044525         DSAP=E0, UI frame     │
│ 13  0.124  Broadcast     Prteon046101 DNS C ID=2478 OP=REGISTER NAME=T │
│ 14  0.001  IBM           61C09Wellfleet DNS C ID=2478 OP=REGISTER NAME=T │
│ 15  0.015  NetBIOS       Prteon046101       DSAP=E0, UI frame     │
│ 16  0.311  Broadcast       IBM  1D2AF8 MAC Active Monitor Present │
│ 17  0.019  Broadcast       IBM  1CC749 MAC Standby Monitor Present│
│ 18  0.013  Broadcast       Prteon045879 MAC Standby Monitor Present│
│ 19  0.018  Broadcast       Prteon043A91 MAC Standby Monitor Present│
│ 20  0.016  Broadcast       IBM  1CB7D8 MAC Standby Monitor Present│
└──────────────────── Frame 13 of 20 ──────────────────────────────┘

  1     2     3     4     5    6DISPLAY  7 PREV  8 NEXT   9   10 NEW
```

Figure 13.7 This Network General trace pinpoints a TCP/IP packet not forwarded across a router.

If the problem is that no data traffic can get from one side of the router to the other, the cause usually is a hardware configuration or hardware failure, as with a bridge.

Repeater Failure Symptoms, Causes, and Troubleshooting

Repeater failure symptoms are candid:

- When a repeater fails, it usually does not allow data traffic to pass. Most of the time, this occurrence is solid, but sometimes it is intermittent.
- Sometimes a repeater failure simulates a main ring path failure symptom, and a hard error (such as beaconing or a wire fault condition) may arise.

A repeater failure is usually related to an internal hardware module failure, and at times to the hardware configuration. Sometimes the physical placement of a repeater may be at fault due to the importance of the Token Ring cabling-length specifications. Also keep in mind that the cabling itself can cause a repeater failure symptom.

The first approach should be a TDR and, in the case of fiber, an OTDR. Also use any repeater unit diagnostics if the manufacturer offers them. One of the best methods of troubleshooting a suspected bad repeater is to remove the unit by bypassing it or relooping the cabling at the repeater entry point. Relooping the cabling can be done with patch cables for the specific cable type.

Gateway Failure Symptoms, Causes, and Troubleshooting

Gateway failure symptoms are rather direct. Usually, either you can access the gateway, or you cannot access the gateway. At times, a gateway session may seem slow or unresponsive, usually due to improper configuration in the LAN gateway design, but it can be related to a possible gateway failure. Also, a LAN-to-host session may lock up intermittently, due to intermittent gateway hardware problems or an improper gateway configuration.

The failure causes can be a little more complex. Some of the most common failure causes are as follows:

- The host is not properly configured as to session setup for the particular gateway.
- The gateway itself is not properly configured in relation to hardware/software for access to the host or allowing ring stations access.
- A particular ring station or group of ring stations cannot access the gateway because they are not properly configured in relation to the software/hardware setup.
- An intermittent gateway hardware problem or an improper gateway configuration may cause a LAN-to-host session to intermittently lock up.

The recommended method for troubleshooting these types of problems is to first thoroughly check the gateway's configuration against the gateway manufacturer's hardware and software setup for use with the LAN and the respective host. Next, verify that ring stations that need to access the gateway are configured properly according to the gateway manufacturer's specifications. Last, make sure that the respective host is properly configured as to session setup and port availability to handle communications to the respective gateway.

If any diagnostics from the manufacturer are available, it always is a good idea to use them for gateway troubleshooting. Also fully reference the gateway manufacturer's instructions when working with any gateway issues.

Understanding Protocol Analysis

This section provides an in-depth look at how to use a protocol analysis session to effectively troubleshoot a network problem within the Token Ring architecture.

As you read, keep in mind the prescribed approach for a general protocol analysis session: capture, view, analyze, check errors, benchmark performance, and focus. This generic approach overlays and directly interrelates with the specific methods of using protocol analysis to troubleshoot a Token Ring network.

It is important to mention that, when approaching the Token Ring protocol model with protocol analysis, you must first analyze the lower layers of communication and then consecutively examine the higher-layer communication processes. This is because the low-level 802.5 Token Ring architectural communications must be at a normal operating state before you can conclusively examine any higher-layer protocols used by applications and NOSs. The integrity of the higher-layer protocol communication is based on proper and fluent low-layer protocol communications.

In performing any type of protocol analysis session on a Token Ring network, you must fully capture network data during peak and off-peak network usage periods. This means you cannot perform protocol analysis on a network in a rushed fashion. The proper method is to use a full-capture approach and to run a protocol analysis session for at least a complete business day. This full-capture approach gives you a complete palette of events occurring on your network. In a multiple-ring environment, each ring should get the full-capture approach.

The next section introduces the proper approach for using protocol analysis to view and troubleshoot the low-level 802.5 communications layer, leads into the higher-layer communication processes, and finally discusses performance testing on a Token Ring network.

Examining and Troubleshooting Low-Level 802.5 Communications

To perform a protocol analysis session on the Token Ring topology, the proper approach is to establish a baseline of the network. A network baseline is the current state of a network's order of operation.

To establish an accurate baseline of your Token Ring network, it is always best to perform a protocol analysis session when your network is not experiencing any failures. Capturing a session of communication from the network when it is operating without any errors provides a true picture of its normal baseline. Then when network failures do occur, you can run a protocol analysis session and examine the captured data for any variation from the established normal network baseline.

By examining any particular variations that occur, you can pinpoint a failure cause within a specific network area or component.

The following sections cover how to use protocol analysis for measuring your network baseline and effectively troubleshooting any deviances from the norm.

802.5 Frame Communication

To establish a baseline or to troubleshoot a failure symptom, you should enter the protocol analysis session by focusing on the 802.5 base data frame communication processes. To recap, the data frame carries the classification of either a MAC frame or an LLC frame.

The LLC frames carry the PDU that encases the actual high-level user data information transmitted on the ring. LLC frames involve multiple frame sequences such as addressing, control, and actual high-layer data information.

Because a defined LLC 802.5 data frame is primarily responsible for transferring the higher-layer data information among RSs, it is not considered responsible for establishing the base Token Ring medium access control communication sequencing. For this reason, when encountering LLC frames, you normally would concentrate on the higher-layer information enveloped with the LLC frame. The higher-layer communication processes are discussed in detail later in this section.

ETHERNET AND TOKEN RING OPTIMIZATION

The 25 MAC frame types handle the actual Token Ring medium access control communication, and this is where you have to focus when examining the 802.5 low-level frame communication processes. When examining an 802.5 MAC data frame you have to correlate the MAC frame type with specific Token Ring communication processes. With a thorough understanding of the Token Ring communication process theory, you should be able to capture a series of MAC frames and decipher what type of Token Ring communication process is currently occurring.

After you understand these two important factors—the MAC frame and the current Token Ring communication process—you can examine and troubleshoot the current state of low-level 802.5 frame communications for proper and fluent communication exchange between the network entities involved. Any deviances from a normal state of a low-level frame communication process may indicate a possible intermittent network component failure.

The following example describes a typical deviance from the normal state of a low-level MAC frame communication process. The Token Ring communication processes presented in Chapter 2 provide the necessary theory to fully understand the following example of typical deviance. The AMP MAC frame is generated to notify all standby monitors that an active monitor is on the ring. Because the Neighbor Notification process requires that the frame be generated every seven seconds, you should be able to see this frame present at a regular interval. If you do not, there is a deviance from the normal state of the MAC frame communication process.

You should be able to isolate a possible intermittent network component failure by examining the captured analysis trace for any deviance from this process, such as a Claim Token MAC frame being generated onto the ring by an RS that had its T(Receive_Notification) timer expire and is attempting to enter the Claim Token Transmit mode. This sequence signifies that the AM or a particular SM has a problem and has dropped off the ring. When this occurs, the protocol analyzer may capture some soft errors present on the ring. The Sniffer trace illustrated by Figure 13.8 depicts an abnormal timing sequence on the ring in the generation of the AMP MAC frame.

By applying the approach displayed in the preceding example to other 802.5 low-level frame communication processes, you can troubleshoot other network failures and isolate a failure cause within a specific network area or component.

```
  SUMMARY Delta
  75  22.385  Broadcast   NwkGnIE004FA          DSAP=00, UI frame
  76  22.995  Broadcast   NwkGnIE004F2          DSAP=00, UI frame
  77  23.015  Broadcast   NwkGnIE002D0  MAC Active Monitor Present
  78  23.025  Broadcast   NwkGnIE004F2  MAC Standby Monitor Present
  79  23.038  Broadcast   NwkGnIE004FA  MAC Standby Monitor Present
  80  23.465  Broadcast   NwkGnIE004F2  MAC Claim Token
  81  23.468  Broadcast   NwkGnIE004FA  MAC Claim Token
  82  23.488  Broadcast   NwkGnIE004FA  MAC Claim Token
  83  23.508  Broadcast   NwkGnIE004FA  MAC Claim Token
  84  23.508  Broadcast   NwkGnIE004FA  MAC Ring Purge
  85  23.512  Broadcast   NwkGnIE004FA          DSAP=00, UI frame
  86  23.512  Config Srv  NwkGnIE004FA  MAC Report New Monitor
  87  23.512  Broadcast   NwkGnIE004FA  MAC Active Monitor Present
  88  23.513  Config Srv  NwkGnIE004F2  MAC Report SUA Change
  89  23.525  Broadcast   NwkGnIE004F2  MAC Standby Monitor Present
  90  23.998  Broadcast   NwkGnIE004F2          DSAP=00, UI frame
  91  24.515  Broadcast   NwkGnIE004FA          DSAP=00, UI frame
  92  25.000  Broadcast   NwkGnIE004F2          DSAP=00, UI frame
  93  25.518  Broadcast   NwkGnIE004FA          DSAP=00, UI frame
  94  26.003  Broadcast   NwkGnIE004F2          DSAP=00, UI frame
                              Frame 94 of 127
  1      2     3     4     5    6DISPLAY  7 PREV   8 NEXT    9   10 NEW
 HELP  MARK               MENUS OPTIONS   FRAME    FRAME         CAPTURE
```

Figure 13.8 An abnormal timing sequence on the ring as displayed in a Sniffer trace.

After examining the 802.5 low-level frame communication processes, the next step is to examine the captured data from the protocol analysis session for any soft- or hard-error conditions that may have been recorded.

Error Recording

During a protocol analysis session, the particular analyzer may capture certain soft and hard errors if they occur on the ring. Depending on the protocol analyzer or network monitoring tool being used, the process may be automatic or it may need to be initiated. All the protocol analysis and monitoring tools mentioned in Chapter 4 dynamically collect most soft and hard errors that occur on a Token Ring network.

Some of the analyzer and monitoring devices allow your captures to be selective by filtering certain specified error patterns; they also enable you to categorize the particular errors in different formats. This troubleshooting approach enables you to gather conclusive and organized testing results.

When you're performing error recording, set alarm triggers for some of the more serious errors or a particular error that you want to observe more closely. Most of the analyzer and monitoring tools mentioned in Chapter 4 offer error alarm triggering.

The next sections describe in detail the soft- and hard-error conditions that can occur on a Token Ring network, and their respective failure causes, along with some recommended troubleshooting methods using protocol analysis.

Soft Error Breakdown

Soft errors are the less-critical type of errors that can occur on the ring, and they usually are temporary disturbances of the normal mode of ring communication.

To recap, when soft errors occur, an RS collects the errors and sends them to the functional REM address. When an RS encounters a soft error, it increments its internal soft error counter and starts a Token Ring protocol timer T(Soft_Error_Report). After two seconds, the timer expires, and the RS generates a Report Soft Error MAC frame.

High occurrences of certain soft errors can cause ring performance degradation and initiate the Ring Recovery process. When the Ring Recovery process occurs, the ring is reset to a stable mode of operation. This process involves reinitiating all the basic ring start-up processes, such as the Token Claiming process and the Neighbor Notification process. Because these processes take place unexpectedly, you can see how ring-performance degradation can occur.

Some soft errors are considered more serious than others. When recording soft errors, be aware of the level of seriousness and the possible failure cause for each type of soft error. Certain soft errors actually point to a possible network component as the failure cause. The Report Soft Error MAC frame that is transmitted contains the soft error type, the reporting RS's NIC address, and its respective NAUN's NIC address.

When performing a protocol analysis session for the purpose of error recording, the proper way to examine a Report Soft Error MAC frame is to note the type of soft error and any associated addresses in the MAC frame; with this information, you can identify certain possible network components as the cause of specific network failures.

As mentioned, the Report Soft Error MAC frame contains the soft error type. The type is indicated by the byte set in the soft error counter field of the Report Soft Error MAC frame. The soft error counter field is a 12-byte field: ten of the bytes represent soft error types; the other two bytes are reserved for future use. The hexadecimal value of a particular soft error byte indicates the actual soft error count for the soft error type. Figure 13.9 displays a soft error report captured by the IBM LAN Manager program.

Chapter 13: Token Ring Fault Isolation 421

Figure 13.9 The IBM LAN Manager reports various Token Ring conditions, including the soft error report shown here.

Soft error types are divided into two different categories: isolating error types and non-isolating error types. Isolating error types are specific errors that the reporting RS internal error counter can collect and isolate to an assigned fault domain. Isolating error types can point to an actual fault domain because the RS that first detects the error is the station that originates the error, and it counts, collects, and generates the Report Soft Error MAC frame.

Non-isolating error types are errors that a certain nonspecific reporting RS can detect, collect, and generate, without any specific, defined error source information. Because the particular reporting RS is not defined as the station that originated the error, the station and its NAUN cannot be conclusively considered part of an assigned fault domain.

The following is a description of isolating error types, their possible associated failure causes, and the recommended troubleshooting methods:

- **Internal Error.** These errors signify that the reporting RS has encountered a recoverable internal error. If this particular error is recorded frequently, the reporting station NIC may be operating in marginal condition. Any available diagnostics should be run on the particular RS, and to be conclusive you can remove the station from the ring and rerun a protocol analysis session. If one internal error is encountered, the NIC may have failed and should be troubleshot.

- **Burst Error.** These errors signify that the reporting RS encountered a signal error or transition has been detected in the Token Ring cabling medium. Normally, these errors occur when RSs leave or enter the ring, which causes ring reconfigurations. If the error is due to a ring reconfiguration, you can check the protocol analysis session trace for the Neighbor Notification process occurring directly before the burst error; for example, you should see a Report NAUN Change MAC frame present before the error. If the burst error count exceeds the level of 20 in one error packet and no stations have entered or left the ring, this may indicate a bad lobe cable which should be checked with a TDR.

Basically, if this particular error is recorded frequently and no ring reconfigurations are occurring, it is possible that the cabling medium has a problem. In this case, troubleshoot the fault domain involved as described earlier in this chapter.

- **Line Error.** These errors signify that the reporting RS checksum process has detected a checksum error in a specific received data frame or token, after transmission of the respective token or data frame. When this error occurs, it usually is related to ring recoveries or simple ring reconfiguration. Sometimes the presence of a line error can be due to a failure cause located in the reporting station's NAUN. If the line error count exceeds the level of 20 in one error packet and no stations have entered or left the ring, this may indicate a bad NIC which should be troubleshot. If line errors arise often, test the reporting station's NAUN. This can be done with diagnostics or by removing the station from the ring and rerunning a protocol analysis session.

- **Abort Delimiter Transmitted Error.** This error signifies that the reporting RS has encountered a recoverable internal error that forced it to transmit an Abort Delimiter frame. If this error is recurrent at rates of more than 10 in one error packet or just is continuously being generated from one ring station, the reporting station NIC may be operating in marginal condition. Again, diagnostics should be run on the particular RS. To be conclusive, the suspected station can be removed from the ring and a protocol analysis session run.

- **AC Error.** This error indicates that the reporting RS's NAUN could not successfully set the address recognized or frame copied bits in the newly transmitted frame, even though it has actually completed the copy of the bits on its last frame received. If this error happens often, it is possible that the reporting station's NAUN has a failure. It is also possible that a common destination station is returning the frame improperly to the source. If this error is captured at counts of even one in an error packet, the NAUN and destination devices of the reporting station should be tested with diagnostics or by removing the stations from the ring and rerunning a protocol analysis session. On router- and bridge-based networks, if a large group of ring stations is experiencing this problem on one common ring, check the router and bridge NICs through diagnostics.

The following is a description of non-isolating error types and their possible associated failure causes and recommended troubleshooting methods:

- **Lost Frame Error.** This error indicates that an originating RS generated a frame onto the ring to a specific address and did not receive the frame back. This error may be detected by either the AM or the originating RS. Because the RS did not receive the frame back, it cannot release the token, which causes the AM to initiate ring recovery and issue a new token. Also because the station did not receive the frame back, the source that may have caused the frame to become lost is not directly identifiable.

  If this type of error occurs frequently, troubleshoot the fault domain surrounding the reporting RS, and rerun the protocol analysis session to identify any repetitive patterns of this error.

- **Receiver Congestion Error.** This error indicates that the reporting RS could not receive a frame addressed to its address. This usually occurs because of lack of buffer space within the NIC on the destination RS. The destination station NIC may be at fault, but this error normally occurs because a specific network software application is causing the particular destination RS to be flooded with data too frequently.

  Receiver congestion errors occur often on certain network file servers. If the cause is related to the flooding of data and is a frequent occurrence, and something is not eventually done to alleviate the problem, the NOS may have operational failures. This problem usually can be remedied in either of two ways: the network software application access can be redesigned, or an NIC with larger buffer space can be installed in the particular destination RS.

- **Frame Copied Error.** This error signifies that the reporting RS has copied a frame that may have the same address as its own—a duplicate address. It also is possible that the frame was corrupted on the ring. If this error occurs frequently, and there is not an assigned duplicate Token Ring address on the ring, check the reporting RS's adapter.

- **Frequency Error.** This error signifies that the reporting RS is attempting to receive a frame that does not contain the proper ring-clock frequency. Because the active monitor is responsible for maintaining the Ring Master

Clock, it is possible that the active monitor has encountered an error. If this error occurs frequently, check the AM and the reporting RS's respective NAUN. It is also possible that a power problem or MRP with bad grounding can induce intermittent frequency errors. Again, run any available diagnostics, remove any suspected RS from the ring, and rerun a protocol analysis session.

- **Token Error.** A token error is generated only by the AM in the event that it does not detect a token on the ring. Because the AM cannot pinpoint the reason for the token being lost, the cause cannot directly be associated with any particular network component. The AM initiates ring recovery and issues a new token. Also, when a token error occurs because of the ring recovery process, it is highly possible that other RSs will detect and generate burst, line, and lost frame errors onto the ring. If token errors occur frequently, continue to run a protocol analysis session to identify any repetitive patterns of this error.

When soft errors occur on a Token Ring network, they are not always caused by an actual failure on the network; sometimes they are triggered by a simple ring reconfiguration. Because of the Token Ring architecture's intricacies, it also was designed with a sophisticated scheme for error handling. This scheme allows the Token Ring architecture to recover from some of the less-serious operational failures. The key to successful analysis of soft errors is to be aware of high occurrences and the associated ring performance degradation that can occur. Again, with a thorough approach to protocol analysis, you can be conclusive as to your testing results by identifying any clear communication trends involving soft errors.

Hard Error Breakdown

Hard errors that occur on the ring are more critical than soft errors. A hard error is an actual solid failure with a specific network component. On a Token Ring network, a hard error takes the form of a failure symptom by the beaconing process. When a hard error occurs, the fault area usually must be bypassed for the ring to operate. The bypass may occur dynamically due to the inherent beaconing process built into the Token Ring architecture.

To recap, when an RS detects a hard error, it enters the beaconing process to attempt a dynamic ring recovery. At times, the fault area causing the hard error cannot be bypassed, and the specific fault area (such as a defined fault domain, lobe area, or network component) must be removed from the ring configuration to reestablish normal ring operation.

By using protocol analysis, you most likely can identify any hard errors quickly. Some protocol analysis and ring monitoring devices actually can enter a beaconing ring, enabling you to troubleshoot and quickly identify any hard errors causing a ring failure.

All the protocol analysis and ring monitoring devices mentioned in Chapter 4 can detect the beaconing process and locate the network fault area to a specified fault domain, lobe area, or network component.

If you encounter a hard error during a protocol analysis session, the first step is to examine the Beacon MAC frame. The Beacon MAC frame contains three important fields related to fault isolation: the reporting RS, the reporting station's NAUN, and the beacon type. The reporting RS and the NAUN are the logical assigned fault domain. The beacon type field further identifies the most likely failure cause within the fault domain. The four beacon types are:

1. **Ring Recovery Mode Set.** This indicates that the ring already is in ring recovery.
2. **Signal Loss Error.** This beacon type indicates that there most likely is a cable fault in the cabling medium internal to the assigned fault domain. If this beacon type recurs, troubleshoot the assigned fault domain cabling medium as discussed earlier in this chapter.
3. **Streaming Signal/Not Claim Token MAC Frame.** This beacon type indicates that most likely a failure is with one of the RSs involved in the fault domain. The error is inconclusive as to which RS is at fault. The best bet here is to troubleshoot the complete assigned fault domain as discussed earlier in this chapter.
4. **Streaming Signal/Claim Token MAC Frame.** This beacon type also signifies a failure with one of the RSs in the assigned fault domain. It is, however, inconclusive as to which RS is at fault. Again, troubleshoot the complete assigned fault domain as discussed earlier in this chapter.

The second step when troubleshooting a hard error is to isolate the failure cause to one of the two lobe areas defined in the assigned fault domain and then isolate the failure cause to a specific network component.

In summary, the proper approach for troubleshooting hard errors in a Token Ring network is to focus on the assigned fault domain addresses and beacon type by using protocol analysis and then integrate the manual fault-isolation methods for troubleshooting an assigned fault domain and lobe areas, as detailed earlier in this chapter.

Token Ring Rotation Time

When examining the physical layer health of a Token Ring network, it is advantageous to have a reading on the Token Rotation Time (TRT). Token Rotation Time is a good indication of how fast token ring frames are being processed on a ring. The TRT value is actually a measurement of how long a single token takes to circle one individual Token Ring network. This measurement statistic is considered separate for every individual Token Ring network within an internetwork of multiple rings. The normal TRT value on a healthy 4Mbps or 16Mbps ring should be between 10 and 150 microseconds.

The TRT value on a ring can be measured by certain protocol analyzers. If the value is out of the normal range of 10 to 150 microseconds, it may indicate that this particular ring has a problem with processing frames. The TRT value does not tell you what is wrong on the ring, but it may indicate that the ring you are analyzing has some sort of problem that you should investigate. In other words, an abnormal TRT value pushes you to examine a ring in more depth.

Instances do occur in which rings manifest problems by periodically displaying high TRT levels. On a healthy ring, the TRT usually is extremely solid—between 10 and 150 microseconds—which indicates a basic, healthy platform for normal ring communications.

As certain levels of traffic increase and certain internetwork changes occur on a Token Ring network, keep an eye on the TRT. It is an important indicator regarding the overall physical condition of the network.

Examining and Troubleshooting High-Layer Communication Problems

After verifying that the 802.5 base frame communication processes are proper and fluent and that the ring has been analyzed for soft- and hard-error occurrences, examine the higher-layer communication processes.

When using a protocol analyzer to troubleshoot the higher-layer communication processes, first perform a full-capture session. Next, view the high-layer protocol communication that occurs concurrently between general RSs and the communication between general RSs and the network file server.

What you actually are examining is the application and NOS communication process between the respective RSs. All applications and NOSs use a predefined protocol for exchanging information. These are unique (to the application or NOS) protocol methods and nomenclature for communication among network nodes. You have to become familiar with the involved application or NOS protocol for communicating. Also be aware that certain applications may use multiple layers of the Token Ring protocol model for transmission.

IBM's PC LAN program uses the session layer for the NetBIOS protocol, for example, and then sets up at the application layer a communication channel on which the IBM SMB protocol communicates. When analyzing this type of communication session, be sure to examine the NetBIOS and SMB communication processes. This requires that you be aware and understand the respective protocol communication commands for each of the assigned high-layer protocols.

Whatever application protocol is involved, everything that occurs between network nodes at the higher layers concerning application and NOS communication is based on some sort of file access process. An application or NOS can do only so many things when it comes to file access: it can open a file, read a file, write to file, close a file, create a file, delete a file, and so on. After you understand the basic processes that occur with file access, you can apply them to protocol analysis. If during protocol analysis, you see an RS attempting to open a file, and it continually is denied access, you can identify the problem as a security problem. Or you may see an RS encountering a write-to-file error due to lack of available disk space on the file server. The same analysis approach can be applied to many different file access scenarios.

The Sniffer trace in Figure 13.10 depicts a bindery error related to a file access problem on a Novell file server. After you understand the application/NOS protocols involved in your network and their basic file access communication processes, you can use a protocol analyzer to examine the higher layers in the Token Ring protocol model for proper and fluent communication processes.

```
┌─ SUMMARY Delta ──────────────────────────────────────────┐
│  4 0.001  IBM         25D10ANovell Ser..  NCP R  Bindery error
│  5 0.057  Novell Ser..IBM    3A5AFC       NCP C  F=BAB6 Read 1024 at 410603
│  6 0.002  IBM         3A5AFCNovell Ser..  NCP R  OK 1024 bytes read
│  7 0.003  Novell Ser..IBM    3A5AFC       NCP C  F=BAB6 Read 1024 at 410603
│  8 0.002  IBM         3A5AFCNovell Ser..  NCP R  OK 1024 bytes read
│  9 0.010  Novell Ser..IBM    3A5AFC       NCP C  F=BAB6 Read 4 at 73
│ 10 0.000  IBM         3A5AFCNovell Ser..  NCP R  OK 4 bytes read
│ 11 0.023  Novell Ser..IBM    3A5AFC       NCP C  F=BAB6 Read 4 at 73
│ 12 0.000  IBM         3A5AFCNovell Ser..  NCP R  OK 4 bytes read
└──────────────────── Frame 4 of 47 ───────────────────────┘
┌─ DETAIL ─────────────────────────────────────────────────┐
│ NCP:   ---- Service a Queue Job Reply ----
│ NCP:
│ NCP:   Request/sub-function code = 23,113 (reply to frame 3)
│ NCP:
│ NCP:   Completion code = D5 (Bindery error)
│ NCP:   Connection status flags = 00 (OK)
│ NCP:   [Normal end of NetWare "Service a Queue Job Reply" packet.]
│ NCP:
└──────────────────── Frame 4 of 47 ───────────────────────┘
                    Use TAB to select windows
  1      2    3   4 ZOOM   5    6 DISPLAY  7 PREV   8 NEXT    9   10 NEW
 HELP   MARK         IN       MENUS OPTIONS  FRAME   FRAME         CAPTURE
```

Figure 13.10 The Sniffer analyzer shows a bindery error on a Novell NetWare file server.

Performance Testing

Abnormal high network bandwidth usage can cause considerable performance degradation on a Token Ring network. This degradation can be in the form of several different failure symptoms, a specific network application operating slowly, the whole network operating slowly, logon failures, or soft- or hard-error conditions.

When benchmarking the actual performance of a Token Ring network, the first step is to monitor the network bandwidth utilization at an overall baseline view, and then to measure the network bandwidth used by each of the individual RSs. Most of the protocol analyzers and ring-monitoring tools mentioned in Chapter 4 enable you to look at the overall baseline network bandwidth and at individual RS levels. Some of the units offer both graphical and numeric display modes for network bandwidth.

When using a protocol analyzer or a ring-monitoring tool to view the overall baseline network bandwidth, be aware of the actual maximum bandwidth available on the Token Ring cabling medium. If the network is running at

4Mbps, for example, the maximum available bandwidth is about 4,500 bytes; if your network is running at 16Mbps, the maximum available bandwidth is about 18,000 bytes.

After you are aware of the maximum available bandwidth, you can determine how much of the available network bandwidth is being consumed by network traffic. Remember that if you are viewing network bandwidth, you must apply the full-capture method (discussed earlier in this chapter) for monitoring the network during peak and off-peak network usage periods to get conclusive testing results. This is extremely important when measuring network bandwidth because your network bandwidth is a usage factor that fluctuates frequently throughout the business day. For example, certain network failures may occur due to a large number of users attempting to access a specific network application at the same time. This typically occurs at certain times of the business day. When monitoring the network with a full-capture approach, you probably can capture this type of network access trend if it is present on the network.

If you are experiencing any abnormal high network bandwidth usage causing performance problems, the cause usually is either a network application problem or is related to a specific RS experiencing a failure.

After you benchmark the network bandwidth utilization at an overall baseline view, the next step is to benchmark the network bandwidth usage of each individual RS. Because you have established the overall baseline of the consumed network bandwidth, you now can use the protocol analyzer or ring monitoring tool to look at the individual RS. By looking closely at individual RSs, you can identify any network bandwidth abnormalities of particular stations. As discussed earlier, certain RSs may absorb an abnormal amount of network bandwidth due to redundant communication traffic between the RS and the file server. Sometimes these failures are related to the application or the NOS, or the particular RS may have an internal failure causing the problem.

The best approach to use if you encounter a particular RS absorbing abnormal bandwidth is to first troubleshoot the 802.5 low-layer and then the high-layer communication processes for normal and fluent communication, as described earlier. If you suspect that the RS is the failure cause, use the methods discussed earlier in this chapter.

Another approach is to load the network. Loading the network by means of one of the traffic-generation features is a useful troubleshooting technique when you are experiencing intermittent problems on a Token Ring network. By

ETHERNET AND TOKEN RING OPTIMIZATION

carefully loading the network with additional network traffic, you can benchmark its tolerance and performance in response to additional traffic, for performance-tuning purposes. This testing technique also can be used to flush out certain types of intermittent failure causes; by generating additional network traffic, you can stress the network enough to cause certain marginal network component failures to surface.

You have to be careful when using this technique. First, you must be aware of the current network usage and any possible impacts to the network user community. Second, you really have to understand all the Token Ring network bandwidth considerations mentioned earlier, including the actual maximum bandwidth available, the overall network bandwidth baseline view, and individual RS bandwidth consumption.

If you use this technique properly, it can be extremely useful for both troubleshooting Token Ring network problems and for performance tuning. Figure 13.11 shows the Sniffer Analyzer Traffic Generator screen displaying traffic being generated onto a Token Ring network.

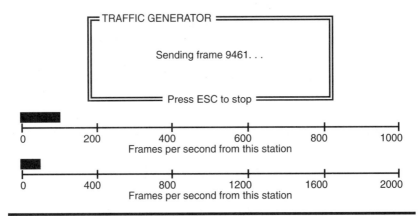

Figure 13.11 Generating additional network traffic, as depicted in this Sniffer Analyzer screen, sometimes aids in troubleshooting.

Chapter 14 presents a series of detailed Token Ring network troubleshooting flow guides that encompass some of the troubleshooting approaches introduced in this chapter.

CHAPTER 14

Token Ring Troubleshooting Flow Guides

As you saw in Chapter 13, "Token Ring Fault Isolation," many fault symptoms and causes are associated with failures of fault domains, lobe areas, and network components. When attempting to troubleshoot these areas in the Token Ring architecture, you must make many correct decisions when vectoring to the path that leads to the cause of your system's failure. Your troubleshooting skills will become more effective as your vectoring decisions become more astute and precise.

The following flow guides were created to help your vectoring decision-making by simulating the correct thought process for fault-isolation vectoring when troubleshooting a Token Ring network.

Take the time to carefully read and follow each step before you take any of the defined actions in a flow guide you are currently following. Also, make sure to thoroughly read any NOTE in the flow guides. While you are using the flow guides, it is a good idea to take memos on your troubleshooting steps and results.

14.1 Network Problem Entry Flow Guide

The network problem entry flow guide is the entry point for approaching the specific network area or component flow guides included in this chapter. From the 14 main network failure symptom choices that follow, decide which one most closely relates to the failure symptom you have encountered in the particular network area and follow the vector to the respective chapter section. If for some reason you feel that your particular failure symptom is associated with a certain network component, you can at your discretion vector directly to the respective flow guide.

While deciding, also note if the failure symptom fits logically into one of the following network areas:

- All network users
- A group of network users
- One network user

In addition, note whether the failure symptom is classified as solid or intermittent.

Main Network Failure Symptoms

1. A ring station, group of ring stations, or the complete network is hanging or freezing.

   (Vector to flow guide 14.6.)

2. A ring station or group of ring stations cannot access any ring resources, such as the main network file server.

   (Vector to flow guide 14.4.)

3. The network is encountering a specific soft or hard error on the network.

   (Vector to flow guide 14.15.)

4. The network is experiencing any of the following failures: the whole network is operating slowly; a specific network application is operating slowly; or network log-on failures are occurring.

Chapter 14: Token Ring Troubleshooting Flow Guide

(Vector to flow guide 14.15.)

5. You are having a problem accessing or using a particular application/group of applications, or certain directories/files, on the network file server.

   (Vector to flow guide 14.14.)

6. A particular network operating system feature or set of NOS features on the network file server is not working.

   (Vector to flow guide 14.14.)

7. A network peripheral cannot be used or accessed.

   (Vector to flow guide 14.10.)

8. A network printer or printers cannot be used or accessed.

   (Vector to flow guide 14.12.)

9. You are experiencing problems accessing or using a network server other than the main network file server, such as database, fax, communication, or print server.

   (Vector to flow guide 14.14.)

10. You are having a problem accessing or using other rings in an internetwork that are connected to the local ring through a bridge.

    (Vector to flow guide 14.7.)

11. You are having a problem accessing or using other rings in an internetwork that are connected to the local ring through a router.

    (Vector to flow guide 14.8.)

12. You are experiencing a problem accessing or using a host connection connected by means of a gateway on the local ring or a ring in an internetwork.

    (Vector to flow guide 14.13.)

13. The complete network is hanging or freezing, and the problem appears to be related to a repeater.

    (Vector to flow guide 14.9.)

14. A network-sharable or non-sharable modem cannot be used/accessed, or there is a problem accessing the ring from a remote modem connection.

    (Vector to flow guide 14.11.)

14.2 Fault Domain and Lobe Area Problem Flow Guides

Is the failure symptom isolated to a fault domain (for example, two lobe areas/two respective ring stations or network devices)?

(Vector to sub-flow guide 14.2.1.)

Is the failure symptom already located to a specific lobe area?

(Vector to sub-flow guide 14.2.2.)

14.2.1 Failure Symptom Is Located to a Fault Domain

Remove one of the lobe cables involved in the fault domain from the MAU or wiring hub. Retest the ring.

Is the failure symptom gone?

[YES]　You have located the problem to the removed lobe area.
(Vector to sub-flow guide 14.2.2 and troubleshoot the removed lobe area.)

If problems still exist after following sub-flow guide 14.2.2, vector back up to this sub-flow guide (14.2.1); then go directly to the next step to troubleshoot the other lobe area in the fault domain as a possible fault.

[NO]　Reconnect the first suspect lobe area cable and disconnect the second lobe area cable and retest.

Is the failure symptom gone?

[YES]　You have located the problem to the removed lobe area.

(Vector to sub-flow guide 14.2.2 and troubleshoot the removed lobe area.)

[NO]　If problems still exist, first attempt restarting at the beginning of sub-flow guide 14.2.1. If you end up back at this same point, vector to flow guide 14.15.

Chapter 14: Token Ring Troubleshooting Flow Guide **435**

NOTE: Remember that if you defined this fault domain from data captured during a protocol analysis session, the Beacon MAC Frame should be examined. If the Beacon type field is classified as a Signal Loss Error, a cable involved in the fault domain may be at fault.

14.2.2 Failure Symptom Is Located to a Specific Lobe Area

Disconnect the suspected lobe cable from its original MAU or wiring hub port and connect it to another MAU or wiring hub port. Retest the ring.

Is the failure symptom gone?

[YES] The original specific MAU or wiring hub port is bad. Troubleshoot the specific MAU or wiring hub port by vectoring to flow guide 14.4 (MAU).

[NO] Test the lobe cable with a TDR or a ring cable tester. If any faults are found with the cable, verify the cable fault by vectoring to flow guide 14.3 (Cable). If no cable faults exist, go to the next step.

Have you thoroughly troubleshot the ring station or network peripheral involved in this lobe area?

[YES] Troubleshoot the respective NIC by vectoring to flow guide 14.5 (NIC).

[NO] Troubleshoot the respective ring station or network peripheral by vectoring to either flow guide 14.6 (Ring Station) or 14.10 (Network Peripheral).

NOTE: If you tried troubleshooting all the network components in the respective lobe area ring station, network peripheral, NIC, MAU or wiring hub, and cabling, and the failure symptom still exists on the ring, attempt to gather more conclusive fault-isolation data by vectoring to flow guide 14.15.

14.3 Cable Problem Flow Guides

Does the failure symptom you are troubleshooting in a specific lobe area appear to be related to a lobe cable?

(Vector to flow guide 14.3.1.)

Does the failure symptom you are troubleshooting with a group of ring stations/network peripherals or the complete Token Ring network appear to be related to the main ring path?

(Vector to flow guide 14.3.2.)

14.3.1 A Lobe Cable Appears to Be Causing a Failure Symptom in a Lobe Path

Remove the lobe cable from the MAU or wiring hub port and the NIC. Test the lobe cable with either a TDR or a ring cable-specific tester.

Did testing the cable find any faults in the cable?

[YES]   The suspected bad cable is faulty. Resolve the problem by replacing the respective lobe cable in the lobe area, and retest the ring station or network peripheral for proper operation. If the failure symptom is gone, record the problem in the network maintenance and service log. If problems still exist, go to the next step.

[NO]   If no faults are found by testing the lobe cable, then another network component such as the MAU or wiring hub port, ring station, network peripheral, or an NIC in the suspected bad lobe area is probably at fault. Re-attach the original lobe cable into the lobe path and re-troubleshoot the respective lobe path by vectoring to flow guide 14.2.

If you definitely feel the original lobe cable has a problem, it may be best to keep the newly replaced lobe cable attached, rather than replace the original lobe cable, before resuming troubleshooting by vectoring to flow guide 14.2. This will be a judgment call on your part.

14.3.2 The Main Ring Path Calling Appears to be Causing a Problem with a Group of Ring Stations or the Complete Token

Does the ring contain a repeater?

[YES]   If you have not troubleshot the repeater, and you feel it may be introducing a problem into the main ring path, vector to flow guide 14.9. If you are confident it is not the problem, go to the next step.

[NO]   Disconnect the first MAU in the MAU rack from the ring by disconnecting its RI and RO cables.

NOTE If your main ring path is configured in such a way that your MAUs are spread out and are not properly centrally located in a MAU rack, the following procedure may be more difficult.

Also, in the case of a wiring hub, you may have to take a unique approach, such as removing the respective wiring hub modules from the wiring hub. Do not overlook the manufacturer's instructions. Check for any available specific MAU connection diagnostics.

Next, test the first MAU by verifying that the ring stations connected to it can properly perform ring insertion.

Did the first MAU test OK?

[YES]   Disconnect the second MAU from the ring and connect it to the first MAU. Next, test the new ring configuration operation (first and second MAU) by verifying that the ring stations connected to it can properly perform ring insertion.

NOTE Continue the troubleshooting method of disconnecting the next physical MAU in the MAU rack from the original ring configuration and adding it to the new ring configuration until a problem is encountered.

ETHERNET AND TOKEN RING OPTIMIZATION

If adding a network component, such as a MAU or main ring path cabling section, to the new ring configuration causes a problem, go to the next step. If no problems are found in any of the main ring path components, vector to flow guide 14.15.

[NO]   Replace both the MAU and main ring path cabling sections that were added to the new ring configuration and caused the failure symptom to arise. Retest the ring.

Retesting the ring should be done by putting aside the suspected bad MAU and main ring cabling path section and then reconnecting the rest of the network to the new ring configuration.

If no further problems are encountered, record the problem in the network maintenance and service log. If problems still exist, restart troubleshooting back from the last MAU that tested properly. More than one failure may be on the network. If you continue to arrive back at this point, vector to flow guide 14.15.

14.4 Multistation Access Unit (MAU) and Wiring Hub Problem Flow Guides

Does the failure symptom appear to be related to a specific MAU or hub port failure?

(Vector to sub-flow guide 14.4.1.)

Do the failure symptoms that appear to be related to a suspected bad MAU or wiring hub module occur with multiple users or the complete Token Ring network?

(Vector to sub-flow guide 14.4.2.)

NOTE

Because this flow guide is generic as to the MAU and wiring hub manufacturer, for some of the troubleshooting steps mentioned in this flow guide you should also reference the respective manufacturer's documentation for any predefined methods for checking configuration and for diagnostic testing.

In the case of some wiring hubs, you may have certain diagnostics available that can help you locate a specific problem. If this type of diagnostics is available, attempt to use it for fault isolation.

14.4.1 A Specific MAU or Hub Port Appears to be Encountering a Failure

Move the lobe cable from the suspected bad port to another port on the same MAU or wiring hub module. Before you move the lobe cable, make sure the new port is functioning. Next, retest the respective ring station or network peripheral on the new MAU or wiring hub port.

Did physically changing the port get rid of the failure symptom?

[YES]   The suspected bad port is bad. Replace the respective MAU or hub module and retest the ring station or network peripheral for proper operation. If the failure symptom is gone, record the problem in the network maintenance and service log. If problems still exist, go to the next step.

[NO]   If a failure still exists with the same ring station or network peripheral, re-attach the lobe cable to the original port and troubleshoot the respective lobe area for the assigned MAU or wiring hub port by vectoring to flow guide 14.2.

14.4.2 A Suspected Bad MAU or Wiring Appears to be Causing Failure Symptoms with Multiple Token Ring

Whether the failure symptom is solid or intermittent, remove the suspected bad MAU or wiring hub module and associated main ring path cabling sections from the ring configuration and then retest the ring.

Are the failure symptoms now gone?

[YES]   The respective MAU, wiring hub module, or a main ring path cabling section is at failure. Replace the removed unit and cables with another unit and cables. Retest the new ring configuration. If no further problems are encountered, record the problem in the network maintenance and service log. If problems still exist, go to the next step.

Even if your problem is now fixed, if you feel that one of the main ring path cabling sections did cause the problem, you can verify the problem by vectoring to flow guide 14.3. If you want to verify the MAU or wiring hub failure, you can do so with any available manufacturer diagnostics.

[NO]   If failure symptoms still exist, reinsert the original MAU or wiring hub module and respective cables into the ring configuration.

Have you troubleshot and verified the integrity of the main ring path cabling?

[YES]   Run a protocol analysis session to gain more conclusive fault isolation data by vectoring to flow guide 14.15.

[NO]   Troubleshoot the main ring path cabling by vectoring to flow guide 14.3.

14.5 NIC Problem Flow Guides

Did you arrive at this flow guide because of NIC failure indications from running a protocol analysis session?

\Vector to sub-flow guide 14.5.1.)

Did you arrive at this flow guide after troubleshooting a lobe area, ring station, network file server, MAU/wiring hub, cable, or network peripheral?

(Vector to sub-flow guide 14.5.2.)

Because this flow guide is generic as to the NIC manufacturer, for some of the troubleshooting steps mentioned in this flow guide you should also reference the NIC manufacturer's documentation for any predefined methods for checking NIC configuration and for bridge testing.

14.5.1 Error Indication Occurs in a Protocol Analysis Session

Whether the error is a hard error indicated by a Beacon MAC frame or a soft error that indicates a possible NIC failure, swap the respective NIC and rerun another thorough protocol analysis session on the ring.

After swapping the NIC and rerunning the new protocol analysis session, did the error go away?

[YES]   Leave the newly replaced NIC in the ring station or device and record the problem in the network maintenance and service log.

[NO]   Replace the original NIC back into the ring station or network peripheral; vector to flow guide 14.15; and rerun a protocol analysis session on the ring. Sometimes when you rerun a protocol analysis session, the failure cause becomes more clear by moving to another Token Ring address.

If after you rerun another protocol analysis session the error does not move to another device and is still identifying the particular NIC address as a failure cause, troubleshoot the assigned lobe area for the respective NIC by vectoring to flow guide 14.2.

14.5.2 Vectoring from Lobe Area, Ring Station, Network File Server, MAU/Wiring Hub, Cable, or Network Peripheral Flow Guide

Is the failure symptom that led you to this flow guide classified as solid or intermittent?

    [SOLID]   Go to **S1**.

    [INTERMITTENT]   Go to **S2**.

    [S1]   **Solid**. Thoroughly check all the following areas:

1. Check all NIC hardware/software configuration parameters:
   - I/O address
   - IRQ
   - DMA
   - Token Ring address
   - Slot settings (32-, 16-, or 8-bit card)
   - NIC microcode level
   - Primary or secondary setting
   - Speed settings
2. Check the ring station for the respective NIC for proper NIC software driver microcode and a good RPL PROM.
3. Check for possible NIC incompatibilities with the particular ring station, MAU, cable type, or the STP/UTP cabling connector.

Did you find any problems in any of the three areas?

    [YES]   Take the necessary action to resolve the problem and retest the ring station or network peripheral for proper operation. If the failure symptom is gone, record the problem in the network maintenance and service log. If the problem still exists after retesting, go to the next step.

[NO] Run any available NIC diagnostics from the NIC manufacturer or elsewhere to be conclusive. Whether the diagnostics pinpoint a failure or not, swap the original NIC in the ring station or network device and retest the ring station or network peripheral for proper operation; vector to flow guide 14.15; and rerun a protocol analysis session on the ring. If the failure symptom goes away, record the problem in the network maintenance and service log.

If, after rerunning another protocol analysis session, an error occurs with the assigned ring station or network peripheral and the specific failure symptom does not go away, replace the original NIC and troubleshoot the assigned lobe area for the respective NIC by vectoring to flow guide 14.2.

If you definitely feel the original NIC has a problem, it may be best to keep the newly replaced NIC in the respective ring station (rather than replacing the original NIC) before resuming troubleshooting by vectoring to flow guide 14.2. This is going to be a judgment call on your part.

[S2] **Intermittent**. In the case of an intermittent problem with an NIC, first attempt to run any available NIC diagnostics. Then regardless of the diagnostic testing results, swap the original NIC in the ring station or network peripheral and check its general operation. Also, vector to flow guide 14.15 and rerun a protocol analysis session on the ring.

If the protocol analysis session does not record any errors associated with the Token Ring address involved, and the intermittent problem does not reappear, record the problem in your network maintenance and service log.

If, after you swap the NIC, the failure symptom still exists, replace the original NIC and troubleshoot the assigned lobe area for the respective NIC by vectoring to flow guide 14.2.

444 ETHERNET AND TOKEN RING OPTIMIZATION

If you definitely feel the original NIC has a problem, it may be best to keep the newly replaced NIC in the respective ring station rather than replace the original NIC before resuming troubleshooting by vectoring to the main menu and choosing 14.2. This will be a judgment call on your part.

14.6 Ring Station Problem Flow Guides

Are all the ring stations on the network experiencing the failure symptom?

(Vector to sub-flow guide 14.6.1.)

Is just a group of ring stations experiencing the failure symptom?

(Vector to sub-flow guide 14.6.2.)

Is just one ring station experiencing the failure symptom?

(Vector to sub-flow guide 14.6.3.)

This flow guide is generic as to the ring station/PC manufacturer. For some of the troubleshooting steps mentioned in this flow guide, you should also reference the PC manufacturer's documentation for any predefined methods for checking PC configuration and for PC testing.

14.6.1 All the Ring Stations Have the Symptom

Are all the ring stations running the same application or using the same directories or files on a particular file server when experiencing the symptom?

 [YES]   Vector to flow guide 14.14 and troubleshoot possible file server application or directory/file problems.

Chapter 14: Token Ring Troubleshooting Flow Guide

[NO] Go to the next step.

Have you troubleshot and verified the integrity of the main ring path cabling?

[YES] Run a protocol analysis session to gather more conclusive results by vectoring to flow guide 14.15.

[NO] Troubleshoot the main ring path cabling by vectoring to flow guide 14.3 (Cable).

14.6.2 A Group of Ring Stations Has the Symptom

Is the group of ring stations running the same application or using the same directories or files on a particular file server when experiencing the symptom?

(Vector to flow guide 14.14 and troubleshoot possible file server application or directory/file problems.)

Is the group of users located on the same MAU or wiring hub module?

[YES] Troubleshoot a possible MAU or wiring hub failure by vectoring to flow guide 14.4.

[NO] Recheck the ring stations involved for proper software and hardware configuration setup and requirements.

- Make sure that all the necessary directories and files are on the local drives in the ring stations and are set up correctly.

- Make sure that all the necessary hardware is installed in the ring stations and is configured correctly.

Check the network operating system manuals for station setup concerning both software and hardware prerequisites.

Are any identifiable hardware or software configuration setup problems present with the involved ring stations?

[YES]   Take the necessary action to resolve the configuration problem and retest the ring stations for proper operation. If the failure symptom is gone, record the problem in the network maintenance and service log. If a failure symptom still exists, go to the next step.

[NO]   If the problem strongly appears to be network file server-to-ring station related to ring insertion, vector to flow guide 14.14.

If you cannot be conclusive, vector to flow guide 14.15 and run a protocol analysis session on the ring.

14.6.3 One Ring Station Has the Symptom

Is the ring station always running the same application or using the same directory or file on a particular file server when experiencing the symptom?

[YES]   Vector to flow guide 14.14 and troubleshoot possible file server application or directory/file problems.

[NO]   Move the ring station to another port on the MAU or wiring hub and recheck the ring station operation.

Did moving the ring station to another port resolve the problem?

[YES]   Vector to flow guide 14.4 and troubleshoot possible MAU or wiring hub problems.

[NO]   Troubleshoot the respective lobe cable involved by vectoring to flow guide 14.3. If troubleshooting the lobe cable does identify any problems with the lobe cable, vector back to this flow guide by choosing flow guide 14.6; then vector to sub-flow guide 14.6.3 and jump directly to the next step.

Next, test the respective ring station for proper software and hardware configuration setup and requirements.

Chapter 14: Token Ring Troubleshooting Flow Guide

- Make sure that all the necessary directories and files are on the local drive in the ring station and are set up correctly.
- Make sure that all the necessary hardware is installed in the ring station and is configured correctly.

Check the network operating system manuals for station setup concerning both software and hardware prerequisites.

Did rechecking the ring station software and hardware requirements locate any incorrect configuration setup problems?

[YES]   Take the necessary action to resolve the configuration problem and retest the ring station for proper operation. If the failure symptom is gone, record the problem in the network maintenance and service log. If the problem still exists and it strongly appears to be network file server-to-ring station related to ring insertion, vector to flow guide 14.15 and troubleshoot the high-level communication process. If it does not appear to be file server related, go to the next step.

[NO]   Attempt to run any available PC diagnostics. Also try to troubleshoot the PC for any I/O board conflicts as discussed in the Ring Station Problems section of Chapter 13.

Did running the diagnostics or troubleshooting the PC find any problems?

[YES]   Take the necessary action to resolve the problem and retest the ring station for proper operation. If the failure symptom is gone, record the problem in the network maintenance and service log. If the problem still exists after retesting, go to the next step.

[NO]   Vector to flow guide 14.5 and troubleshoot the respective ring station for a NIC problem.

Many new ring stations are being manufactured with internal NICs within the PC motherboard hardware architecture. If the ring station you are troubleshooting has this configuration, you should just attempt to replace the motherboard rather than vectoring to 14.5 and troubleshooting the NIC.

14.7 Bridge Problem Flow Guides

Is the failure symptom that no data traffic can get from one side of the bridge to the other, or is data intermittently getting corrupted when passing through the bridge?

(Vector to sub-flow guide 14.7.1.)

Is the failure symptom that only partial data traffic can pass across the bridge?

(Vector to sub-flow guide 14.7.2.)

Is the failure symptom that an overloaded bandwidth condition is present on a certain ring?

(Vector to sub-flow guide 14.7.3.)

NOTE

This flow guide is generic as to the bridge manufacturer. For some of the troubleshooting steps mentioned in this flow guide, you should also reference the bridge manufacturer's documentation for any predefined methods for checking bridge configuration and for bridge testing.

14.7.1 No Data Traffic Can Get from One Side of the Bridge to the Other, or Data is Intermittently Getting Corrupted when Passing through the Bridge

Thoroughly check the software and hardware configuration of the bridge.

Are any incorrect configuration parameters present in the bridge?

    [YES]   Take the necessary action to resolve the problem and retest the bridge for proper operation. If the failure symptom is gone, record the problem in the network maintenance and service log. If the problem still exists after retesting, go to the next step.

    [NO]   Attempt to run bridge diagnostics.

Chapter 14: Token Ring Troubleshooting Flow Guide

Did running the diagnostics produce any errors that identify a bridge failure?

    [YES]   Take the necessary action to resolve the problem and retest the bridge for proper operation. If the failure symptom is gone, record the problem in the network maintenance and service log. If the problem still exists after retesting, go to the next step.

    [NO]   A problem may still exist with the bridge, but to get more conclusive fault-isolation data, vector to flow guide 14.15.

If after using this flow guide you cannot conclusively locate the problem and you continue to find failure symptoms that point to a bridge problem, reference the manufacturer's instructions.

14.7.2 Only Partial Data Traffic Can Pass Across the Bridge

Thoroughly check the software and hardware configuration of the bridge.

Are any incorrect configuration parameters in the bridge?

    [YES]   Take the necessary action to resolve the problem and retest the bridge for proper operation. If the failure symptom is gone, record the problem in the network maintenance and service log. If the problem still exists after retesting, go to the next step.

    [NO]   Check the ring for source-routing problems with certain ring stations. Thoroughly examine the Routing Information field of the frames that are not being passed through the bridge.

Particular ring stations can have a software application configuration problem in relation to the source-routing field that they are directly transmitting.

Did examining the ring for source-routing problems locate any specific problems with a certain ring station's Routing Information field?

[YES] Take the necessary action to resolve the source-routing problems with the respective ring station's source-routing parameters; then retest the bridge for proper operation. If the failure symptom is gone, record the problem in the network maintenance and service log. If the problem still exists after retesting, go to the next step.

[NO] Gather more conclusive fault-isolation data by thoroughly examining the Routing Information field from all the frames not being passed through the bridge. Vector to flow guide 14.15.

If, after using this flow guide, you cannot conclusively locate the problem and you continue to find failure symptoms that point to a bridge problem, reference the manufacturer's instructions.

14.7.3 An Overlooked Bandwidth Condition is Present on a Certain Ring

Thoroughly check the bridge for any incorrect configuration parameters that can control the amount of traffic to be forwarded to another ring.

Are any incorrect configuration parameters present in the bridge?

[YES] Take the necessary action to resolve the problem and retest the bridge for proper operation. If the failure symptom is gone, record the problem in the network maintenance and service log. If the problem still exists after retesting, go to the next step.

[NO] Check the source ring for source-routing problems with certain ring stations. Thoroughly examine the Routing Information field of the frames possibly causing bandwidth problems in the destination ring.

Chapter 14: Token Ring Troubleshooting Flow Guide

A particular ring station can have a software application configuration problem in relation to the source-routing field that it is directly transmitting.

Did examining the ring for source-routing problems locate any specific problems with a certain ring station's Routing Information field?

[YES]   Take the necessary action to resolve the source-routing problems with the respective ring station's source-routing parameters, then retest the bridge for proper operation. If the failure symptom is gone, record the problem in the network maintenance and service log. If the problem still exists after retesting, go to the next step.

[NO]   Attempt to gather more conclusive fault-isolation data by vectoring to flow guide 14.15.

Thoroughly examine the Routing Information field from all the frames for incorrect addressing information for source routing that may be causing an overhead problem from one ring to another. Look closely at the percentage of frames being forwarded that are overloading the destination ring with traffic.

If, after using this flow guide, you cannot conclusively locate the problem and continue to find failure symptoms that point to a bridge problem, reference the manufacturer's instructions.

14.8 Router Problem Flow Guides

Is the failure symptom that particular protocols are not being passed through to another ring?

(Vector to sub-flow guide 14.8.1.)

Is the failure symptom that no data traffic can get from one side of the router to the other, or that data is intermittently getting corrupted when passed through the router?

(Vector to sub-flow guide 14.8.2.)

Is the failure symptom that only partial data traffic can pass across the router?

(Vector to sub-flow guide 14.8.3.)

Is the failure symptom that an overloaded bandwidth condition is present on a certain ring?

(Vector to sub-flow guide 14.8.4.)

This flow guide is generic as to the router manufacturer. For some of the troubleshooting steps mentioned in this flow guide, reference the router manufacturer's documentation for any predefined methods for checking router configuration and for router testing.

14.8.1 Particular Protocol are Not Being Passed through Another Ring

Thoroughly check the router's software and hardware configuration, as related to the router's protocol-routing table.

Are any incorrect configuration parameters present in the router's protocol-routing table, as related to the specific protocol that is not properly being passed through to the destination ring?

    [YES]   Take the necessary action to resolve the problem and retest the router for proper operation. If the failure symptom is gone, record the problem in the network maintenance and service log. If the problem still exists after retesting, go to the next step.

    [NO]   Attempt to run router diagnostics.

Did running the diagnostics produce any errors that identify a router failure?

    [YES]   Take the necessary action to resolve the problem and retest the router for proper operation. If the failure symptom is gone,

Chapter 14: Token Ring Troubleshooting Flow Guide

record the problem in the network maintenance and service log. If the problem still exists after retesting, go to the next step.

[NO] A configuration problem may still exist with the router, but to get more conclusive fault-isolation data, vector to flow guide 14.15.

NOTE

When running a protocol analysis session on the ring, keep in mind that a router's main purpose is to connect rings that need to share the same protocols; they must understand and be configured for the protocol that they are forwarding.

If, after using this flow guide, you cannot conclusively locate the problem and you continue to find failure symptoms that point to a router problem, reference the manufacturer's instructions.

14.8.2 No Data Traffic Can Get from One Side of the Router to the Other, or Data is Intermittently Getting Corrupted when Passed through the Router

Thoroughly check the software and hardware configuration of the router.

Are any incorrect configuration parameters present in the router?

[YES] Take the necessary action to resolve the problem and retest the router for proper operation. If the failure symptom is gone, record the problem in the network maintenance and service log. If the problem still exists after retesting, go to the next step.

[NO] Attempt to run router diagnostics.

Did running the diagnostics produce any errors that identify a router failure?

[YES] Take the necessary action to resolve the problem and retest the router for proper operation. If the failure symptom is gone, record the problem in the network maintenance and service log. If the problem still exists after retesting, go to the next step.

454 ETHERNET AND TOKEN RING OPTIMIZATION

[NO]   A problem with the router may still exist, but to get more conclusive fault-isolation data, vector to flow guide 14.15.

If, after using this flow guide, you cannot conclusively locate the problem and continue to find failure symptoms that point to a router problem, reference the manufacturer's instructions.

14.8.3 Only Partial Data Traffic Can Pass across the Router

Thoroughly check the software and hardware configuration of the router.

Are any incorrect configuration parameters present in the router?

[YES] Take the necessary action to resolve the problem and retest the router for proper operation. If the failure symptom is gone, record the problem in the network maintenance and service log. If the problem still exists after retesting, go to the next step.

[NO]   Check the ring for source-routing problems with certain ring stations. Thoroughly examine the Routing Information field of the frames that are not being passed through the router.

A particular ring station can have a software application configuration problem in relation to the source-routing field that it is directly transmitting.

Did examining the ring for source-routing problems locate any specific problems with a certain ring station's Routing Information field?

[YES] Take the necessary action to resolve the source-routing problems with the respective ring station's source-routing parameters, and then retest the router for proper operation. If the failure symptom is gone, record the problem in the network maintenance and service log. If the problem still exists after retesting, go to the next step.

[NO] Attempt to gather more conclusive fault-isolation data by thoroughly examining the Routing Information field from all the frames that are not being passed through the router. Vector to flow guide 14.15.

If, after using this flow guide, you cannot conclusively locate the problem and continue to find failure symptoms that point to a router problem, reference the manufacturer's instructions.

14.8.4 An Overloaded Bandwidth Condition is Present on a Certain Ring

Thoroughly check the router for any incorrect configuration parameters that can control the amount of traffic to be forwarded to another ring.

Are any incorrect configuration parameters present in the router?

[YES] Take the necessary action to resolve the problem and retest the router for proper operation. If the failure symptom is gone, record the problem in the network maintenance and service log. If the problem still exists after retesting, go to the next step.

[NO] Check the source ring for source-routing problems with certain ring stations. Thoroughly examine the Routing Information field of the frames possibly causing bandwidth problems in the destination ring.

A particular ring station can have a software application configuration problem in relation to the source-routing field that it is directly transmitting.

ETHERNET AND TOKEN RING OPTIMIZATION

Did examining the ring for source-routing problems locate any specific problems with a certain ring station's Routing Information field?

[YES]   Take the necessary action to resolve the source-routing problems with the respective ring station's source-routing parameters, and then retest the router for proper operation. If the failure symptom is gone, record the problem in the network maintenance and service log. If the problem still exists after retesting, go to the next step.

[NO]   Attempt to gather more conclusive fault-isolation data. Vector to flow guide 14.15.

Thoroughly examine the Routing Information field from all the frames for incorrect addressing information for source routing that may be causing an overhead problem from one ring to another. Look closely at the percentage of frames being forwarded that are overloading the destination ring with traffic.

If, after using this flow guide, you cannot conclusively locate the problem and continue to find failure symptoms that point to a router problem, reference the manufacturer's instructions.

14.9 Repeater Problem Flow Guide

Is the failure symptom that no data traffic can get from one side of the repeater to the other, or that a hard error such as a beaconing condition is present on the ring?

(Vector to sub-flow guide 14.9.1.)

This flow guide is generic as to the repeater manufacturer. For some of the troubleshooting steps mentioned in this flow guide, you should also reference the repeater manufacturer's documentation for any predefined methods for checking repeater configuration and for repeater testing.

14.9.1 No Data Traffic Can Get from One Side of the Repeater to the Other, or a Hard Error Such as a Beaconing is Present on the Ring

NOTE

If a repeater is the suspected problem, first attempt to troubleshoot the problem by testing the main ring path cabling section that normally passes through the repeater. Do this by disconnecting the attached cable sections and relooping the cabling sections at the repeater entry points with patch cables. With fiber optics cabling, this may be more difficult.

Bypass the repeater and test the main ring path cabling segments with a TDR (or OTDR in the case of fiber).

With the repeater disconnected, did testing the cable produce any cable faults?

    [YES]   Most likely a problem exists with the main ring path cabling. If you are not sure what portion of the main ring path section is bad, vector to flow guide 14.3.
                If you are sure as to which portion of the main ring cabling path section is bad, replace that section. Then reattach the repeater and retest the ring. If the failure symptom is gone, record the problem in the network maintenance and service log. If the problem still exists after retesting, go to the next step.

    [NO]   Attempt to run any available repeater diagnostics.

Did running the diagnostics produce any errors that identify a repeater failure?

    [YES]   Take the necessary action to resolve the problem and retest the repeater for proper operation. If the failure symptom is gone, record the problem in the network maintenance and service log. If the problem still exists after retesting, go to the next step.

    [NO]   Thoroughly check the repeater configuration.

ETHERNET AND TOKEN RING OPTIMIZATION

Are any incorrect configuration parameters present in the repeater?

[YES]   Take the necessary action to resolve the problem and retest the repeater for proper operation. If the failure symptom is gone, record the problem in the network maintenance and service log. If the problem still exists after retesting, go to the next step.

[NO]   Check the actual physical placement of the repeater with respect to its specification for distance requirements within the Token Ring cabling system.

Sometimes the physical placement of a repeater can cause failure symptoms that point to the main ring path cabling being at fault. Consult the repeater manufacturer for instructions as to distance requirements.

Is the repeater incorrectly placed as to its specifications?

[YES]   Take the necessary action to resolve the problem and retest the repeater for proper operation. If the failure symptom is gone, record the problem in the network maintenance and service log. If the problem still exists after retesting, go to the next step.

[NO]   A problem may still exist with the repeater, but to get more conclusive fault-isolation data, vector to flow guide 14.15.

If, after using this flow guide, you cannot conclusively locate the problem and continue to find failure symptoms that point to a repeater problem, reference the manufacturer's instructions.

14.10 Network Peripheral Problem Flow Guides

NOTE

If devices such as modems, printers, or fax boards are connected to a ring station or a file server, they are not actually considered network peripherals because they do not contain their own NICs. If the peripheral you are troubleshooting does not contain its own internal NIC, vector to the applicable flow guide. (For example, suppose a modem or printer is connected to a ring station or file server, and the ring station or file server contains the NIC. In this instance, you would vector to either the modem or printer problem flow guide.) But if the device does contain its own internal NIC, this flow guide is applicable.

Did you arrive at this flow guide because of NIC failure indications from running a protocol analysis session?

(Vector to sub-flow guide 14.10.1.)

Did you arrive at this flow guide because you have identified a failure symptom that appears to be directly related to a problem with a specific network peripheral?

(Vector to sub-flow guide 14.10.2.)

NOTE

As discussed in Chapter 13, a network peripheral failure symptom usually differs from that of a standard ring station. But because both a network peripheral and a standard ring station contain an NIC and both access the ring through the 802.5 rules, they both can be assumed to have the same logical network area of fault components, which is the respective network peripheral's lobe area, specifically the network peripheral, NIC, lobe cable, and MAU or hub port.

Some of the network peripherals access the Token Ring network with NIC and hardware/software components; others just use NIC hardware with firmware contained within PROM chips. Both configurations allow the assigned network peripheral to access the ring through standard ring insertion, and they both operate according to the Token Ring architecture operating-mode principles.

This flow guide is generic as to the network peripheral manufacturer. For some of the troubleshooting steps mentioned in this flow guide, you should also reference the network peripheral manufacturer's documentation for any predefined methods for checking network peripheral configuration and for network peripheral testing.

14.10.1 Error Indication Occurs in a Protocol Analysis Session

Whether the error is a hard error indicated by a Beacon MAC frame or a soft error that indicates a possible NIC failure in the network peripheral, swap the respective NIC and rerun another thorough protocol analysis session on the ring.

Some types of network peripherals have an NIC physically built into the motherboard. If this is the case, you may have to replace the whole unit. Reference the manufacturer's instructions.

After you swapped the NIC and reran a protocol analysis session, did the error go away?

[YES]   Leave the newly replaced NIC in the network peripheral and record the problem in the network maintenance and service log.

[NO]   Return the original NIC back into the network peripheral; vector to flow guide 14.15; and rerun a protocol analysis session on the ring. Sometimes, by rerunning a protocol analysis session, the failure cause becomes more clear by moving to another Token Ring address.

Chapter 14: Token Ring Troubleshooting Flow Guide

NOTE

If after rerunning a protocol analysis session the error does not move to another device and is still identifying the particular NIC address as a failure cause, troubleshoot the assigned lobe area for the respective NIC by vectoring to flow guide 14.2.

If, after using this flow guide, you cannot conclusively locate the problem and continue to find failure symptoms that point to a network peripheral problem, reference the manufacturer's instructions.

14.10.2 A Failure Symptom Appears to be Directly Related to a Problem with a Specific Network Peripheral

Is the network peripheral involved in some network communications with a particular application, or is it using the same directory or file on a particular file server when experiencing the symptom?

  [YES]   Vector to flow guide 14.14 and troubleshoot a possible file server application or directory/file problem that may be related to the network peripheral operation.

  [NO]   Move the network peripheral to another port on the MAU or wiring hub and recheck the network peripheral operation.

Did moving the network peripheral to another port resolve the problem?

  [YES]   Vector to flow guide 14.4 and troubleshoot a possible MAU or wiring hub problem.

  [NO]   Troubleshoot the respective lobe cable involved by vectoring to flow guide 14.3. If troubleshooting the lobe cable does not identify any problems with the lobe cable, vector back to this flow guide (14.10); then vector to sub-flow guide 14.10.2 and jump directly to the next step.

  Next, test the respective network peripheral for proper software and hardware configuration setup and requirements:

- If the network peripheral has local disk storage, make sure that all the necessary directories and files for the network peripheral are set up correctly.
- Make sure that all the necessary hardware is installed in the network peripheral and that it is configured correctly.

Check the network operating system manuals for network peripheral setup concerning both software and hardware prerequisites.

Did rechecking the network peripheral software and hardware requirements find any incorrect configuration-setup problems?

[YES]   Take the necessary action to resolve the configuration problem and retest the network peripheral device for proper operation. If the failure symptom is gone, record the problem in the network maintenance and service log. If the problem still exists, go to the next step.

[NO]   Attempt to run any available network peripheral diagnostics. Also try to troubleshoot the network peripheral for any I/O board conflicts.

Did running the diagnostics or troubleshooting the network peripheral find any problems?

[YES]   Take the necessary action to resolve the problem and retest the network peripheral for proper operation. If the failure symptom is gone, record the problem in the network maintenance and service log. If the problem still exists after retesting, go to the next step.

Has the NIC in the assigned network peripheral been troubleshot?

[YES]   A network file server-to-network peripheral related problem may exist as to ring insertion or protocol communication. Perform a protocol analysis session and focus closely on the

Chapter 14: Token Ring Troubleshooting Flow Guide   **463**

communication between the network file server and the assigned network peripheral. Vector to flow guide 14.15.

[NO]   Vector to flow guide 14.5 and troubleshoot the respective network peripheral station for a NIC problem.

NOTE Many network peripherals are being manufactured with internal NICs within the respective logic board hardware architecture. If the network peripheral you are troubleshooting has this configuration, attempt to replace the motherboard rather than vectoring to 14.5 and troubleshooting the NIC.

If, after using this flow guide, you cannot conclusively locate the problem and continue to find failure symptoms that point to a network peripheral problem, reference the manufacturer's instructions.

14.11 Modem Problem Flow Guides

Are you having a problem accessing or using a modem connected to the ring as a shared modem?

(Vector to sub-flow guide 14.11.1.)

Are you having a problem accessing or using a modem connected to a specific ring station or file server as an unshared modem?

(Vector to sub-flow guide 14.11.2.)

Are you having a problem accessing or using a modem connected to a ring from a remote location?

(Vector to sub-flow guide 14.11.3.)

NOTE If the respective modem is connected to a ring station or a file server, it is not actually considered a network peripheral because it does not contain its own NIC. In this case, the following flow guide is applicable.

If the modem does contain its own NIC, you should troubleshoot the problem as a network peripheral by vectoring to flow guide 14.10. If, after troubleshooting the problem as a network peripheral, you feel that the modem or modem-sharing software is at fault, vector back to this flow guide (14.11).

This flow guide is generic as to the modem and modem network-sharing software manufacturer. For some of the troubleshooting steps in this flow guide, you should also reference the manufacturer's documentation for any predefined methods for checking configuration and for testing.

14.11.1 You Have a Problem Accessing or Using a Modem Connected to the Ring as a Shared Modem

Check the ring station or file server to which the modem is connected, and the modem itself, to make sure that they are configured with all the proper hardware and software components and the correct configuration parameters. Also check the network file server for all the correct modem-sharing software and proper configuration.

Are any incorrect configuration parameters present in either the respective ring station, modem, or network file server?

[YES] Take the necessary action to resolve the problem, and retest the modem for proper operation. If the failure symptom is gone, record the problem in the network maintenance and service log. If the problem still exists after retesting, go to the next step.

[NO] Attempt to run any available modem diagnostics and troubleshoot the modem link cables and phone lines.

Did running the diagnostics, checking the link, or checking the phone lines produce any errors?

[YES] Take the necessary action to resolve the problem and retest the modem for proper operation. If the failure symptom is gone, record the problem in the network maintenance and service log. If the problem still exists after retesting, go to the next step.

[NO]   A configuration problem may still exist with the modem or the modem network-sharing software. Reference the instructions from the respective modem and modem-software manufacturers.

14.11.2 You Have a Problem Accessing or Using a Modem Connected to a Specific Ring Station or File Server as an Unshared Modem

Check the ring station or file server to which the modem is connected, and the modem itself, to make sure that they are configured with all the proper hardware and software components and the correct configuration parameters.

Are any incorrect configuration parameters present in either the respective ring station, file server, or modem?

[YES]   Take the necessary action to resolve the problem and retest the modem for proper operation. If the failure symptom is gone, record the problem in the network maintenance and service log. If the problem still exists after retesting, go to the next step.

[NO]   Attempt to run any available modem diagnostics and troubleshoot the modem link cables and phone lines.

Did running the diagnostics, checking the link, or checking the phone lines produce any errors?

[YES]   Take the necessary action to resolve the problem and retest the modem for proper operation. If the failure symptom is gone, record the problem in the network maintenance and service log. If the problem still exists after retesting, go to the next step.

[NO]   A configuration problem may still exist with the modem. Reference the respective modem manufacturer's instructions.

14.11.3 You Have a Problem Accessing or Using a Modem Connected to a Ring from a Remote Location

Check the local and host ring stations to which the modems are connected, and the modems themselves, to make sure that they are configured with all the proper hardware and software components and the correct configuration parameters. Also check the host network file server for all the correct modem-sharing software and proper configuration.

Are any incorrect configuration parameters present in either the respective ring stations, modems, or host network file server?

- [YES] Take the necessary action to resolve the problem and retest the modems for proper operation. If the failure symptom is gone, record the problem in the network maintenance and service log. If the problem still exists after retesting, go to the next step.

- [NO] Attempt to run any available modem diagnostics and troubleshoot the host and remote modems, link cables, and phone lines.

Did running the diagnostics, checking the link cables, or checking the phone lines produce any errors?

- [YES] Take the necessary action to resolve the problem and retest the modems for proper operation. If the failure symptom is gone, record the problem in the network maintenance and service log. If the problem still exists after retesting, go to the next step.

- [NO] A configuration problem may still exist with the modems or the modem network-sharing software. Reference the instructions of the respective modem and modem-software manufacturers.

14.12 Printer Problem Flow Guides

Are you having a problem accessing or using a printer connected to the ring as a shared printer?

(Vector to flow guide 14.12.1.)

Chapter 14: Token Ring Troubleshooting Flow Guide   467

Are you having a problem accessing or using a printer connected to a specific ring station or file server as an unshared printer?

(Vector to flow guide 14.12.2.)

If this printer is connected to a ring station or a file server, it is not actually considered a network peripheral because it does not contain its own NIC. In this case, the following flow guide is applicable.

If it does contain its own NIC, you should troubleshoot the problem as a network peripheral by vectoring to flow guide 14.10. If, after troubleshooting the problem as a network peripheral, you feel that the printer or printer-sharing software may be at fault, vector back to this flow guide (14.12).

This flow guide is generic as to the printer and printer network-sharing software manufacturer. For some of the troubleshooting steps in this flow guide, you should also reference the manufacturer's documentation for any predefined methods for checking configuration and for testing.

14.12.1 You Have a Problem Accessing or Using a Printer Connected to the Ring as a Shared Printer

Check the ring station, file server, or print server to which the printer is connected, and the printer itself, to make sure that they are configured with all the proper hardware and software components and the correct configuration parameters. Also check the network file server or print server for all the correct printer-sharing software and proper configuration.

ETHERNET AND TOKEN RING OPTIMIZATION

Are any incorrect configuration parameters present in either the respective ring station, network file server, print server, or printer?

[YES]   Take the necessary action to resolve the problem and retest the printer for proper operation. If the failure symptom is gone, record the problem in the network maintenance and service log. If the problem still exists after retesting, go to the next step.

[NO]   Attempt to run any available printer diagnostics and test the printer cabling.

Did running the diagnostics and testing the printer cabling produce any errors?

[YES]   Take the necessary action to resolve the problem and retest the printer for proper operation. If the failure symptom is gone, record the problem in the network maintenance and service log. If the problem still exists after retesting, go to the next step.

[NO]   A configuration problem may still exist with the printer or the printer network-sharing software. Reference the instructions of the respective printer and printer-software manufacturers.

14.12.2 You Have a Problem Accessing or Using a Printer Connected to a Specific Ring Station or File Server as an Unshared Printer

Check the ring station or file server to which the printer is connected, and the printer itself, to make sure that they are configured with all the proper hardware and software components and the correct configuration parameters.

Are any incorrect configuration parameters present in either the respective ring station or the printer?

[YES]   Take the necessary action to resolve the problem and retest the printer for proper operation. If the failure symptom is gone, record the problem in the network maintenance and service log. If the problem still exists after retesting, go to the next step.

[NO]   Attempt to run any available printer diagnostics and test the printer cabling.

Did running the diagnostics and testing the printer cabling produce any errors?

[YES] Take the necessary action to resolve the problem and retest the printer for proper operation. If the failure symptom is gone, record the problem in the network maintenance and service log. If the problem still exists after retesting, go to the next step.

[NO]   A configuration problem may still exist with the printer or the printer network-sharing software. Reference the instructions of the respective printer and printer-software manufacturers.

14.13 Gateway Problem Flow Guides

Is the whole network having a problem accessing or using a host gateway connected to a local ring?

(Vector to sub-flow guide 14.13.1.)

Is just one ring station or a group of ring stations having a problem accessing or using a host gateway connected to a local ring?

(Vector to sub-flow guide 14.13.2.)

Is there a problem accessing or using a host gateway from a non-local ring bridged, routed, or connected through a remote connection?

(Vector to sub-flow guide 14.13.3.)

Is the failure symptom that gateway sessions appear to be running slowly or unresponsively?

(Vector to sub-flow guide 14.13.4.)

Are LAN-to-host sessions intermittently locking up or freezing?

(Vector to sub-flow guide 14.13.5.)

NOTE

This flow guide is generic as to the gateway and gateway-sharing software manufacturers. For some of the troubleshooting steps mentioned in this flow guide, you should also reference the manufacturer's documentation for any predefined methods for checking configuration and for testing.

14.13.1 The Entire Network Has a Problem Accessing or Using a Host Gateway Connected to a Local Ring

Thoroughly check the gateway's configuration as to the gateway manufacturer's hardware and software setup for use with the LAN and the respective host.

Are any incorrect configuration parameters present in the gateway's configuration as to the hardware and software setup for use with the LAN or the host?

    [YES]   Take the necessary action to resolve the problem and retest the gateway for proper operation. If the failure symptom is gone, record the problem in the network maintenance and service log. If the problem still exists after retesting, go to the next step.

    [NO]   Check all the ring stations that need to access the gateway for the proper configuration as to the gateway manufacturer's specifications.

Are any incorrect configuration parameters present in the ring station's configuration as to hardware and software setup for use with the gateway?

    [YES]   Take the necessary action to resolve the problem and retest the gateway for proper operation. If the failure symptom is gone, record the problem in the network maintenance and service log. If the problem still exists after retesting, go to the next step.

    [NO]   Check the host to make sure that it is properly configured as to session setup and port availability to handle communications to the respective gateway.

Chapter 14: Token Ring Troubleshooting Flow Guide

Are any incorrect configuration parameters present in the host's configuration as to hardware and software setup for use with the LAN ring stations or the gateway?

[YES] Take the necessary action to resolve the problem and retest the gateway for proper operation. If the failure symptom is gone, record the problem in the network maintenance and service log. If the problem still exists after retesting, go to the next step.

[NO] Attempt to run any available gateway diagnostics.

Did running the diagnostics produce any errors?

[YES] Take the necessary action to resolve the problem and retest the gateway for proper operation. If the failure symptom is gone, record the problem in the network maintenance and service log. If the problem still exists after retesting, go to the next step.

[NO] A configuration problem may still exist with the gateway or the LAN gateway software. Reference the instructions of the respective gateway and gateway software manufacturers.

14.13.2 One Ring Station or a Group of Ring Stations Has a Problem Accessing or Using a Host Gateway Connected to a Local Ring

Check all the ring stations experiencing the problem for the proper configuration as to the gateway manufacturer's specifications.

Are any incorrect configuration parameters present in the ring stations' configuration as to the hardware and software setup for use with the gateway?

[YES] Take the necessary action to resolve the problem and retest the gateway for proper operation. If the failure symptom is gone, record the problem in the network maintenance and service log. If the problem still exists after retesting, go to the next step.

[NO] Check the host to make sure that it is properly configured as to session setup and port availability to handle communications for all the ring stations that are experiencing the problem.

Are any incorrect configuration parameters present in the host's configuration as to the hardware and software setup for use with the LAN ring stations?

[YES] Take the necessary action to resolve the problem and retest the gateway for proper operation. If the failure symptom is gone, record the problem in the network maintenance and service log. If the problem still exists after retesting, go to the next step.

[NO] Attempt to run any available gateway diagnostics.

Did running the diagnostics produce any errors?

[YES] Take the necessary action to resolve the problem and retest the gateway for proper operation. If the failure symptom is gone, record the problem in the network maintenance and service log. If the problem still exists after retesting, go to the next step.

[NO] A configuration problem may still exist with the gateway or the LAN gateway software. Attempt to get more conclusive fault-isolation data concerning the communication between the gateway and the ring stations experiencing the problem. Vector to flow guide 14.15.

If, after using this flow guide, you cannot conclusively locate the problem and you continue to find failure symptoms that point to a gateway problem, reference the manufacturer's instructions.

14.13.3 You Have a Problem Accessing or Using a Host Gateway from a Non-Local Ring Bridged, Routed, or Connected through a Remote Connection

First, verify that the particular bridge, router, or remote connection link is functioning properly. If necessary, vector to the respective flow guide for the particular device: flow guides 14.7 Bridge; 14.8 Router; and 14.11 Modem.

Chapter 14: Token Ring Troubleshooting Flow Guide

Are there any problems with the linking devices, specifically the bridge, router, or communication (modem) devices/links?

    [YES]   Take the necessary action to resolve the problem and retest the gateway for proper operation. If the failure symptom is gone, record the problem in the network maintenance and service log. If the problem still exists after retesting, go to the next step.

    [NO]   If no problems can be conclusively located to those respective devices, attempt to get more conclusive fault-isolation data on the complete LAN communication process relating to the gateway by vectoring to flow guide 14.15.

14.13.4 The Gateway Sessions Appear to be Running Slowly or Unresponsively

Check all the gateway's operational-mode configurations for the proper configuration as to the gateway manufacturer's specifications.

Are any incorrect configuration parameters in any of the gateway's configurations for the hardware and software setup for use with the LAN/host?

    [YES]   Take the necessary action to resolve the problem and retest the gateway for proper operation. If the failure symptom is gone, record the problem in the network maintenance and service log. If the problem still exists after retesting, go to the next step.

    [NO]   Check the host to make sure its session setup and port availability are properly configured to handle communications for all the ring stations that are experiencing the problem.

Are any incorrect configuration parameters present in the host's configuration as to session and port capacity for use with the LAN layout of ring stations set up to use the gateway?

    [YES]   Take the necessary action to resolve the problem and retest the gateway for proper operation. If the failure symptom is gone, record the problem in the network maintenance and service log. If the problem still exists after retesting, go to the next step.

    [NO]   Attempt to run any available gateway diagnostics.

Did running the diagnostics produce any errors?

[YES]   Take the necessary action to resolve the problem and retest the gateway for proper operation. If the failure symptom is gone, record the problem in the network maintenance and service log. If the problem still exists after retesting, go to the next step.

[NO]   A configuration problem may still exist with the gateway or the LAN gateway software. Attempt to get more conclusive fault-isolation data as to the communication between the gateway and the ring stations that are experiencing the problem. Vector to flow guide 14.15.

If, after using this flow guide, you cannot conclusively locate the problem and you continue to find failure symptoms that point to a gateway problem, reference the manufacturer's instructions.

14.13.5 LAN-to-Host Sessions are Intermittently Locking Up or Freezing

Attempt to run any available gateway diagnostics.

Did running the diagnostics produce any errors?

[YES]   Take the necessary action to resolve the problem and retest the gateway for proper operation. If the failure symptom is gone, record the problem in the network maintenance and service log. If the problem still exists after retesting, go to the next step.

[NO]   A configuration problem may still exist with the gateway or the LAN gateway software.

Thoroughly check the gateway's configuration as to the gateway manufacturer's hardware and software setup for use on the LAN and the respective host.

Are any incorrect configuration parameters present in the gateway's configuration as to the hardware and software setup for use with the LAN or the host?

[YES] Take the necessary action to resolve the problem and retest the gateway for proper operation. If the failure symptom is gone, record the problem in the network maintenance and service log. If the problem still exists after retesting, go to the next step.

[NO] Attempt to get more conclusive fault-isolation data as to the communication between the gateway and the ring stations that are experiencing the problem. Vector to flow guide 14.15.

If, after using this flow guide, you cannot conclusively locate the problem and continue to find failure symptoms that point to a gateway problem, reference the manufacturer's instructions.

14.14 File Server Problem Flow Guides

Is there a problem on the network file server with a ring station, group of ring stations, the complete network, or a network peripheral accessing or using a particular application/group of applications, or certain directories/files?

(Vector to sub-flow guide 14.14.1.)

Is a particular network operating system (NOS) feature or set of NOS features on the network file server not working?

(Vector to sub-flow guide 14.14.2.)

Is there a problem accessing or using an extra network server other than the main network file server (for example, database, fax, communication, print server)?

(Vector to sub-flow guide 14.14.3.)

Does there appear to be a problem with abnormal network bandwidth between a particular ring station/group of ring stations and the network file server, or between a network peripheral and the network file server?

(Vector to sub-flow guide 14.14.4.)

NOTE: This flow guide is generic as to the NOS (such as Novell, IBM LAN Server, Microsoft LAN Manager, and Banyan VINES). When you reference some of the troubleshooting steps in this flow guide, you should also reference the NOS manufacturer's documentation for any predefined methods for checking NOS configuration, hardware/software requirements, and for NOS diagnostics and testing.

14.14.1 There is a Problem with a Ring Station, a Group of Ring Stations, the Entire Network, or a Network Peripheral Accessing or Using a Particular Application/Group of Applications, or Certain Directories/Files on the Network File Server

First, check the network file server and any symptomatic ring stations for the following software and hardware configuration setup parameters and requirements:

- Make sure that the NOS network shell software, NOS NIC drivers, CONFIG.SYS, AUTOEXEC.BAT, and all the necessary network operating system files are set up for the respective NOS specialized configuration and NOS hierarchical directory structure.

- Check the NOS directory structure as it relates to the ring station and any respective network peripheral access.

Chapter 14: Token Ring Troubleshooting Flow Guide   477

- Check all the NOS security rights configurations.
- Make sure that all the necessary directories/files for all NOS applications on the network drive and ring station drives are set up correctly.
- Make sure that all the necessary hardware is installed in the file server/ring stations, configured correctly, and functioning properly.

Check the respective NOS manuals for file server setup concerning network software vendor requirements for both software and hardware prerequisites and their respective configurations.

Are there any identifiable hardware or software configuration setup problems with the network file server?

[YES]   Take the necessary action to resolve the configuration problem and retest the ring for proper operation. If the failure symptom is gone, record the problem in the network maintenance and service log. If the failure symptom still exists, go to the next step.

[NO]   If there appears to be no problem with the file server or its setup, attempt to gather more conclusive fault-isolation data by running a protocol analysis session on the ring. Vector to flow guide 14.15 and focus on the problem by capturing and viewing the high-layer communication processes.

If, after using this flow guide, you cannot conclusively locate the problem and continue to find failure symptoms that point to the network file server problem, reference the instructions of both the NOS software and the particular file server/hardware manufacturers.

ETHERNET AND TOKEN RING OPTIMIZATION

14.14.2 A Particular NOS Feature or Set of NOS Features on the Network File Server is Not Working

First, fully reference the respective NOS manuals for operation of the NOS feature or features.

In checking the NOS manuals, did you find any operational instructions to resolve your problem?

- [YES] Take the necessary action to resolve the problem and retest the NOS feature for proper operation. If the failure symptom is gone, record the problem in the network maintenance and service log. If the failure symptom still exists, go to the next step.

- [NO] Check the NOS manuals for file server setup concerning network software vendor requirements for both software and hardware prerequisites and their respective configurations.

Are there any identifiable hardware or software configuration setup problems with the network file server?

- [YES] Take the necessary action to resolve the configuration problem and retest the NOS feature for proper operation. If the failure symptom is gone, record the problem in the network maintenance and service log. If the failure symptom still exists, go to the next step.

- [NO] Contact your NOS support channel for assistance in using and configuring this particular NOS feature.

14.14.3 There Is a Problem Accessing or Using an Extra Network Server Other than the Main Network File Server (for Example, Database, Fax, Communication, or Print Server)

Is the file server involved on a non-local ring that is bridged, routed, or connected through a remote connection?

[YES] Go to **S1**.

[NO] Go to **S2**.

[S1] File server is on a non-local ring that is bridged, routed, or connected through a remote connection. First, verify that the particular bridge, router, or remote connection link is functioning properly. If necessary, vector to the respective flow guide for the particular device: flow guides 14.7 Bridge; 14.8 Router; 14.11 Modem.

Are there any problems with the linking devices, specifically the bridge, router, or communication (modem) devices/links?

[YES] Take the necessary action to resolve the problem and retest the respective network file server for proper operation. If the failure symptom is gone, record the problem in the network maintenance and service log. If the problem still exists after retesting, go to the next step.

[NO] Go to **S2** and follow the troubleshooting steps as though the remote file server were actually located on the local ring.

[S2] File server is on the local ring. First, check the network file server for the following software and hardware configuration setup parameters and requirements.

- Make sure that the NOS network shell software, NOS NIC drivers, CONFIG.SYS, AUTOEXEC.BAT, and all the necessary network operating system files are set up for the respective NOS specialized configuration and NOS hierarchical directory structure.

480 ETHERNET AND TOKEN RING OPTIMIZATION

- Check the NOS directory structure as it relates to the ring station and any respective network peripheral access.
- Check all the NOS security rights configurations.
- Make sure that all the necessary directories/files for any NOS applications on the network drive are set up correctly.
- Make sure that all the necessary hardware is installed in the file server, is configured correctly, and is functioning properly.

Check the respective NOS and software application manuals for file server setup concerning network software vendor requirements for both software and hardware prerequisites and their respective configurations.

Are there any identifiable hardware or software configuration setup problems with the network file server?

[YES] Take the necessary action to resolve the configuration problem and retest the ring for proper operation. If the failure symptom is gone, record the problem in the network maintenance and service log. If the failure symptom still exists, go to the next step.

[NO] If no problem appears to be with the file server or its setup, attempt to gather more conclusive fault-isolation data by running a protocol analysis session on the ring. Vector to flow guide 14.15 and focus on the problem by capturing and viewing the high-layer communication processes.

If, after using this flow guide, you cannot conclusively locate the problem and continue to find failure symptoms that point to the network file server problem, reference the instructions of both the NOS software and the particular file server/hardware manufacturers.

14.14.4 There Appears to be a Problem with Abnormal Network Bandwidth between a Particular Ring Station/Group of Ring Stations, or a Network Peripheral, and the Network File Server

First, check the network file server for the following software and hardware configuration setup parameters and requirements:

- Make sure that the NOS network shell software, NOS NIC drivers, CONFIG.SYS, AUTOEXEC.BAT, and all the necessary network operating system files are set up for the respective NOS specialized configuration and NOS hierarchical directory structure.
- Check the NOS directory structure as it relates to the ring station and any respective network peripheral access.
- Check all the NOS security rights configurations.
- Make sure that all the necessary directories/files for all NOS applications on the network drive are set up correctly.
- Make sure that all the necessary hardware is installed in the file server, is configured correctly, and is functioning properly.

Check the respective NOS and software application manuals for file server setup concerning network software vendor requirements for both software and hardware prerequisites and their respective configuration.

Are there any identifiable hardware or software configuration setup problems with the network file server?

    [YES]   Take the necessary action to resolve the configuration problem and retest the ring for proper operation. If the failure symptom is gone, record the problem in the network maintenance and

ETHERNET AND TOKEN RING OPTIMIZATION

service log. If the failure symptom still exists, go to the next step.

[NO]   Check the file server NIC buffer space specifications to see if they meet the NOS and software application manufacturers' requirements for the ring user population and access.

Is the file server's NIC low on required buffer space for the NOS or particular application's operation?

[YES] Take the necessary action to resolve the problem and retest the ring for proper operation. If the failure symptom is gone, record the problem in the network maintenance and service log. If the failure symptom still exists, go to the next step.

[NO]   Attempt to gather more conclusive fault-isolation data by running a protocol analysis session on the ring. Vector to flow guide 14.15 and focus on the problem by capturing and viewing the high-layer communication processes and the baseline network bandwidth.

If, after using this flow guide, you cannot conclusively locate the problem and continue to find failure symptoms that point to a network file server problem, reference the instructions of both the NOS software and the particular file server/hardware manufacturers.

14.15 Protocol Analysis Flow Guides

Did you arrive at this flow guide because you need to troubleshoot a network failure symptom that requires running a protocol analysis session to examine the low-layer 802.5 frame communication processes?

(Vector to sub-flow guide 14.15.1.)

Did you arrive at this flow guide because you are encountering a specific soft or hard error on the network, or the network is freezing or hanging?

(Vector to sub-flow guide 14.15.2.)

Chapter 14: Token Ring Troubleshooting Flow Guide

Did you arrive at this flow guide because you need to troubleshoot a network failure symptom that requires running a protocol analysis session to examine the high-layer network frame communication processes?

(Vector to sub-flow guide 14.15.3.)

Is the network experiencing any of the following failure symptoms: The whole network is operating slowly; a specific network application is operating slowly; or logon failures are occurring?

(Vector to sub-flow guide 14.15.4.)

While using these flow guides, keep in mind the prescribed approach for a general protocol analysis session: capture, view, analyze, check errors, benchmark performance, and focus.

14.15.1 Perform a Protocol Analysis Session to Examine the Low-Layer 802.5 Frame Communication Processes

First, start the protocol analysis session by establishing the network baseline of operations. Set up the protocol analyzer to perform a full capture.

If the higher-layer protocols are clouding your testing results, you can filter them out, so as to focus more closely on the low layers.

Closely examine the 802.5 low-level frame communication processes. Interrogate all the base 802.5 MAC data frames as to how they respectively correlate with the time-related Token Ring communication processes captured in the protocol analysis session.

ETHERNET AND TOKEN RING OPTIMIZATION

Scrutinize the current state of low-level 802.5 frame communications exchange between the network entities involved for proper and fluent protocol exchange. Specifically, if you are troubleshooting a certain network component, such as a gateway, router, bridge, ring station, file server, or network peripheral, look for the low-level 802.5 frame communication processes associated with that specific network device's Token Ring address.

In other words, are there any noticeable deviations from a normal state of low-level frame communication process that may indicate a possible failure within a fault domain or a specific network component? (Refer to the Token Ring communication processes presented in Chapter 12.)

Did you find any deviations from the normal state of low-level 802.5 frame communication processes that indicate a possible failure within a fault domain or a specific network component failure?

   [YES]   Take the necessary action to resolve the problem by vectoring to the flow guide for that specific network component (such as 14.6 Ring Station, 14.10 Network Peripheral, 14.14 File Server, and so on).
   If you are not completely conclusive as to a specific network component that may be related to the failure symptom, vector to flow guide 14.2 and troubleshoot the respective Token Ring addresses associated in the frames (that is, the possible fault domain) that deviate from the normal state of communication.
   If, after vectoring to the respective fault domain, network area, or network component, you find a problem, resolve the problem and retest the ring by vectoring back to this flow guide (14.15). Rerun another baseline session to test the ring. If there are no more deviations from the normal state of operations, record the problem in the network maintenance and service log. If the problem still exists after rerunning another session, go to the next step.

   [NO]   Vector down to the next sub-flow guide, 14.15.2.

14.15.2 Encountering Specific Soft or Hard Errors on the Network, or the Whole Network is Freezing or Hanging

NOTE Abnormally high network bandwidth usage can cause performance degradation that can present itself in the form of soft or hard error conditions. If you immediately suspect high bandwidth as a problem, first vector down to sub-flow guide 14.15.4 and analyze the network bandwidth. If at this point you feel that the bandwidth is within normal parameters, continue with the following steps. Remember that by using any available error alarm triggering features with your protocol analyzer, you can observe more dynamically any particular errors as they occur.

Examine the captured data from the respective protocol analysis session for any recorded soft or hard error conditions.

If any soft errors are recorded, go to **S1**.

If any hard errors are recorded, go to **S2**.

   [S1]   Soft Error Vectoring

NOTE Soft errors are the less-critical type of errors that can occur on the ring, and they do not always indicate a definite problem with any associated network component through a Token Ring address. They may, however, indicate a marginal failure with that network component. When following any recommended vectors in the following soft error vectors, use your own thought processes as to the seriousness of the failure symptom that is occurring before taking any corrective action.

When examining the type of soft error captured during the protocol analysis session, look closely at the Report Soft Error MAC frame for the following information: the type of soft error and both associated addresses in the MAC frame.

The Report Soft Error MAC frame contains the soft error counter field, which is a 12-byte field: 10 of the bytes actually represent soft error types, and the other two are reserved for future use. The hexadecimal value of a particular soft error byte indicates the actual soft error count for the soft error type.

ETHERNET AND TOKEN RING OPTIMIZATION

Examine the respective Report Soft Error MAC frame captured during the protocol analysis session for the type of soft error and both associated addresses in the MAC frame.

Place your captured soft error type into one of the following ten soft error type categories, and go to that soft error type. Next, use the address information along with the presented isolation solution to identify the soft error failure cause.

The ten soft error types are as follows:

- **Internal error.** Troubleshoot the addresses in the assigned fault domain by vectoring to flow guide 14.2. The reporting station NIC may be the failure cause.
- **Burst error.** These errors can occur when ring stations leave or enter the ring, causing ring reconfigurations, which are not serious. Check the protocol analysis session trace for ring reconfigurations occurring directly before the burst error. If no ring reconfigurations are occurring, troubleshoot the addresses in the assigned fault domain by vectoring to flow guide 14.2.
- **Line error.** These errors also can occur when ring stations leave or enter the ring, which causes ring reconfigurations, or because of simple ring recoveries. Check the protocol analysis session trace for the ring reconfigurations occurring directly before the line error. If no ring reconfigurations or ring recoveries are occurring, troubleshoot the addresses in the assigned fault domain by vectoring to flow guide 14.2. The presence of a line error can be due to a failure cause located in the reporting station's NAUN.
- **Abort delimiter transmitted error.** Troubleshoot the addresses in the assigned fault domain by vectoring to flow guide 14.2. The reporting station NIC may be the failure cause.
- **AC error.** Troubleshoot the addresses in the assigned fault domain by vectoring to flow guide 14.2. The presence of an AC error can be due to a failure cause located in the reporting station's NAUN.
- **Lost frame error.** Troubleshoot addresses in the assigned fault domain by vectoring to flow guide 14.2.
- **Receiver congestion error.** Troubleshoot the addresses in the assigned fault domain by vectoring to flow guide 14.2. A receiver congestion error

usually occurs because of lack of buffer space within the NIC on the destination ring station.

- **Frame copied error.** Check the ring for duplicate address as related to the reporting ring station's adapter. If no duplicate address is found, troubleshoot the addresses in the assigned fault domain by vectoring to flow guide 14.2.
- **Frequency error.** Troubleshoot the station assigned the active monitor role and the reporting ring station's NAUN for a possible failure by vectoring to flow guide 14.6.
- **Token error.** Troubleshoot the addresses in the assigned fault domain by vectoring to flow guide 14.2.

> **NOTE**
> When experiencing intermittent problems such as soft errors on a Token Ring network, you can use traffic-generation techniques to load the network with additional traffic to flush out certain types of intermittent failure causes. By generating additional network traffic, you can stress the network enough to cause certain marginal network component failures to surface.
>
> If a particular soft error occurs frequently and you have thoroughly analyzed the respective soft error and followed the recommended troubleshooting steps, yet cannot conclusively locate a failure cause for the error, vector down to sub-flow guide 14.15.4 and analyze the network bandwidth.

[S2]   Hard Error Vectoring

> Hard errors are the more critical category of errors that can occur on the ring. They are actual solid failures with a specific network component and take the form of a failure symptom by the beaconing process.

NOTE If you encounter a hard error in a protocol analysis session, the first step is to examine the Beacon MAC frame for the following information:

- The assigned fault domain addresses: reporting ring station and the reporting station's NAUN.

- The Beacon type. When a hard error occurs and a Beacon MAC frame is captured, troubleshoot the addresses in the assigned fault domain by vectoring to flow guide 14.2. If the Beacon type is a signal loss error, the failure cause is most likely a cable fault in the cabling medium internal to the assigned fault domain.

> If a hard error occurs frequently, and you have thoroughly analyzed the Beacon MAC frame and followed the recommended troubleshooting steps for the fault domain and yet cannot conclusively locate a failure cause for the error, vector down to sub-flow guide 14.15.4 and analyze the network bandwidth.

14.15.3 Perform a Protocol Analysis Session to Examine the High-Layer Network Frame Communication Processes

Have you verified that the 802.5 base frame communication processes are proper and fluent as to low-level protocol exchange?

[YES] Go to S1.

[NO] Vector back to sub-flow guide 14.15.1 and troubleshoot the low-level 802.5 base communication processes.

[S1] First, perform a full-capture session. Next, view the high-layer protocol communication that occurs concurrently between the network components—the ring stations, network peripherals, gateways, bridges, routers, and file servers—involved in the high-layer communication processes that you are troubleshooting. Closely examine the application and NOS communication process between the respective network components.

Chapter 14: Token Ring Troubleshooting Flow Guide   489

NOTE

Certain applications may use multiple layers of the Token Ring protocol model for transmission. Check all the higher layers.

Are the involved network components and their respective application/NOS communication processes exchanging the correct assigned protocol?

- **[YES]** Reference the NOS and software application manufacturers' manuals and if necessary contact your NOS and software support channel for assistance with troubleshooting any suspected high-layer communication process.

- **[NO]** Does the incorrect protocol exchange appear to be related to some sort of file access process problem with a particular NOS or software application?

- **[YES]** Reference the NOS and software application manufacturers' manuals and if necessary contact your NOS and software support channel for assistance with troubleshooting any suspected high-layer communication process.

- **[NO]** Check the network components involved in the specific high-layer communication process that you are troubleshooting for a possible failure by vectoring to the flow guide for that particular specific network component (for example, 14.6 Ring Station, 14.10 Network Peripheral, 14.14 File Server, and so on).

If you are not completely conclusive as to a specific network component that may be related to the failure symptom, vector to flow guide 14.2 and troubleshoot the respective Token Ring addresses associated in the high-layer frames that appear to be involved with failure symptoms.

If, after vectoring to the respective fault domain, network area, or network component, you find a problem, resolve the problem and retest the ring by vectoring back to this flow guide (14.15) and rerun another baseline session to test the ring. Then reexamine the high-layer communication processes for any deviations from the previous testing results.

If everything appears normal, record the problem in the network maintenance and service log. If the problem still exists, contact your NOS and software support channel for assistance with troubleshooting any suspected high-layer communication process.

14.15.4 The Network is Experiencing One or More of the Following Failure Symptoms: The Whole Network is Operating Slowly; a Specific Network Application is Operating Slowly; or Logon Failures are Occurring

First, set up the protocol analyzer or network monitoring tool to monitor the network bandwidth utilization at an overall baseline view.

Is the overall network baseline within normal operating levels of a previously established baseline for your network?

> If you do not have a previously established baseline for your network, attempt to identify that a reasonable portion of the available maximum bandwidth is still available for use.

[YES] Vector back to the beginning of this flow guide (14.15) and follow the subsections of this complete flow guide. (That is, examine the low-layer 802.5 frame communication processes; check for specific soft or hard errors on the network; and examine the high-layer network frame communication processes.)

[NO] Check the overall baseline network bandwidth as to individual ring stations and all other network components' level usage. Attempt to locate a particular ring station or other network component that may be absorbing abnormal bandwidth.

Chapter 14: Token Ring Troubleshooting Flow Guide

Can you locate any particular ring stations or other network components that may be absorbing abnormal bandwidth?

[YES] If you have not troubleshot the high-level communication process on the ring, vector back to sub-flow guide 14.15.3 and thoroughly troubleshoot the high-level communication process for any NOS or application communication processes that may be absorbing abnormal bandwidth. After analyzing the high-layer communication process, vector back to this sub-flow guide (14.15.4) and remeasure the baseline network bandwidth.

If you have troubleshot the high-level communication processes, go to the next step.

[NO] Even though you cannot specifically locate any particular ring stations or other network components that may be absorbing abnormal bandwidth, still check any ring stations or network components that are suspect by vectoring to the flow guide for that particular specific network component (for example, 14.6 Ring Station, 14.10 Network Peripheral, 14.14 File Server, and so on).

If you are not completely conclusive as to a specific network component that may be related to the failure symptom, vector to flow guide 14.2 and troubleshoot the respective Token Ring addresses associated with high bandwidth usage.

If, after vectoring to the respective fault domain, network area, or network component, you find a problem, resolve the problem and retest the ring by vectoring back to this flow guide (14.15) and vector directly back to sub-flow guide 14.15.4. Rerun another baseline bandwidth test session to reexamine the ring for bandwidth usage.

If everything appears normal, record the problem in the network maintenance and service log. If the problem still exists, contact your NOS and software support channel for assistance with troubleshooting any suspected network bandwidth issues.

NOTE

If you have benchmarked the network bandwidth utilization at overall baseline view and usage of the individual ring stations and other network components, and you still have a bandwidth problem that you cannot locate, contact your NOS and software support channel for assistance with troubleshooting any suspected bandwidth problem.

CHAPTER 15

Architecture

The Ethernet architecture was designed by Digital Equipment Corp. with participation from Xerox and Intel Corp. International standards for the Ethernet architecture are defined by the Institute of Electrical and Electronics Engineers (IEEE) and other groups, such as the American National Standards Institute (ANSI). The term Ethernet is used frequently in both baseband and broadband environments because certain varieties of its specification work in both modes.

Ethernet itself can be confusing, given the fact that several Ethernet frame types exist, such as standard 802.3 or standard Ethernet II. The different Ethernet frame types are presented later in this chapter. The variations in the physical design of Ethernet environments include the following industry specifications considered part of the Ethernet topology.

The most common Ethernet version is the standard 10Mbps Ethernet, normally labeled as 10BASE5, 10BASE2, or 10BASE-T, all of which operate in baseband mode. Of these, the most common Ethernet is the 10BASE-T environment, which utilizes 10Mbps baseband transmission over unshielded twisted pair wiring, normally designed in a star layout from wiring centers and using phone-type wiring cabling.

The second most common type of standard Ethernet transmission is the 10BASE2 type. 10BASE2 wiring is based on coaxial cable, which is designed to be laid out in a bus form. The maximum segment length is about 185 meters. Because the cable width used is thinner in the 10BASE2 environment, 10BASE2 is frequently referred to as *Thin Ethernet*, or simply *ThinNet* or *CheapNet*. (The term CheapNet is used because the cabling is less expensive.) Thin Ethernet is less cumbersome to work with from a general layout standpoint than 10BASE5.

The 10BASE5 specification is called standard Ethernet and also uses the bus layout. The 10BASE5 cable is much thicker and is nicknamed ThickNet. The thicker cable allows for 500-meter-long segments and more protection from electrical interference.

The least frequently seen version of Ethernet is an older specification called 10Broad36 Ethernet, which is a 10Mbps broadband transmission network that supports broadband frequency transmission over cables 3,600 meters in length. Ethernet transmission also is seen across fiber optic cabling in a point-to-point star layout fashion from fiber-optic hubs or repeaters. This type of Ethernet layout is called a 10BASE-F network, which is a fiber-optic link of up to 1.3 miles in length. It also runs at 10Mbps.

Of this topology, the most common types in most Ethernet environments today are 10BASE-T, 10BASE2, and 10BASE5. The 10BASE-T specification is seen frequently because it is supported through most twisted pair phone cabling systems and is much easier to implement from a wiring standpoint.

The access control method in the Ethernet environment is based on collision detection with a sensed approach from devices called transceivers within the topology. This technology is called Carrier Sense Multiple Access with Collision Detection (CSMA/CD). The architecture is similar to some of the AppleTalk networks, such as LocalTalk.

Because of the many varieties of Ethernet, you must be aware of the exact type of Ethernet configuration you are troubleshooting.

Understanding Design and Layout

The design and layout of an Ethernet network depend on the type of Ethernet topology and how it corresponds to particular computing environments. The following subsections discuss the three major Ethernet types—Thin Ethernet,

Thick Ethernet, and Twisted Pair Ethernet—and their respective design and layout schemes.

Thin Ethernet 10BASE2

Thin Ethernet is described by the IEEE 10BASE2 media specification. Thin Ethernet, frequently called ThinNet, allows for up to 185 meters or 607 feet in total length per segment. Some manufacturers support distance variations beyond the specification's 185 meters, depending on the devices used on the Ethernet, such as network interface cards (NICs) and wiring hubs.

Each network segment is considered a separate network within an Ethernet environment. The Thin Ethernet segment specification was designed to accommodate a maximum of approximately 30 users or workstations per segment, which is usually composed of a coaxial cable. The coaxial cable used for Thin Ethernet is based on the RG-58 coaxial cable type. The cable is wired from node to node (the specific workstation PCs or LAN device) throughout the segment to form an individual Ethernet LAN. Figure 15.1 pictures a group of workstations connected by a long cable physically wired as a bus.

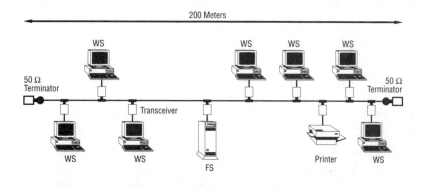

Figure 15.1 Workstations connected by a long cable physically wired as a bus.

Thin Ethernet media type is based on a bus-type layout. The coaxial cable is laid along the route of the workstations or LAN devices. At the end of each long strand of RG-58 cable is a termination point; but along the cable is a point where each workstation connects to the bus. The individual Thin Ethernet cabling segments are terminated at each end by a 50-ohm terminator.

ETHERNET AND TOKEN RING OPTIMIZATION

The Ethernet topology is described as a bus because all devices on the network are connected in parallel to the connectors in the cable. Any data transmitted on the cable propagates throughout the entire cable and is "seen" by each device on the network. (On a bus, all devices can communicate with each other directly without consecutively passing a token.) This contrasts distinctly with Token Ring, where a signal is relayed from one station to the next. At any given moment, one device is sending, and another is receiving. The rest of the devices on the network wait in a receive state for a frame to reach them.

A transceiver connects each PC workstation or LAN device to the coaxial cable. A transceiver is the device that allows the workstation or LAN device and its NIC within the workstation to actually connect to the cabling medium and communicate with the other Ethernet stations. A transceiver is sometimes called a Medium Attachment Unit (MAU) because it attaches the workstation or LAN device to the cabling medium.

The transceiver works with the cabling system to detect events, called collisions, in the Ethernet medium access protocol. The transceiver allows the workstation or LAN device to logically and electrically connect to the Ethernet cabling medium. (This is discussed later in this section.)

Some NICs include their own on-board transceivers physically designed into the NIC. When an NIC card does not employ an on-board transceiver design, a separate transceiver device attaches the NIC card to the cabling medium.

The distance between any transceiver on a Thin Ethernet segment should be at least 1.6 feet. The connection on most transceivers is usually provided by a T-Connector with a BNC-type connection, described later in greater detail. However, external transceivers also can be used. Figure 15.2 shows an external Thin Ethernet transceiver.

Each workstation along a segment includes an NIC. The NIC used in Ethernet includes certain software and hardware routines in the chipsets on the card that allow the card to access the Ethernet medium. The cabling medium access technology used in Ethernet is CSMA/CD. An NIC installed on an individual Thin Ethernet network can access the cabling medium and work with the rest of the workstations along the bus.

Each individual Thin Ethernet segment in a Thin Ethernet environment is considered a separate Ethernet network, but these segments can be a common network if combined by a repeater. A complete Ethernet layout can have up to four repeaters connecting five segments installed in the complete network layout. This limits a complete Thin Ethernet environment to a length of 925 meters, but basic repeaters are available that extend the Thin Ethernet segment. Extensions for a segment can usually be obtained to over 400 feet with basic RG-58 cabling.

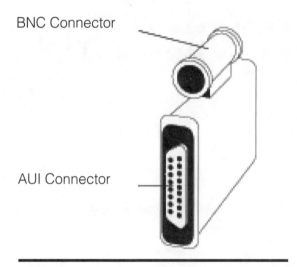

Figure 15.2 An external Thin Ethernet transceiver.

In the Ethernet environment, the most common repeater device is called a multiport repeater, which can allow the individual Ethernet segments to be extended to other Ethernet segments in a fan-out star layout.

For cabling medium access with the CSMA/CD access protocol, there are some differences in the Ethernet environment when networks are separated by a multiport repeater. Multiport repeaters can allow multiple Ethernet segment networks to connect to each other to create a combined network fan-out effect of individual network Ethernet segments. These devices usually provide signal regeneration between ports. This type of wiring scheme provides a linear segment approach to network transmissions but with a star layout.

In Thin Ethernet environments that use repeaters, transceivers (whether internal to NICs or external) usually do not use a technology called Signal Quality Error (SQE). SQE is used for collision detection and is discussed later.

Note that the multirepeater approach still conforms to a straight bus format on each segment drop from the repeater, with each workstation or LAN device splicing into the segment drops through its transceiver/BNC connector. This layout looks like a star, but is still a bus, as pictured in figure 15.3. This is an organized environment and usually provides excellent layout in large installations and reliable data communications for high-end applications.

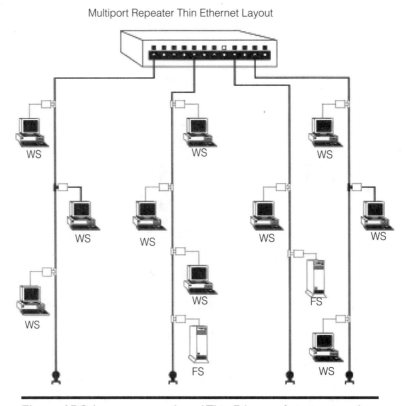

Figure 15.3 A concentrator-based Thin Ethernet functions as a bus.

Thick Ethernet 10BASE5

Thick Ethernet is described by the IEEE 10BASE5 media specification. Thick Ethernet supports a segment length up to 500 meters for individual Ethernet segments and accommodates 100 stations on each segment.

Connecting segments to increase the segment length is accomplished with repeaters. No more than four repeaters should be in a complete layout scheme, limiting a complete Thick Ethernet environment to a length of 2500 meters (five individual Ethernet segments joined by four repeaters). As in ThinNet, a 50-ohm termination also is required at the end of each cable segment in a Thick Ethernet. This can be done with what is called an N Series Coaxial connector.

The Thick Ethernet cabling medium also is accessed by workstation and LAN device NICs via a transceiver. The transceiver in a Thick Ethernet layout is always external to the workstation or LAN device. It provides the standard signal conversion, which matches the NICs on the workstations and LAN devices to the Thick Ethernet cabling medium. These transceivers also are referred to as MAUs.

The transceivers (or MAUs) in Thick Ethernet are most commonly connected to the cabling through a device called a vampire tap. The vampire tap drills teeth into the cable to connect to the shield and the center conductor of the coaxial cable.

The usual minimum allowable distance between transceivers in Thick Ethernet is 2.5 meters or 8.2 feet. The transceiver has a special port on it, an Attachment Unit Interface (AUI) port. The AUI port connects to a drop cable connection that allows the ThickNet cabling transceiver AUI port to connect to the NIC in the workstation or LAN device.

The standard maximum length of each drop cable is 165 feet. The NICs that work with this type of configuration in ThickNet have a DB15 connector on the back of their NIC as a port. Certain devices, such as repeaters and wiring hubs that are used in Thick Ethernet layouts, also employ this type of DB15 connector. This allows newer Ethernet layouts and older Thick Ethernet to be integrated. Thus Thick Ethernet, Thin Ethernet, and even 10BASE-T twisted pair Ethernet are frequently combined together through new internetwork devices such as repeaters, bridges, routers, and intelligent wiring hubs to form common and compatible Ethernet computing environments.

In Thick Ethernet it is more common to see the transceivers use the SQE technology for collision detection.

The Thick Ethernet cabling standard provides reliable data communications, but it is difficult to work with from a network design, layout, installation, and troubleshooting standpoint because of the actual width size of the coaxial cable. Thick Ethernet uses a clear bus technology, as displayed in Figure 15.4.

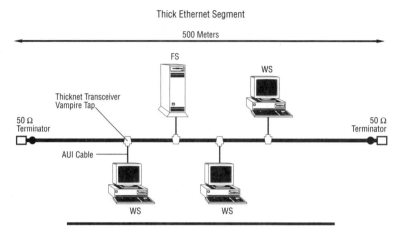

Figure 15.4 Thick Ethernet uses a bus technology.

Twisted Pair Ethernet 10BASE-T

A twisted pair cabling Ethernet environment is known as 10BASE-T and is the most common standard in the networking industry today. The overall layout is a star-type design. Twisted pair Ethernet is based on unshielded twisted pair (UTP) type 3 telephone cabling on a variety of quality levels. Level 3, 4, and 5 UTP cables are the types most commonly employed with 10BASE-T.

Workstations and LAN devices normally connect through a standard RJ-45 phone type connector, usually built into 10BASE-T NICs. UTP cabling connects the workstation to an intelligent wiring hub or repeater with a direct UTP connection port. Normally, the transceiver is internal and mounted on the NIC, but it is possible to use an external UTP transceiver, allowing Thick AUI and Thin BNC NIC cards to connect to a UTP-based wiring hub device. It is therefore possible to use a single type of Ethernet card throughout a mixed Ethernet that combines coaxial cable and UTP, provided the card is equipped with an AUI connector.

The star layout approach normally is configured to work with a multiport repeater or intelligent wiring hub. A UTP cable connects each device to the hub in a star configuration, as pictured in Figure 15.5.

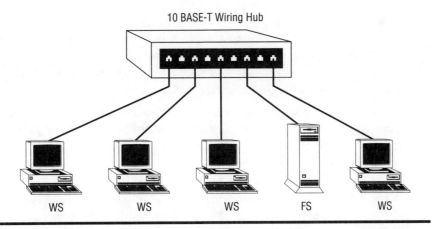

Figure 15.5 A UTP cable connects each device to the hub in a star configuration.

The 10BASE-T technology has electrical differences, including an electrical charge on the wire, that change the manner in which the signal is propagated across the network. The wiring hubs or multiport repeaters include a more complex regeneration scheme and provide port partitioning and switching. (This is discussed more in the next chapter.) Due to some of the electrical differences, transceivers in the 10BASE-T environments normally do not work in the same way with the collision detection system as accurately as the standard Thick or Thin Ethernet transceivers.

The resulting network topology of the 10BASE-T environment is a distributed star that allows for each UTP drop cable from a wiring hub to be up to 100 meters long. This is physically unlike Thin and Thick Ethernet, but it can be managed more easily because all the cables throughout the 10BASE-T environment are dropped to the workstations from the hub. Network management can be performed from the hub in a 10BASE-T environment with much the same feel as that of a standard Token Ring environment.

Overview of the Main Ethernet Types

Whether ThickNet, ThinNet, or Twisted Pair, all Ethernet propagation is based on one major cabling medium access protocol for communicating: CSMA/CD.

The layout can be either a bus or star, but there is always going to be a CSMA/CD medium access control.

Depending on the size of the network, there may be repeaters or wiring hubs for extension and connection between multiple Ethernet segments. The NICs throughout the Ethernet environment are intelligent, but do not include some of the high-end recovery mechanisms found in the Token Ring environment. Because of this, the overhead bandwidth levels of physical layer communications are not as high as they are for Token Ring.

In 10BASE5 and 10BASE2 environments, the transceiver is called an MAU. In the 10BASE2 environment, the MAU commonly is built into the NIC, as part of its design. In the 10BASE5 type, the MAU is always external to the NIC. The main type of drop cable to the workstation or LAN device NIC connection in the 10BASE5 ThickNet environment is normally the AUI cable type. In 10BASE2 type Ethernets, the BNC connector is most common. It is also common to see AUI and BNC connection points on internetworking Ethernet devices such as 10BASE-T wiring hubs to allow for interfacing between Twisted Pair, Thick Ethernet, and Thin Ethernet environments.

This integration of multiple Ethernet type environments is also a common progression by the Ethernet NIC manufacturers who design most NICs with AUI, BNC, and RJ-45 UTP connectors so that there is easy integration among any of the main Ethernet environments—10BASE5, 10BASE2, and 10BASE-T.

Both the Thick and Thin Ethernet types require a 50-ohm terminator for the cabling bus termination. Twisted Pair Ethernet uses internal engineering to form a cabling star layout, and each termination point is provided at the NIC or the hub port.

The individual segments in Thick and Thin Ethernet can be connected to each other through a point-to-point connection with repeaters. In Twisted Pair layouts, it is more common to see intelligent wiring hubs, which create a common segment through the star approach. Some repeaters and wiring hubs also can link segments in the ThinNet, ThickNet, and Twisted Pair environments. Repeater or hub connections count in the number of workstations in an Ethernet environment. If multiple Ethernet networks are going to interconnect to form one common Ethernet, this can be done through a repeater or a custom wiring hub propagation device.

It also is possible for multiple Ethernet networks to be combined to form Ethernet internetworks through bridges and routers. Ethernet bridging and routing theories are discussed later. Other high-end devices are in the Ethernet environment, such as gateways and network peripherals; these are discussed as required throughout this chapter. Figure 15.6 shows a conceptual picture of an Ethernet internetwork.

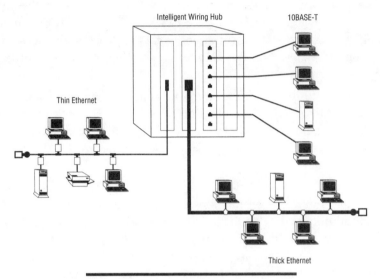

Figure 15.6 An Ethernet internetwork.

When deciding on an Ethernet type, remember that an Ethernet network can be designed in two different network layouts: bus or star. An Ethernet network also supports up to four types of cabling schemes: Thin, Thick, UTP, and Fiber. This allows for flexibility when designing an internetwork based on Ethernet. For example, it is possible to configure a Thick Ethernet backbone that connects to Thin and Twisted Pair Ethernet network environments; just keep in mind the basic common factors and differences between the Ethernet types.

CSMA/CD

Carrier Sense Multiple Access with Collision Detection (CSMA/CD) is a protocol access algorithm developed for the Ethernet architecture. This technology enables PC workstations or LAN devices (nodes) that want to transmit on the Ethernet cabling medium to identify whether communication is occurring. To understand how CSMA/CD functions, it is useful to pick apart the name.

Ethernet stations are supposed to transmit only when no other traffic is on the cable. Carrier Sensing describes the capability of Ethernet NICs to listen to the network for any data communication signals.

The event cycle of the access method of CSMA/CD operates in the following manner. A node waits to transmit on a network, listening to the network to determine whether any data transmission is taking place on the network. If no transmission or carrier is on the network at the time, the station attempts to send its transmission or message.

Ethernet is a Multiple Access network, meaning that any station can attempt to transmit any time the network is not in use. If by chance two stations are listening at the same time and attempt to start their transmission so that the transmission occurs at approximately the same interval on the network, a collision may occur.

If a collision occurs, Collision Detection is performed. Any station that determines that multiple transmissions are interfering or "colliding" with each other sends additional data on the network to initiate a process called jamming. This ensures that the collision is propagated throughout the network to all the other Ethernet stations that may attempt to transmit. That station then remains quiet for a period of time and determines whether it can transmit again. The period of time varies and usually is determined by the hardware and software operation algorithms in the Ethernet NIC.

With basic Thin Ethernet type NICs, a node waits approximately nine microseconds before attempting to transmit. This allows the workstations to stabilize throughout the network. As higher traffic (bandwidth or utilization increases) levels occur on the network, longer delays can occur between stations before they can transmit on the network. This is why a standard number of network nodes is recommended per network. This also varies from an analyst's standpoint depending on the application level on the network. Figure 15.7 shows a collision detection event occurring between two Ethernet workstations on a Thin Ethernet segment.

As more workstations attempt to access the network, throughput on the network can decrease, and the overall traffic across the network shows this. There is a point when actual data throughput can decrease on an Ethernet network due to high packet collisions in relation to the CSMA/CD algorithm. If collisions are over 1% of overall traffic, a problem might exist on the network with an NIC or something of that nature. This type of problem is discussed in the troubleshooting chapter.

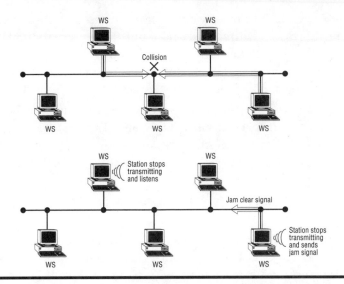

Figure 15.7 A collision detection event between two Ethernet workstations.

The approach of the CSMA/CD access protocol is to facilitate nodes to transmit on the network when there is the least amount of traffic possible. Within this protocol, workstations should be able to identify whether a certain transmission is occurring and then attempt to transmit. In essence, the nodes sense the carrier, allowing for carefully sequenced access for multiple stations. The following is a presentation of the detailed operation of CSMA/CD.

CSMA/CD Detailed Operation Transmission Access Approach

In the Ethernet topology there is a specific set of sequences and events that occur for CSMA/CD to operate. This access method is unique and provides a balanced approach and availability to the Ethernet medium. The following is the breakout for this type of access.

For the key transmission access approach, the following discussion presents how stations attempt to access the Ethernet cabling medium:

- All stations are in a constant listen mode for the Ethernet carrier signal.

    Before an Ethernet station transmits it will listen. Called the *slot time*, this is normally 512 bit times or approximately 51.2 microseconds. The slot time is normally within this value, but there are variations on some Ethernet NICs. If no carrier is sensed, the Ethernet NIC will then attempt to transmit on the Ethernet medium. If an Ethernet node transmits at the same time that another Ethernet node transmits, a collision may occur.

I f the carrier is present, it should be noted that the Ethernet NIC node will wait to transmit for a specified wait time. This may also vary by NIC manufacturer. There was some variance allowed in design in this area. The standard wait time is normally 9.6 microseconds. This is also called the *defer time*.

- Once a node transmits, if a collision does occur, the following event may take place.

    All stations involved in collisions on a particular occurrence will back off and transmit a 32- to 48-bit time jam signal on the network. This particular jam signal should stop within the 32- to 48-bit time. If it does not stop, jabber may occur.

    Once the jam is heard on the network, all stations that would normally attempt to transmit will hear the jam and not transmit.

    Colliding stations will increment a counter and attempt to perform a back-off algorithm, and then eventually reattempt transmission. It should be noted that after an excessive number of re-attempts, the station may abort the transmission. Normally this count is 16 attempts.

CSMA/CD Receiving Approach

The following is a discussion of how stations on an Ethernet topology configuration will interrogate information upon receiving:

- All stations on the segment will investigate the frames that pass the node point.

    The first investigation step is to decide whether or not the destination address is a match for the respective node. It should be noted that the destination match can be the specific destination address, a broadcast ID, or a common multicast match address.

    If the address matches for one of the areas noted above, the station will then investigate the integrity of the packet for a valid frame size and a valid CRC field. If these particular fields are okay, the station and the NIC will then pass the packet up to the upper protocol sockets for process.

I f the particular integrity does not check for the frame size or the CRC, the end node NIC process will not process the packet to the upper layer protocol sockets, and eventual retransmissions or loops on request from the original source station may occur. This can be picked up on an analyzer.

Collisions

A *collision* on an Ethernet network can be defined as the result of two or more Ethernet nodes attempting to transmit on the Ethernet medium at the same time and having their data transmission collide. Collisions are normal events unless the traffic level of collisions on a single Ethernet network rises above 1%. When a collision occurs, the frames may get corrupted, and certain nodes may detect this occurrence as a runt type frame.

According to CSMA/CD theory, only one computer should normally be able to transmit across the Ethernet medium at any given time. It is the responsibility of sections of the transceivers and NICs of an Ethernet node to detect a network communication session or collision. Standard Thick and Thin Ethernet transceivers and NIC cards usually have the capability to monitor collision events on the cabling medium. This is due to the early implementation of SQE testing in the Ethernet networks that use the Ethernet II frame transmission standard.

Older Ethernet II NICs and transceivers would normally transmit a signal, called *heartbeat*, to test the collision detection circuitry in MAUs and transceivers. The SQE testing conflicts with the operation in most of today's Ethernet 802.3 standard NIC frame transmission devices, such as repeaters. The differences between Ethernet frame specification types is discussed later in this section. In most Thin and Twisted Pair Ethernet networks, NICs or transceivers that have SQE capability normally have the SQE function disabled.

Some transceivers have technology that can alert a troubleshooter with LEDs. At times, stations transmit a signal to attempt to jam the network for collision prevention, and then do not stop the jamming signal. This is considered excessive jabber and at that time certain jabber can be detected by certain types of transceivers and MAUs.

Addressing of the Ethernet Environment

Every node on an individual Ethernet network has a unique physical hardware address for its NIC. The Ethernet addressing scheme is assigned by the manufacturer of the NIC with a 6-byte hexadecimal address. The first three bytes in the left-most end of the address contain a unique NIC manufacturer identification. Each manufacturer then assigns three bytes at the right-most end to be unique to the particular card's network physical address. As a result, each Ethernet NIC is assigned a hard-coded ID different from every other Ethernet NIC. The following is a breakout of an Ethernet address frame format in Figure 15.8.

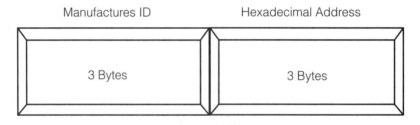

Figure 15.8 An Ethernet address frame format.

Understanding Data Transmission Methodology for Ethernet

The Ethernet topology uses Manchester Encoding, a standard bi-phase encoding technique in which the first half of a byte period is blended with the second half of a byte period. Just as with Token Ring, a clock signal also is built in for synchronization between the first half and the second half of the byte signal. The clock signal blends with the data to produce a resultant code for physical transmission on the cabling medium.

Understanding Physical and Higher Layer Management of the Ethernet Environment

The inherent design of physical layer management of the Ethernet network environment is not as complex as Token Ring topology. For example, standard Ethernet NICs do not include error recovery techniques in the chipsets.

Despite that relative simplicity, several network management approaches should be used for an Ethernet network. First, there should always be a physical layer management approach with either a protocol analyzer or another network management tool that can monitor collision levels and other error types such as CRC errors. Chapter 17 discusses the Ethernet physical error types and applied troubleshooting methodologies. The bandwidth or utilization level also should be monitored. A physical layer tool (such as the network monitors and protocol analysis tools discussed in Part One of this book, "Network Optimization") can be referenced for these type of tools.

For network management of the Ethernet lower and higher layers, the most popular trend for fault management and detection of problems is the Simple Network Management Protocol (SNMP) from the TCP/IP protocol suite. The SNMP protocol was developed in the Internet community and is frequently used in Ethernet networks for general network management. Multiple versions of the SNMP protocol currently exist. This is especially true when the TCP/IP full protocol suite itself is implemented in a network architecture.

A large portion of intelligent hub products use SNMP for management communication in a network, enabling network managers to establish seamless management of the entire network. Most hub manufacturers are using the SNMP network management approach. NICs, multiport repeaters, and wiring hubs for Ethernet are being designed and shipped with internal SNMP Management Information Based (MIB) agents. An SNMP MIB agent is a firmware agent that exchanges SNMP management messages with a central SNMP protocol monitoring console.

In most networks to be managed with SNMP, an SNMP management console is placed on one portion of the network; then all the devices that have SNMP agents designed within the hardware and software operations can respond to commands transmitted with the SNMP protocol from the master console. The master console may query the devices and pick up different statistics throughout the network to update its internal database on the general operation of the internetwork. This is more commonly seen in larger Ethernet internetworking environments, that is, those with more than one network.

From a network optimization and troubleshooting standpoint, an analyst should be able to decode the SNMP protocol with an analyzer. The approach is to obtain all the specifications on commands used from the SNMP type across the network, and to connect to the Ethernet network and monitor the SNMP protocol for fluency. This book does not cover the scope of SNMP discrete types and commands, but for more information on the SNMP protocol, see the reference section of this book. Figure 15.9 displays a conceptual implementation of protocol analyzers and SNMP agents across an Ethernet internetwork to provide physical and upper layer management.

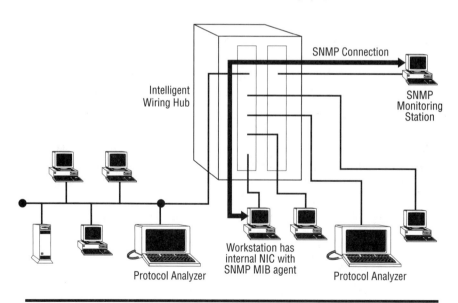

Figure 15.9 Implementation of protocol analyzers and SNMP agents across an Ethernet internetwork.

Understanding Ethernet Frame Types

The Ethernet frame is responsible for carrying and transmitting the higher layer data across the network. The Ethernet physical frame has headers and trailer fields that envelop the actual data portion in its frame. This is how information is packaged for transfer from one Ethernet node to another in network communication. The actual physical entity is usually termed a packet, and the packet uses one of the Ethernet frame specifications to envelop the network data.

Ethernet NICs then transmit the packet from the Ethernet node to its destination. Communication synchronization methods within the different Ethernet frame types include error checking and address identification for Ethernet network transmission.

The header and trailer portions of the different Ethernet frame types define the way data packets are carried across the network. Each frame type differs slightly in how it actually codes and decodes the packets sent between the different node NICs in an Ethernet network.

Several frame types are employed in an Ethernet environment, including the standard Ethernet II frame type, RAW 802.3 Ethernet, and the IEEE 802.2 SNAP Ethernet frame type. As mentioned earlier, the Ethernet frame types were mainly developed by Xerox, Digital Equipment, and Intel as a consortium to put together the complete Ethernet networking composite. All the different frame types have certain common fields, including an Ethernet node source and destination address, a data field, and a network error checking field.

The following is a breakdown of the different Ethernet frame types and their descriptions.

Ethernet II

Ethernet II is the original Ethernet frame type developed by the Digital/Intel/Xerox consortium. This frame type is composed of a preamble, a destination and source address, a data area, and a frame check sequence. The preamble is an 8-byte area where the fixed data pattern is implemented for synchronization in and out of the NIC. The destination and source addresses inside the standard Ethernet II frame type are 6 bytes each. Within those 6-byte areas is the Ethernet frame address for the source and destination nodes.

A data area also exists within the Ethernet II frame that can be anywhere from 46 to 1,500 bytes. This is considered a variable length frame, because the data is variable. It is possible to have a routing information field, and certain bytes are set within the addressing area of the Ethernet frame, if that is the case.

A frame check sequence is always in a standard Ethernet II frame; it is always a 4-byte sequence that allows for checking of frame synchronization between two Ethernet node transmissions. The Ethernet II frame specification includes a 2-byte type field.

The total allowable length for the complete Ethernet II packet is from 64 to 1,518 bytes. Anything under or over that range is considered a runt or a long frame type for the Ethernet II frame category. The troubleshooting of Ethernet long and runt frame problems is discussed in Chapter 17.

RAW 802.3 Ethernet

The IEEE developed its own standard for Ethernet. Labeled standard 802.3 Ethernet frame type, it is close to Ethernet II but varies in its overall structure. A variation of the original design from the IEEE also exists, called RAW 802.3. Most of the differences are in terminology. However, a significant difference between the original Ethernet II and the 802.3 RAW frame type is the substitution of a frame length field for the Ethernet II type field. This allows the NIC to do a different type of processing than for the RAW Ethernet 802.3 type.

The RAW 802.3 frame breakdown is as follows. A preamble is 7 bytes long and is responsible for synchronization on transmission and reception of data at the NIC. The preamble also has a 1-byte-long start frame delimiter field that assists in synchronization of the Ethernet frame in and out of the NIC.

Physical source and destination address fields are 6 bytes each in length. Then a length field is 2 bytes in length and identifies the length of the frame. The cyclic redundancy check (CRC) field area for the error checking between node transmission is 4 bytes. Finally, there is the field for the data, which internally can range from 46 bytes to 1,500 bytes in length.

Because the standard Ethernet II frame type and RAW 802.3 differ in structure, it should be clear that the network and higher layers may process the frame types differently. In the 802.3 RAW format, the Ethernet topology pads the data length at times.

IEEE Standard 802.3 Ethernet

Only one real difference exists between the 802.3 standard frame type accepted by the IEEE and the nonstandard RAW 802.3 type. The latter allows for not using a 802.2 Logical Link Control (LLC) header inside the data field. The 802.2 is a connection protocol standard defined by the IEEE and is explained in the following paragraph. In a standard 802.3 frame type, an 802.2 header is inside the data field to package the data. The 802.2 header includes a destination service access point, a source service access point, and a control field internally to envelop the data fields. The actual data is placed inside the 802.2 LLC data header.

The nonstandard 802.3 RAW does not have to include the 802.2 LLC data header, but includes a length field and then has the data contained within the 802.3 RAW data field. This is where the term RAW comes from—it carries the data RAW inside, without an LLC header. Figure 15.10 is a comparison of the main Ethernet frame types.

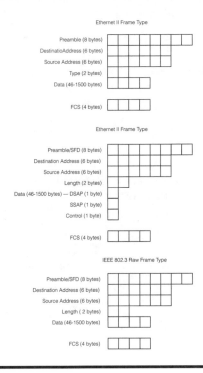

Figure 15.10 A comparison of the main Ethernet frame types.

Defining Protocols Used in Ethernet Frame Transfer

The following protocols are used in Ethernet frame types for varying reasons. The 802.2 LLC standard is considered separate as a protocol, but is used in standard 802.3 frames to envelop data. The Subnetwork Access Protocol (SNAP) frame type is often used to carry Ethernet frame data across other topologies, such as Token Ring. These two protocols are described in the following sections.

Logical Link Control

The LLC layer is described by the IEEE 802.2 standard. It is a communication-carrying protocol that provides reliable transmission of information across a LAN. The route across the network is defined by the MAC layer of the particular topology. The LLC protocol can be used to envelop data and provide flow control in the transfer of data.

Node and internal processes that use the LLC protocol for data transfer are defined as source and destination Service Access Points (SAPs). Both the source and destination address normally are specified in the 802.2 LLC protocol. Each process between a destination and source node address may have a unique SAP. That SAP address can be up to 8 bytes in length.

Three different types of communication can occur in an LLC environment; a control field identifies what the type of the communication is for the LLC frame. This LLC frame normally is carried by a physical frame as the general Protocol Data Unit (PDU) for holding the data communicated from node to node. In the Ethernet 802.3 standard, the LLC header is used to carry data and is enveloped within the data fields of 802.3 frames.

The LLC Protocol has the following three type fields:

- Type 1 is an unacknowledged connectionless service, where the sending and receiving stations send their datagrams from point to point. Broadcasts are supported by this type, but no acknowledgment is required, and no connection is actually maintained.

- Type 2 of LLC communication involves a logical connection between the SAP addresses; full flow control acknowledgment and error control takes place between their connection.
- Type 3 uses an acknowledgment when required, but no actual connection maintenance takes place. Type 3 is acknowledged connectionless service.

An LLC session involves the establishment of a virtual connection between two network nodes. Normally, this is a connectionless approach with Type 1 communications for LLC. The destination service access point (DSAP) and the source service access point (SSAP) have preassigned codes and indicate the subprotocol for the rest of the frame. Internally, that code may indicate, for instance, NetBIOS with a hex ID with the SAP, which indicates what protocol is enveloped in the data field inside the PDU of the LLC headers.

The control field also may have information relating to whether the LLC frame is Informational (I), Supervisory (S), or Unnumbered (U). It is usually in one of these three categories that LLC communication occurs, and the LLC frame is labeled as one of the three types.

If an LLC frame format is labeled Informational, data is going to be inside the PDU, and there always will be a sequence number and sequence assigned to the communication.

If the LLC frame format is labeled Supervisory, it assumes that the node-to-node communication has some sort of command or response involved. Certain types of sub-actions within Supervisory can be labeled, such as receive ready, receive not ready, and reject. This activity represents the flow control strength of LLC.

If the LLC frame is labeled an Unnumbered communication, the LLC frame is usually involved in a mode of connection control. The following modes may occur: Asynchronous Balance Mode (ABM), Disconnect Mode (DISC), Disconnected Mode (DM), Unnumbered Acknowledgment (UA), Frame Reject (FRMR), Exchange Information (XID), Testing (TEST), and Unnumbered Information.

Overall, Information, Supervisory, and Unnumbered are the categories in the control field that may be present in LLC frames, and this can be identified within the frame type with a protocol analyzer. Figure 15.11 displays an LLC PDU.

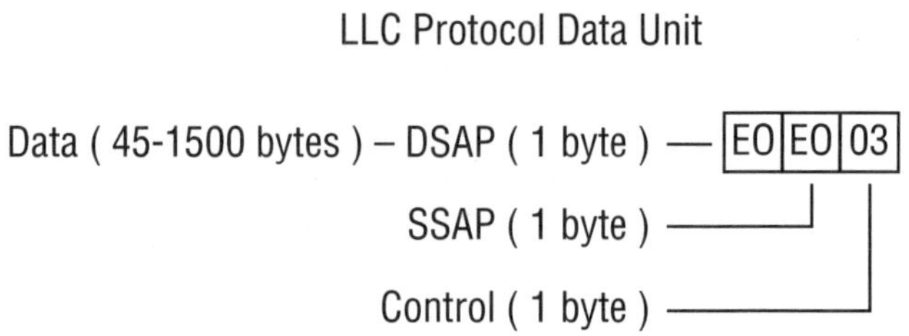

ETHERNET AND TOKEN RING OPTIMIZATION

LLC Protocol Data Unit

Data (45-1500 bytes) – DSAP (1 byte) — | E0 | E0 | 03 |
SSAP (1 byte)
Control (1 byte)

Figure 15.11 An LLC PDU.

Subnetwork Address Protocol

One more frame protocol in the Ethernet environment is Subnetwork Address Protocol, better known as SNAP. Normally within an 802.LLC header, it is common to pick up SNAP frame types inside the LLC header. This is an encapsulation protocol used frequently when Ethernet frames have to be carried across a Token Ring environment. Within the 802.2 standard LLC frame in the data frame, after the LLC headers, there may a SNAP header. The SNAP header includes other data internally, such as general Ethernet protocols and higher layer information.

The breakdown for the SNAP header is as follows. Normally a protocol ID is 3 bytes in length, and then there is a 2-byte Ethertype ID for the Ethertype environment. Encapsulated further is the data.

In an 802.2 SNAP frame is the physical frame headers and trailers, which then envelop an LLC PDU. The LLC PDU in turn envelops a SNAP header. SNAP headers include protocol identification and Ethertype breakout fields for the SNAP frame. Then the actual data is layered within the SNAP frame.

The SNAP frame is mainly used within the LLC PDU to carry other protocols. This allows for another encapsulation. Figure 15.12 shows the SNAP frame format.

This chapter discussed the frame types within Ethernet. Analysts should be aware of multiple Ethernet types and multiple Ethernet frame types when examining Ethernet internetworks. This discussion also encompassed the Ethernet access protocols and most of the general breakdowns of Ethernet physical layer operations in its design and layout. This is considered the general architecture of Ethernet. The following chapters now discuss the major devices and specifications in the Ethernet environment.

Total Ethernet Frame Structure with SNAP Encapsulation

```
Preamble/SFD ( 8 bytes )
Destination Address ( 6 bytes )
Source Address ( 6 bytes )
Length ( 2 bytes )
Data ( 45-1500 bytes ) – DSAP ( 1 byte )
               SSAP ( 1 byte )
               Control ( 1 byte )        SNAP Internal
        Organization Code ( 3 bytes )    Frame Structure
           Ethernet Type ( 2 bytes )

FCS ( 4 bytes )
```

SNAP Encapsulation Concept

| 802.3 | LLL | SNAP | LLC | 802.3 |

Figure 15.12 SNAP frame format.

CHAPTER 16

Devices and Specifications

In troubleshooting networking problems, keep a close eye on the specifications of any Ethernet devices on the network. Network devices must be working according to their design specifications. All Ethernet devices need to be configured properly to work with each other as far as their communication and general performance.

This chapter will examine some of the key Ethernet devices in today's internetworking environment. This section begins by discussing the specifications for the cabling and layout for the different Ethernet types and their environments. Next, some of the specifications for Ethernet NICs, wiring hubs, bridges, routers, and repeaters will be discussed, with some of the major product platforms in the industry presented as examples.

Exploring Ethernet Cabling and Layout Specifications

There are four main cabling schemes in the Ethernet environment: Thick Ethernet, Thin Ethernet, Twisted Pair Ethernet, and Fiber Optic Ethernet. Clear differences exist among the types in specification, layout, and node capacity, leading to performance differences.

The transmission speed of all the Ethernet types is always 10Mbps. The layout design for each type has either a bus or star configuration. The following sections outline the significant properties of the four Ethernet types, and their specification and layout.

Thick Ethernet—10BASE5

- Transmission—10Mbps baseband.
- Bus layout.
- The type of cable used in the Thick Ethernet environment is normally a wide 0.4-inch-diameter coaxial cable.
- The maximum segment length per Thick Ethernet segment is 500 meters.
- The actual termination in a Thick Ethernet environment must be done by a 50-ohm terminator.
- Repeaters and other devices such as wiring hubs can be used to extend the segment distance.
- Workstations and LAN devices attach to the network cabling medium through external transceivers or MAUs.
- The connector type used for connection of the transceiver to the cabling medium is provided via a vampire tap.
- A Thick Ethernet segment can support up to 100 workstations or LAN devices.
- Thick Ethernet cabling allows for more insulation from electrical interference.

Thin Ethernet—10BASE2

- Transmission—10Mbps baseband.
- Bus layout.
- The most common cable type in this environment is RG58A.
- The maximum segment length per Thin Ethernet segment is 185 meters.
- Termination in a Thin Ethernet environment must be done by a 50-ohm terminator.
- Repeaters and other devices such as wiring hubs can be used to extend the segment distance.
- Workstations and LAN devices attach to the network cabling medium through transceivers or MAUs. These may be external or internal to the NIC.
- The connector type used for connection of the transceiver to the cabling medium is provided by a BNC-T adapter.
- There should only be 30 workstations or LAN devices connected through transceivers per Thin Ethernet segment.

Twisted-Pair Ethernet—10BASE-T

- Transmission—10Mbps baseband.
- Star layout.
- The most common cable type is 24 AWG, unshielded twisted-pair standard telephone wire. The are different levels of UTP wiring that range in their category of quality. The levels used for Ethernet are category three to five.
- Central wiring hubs are utilized as concentrators to interconnect individual 10BASE-T drop cables to workstations and LAN devices.
- The maximum segment length per UTP Ethernet drop cable is 100 meters. This may vary depending on the wiring hubs and NIC manufacturer.
- UTP-based Ethernet NICs usually come with internal UTP transceivers. It is possible to acquire external UTP transceivers so standard Thick or Thin Ethernet NICs can work in a UTP scheme.

- An RJ-45 modular jack is often used as the NIC connector, with positive and negative transmit and receive pairs based on 8-pin connections.
- UTP cabling is easy to install and maintain, and is cost effective. It is susceptible to electrical interference and must be installed according to specification.

Fiber Optic Ethernet—10BASE-F

- Transmission—10Mbps baseband.
- Star layout.
- The cable is usually 50- or 100-micron fiber-optic cable.
- Central fiber-optic wiring hubs or Multiport repeaters are utilized as concentrators to interconnect individual 10BASE-F drop cables to workstations and LAN devices.
- The maximum segment length per fiber-optic Ethernet drop cable is 1.3 miles.
- Fiber-optic cabling allows for complete installation from electrical energy source interference.

Ethernet Cabling Connectors

Depending on the type of Ethernet, different types of cabling connectors may be used for cabling connections to NICs, transceivers, repeaters, and hubs.

All devices intended for use with Thick Ethernet are equipped with a 15-pin AUI or DIX connector. (The name DIX is derived from the names of the firms that were most instrumental in defining Ethernet: Digital, Intel, and Xerox.) A workstation or other device is connected to the Ethernet transceiver by means of an Attachment Unit Interface (AUI) cable, which connects the DIX connector on the Ethernet NIC board to the DIX connector on a transceiver. The transceiver then attaches to the Ethernet coax using either connectors or by means of a vampire tap which drills directly into the cable. A variety of coaxial cable connectors are used to connect coax cables together.

In the Thin Ethernet environment, a BNC T-shaped connector is used to connect the Ethernet cable directly to a connector on the workstation or other device. If there are problems with a cabling segment in a Thin Ethernet environment, the T-type connector is frequently a cause, and should be examined for proper connection to the coax cabling.

10BASE-T Ethernet uses a standard RJ-45 telephone type connector for connection between 10BASE-T NICs and Ethernet UTP-based intelligent wiring hubs.

Depending on the Ethernet environment, it is common to see the different Ethernet type connectors on a common wiring hub for interconnection between type environments. For example, you'll often see on the back of a normal 10BASE-T wiring hub a DIX connector for a Thick Ethernet AUI connection, and a BNC connection for a standard Thin Ethernet connection capability. This allows different Ethernet type environments to be integrated for internetworking. With Ethernet NICs, it is common to have connectors for RJ-45 connections, BNC connectors, and AUI connectors all on one board.

Figure 16.1 presents some of the major connectors found throughout the different Ethernet type environment, including the Thick Ethernet DIX connector, the Thin Ethernet connector, and the 10BASE-T RJ-45 UTP-based connector.

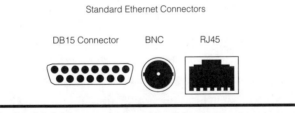

Figure 16.1 Major connectors in Ethernet environments.

Wiring Hubs for the Ethernet Environment

In the Thick Ethernet and Thin Ethernet environments, repeaters are used to connect segments with each other. When multiport repeaters are used, the repeaters can be regarded as wiring hubs between different Ethernet segments. Multiport repeaters are frequently labeled as FAN-OUT boxes because they create a star-type layout when connecting multiple bus-type Ethernet segments.

The Twisted Pair Ethernet (10BASE-T) environment has a range of wiring hubs. In 10BASE-T Ethernet, the cabling drop runs from each NIC all come back to one point, the ports on the wiring hub. This creates a star physical topology. By centralizing the node cabling to a wiring hub, this allows for easier troubleshooting and network management. The wiring hub is an excellent place to have intelligent technology to manage a complete internetworking environment. Think of the wiring hub in a 10BASE-T layout as the intersection for traffic.

Ethernet hub manufacturers are implementing features in the hub technology to manage the Ethernet nodes which they support. Each Ethernet node that is connected to an intelligent wiring hub is considered a port that can be monitored. A range of network management techniques are now being designed in the hub. Many of these are based on SNMP technology. An intelligent wiring hub can monitor each port for its function at the physical level, general traffic level and data communication patterns observed. Both standard LEDs and complex software network management platforms are used for monitoring.

There is a range of intelligent hubs to accommodate the Ethernet environment. Most early designs for intelligent hubs were configured for the Ethernet topology, because Ethernet was considered the most widely based topology that was utilizing UTP-based wiring schemes. Token Ring intelligent wiring hubs and smart MAUs evolved later. (There is a discussion of UTP-based hubs for the Token Ring topology in the Token Ring section of this book.)

Individual segment switching is another new Ethernet technology. Segment switching is accomplished through the implementation of Ethernet switches. Ethernet switches can route traffic quickly between different Ethernet segments and certain key end nodes such as servers. This makes more effective use of the Ethernet available bandwidth on a per-transfer basis.

The standard Ethernet Carrier Sense Multiple Access Collision Detection (CSMA/CD) protocol works well until there is an overload of high utilization. Although the 10Mbps throughput normally is sufficient, at times a network may experience data throughput problems when there is a high level of data communication on an individual Ethernet segment.

Segment switching is accomplished through directly connecting an Ethernet switch to the site hubs. It can also be implemented in most intelligent hubs by adding an internal module. Most manufacturers have developed some variation of this design.

Overall, Ethernet switching allows for increased bandwidth and more direct conversations between each node. As the network grows and migrates over time, load balancing techniques can be performed by strategically placing nodes and segments on certain ports in an Ethernet switch.

As the utilization of an individual node or segment increases, a properly implemented switch can balance the network workload. This enables applications to run faster, because switching between different segments can be done dynamically. For example, certain file servers can be placed together in consecutive ports to allow less segment traffic for server-to-server sessions.

When an Ethernet switch is implemented, it usually creates one large Ethernet segment. Note that Ethernet switching is now supported in routing environments that rely on certain addressing schemes such as TCP/IP, but this usually involves a more complex addressing scheme in the switch.

Thus the effective bandwidth on a 10Mbps network with today's technology can be increased to 100Mbps in an Ethernet switching environment. Because physical layer Ethernet switching is simple and faster, it challenges any current Ethernet 10Mbps network implementations.

Another emerging Ethernet technology is the hub card. This approach implements the Ethernet wiring hub technology in an NIC that can be configured in a PC or file server. The Ethernet hub card has multiple ports on the back of the card; these allow different Ethernet segments to connect and interswitch. This effectively creates a hub inside a PC or a file server.

This is an excellent approach for small sites where only minor Ethernet nodes are implemented. It is easy to take a hub card with four to eight ports and implement it within a PC. Different nodes can share a 10BASE-T environment via UTP cable connections. This area is emerging as an attractive option for small Ethernet networks.

Many Ethernet vendors have developed significant wiring hubs. The following is just a sample:

- Cabletron's Multi Media Access Center (MMAC) wiring hubs
- Bay Network's System 5000 Enterprise wiring hubs

ETHERNET AND TOKEN RING OPTIMIZATION

- ChipCom Ethernet wiring hubs
- Networth Ethernet wiring hubs
- 3COM NetBuilder Ethernet wiring hubs

Figures 16.2 and 16.3 shows the Bay Networks 5000 system and the 3COM NetBuilder systems deployed in an Ethernet environment.

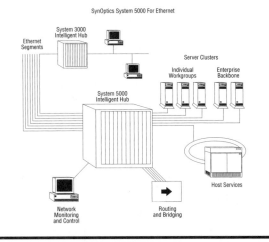

Figure 16.2 Bay Networks' System 5000 for Ethernet.

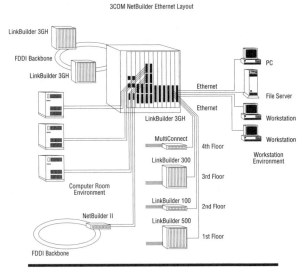

Figure 16.3 A 3COM NetBuilder for Ethernet.

Ethernet Technology Advances

Ethernet technology is breaking new ground. The name of the game is performance. The technology that is now being offered through switching products and 100Mbps Fast Ethernet has brought relief to Ethernet segments that have been experiencing performance problems. Network performance in the Ethernet topology is no longer held hostage to high traffic levels.

Fast Ethernet implements a 100Mbps transmission rate using standard Ethernet access control methods. The original proposals for this technology focused on allowing CSMA/CD Fast Ethernet to run 100Mbps across unshielded twisted pair environments. These proposals have now become a reality due to support from vendors such as DEC, 3COM, Intel, Bay Networks, and Kalpana.

The Fast Ethernet approach is rivaled by other manufacturers, such as IBM and HP, who are now promoting other new technologies such as the 100BASE VG ANYLAN. The 100BASE VG ANYLAN technology allows Ethernet and Token Ring topologies to interconnect on a new 100Mbps platform. This technology is discussed in the Token Ring section of this book.

Understanding Ethernet Switching

One of the new areas of Ethernet switching design incorporates a technology that is labeled "cut through" switching or "on the fly" switching. This technology allows for a packet that is being sent between two particular Ethernet segments to enter a high-speed Ethernet switch. The switch is then able to interpret the packet as an incoming packet and quickly determine its destination point within the switch. This is first done through the quick examination of the physical source and destination address in the Ethernet frame headers. Some of the Ethernet switches available today allow for address filtering or even a high protocol type and frame pattern match filtering between particular types of packets. This allows for the capability to filter on the Ethernet physical address, the protocol address, or even a pattern of data within the particular data field. The Ethernet cut-through mode allows for a faster transfer than the optional "store and forward" mode.

The cut-through mode allows the switching device to read the physical header and immediately transfer the packet out to the destination data port before the trailing port of the original packet actually enters the switch. Essentially the leading edge of the packet is immediately read and forwarded to its destination port before the full packet is even transferred into the switch on the trailing edge.

The store-and-forward mode is optional and is normally only used for error checking. This mode basically takes the packet and stores it in memory. The packet is then checked for error integrity before it is forwarded to its final destination data port in the switch. This allows for error integrity checking.

If there is a possibility of an error on the Ethernet segment that filters through, the switch can analyze the error by going into a quick store and forward mode.

The packet is stored quickly and analyzed for any type of error category, then simply discarded. This may cause the end node on the segment that was sending the frame to retransmit the frame. This process does reduce the possibility of errors filtering over from one segment to another data port. This error detection ability allows for low levels of bad CRC and short packets to filter in from one segment to another data port.

Overall, the combination of cut-through and store-and-forward technology allows for latency characteristics, high performance between Ethernet segments, along with a high error checking capability.

Most manufacturers producing Ethernet-based switches are using configurations that implement small groups of 8-, 16-, or 32-port devices. They have also incorporated the capability to cascade the switches in building blocks, which allows for expansion and high-speed connectivity between the switches. The capability to allow for the connecting of switches is offered in what is called full duplex Ethernet mode. This allows for a port-to-port connection between switches in a full duplex mode.

When Ethernet was introduced, the configuration was in half duplex mode. This was partially because the initial design to run over coaxial cabling. However, with the advances in 10Base-T cabling which allows for four wires to be utilized between respective end nodes, Ethernet can now be used in a full duplex operation. It should be noted that 10Base-T is still seen implemented in half duplex mode, but with the new standards in the wiring scheme of 10Base-T, full duplex will become more popular. Full duplex incorporates the capability for Ethernet ports on a particular high-speed Ethernet switch to transmit and receive at the same time. This provides collision-free communication between those respective ports, as the ports are considered dedicated. It also allows for conversations to occur in two different directions. Vendors strong in this development include Kalpana, Bay Networks, IBM, Thomas-Conrad, Cabletron, and Digital Equipment. It has recently been found that the full duplex works very well between port-to-port capability and high-speed switching environments.

Some Ethernet switches available today offer extremely high performance. They have the capability to essentially increase bandwidth and handle a large number of ports. Most of the switches in the industry can be configured with a capability of cascading and still internally handle well over 100 ports. This is partially accomplished through the switch backplane design. Some switches have more than 5 GB of bandwidth capacity designed into the internal backplane.

The ability to quickly and easily implement some switches in the design of an internetwork is a big plus. The switches are basically plug-and-play. The integration of a switch usually incorporates the highest speed switch at the site as the centerpiece of the internetwork. All the key internetwork hubs and other site switches are normally brought into the centerpiece high-speed switch in cascaded fashion as individual tiered switches for departmental installation.

Site hubs and other switches usually can connect in full duplex to the centerpiece high-speed switch to allow for high-speed internetwork access. This type of implementation will usually require other devices to be upgraded to allow for full duplex operation. Some of the new switches allow for high-speed Ethernet port connections directly to end node devices. Normally these high-speed ports are used for servers and site-based routers. These ports can be configured for 10Mbps up to 200Mbps full duplex operation.

Some switch manufacturers, such as Kalpana and Bay Networks, offer the capability to integrate with ATM configurations. Kalpana uses a direct port expansion capability from its Pro 16 stack switch at 200Mbps full duplex. Bay Networks offers the ability to create virtual networks between the switches and key hub points in an internetwork. This is accomplished through high-end network management schemes built within the switch and the ability to interface with ATM connections.

Today, most Ethernet switches offer extra features such as the capability to support loop preventing protocols such as the Spanning Tree protocol, 802.1. Managing the switch environment has also definitely become an area of focus. Most of the switches have the capability to be managed by a true Simple Network Management Protocol (SNMP) system. This is accomplished through the implementation of remote monitoring Management Information Bases (MIBs) that are built within the switch. The switches are designed with this

530 ETHERNET AND TOKEN RING OPTIMIZATION

capability so they can be implemented in a full SNMP and Remote Monitoring (RMON) environment. This way they can be supported by key SNMP and RMON monitoring tools. These tools are usually third-party developed and use the SNMP protocol for probing MIB data across internetworks. Through the implementation of SNMP-compliant MIBs and RMON agents, most Ethernet switch systems can now be managed by network management platforms such as Hewlett Packard's OpenView and LANprobes, Optivity from Bay Networks, and other network management applications in the Windows arena.

Overall, Ethernet switches today allow a high increase in performance, allow departmental LANs to become a reality, and allow distributive work group management to become a real plus. Figure 16.4 shows an Ethernet switch implementation.

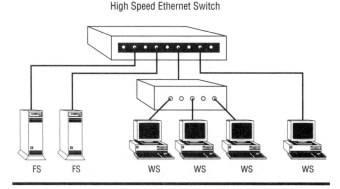

Figure 16.4 An Ethernet wiring hub switch implementation.

Understanding 100Mbps Ethernet Transmission

At this point, 100Mbps Ethernet is a reality and is considered a good approach for communicating across LAN and WAN environments. It should be noted that a complete Ethernet LAN can be based on 100Mbps NICs or the technology can be used just for switch-based ports. There are several options when implementing 100Mbps technology in the Ethernet topology.

The 100BASE-TX design is the most capable high-speed Ethernet topology version for real implementation when requiring an upgrade from 10BASE-T

Chapter 16: Devices and Specifications

configurations. Specifically, the Media Independent Interface (MII) provides MAC layer connectivity between the new 100BASE-T environment and current 10BASE-T layouts. The most common way to migrate from the familiar 10BASE-T Ethernet to 100Mbps Ethernet is to use Category 5 UTP cable or 2 pair (Type 1) Shielded Twisted Pair (STP) cable.

The 100BASE-T4 specification is frequently found in sites that cannot upgrade existing wiring. The specification allows the use of category 3, 4 or 5 UTP-based cable. It should be noted that the category 3 and 4 cable levels of the UTP categories does not offer the high integrity that the 100 BASE-TX specification allows in data transmission.

The 100BASE-FX specification allows for 100Mbps data flow over fiber-optic cable. Due to the fiber technology, site cabling lengths can achieve much longer runs. The costs involved with 100Mbps technology components are relatively conservative, and the industry seems to support all the standards fairly well. It should be noted though, that when going to 10BASE-T, the extension of the 100Mbps direct segments has to be limited.

Depending on the type used, the direct segment may have to dropped from as high as 2500 meters down to a little more than 200 meters. If the 10BASE-T4 configuration is going to be used, an almost perfect cabling implementation will be required. Specifically, the four cables that are internal to a T4 cable layout will operate over category 3, but if the pairs are not terminated in almost a perfect configuration, actual implementation problems may arise when using data rates up to 100Mbps.

One of the toughest issues in 100Mbps CSMA/CD technology is the extremely short slot time that the NICs use to allow for detecting a collision. In a 10Mbps Ethernet, the slot time is approximately 51.2 microseconds. In the 100Mbps technology, there is some variation in the actual slot time, but it is much shorter in duration. This allows for 512 bits of data in listening time. Due to the fact that 100Mbps data speeds throughput is about 10 times greater in overall throughput, the ability to insure that collision notifications are received must end at a shorter slot of time.

This is what limits the overall length of the segment. To conform with this, the actual Hops of the repeater configuration drops from approximately four repeaters connecting five segments, down to approximately only two repeaters allowing a three-Hop segment. In essence, the slot time of the NIC will actually stay the same at about 512 bits, but what actually occurs is the length of the overall segment must be shorter to allow for this slot time difference.

ETHERNET AND TOKEN RING OPTIMIZATION

In going to a full duplex operation, certain layout concerns may arise. When using a switch-to-switch connection, or direct server connection on a full duplex port, all four wires of the cable are usually required. This is due to the requirement for two-way conversations to occur at the same time. The capacity of the Ethernet direct connection is actually doubled and collisions are virtually eliminated, but the criticality of the data is much more serious. Full duplex Ethernet can coexist with half duplex Ethernet, but the wiring scheme must be configured properly. Vendors that have made advances in this area include Kalpana, Bay Networks, and Grand Junction.

When incorporating direct connections for servers at 100Mbps, it is not possible to achieve a true 100Mbps connection. This is because the average packet size of most Ethernet LANs today is still under 1000 bytes. As packet size capabilities increase in network operating systems and applications, high-speed Ethernet technology configurations will be able to handle the throughput. The highway will be in place for the NOS and applications when they are ready to start transferring the larger packet sizes.

It has been found through testing at different vendors' environments that a true 50Mbps throughput sometimes is not even achieved when a server with a 100Mbps NIC is connected to a switch data port that can handle 100Mbps. This is due to limitations that may be in place in the server related to the bus, the memory and processing speeds. For example, when various EISA NICs were used in different transfer technologies of certain servers connected directly to a 100Mbps port on a particular switch, data rates were only maintained anywhere from 25Mbps to 50Mbps. When 100Mbps PCI NICs PCI server buses were used, actual data rates increased 35Mbps to 75Mbps.

Overall, the 100Mbps Fast Ethernet technology does offer high-speed data flow, creating a larger effective throughput capability on today's Ethernet internetworks. The technology is also fairly easy to implement and is supported by a variety of vendors.

Using Network Interface Cards

Ethernet NICs have evolved from 8-bit cards to the 16-bit, 32-bit, and new 100Mbps EISA and PCI bus type NICs. The bit size of a card refers to the number of data bits that can be transferred through the PC data bus in a given transfer operation.

Today 32-bit cards are popular for EISA-based machines, but the new 100Mbps Fast Ethernet technology is causing a large increase in 100Mbps NICs.

Due to the traffic levels on today's networks, and some of the high throughput applications, higher throughput cards are now required for Ethernet NICs. Applications such as imaging absolutely require a 32-bit Ethernet card.

With increasing demand, the hardware platforms in the PCs to support Ethernet transfer must be robust. The newest technology being implemented across workstations and file server platforms is the 100Mbps PCI card. The 100Mbps cards are much faster than a standard ISA and EISA bus and allow for a high transfer rate with devices and servers.

Overall, network throughput for performance is not only determined by the application or by the transmission speed. At times, it is very dependent on the NIC and the PC bus design. A 16-bit card is much less expensive than a 32-bit card, but a 32-bit card achieves much higher performance. It offloads a lot of CPU cycles from the PC or file server that has to transmit through it, and frees up the device for other processes.

The new Ethernet NIC drivers are optimized to achieve high throughput and reduce the CPU cycles that the card requires. Some of these cards are termed bus mastering or parallel tasking cards. When implementing an NIC across the Ethernet environment, a designer should take a close look at the card's cost versus power.

Ethernet adapters are now available for the Personal Computer Memory Card International Association (PCMCIA) adapter slots found in most new portable PCs. These adapters are the size of a credit card. The performance of these adapters is still being benchmarked, but this is the technology that is going to be used for portability.

There is different technology available depending on the manufacturer, and it is important to adhere to the specifications when implementing the card.

The following list is an example of products that offer new technology in the Ethernet NIC arena:

- NE3200 from Eagle Technology
- EtherTwist EISA 32 BIT NIC from Hewlett-Packard
- Intel's EtherExpress 32-BIT and 100Mbps NICs

ETHERNET AND TOKEN RING OPTIMIZATION

- SMC Ethernet NICs
- 3COM Parallel Tasking NICs
- EtherCard Plus Elite32 and Elite32T

Ethernet Bridges

Bridges are devices that operate at the data link layer and relay and forward frames based on the network address. In the Ethernet environment, transparent bridging is considered the primary approach for bridging.

With transparent bridging, the bridges are responsible for routing traffic through the internetwork. This contrasts sharply with Token Ring's source routing approach, in which the source of a transmission must specify the complete route used to route frames through the internetwork. Transparent bridging methodology gets its name from the fact that the intelligence is internal to the bridge, and the other networks are transparent to the sending and destination nodes. This makes the transfer from network segment to network segment across multiple Ethernet networks transparent to the workstations communicating.

A transparent bridge has to maintain address tables that describe the various segments of the internetwork so it can transfer and forward packets across its network connections. Forwarding packets involves the following. When a workstation on network 1 wants to transmit to a workstation on network 2, it will send a packet to the bridge, and the bridge identifies whether the particular packet needs to be routed across the bridge. If a routing information byte is set within the packet data, the bridge routes it over the internetwork to the workstation on the network that is identified.

The bridge normally maintains a table on the addresses throughout the network. This is called a *bridge learning approach*, and a transparent bridge will maintain a workstation-to-network address as it transmits on its I/O ports from network to network. The database of addresses is maintained and is developed and increased every time the bridge processes a frame. This process is called *learning*.

Control of the environment is very important with a transparent bridge. A feature is usually employed within transparent bridging to make sure no loops are present where networks are sending packets through the bridge at multiple times. This process is ensured through the Spanning Tree Algorithm (STA).

The STA method has two impacts on bridging. It ensures that the best possible path is being used, and it inherently stops looping (when a frame arrives on a ring from two different paths).

The STA method determines the best possible path by first selecting the highest priority bridge within the internetwork as a "root bridge." Next, every other bridge identifies the port that is logically the closest to the root bridge as a "root port." The selection process follows as the individual LANs next pick the closest bridge to the root bridge as their designated bridge. When the election of the main bridge components is complete, the main logical route, or tree-branching scheme, is considered defined. The algorithm will look for redundant paths (multiple paths to one network), and it locks the root ports on those designated bridges. This establishes a nonlooping multiple network path. Bridges developed for the Ethernet environment include:

- 3COM NetBuilder bridges
- VitaLink TransLAN bridges
- Bay Networks' LattisNet bridges

Figure 16.5 shows a Bay Networks LattisNet bridge configuration.

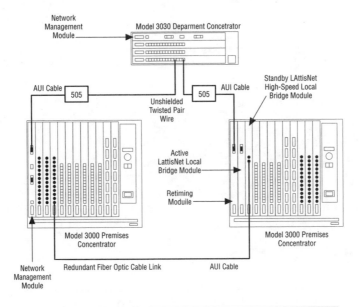

Figure 16.5 A Bay Networks LattisNet bridge configuration.

Understanding Ethernet Routers

The function of a router is to filter or not filter specific protocols between Ethernet networks. Ethernet routers operate at the network layer in OSI. Routers are complex devices that look closely at the data link and network layers to identify any address filters or protocol filters present. In an Ethernet environment, routers normally rely on the Internet addressing scheme used in the TCP/IP environment. Troubleshooting a router in an Ethernet network frequently uncovers the configuration as the cause.

As networks grow in size, so does the complexity of their protocols. The key devices utilized today to interconnect individual networks are routers. Routers are used for interconnection because they employ the intelligence required for dynamically selecting the optimum path between segments. Routers also provide excellent redundancy and applied securities between individual networks. As small networks grow into large ones, there will be a need to filter data traffic more carefully to departmentalize an internetworking environment. Figure 16.6 shows an example of using a router to departmentalize an internetwork.

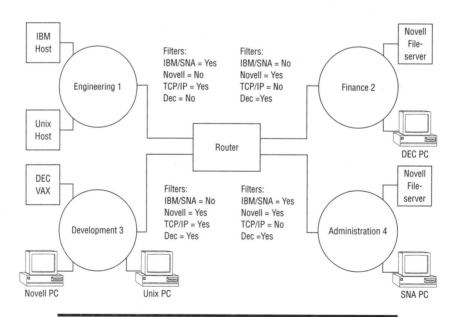

Figure 16.6 Using a router to departmentalize an internetwork.

Chapter 16: Devices and Specifications

Overall, routers allow for the design of interconnecting different topologies and protocols, but can provide separation of computing methodologies.

In using the network layer for filtering, routers can be protocol specific, but they can also be specific with an Ethernet address for filtering. They can identify whether a specific protocol can be forwarded to a segment or area based on preset filtering. They also can identify the physical header address and make applied forwarding decisions based upon the destination address in the frame. Routers are an effective technology for preventing specific protocol broadcast traffic from passing between different Ethernet networks. The following list points out key developments in router technology for the Ethernet environment:

- Novell NetWare Multiprotocol Router (MPR)
- Digital Equipment Corp. DECbrouter 90
- Cisco Systems Router 7000
- Bay Networks (Wellfleet) Routers

An implementation of the Novell MPR, DECbrouter 90, and the Cisco 7000 routers are shown in Figures 16.7, 16.8, and 16.9, respectively.

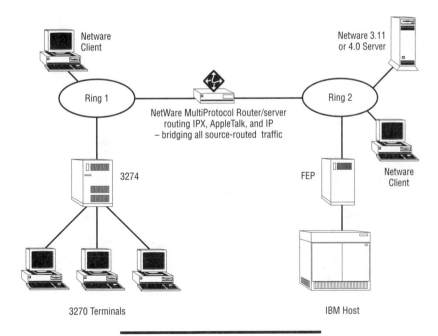

Figures 16.7 The Novell MPR router.

538 ETHERNET AND TOKEN RING OPTIMIZATION

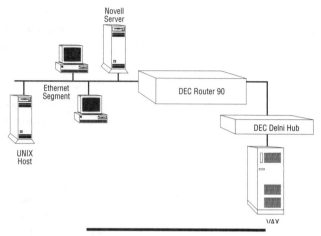

Figure 16.8 The DECbrouter 90.

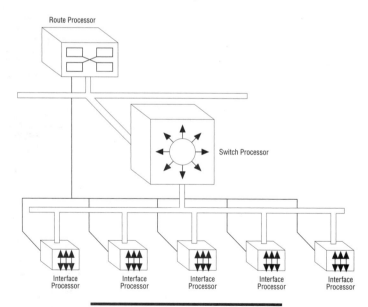

Figure 16.9 The Cisco 7000 router.

Understanding Ethernet Repeaters

In the Ethernet environment, repeaters are used to propagate a signal from one Ethernet segment to another. Ethernet repeaters normally have much intelligence built in, typically with general fault LEDs and port activity monitoring for Ethernet conversations.

Collisions can usually be monitored fairly easily on an Ethernet repeater. An Ethernet repeater almost acts as a hub between different Ethernet segments. The focus of an Ethernet repeater is to propagate the signal from one Ethernet segment to another. Normally diagnostic LEDs are in place that will indicate collisions and jam signals as they occur. Faults may even be monitored on a normal Ethernet repeater.

Among the standard repeaters used in the Ethernet environment today are the 3COM and IMC Networks product lines. An Ethernet implementation of the 3COM repeaters is shown in Figure 16.10.

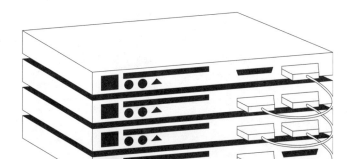

Figure 16.10 An Ethernet implementation of the 3COM repeaters.

CHAPTER 17

Ethernet Fault Isolation

Ethernet was not designed with the troubleshooting capabilities built into the physical layer like the Token Ring. Thus fault-isolation processes for Ethernet require more basic troubleshooting than is required for Token Ring.

For example, when a Token Ring NIC fails, it sends an error frame that can be decoded by an analyzer for specific cause of the error. If an NIC fails in an Ethernet environment, it may send a corrupted frame onto the network, but it does not have any specific information as to the possible cause. The Token Ring topology is designed to attempt auto-recovery from most errors. In Ethernet, fault isolation usually requires more manual intervention through the troubleshooting process.

The capability of Token Ring to detect and recover from many problems comes at the cost of additional traffic overhead. Ethernet physical layer operations require less overhead. The shortcoming is the fact that the troubleshooting process requires more of a calculated approach by the technician or analyst working with the network problem.

This chapter details the specific fault-isolation techniques that should be used for an Ethernet network. Specific information is presented on how to troubleshoot the different cabling types. Methodologies are discussed for isolating failures that may occur with the major hardware platforms for Ethernet, such as wiring hubs, bridges, routers, and repeaters.

Checking for a properly functioning cabling infrastructure is a good place to begin troubleshooting any network at the physical layer, but it is especially important in Ethernet. This chapter uses a bottom-up approach to troubleshooting problems. The approach starts with the cabling and advances to NICs and the other Ethernet active devices. The first section of this chapter is a description of fault-isolation techniques for the Ethernet cabling environment. Before starting, remember to evaluate the overall Ethernet network layout and configuration. A frequent cause of an Ethernet network failure is non-compliance with a specification of the type of Ethernet implemented.

Troubleshooting Ethernet Cabling Environments

Within any type of Ethernet environment, the use of a Time Domain Reflectometer (TDR) is a good way to approach troubleshooting the physical layer for proper cable quality. Although specialized TDRs are available, many protocol analyzers also provide TDR analysis functionality. Normally, however, the TDRs within protocol analyzers are not as advanced as standalone TDRs, such as the ones recommended from Microtest Inc.

The goal should always be to verify whether there are any opens or shorts across an Ethernet cabling segment or individual drop cable. One of the key areas to note is proper termination of the T-connections and the 50-ohm transmitters on each end of the cable. Improper termination is especially a problem in Thin Ethernet networks. Problems are frequently found with bad termination at the segment ends and on node BNC T-connectors.

When laying Ethernet cable, it is important to keep it separate from electrical devices such as fluorescent lights, air conditioning, high-voltage AC, and other types of interference. When interference is close to an Ethernet cabling segment, especially an unshielded twisted pair (UTP) run, problems can occur in the quality of the Ethernet signal. UTP cabling is quite susceptible to electromagnetic interference from most energy sources.

The lengths of the cable should be checked with a TDR. Make sure that you follow the specifications for cable length presented in Chapter 16.

Proper functioning of Ethernets requires high-quality wiring components, particularly the connectors. This problem is particularly acute with thin coaxial cable, and T-connectors should be of especially high quality, preferably meeting military specifications. Every portion of the cabling infrastructure needs to be solid.

TDR Testing Methodologies for Ethernet

A TDR is the most effective device for troubleshooting Ethernet cabling; it can measure the full continuity across an Ethernet cabling environment by measuring the true DC resistance.

A good TDR also can discover whether any cable crimps or kinks exist by measuring the signal reflections. In many cases, the TDR can identify the probable problem type and how far along the cable the fault is located. When an open, short, or other problem in the cable is detected, the TDR usually indicates this and gives the approximate distance to the failure point. The node connections of the cabling are especially critical. The BNC T-connectors within the Thin Ethernet environment frequently fail because of the quality of the BNC crimp and sometimes the quality of the connection point.

Transceivers frequently fail and can give the impression of a bad cable. A transceiver can be troubleshot with a TDR. A TDR attempts the connection; if a failure occurs, the transceiver can be replaced with another one, and the test can be rerun on the TDR.

Attenuation describes the degree to which the strength of a signal is reduced as the signal is transmitted through a cable. Some cable faults can increase attenuation, resulting in an unacceptable loss of signal strength. Some TDRs can analyze the attenuation of the cable to make sure that the transmission link is operating properly. Attenuation is usually a negative number referenced by the DB or decibel rating on the network. Most negative attenuation measurements are displayed on the TDR being used.

As you can see, TDR is a valuable tool for accurately testing Ethernet cabling segments. The following sections give specifics for the different Ethernet cabling types.

Thick Ethernet Cable Testing

First make sure that the cabling has a proper segment length. Next, count the transceivers to ensure that the device limit for the segment is not exceeded. Finally, check for the proper distance between transceivers. To test a Thick Ethernet cable segment, remove one of the end terminators from the segment. Next, follow your TDR's directions to test the segment for 50-ohm impedance from coax middle wire to the cabling shield. If the impedance is incorrect, the TDR reports the problem type and location. (Depending on the TDR, the procedure and results may vary for testing.)

In many cases, transceivers are connected to the thick coax using a technique called a vampire tap, in which pins from the transceiver actually drill into the cable to contact the shield and center conductor. Some Thick Ethernet cabling failures can be traced to bad vampire taps. A TDR may point to the tap by indicating a certain length of segment failure. It is possible to test the vampire tap's quality of connection to the Thick Ethernet cable. If the vampire tap is bad, it can be checked with a simple ohmmeter device. First, remove the screws in the outside shell of the tap. Remove the shell cover and locate the one middle and two outer braided pick pins. Use an ohmmeter to check for approximately 25 ohms from the middle pin to one of the outer pins. If the resistance varies more than 10% in any direction, the vampire tap should be replaced.

Thin Ethernet Cable Testing

Always begin troubleshooting Thin Ethernets by checking for proper termination. This can be done with a voltmeter/ohmmeter to determine that both ends of the cable segment are terminated with the proper 50-ohm resistor.

When cable faults in a Thin Ethernet segment are located with a TDR and do not have a specific length location, it is usually a bad BNC connector. The bad connector can be isolated promptly by moving a known good terminator from workstation to workstation. Start the test at one end node and apply the BNC connector. Next, make sure that at least one end section of the segment is properly terminated. (Note that certain TDRs have their own termination devices and procedures.) Last, run a TDR quality check.

If the TDR still shows a problem, reconnect the original BNC connector, proceed to the next node, and follow the same procedure. When the TDR problem reading goes away, a bad BNC connector or cable end crimp may have been located. You also can follow this procedure for Thick Ethernet, but it is more cumbersome because of the coax width and vampire tap clamp removal.

Testing Unshielded Twisted Pair Ethernet Cabling Environments

In a UTP-based environment, it becomes more critical to monitor the cabling environment to ensure that it is not located next to any type of electrical interface. This is because the cabling of Type 3 telephone-based cable is usually more susceptible to interference.

Impedance is very important. This is the resistance in matching between different cabling connections within unshielded twisted pair environments. The impedance can be mismatched if problems exist with the data and voice wiring in an Ethernet installation.

Most UTP cabling is connected using punch blocks. Often the punch blocks for both the data and voice circuits in a building are located in the same telephone closet. If the data and voice punch blocks are in close proximity, interference and crosstalk can result. Always attempt to place the data and punch blocks in separate locations.

Connections between cabling segments are called *cross connects*. The number of cross connects should be kept to a minimum, because the impedance can be changed in the overall cable drop run. It may not be possible to run a full specification length for a drop cable for the Ethernet type. This is a common problem in the UTP Ethernet environment.

Another area to look for when troubleshooting a Twisted Pair Ethernet environment is that the RJ-45 connections on the end of the UTP cable are solid and are punched into all the proper wiring pairs in the UTP cable. Loose or improperly installed connectors cause interference that can make TDR indicate a cable fault.

At times, a bad UTP cable or RJ-45-45 end may cause errors in intelligent wiring hubs. Check that all wiring hub ports are active and the proper LEDs are illuminated throughout the 10BASE-T environment.

Proper capacitance of the signal is a concern in UTP environments: if the cable is operating, all the conductive outlays of the cabling environment should be properly insulated within the cable. Capacitance should always be kept to a minimum within the cabling environment. A good TDR usually pinpoints problems in capacitance.

As with all data cabling, the cabling length of UTP cable must be proper and within specification.

The major concerns in UTP Ethernet-based network cabling are proper length layouts and proper layout and termination in the UTP wiring paths. It is important to properly lay out the cabling path to reduce any possibility of electrical noise entering the UTP cabling medium and causing crosstalk. Figure 17.1 shows a proactive TDR testing concept.

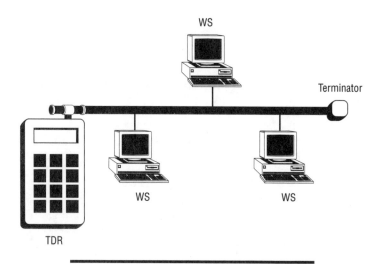

Figure 17.1 A proactive TDR testing concept.

Cabling Problems and Protocol Analysis

When troubleshooting cabling, it is important to look at the network's overall performance with a protocol analyzer. Certain packet types that can be captured in an Ethernet network can point to bad cabling segments or connectors. It is essential to understand the utilization levels to determine if the cabling used can support the number of users and the layout of the environment. The section, "Examining Protocol Analysis for Ethernet," later in this chapter, covers these issues.

Troubleshooting Ethernet Transceivers or MAUs

When troubleshooting an Ethernet transceiver or MAU, remember that the transceiver is responsible for matching the NIC signals with the cabling medium standard signal. Depending on the NIC, this may require an internal on-board NIC transceiver or external separate unit. If the unit is internal to the NIC, follow the NIC methodologies for troubleshooting. If the transceiver is external, the MAU unit needs to be monitored for proper connection and operation. If a transceiver fails, the problem usually is not intermittent.

When a solid failure occurs, it does not allow the Ethernet node to connect to the network. In this case, the unit should be replaced and a network connection should be re-attempted. If the problem is intermittent, the transceiver may have LEDs that indicate failures. Certain Thick and Thin transceivers need to have SQE testing turned off when connecting to certain active wiring hubs and repeaters. The SQE may cause a false collision problem across an Ethernet environment. Figure 17.2 shows a Thick Ethernet transceiver injecting an unwanted SQE signal into an active repeater.

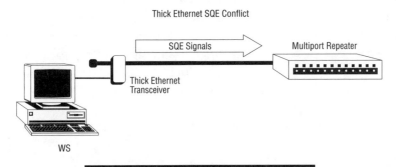

Figure 17.2 A Thick Ethernet SQE conflict.

Specific intermittent failures that a transceiver can cause are Ethernet packet corruption through transmission, which may be read by testing devices as high collisions, CRC, or excessive jamming. If an analyzer or another testing device indicates a problem with the physical Ethernet address, the cabling, connector, NIC, or the transceiver related to the address may have failed. To test the transceiver, simply replace the unit and retest the network to see if the address is still showing Ethernet packet errors.

Troubleshooting Thick and Thin Ethernet Repeaters

Depending on the layout of the environment, repeaters must be checked for proper network placement. The ports on the repeater must have solid connections to the different Ethernet segments. Pay close attention to the connectors and wiring specifications for each port on a repeater. Because Ethernet multiport repeaters connect to different Ethernet segments, each segment must be operational. An individual segment can inject failures across other segments connected to a multiport repeater.

With basic repeaters, watch for any LED indication that the unit provides, such as port activity. If there is a problem, check the cabling and connector points for connection to the repeater. Examine the port connectors closely for any loose wires or cabling ends. If no problem is found, attempt to use another port, if available. Run any diagnostics available for the repeater. If failures are still present, attempt replacement of the repeater unit.

If the unit is a multiport repeater, follow the steps mentioned earlier for basic repeaters. Usually, a failure is indicated on an LED mounted on the multirepeater. If a problem is present, remove the segment runs connected to repeater ports one by one. Watch for the failure-indicating LED to stop illuminating. If it goes out when a segment is removed, it is possible that a bad segment has been located that was injecting a group segment problem.

Repeaters are usually not complicated to troubleshoot. They illustrate how Ethernet troubleshooting is more manual than Token Ring. It helps to remember that most Ethernet repeaters of this type have a series of diagnostic indicators on the front panel to indicate error.

Troubleshooting 10BASE-T Wiring Hubs and Repeaters

Within the 10BASE-T Ethernet-based environment, it is critical to be aware of the complete UTP cabling integration within the wiring hub or repeater. Usually, the UTP wiring hub or repeater is responsible for propagating the signal between the different drop runs in the UTP-based environment. The signal transitions are more critical, and the timing also is more tightly monitored. Be aware of the technical components in place within a UTP-based hub. A UTP-based wiring design has high-end electronics and more of an intelligence-based environment.

In Ethernet 10BASE-T, when integrating with a Thin or Thick environment, some integration problems can occur. There is the possibility of active regeneration hub signals within a UTP-based environment conflicting with the standard CSMA/CD technology detection systems in Thin and Thick Ethernet networks. Remember, any NICs or transceivers should normally have SQE options set as inactive when implemented in 10BASE-T Ethernet networks.

Watch for proper connection points at the hub and repeater ports in 10BASE-T networks. Normally, the Thin and Thick Ethernet cabling segments are matched carefully from an impedance standpoint on the outside of the unit or within the modules of a UTP-based hub or repeater.

Sometimes certain timing errors can arise when active regeneration devices such as 10BASE-T hubs and repeaters are mixed with older standard Ethernet NICs. This is usually not a problem, but if intermittent high collision bursts occur, follow the basic path of working up the ladder by checking the cabling, connectors, transceivers, and hub or repeater ports for proper configuration and operation. Be aware of the differences in the Ethernet types and make sure that devices are properly configured.

When examining a 10BASE-T Ethernet wiring hub or repeater, first make sure that all its LED indicators are showing proper operation and are properly configured without errors. If a network management platform is available for the 10BASE-T Ethernet wiring hub or repeater, it should be implemented so that the troubleshooting can follow the manufacturer's technical approach. Figure 17.3 shows how an Ethernet module indicates excessive collisions on multiple ports.

10BASE-T intelligent wiring hubs and repeaters also use technology to monitor the port channels for any physical layer errors that occur in Ethernet. These error types may include high collision rates, CRC errors, long and short frame types, jamming, or any general illegal length frame processes. When implementing high intelligence devices among basic Ethernet components that have been around for years, certain conflicts may occur and result in signal errors.

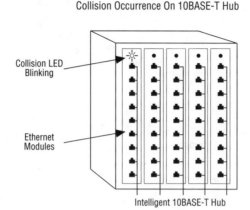

Figure 17.3 An Ethernet module indicating excessive collisions on multiple ports.

The best approach is to engage the network management platform or diagnostic platform from the manufacturer; an example is found in the Bay Networks Ethernet wiring hub environment. This environment has a high-end network management platform called Optivity that is usually implemented along with a hub. It is always better to have this running along with a hub from a standard troubleshooting and proactive standpoint.

The most comprehensive step that can be performed when troubleshooting 10BASE-T Ethernet environments is protocol analysis. Using an analyzer to examine active regeneration devices (such as wiring hubs and repeaters) in UTP-based networks is proactive. Specialized tests examine the Ethernet environment for errors that can be pointed back to the cause of failure. At times, an analyzer picks out a group of errors that relate to addresses all on one hub or repeater. This identifies the device as suspect.

Troubleshooting Ethernet NICs

In the Ethernet environment, the NIC is not as complex as in Token Ring because fewer overhead processes occur. When troubleshooting an Ethernet NIC, the focus is protocol analysis. When an Ethernet NIC fails, it may transmit a group of different problem-type packets. An analyzer or sophisticated network management system must be used to detect whether the NIC is generating problem packets on the network.

Chapter 17: Ethernet Fault Isolation 551

When troubleshooting Ethernet NICs, examine the packet types with a protocol analyzer. This is the only way to discover whether an Ethernet NIC is truly working properly. In Chapter 3, the types of Ethernet problem packets (such as long/short frames, CRC, high local/remote collisions) are presented in detail. By using an analyzer to capture these types of packets, it may be possible to identify a failed Ethernet NIC.

When troubleshooting an Ethernet NIC, be aware of all the specifications for the card and the applied configurations. These range from interrupts on the card via jumper or software settings, to the actual port configuration. It is important to verify the NIC's Interrupt Request (IRQ) and I/O Address.

Some manufacturers design an Ethernet NIC with Thick, Thin, or UTP Ethernet on-board transceivers internal to the NIC board. Make sure that the proper jumpers are set on the NIC. If an NIC is set for Thick Ethernet but is connected to a Thin Ethernet, the connection does not work. In this situation, the AUI port would be active instead of the required BNC connection for Thin Ethernet. Figure 17.4 illustrates this conflict. Refer to the manufacturer's documentation for valid configuration and settings.

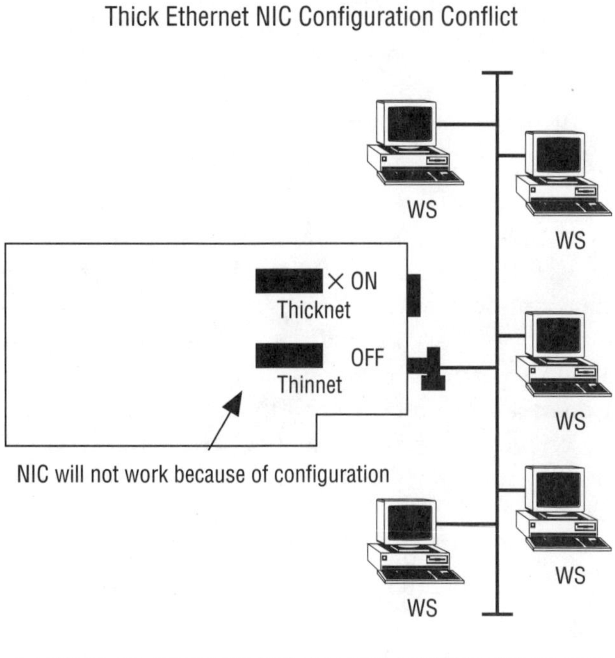

Thick Ethernet NIC Configuration Conflict

Figure 17.4 Thick Ethernet NIC configuration conflict.

The first testing approach for suspected failures on Ethernet NICs is protocol analysis. When a protocol analysis session isolates a problem to a particular NIC address, the second step is diagnostics. If any manufacturer diagnostics are provided with the NIC, they should be employed. The last step is to replace the NIC and re-analyze the Ethernet network for errors related to the new NIC address. The methodologies for analysis of certain Ethernet NIC errors are discussed in the protocol analysis section of this book.

Troubleshooting Ethernet Workstations and File Servers

After encountering a problem with an Ethernet node, categorize the problem as solid or intermittent. Also research whether the node has been operating okay for a while, or if it has recently been involved in a new installation or any hardware/software modifications.

As you troubleshoot an Ethernet node problem in a workstation or file server, use the following logical guidelines:

- If a protocol analysis session raises suspicions about a node, replace the NIC and then the transceiver. Then re-analyze the network while filtering on the new address to check for errors. The protocol analysis section of this book discusses this process.

- When a solid hardware failure occurs, troubleshoot the PC by running advanced local PC diagnostics. If the diagnostics do not locate a failure, troubleshoot the PC by swapping out the I/O boards one by one and retesting. Check all necessary I/O and PC configurations. Sometimes the PC settings can be corrected simply by going through the configuration process. If none of these methods locates the failure, recheck the NIC as a possible cause of failure. Software configuration errors within an Ethernet PC can cause jabber problems. All the necessary network filesincluding Ethernet NIC drivers, network shell drivers, AUTOEXEC.BAT, and CONFIG.SYSmust be in the correct file structure and must be uncorrupted.

- If a software configuration or corruption failure is suspected, first check to make sure that all the files are in the correct file structure and directory placement.

- If file corruption is suspected, attempt to reload and reconfigure the suspect file or files. As always, network documentation and vendor software manuals are helpful in this process.

A file server contains the same important network files as a standard Ethernet workstation, such as the network shell software, CONFIG.SYS, and AUTOEXEC.BAT, with the addition of a network operating system (NOS) and its specialized configuration and drivers. Always make sure that no incompatibilities exist between the NOS revision, configuration, file structure, security settings, and the Ethernet network shell software revision or configuration. When this type of problem occurs, attempt to focus closely on these possible causes. Your best aid is the network software vendor documentation and the general network documentation.

To ensure network integrity, after taking any measures during troubleshooting an Ethernet workstation or file server node, rerun the protocol analysis session.

Troubleshooting Ethernet Bridges and Routers

When troubleshooting a bridge or router in the Ethernet topology, there is only one key diagnostic tool—the protocol analyzer. When a bridge or router is used, Ethernet packets are being transferred from one Ethernet network to another network. For troubleshooting purposes, it is important to understand the route an Ethernet packet takes on an internetwork transfer. A protocol analyzer enables you to capture internetwork packets and decode their address and routing fields.

The addressing fields include key information on the source network/node and destination network/node. The routing field portion of an Ethernet packet contains valuable information on the route between the source and destination networks, the absolute time consumed in transfer, and the number of individual Ethernet networks traversed.

The most frequent problems with bridges are incorrect configuration setups and corrupted internetwork address tables. As mentioned in the Ethernet networks section, the primary method used for bridging is called transparent. A transparent bridge must maintain address tables on the Ethernet internetwork node locations that it transfers. At times, an Ethernet bridge can fail and not

ETHERNET AND TOKEN RING OPTIMIZATION

properly maintain the address table. One sure way to analyze whether a bridge is directing Ethernet packets properly is an end-to-end analysis. A set of protocol analyzers can be positioned on both sides of certain bridges when a packet is being transferred across an internetwork. The packet can be decoded on both sides of multiple bridges, and the analysts can pinpoint whether the bridges involved in an internetwork transfer are properly directing and transferring the packet through a correct route. Figure 17.5 shows a conceptual example of an incorrect route transfer caused by a bridge.

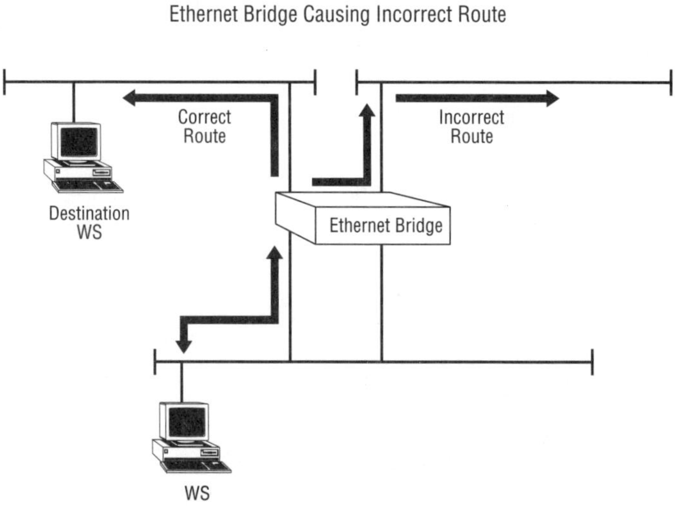

Figure 17.5 Ethernet bridge causing an incorrect route.

A protocol analyzer is invaluable with Ethernet routers because internetwork transferred packets can be captured, and the routing protocol frames can be decoded. Routing protocols are used between routers in an internetwork to update multiple routers of each other's location and operation. Certain routing protocols can be decoded to show the number of networks traversed in a packet transfer. For example, in the Novell suite, an analyst can capture a Novell RIP packet and decode the layers to identify the hops field for the number of Novell networks hopped in a transfer.

The network and transport layers in certain protocol suites also carry valuable information on Ethernet internetwork transfers through routers. For example, in the TCP/IP suite, the IP layer includes a Time-To-Live (TTL) field

Chapter 17: Ethernet Fault Isolation

that, when captured at low levels, may show a routing loop or a high propagation delay in an Ethernet internetwork. A routing loop can be defined as a condition that occurs when a packet continuously routes around an internetwork until it is discarded by a router. When an IP packet in IP internetworks starts to transfer it has a certain value, for example, 64.

As mentioned in the Network Optimization section of this book, if any IP packets pass a router with the TTL value of zero, it is discarded from the internetwork by the router.

Most routers in an Ethernet internetwork use the IP addressing scheme to transfer and route packets. If a router fails in an Ethernet internetwork, it may cause an Ethernet packet to be misdirected and loop the internetwork. A technique to capture a routing loop problem is to use a set of protocol analyzers to capture IP packets on both sides of certain routers. For example, say an Ethernet internetwork has only 11 routers. A protocol analyzer session is started. A group of IP internetwork packets are captured with a very low TTL value, 2 to 1. It is likely that a router is causing a loop. The analyzers may have to be repositioned multiple times to catch a router that continually loops a packet. This is a problem when internetwork routers and bridges are misconfigured.

Another cause of problems in an Ethernet router is an incorrect Internet address setting. It is a complex task to set up an internetwork address system for IP routing. It requires careful attention to documentation and project coordination. When an IP device cannot be reached in an Ethernet internetwork, a router might be the cause.

To test connectivity to the device and router, an IP workstation can be used to invoke an IP PING test. This test queries the router and node through the Internet Control Message Protocol (ICMP). (See Part One of this book, "Network Optimization," for more detail.) If the router cannot be queried or pinged, it should be checked for configuration and operation.

Most problems in Ethernet router internetworks are caused by misconfiguration. An example of basic misconfiguration is if a router is passing only one protocol type. The problem is most likely an incorrect protocol filter setting in the router to filter the particular protocol.

Most bridges and routers used in the Ethernet environment have a group of diagnostic LEDs to display packet transfer and port activity information. The operational status of an Ethernet bridge or router port can sometimes be determined by the state of these indicators. The manufacturer's manuals need to be referenced before any action is taken on an LED indication of the bridge's or router's status.

The general troubleshooting process for problems that appear to be related to a bridge or router operation on an Ethernet internetwork is as follows:

1. Thoroughly check the configuration and address of the bridge or router.
2. Any available diagnostics should be performed to locate the cause.
3. Use a protocol analyzer.

The routing protocols and addressing fields of internetwork transferred packets may point to an immediate cause of failure. Also, when experiencing problems with partial transfers and slow throughput, use the techniques mentioned in Part One of this book.

Ethernet Network Peripheral Problems

In today's networks, peripherals are becoming much more sophisticated. New LAN-attached products are appearing almost daily. Examples are network printers with their own Ethernet NIC card so that they do not need to attach to a workstation or file server.

These devices are not simple peripherals any more—they are now actual nodes on the Ethernet network. Because they contain their own NICs, they also have a unique Ethernet node address. This also means that these devices function as standard Ethernet nodes. An Ethernet network peripheral failure can cause Ethernet errors at the physical layer to be generated on an Ethernet segment. Follow the instructions for troubleshooting and analysis in the Ethernet protocol analysis chapter of this book. Because network peripherals are new entities to the standard Ethernet network, a protocol analysis session is recommended. Ethernet network peripheral devices should be monitored for proper workload characterizations, just as a standard Ethernet workstation node.

Exploring Gateway Failure Symptoms, Causes, and Troubleshooting

Gateway failure symptoms are rather straightforward (see Part Two of this book for additional detail). You may or may not be able to access the gateway. At times, a gateway session may seem slow or unresponsive.

The problems may be due to improper configuration in the LAN gateway design, but they also can be related to a possible host or gateway failure. At times, a LAN-to-host session may lock up intermittently, due to intermittent gateway or host hardware problems or an improper gateway configuration.

In an Ethernet network, if the IP addressing scheme is implemented, the gateway IP address must be correct when configuring it for access from Ethernet nodes.

To ensure operation on an Ethernet network, first check both the host and gateway configuration and addressing to ensure that they are properly set up for session setup and transfer. The recommended method for troubleshooting Ethernet gateway problems is to verify the Ethernet node's access processes with the gateway through protocol analysis. It is essential to monitor the gateway and attached Ethernet workstations with protocol analysis filtering. Watch for proper session setup, connection, transfer, and breakdown. Refer to the Network Optimization section of this book, which discusses techniques for analyzing proper connection and session setup on a network.

If any diagnostics from the manufacturer are available, it is a good idea to use them for gateway troubleshooting. You also should reference the gateway manufacturer's instructions when working with any gateway problems.

Examining Protocol Analysis for Ethernet

When an Ethernet network is not performing well, the evaluation weapon of choice should be a protocol analyzer. With it, you can fully examine the physical layer health of the network. Carefully follow the network baselining steps in Chapters 1 and 3.

Ethernet physical layer health can be checked by monitoring the collision and error rates of the Ethernet physical layer. By looking at the overall health of the physical layer, you can determine whether the network has a sound infrastructure. Upper layer protocols such as Novell's NetWare Core Protocol (NCP) and TCP/IP need a sound infrastructure to operate properly.

If the physical layer of the network is not healthy and causes excessive error or collision problems, function of the upper layer protocol communication will be impaired, and the complete network cannot operate normally. For example, if a high number of local collisions are on the Ethernet, bandwidth gets consumed and operational time normally used for upper layer frame fluency is chewed up by lower level errors. Frame fluency can best be described as the workstation's receipt of requested packets or frames from a file server in a normal or timely manner. Simply put, response isn't what users expect it to be. This specific situation can be seen with a protocol analyzer. The Network Optimization section of this book presents a technique on how to monitor response time. NetWare request and reply commands would not operate fluently because of excessive collisions at the physical layer.

Six specific low-level error conditions on an Ethernet can cause problems. These errors presented in the following list can be captured through protocol analysis:

- Local collisions
- Remote collisions
- Late collisions
- CRC errors/alignment
- Long frames/short frames
- Jabber

Using a protocol analyzer, you can watch the pure Ethernet physical layer traffic level. These would be packets without any higher layer data. Basically, they are one of the error frame types in the preceding list. If the physical layer traffic level rises above the 2% to 3% level, the pure physical layer packets should be filtered and analyzed.

Although any one or a combination of the six error conditions can exist on an Ethernet network, experience shows that local collisions are the most common. A normal Ethernet collision rate should be less than 1% of overall network traffic, and the overall error rate of all conditions should not exceed 2% of the available bandwidth.

Any reasonably populated Ethernet segment will have network collisions, due to the characteristics of the CSMA/CD access control method. Ethernet nodes listen and receive, and if multiple nodes try to communicate at the same time, collisions occur. If physical-layer hardware problems are present in the cabling scheme, NICs, or hub design, the collision rate can exceed the normal range. This is when trouble begins.

To discover the condition of an Ethernet, connect a protocol analyzer to the network. As mentioned, most protocol analyzers have an Ethernet connection for 10BASE-T, BNC, or other standard connectors for their built-in network adapter cards.

The first step is to filter on the different types of collision and error frames. Certain protocol analyzers trap the collision and error rate efficiently. As a rule, Network General's Sniffer is excellent. Its Ethernet Monitor Test taps on the collision and error rates, which is extremely useful for monitoring the network's overall physical health.

After the physical layer's health is tested, the next area to examine is the fluency of the upper layer protocols. For example, in the NetWare suite, it is important to review NCP request-to-reply fluency. The Network Optimization section of this book presents the analysis methodologies for multiple upper layer protocols. It is important to have a firm grasp of the NetWare protocol suite, particularly the Internetwork Packet Exchange (IPX), Sequenced Packet Exchange (SPX), and the NCP documented commands.

Using a protocol analyzer, you can examine the fluency of a NetWare conversation between workstations and file servers across the network. For example, it is normal to have a workstation request a certain file from a file server and have the file server reply without any errors. But if the workstation requests the file, and the file server replies with Cannot Find File or Bindery Error, this indicates a nonfluent condition.

Another example of Novell-related upper layer analysis for performance evaluation is to use a protocol analyzer to filter on the NetWare protocol layers. Next, observe the overall numbers of Requests Being Processed packets, which are NCP-type frames generated from a NetWare file server. A high number of these packets, over 2 to 3% of overall traffic, indicates that the server has an internal performance problem. This problem could mean the server needs more memory or disk capacity, or some other server-specific problem.

Error Detection in the Ethernet Physical Layer Environment

To expand the discussion on the error types in the Ethernet environment, the following sections describe the main error types that can be captured through a protocol analysis session.

Local Collisions

A *local collision* is an Ethernet packet that usually is less than 64 bytes in length and may contain a garbled CRC field. A local collision will be on the local segment. Collisions on a network are considered normal, especially in the CSMA/CD access method. Stations are supposed to collide; and when transmissions collide, they are supposed to listen and wait to retransmit. But certain levels are considered problems. When collisions are more than 1% of overall traffic, it is considered an issue.

Normally if no problems exist on a network, a minor collision rate from one station does not indicate a major problem in general network communications. However, if the rate of collisions is over 1% of all traffic on an Ethernet, the NIC address captured should be recorded, and the adapter should be troubleshot.

Although a high collision rate from one particular station can be a minor component of overall traffic levels, it should be addressed immediately. From a troubleshooting standpoint, if a high collision rate is transmitted from one station that is over the 1% traffic level of the overall bandwidth used, that station card should be replaced or the connector should be checked within that particular station. Check the connections on the cabling connectors first; then replace the NIC board. The network should be reanalyzed to determine whether the error is still present on the network.

Excessive collisions from stations on a network can consume bandwidth and cause a transmission problem across a complete network. In such cases, it is important that the collision problem be troubleshot, and the cause corrected. High collision rates from multiple stations on the Ethernet network may indicate cabling, transceiver, or repeater problems; the complete network segment should be analyzed and troubleshot.

If one area of a network has multiple adapters transmitting CRC or collision errors in composite, that particular area of the network usually has a common factor such as a repeater or wiring hub module. This is where the trial-and-error method takes place, but a protocol analyzer is invaluable because it picks up the addresses with the collision rates. At that point, if those addresses are itemized and found to be in the same area of the network, any common device should be located and replaced.

Remote Collisions

A *remote collision* is a collision packet usually less than 64 bytes in size with a corrupted CRC field value. These are packets that have filtered over from another segment. This may indicate that a specific node's NIC or transceiver on another side of a repeater has a problem. A bridge or router isolates all collisions to their respective local segment. Most protocol analyzers can detect when a collision is not local if the address fields are valid and not local. Sometimes false readings can occur in this area.

If a valid high remote collision is detected with an analyzer, you are going to have a tough troubleshooting session. If the cause of a node and segment problem is to be located specifically, it will require systematic troubleshooting by checking all the Ethernet segments attached to a repeater for their individual health at the physical layer. When a local collision is found on a particular segment, the next step is to locate the bad node and follow the replace-and-reanalyze approach.

Late Collisions

A late collision is a collision packet usually larger than 64 bytes with a corrupted CRC field value. This is a packet that will clearly be on the local segment. If a collision occurs with less than the normal 64 bytes of transmission of a particular station generation, this means that there is a normal collision occurrence upon transmission.

However, if the collision occurs with greater than 64 bytes of data on an Ethernet station transmission, this is considered "late," because it did not occur before the 64-byte transmission ratio. Late collisions can cause a high number of bytes to be transmitted in a train fashion because more bytes are on the network than with a normal collision under 64 bytes.

More often this indicates that the station's NIC transmitting the collision cannot hear properly to stop its transmission and is going to continue to broadcast high collision rates on the network. This also may be captured as a form of excessive jamming. This usually is a problem with an NIC, and the card should be replaced and the network reanalyzed.

Cyclic Redundancy Check/Alignment Errors

On any Ethernet network, a CRC error can be captured in an analysis session. A CRC error is picked up by a protocol analyzer when the Ethernet packet has a byte-positioning problem. The Ethernet packet is responsible for checking its transfer from station to station through general network communications with a CRC field. The CRC field is a math algorithm field used for calculating an Ethernet's packet contents for proper communication from station to station.

Normally, a sending station sends out a packet that has a CRC pattern in it that is supposedly standard. The receiving or destination station within an Ethernet network recalculates the frame contents to correlate whether it matches the proper CRC value. If a problem occurs in the error calculation and a difference arises, the packet possibly is corrupted and a CRC error may be generated by the station onto the network. If a CRC error generation is picked up, the analyzer usually records that CRC error and indicates that the sending station or the destination station has a corruption in packet transmission.

At times, CRC and alignment errors may be recorded as the same type of error. This is because they both really indicate a byte-alignment problem in transmissions. If CRC errors are recorded in a protocol analysis session above the 2 to 3% level of overall traffic on a network, they are considered excessive. The group of stations involved in a transfer on occurrence of a specific node sending of CRC transmissions may have a problem. All the addresses of transmitting nodes captured in a trace with frames in front and after the CRC error frame should be noted for the record. The problem may be in the group of stations. It is possible that a node NIC, transceiver, respective cabling, or even a connected repeater or wiring hub port has failed. But relax. Usually the station sending the CRC error will have a bad NIC or transceiver.

If CRC errors are high on a particular Ethernet segment, cable connections may have problems or improper grounding may exist throughout the network. The cabling and connections should be checked first. If the problem is still present, the NIC should be replaced. The BNC T-connector, the tap connector, and transceivers also can be one of the primary causes for this type of problem. But the most probable cause is the NIC sending the CRC. After checking the cabling infrastructure, replace the NIC. Next, the network should be reanalyzed to check for any errors related to the new NIC address. If problems are still present, multiport repeaters and wiring hubs should also be checked as a cause for the CRC errors.

It is possible to attribute this problem to one particular network station's NIC. The most certain way to isolate this is through a protocol analysis session. Look closely for a high number of CRC errors, because a high frequency indicates a definite problem for the sending station.

Long and Short Packets

Ethernet frame types have certain rules. Depending on the packet type, frames can be from 64 to 1518 bytes in length. With the proper protocol analyzer, you can pick up two types of packets called short frames (runts) and long packets. A short or runt packet is any packet smaller than 64 bytes. Long packets are those larger than 1518 bytes. These are considered problems on a network and an analyst should use a protocol analyzer to capture multiple transmissions of the occurrence.

It is possible for an NIC, transceiver, or even a corrupted LAN driver to generate long and short frames. The cause is usually isolated to the failing NIC. Captured long or short packets may not include reliable address fields. The analyst should identify the addresses attempting to communicate in the trace that are right before and after the long or short packets. Next, one by one, remove the suspect nodes and reanalyze the network until the problem subsides. After the node area is located, the NIC, transceiver, and NIC driver should be troubleshot.

Jabber

At times, Ethernet NICs and external transceivers also generate a problem called jabbering. This is when garbled bits of data are emitted within the frame sequence in a continuous transmission fashion. The packet length is usually over 1,518 bytes. This can be identified by a protocol analyzer as a CRC error. When nodes detect collisions, they emit a normal jam signal on the network segment to clear transmission. Sometimes certain nodes attempt to keep jamming the network due to high collision rates above normal; this also can be captured as high CRC or late collision error rate. The cause can be overloaded traffic levels.

If the bandwidth utilization levels are normal or low for the particular Ethernet segment, it is possible that the collision detection pair of a jamming node's NIC or transceiver cannot hear the network signal, and may not know a collision has stopped. If this occurs, it continues to jam the network.

ETHERNET AND TOKEN RING OPTIMIZATION

If a certain node on an Ethernet segment emits a lot of jabber, the node's NIC and transceiver should be troubleshot through consecutive replacement and reanalysis.

As mentioned in Part Two of this book, if an Ethernet network has intermittent high network bandwidth usage that causes performance problems, the cause can be re-created by loading the network with traffic-generation features in a protocol analyzer.

Be careful when using this technique. First, you must be aware of the current network usage and any possible impacts to the network user community. Second, you have to understand all the Ethernet network bandwidth considerations discussed earlier, including the actual maximum bandwidth available, the overall network bandwidth baseline view, and individual Ethernet node bandwidth consumption.

Make sure that a proper baseline is performed on the lower and upper layers of the Ethernet. Follow the baseline directions and methodologies presented in Part One of this book.

Interactive Troubleshooting Errors for Physical Ethernet Table

Error Type	Possible Causes
High local collision errors over 1% of overall traffic	Overloaded segments
	Cable segment quality problem or possibly too long for specifications Remote segment may be overloaded
	There may also be a bad repeater passing over packet traffic collision related to a remote segment
	Remote segment cable problem
Long or short packets illegal for length specification:	This problem is usually caused by a possible bad NIC driver, NIC component, or even a transceiver
Late collisions	The cable may be too long for general specifications
Jabber	Possible bad NIC or transceiver
CRC alignment errors	Bad NIC, possible bad drivers, cable, or connection quality within the particular segment run

The Advantages and Disadvantages of Ethernet

The Ethernet topology provides an excellent infrastructure for data transfer at high speeds, but there are advantages and disadvantages to the Ethernet topology.

Advantages of Ethernet

The Ethernet topology is extremely easy to configure and implement. It is well supported by a large group of manufacturers and is fairly workable for most design concerns.

Because Ethernet has been in place so long in the industry, it is a very strongly supported topology by many vendors and different technical software companies for application support.

Disadvantages of Ethernet

The Ethernet topology performs well at certain traffic levels, but it should be noted that throughput will decrease on heavier traffic loads. It was found through a large set of studies that when bandwidth exceeds the 50% to 60% level, throughput will start to decrease on a natural curve.

It should also be noted that the bus-type topologies of Ethernet, specifically Thicknet and ThinNet, are more difficult to troubleshoot. This is due to the coaxial cabling systems, which are more prone to physical error problems.

Problems with device connection quality are a common problem because of the bus layout. When the bus layout is implemented, it is a concern because sometimes the complete segment has to be taken down to troubleshoot physical error issues.

Ways to Make Ethernet Perform

There are different ways to improve the protocol operation of the Ethernet topology. The following is a breakout of these steps.

Adhere to Specifications

By adhering to specifications of the Ethernet product configurations, performance can be improved. Limit segment cable length to slightly shorter than the maximum specification for each topology configuration. Limit the node count to slightly short of the maximum node configuration for each topology type. Application traffic that is large and bursty in nature should be separated from application traffic that is more interactive in nature and considered chatty. Large file transfers can possibly cause bursty type traffic, including high frame-per-second rates combined with large packets. This type of application traffic should be on separate segments in switched configurations. In reference to interactive traffic that again is chatty in nature for some application layer protocols, this traffic type would be best placed on separate segments for general office applications.

Implement Uniform NIC Type Drivers and Ethernet Frame Types

Protocol communication on an Ethernet topology network can be ensured for better performance by making sure that all of the NIC drivers across the particular segment are compatible. This is extremely important because older revision NIC drivers may cause different problems at the Ethernet frame level. It should also be noted that Ethernet frame types should be compatible. Specifically, Ethernet II, Ethernet 802.3 RAW, and Ethernet 802.3 IEEE frames should be bound to the proper hosts and end nodes and be compatible across the segment.

Implement Adequate Resources in All Key End Nodes

A good Ethernet network performance rating can also be ensured by making sure that all of the key end nodes have the proper memory and resource configuration for the protocol operation being applied. This is relevant today because some of the multiple applications and protocol stack environments may require a higher memory level to adequately perform in the network. At times when memory levels are low in a general platform configuration for the NIC or actual hardware platform of the particular device, this may cause excessive retransmission levels at the upper protocol layers and again bring down effective throughput and performance.

Attempt to Increase Packet Size in all Key End Nodes, and Bridges/Routers that Can Pass Packet Size on a High Frame Per Second Rate Without Bottlenecks Occurring

Specifically, it may be possible to provide a higher transfer rate on the Ethernet segment by increasing end node transmission and receive packet size, but first this must be insured by implementing compatible NICs with a uniform packet size. Once this is done, it may be possible to eventually increase packet size on end nodes to improve performance. If high-end technology is chosen for the NICs that can produce a high packet-per-second rate, this will combine with increased packet size to produce better performance. Ideal conditions would be to transmit the most amount of data in the least amount of time with true integrity.

The next chapter presents a group of extensive, component-level troubleshooting flow guides for the Ethernet environment.

CHAPTER 18

Ethernet Troubleshooting Flow Guides

As you saw in Chapter 17, a group of errors is associated with the Ethernet topology that can lead you to troubleshoot different areas of the network. A finite amount of failure symptoms can occur in Ethernet, but the causes associated may be in a range of possible network components. In the Token Ring section of this book, a set of unique troubleshooting guides was presented that lead you through the complex path of troubleshooting a Token Ring. This chapter offers the same approach for the Ethernet topology.

The following flow guides for Ethernet will assist you when vectoring through the troubleshooting of an Ethernet network.

Take the time to carefully read and follow each step before you perform any of the defined actions in a flow guide. Also, make sure that you thoroughly read any NOTE in the flow guides.

While you are using the flow guides, it is a good idea to take notes on your troubleshooting steps and results.

Network Problem Entry Flow Guide

The network problem entry flow guide is the entry point for approaching the specific network area or component flow guides included in this chapter. From the 16 main network failure symptom choices that follow, decide which one most closely relates to the failure symptom you encountered in the particular network area and follow the vector to the respective chapter section. If for some reason you feel that your particular failure symptom is associated with a certain network component, you can at your discretion vector directly to the respective flow guide.

While deciding, also note if the failure symptom fits logically into one of the following network areas:

- All Ethernet internetwork users
- All users on a specific Ethernet segment
- A group of network users on different Ethernet segments
- A group of network users on the same Ethernet segment
- One network user on a specific Ethernet Segment

In addition, note whether the failure symptom is classified as solid or intermittent.

18.1 Main Ethernet Network Failure Symptom Flow Guide

1. On an Ethernet segment, nodes are not operating, or are hanging or freezing during operation.

   (Vector to flow guide 18.2.)

2. The network is encountering a high count of Ethernet frame errors.

   (Vector to flow guide 18.15.)

Chapter 18: Ethernet Troubleshooting Flow Guides   571

3. The network is experiencing any of the following failures: the whole network is operating slowly; a specific network application is operating slowly; or network logon failures are occurring.

   (Vector to flow guide 18.15.)

4. You are having a problem accessing or using a particular application/group of applications or certain directories/files on the network file server.

   (Vector to flow guide 18.14.)

5. A particular network operating system feature or set of NOS features on the network file server is not working.

   (Vector to flow guide 18.14.)

6. An Ethernet station node or network peripheral cannot be used or accessed.

   (Vector to flow guide 18.5 Ethernet Node, or 18.10 Network Peripheral.)

7. A network printer or printers cannot be used or accessed.

   (Vector to flow guide 18.12.)

8. You are experiencing problems accessing or using a network server other than the main network file server, such as database, fax, communication, or print server.

   (Vector to flow guide 18.14.)

9. You are having a problem accessing or using other segments in an internetwork that are connected through a common bridge.

   (Vector to flow guide 18.7.)

10. You are having a problem accessing or using other segments in an internetwork that are connected through a router.

    (Vector to flow guide 18.8.)

11. You are having a problem accessing or using other segments in an internetwork that are commonly connected by an intelligent hub or repeater.

    (Vector to flow guide 18.4.)

12. You are experiencing a problem accessing or using a host connection connected by means of a gateway on the local segment or a segment in an internetwork.

ETHERNET AND TOKEN RING OPTIMIZATION

(Vector to flow guide 18.13.)

13. The complete network is hanging or freezing, and the problem appears to be related to a common intelligent hub.

    (Vector to flow guide 18.4.)

14. The complete network is hanging or freezing, and the problem appears to be related to a common repeater.

    (Vector to flow guide 18.4.)

15. A network-sharable or non-sharable modem cannot be used or accessed, or there is a problem accessing the segment from a remote modem connection.

    (Vector to flow guide 18.11.)

16. The complete network is hanging or freezing, and the problem appears to be related to a common Thick or Thin repeater.

    (Vector to flow guide 18.9.)

18.2 Ethernet Segment Area Problem Flow Guides

Ethernet segments are not operating, or are hanging or freezing during operation.

Is the failure symptom being experienced on multiple Ethernet segments?

(Vector to sub-flow guide 18.2.1.)

Is the failure symptom isolated to a specific Ethernet segment (for example, one Thin Ethernet segment cabling run from a repeater)?

(Vector to sub-flow guide 18.2.2.)

18.2.1 Failure Symptom Is Experienced on Multiple Ethernet Segments

On a group of Ethernet segments, nodes are not operating or are hanging or freezing during operation.

Remove one of the segment runs involved in the failure area from the repeater or wiring hub. Retest the internetwork.

Is the failure symptom gone?

    [YES]   You have located the problem to the removed segment area. (Vector to sub-flow guide 18.2.2 and troubleshoot the removed segment.)

    [NO]   Remove the next segment and retest the network. Continue the process of removing segments and then retesting the complete internetwork for the error. Attempt to locate the problem to one segment.

Have you located the problem to a removed Ethernet segment?

    [YES]   Vector to sub-flow guide 18.2.2 and troubleshoot the removed segment.

    [NO]   If the problem still exists with any of the segments attached separately to a repeater or wiring hub, troubleshoot the hub or repeater. (Vector to flow guide 18.4 and troubleshoot the repeater or wiring hub.)

NOTE

If problems still exist after following sub-flow guide 18.2.2, vector back to this sub-flow guide (18.2.1) and attempt to retroubleshoot the problem to a specific segment. If problems then still exist, vector to flow guide (18.4) and attempt to troubleshoot the problem to a repeater or wiring hub fault.

If you defined this area of the Ethernet internetwork from data captured during a protocol analysis session, the errors should be troubleshot for their specific error type and category. The error type may point to either a local or remote Ethernet segment problem.

18.2.2 Failure Symptom Is Located on a Specific Ethernet Segment

On a specific Ethernet segment, nodes are not operating, or are hanging or freezing during operation.

Disconnect the suspected Ethernet segment from its original repeater or wiring hub port and connect it to another repeater or wiring hub port. Retest the internetwork.

Is the failure symptom gone?

[YES] The original specific repeater or wiring hub port is bad. Troubleshoot the specific repeater or wiring hub port by vectoring to flow guide 18.4.

[NO] Test the segment cabling with a TDR by vectoring to flow guide 18.3 (Cable). If no cable faults are found in flow guide 18.3, come back here and go to the next step.

Have you found any symptoms that point to one specific Ethernet node or network peripheral involved in this segment area?

[YES] Troubleshoot the respective node by vectoring to flow guide 18.5 (Ethernet Station Node).

[NO] Troubleshoot the Ethernet segment by providing an end termination to isolate the segment as a single Ethernet, then perform a protocol analysis session to locate a specific bad Ethernet node area on the segment. Vector to the Protocol Analysis flow guide 18.15.

If you tried troubleshooting all the network components in the respective segment area—Ethernet node stations, network peripheral, transceivers, NIC, repeaters or wiring hub, and cabling—and the failure symptom is still present on the segment, gather more conclusive fault isolation data by vectoring to flow guide 18.15 Protocol Analysis.

18.3 Ethernet Cabling Problem Flow Guides

Does the cable failure symptom occur in a complete Ethernet segment?

(Vector to flow guide 18.3.1.)

Does the cable failure symptom appear to be related to a specific drop cable for one Ethernet node?

(Vector to flow guide 18.3.2.)

18.3.1 A Complete Ethernet Segment Cabling Run Is in Question

Remove one of the end termination points and test the cable segment with a TDR.

Did testing the cable find any faults in the segment without a specific length of failure?

[YES] Record the failure type and length. Measure the distance and locate the problem area.

(a) If a specific node is present at the failure point, troubleshoot the problem by checking the connection quality of the BNC-T connector for Thin Ethernet or measuring the pin impedance in the vampire tap for Thick Ethernet. If a problem is found, replace the bad device. If no problems are found, proceed to troubleshoot the respective node by vectoring to flow guide 18.5 (Ethernet Station Node).

(b) If the length of distance points to a problem where no Ethernet node is present, the suspected bad area cable might be faulty. Check for kinks or bends and action to resolve the problem by replacing the respective segment of cable. Next, retest the segment run with a TDR. If the failure symptom is gone, record the problem in the network maintenance and service log. If problems still exist, go to 18.15 and perform a baseline analysis.

[NO]   Troubleshoot the Ethernet segment by providing an end termination to isolate the segment as a single Ethernet, then perform a protocol analysis session to locate a specific bad Ethernet node area on the segment. Vector to the Protocol Analysis flow guide 18.15.

18.3.2 A Specific Ethernet Drop Cable Is in Question

The cable failure symptom appears to be related to a specific drop cable for one Ethernet node.

Remove the drop cable and properly test it with a TDR.

Did testing find any faults in the cable?

[YES]   Replace the cable and retest the new cable. If no problems are found after replacing the cable, record the failure in the network maintenance and service log. If problems still exist, proceed in the troubleshooting process by vectoring to flow guide 18.5 (Ethernet Station Node).

[NO]   Troubleshoot the Ethernet device transceiver by vectoring to flow guide 18.5 (Ethernet Station Node).

18.4 Ethernet Multiport Repeater and Wiring Hub Problem Flow Guides

Does the failure symptom appear to be related to a specific repeater or wiring hub port failure?

(Vector to sub-flow guide 18.4.1.)

Do the failure symptoms that appear to be related to a suspected bad repeater or wiring hub module occur with multiple ports or the complete Ethernet internetwork?

(Vector to sub-flow guide 18.4.2.)

NOTE

Because this flow guide is generic as to the repeater and wiring hub manufacturer, for some of the troubleshooting steps mentioned in this flow guide, you should also refer to the respective manufacturer's documentation for any predefined methods for checking configuration and diagnostic testing. In the case of some wiring hubs, you may have certain diagnostics available that help you locate a specific problem. If this type of diagnostic is available, use it for fault isolation.

18.4.1 A Specific Repeater or Hub Port Is Encountering a Failure

Move the drop cable (10BASE-T) or segment cable (Thick or Thin Ethernet) from the suspected bad port to another port on the same repeater or wiring hub module. Before you move the cable, make sure that the new port is functioning. Next, retest the respective Ethernet node (10BASE-T) or Ethernet segment (Thick or Thin Ethernet) on the new repeater or wiring hub port.

Did physically changing the port get rid of the failure symptom?

[YES] The suspected port is bad. Replace the respective repeater or hub module and retest the Ethernet node or segment for proper operation. If the failure symptom is gone, record the problem in the network maintenance and service log. If problems still exist, go to the next step.

[NO] If a failure still exists with the same Ethernet node or segment, re-attach the cabling segment to the original port. For 10BASE-T, troubleshoot the respective Ethernet node segment area by vectoring to flow guide 18.5 (Ethernet Station Node). For Thick or Thin Ethernet, troubleshoot the specific segment cabling by vectoring to flow guide 18.3.

18.4.2 A Suspected Bad Repeater or Wiring Hub Module Is Causing Failure Symptoms with Multiple Users or the Complete Ethernet Internetwork

Regardless of whether the failure symptom is solid or intermittent, run full manufacturer's diagnostics on the repeater or hub. Next, remove the suspected bad repeater or wiring hub module and associated cabling sections to other hubs or repeaters from the internetwork configuration and then retest the internetwork operations.

Are the failure symptoms now gone?

[YES] The respective repeater, wiring hub module, or internetwork cabling section is at failure. Replace the removed unit and cables with another unit and cables. Retest the new configuration. If no original problems are encountered, record the problem in the network maintenance and service log. If problems are still present, go to the next step.
Even if your problem is now fixed, if you feel that one of the cabling sections caused the problem, you can verify the problem by testing the internetwork cabling run with a TDR. If you want to further verify the repeater or wiring hub failure, you can do so with any available manufacturer diagnostics.

[NO] If failure symptoms are still present, reinsert the original repeater or wiring hub module and respective cables into the network configuration. Go to the next step.

Have you troubleshot and verified the integrity of the main internetwork cabling?

[YES] Again, run full diagnostics on the repeater or hub and engage a protocol analysis session to gain more conclusive fault isolation data by vectoring to flow guide 18.15.

[NO] Troubleshoot the main internetwork segment cabling by vectoring to flow guide 18.3.

18.5 Ethernet Station Node Problem Flow Guides

Are all the Ethernet station nodes on the network experiencing the failure symptom?

(Vector to sub-flow guide 18.5.1.)

Is a group of Ethernet station nodes experiencing the failure symptom?

(Vector to sub-flow guide 18.5.2.)

Is just one Ethernet station node experiencing the failure symptom?

(Vector to sub-flow guide 18.5.3.)

NOTE

This flow guide is generic as to the Ethernet station/PC manufacturer. For some of the troubleshooting steps mentioned in this flow guide, you also should refer to the PC manufacturer's documentation for any predefined methods for checking PC configuration and for PC testing.

If devices such as modems, printers, or fax boards are connected to an Ethernet workstation or a file server, they are not actually considered network peripherals because they do not contain their own NICs. If the peripheral you are troubleshooting does not contain its own internal NIC, vector to the applicable flow guide. (For example, suppose that a modem or printer is connected to an Ethernet workstation or file server, and the Ethernet station node or file server contains the NIC. In this case, you would vector to either the modem or printer problem flow guide.) But if the device does contain its own internal NIC, this flow guide is applicable because it is actually a standard Ethernet node.

18.5.1 All the Ethernet Station Nodes Are Experiencing the Symptom

Are all the Ethernet station nodes running the same application or using the same directories or files on a particular file server when experiencing the symptom?

ETHERNET AND TOKEN RING OPTIMIZATION

[YES]   Vector to flow guide 18.14 and troubleshoot possible file server application or directory/file problems.

[NO]   Go to the next step.

Have you troubleshot and verified the integrity of the main segment areas?

[YES]   Run a protocol analysis session to gather more conclusive results by vectoring to flow guide 18.15.

[NO]   Troubleshoot the main segment areas by vectoring to flow guide 18.2 (Segment Areas).

18.5.2 A Group of Ethernet Station Nodes Is Experiencing the Symptom

Is the group of Ethernet station nodes running the same application or using the same directories or files on a particular file server when experiencing the symptom?

[YES]   (Vector to flow guide 18.14 and troubleshoot possible file server application or directory/file problems.)

[NO]   Go to the next step

Is the group of users located on the same repeater or wiring hub module?

[YES]   Troubleshoot a possible repeater or wiring hub failure by vectoring to flow guide 18.4.

[NO]   Recheck the Ethernet station nodes involved for proper software and hardware configuration setup and requirements.

- Make sure that all the necessary directories and files are on the local drives in the Ethernet station nodes and are set up correctly.

- Make sure that all the necessary hardware is   installed   in the Ethernet station nodes and is configured correctly.

Check the network operating system manuals for station setup concerning both software and hardware prerequisites.

Are any identifiable hardware or software configuration setup problems present with the involved Ethernet station nodes?

[YES]   Take the necessary action to resolve the configuration problem and retest the Ethernet station nodes for proper operation. If the failure symptom is gone, record the problem in the network maintenance and service log. If a failure symptom is still present, go to the next step.

[NO]   If the problem strongly appears to be network file server-to-workstation related as to network access, vector to flow guide 18.14.
If you cannot be conclusive, vector to flow guide 18.15 and run a protocol analysis session on the segment.

18.5.3 One Ethernet Station Node Is Experiencing the Symptom

Is the Ethernet station node always running the same application or using the same directory or file on a particular file server when experiencing the symptom?

[YES]   Vector to flow guide 18.14 and troubleshoot possible file server application or directory/file problems.

[NO]   Move the Ethernet station to another port on the repeater or wiring hub and recheck the node operation.

Did moving the Ethernet station node to another port resolve the problem?

[YES]   Vector to flow guide 18.4 and troubleshoot possible repeater or wiring hub problems.

[NO]   Troubleshoot the respective node by replacing the transceiver if it is external and then retesting for the failure. If the transceiver is in an NIC on-board, jump to the NIC flow guide 18.6. If the transceiver checks OK, check the drop cable involved by vectoring to flow guide 18.3. If troubleshooting the drop cable identifies any problems with the segment cable, vector back to this flow guide by choosing flow guide NIC 18.6, then vector to sub-flow guide 18.5.3 and jump directly to the next step.

Next, test the respective Ethernet station node for proper software and hardware configuration setup and requirements.

- Make sure that all the necessary directory and files are on the local drive in the Ethernet station node and are set up correctly.
- Make sure that all the necessary hardware is installed in the Ethernet station node and is configured correctly.

Check the NOS manuals for station setup concerning both software and hardware prerequisites. Did rechecking the Ethernet station node software and hardware requirements locate any incorrect configuration setup problems?

[YES] Take the necessary action to resolve the configuration problem and retest the Ethernet station node for proper operation. If the failure symptom is gone, record the problem in the network maintenance and service log. If the problem is still present and it strongly appears to be network file server-to-Ethernet station node related as to network access, vector to flow guide 18.15 and troubleshoot the high-level communication process. If it does not appear to be file server related, go to the next step.

[NO] Attempt to run any available PC diagnostics. Also try to troubleshoot the PC for any I/O board conflicts as discussed in the station node problems section of Chapter 17.

Did running the diagnostics or troubleshooting the PC find any problems?

[YES] Take the necessary action to resolve the problem and retest the Ethernet station node for proper operation. If the failure symptom is gone, record the problem in the network maintenance and service log. If the problem still exists after retesting, go to the next step.

[NO] Vector to flow guide 18.6 and troubleshoot the respective Ethernet station node for an NIC problem.

Chapter 18: Ethernet Troubleshooting Flow Guides

NOTE

Many new Ethernet station nodes are being manufactured with internal NICs within the PC motherboard hardware architecture. If the Ethernet station node you are troubleshooting has this configuration, attempt replacing the motherboard rather than vectoring to 18.6 and troubleshooting the NIC.

18.6 Ethernet NIC Problem Flow Guides

Did you arrive at this flow guide because of NIC failure indications from running a protocol analysis session?

    [YES]   Vector to sub-flow guide 18.6.1.

    [NO]   Go to the next step.

Did you arrive at this flow guide after troubleshooting a segment area, Ethernet station node, network file server, repeater/wiring hub, cable, or network peripheral?

    [YES]   Vector to sub-flow guide 18.6.2.

    [NO]   Go to the next step.

NOTE

Because this flow guide is generic as to the NIC manufacturer, for some of the troubleshooting steps mentioned in this flow guide, you also should refer to the NIC manufacturer's documentation for any predefined methods for checking NIC configuration and bridge testing.

18.6.1 Error Indication in a Protocol Analysis Session

Regardless of whether the error is by a collision, CRC, long/short, or jabber-related error type transmission that indicates a possible NIC failure, swap the respective NIC and rerun another thorough protocol analysis session on the segment.

After swapping the NIC and rerunning the new protocol analysis session, did the error go away?

    [YES]   Leave the newly replaced NIC in the Ethernet station node or device and record the problem in the network maintenance and service log.

    [NO]   Place the original NIC back into the Ethernet station node or network peripheral; vector to flow guide 18.15; and rerun a protocol analysis session on the segment. Sometimes when you rerun a protocol analysis session, the failure cause becomes more clear by moving to another Ethernet address.

If, after you rerun another protocol analysis session, the error does not move to another device and is still identifying the particular NIC address as a failure cause, troubleshoot the assigned segment area for the respective NIC by vectoring to flow guide 18.2.

18.6.2 Vectoring from Segment Area, Ethernet Station Node, Network File Server, MAU/Transceiver, Repeater/Wiring Hub, Cable, or Network Peripheral Flow Guide

Is the failure symptom that led you to this flow guide classified as solid or intermittent?

    [SOLID]   Go to **S1**.

    [INTERMITTENT]   Go to **S2**.

    [S1] Solid.   Thoroughly check all the following areas:

1. Check all NIC hardware/software configuration parameters:
   - I/O address
   - IRQ

- DMA
- Slot settings (32-, 16-, or 8-bit card)
- NIC microcode level

Check the Ethernet station node for the respective transceiver setting. Also check the NIC for proper NIC software driver microcode and proper revision PROMS on the NIC.

2. Check for possible NIC incompatibilities with the particular Ethernet station node, transceiver port, standard port connectivity with external transceiver/MAU, cable type, or the cabling connector.

Did you find any problems in any of the areas?

[YES] Take the necessary action to resolve the problem and retest the Ethernet station node or network peripheral for proper operation. If the failure symptom is gone, record the problem in the network maintenance and service log. If the problem still exists after retesting, go to the next step.

[NO] Run any available NIC diagnostics from the NIC manufacturer or from elsewhere to be conclusive. Regardless of whether the diagnostics pinpoint a failure, swap the original NIC in the Ethernet station node or network device and retest the Ethernet station node or network peripheral for proper operation; vector to flow guide 18.15; and rerun a protocol analysis session on the segment. If the failure symptom goes away, record the problem in the network maintenance and service log.

If, after rerunning another protocol analysis session, an error occurs with the assigned Ethernet station node or network peripheral and the specific failure symptom does not go away, replace the original NIC and troubleshoot the assigned segment area for the respective NIC by vectoring to flow guide 18.2.

If you definitely feel the original NIC has a problem, it may be best to keep the newly replaced NIC in the respective Ethernet station node (rather than replacing the original NIC) before resuming troubleshooting by vectoring to flow guide 18.2. This will to be a judgment call on your part.

[S2]　**Intermittent**. In the case of an intermittent problem with an NIC, first attempt to run any available NIC diagnostics. Then, regardless of the diagnostic testing results, swap the original NIC in the Ethernet station node or network peripheral and check its general operation. Also, vector to flow guide 18.15 and rerun a protocol analysis session on the segment.

If the protocol analysis session does not record any errors associated with the Ethernet address involved, and the intermittent problem does not reappear, record the problem in your network maintenance and service log.

If, after the swap, the NIC failure symptom is still present, replace the original NIC and troubleshoot the assigned segment area for the respective NIC by vectoring to flow guide 18.2.

> If you definitely feel that the original NIC has a problem, it might be best to keep the newly replaced NIC in the respective Ethernet station node rather than replace the original NIC before resuming troubleshooting by vectoring to the main menu and choosing 18.2. This is going to be a judgment call on your part.

18.7 Ethernet Bridge Problem Flow Guides

No data traffic can get from one side of the bridge to the other, or data is intermittently getting corrupted when passing through the bridge.

(Vector to sub-flow guide 18.7.1.)

Only partial data traffic can pass across the bridge.

(Vector to sub-flow guide 18.7.2.)

An overloaded bandwidth condition is present on a certain segment.

(Vector to sub-flow guide 18.7.3.)

This flow guide is generic as to the bridge manufacturer. For some of the troubleshooting steps mentioned in this flow guide, you also should refer to the bridge manufacturer's documentation for any predefined methods for checking bridge configuration and for bridge testing.

18.7.1 No Data Traffic Can Get from One Side of the Bridge to the Other, or Data Is Intermittently Getting Corrupted when Passing Through the Bridge

Thoroughly check the software and hardware configuration of the bridge. If in an Ethernet and TCP/IP addressing environment, check for the correct TCP/IP address. Attempt an ICMP ping test.

Are any incorrect configuration parameters present in the bridge?

    [YES]   Take the necessary action to resolve the problem and retest the bridge for proper operation. If the failure symptom is gone, record the problem in the network maintenance and service log. If the problem still exists after retesting, go to the next step.

    [NO]   Attempt to run bridge diagnostics.

Did running the diagnostics produce any errors that identify a bridge failure?

    [YES]   Take the necessary action to resolve the problem and retest the bridge for proper operation. If the failure symptom is gone, record the problem in the network maintenance and service log. If the problem still exists after retesting, go to the next step.

    [NO]   A problem may still exist with the bridge, but to get more conclusive fault isolation data, vector to flow guide 18.15.

If after using this flow guide you cannot conclusively locate the problem and continue to find failure symptoms that point to a bridge problem, refer to the manufacturer's instructions.

18.7.2 Only Partial Data Traffic Can Pass Across the Bridge

Thoroughly check the software and hardware configuration of the bridge. Check the current address table through software management if possible. It may be that the destination network address is not stored.

Are any incorrect configuration parameters in the bridge?

[YES]   Take the necessary action to resolve the problem and retest the bridge for proper operation. If the failure symptom is gone, record the problem in the network maintenance and service log. If the problem still exists after retesting, go to the next step.

[NO]   Check the internetwork for address update problems with certain Ethernet station nodes, specifically file servers and other bridges.

Particular Ethernet station nodes can have a software application configuration problem in relation to the source-routing field that they are directly transmitting.

Did examining the internetwork locate any specific problems with a certain Ethernet station node's or network's addressing?

[YES]   Take the necessary action to resolve the addressing problems with the respective Ethernet station node's or network's parameters; then retest the bridge for proper operation. If the failure symptom is gone, record the problem in the network maintenance and service log. If the problem still exists after retesting, go to the next step.

[NO]   Attempt to gather more conclusive fault-isolation data by thoroughly examining the packet transfer from source and destination nodes that is attempting to pass across the bridge. Vector to flow guide 18.15, and utilize protocol analysis techniques.

If after using this flow guide you cannot conclusively locate the problem and continue to find failure symptoms that point to a bridge problem, refer to the manufacturer's instructions.

18.7.3 An Overloaded Bandwidth Condition Is Present on a Certain Segment

Thoroughly check the bridge for any incorrect configuration parameters that can control the amount of traffic to be forwarded to another segment.

Check for proper address filters settings. Also check for Spanning Tree Algorithm settings; the bridge might be forwarding extra packets because of looping data in the internetwork.

Are any incorrect configuration parameters present in the bridge?

[YES] Take the necessary action to resolve the problem and retest the bridge for proper operation. If the failure symptom is gone, record the problem in the network maintenance and service log. If the problem still exists after retesting, go to the next step.

[NO] Check the bridge address tables for problems with certain Ethernet station node location mismatches.

A particular Ethernet station node can have a software application configuration problem in relation to the destination network to which it is directly transmitting. Sometimes the proper network may not be referenced from the node.

ETHERNET AND TOKEN RING OPTIMIZATION

Did examining the bridge address table locate any specific problems with a certain Ethernet station node's addressing?

[YES]   Take the necessary action to resolve the addressing with the respective Ethernet station node's parameters; then retest the bridge for proper operation. If the failure symptom is gone, record the problem in the network maintenance and service log. If the problem still exists after retesting, go to the next step.

[NO]   Attempt to gather more conclusive fault-isolation data by vectoring to flow guide 18.15.

NOTE

When performing a protocol analysis session on an attempted bridge transfer across segments, check for any excessive broadcast storms coming from the bridge. A bridge may be transmitting extra or excessive packets to locate a network. This is usually caused by a configuration or software revision problem with the bridge or multiple bridges in an Ethernet internetwork.

If after using this flow guide you cannot conclusively locate the problem and continue to find failure symptoms that point to a bridge problem, refer to the manufacturer's instructions.

18.8 Ethernet Router Problem Flow Guides

Particular protocols are not being passed through to another segment.

(Vector to sub-flow guide 18.8.1.)

No data traffic can pass from one side of the router to the other, or data is intermittently getting corrupted when passed through the router.

(Vector to sub-flow guide 18.8.2.)

Only partial data traffic can pass across the router.

(Vector to sub-flow guide 18.8.3.)

An overloaded bandwidth condition is present on a certain segment.

(Vector to sub-flow guide 18.8.4.)

Chapter 18: Ethernet Troubleshooting Flow Guides 591

This flow guide is generic as to the router manufacturer. For some of the troubleshooting steps mentioned in this flow guide, consult the router manufacturer's documentation for any predefined methods for checking router configuration and for router testing.

18.8.1 Particular Protocols Are Not Being Passed Through to Another Segment

Thoroughly check the router's software and hardware configuration, as related to the router's protocol-routing table.

Are any incorrect configuration parameters present in the router's protocol-routing table, as related to the specific protocol not properly being passed through to the destination segment?

    [YES]   Take the necessary action to resolve the problem and retest the router for proper operation. If the failure symptom is gone, record the problem in the network maintenance and service log. If the problem still exists after retesting, go to the next step.

    [NO]   Attempt to run router diagnostics.

Did running the diagnostics produce any errors that identify a router failure?

    [YES]   Take the necessary action to resolve the problem and retest the router for proper operation. If the failure symptom is gone, record the problem in the network maintenance and service log. If the problem still exists after retesting, go to the next step.

    [NO]   A configuration problem may still exist with the router, but to get more conclusive fault-isolation data, vector to flow guide 18.15.

When running a protocol analysis session on the segments involved in the router transfer, keep in mind that a router's main purpose is to connect Ethernet segments that need to share the same protocols; they must understand and be configured for the protocol that they are forwarding.
If after using this flow guide, you cannot conclusively locate the problem and continue to find failure symptoms that point to a router problem, refer to the manufacturer's instructions.

18.8.2 No Data Traffic Can Pass from One Side of the Router to the Other, or Data Is Intermittently Getting Corrupted When Passed Through the Router

Thoroughly check the software and hardware configuration of the router. If in an Ethernet and TCP/IP addressing environment, check for the correct TCP/IP address. Attempt an ICMP ping test.

Are any incorrect configuration parameters present in the router?

- **[YES]** Take the necessary action to resolve the problem and retest the router for proper operation. If the failure symptom is gone, record the problem in the network maintenance and service log. If the problem still exists after retesting, go to the next step.

- **[NO]** Attempt to run router diagnostics.

Did running the diagnostics produce any errors that identify a router failure?

- **[YES]** Take the necessary action to resolve the problem and retest the router for proper operation. If the failure symptom is gone, record the problem in the network maintenance and service log. If the problem still exists after retesting, go to the next step.

- **[NO]** A problem with the router may still exist, but to get more conclusive fault-isolation data, vector to flow guide 18.15.

> If after using this flow guide, you cannot conclusively locate the problem and continue to find failure symptoms that point to a router problem, refer to the manufacturer's instructions.

18.8.3 Only Partial Data Traffic Can Pass Across the Router

Thoroughly check the software and hardware configuration of the router.

Chapter 18: Ethernet Troubleshooting Flow Guides   593

Are any incorrect configuration parameters present in the router's network-to-address routing table, as related to the specific network address of a nodes packet not properly being passed through to the destination segment?

Are any incorrect configuration parameters present in the router?

> [YES] Take the necessary action to resolve the problem and retest the router for proper operation. If the failure symptom is gone, record the problem in the network maintenance and service log. If the problem still exists after retesting, go to the next step.
>
> [NO]   Check the segment for address problems with certain Ethernet station nodes, specifically file server routing update tables. Thoroughly examine the routing tables in a file server for addressing updates different from the router that has the problem. The router and the file server may have an address conflict.

> A particular Ethernet station node or file server can have a software router update configuration problem in relation to the network addresses to which it is directly transmitting.

Did examining the network addressing locate any specific problems with a certain Ethernet station node's or file server's routing update tables?

> [YES] Take the necessary action to resolve the network addressing problems with the respective Ethernet station node's or file server's parameters; then retest the router for proper operation. If the failure symptom is gone, record the problem in the network maintenance and service log. If the problem still exists after retesting, go to the next step.
>
> [NO]   Attempt to gather more conclusive fault-isolation data by thoroughly examining the routing transfer between Ethernet nodes and segments by vectoring to flow guide 18.15.

> If after using this flow guide you cannot conclusively locate the problem and continue to find failure symptoms that point to a router problem, refer to the manufacturer's instructions.

18.8.4 An Overloaded Bandwidth Condition Is Present on a Certain Segment

Thoroughly check the router for any incorrect configuration parameters that can control the amount of traffic to be forwarded to another segment.

Check for proper Spanning Tree Algorithm and router-to-router communication settings.

Are any incorrect configuration parameters present in the router?

[YES]   Take the necessary action to resolve the problem and retest the router for proper operation. If the failure symptom is gone, record the problem in the network maintenance and service log. If the problem still exists after retesting, go to the next step.

[NO]   Check the source network segment routing problems related to destination address settings in certain Ethernet station nodes.

> A particular Ethernet station node can have a software application configuration problem. At times, this issue can cause a constant transmission to a certain Ethernet network segment.

Did examining the segment locate any specific address problems with a certain Ethernet station node's routing transfers?

[YES]   Take the necessary action to resolve the problems with the respective Ethernet station node's routing parameters and then

Chapter 18: Ethernet Troubleshooting Flow Guides

retest the router for proper operation. If the failure symptom is gone, record the problem in the network maintenance and service log. If the problem still exists after retesting, go to the next step.

[NO]   Attempt to gather more conclusive fault-isolation data. Vector to flow guide 18.15.

NOTE

Look closely at the percentage of frames being forwarded that are overloading the destination segment with traffic to see if they are related to a specific node or process. There may be an unneeded broadcast.

Specifically as with a bridge, check for Spanning Tree Algorithm and router-to-router settings. The bridge may be forwarding extra packets because of looping data in the internetwork. These issues can cause an Ethernet internetwork broadcast storm.

If after using this flow guide you cannot conclusively locate the problem and continue to find failure symptoms that point to a router problem, refer to the manufacturer's instructions.

18.9 Basic Thick and Thin Repeater Problem Flow Guide

No data traffic can get from one side of the repeater to the other.

(Vector to sub-flow guide 18.9.1.)

NOTE

This flow guide is generic as to the repeater manufacturer. For some of the troubleshooting steps mentioned in this flow guide, you also should refer to the repeater manufacturer's documentation for any predefined methods for checking repeater configuration and for repeater testing.

18.9.1 No Data Traffic Can Pass from One Side of the Repeater to the Other

NOTE If a repeater is the suspected problem, attempt to try another port on the repeater if available. Next, troubleshoot the problem by testing the main cabling sections that normally pass through the repeater. Do this by disconnecting the attached cable segments and relooping the cabling sections at the repeater entry points with patch cables. With fiber optics cabling, this may be more difficult.

Bypass the repeater and test the main cabling segments with a TDR (or OTDR in the case of fiber).

With the repeater disconnected, did testing the cable produce any cable faults?

[YES]   Most likely a problem exists with the located segment cabling. If you are not sure what portion of the segment area is bad, vector to flow guide 18.2.
 If you are sure which portion of the main cabling path section is bad, replace that section. Then reattach the repeater and retest the segment. If the failure symptom is gone, record the problem in the network maintenance and service log. If the problem still exists after retesting, go to the next step.

[NO]   Attempt to run any available repeater diagnostics.

Did running the diagnostics produce any errors that identify a repeater failure?

[YES]   Take the necessary action to resolve the problem and retest the repeater for proper operation. If the failure symptom is gone, record the problem in the network maintenance and service log. If the problem still exists after retesting, go to the next step.

[NO]   Thoroughly check the repeater configuration.

Chapter 18: Ethernet Troubleshooting Flow Guides 597

Are any incorrect configuration parameters present in the repeater?

[YES]　Take the necessary action to resolve the problem and retest the repeater for proper operation. If the failure symptom is gone, record the problem in the network maintenance and service log. If the problem still exists after retesting, go to the next step.

[NO]　Check the actual physical placement of the repeater with respect to its specification for distance requirements within the Ethernet cabling system.

Sometimes the physical placement of a repeater can cause failure symptoms that point to a specific Ethernet segment cabling being at fault. Consult the repeater manufacturer for instructions as to distance requirements.

Is the repeater incorrectly placed as to its specifications?

[YES]　Take the necessary action to resolve the problem and retest the repeater for proper operation. If the failure symptom is gone, record the problem in the network maintenance and service log. If the problem still exists after retesting, go to the next step.

[NO]　A problem still may exist with the repeater. To get more conclusive fault-isolation data, vector to flow guide 18.15.

If after using this flow guide you cannot conclusively locate the problem and continue to find failure symptoms that point to a repeater problem, refer to the manufacturer's instructions.

18.10 Ethernet Network Peripheral Problem Flow Guides

NOTE If devices such as modems, printers, or fax boards are connected to an Ethernet station node or a file server, they are not actually considered network peripherals because they do not contain their own NICs. If the peripheral you are troubleshooting does not contain its own internal NIC, vector to the applicable flow guide. (For example, suppose that a modem or printer is connected to an Ethernet station node or file server, and the Ethernet station node or file server contains the NIC. In this case, you would vector to either the modem or printer problem flow guide.) If the device does contain its own internal NIC, this flow guide is applicable.

Did you arrive at this flow guide because of NIC failure indications from running a protocol analysis session?

(Vector to sub-flow guide 18.10.1.)

Did you arrive at this flow guide because you identified a failure symptom that appears to be directly related to a problem with a specific network peripheral?

(Vector to sub-flow guide 18.10.2.)

NOTE As discussed in Chapter 17, a network peripheral failure symptom usually differs from that of a standard Ethernet station node. However, both a network peripheral and a standard Ethernet station node contain an NIC and access the segment through the Ethernet rules. Because of this, they both can be assumed to have the same logical network area of fault components, which is the respective network peripheral's segment area, specifically the network peripheral, the NIC, the segment cable, and the repeater or wiring hub port.

Chapter 18: Ethernet Troubleshooting Flow Guides

NOTE

Some network peripherals access the Ethernet network with NIC and hardware/software components; others just use NIC hardware with firmware contained within PROM chips. Both configurations allow the assigned network peripheral to access the segment through standard network access, and they both operate according to the Ethernet CSMA/CD operating-mode principles. This flow guide is generic as to the network peripheral manufacturer. For some of the troubleshooting steps mentioned in this flow guide, you should also refer to the network peripheral manufacturer's documentation for any predefined methods for checking network peripheral configuration and for network peripheral testing.

18.10.1 Error Indication in a Protocol Analysis Session

Whether the error is a CRC, Collision, Long/Short, or Jabber indicated by an Ethernet physical frame, it still indicates a possible NIC failure in the network peripheral. Swap the respective NIC and rerun another thorough protocol analysis session on the segment.

NOTE

Some types of network peripherals have an NIC physically built into the motherboard. If this is the case, you may have to replace the whole unit. Refer to the manufacturer's instructions.

After you swapped the NIC and reran a protocol analysis session, did the error go away?

[YES] Leave the newly replaced NIC in the network peripheral and record the problem in the network maintenance and service log.

[NO] Replace the original NIC in the network peripheral; vector to flow guide 18.15; and rerun a protocol analysis session on the segment. Sometimes by rerunning a protocol analysis session, the failure cause becomes more clear by moving to another Ethernet address.

NOTE

If, after rerunning a protocol analysis session, the error does not move to another device and is still identifying the particular NIC address as a failure cause, troubleshoot the assigned segment area for the respective NIC by vectoring to flow guide 18.2.

If after using this flow guide you cannot conclusively locate the problem and continue to find failure symptoms that point to a network peripheral problem, refer to the manufacturer's instructions.

18.10.2 A Failure Symptom Appears to be Directly Related to a Problem with a Specific Network Peripheral

Is the network peripheral involved in some network communications with a particular application, or is it using the same directory or file on a particular file server when experiencing the symptom?

- [YES] Vector to flow guide 18.14 and troubleshoot a possible file server application or directory/file problem that may be related to the network peripheral operation.

- [NO] Move the network peripheral to another port on the repeater or wiring hub and recheck the network peripheral operation.

Did moving the network peripheral to another port resolve the problem?

- [YES] Vector to flow guide 18.4 and troubleshoot a possible repeater or wiring hub problem.

- [NO] Troubleshoot the respective node segment cable drop area involved. First, check and replace any external transceivers and then retest. If problems still exist, check the cable drop by vectoring to flow guide 18.3. If troubleshooting the segment cable does not identify any problems with the segment cable, vector back to this flow guide (18.10); then vector to sub-flow guide 18.10.2 and jump directly to the next step.

Next, test the respective network peripheral for proper software and hardware configuration setup and requirements.

Chapter 18: Ethernet Troubleshooting Flow Guides

- If the network peripheral has local disk storage, make sure that all the necessary directories and files for the network peripheral are set up correctly.
- Make sure that all the necessary hardware is installed in the network peripheral and is configured correctly.

> Check the NOS manuals for network peripheral setup concerning both software and hardware prerequisites.

NOTE

Did rechecking the network peripheral software and hardware requirements find any incorrect configuration setup problems?

[YES]   Take the necessary action to resolve the configuration problem and retest the network peripheral device for proper operation. If the failure symptom is gone, record the problem in the network maintenance and service log. If the problem is still present, go to the next step.

[NO]   Attempt to run any available network peripheral diagnostics. Also try to troubleshoot the network peripheral for any I/O board conflicts.

Did running the diagnostics or troubleshooting the network peripheral find any problems?

[YES]   Take the necessary action to resolve the problem and retest the network peripheral for proper operation. If the failure symptom is gone, record the problem in the network maintenance and service log. If the problem still exists after retesting, go to the next step.

Has the NIC in the assigned network peripheral been troubleshot?

[YES]   There may be a network file server-to-network peripheral related problem as to network access or protocol communication. Perform a protocol analysis session and focus closely on the communication between the network file server and the assigned network peripheral. Vector to flow guide 18.15.

ETHERNET AND TOKEN RING OPTIMIZATION

[NO]   Vector to flow guide 18.6 and troubleshoot the respective network peripheral station for an NIC problem.

NOTE

Many network peripherals are being manufactured with internal NICs within the respective logic board hardware architecture. If the network peripheral you are troubleshooting has this configuration, just attempt replacing the motherboard rather than vectoring to 18.6 and troubleshooting the NIC.

If after using this flow guide you cannot conclusively locate the problem and continue to find failure symptoms that point to a network peripheral problem, refer to the manufacturer's instructions.

18.11 Modem Problem Flow Guides

You cannot access or use a modem connected to the segment as a shared modem.

(Vector to sub-flow guide 18.11.1.)

You cannot access or use a modem connected to a specific Ethernet station node or file server as an unshared modem.

(Vector to sub-flow guide 18.11.2.)

You cannot access or use a modem connected to a segment from a remote location.

(Vector to sub-flow guide 18.11.3.)

NOTE

If the respective modem is connected to an Ethernet station node or a file server, it is not actually considered a network peripheral because it does not contain its own NIC. In this case, the following flow guide is applicable.

If the modem does contain its own NIC, you should troubleshoot the problem as a network peripheral by vectoring to flow guide 18.10. If, after troubleshooting the problem as a network peripheral, you feel that the modem or modem-sharing software may be at fault, vector back to this flow guide (18.11).

This flow guide is generic as to the modem and modem network-sharing software manufacturer. For some of the troubleshooting steps in this flow guide, you also should refer to the manufacturer's documentation for any predefined methods for checking configuration and for testing.

18.11.1 You Cannot Access or Use a Modem Connected to an Ethernet Segment as a Shared Modem

Check the Ethernet station node or file server to which the modem is connected, and the modem itself, to make sure that they are configured with all the proper hardware and software components and the correct configuration parameters. Also, check the network file server for all the correct modem-sharing software and proper configuration.

Are any incorrect configuration parameters present in either the respective Ethernet station node, modem, or network file server?

    [YES]   Take the necessary action to resolve the problem, and retest the modem for proper operation. If the failure symptom is gone, record the problem in the network maintenance and service log. If the problem still exists after retesting, go to the next step.

    [NO]   Attempt to run any available modem diagnostics and troubleshoot the modem link cables and phone lines.

Did running the diagnostics, checking the link, or checking the phone lines produce any errors?

    [YES]   Take the necessary action to resolve the problem and retest the modem for proper operation. If the failure symptom is gone, record the problem in the network maintenance and service log. If the problem still exists after retesting, go to the next step.

    [NO]   A configuration problem may still exist with the modem or the modem network-sharing software. Refer to the instructions of the respective modem and modem-software manufacturers.

18.11.2 You Cannot Access or Use a Modem Connected to a Specific Ethernet Station Node or File Server as an Unshared Modem

Check the Ethernet station node or file server to which the modem is connected and the modem itself to make sure that they are configured with all the proper hardware and software components and the correct configuration parameters.

Are any incorrect configuration parameters present in the respective Ethernet station node, file server, or modem?

- [YES] Take the necessary action to resolve the problem and retest the modem for proper operation. If the failure symptom is gone, record the problem in the network maintenance and service log. If the problem still exists after retesting, go to the next step.

- [NO] Attempt to run any available modem diagnostics and troubleshoot the modem link cables and phone lines.

Did running the diagnostics, checking the link, or checking the phone lines produce any errors?

- [YES] Take the necessary action to resolve the problem and retest the modem for proper operation. If the failure symptom is gone, record the problem in the network maintenance and service log. If the problem still exists after retesting, go to the next step.

- [NO] A configuration problem may still exist with the modem. Refer to the respective modem manufacturer's instructions.

18.11.3 You Cannot Access or Use a Modem Connected to an Ethernet Segment from a Remote Location.

Check the local and host Ethernet station nodes to which the modems are connected and the modems themselves to make sure that they are configured with all the proper hardware and software components and the correct configuration parameters. Also check the host network file server for all the correct modem-sharing software and proper configuration.

Are any incorrect configuration parameters present in the respective Ethernet station nodes, modems, or host network file server?

[YES] Take the necessary action to resolve the problem and retest the modems for proper operation. If the failure symptom is gone, record the problem in the network maintenance and service log. If the problem still exists after retesting, go to the next step.

[NO] Attempt to run any available modem diagnostics and troubleshoot the host and remote modems, link cables, and phone lines.

Did running the diagnostics, checking the link cables, or checking the phone lines produce any errors?

[YES] Take the necessary action to resolve the problem and retest the modems for proper operation. If the failure symptom is gone, record the problem in the network maintenance and service log. If the problem still exists after retesting, go to the next step.

[NO] A configuration problem may still exist with the modems or the modem network-sharing software. Refer to the respective modem and modem software manufacturer's instructions.

18.12 Printer Problem Flow Guides

You cannot access or use a printer connected to the segment as a shared printer.

(Vector to flow guide 18.12.1.)

You cannot access or use a printer connected to a specific Ethernet station node or file server as an unshared printer.

(Vector to flow guide 18.12.2.)

NOTE

If this printer is connected to an Ethernet station node or a file server, it is not actually considered a network peripheral because it does not contain its own NIC. In this case, the following flow guide is applicable.

If it does contain its own NIC, you should troubleshoot the problem as a network peripheral by vectoring to flow guide 18.10. If, after troubleshooting the problem as a network peripheral, you feel that the printer or printer-sharing software may be at fault, vector back to this flow guide (18.12).

This flow guide is generic as to the printer and printer network-sharing software manufacturer. For some of the troubleshooting steps in this flow guide, you should also refer to the manufacturer's documentation for any predefined methods for checking configuration and for testing.

18.12.1 You Cannot Access or Use a Printer Connected to the Segment as a Shared Printer

Check the Ethernet station node, file server, or print server to which the printer is connected and the printer itself, to make sure that they are configured with all the proper hardware and software components and the correct configuration parameters. Also check the network file server or print server for all the correct printer-sharing software and proper configuration.

Are any incorrect configuration parameters present in the respective Ethernet station node, network file server, print server, or printer?

[YES] Take the necessary action to resolve the problem and retest the printer for proper operation. If the failure symptom is gone, record the problem in the network maintenance and service log. If the problem still exists after retesting, go to the next step.

[NO] Attempt to run any available printer diagnostics and test the printer cabling.

Did running the diagnostics and testing the printer cabling produce any errors?

[YES]   Take the necessary action to resolve the problem and retest the printer for proper operation. If the failure symptom is gone, record the problem in the network maintenance and service log. If the problem still exists after retesting, go to the next step.

[NO]   A configuration problem may still exist with the printer or the printer network-sharing software. Refer to the instructions of the respective printer and printer software manufacturers.

18.12.2 You Cannot Access or Use a Printer Connected to a Specific Ethernet Station Node or File Server as an Unshared Printer.

Check the Ethernet station node or file server to which the printer is connected, and the printer itself, to make sure that they are configured with all the proper hardware and software components and the correct configuration parameters.

Are any incorrect configuration parameters present in either the respective Ethernet station node or the printer?

[YES]   Take the necessary action to resolve the problem and retest the printer for proper operation. If the failure symptom is gone, record the problem in the network maintenance and service log. If the problem still exists after retesting, go to the next step.

[NO]   Attempt to run any available printer diagnostics and test the printer cabling.

Did running the diagnostics and testing the printer cabling produce any errors?

[YES]   Take the necessary action to resolve the problem and retest the printer for proper operation. If the failure symptom is gone, record the problem in the network maintenance and service log. If the problem still exists after retesting, go to the next step.

[NO]   A configuration problem may still exist with the printer or the printer network software. Refer to the respective printer and printer software manufacturer's instructions.

18.13 Gateway Problem Flow Guides

The whole network has trouble accessing or using a host gateway connected to a local segment.

(Vector to sub-flow guide 18.13.1.)

Is just one Ethernet station node or a group of Ethernet station nodes having trouble accessing or using a host gateway connected to a local segment?

(Vector to sub-flow guide 18.13.2.)

Is there a problem accessing or using a host gateway from a non-local segment that is bridged, routed, or connected through a remote connection?

(Vector to sub-flow guide 18.13.3.)

Do gateway sessions appear to be running slowly or unresponsively?

(Vector to sub-flow guide 18.13.4.)

Are LAN-to-host sessions intermittently locking up or freezing?

(Vector to sub-flow guide 18.13.5.)

This flow guide is generic as to the gateway and gateway-sharing software manufacturers. For some of the troubleshooting steps mentioned in this flow guide, you should also refer to the manufacturer's documentation for any predefined methods for checking configuration and for testing.

18.13.1 The Complete Network Has Trouble Accessing or Using a Host Gateway Connected to a Local Segment.

Thoroughly check the gateway's configuration as to the gateway manufacturer's hardware and software setup for use with the LAN and the respective host.

Double-check all address assignments if in a TCP/IP addressing scheme. Are any incorrect configuration parameters present in the gateway's configuration as to the hardware and software setup for use with the LAN or the host?

[YES]   Take the necessary action to resolve the problem and retest the gateway for proper operation. If the failure symptom is gone, record the problem in the network maintenance and service log. If the problem still exists after retesting, go to the next step.

[NO]   Check all the Ethernet station nodes that need to access the gateway for the proper configuration as to the gateway manufacturer's specifications and TCP/IP addressing.

Are any incorrect configuration parameters present in the Ethernet station node's configuration as to hardware and software setup for use with the gateway?

[YES]   Take the necessary action to resolve the problem and retest the gateway for proper operation. If the failure symptom is gone, record the problem in the network maintenance and service log. If the problem still exists after retesting, go to the next step.

[NO]   Check the host to make sure that it is properly configured as to session setup and port availability to handle communications to the respective gateway.

Are any incorrect configuration parameters present in the host's configuration as to hardware and software setup for use with the LAN Ethernet station nodes or the gateway?

[YES]   Take the necessary action to resolve the problem and retest the gateway for proper operation. If the failure symptom is gone, record the problem in the network maintenance and service log. If the problem still exists after retesting, go to the next step.

[NO]   Attempt to run any available gateway diagnostics.

Did running the diagnostics produce any errors?

[YES]   Take the necessary action to resolve the problem and retest the gateway for proper operation. If the failure symptom is gone, record the problem in the network maintenance and service log. If the problem still exists after retesting, go to the next step.

[NO]   A configuration problem may exist with the gateway or the LAN gateway software. Refer to the instructions of the respective gateway and gateway software manufacturers.

18.13.2 One Ethernet Station Node or a Group of Ethernet Station Nodes Has Trouble Accessing or Using a Host Gateway Connected to a Local Segment

Check the Ethernet station node(s) experiencing the problem for the proper configuration as to the gateway manufacturer's specifications and TCP/IP addressing setup.

Are any incorrect configuration parameters present in the Ethernet station nodes' configuration as to the hardware and software setup for use with the gateway?

[YES]   Take the necessary action to resolve the problem and retest the gateway for proper operation. If the failure symptom is gone, record the problem in the network maintenance and service log. If the problem still exists after retesting, go to the next step.

[NO]   Check the host to make sure that it is properly configured as to session setup and port availability to handle communications for all the Ethernet station nodes experiencing the problem.

Are any incorrect configuration parameters present in the host's configuration as to the hardware and software setup for use with the LAN Ethernet station nodes?

[YES]   Take the necessary action to resolve the problem and retest the gateway for proper operation. If the failure symptom is gone,

Chapter 18: Ethernet Troubleshooting Flow Guides

record the problem in the network maintenance and service log. If the problem still exists after retesting, go to the next step.

[NO]   Attempt to run any available gateway diagnostics.

Did running the diagnostics produce any errors?

[YES]   Take the necessary action to resolve the problem and retest the gateway for proper operation. If the failure symptom is gone, record the problem in the network maintenance and service log. If the problem still exists after retesting, go to the next step.

[NO]   A configuration problem may still exist with the gateway or the LAN gateway software. Attempt to get more conclusive fault-isolation data concerning the communication between the gateway and the Ethernet station nodes experiencing the problem. Vector to flow guide 18.15.

If after using this flow guide you cannot conclusively locate the problem and continue to find failure symptoms that point to a gateway problem, refer to the manufacturer's instructions.

18.13.3 You Have Trouble Accessing or Using a Host Gateway from a Non-local Segment Bridged, Routed, or Connected Through a Remote Connection

First, verify that the particular bridge, router, or remote connection link is functioning properly. If necessary, vector to the respective flow guide for the particular device: 18.7 Bridge; 18.8 Router; and 18.11 Modem.

Are any problems with the linking devices, specifically the bridge, router, or communication (modem) devices/links?

[YES]   Take the necessary action to resolve the problem and retest the gateway for proper operation. If the failure symptom is gone,

record the problem in the network maintenance and service log. If the problem still exists after retesting, go to the next step.

[NO]   If no problems can be conclusively located to those respective devices, attempt to get more conclusive fault-isolation data on the complete LAN communication process relating to the gateway by vectoring to flow guide 18.15.

18.13.4 The Gateway Sessions Are Running Slowly or Are Unresponsive

Check all the gateway's operational-mode configurations for the proper configuration as to the gateway manufacturer's specifications.

Are any incorrect configuration parameters in any of the gateway's configurations for the hardware and software setup for use with the LAN/host?

[YES]   Take the necessary action to resolve the problem and retest the gateway for proper operation. If the failure symptom is gone, record the problem in the network maintenance and service log. If the problem still exists after retesting, go to the next step.

[NO]   Check the host to make sure that its session setup and port availability are properly configured to handle communications for all the Ethernet station nodes experiencing the problem.

Are any incorrect configuration parameters present in the host's configuration as to session and port capacity for use with the LAN layout of Ethernet station nodes set up to use the gateway?

[YES]   Take the necessary action to resolve the problem and retest the gateway for proper operation. If the failure symptom is gone, record the problem in the network maintenance and service log. If the problem still exists after retesting, go to the next step.

[NO]   Attempt to run any available gateway diagnostics.

Did running the diagnostics produce any errors?

[YES]   Take the necessary action to resolve the problem and retest the gateway for proper operation. If the failure symptom is gone,

Chapter 18: Ethernet Troubleshooting Flow Guides

record the problem in the network maintenance and service log. If the problem still exists after retesting, go to the next step.

[NO] A configuration problem may still exist with the gateway or the LAN gateway software. Attempt to get more conclusive fault-isolation data as to the communication between the gateway and the Ethernet station nodes experiencing the problem. Vector to flow guide 18.15.

If after using this flow guide you cannot conclusively locate the problem and continue to find failure symptoms that point to a gateway problem, refer to the manufacturer's instructions.

18.13.5 LAN-to-Host Sessions Are Intermittently Locking Up or Freezing

Attempt to run any available gateway diagnostics.

Did running the diagnostics produce any errors?

[YES] Take the necessary action to resolve the problem and retest the gateway for proper operation. If the failure symptom is gone, record the problem in the network maintenance and service log. If the problem still exists after retesting, go to the next step.

[NO] A configuration problem may still exist with the gateway or the LAN gateway software.

Thoroughly check the gateway's configuration as to the gateway manufacturer's hardware and software setup for use on the LAN and the respective host.

Are any incorrect configuration parameters present in the gateway's configuration as to the hardware and software setup for use with the LAN or the host?

[YES] Take the necessary action to resolve the problem and retest the gateway for proper operation. If the failure symptom is gone,

record the problem in the network maintenance and service log. If the problem still exists after retesting, go to the next step.

[NO] Attempt to get more conclusive fault-isolation data as to the communication between the gateway and the Ethernet station nodes experiencing the problem. Vector to flow guide 18.15.

If after using this flow guide you cannot conclusively locate the problem and continue to find failure symptoms that point to a gateway problem, refer to the manufacturer's instructions.

18.14 File Server Problem Flow Guides

Is there a problem on the network file server with an Ethernet station node, a group of Ethernet station nodes, the complete network, or a network peripheral accessing or using a particular application/group of applications, or certain directories/files?

(Vector to sub-flow guide 18.14.1.)

A particular NOS feature or set of NOS features on the network file server are not working.

(Vector to sub-flow guide 18.14.2.)

You have a problem accessing or using an extra network server other than the main network file server (for example, database, fax, communication, print server).

(Vector to sub-flow guide 18.14.3.)

There appears to be a problem with abnormal network bandwidth between a particular Ethernet station node/group of Ethernet segments and the network file server, or between a network peripheral and the network file server.

(Vector to sub-flow guide 18.14.4.)

Chapter 18: Ethernet Troubleshooting Flow Guides

NOTE: This flow guide is generic as to the NOS (such as Novell, IBM LAN Server, Microsoft LAN Manager, and Banyan VINES). When you reference some of the troubleshooting steps in this flow guide, you also should refer to the NOS manufacturer's documentation for any predefined methods for checking NOS configuration, hardware/software requirements, and for NOS diagnostics and testing.

18.14.1 There Is a Problem with an Ethernet Station Node, a Group of Ethernet Station Nodes, the Complete Network, or a Network Peripheral Accessing or Using a Particular Application/Group of Applications, or Certain Directories/Files on the Network File Server

First, check the network file server and any symptomatic Ethernet station nodes for the following software and hardware configuration setup parameters and requirements.

- Make sure that the NOS network shell software, NOS NIC drivers, CONFIG.SYS, AUTOEXEC.BAT, and all the necessary network operating system files are set up for the respective NOS specialized configuration and NOS hierarchical directory structure.
- Check the NOS directory structure as it relates to the Ethernet station node and any respective network peripheral access.
- Check all the NOS security rights configurations.
- Make sure that all the necessary directories/files for all NOS applications on the network drive and Ethernet station node drives are set up correctly.
- Make sure that all the necessary hardware installed in the file server/Ethernet station nodes is configured correctly and is functioning properly.

NOTE

Check the respective NOS manuals for file server setup concerning network software vendor requirements for both software and hardware prerequisites and their respective configurations.

Are there any identifiable hardware or software configuration setup problems with the network file server?

[YES] Take the necessary action to resolve the configuration problem and retest the segment for proper operation. If the failure symptom is gone, record the problem in the network maintenance and service log. If the failure symptom is still present, go to the next step.

[NO] If there appears to be no problem with the file server or its setup, attempt to gather more conclusive fault-isolation data by running a protocol analysis session on the segment. Vector to flow guide 18.15 and focus on the problem by capturing and viewing the high-layer communication processes.

NOTE

If after using this flow guide you cannot conclusively locate the problem and continue to find failure symptoms that point to the network file server problem, refer to both the NOS software and the particular file server/hardware manufacturer's instructions.

18.14.2 A Particular NOS Feature or Set of NOS Features on the Network File Server Is Not Working

First, fully refer to the respective NOS manuals for operation of the NOS feature(s).

Chapter 18: Ethernet Troubleshooting Flow Guides 617

In checking the NOS manuals, did you find any operational instructions to resolve your problem?

[YES] Take the necessary action to resolve the problem and retest the NOS feature for proper operation. If the failure symptom is gone, record the problem in the network maintenance and service log. If the failure symptom is still present, go to the next step.

[NO] Check the NOS manuals for file server setup concerning network software vendor requirements for both software and hardware prerequisites and their respective configurations.

Are there any identifiable hardware or software configuration setup problems with the network file server?

[YES] Take the necessary action to resolve the configuration problem and retest the NOS feature for proper operation. If the failure symptom is gone, record the problem in the network maintenance and service log. If the failure symptom is still present, go to the next step.

[NO] Contact your NOS support channel for assistance in using and configuring this particular NOS feature.

18.14.3 You Have Trouble Accessing or Using an Extra Network Server Other Than the Main Network File Server (For Example, Database, Fax, Communication, or Print Server)

Is the file server involved on a non-local segment that is bridged, routed, or connected through a remote connection?

[YES] Go to **S1**.

[NO] Go to **S2**.

[S1] File server is on a non-local segment that is bridged, routed, or connected through a remote connection. First, verify that the particular bridge, router, or remote connection link is functioning properly. If necessary, vector to the respective flow guide for the particular device: flow guides 18.7 Bridge; 18.8 Router; 18.11 Modem.

Are there any problems with the linking devices, specifically the bridge, router, or communication (modem) devices/links?

[YES]   Take the necessary action to resolve the problem and retest the respective network file server for proper operation. If the failure symptom is gone, record the problem in the network maintenance and service log. If the problem still exists after retesting, go to the next step.

[NO]   Go to **S2** and follow the troubleshooting steps as though the remote file server were actually located on the local segment.

[S2]   File server is on the local segment. First, check the network file server for the following software and hardware configuration setup parameters and requirements.

- Make sure that the NOS network shell software, NOS NIC drivers, CONFIG.SYS, AUTOEXEC.BAT, and all the necessary network operating system files are set up for the respective NOS specialized configuration and NOS hierarchical directory structure.

- Check the NOS directory structure as it relates to the Ethernet station node and any respective network peripheral access.

- Check all the NOS security rights configurations.

- Make sure that all the necessary directories/files for any NOS applications on the network drive are set up correctly.

- Make sure that all the necessary hardware is installed in the file server, is configured correctly, and is functioning properly.

Check the respective NOS and software application manuals for file server setup concerning network software vendor requirements for both software and hardware prerequisites and their respective configurations.

Are there any identifiable hardware or software configuration setup problems with the network file server?

[YES]   Take the necessary action to resolve the configuration problem and retest the segment for proper operation. If the failure symptom is gone, record the problem in the network maintenance and service log. If the failure symptom is still present, go to the next step.

[NO]   If there appears to be no problem with the file server or its setup, attempt to gather more conclusive fault-isolation data by running a protocol analysis session on the segment. Vector to flow guide 18.15 and focus on the problem by capturing and viewing the high-layer communication processes.

If after using this flow guide you cannot conclusively locate the problem and continue to find failure symptoms that point to the network file server problem, reference both the NOS software and the particular file server/hardware manufacturer's instructions.

18.14.4 There Appears to Be a Problem with Abnormal Network Bandwidth Between a Particular Ethernet Station Node/Group of Ethernet Segments or Network Peripheral and the Network File Server

First, check the network file server for the following software and hardware configuration setup parameters and requirements:

- Make sure that the NOS network shell software, NOS NIC drivers, CONFIG.SYS, AUTOEXEC.BAT, and all the necessary NOS files are set up for the respective NOS specialized configuration and NOS hierarchical directory structure.

- Check the NOS directory structure as it relates to Ethernet station node and any respective network peripheral access.
- Check all the NOS security rights configurations.
- Make sure that all the necessary directories/files for all NOS applications on the network drive are set up correctly.
- Make sure that all the necessary hardware is installed in the file server, is configured correctly, and is functioning properly.

> Check the respective NOS and software application manuals for file server setup concerning network software vendor requirements for both software and hardware prerequisites and their respective configuration.

Are there any identifiable hardware or software configuration setup problems with the network file server?

[YES]   Take the necessary action to resolve the configuration problem and retest the segment for proper operation. If the failure symptom is gone, record the problem in the network maintenance and service log. If the failure symptom is still present, go to the next step.

[NO]   Check the file server NIC buffer space specifications to see if they meet the NOS and software application manufacturers' requirements for the segment user population and access.

Is the file server's NIC low on required buffer space for the NOS or particular application's operation?

[YES]   Take the necessary action to resolve the problem and retest the segment for proper operation. If the failure symptom is gone, record the problem in the network maintenance and service log. If the failure symptom is still present, go to the next step.

[NO]   Attempt to gather more conclusive fault-isolation data by running a protocol analysis session on the segment. Vector to flow guide 18.15 and focus on the problem by capturing and viewing the high-layer communication processes and the baseline network bandwidth.

NOTE: If after using this flow guide you cannot conclusively locate the problem and continue to find failure symptoms that point to a network file server problem, reference both the NOS software and the particular file server/hardware manufacturer's instructions.

18.15 Protocol Analysis Flow Guides

Did you arrive at this flow guide because you need to troubleshoot a network failure symptom that requires running a protocol analysis session to examine the low-layer Ethernet frame communication processes?

(Vector to sub-flow guide 18.15.1.)

Did you arrive at this flow guide because you are encountering a specific error on the network, or the network is freezing or hanging?

(Vector to sub-flow guide 18.15.2.)

Did you arrive at this flow guide because you need to troubleshoot a network failure symptom that requires running a protocol analysis session to examine the high-layer network frame communication processes?

(Vector to sub-flow guide 18.15.3.)

Is the network experiencing any of the following failure symptoms: The whole network is operating slowly; a specific network application is operating slowly; or log-on failures are occurring?

(Vector to sub-flow guide 18.15.4.)

> While using these flow guides, keep in mind the prescribed approach for a general protocol analysis session: capture, view, analyze, check errors, benchmark performance, and focus. Refer to the Network Optimization section of this book.

18.15.1 Performing a Protocol Analysis Session to Examine the Low-Layer Ethernet Frame Communication Processes

First, start the protocol analysis session by establishing the network baseline of operations. Set up the protocol analyzer to perform a full capture.

> If the higher-layer protocols are clouding your testing results, you can filter them out, so as to focus more closely on the low layers.

Closely examine the low-level Ethernet frame communication processes. Interrogate all the base Ethernet frames as to how they respectively correlate with the time-related communication processes captured in the protocol analysis session.

Scrutinize the current state of low-level Ethernet frame communications exchanged between the network entities involved for protocol exchange. Specifically, if you are troubleshooting a certain network component, such as a gateway, router, bridge, Ethernet station node, file server, or network peripheral, look for the exact amount and low-level Ethernet error frame type associated with that specific network device's Ethernet address. Chances are you have captured an Ethernet error type. Check for the error type and reference Chapter 17 for an error type description.

In other words, are any noticeable high counts of an Ethernet frame error type associated with an address related to a specific segment area or Ethernet station node?

Chapter 18: Ethernet Troubleshooting Flow Guides 623

Did you find an Ethernet error type correlation to an address or segment area on the internetwork?

[YES] Take the necessary action to resolve the problem by vectoring to the flow guide for that specific network component (such as 18.2 Segment Areas; 18.5 Ethernet Station Node; 18.10 Network Peripheral; 18.14 File Server; and so on).

If you are not completely sure as to a specific network node, but you know the segment area that may be related to the failure symptom, vector to flow guide 18.2 and troubleshoot the respective addresses associated in the frames (that is, the possible segment area) that deviate from the normal state of communication. If, after vectoring to the respective segment area or network component, you find a problem, resolve the problem and retest the internetwork by vectoring back to this flow guide (18.15). Rerun another baseline session to test the segments involved. If no more deviances from the normal state of operations occur, record the problem in the network maintenance and service log. If the problem still exists after rerunning another session, go to the next step.

[NO] Vector down to the next sub-flow guide, 18.15.2.

18.15.2 You Encounter a Specific Error on the Network, or the Whole Network Is Freezing or Hanging

NOTE

Abnormal high network bandwidth usage can cause performance degradation on the network, which can present itself in the form of error conditions. If you immediately suspect high bandwidth as a problem, vector down to sub-flow guide 18.15.4 and analyze the network bandwidth. If at this point you feel that the bandwidth is within normal parameters, continue with the following steps. Remember that by using any available error alarm triggering features with your protocol analyzer, you can observe more dynamically any particular errors as they occur.

Examine the captured data from the respective protocol analysis session for any recorded error conditions.

Ethernet Error Vectoring

NOTE Errors are not always critical. Only certain levels, for example, collisions recorded above 1% of overall traffic, that are related to a specific address may indicate a marginal failure with that network component. So when following any recommended vectors in the following error vectors, use your own logical thought processes as to the seriousness of the failure symptom occurring before taking any corrective action.

NOTE When examining the type of error captured during the protocol analysis session, look closely at the error frame for the following information and take notes on the type of error and any associated Ethernet addresses in the error frame.

Examine the respective error frame captured during the protocol analysis session for the type of error and both associated addresses in the frame.

Place your captured error type into one of the following six error type categories, and go to that Ethernet error type. Next, use the address information along with the presented isolation solution to identify the error failure cause.

The Ethernet frame error types are as follows:

Local Collision Error. Troubleshoot the addresses in the assigned node by vectoring to flow guide 18.5 and 18.6. Keep in mind that the reporting station NIC may be the failure cause.

Remote Collision Error. Troubleshoot the other segments for local collision levels that were attached to the internetwork involved in active data transfers when the error occurred. If a segment is located with a collision level above 1% of all traffic, follow the preceding local collision process.

CRC Error. Troubleshoot the addresses in the assigned node by vectoring to flow guide 18.5 and 18.6. Keep in mind that the reporting station NIC may be the failure cause.

Long or Short Frame Error. Troubleshoot addresses in the assigned node by vectoring to flow guide 18.5 and 18.6. Keep in mind that the reporting station NIC may be the failure cause.

Jabber Error. Check and replace the nodes transceiver that is transmitting a high jabber and then retest. If problems are still present, troubleshoot the addresses in the assigned node by vectoring to flow guide 18.5 and 18.6. Keep in mind that the reporting station NIC may be the failure cause.

NOTE

When experiencing intermittent problems such as high errors on an Ethernet network, you can use traffic-generation techniques to load the network with additional traffic to flush out certain types of intermittent failure causes. By generating additional network traffic, you can stress the network enough to cause certain marginal network component failures to surface.

If a particular error occurs frequently and you have thoroughly analyzed the respective error and followed the recommended troubleshooting steps, and still cannot conclusively locate a failure cause for the error, vector down to sub-flow guide 18.15.4 and analyze the network bandwidth.

18.15.3 Perform a Protocol Analysis Session to Examine the High-Layer Network Frame Communication Processes.

Have you verified that the Ethernet low-level base frame communication processes are proper and fluent as to low-level protocol exchange?

[YES]   Go to S1.

[NO]   Vector back to sub-flow guide 18.15.1 and troubleshoot the low-level Ethernet base communication processes.

[S1]   First, perform a full-capture session. Next, view the high-layer protocol communication that occurs concurrently between the network components—the Ethernet station nodes, network peripherals, gateways, bridges, routers, file servers, and so on—involved in the high-layer communication processes that you are troubleshooting. Closely examine the application and network operating system communication process between the respective network components.

Keep in mind that certain applications may use multiple layers of the OSI or specific protocol model for transmission. Check all the higher layers. Refer to the Network Optimization section of this book.

Are the involved network components and their respective application/NOS communication processes exchanging the correct assigned protocol?

[YES]   Refer to the NOS and software application manufacturers and if necessary, contact your NOS and software support channel for assistance with troubleshooting any suspected high-layer communication process.

[NO]   Does the incorrect protocol exchange appear to be related to some sort of file access process problem with a particular NOS or software application?

[YES]   Refer to the NOS and software application manufacturers and if necessary, contact your NOS and software support channel for assistance with troubleshooting any suspected high-layer communication process.

[NO]   Check the network components involved in the specific high-layer communication process that you are troubleshooting for a possible failure by vectoring to the flow guide for that particular specific network component (for example 18.5 Ethernet Station Node; 18.10 Network Peripheral; 18.14 File Server; and so on).

If, you are not completely conclusive as to a specific network component, that may be related to the failure symptom, vector to flow guide 18.2 and troubleshoot the respective Ethernet addresses associated in the high-layer frames that appear to be involved with failure symptoms.

If, after vectoring to the respective segment area or network component, you find a problem, resolve the problem and retest the Ethernet internetwork by vectoring back to this flow guide (18.15) and rerun another baseline session to test the segment. Then reexamine the high-layer communication processes for any deviances from the previous testing results.

If everything appears normal, record the problem in the network maintenance and service log. If the problem is still present, contact your NOS and software support channel for assistance with troubleshooting any suspected high-layer communication process.

18.15.4 The Network Is Experiencing One or More of the Following Failure Symptoms: The Whole Network Is Operating Slowly; a Specific Network Application Is Operating Slowly; or Logon Failures Are Occurring

First, set up the protocol analyzer or network monitoring tool to monitor the network bandwidth utilization at an overall baseline view.

Is the overall network baseline within normal operating levels of a previously established baseline for your network?

If you do not have a previously established baseline for your network, attempt to identify that a reasonable portion of the available maximum bandwidth is still available for use.

[YES] Vector back to the beginning of this flow guide (18.15) and follow the subsections of this complete flow guide. (That is, examine the low-layer frame communication processes, check for specific Ethernet errors on the network, and examine the high-layer network frame communication processes.)

ETHERNET AND TOKEN RING OPTIMIZATION

[NO]   Check the overall baseline network bandwidth as to individual Ethernet station nodes and all other network components' level usage. Attempt to locate a particular Ethernet station node or other network component that may be absorbing abnormal bandwidth.

Can you locate any particular Ethernet station nodes or other network components that may be absorbing abnormal bandwidth?

[YES]   If you have not troubleshot the high-level communication process on the segment, vector back to sub-flow guide 18.15.3 and thoroughly troubleshoot the high-level communication process for any NOS or application communication processes that may be absorbing abnormal bandwidth. After analyzing the high-layer communication process, vector back to this sub-flow guide (18.15.4) and remeasure the baseline network bandwidth.

If you have troubleshot the high-level communication processes, go to the next step.

[NO]   Even though you cannot specifically locate any particular Ethernet station nodes or other network components that may be absorbing abnormal bandwidth, still check any Ethernet station nodes or network components that are suspect by vectoring to the flow guide for that particular specific network component (for example, 18.5 Ethernet Station Node; 18.10 Network Peripheral; 18.14 File Server; and so on).

If you are not completely sure that a specific network component is related to the failure symptom, vector to flow guide 18.2 and troubleshoot the respective segment areas on the Ethernet internetwork associated with high bandwidth usage.

If, after vectoring to the respective fault domain, network area, or network component, you find a problem, resolve the problem and retest the segment by vectoring back to this flow guide (18.15); then vector directly back to sub-flow guide 18.15.4. Rerun another baseline bandwidth test session to reexamine the segment for bandwidth usage.

If everything appears normal, record the problem in the network maintenance and service log. If the problem is still present, contact your NOS and software support channel for assistance with troubleshooting any suspected network bandwidth issues.

If you have benchmarked the network bandwidth utilization at overall baseline view and usage of the individual Ethernet station nodes and other network components, and you still have a bandwidth problem that you cannot locate, contact your NOS and software support channel for assistance with troubleshooting any suspected bandwidth problem.

APPENDIX A

Glossary

802.3 See Ethernet frame normal.

802.5 An IEEE standard for the Token Ring access method and physical layer specifications.

4Mbps A Token Ring-specified speed for data transmission that uses frame sizes of approximately 4,500 bytes.

16Mbps A Token Ring-specified speed for data transmission that uses frame sizes of approximately 18,000 bytes, along with ETR.

10BASE2 See Thin Ethernet.

10BASE-T The specification for unshielded twisted-pair Ethernet.

Abort sequence frame A frame sequence used to clear the ring when a problem exists with a frame.

Absolute time The actual time stamped on a particular frame transmission across the network involved.

ETHERNET AND TOKEN RING OPTIMIZATION

Active monitor (AM) The main communication manager on the ring; the AM is responsible for maintaining key transfer of data and control information balanced between all stations on the ring.

Adjusted ring length (ARL) The final maximum length of certain cabling segments in the Token Ring topology, derived by calculations involving distance in relation to the number of MAUs, repeaters, and wiring closets in the network.

Advanced program-to-program communications (APPC) Part of the SNA protocol, establishing the conditions that enable programs to communicate across the network. This capability, involving LU6.2 and its associated protocols, enables communication between two or more processes in an SNA network without the involvement of a common host system or of terminal emulation.

AppleTalk A set of communication protocols used to define networking on an AppleShare network. Based on the OSI model, AppleTalk is comparable to other communication protocols in that they specify communications that range from application interfaces to media access.

Application efficiency examination An optimization technique used when a particular application has a problem on the network.

Attachment Unit Interface (AUI) In Thick Ethernet cabling, a standard port or drop cable connection that allows the cabling transceiver to have a port that connects the network interface card.

AUTOEXEC.BAT A special file used to customize the DOS workstation environment.

Average utilization. The amount of use on a network over a specified standard period of time.

Bandwidth utilization The total capacity actually being used on the network.

Banyan VINES Banyan's Virtual Internetworking System.

Chapter 2: Introduction to Topologies

Banyan VINES System Protocols   A set of protocols used for internetworking in the LAN and WAN environment for the Banyan VINES operating system.

Baseband transmission   A form of data transmission used to send unmodulated digital pulses over the network cabling by sending only one signal frequency over the line at a time.

Baselining   Examining the current state of operations of the network.

Beaconing   A Token Ring communication process that occurs when a ring station generates a warning signal onto the ring if it sees a hard error occur with itself or its NAUN.

BPDU (hello Bridge Protocol Data Units)   A protocol used by the spanning tree algorithm to control transmission of data.

Bridge   A device that connects local area networks via the data link layer of the OSI model.

Broadcasting   An addressing method by which a station on the ring communicates to one or more stations through a common address that the destination stations share.

Broadcast storm.   When high broadcast levels (over 10% and as high as 20% to 25%) are generated by problems in a network or in the network's devices.

Building blueprints   A set of documents that shows the physical layout of a particular building.

Cabling   The physical medium that connects transmission points within a local area network.

Cabling connector   A physical link that connects two points within the cabling section of a local area network.

Carrier Sense Multiple Access/Collision Detection (CSMA/CD)   The access approach used throughout the Ethernet environment.

Central Processing Unit (CPU)   The part of a computer containing the circuits required to interpret and execute instructions.

Channel Service Unit (CSU) A device that interfaces a T1 line to a local loop.

Collapsed backbone The situation where the external networks throughout an internetwork actually join within the backplane of a large comprehensive router.

Collision The result of two or more workstations attempting to transmit on the Ethernet medium at the same time and having their data transmission collide.

CONFIG.SYS file A special file used to configure the DOS workstation environment.

Configuration report server (CRS) A ring management server role whose main responsibility is to collect important statistical information from the ring and to forward that information to the LAN Manager console.

Cyclic redundancy check (CRC) A 32-bit sequence within a Token Ring data frame that is an error-checking method involving a calculation of the bit transmission at the sending and receiving ends of each ring station.

Data frame A variable-length frame that carries ring control or data information. The frame then carries the designation of a MAC frame (control) or an LLC frame (data).

Data Service Unit (DSU) A device that converts RS232 terminal signals to line codes for local loop transmission.

DECnet A set of networking protocols developed by Digital Equipment Corp. (DEC) and used in the VAX family of computers for data exchange. Although DECnet is currently a proprietary protocol, DEC is merging its protocols with OSI protocols.

Delta time See Interpacket time.

Destination ring station A station that is the intended receiver of a particular frame generated and transmitted by an originating ring station.

Chapter 2: Introduction to Topologies

Differential Manchester Encoding   A form of data transmission communicated on the ring medium using a specialized bit-encoding scheme.

DLC.LAN   The portion of the data link layer of Token Ring that encodes, decodes, and routes MAC and LLC information.

DLC.LANMGR   A manager function within the DLC.LAN responsible for managing the control of information between both the LLC and MAC layers at the data link level.

Downstream   The normal direction of data flow on the Token Ring network.

Duplicate address   An address at the physical or upper-protocol layer that is the same as the address of another active ring station on the ring.

Dynamic routing   Utilized when routers are updating each other with general information changes and operation changes on the networks involved.

Early token release (ETR)   A ring-access technique that lets two data frames travel on the ring at the same time.

Encapsulation   The enveloping of protocols within other protocols to allow transmission across the respective network.

Ethernet   A network topology and access protocol scheme originally developed by DEC, Intel, and Xerox, now marketed primarily by DEC and 3Com.

Ethernet frame (Normal, 802.3)   Accepted by the IEEE; differs from the raw non-standard 802.3 in that it usually includes an 802.2 field envelope.

Ethernet 2 frame type   The original Ethernet frame type generated by the IEEE, composed of a preamble, destination and source address, data area, and frame check sequence.

ETHERNET AND TOKEN RING OPTIMIZATION

Fault domain The logical area of a fault error as determined by the Token Ring architecture.

Fault isolation vectoring The art of deciding the correct direction to follow when troubleshooting a LAN problem.

Fiber Data Distributed Interface (FDDI) A network topology that runs at 100Mbps. The topology is a token-passing network very similar to IEEE 802.5.

Fiber optic cabling Cable that uses light rather than electricity to transfer information.

File throughput The amount of data passed in a block of time.

Flow guide A logical, non-graphical, written troubleshooting flow chart.

Frame Same as Packet description, except usually does not have higher layer data internal.

Frame fluency The workstation's receipt of requested packets or frames from a file server in a normal or timely manner. See Network Transfer Integrity.

Functional addressing An addressing method by which a station that has widely used functions can be assigned a predefined address so that other stations can communicate with it.

Gateway A hardware/software package that runs on the OSI application layer and enables incompatible protocols to communicate. Includes X.25 gateways. Usually connects PCs to a host machine, such as an IBM mainframe.

Group addressing An addressing method by which one or more stations are addressed.

Hard errors The more serious type of errors that can occur on the ring. A hard error is considered an actual solid failure and impairs the normal mode of ring operation.

Header frames Define the way the data packets are carried across the network, and how they are decoded and coded between the different network interface cards in a network environment.

Hub A wiring center for a LAN or WAN cabling or node scheme.

IBM cabling types A set of cabling types designed for the Token Ring topology as specified by IBM.

IBM data connector The IBM standard data connector that has internal self-shorting bars, which automatically loop the cabling back to form an electrical ring.

IBM NetView Network-monitoring software for SNA networks.

IBM Network Management (IBMNM) protocol A specific communication protocol used to communicate among the Token Ring architectural ring management roles.

IBM Server Message Block (SMB) A distributed file-system network protocol from IBM and Microsoft that enables one computer to use the files and peripherals of another as if they were local.

IBM Systems Network Architecture (SNA) An IBM network architecture defined in terms of its functions, formats, and protocols.

IBM Token Ring planning forms A set of IBM forms for planning and maintaining Token Ring network configurations.

Individual addressing An addressing method by which each station is addressed uniquely across the ring.

Institute of Electrical and Electronics Engineers (IEEE) A body of engineers that establishes networking standards for cabling, electrical topology, physical topology, and access schemes.

Intermittent failure A failure symptom that cannot be re-created at will; it might occur any time.

Internetwork Two or more networks connected by an internal or external router that connect across common or multiple topologies and communicate with common or multiple protocols for full interoperability.

Internetwork Packet Exchange (IPX)   A Novell NetWare protocol that enables the exchange of message packets on an internetwork.

Interpacket time (or delta time)   The amount of time between two consecutive frames on a respective network.

I/O board   Hardware that enables the transfer of data into and out of a computer.

Jabbering   When garbled bits of data are emitted within the Ethernet frame sequence. This occurs when an NIC card continues to jam an Ethernet segment.

Jam   A signal sent by an Ethernet card to clear a collision on an Ethernet segment.

Jumper cables   Cables usually used between ports on a patch panel.

LAN Bridge Server (LBS)   A ring management server role whose main responsibility is to monitor important statistical information about data routed between two or more rings connected by a bridge.

LAN drivers   Software or firmware that translates operating system requests (such as input/output requests) into a recognizable format for specific hardware, such as adapters.

LAN Reporting Mechanism (LRM)   A ring management server function responsible for maintaining communication between a LAN Manager console and remote management servers.

Late collision   See Collision, Remote.

Layer   A subsection of an overall network communication session.

Lobe   The complete composite of network components in a specific lobe area that physically connects to a specific MAU or wiring hub.

Lobe area One logical arm of a specified network node, including specific network components, such as a ring station, an NIC, a lobe cable, and an MAU or wiring hub port.

Lobe cable The section or sections of cable that attach a ring station or network device to an MAU or wiring hub.

Lobe path See Lobe Area.

Local administration The means of assigning ring stations unique individual addresses defined by a group or person other than the IEEE.

Local area network (LAN) A system that links computers together to form a network, usually by using a wiring-based cabling scheme. LANs connect personal computers and electronic office equipment, enabling users to communicate, share resources such as data storage and printers, and access remote hosts or other networks.

Local collision error An Ethernet frame with less than 64 bytes and a bad CRC.

Logical Link Control (LLC) The data frame sequence type used in Token Ring data frames that contains actual user data information to be transmitted.

Logical Link Control (LLC) Layer The IEEE 802.2 Standard; considered a communication-carrying protocol across local area networks.

Long frame errors Ethernet frames larger than 1,518 bytes.

Main ring path The logical path that interconnects a series of network components and cabling sections to form the logical ring.

Main ring path cabling The cabling sections that make up the physical path that forms the main ring path.

Mature, technically migrated network A network that has grown over a long period of time and has undergone a number of modifications.

MAU Ethernet See Medium Attachment Unit.

ETHERNET AND TOKEN RING OPTIMIZATION

MAU Token Ring See Multistation Access Unit.

MAU charger An IBM device used to open relays in the IBM MAU.

MAU rack layout A document that depicts the physical and logical layout of a MAU rack.

Maximum lobe length The maximum length of a lobe cable before it loses transmission quality and capability.

Medium Access Control (MAC) The data sequence used in Token Ring data frames that contains the information for managing the flow of traffic on the ring.

Medium Attachment Unit (MAU) or Transceiver Connects different Ethernet nodes together in an organized fashion across an individual Ethernet segment; allows multiple Ethernet segment nodes to connect to each other to create a segment.

Memory The active part of computer storage used when a computer runs a program or a command.

Modem A device that enables the transmission and reception of digital information over telephone lines.

Multistation Access Unit (MSAU or MAU) An access device used to connect the main cabling structure to devices in use on a Token Ring network.

Nearest Active Upstream Neighbor (NAUN). The first active upstream ring station from any particular active ring station.

Neighbor notification. A Token Ring communication process that involves a logical consecutive procedure enabling every ring station to be informed of its NAUN's address.

NetBIOS (Network Basic Input/Output System) A programmable entry into the network that enables systems to communicate over network hardware using a generic networking interface that can run over multiple transports or media.

Chapter 2: Introduction to Topologies

Network architecture The design of the way the network topology is integrated with the network protocols.

Network area Any particular logically defined area of the network, such as a group of ring stations, a set of MAUs, and so forth.

Network baseline The actual measurement and recording of a network's state of operation over a period of time. The current state of a network's order of operation.

Network baseline study A protocol analysis session performed to obtain the statistical measurements of a network when it is operating under normal conditions.

Network component Any specific hardware or software device connected to the network or part of a specific network area.

Network connection The actual network connection sequence involving an initiation from one device for a connection, the final establishment of a true connection, and some sort of transmission that occurs at that point.

Network documentation The necessary documents to maintain a reference of the hardware and software components within a LAN layout.

Network documentation software tools A software package that can gather LAN statistics (such as hardware and software configurations) and create automated records based on the gathered information.

Network file server A computer on the network capable of recognizing and responding to client requests for services. The services can range from basic file and print services to support for complex, distributed applications. For example, a distributed database management system can create a single logical database across multiple servers.

Network file server and ring station documentation A series of written or automated records that maintains an overview of the components of both the file server and ring stations in a Token Ring network environment.

Network interface card (NIC)   A logic card that uses electronic circuitry and software routines to connect a workstation to the cabling medium through a specified access method.

Network maintenance and service log   A written or automated record that maintains a historical log of any problems that occur in the Token Ring network environment.

Network operating system (NOS)   A set of software programs that manages the use of data and resources in a network of connected workstations.

Network optimization   The process of measuring a network's workload characteristics to a defined level and then making necessary modifications to the network's layout, design, and configuration to improve its overall performance.

Network overload   A condition that occurs when the bandwidth exceeds a safe operational condition for that particular network due to its topology, applications, and user profiles.

Network peripherals   Network devices that physically connect to the network by using their own internal NIC, without needing to be attached to a ring station or a file server.

Network protocol   An orderly, predefined method by which devices on a LAN communicate.

Network shell software   The software programs at each workstation that enable the workstation to take advantage of the network's data and resources.

Network transfer integrity   The actual fluency of network frame communication on a given network (also known as frame fluency).

Chapter 2: Introduction to Topologies

NIC agent A set of routines within the Token Ring chipset on the NIC that interpret and route all the data frames transferred between the device and the network.

Node-by-node utilization A key measurement involving breaking down the overall bandwidth utilization between the nodes on the network involved.

Open networking See Internetwork.

Open System Interconnection (OSI) A model for network communications, consisting of seven layers that describe what happens when computers communicate.

Optical time domain reflectometer (OTDR) A device that operates in the same manner as a TDR, except by using a laser as a light source to generate optical pulse signals and by using an optical receiver.

Originating ring station A ring station that generates and transmits a particular frame onto the Token Ring cabling medium.

Packet The actual capsule where higher layer data is implemented and communicated across the networks. See Frame.

Paging through a trace Actually stepping through each particular packet in a full captured data gathering with a protocol analyzer from a respective network.

Patch cables. Cables used between a ring station and a wall plate.

Patch panel A physical panel, usually contained within a wiring closet, used as a patch board for running a group of cables to one area, and providing the flexibility to move lobe cables from one MAU to another easily.

Patch panel layout A document that depicts the physical layout and logical cable wiring scheme of a patch panel.

Peak utilization The highest peak of utilization reached during a specified time.

ETHERNET AND TOKEN RING OPTIMIZATION

Performance tuning   Using the statistics gathered in a protocol analysis session and making any necessary modifications to the software or hardware design components of a LAN to improve operational performance.

Phantom DC current   A current generated during Ring Insertion by an NIC to a specific MAU port to open the MAU port relay.

Physical bus   A network topology with a straight bus formed segment with individual tap points for nodes.

Physical star   A network topology with a central hub and radiating spokes.

Priority access   A Token Ring communication process that involves a qualifying method by which all ring stations attain a certain priority for their turn to gain control of the token.

Problem reversal theory   A troubleshooting theory based on taking known testing results and reversing the respective troubleshooting procedure to re-create the problem for verification before implementing the newly tested network component.

Project management   The planning, organizing, accurate implementation, and regulation of a company's internal and external resources to accomplish specific goals for an overall project.

Protocol analysis   The process of capturing, viewing, and analyzing the way a communication protocol operates in a particular network architecture.

Protocol analysis session   A specific instance of using a protocol analyzer to capture, decode, and examine data involved in communication across a live network.

Protocol analyzer   A device that can capture, decode, and display packets of data from a network. These tools enable you to optimize and view data on your network to help you understand how that data is performing.

Chapter 2: Introduction to Topologies

Protocol suite The subset of internal protocols contained within a protocol utilized in a particular network.

Protocols The actual transmission tools used to get data from one point to another within the internetwork.

Raw 802.3 An Ethernet frame type close to 802.3 standard that does not have to include the 802.2 data envelope; includes a frame length field and then carries the data within raw.

Relative time The amount of time between two specific network events or trace frames being analyzed.

Remote collision error A collision that occurs when less than the normal 64 bytes of data are in the frame and the CRC is bad, and the packet has remote address fields.

Remote program load (RPL) PROM A PROM that enables a diskless ring station to attach to a network file server.

Repeater A device that amplifies and then regenerates a signal to extend the distance of a local area network.

Response time The amount of time required for a specific network operation to occur. The effective amount of time that an actual node responds to another node within internetwork communication, in response to a particular request for data.

Ring cable tester A device designed specifically for testing the Token Ring topology cabling.

Ring error monitor (REM) A ring management server role whose main responsibility is to collect soft and hard errors from all stations that generate errors on the ring.

Ring In (RI) The port on the left side of the MAU, used for access from another MAU and the associated ring cabling section. Also called the entrance method to another MAU or wiring hub module.

Ring Insertion The five-phase process that a ring station goes through to attach itself to a Token Ring network.

Ring Out (RO) The port on the right side of the MAU, used to access another MAU and the associated ring cabling section. Also called the exit method from one MAU or wiring hub module to another.

Ring parameter server (RPS) A ring management server role whose main responsibility is to communicate ring initialization parameters to all new ring stations attaching to the ring.

Ring purge A Token Ring communication process that can be defined as the attempted resetting of the ring to Normal Repeat mode.

Ring station (RS) A PC that contains the necessary hardware, software, and functions to enable it to access a Token Ring network as a node.

Router A software and hardware connection between two or more networks, usually of similar design, that enables traffic to be routed from one network to another based on the intended destinations of the traffic. A router can connect networks that use different network adapters or transmission media as long as both sides of the connection use the same protocols. If a router is located in a server, it is called an internal router; if located in a workstation, it is called an external router.

Router protocols Internetwork protocols used in certain internetworking environments to allow for communication and calculation of routes between respective subnetwork routers.

RS232 A set of interface standards that dictates how asynchronous devices, such as PCs and terminals, communicate over telephone wire. Based on a 25-pin architecture that permits 19.2Kbps data transfer.

Shielded twisted pair (STP) A cable consisting of two twisted-pair conductors insulated by a metal-backed mylar substance.

Short (or Runt) frame error Any frame under 64 bytes in size.

Chapter 2: Introduction to Topologies

Signal Quality Error Test (SQE)   Used to test collision detect circuitry in older Ethernet layouts.

Simple Network Management Protocol (SNMP)   Developed for TCP/IP networks.

Soft error   The less serious type of error that occurs on the ring. It usually does not impair the normal mode of ring operation.

Solid failure. A failure symptom that can be recreated at will.

Source routing   A means of data transmission by which the node generating the transmission determines the route that the data follows.

Source routing bridge   A bridge that can understand and forward frames with source-routing data fields.

Spanning tree algorithm (STA)   A method to determine a packet's best path when multiple path routes are within an internetwork.

Standby monitors (SM)   All general ring stations (RSes) on the ring.

Subnetwork Access Protocol (SNAP)   An encapsulation protocol used frequently when Ethernet frames have to be carried across a Token Ring environment.

Synchronous Data Link Control (SDLC)   A code-independent IBM-defined link-control protocol.

Thick Ethernet   Allows for up to 500 meters for a complete Ethernet segment and accommodates 100 stations on each segment.

Thin Ethernet   Allows for up to 200 meters in a total length per segment; usually composed of a coaxial cable based on RG-58 coaxial cable type.

Throughput   The amount of information passed in a block of time over the given wire between the workstation and the file server.

Time domain reflectometer (TDR)   A device that generates and transmits a specific signal down a cable and then monitors the cable for a signal reflection.

Token claiming   A Token Ring communication process that occurs when standby monitors go into contention to win the active monitor role.

Token frame   A three-byte frame that circulates the ring as a control signal.

Token Ring   A network that employs a ring topology and uses a token-passing method for ring access.

Token Ring addressing schemes   Set addressing methods dictated by the Token Ring architecture.

Token Ring architecture management roles   Management ring station roles predefined by the Token Ring architecture.

Token Ring protocol timers   A set of clock utilities included in the Token Ring architecture, used for synchronizing the protocols that interrelate on the ring.

Topology   The physical layout of a network.

Trace   A data record made by a protocol analyzer that can be reviewed by an analyst to decode a specific protocol.

Transceiver   See Medium Attachment Unit (Ethernet).

Transmission Control Protocol/Internet Protocol (TCP/IP)   A protocol suite developed for the United States Department of Defense (DoD) to permit different types of computers to communicate and exchange information. TCP/IP is currently mandated as an official DoD protocol and is also widely used in the UNIX community.

Twisted-pair Ethernet environment   Based on unshielded twisted pair cable on a variety of levels, normally wired in a star-type manner.

Universal administration   The means of assigning ring stations unique individual addresses defined by the IEEE.

Unshielded twisted pair (UTP)   A cable consisting of two uninsulated twisted-pair conductors; common telephone wire.

Chapter 2: Introduction to Topologies

Upstream   The direction on a Token Ring network contrary to the normal direction of data flow (that is, downstream).

VINES   See Banyan VINES.

Wall plate   A plate usually used for mounting an internal building cable connector on a physical wall.

Wiring closet   A room that usually contains the patch panel and MAU racks. Some large Token Ring installations require multiple wiring closets.

Wiring hubs   Access devices that also connect the main cabling structure to the devices used on the network, but that typically use a cage construction and enable multiple topologies and cabling types to be intermixed through specialized hardware and software.

Workload characterization   The particular character of the network in relation to its statistical points when a certain workload is applied.

X.25   CCITT recommendations that define a protocol for communication between packet-switched public data networks and user devices in the packet-switched mode.

XNS (Xerox Networking System)   A set of transmission protocols developed by Xerox.

APPENDIX B

Other Reference Material

1. IBM Token Ring Network Architecture Reference, Document SC30-3374-02.
2. IBM Token Ring Network Problem Determination Guide, Document SX27-3710-3.
3. IBM Cabling System Planning and Installation Guide, Document GA27-3361-5.
4. IBM Token Ring Network Installation Guide, Document GA27-3578-2.
5. The Institute of Electrical and Electronics Engineers, Inc., Token Ring Access Method and Physical Layer Specifications, IEEE STD 802.5-1989.
6. Using the IBM Cabling System with Communication Products, Document GA27-3620.
7. IBM Token Ring Network Introduction and Planning Guide, Document GA27-3677.
8. J. Ranade and G. Sackett, Introduction to SNA Networking, McGraw-Hill, 1989.
9. IEEE Standard (ANSI) 1992 Carrier Sense with Collision Detection

(CSMA) Access Method and Physical Layer Specification. Institute of Electrical Engineers, 1992.

10. IEEE 802.3 (ANSI) Supplement to CSMA/CD, Supplements, Consideration for 10Mbps Baseband Networks, Twisted Pair MAU, 10BASE-T: Institute of Electrical and Electronics Engineers, Inc.

11. Digital Equipment Corp. DECnet Phase IV Routing Layer Functional Specification, 1993.

12. Banyan Systems Inc., VINES Architectural Definition, 1988.

13. Apple Computer Inc., AppleTalk Phase 2 Protocol Specification, 1989.

14. Novell Inc., NetWare 386 Technical Overview, 1989.

15. Novell Inc., NetWare Theory of Operations, 1987.

16. Request For Comments (RFCs) 894, 1042, 877, 791, 793.

Index

10BASE2 standard. *See* Thin Ethernet 10BASE2 networks

10BASE5 standard. *See* Thick Ethernet 10BASE5 cable; Thick Ethernet 10BASE5 networks

10BASE-F standard. *See* Fiber Optic 10BASE-F networks

10BASE-T standard, 12, 631. *See also* Twisted-pair 10BASE-T Ethernet networks

10Broad36 standard, 11, 494. *See also* Ethernet networks

100Mps VG AnyLAN, 328-329

802.2 standard. *See* LLC (Logical Link Control) protocol

802.3 standard, 10, 11-12. *See also* Ethernet networks

802.5 standard, 10-11 , *See also* Token Ring networks

history of, 10

standard frame format, 358-368

in troubleshooting, 417-419

A

abort delimiter transmitted errors, 422

Abort Retry error messages, NetWare, 279-283

abort sequence frames

802.5 standard format, 360-365

defined, 631

described, 332-333

absolute time, 38, 631

AC errors, 422-423

Access Control field, 348, 359

Acknowledgment Number (TCP) field, 204

active MAUs (Multistation Access Units), 375-376

active monitor (AM), 632

Active Monitor Present frame, 366

Address Resolution Protocol (ARP). *See* ARP (Address Resolution Protocol); Proxy ARP; Reverse Address Resolution Protocol (RARP)

addresses

assigning symbolic names to Token Ring, LANVision, 82

in broadcast level examination, 119-120

differences among layers for, 146

duplicate

defined, 635

detecting and correcting, 122-123

problems caused by, 121-122

masking of, 207

in protocol analysis of TCP/IP Internet layer, 205-206

Service Access Point, 157

Token Ring

constantly changing, 390

Fluke 670 global naming feature, 109

types of, 322

types contained in packets, 152-153

addressing. *See also* functional addressing

ARP and, 192

Ethernet environment, 508

group, defined, 636

individual, defined, 637

internetwork, 146

addressing schemes

Token Ring

defined, 648

described, 322

Internet, 193

adjusted ring length (ARL), 372, 632

ADSP (AppleTalk Data Stream Protocol), 215

Advanced Monitoring for Token Ring and Etn, 59-60

AEP (AppleTalk Echo Protocol), 215

AFP (AppleTalk Filing protocol), 217

Agent

defined, 643

Token Ring, 316

alarms

Microtest Pair Scanner Management software, 102

products supporting

LANVision, 82

LANWatch Network Analyzer, 78

alignment errors, 562-563

AM (active monitor)

contention for, 334

defined, 632

generation of new tokens by, 13

responsibilities, 334-337

Ring Purge initiation by, 350

Antel Optronics AOC10 OTDR, 113-115

AppleTalk Data Stream Protocol (ADSP), 215

AppleTalk Filing Protocol (AFP), 214

AppleTalk protocol suite

defined, 632

items to analyze in, 216-217

overview, 214

protocol types, 214-215

routing information, 238-239

653

ETHERNET AND TOKEN RING OPTIMIZATION

application access events
  application efficiency measurements, 22
  in network timing optimization, 38
application efficiency examination, 632
application layer
  AppleTalk protocols, 214
  DECnet network, 185
  described, 16
  SMB communication on, 179
application load factor analysis tables, 140
application tuning, 44-45
applications
  Application layer and, 16
  characterizing, 139-140
  communications between workstations and servers, 34-35
  measuring efficiency of, 21-23
  NetBIOS Name Service function and, 179-180
  network retransmissions caused by, 126
  testing using LAN Network Probe, 85
  troubleshooting
    abnormal bandwidth usage, 429
    upper layer communications, 426-430
architecture. See network architecture; topologies
ArcNet cable, cable testers supporting, 102
ARL (adjusted ring length), 372
ARP (Address Resolution Protocol). See also Proxy ARP; Reverse Address Resolution Protocol (RARP)
  Banyan VINES environments, 220
  described, 192
  protocol analysis of, 205, 236-237
  in TCP/IP environments, 205, 211
ARPANET (Advanced Research Project Agency Network), 190-191
ASP (AppleTalk Session Protocol), 215, 217
asynchronous bandwidth allocation, 330-331

ATM (asynchronous transfer mode) networks, 113, 326-327
ATP (AppleTalk Transaction Protocol), 215
Attachment Unit Interface (AUI), 522, 632
attenuation, cable faults causing, 543
AUI cabling connectors, 522
Auto-Baseliner, Network Strategies, 66-67
AUTOEXEC.BAT file, 128, 406, 552, 553, 632
average utilization, 298, 632. See also bandwidth utilization

B

backbone, collapsed, 227, 327, 634
bandwidth allocation management, 330
bandwidth utilization. See also node-by-node utilization; traffic
  4Mps vs. 16Mps Token Ring, 323
  broadcast levels in, 118-119
  composite, 31
  defined, 632
  displaying, 59, 85
  Ethernet vs. Token Ring networks, 502
  excessively high, 428-429
  file server problems, 407
  logon sequence inefficiency and high, 144
  in network design testing, 285-286
  network overloads and, 133-135
  in performance tuning methodology, 52
  testing using Microtest Scanners, 102, 104-105
Banyan VINES System protocol suite
  defined, 633
  described, 218-223
  items to analyze in, 220-223
  protocol types, 219-220
Banyan VINES (Virtual Internetworking System), 632
baseband transmission, 10-11, 493, 633

baselining
  after product implementations, 47-48
  bandwidth utilization, 133-135
  before network modifications, 289
  defined, 633
  described, 30-31
  full capture approach, 283-289
  graphed results of sample, 34-35
  products for, 66-67, 88-90
Bay 5000 hubs, 62
Beacon MAC frames, 13, 350, 390, 425
beaconing
  defined, 633
  described, 350-351
  error conditions, TDRs detecting, 99
  in fault isolation to fault domains, 351-353
  hard errors and, 424-425
  manuallly troubleshooting solid, 390
BERT (byte error rate testing, 71, 74
BGP (Border Gateway Protocol), 232-233
bindery error packets, 173-174
BindView NCS software, 251
bitstream. See also data frames
block sizes
  in application tuning, 44
  examining, 35-37
  identifying optimum, 23-24
  reducing to correct overloads, 15
blueprints, building, 244-245, 633
BNC connectors, 523, 544
Border Gateway Protocol (BGP), 232-233
BPDU (hello Bridge Protocol Data Units), 381, 633
bridges
  block sizes vs. throughput, 36-37
  defined, 633
  described, 379-385
  Ethernet networks, 534-535
  IBM Network Manager querying of, 68

Index

LBS monitoring of data routed over, 338
in packet routing information, 153
purpose of, 318
source-routing
congested, 309-314
defined, 647
LANPharaoh and, 76
troubleshooting
Ethernet, 553-556
flow guides, 448-451, 586-590
Token Ring, 409-412
broadband networks, 10-11
broadcast storms, 119, 154, 633
broadcasts
analyzing packets for information on, 154
defined, 633
levels of
bandwidth limitations and, 118-119
described, 118-119
of NetWare server availability, 168-169
in protocol analysis, 145
single-route and all-route, 380
brouters, 384
building blueprints, 244-245, 633
burst errors, 421-422
Burst Mode, NCP Packet, 168
bus topology, 494, 496, 565, 644
byte error rate testing (BERT), 71, 74
Bytex Ring Out Cable Tester, 105-108

C

Cable Management Systems (CMS) database, 100
cable signal fault signatures (CSFSs), 98, 102
cable test equipment
Bytex Ring Out Cable Tester, 205-208
Fluke 670/2 LANmeters, 108-109
Frame Scope 100/155 cable testers, 109-113
IBM Cable Tester, 113

Microtest Scanners, 100-105
cables
broadcasts updating naming or addressing, 145
Ethernet
preventing interference on, 542
test equipment for, 100-105, 108-109, 110
lengths of, 371-373, 494, 495, 543
patch, 373-374, 643
tracing, 102
cabling
802.3/Ethernet, disadvantage of, 12
block sizes and, 37
defined, 633
documenting locations of, 247
Ethernet, 520, 521, 521-522, 522
IBM cable types, 369-371
main ring path, 317, 639
MT350 Scanner and documenting, 101
repeater failure symptoms caused by, 414
testing, 86
Token Ring. See also IBM cable types
beaconing and, 352
described, 318
hard errors and, 354
troubleshooting
Ethernet, 542-546
Ethernet flow guides, 575-576
TDRs, using, 98-99, 99
Token Ring, 106, 392-394, 436-438
verfication analysis of ATM, 113
cabling connectors. See connectors, cabling
Carrier Sense, 11. See also CSMA/CD (Carrier Sense Multiple Access with Collision Detection)
case studies, 294-313
The Central Bank of the South case study, 268-272
certification, network, 110-111
Change Parameters MAC frame, 367

Channel Service Unit (CSU), 634
Checksum (ICMP) field, 200
Checksum (TCP) field, 204
Checksum (UDP) field, 200
Cisco's Interior Gateway Routing Protocol (IGRP), 233-234
CitiSteel USA case study, 272-279
Claim Token MAC frame, 347, 367
Class A to E Network Addresses, 193-194
CMOT (Common Management over TCP/IP) protocol, 212
coaxial cable, 12, 494, 522-523, 544
Code Bits (TCP) field, 204
Code (ICMP) field, 199
collapsed backbone, 227, 327, 634
collision detection, 11-12, 494
collisions. See also CSMA/CD (Carrier Sense Multiple Access with Collision Detection); local collision errors; remote collision errors
caused by
bad Ethernet hub, 275
SQE "Heartbeat" feature, 307-308
defined, 634
described, 507
Ethernet repeaters monitoring, 539
full duplex 10BASE-T vs., 528
indicated on wiring hub LEDs, 549, 550
late, 562
Command Terminal (CTERM) protocol, 186
communication link sizing, 7-8, 25-26
communication parameters, workstation, 46-47
Complete Internetwork Overlay drawings, 258-259
components, network
defined, 641
in failures isolated to lobe areas, 390-391
implementing changes to, in performance tuning, 52
packet type determination by, 45

Token Ring, self-diagnostic
    capabilities of, 14
verifying interoperability of, 26-
    28
configuration report servers (CRSs),
    337, 346, 634
configurations
  bridge, 382-383
  changes to, verifying effect of, 28
  documenting server and
    workstation, 246-250
  faulty
    Ethernet NICS, 551
    gateway failures and, 415
    RS, 403
    Token Ring NICs, 402
  memory, 43-44
  response time problems and, 20,
    21
configuring
  applications for improved
    performance, 22, 44-45
  Ethernet networks, ease of, 565
  LAN Network Probe operating
    environment, 87
  lobe cables, 252-253
connections, network
  in DECnet protocol analysis, 188
  defined, 641
  keep-alive transmissions for, 144-
    145
  in LLC sessions, 158
  in multiprotocol analysis, 155
  NetBIOS session, 184
  in protocol analysis, 143-144
  in SNA sessions, 183
  SPX fields and, 170
  TCP, 201
connectors, cabling
  BNC, 523, 544
  checking RJ45, 545
  coaxial, 522-523, 544
  defined, 633
  described, 373-374
  Ethernet networks, 522-523
  Token Ring networks, 373-374,
    393-394

continuity tests, DC, 107, 113. See
    also loopback tests
cross connects, 545
crossed conductors, 393
crosstalk, 392-393
CSFSs (cable signal fault
    signatures), 98, 102
CSMA/CD (Carrier Sense Multiple
    Access with Collision Detection)
  100Mbps networks, 531
  in all Ethernet propagation, 5012
  defined, 633
  described, 11-12, 503-505
  receiving, 506-507
  in segment switching, 524
  transmission access, 505-506
cut through switching, 527
cyclic redundancy checks (CRCs),
    14, 562-563, 634

D

data. See also data frames; packets;
    transactions
  capturing and analyzing, 50, 55
  Presentation layer processing of,
    16
Data Access Protocol (DAP), 186
data communication tests, 99, 102
Data Field (UDP) field, 200
data flow layer, SNA, 176. See also
    session layer
data frames. See also data; packets
  802.5 standard format, 360-365
  Data Link layer and, 16
  defined, 634
  number permitted
    simultaneously on Token Rings,
    323-324
  Token Ring, 332
Data (IP) field, 198
data link layer, 16, 175, 185, 365-366
data loop tests, 103
Datagram Address and ICMP
    fields, 200
Datagram Service, NetBIOS, 177-
    178, 180
Datagrams, 191
DB9 connectors, 373-374

DDP (Datagram Delivery Protocol),
    214
DECnet protocol suite
  defined, 634
  described, 185-189
  items for protocol analysis, 187-
    189
  protocol types within, 188-189
  Re-transmission Lost errors, 305-
    309
  routing information protocols,
    239-240
DECnet Routing Protocol (DRP),
    186, 188
Dedicated Token Ring (DTR), 325-
    328
DEFAULT LANalyzer test suite,
    291-292, 298
delay packets, Novell, 171-172, 276,
    281-282
delay patterns, ring, 336
delta time. See interpacket time
The Delaware Group case study,
    305-309
destination ring stations, 379-380,
    634
Destination Service Access Points
    (DSAPs), 157
deterministic networks, 14
diagnostic packets, DECnet, 188
Differential Manchester Encoding,
    331-332, 508, 635
Digital Equipment Corporation, 10,
    493
Distance Vector routing protocols,
    228-229, 230, 233
Distributed Sniffer System (DSS),
    57, 62-63
DIX cabling connectors, 522
DLC.LAN, 365-366, 635
DLC.LANMGR, 635
DLC.MGR, 365-366
DNS (Domain Name Service)
    protocol, 211
documentation, network
  cabling, 101
  defined, 641
  documentation tools, 251-252
  Ethernet-specific, 258-260

Index

file servers and workstations, 246-250

layout documents, building blueprints, 244-245

network vendor and personal resource tables, 249-250

overview, 243-244

of performance tuning, 52

software tools for, 641

test result, TDR saving and printing features, 99

Token Ring-specific, 252-258

Dolphin ESP analyzers, 90-91

DominoLAN Internetwork and WAN analyzers, 72-75

downstream direction, 321, 635

DTR (Dedicated Token Ring), 325-328

Dual Attached Station (DAS) configurations, 331

Duplicate Address Test MAC frame, 344, 367

duplicate addresses

defined, 635

detecting and correcting, 122-123

gateway, 269-271

IPX, 170

problems caused by, 121-122

ring insertion check for, 344

E

early token release (ETR), 323

Echo Request/Reply message, ICMP, 206

Edward Fred Morris (EFM) company scenario, 263-266

802.2 standard. See LLC (Logical Link Control) protocol

802.3 standard, 10, 11-12. See also Ethernet networks

802.5 standard, 10, 358-368. See also Token Ring networks

encapsulation

defined, 149, 635

of SMB in SPP in Banyan VINES environments, 220

of TCP within IP protocol, 189-190

as transmission vehicle between nodes, 149-150

encapsulation and connection protocols, 157-159

End Systems (ES), 233

Ending Delimiter field, 359-360

envelopment of protocols. See encapsulation

error messages, network, 145

error recording, 419-420

error-checking

cyclic redundancy checks for, 14

in Data Link layer, 16

SPX protocol and, 162

store and forward mode switching and, 528

errors. See also BERT (byte error rate testing); hard errors; soft errors

capturing and recording, 32-33, 90

Ethernet

CRC and alignment, 562-563

monitoring of physical layer, 549

protocol analysis of physical layer, 559-564

file transfer, 40-42

isolating, types of, 421-423

LAT protocol, 187-189

local collision, 560, 639

logging, 67-69

long frame, 563, 639

network, measuring

HP Network Advisor, 95

LANWatch Network Analyzer, 78

in optimization, 42-43

non-isolating, types of, 423-424

Novell bindery, 173-174

in protocol analysis, 145

REM gathering of statistics for, 338

remote collision, 561, 645

TDRs in detection of, 99

Ethernet II frames, 511-512, 635

Ethernet networks. See also CSMA/CD (Carrier Sense Multiple Access with Collision Detection)

100Mbps transmission, 530-532

addressing on, 508

advantages and disadvatages, 565-567

bandwidth utilization levels, 133, 134

cabling connectors, 522-523

cabling schemes

Fiber Optic Ethernet 10BASE-F, 522

Thick Ethernet 10BASE5, 520

Thin Ethernet 10BASE2, 521

Twisted Pair Ethernet 10BASE-T, 521-522

Demand Priority Access scheme, 328

described, 11-12

design and layout, 494-508

overview, 494-495

Thick Ethernet 10BASE5, 498-500

Thin Ethernet 10BASE2, 495-498

Twisted pair Ethernet 10BASE-T, 500-503

documenting, 258-260

errors on, workload characterization of, 32-33

frame types

Ethernet II, 511-512

IEEE standard 802.3 Ethernet, 513

overview, 511

RAW 802.3 Ethernet, 512

history of, 10-11, 493

MAC packet characterization, 33-34

OSI model and, 17

overview, 493-494

physical and higher layer management, 509-510

protocol analysis of, TCP/IP, 205

routers, 536-538

switching, 527-530

technology advances, 527-532

troubleshooting

bridges/routers, 553-556

cabling, 542-546

flow guides for, 569-629

gateways, 556-557

network peripherals, 556
NICs, 550-552
performance slowdowns, 272-279
protocol analysis in, 557-564
repeaters, 548, 548-550
transceivers/MAUs, 547
workstations/file servers, 552-553
types compared, 501-503
wiring hubs, 523-526
EtherSwitch, Kalpana, 277-279
ETR (early token release), 323
events, network. See also alarms; application access events; file access events
capturing/displaying specific, 55
logging in IBM Network Manager, 67-69
relative time between, 39
expanding Token Ring networks, 317
Exterior Gateway Protocols (EGPs), 228, 232

F

fault domains
beaconing and, 350-351
defined, 636
described, 351-353
NAUNs in isolating failures to, 322
Token Ring advantage in isolating faults to specific, 12
troubleshooting, 389-392, 434-435
fault isolation. See also troubleshooting; troubleshooting flow guides
documentation, importance of network, 243
Ethernet networks, 541-542
HP Network Advisor's Finder Expert System, 97
Network General expert system enhancement, 60-62
Token Ring networks
advantages of, 12, 14
beaconing and fault domains, 351-353

fault isolation vectoring, 636
FDDI (Fiber Data Distributed Interface) networks
defined, 636
as high-speed Token Ring upgrade, 330-331
protocol analyzers for
Domino InternetworkLAN/WAN analyzers, 74
LANHAWK analyzers, 69, 71-72
Fiber Optic 10BASE-F networks, 522, 531
fiber optic cabling
defined, 636
described, 370, 371
troubleshooting
AOC10 OTDR, 114-115
OTDR theory and, 98-99
fields
in 802.5 standard frame formats, 358-368
ICMP, 199-200
IP protocol, 195-198
IPX packet, 161-162, 170
LLC protocol, 157-158
LLC type, 514-515
SPX protocol, 163-164, 170
TCP protocol, 203-204
UDP protocol, 200-201
file access events
in analysis of file search methodology, 146
capturing
errors opening or closing, 40-42
for throughput measurements, 40
insufficient disk capacity and, 279-283
NetWare file failure packets and, 172-173
in troubleshooting, upper layer protocols, 427
file failure packets, NetWare, 172-173
file requests
burst mode, 168
NCP formats, 164, 170-171

file search processes
in measuring application efficiency, 22
NetWare file failure packets and, 172-173
in network transfer integrity measurements, 41-42
protocol analysis of methodology of, 146
retransmissions caused by, 17-18
File Server Not Found error messages, NetWare, 279-283
file server replies. See also response time
interpacket time in examining, 38-39
request-to-reply overlaps and, 128-131
file servers
bindery error packets and, 173
broadcasts of availability from NetWare, 168-169
causing repeated ring insertions, 391
configuring, communication parameters, 46-47
defined, 641
documentation of, 246-250
interprocessing time, network timing and measuring, 37-38
logon sequences, 144
memory configuration, 43-44
Novell network
broadcasts of availability of, 168-169
delay packets and, 171-172
response time measurements
in optimization theory, 20-21
for specific, 124-125
SAP packets, in analysis of, 171
troubleshooting
disk capacity, 279-283
Ethernet, 552-553
Ethernet flow guides, 614-621
flow guides, 475-482
NetWare, 276
Token Ring, 405-407
file throughput. See throughput, file

Index 659

File Transfer Protocol. See FTP (File Transfer Protocol)
files. See also throughput, file
   central role in network communications, 39
   conversion of trace between protocol analyzers, 79
   errors in transfer of, 40-42
   examining packets for specifics of, 153
   request-to-reply overlaps and, 128-129
filtering
   addresses in request-to-reply overlaps, 130
   broadcast packets, 119
   described, 55
   in multiprotocol analysis, 154
   network addressing fields for duplicate addresses, 122
   products supporting
      Dolphin ESP analyzer, 91
      DominoLAN Internetwork Analyzers, 73
      FireBerd analyzers, 69
      LAN Network Probe, 85, 88
      LANdecoder, 80
      LANWatch Network Analyzer, 78
      Sniffer Analyzer, 58
   retransmissions by, capturing, 127
   throughput measurements, in effective, 132
Finder Expert System feature, HP Network Advisor, 95, 97
finite state machines, 354
FireBerd analyzers, 69-71
Flags (IP) field, 196
flow charts, optimization project, 266
flow control
   SNA transmission control layer and, 176
   on TCP/IP networks, 202-203
fluency, network, 43-44, 128-129
Fluke 670/2 LANmeters, 108-109
Foundation Manager Series, Network General, 63-64

Foundation Services (FOUND) protocol, 186
Fragment Offset (IP) field, 197
Fragmentation Required message, ICMP, 206-207
frame copied errors, 423
frame fluency, 636. See also fluency, network; packet fluency
frame relays, analysis of, 71, 74
Frame Scope 803 Network Analyzer, 109-111
frames. See also data frames
   capturing, 75, 109-111
   defined, 636
   detection of improperly transmitted Token Ring, 355
   encapsulation of headers within, 149-150
   Ethernet
      IEEE standard 802.3 Ethernet, 513
      implementing uniform types, 566
      overview, 511
      RAW 802.3 Ethernet, 512
      types compared, 513
      Ethernet II, 511-512, 635
   examining packets for length of, 153
   format breakouts
      802.5 standard, 358-368
      Ethernet address frame, 508
      NCP Packet Burst Mode, 168
      NCP protocol, 165-167
      Novell RIP, 169
      SAP protocol, 168-169
      SNA, 177, 178
      SPX protocol, 163-164
      LLC, 158, 514-516
   in logon sequences, 144
   NetBIOS session connection problems, 184
   routing information fields in, 147, 379-380
   SNA networks, indicating problems in, 183
   SNAP, 516-517
   time, examining packets for, 153
   Token Ring

4Mps vs. 16Mps, 323
   abort sequence, breakout of, 360-365
   AM monitoring of, 336
   in troubleshooting, 417-419
   TRT and processing speed of, 291-292
   types of, 332-333
frequency errors, 423-424
Fresnel Reflections, 99, 115
FTP (File Transfer Protocol), 201, 211
full duplex operation, 326, 528
functional addressing, 322, 339, 636

G

gateways
   defined, 636
   in IP environment, 232
   in TCP/IP development, 191
   troubleshooting, 409-410, 415-416
      access problems, case study of, 268-272
      Ethernet, 556-557
      Ethernet flow guides, 608-614
      flow guides, 469-475
GGP (Gateway-to-Gateway) protocol, 211
Gray Chemical Co. case study, 289-295
group addressing, 322, 636

H

hard errors
   beaconing resulting from, 350-351
   breakdown of, 424-426
   defined, 636
   ring recovery process in, 354
   Token Ring
      NIC failures and, 399
      types of, 33
Header Checksum (IP) field, 197
header frames, 637
Header Length (IP) field, 196
Header Length (TCP) field, 204
headers, packet
   breakouts of, SNAP, 159

encapsulation of, 149-150
IPX packet, 170
as part of packet composite, 36
VINES IP, 221-222
heartbeat signal, 507
Hello timers, 144, 187-188
Hewlett-Packard Network Advisor, 95-97
hop count limit (HCL), 380-381
HOPCOUNT test suite, LANalyzer, 293-294
host acknowledgements, repeated, 209-210
Host to Host (TCP/IP) layer, 191, 208-210
hosts, overloaded IP-based, 207-208
hub cards, Ethernet, 525
hubs. See intelligent hubs; wiring hubs

I

IBM 8218/9 Repeater Cabling forms, 257
IBM 8228 MAU, 316-319, 375
IBM 8230 Controlled Access Unit (CAU), 376
IBM
  development of Token Ring by, 10
  network management scheme, 342
IBM Bridge Planning chart, 258
IBM Cable Tester, 113
IBM cable types, 102-103, 369-371, 637
IBM data connectors, 373, 637
IBM LAN Manager software. See IBM Network Manager software
IBM Netview 6000 system, 342
IBM Network Management (IBMNM) protocol, 333, 637
IBM Network Manager software, 67-69
IBM Physical Location to Adapter Address Locator chart, 255
IBM Ring Sequence chart, 256
IBM Systems Network Architecture (SNA). See SNA (IBM Systems Network Architecture)

IBM Token Ring 8228 Cabling chart, 255
IBM Token Ring planning forms, 254-258, 637
ICMP (Internet Control Message Protocol)
  described, 198-200
  protocol analysis of, 206-208
  in TCP/IP environments, 211
  in troubleshooting Ethernet routers, 555
Identification (IP) field, 196
IDRP (Inter Domain Routing Protocol), 233
IEEE (Institute of Electrical and Electronics Engineers), 10, 15, 637
IEEE standard 802.3 Ethernet frames, 513
IGRP (Cisco's Interior Gateway Routing Protocol), 233-234
individual addressing, 322, 637
Individual Segment Overlay drawings, 259-269
Initialize Ring Station frame, 367
integrity, network transfer. See frame fluency
intelligent hubs. See also wiring hubs
  bad UTP cables or RJ45 connectors, 545
  Ethernet networks, 524-525
  features, 375
  internal Token Rings within, 325
  SNMP network management and, 509
Interior Gateway Protocols (IGPs), 228, 232
internal errors, 421
International Organization for Standardization (ISO), 15
Internet, 190, 192, 232
Internet Addressing protocol, 193
Internet Protocol (IP) layer, 191
internetwork addressing, 146
internetworking route identification, 136, 136-138
internetworks
  analysis of, as component of optimization, 7-8
  defined, 7, 637-638

high broadcast levels over, 119
poor application performance on, 22
protocol analysis of
  Domino InternetworkLAN/WAN analyzers, 72-75
  FireBerd analyzers, 71
  IMB Network Manager, 67-69
  LANVista analyzers, 92
  Network General DSS, 63
routing technology and, 226-228
Token Ring, switching, 326
tuning, 295-304
internetworks. See WANs (wide area networks)
interoperability, verifying, 26-28
interpacket time, 38, 44-45, 638
interprocessing time, 43-44
IP (Internet Protocol)
  field specifics, 195-198
  ICMP protocol, message types, 198-200
  in protocol analysis of TCP/IP Internet layer, 205-206
  TCP
    described, 201-204
    encapsulation within, 189-190
  in TCP/IP environments, 211
  UDP, 200-201
IP Options (IP) field, 197
IPX (Internetwork Packet Exchange) protocol, 160-162, 638
IS to IS routing protocols, 233
ISO (International Organization for Standardization), 15
isolating errors, 421-423

J

jabber, 507, 563-564, 638
jamming, 504, 507
John Steel Ltd. case study, 279-283

K

Kalpana EtherSwitch, 277-279
kit bridges, 381

Index

L

LAI (LAN Automatic Inventory) software, 251
LAMs (lobe attachment modules), 376
LAN Directory software, 251
LAN Manager, 339-341
LAN Manager console, 337
LAN Network Probe, 83-88
LANalyzer. See also LAN Network Probe
   DEFAULT test suite, 291-292, 298
   licensing to NCC, 83
   OVERVIEW test suite, 281-282
   PROTOCOL test suite, 292-293, 298
   SNA OVERVIEW test suite, 293
   TRACKOL test, 307
   Windows 2.x software, 88-90
LANdecoder monitors, 79-83
LANetWareatch Network Analyzer, 77-79
LANHAWK analyzers, 69, 71-72
LANPharaoh Scope, 75-77
LANs (local area networks)
   connection of protocol analyzers to, 54
   defined, 639
   effective throughput on, measuring, 131-133
   OSI model for, 15-17
   response times, mininum standard, 124
LANVision monitors, 79-83
LANVista analyzers, 91-95
LAP (Link Access Protocol), 215
Large Internet Packet (LIP) option, 168
late collisions, 562
layers
   analyzing protocol, 148-151
   defined, 148, 638
   differences in addressing among, 146
   network analysis software, 54
   OSI model
      AppleTalk vs., 215

      Banyan VINES protocols vs., 218-219
      DECnet vs., 185
      described, 16
      NetBIOS vs., 178
      Novell NetWare vs., 159-160
      in OSI model hierarchy, 15
      SNA vs., 175-176, 182
      TCP/IP protocol suite vs., 212
   routing information contained in, 136-137
   TCP/IP
      internal, 192-194
      original, 191-192
LBS (LAN bridge serversprotocol analyzers), 338
level 5 UTP-based cable, 100-105
line errors, 422
Link State Routing protocols, 229
links. See communication link sizing
LIP (Large Internet Packet) option, 168
LLC frames, 360-365, 417-419
LLC (Logical Link Control) protocol
   in Banyan VINES environments, 220
   DECnet, 187
   defined, 639
   described, 157-158
   in Ethernet frame transfer, 514-516
   NetBIOS information, 178-179
   in TCP/IP environments, 212
LLC-layer bridges, 379
lobe areas
   defined, 639
   isolating faults to specific, 389
   troubleshooting, 390-392
   flow guides, 434-435
lobe cables
   cable type specifications for distance of, 372-373
   configuring and labeling, 252-253
   defined, 639
   MAU port connections, 317
   troubleshooting, 39405

lobe length, 372-373, 640
lobe media check, 343
lobe paths. See lobe areas
Lobe Test frame, 367
lobes, 638
local area networks. See LANs (local area networks)
Local Area Transport Protocol (LAT), 187
local collision errors, 560, 639
location vectors, 229
log-on sequences, 38, 144, 285-286
Logical Link Control (LLC). See LLC (Logical Link Control)
logical units, SNA network, 177
logs
   network event, LANVision, 82
   network maintenance and service, 247-249, 642
long frame errors, 563, 639
loopback tests. See also continuity tests, DC
   Frame Scope 802 Analyzer, 110, 112
   of Token Ring cable sections, 103, 107, 113
looping
   BGP detection of, 232
   cause of, 226
   failed Ethernet routers causing, 555
   protocols preventing, 529
   routers permitting, 384
   spanning tree algorithm prevention of, 380
Lost Frame Non-Isolating Error
   in gateway access problem, 271
   troubleshooting, 423
LRM (LAN reporting mechanism), 339

M

MAC frames
   802.5 standard field breakouts, 360-365
   detection in ring insertion process, 343-344
   in troubleshooting, 417-419

types of, 366-368
MAC (media access control) sublayer, 33-34, 157
MAC-layer bridges, 379
MAIL protocol, 220
main ring path, 317, 372, 639
main ring path cabling, 395-396, 639
Maintenance Operations Protocol (MOP), 186-187
maintenance and service logs, network. See logs
management layer, DECnet network, 185
MasterRMON monitoring tool, 82
MATCHMAKER protocol, 220
MAU chargers, 640
MAU rack layouts, 640
MAUs (Multistation Access Units)
  defined, 640
  described, 316-319, 375-378
  documenting, locations of, 247
  in main ring path cable failures, 395-396
  rack layouts, 252-253
  in ring insertion process, 343
  test equipment for, 109
  troubleshooting
    Ethernet, 547
    flow guides, 438-440
    Token Ring, 396-398
measurements
  application efficiency, described, 21-23
  for optimization
    bandwidth utilization, 31, 134-135
    baselining and workload characterization, 30-31
    categories of, 29-35
    error types and levels, 32-33
    file throughput, 39-40
    network error, 42-43
    network packet compatibility, 45-46
    node-by-node utilization, 31-32
    packet fluency, 40-42
    physical layer packet statistics and operations, 33-34

product integration, 47-49
protocol breakdowns, 32
response time, described, 20-21
upper layer packet statistics, 34-35
workstation/file server configuration, 46-47
test model network design performance, 283-288
memory, 24, 43-44, 640
Message Length (UDP) field, 200
messages. See also error messages, network; transmissions, data
  collisions of, on CSMA/CD networks, 11-12
  error-checking of, on Token Ring networks, 14
  ICMP, 198
  Session Service and NetBIOS data, 180
metrics, 226, 230
Microtest Scanners, 100-105
migrations, technical, 4-5, 328
modems, 463-466, 602-605, 640
modifications, network
  analysis of, as component of optimization, 8
  planning, 262-263
  procedure, 289-295
monitoring
  applications, newly deployed, 139-140
  neighbor notification by AM, 335-336
  network retransmissions, 127-128
monitoring tools. See also network analysis software; protocol analyzers
  bandwidth utilization measurements, 31
  DominoLAN Internetwork and WAN analyzers, 73
  Frame Scope 802 Analyzer, 109-111
  LANalyzer, 88-90
  LANdecoder monitors, 79-83
  LANVision, 80-83
  LANVista analyzers, 94
  Master RMON, 82

in measuring effects of migrations, 4-5
Network General DSS, 62
protocol analyzers vs., 2
Sniffer Analyzer feature, 59
MT350 FLASH ROM database, 100
multiport repeaters, 497, 523-524, 576-578
multiprotocol analysis, 151-155. See also protocol analysis
Multistation Access Units (MSAUs or MAUs). See MAUs (Multistation Access Units)

N

Name In Conflict (NIC) frames, 184
Name Service function, NetBIOS, described, 179-180
NAUN (nearest active upstream neighbor), 14, 321-322, 640
NBP (Name Binding Protocol), 215, 216
NCC (Network Communications Corp.). See LAN Network Probe
NCP busy packets. See delay packets, Novell
NCP (NetWare Core Protocol), 164-167, 168, 170-171
Near End Crosstalk (NEXT) testing, 113
neighbor notification
  AM responsibilities for, 335-336
  defined, 640
  described, 348-349
  NAUN addresses in, 321
  in ring insertion process, 344-345
NetBIOS commands, 181
NetBIOS (Network Basic I/O System) protocol
  Agent and, 316
  defined, 640
  protocol analysis of, 183-184
  as protocol within SNA protocol suite, 182
  in TCP/IP environments, 211
  theory, 178-181
NetWare Core Protocol (NCP). See NCP (NetWare Core Protocol)

Index 663

NetWare Link State Protocol. See NLSP (NetWare Link State Protocol)

NetWare networks. See also NCP (NetWare Core Protocol); NLSP (NetWare Link State Protocol); Novell protocol suite
  hop count levels, 293-294
  packet sizes, 168
  problem packets
    bindery error, 173-174
    delay, 171-172, 276
    file failure, 172-173
  troubleshooting, error messages, 279-283

NetWare protocol suite, protocols in, 159

network analysis software. See also monitoring tools; protocol analyzers
  LAN Network Probe, 83-88
  LANalyzer for Windows 2.x, 88-90
  LANdecoder/Vision monitors, 79-83
  LANWatch Network Analyzer, 77-79
  layered model of, 54

network architecture, 3, 247, 641

network baseline studies. See baselining

Network General Sniffer Analyzer, 57-65. See also Auto-Baseliner, Network Strategies

Network HQ software, 251

Network Information and Control Excange (NICE) protocol, 186

Network Interface (TCP/IP) layer, 191

network layer, 16, 205, 214

network maintenance and service logs. See logs

network monitoring tests, 104-105

network operating systems. See operating systems, network

network optimization. See optimization, network

Network Services Protocol (NSP), 186

network shell software. See software, network shell

network transfer integrity. See frame fluency

networks. See also events, network; WANs (wide area networks)
  deterministic vs. probalistic, 14
  expanding, MAU ports and, 317
  mature technically migrated, defined, 639
  in packet routing information, 153
  routing methodology between, analysis of, 147
  single-session analysis of multiple, LANPharoah analyzers, 76
  test model, 283-288
  troubleshooting
    Ethernet flow guides, 570-572
    problem entry fg, 432-433
    when to optimize, 3-5

Next Scanner time domain reflectometer, 105

NEXT testing. See Near End Crosstalk (NEXT) testing

NICs (network interface cards)
  AOC10 OTDR, 114
  defined, 642
  described, 387-388
  Ethernet
    collision monitoring by, 507
    described, 532-534
    hardware addresses, 508
    jabbering caused by, 563-564
    late collisions and, 561
    overview, 496
    uniform drivers for, 566
  Ethernet networks, failures of, 547
  incompatible drivers causing retransmissions, 126
  Landecoder and promiscuous mode, 80
  memory levels, in optimization, 43-44
  packet sizes and, 37
  packet type determination by, 45
  in protocol analyzers
    connecting to LANs via, 54
    FireBerd series, 69

LANPharaoh Scope analyzers, 76
purpose of, 316
Token Ring, RS failures and, 403, 404
troubleshooting, 398-402
  Ethernet, 550-552
  Ethernet flow guides, 583-586
  flow guides, 441-444

NLSP (NetWare Link State Protocol), 169, 234

No Receive (NR) frames, 184

node-by-node utilization, 31, 643. See also bandwidth utilization

nodes. See also ring stations (RSs)
  balancing Token Ring, 295-304
  communication of layers between, 148-149
  disconnection from network, no response to polls, 144-145
  Ethernet
    adequate resources for key, 566
    in CSMA/CD access method, 504
    peripherals as, 556
    generating in chronological order, LAN Network Probe, 87
    investigating usage of large percentages of bandwidth by, 31
    protocol analyzer vs. regular, 54
    SPX enabling error detection and retransmission by, 162
    testing Novell end, 110
    troubleshooting Ethernet, 552-553
    virtual data path between, Network layer, 16

noise, 392-393

non-isolating errors, 423-424

Normal Repeat mode, 349

Novell, 83. See also LANalyzer; NetWare Networks

Novell protocol suite
  items for analysis in, 169-174
  overview, 159-160
  protocol types, 160-169
  routing protocols. See also RIP (Routing Information Protocol)
  NLSP, 234

NSFNET, 190-191

null characters, 324

O

OffNet Sniffer, Network General, 65
open cables, 393
open networking. *See* internetworks
operating systems, network
 communications between workstations and servers, workload characterization, 34-35
 defined, 642
 failures of, router failures masquerading as, 413
 integration of file server, with other, 27
 troubleshooting, upper layer communications, 426-430
operational modes
 described, 55-56
 LAN Network Probe, 83-87
 LANVision, 81
 LANVista analyzer, 93-94
 LANWatch Network Analyzer, 78
 Sniffer Analyzer, 58-59
optical time domain reflectometers (OTDRs). *See also* time domain reflectometers (TDRs)
 Antel Optronics AOC10, 113-115
 defined, 643
 described, 98-99
 in troubleshooting, repeater failures, 415
optimization, network
 defined, 1-2, 642
 determining goals of, 19-29
 techniques
  application characterization, 139-140
  broadcast level examination, 118-120
  duplicate addresses, 121-123
  internetwork route identification, 136-138
  network retransmissions, 126-128
  overloads, 133-135
  request-to-reply overlaps, 128-131

  response time, 123-125
  throughput, network, 131-133
  when to perform
   network modification analysis, 8
   new network implementations, 5-6
   overview, 3-5
   reactive problem analysis, 6-7
   WAN and internetwork analysis, 7-8
Option and Data (TCP) field, 204
originating ring stations, 379-380, 643. *See also* destination ring stations
OSI (Open Systems Interconnection) model, 15-17, 643. *See also* Token Ring Protocol model
OSI-ES to IS routing protocols, 233
OSPF (Open Shortest Path First) protocol, 231
overloads, network, 133-134, 642
OVERVIEW test suite, NetWare, 281-282

P

packet fluency, 40-42. *See also* fluency, network; frame fluency
packet types
 compatibility among protocols used, 45-46
 identifying source of problematic, 147
 incompatibilities causing retransmissions, 126, 127
packets. *See also* data; data frames
 analyzing
  addresses for network, 152-153
  areas for analysis, 152
  broadcast information, 154
  file specifics, 153
  frame length, 153
  protocol information, specific, 154-155
  routing information, 153
  time frames, 153
 block size of data within, examining, 35-37
 broadcast, 119

 capturing
  errors and problems in transmission of, 41
  in LAN Network Probe, 85, 86
  characterization and percentage levels, 292
  defined, 35
  encapsulation of protocols within, 149-150
 Ethernet networks
  bad NICs generating problem, 550-551
  corrupted, 547
  CRC errors in, 562-563
  in high-speed switching, 527
  increasing size of, 567
  long and short, 563
  structure of, 511
 format breakdowns, IPX, 160-162
 fragmentation of IP, 206-207
 Internet. *See* Datagrams
 interpacket time between, 38-39
 MAC, workload characterization of, 33-34
 multiprotocol analysis of
  address categories, 152-153
  broadcast information, 154
  file specifics, 153
  frame length, 153
  protocol information, specific, 154-155
  routing information, 153
  time frames, 153
 network error messages identified by sequences of, 145
 Network layer processing of, 16
 Novell network problem
  bindery error, 173-174
  delay, 171-172
  file failure, 172-173
 protocol analyzer copying of, 54
 received by Ethernet stations, 506-507
 routing information in, 136, 137-138, 227-228
 SNA, 177-178
 upper layer protocol, 34-35
PAP (Printer Access Protocol), 215

Index

PAR (Positive Acknowledgement and Retransmission) protocol, 202, 209-210
patch cables, 373-374, 643
patch panels
 advantage of, 317
 defined, 643
 layouts of, 253-254, 643
path control layer, SNA, 175. See also network layer; transport layer
paths, lobe. See lobe areas
peak utilization, 298, 643
performance
 ensuring product peak, 28-29
 improving Ethernet, 565-567
 measuring, test model network designs, 283-288
 protocol analyzers in examining, overview, 6-7
 slowdowns, troubleshooting, 272-279
 troubleshooting, Token Ring problems in, 428-430
 TRT levels in measurement of, 287, 291-292, 299
Performance feature, IBM Network Manager Trace and, 67-69
performance tuning, 50, 51-53, 644
peripherals, network
 defined, 642
 failures, 408-409
 operations, 408
 troubleshooting
  Ethernet, 556
  Ethernet flow guides, 598-602
  flow guides, 459-463
personnel
 documenting network, 249-250
 in planning optimization projects, 261-262
physical layer. See also network architecture; topologies
 address categories, 152-153
 analysis of
  Banyan VINES protocol suites, 220-221
  Fluke 670 LANmeter, 108-109

Frame Scope 802 Analyzer, 109-111
 in LANalyzer, 90
 AppleTalk protocols, 214
 DECnet, 185, 187
 described, 16
 error conditions, retransmissions and, 127
 Ethernet environments, 509-510
  troubleshooting, 558-559, 559-564
 network errors occuring on, measuring, 42-43
 packet statistics and operations, measuring, 33-34
 SNA, 175
 in TCP/IP protocol analysis, 205
Physical Star Layout Overlay drawings, 260
physical star topology, 319, 500-501, 644
physical units, SNA network, 177
Ping message, ICMP, 206, 555
planning network optimization projects
 overview, 261
 scenario, 263-266
 specific methods for, 262-263
polling, keep-alive transmissions and, 144
ports. See also MAUs (Multistation Access Units)
 analysis of, FireBerd analyzer multiple, 71
 charging requirement for IBM 8228 MAU, 375
 documenting locations of, 247
 relays within, 316-317
 UDP environments, incorrectly configured, 208-209
Positive Acknowledgement and Retransmission protocol. See PAR (Positive Acknowledgement and Retransmission) protocol
Presentation layer, 16
presentation services, SNA, 176
printers. See also peripherals, network
printers, troubleshooting, 466-469, 605-608
Priority Access method, 348

probalistic networks, 14
problem entry sheets, maintenance and service log, 248-249
problem reversal theory, 644
Process and Application TCP/IP layer, 191-192, 210
product vendor tables, 249-250
project management, 644
projects, network optimization, 3-5, 261-266
promiscuous mode NICs, 54
propagation delays, 202, 206
protocol analysis. See also multiprotocol analysis; troubleshooting
 before and after network modfications, 289-295
 broadcast levels, 118-120
 broadcasts in, 145
 defined, 644
 error messages, network, 145
 Ethernet networks, cabling problems and, 546
 experience required for, 313
 file search methodology, 146
 of gateway access problems, 269-271
 of internetwork addressing, 146
 keep-alive connection transmissions, 144-145
 logon sequences in, 144
 methodology, 50-51, 314
 network connections, 143-144
 Network Geneneral DSS and, 62
 overview, 50, 141-142
 packet identification problems, of specific, 147
 of performance slowdowns, 272-279
 of protocol layers, 148-151
 of routing methodologies, 147
 TCP/IP protocol suite, 192-194
 in Token Ring network troubleshooting
  802.5 frame communication, 417-419
  error recording, 419-420
  hard error breakdown, 424-426

higher-layer communications, 426-430
overview, 416
soft error breakdown, 420-424
Token Rotation Time, 426
troubleshooting, Ethernet, 557-564
in troubleshooting, Ethernet flow guides, 621-629
troubleshooting flow guide, 482-491
types of communication requiring optimization, 143
protocol analysis sessions
   defined, 644
   Network General expert system and, 60
   Novell networks, 169-174
   in planning optimization projects, 262-263
protocol analyzers. See also monitoring tools; network analysis software
   application access events, capturing, 22-23
   in network timing optimization, 38
   application characterization, 139-140
   bandwidth utilization measurements, 31, 134
   block size, identifying optimum, 23-24
   block sizes, examining, 36
   broadcast level examination, 119-120
   capturing, abnormal packets, 41
   configuration changes, verifying effects of, 28
   connections, capture of network, 143-144
   defined, 644
   duplicate addresses, resolving, 121, 122-123
   in Ethernet network management, 509-510
   Ethernet troubleshooting, bridges and routers, 553-554
   file throughput measurements, 40
   internetwork route identification, 136-138

interoperability, verifying, 27
interprocessing time measurements, 43-44
keep-alive connection transmissions, detection of, 144-145
log-on sequences, capturing, 38, 144
in multiprotocol analysis, 151-152
NetBIOS commands intercepted by, 181
operating
   components of, 54
   knowledge required for, 53
   operational modes, 55-56
overview, 2
packet type incompatibilities, detecting, 45-46
products
   Digilog LANVista, 91-95
   Dolphin ESP, 90-91
   DominoLAN Internetwork and WAN analyzers, 72-75
   FireBerd analyzers, 69-71
   Fluke 670/2 LANmeters, 108-109
   HP Network Advisor, 95-97
   IBM Network Manager, 67-69
   LANHAWK analyzers, 69, 71-72
   Network General Sniffer Analyzer, 57-65
in reactive problem analysis, 6-7
request-to-reply overlaps, identifying, 130-131
response time measurements, described, 20-21
retransmissions, detecting network, 126
routing protocols and, 227-228
selecting, 56-57
sizing communication links using, overview, 25-26
as Token Ring REMs, 338
as tool for examining
   effects of migrations, 4-5
   performance and timing problems, 6-7
WANs and internetworks, 7-8
upper and lower protocol error measurements, for optimization, 42-43

protocol breakdowns, 32, 89
Protocol Data Units (PDUs), 157, 515-516
Protocol (IP) field, 197
protocol suites
   defined, 645
   network analysis software decifering of, 54
   SNA protocols within, types of, 181-183
   as subset of protocols within protocols, 148
   supported by
      Dolphin ESP analyzers, 90-91
      DominoLAN Internetwork and WAN analyzers, 72-73
      FireBerd analyzers, 70
      Foundation Manager Series, 63-64
      HP Network Advisor, 95-96
      IBM Network Manager, 67
      LAN Network Probe, 83-84, 87
      LANalyzer, 89
      LANPharaoh analyzers, 76
      LANVista analyzers, 92-93
      LANWatch analyzer, 77
      Sniffer Analyzer, 58
PROTOCOL test suite, LANalyzer, 292-293, 298
protocols. See also routing protocols; entries for specific protocols
   addressing parameters vs. physical layer addresses, 146
   analyzing packets for specific information on, 154-155
   connections, differing rules for network, 143-144
   decoded by
      Dolphin ESP analyzer, 91
      LANalyzer for Windows, 90
      LANdecoder/Vision monitors, 79
      LANVision, 82-83
      LANVista analyzer, 94
   decoding of
      by protocol analyst, 150
      SNMP, 510
   defined, 3, 642

Index

developing expertise for, 156
encapsulation of, 149-150
in Ethernet frame transfer, 514-516, 516-517
file attrtibutes incorrect for specific, 146
in higher layer workload characterization, 34-35
keep-alive connection transmissions, 144-145
limiting maximum block size, 36
loop preventing, 529
in OSI model, 15-17
problematic packet types specific to, 147
protocol suites as subsets within, 148
repeater specificity for, 386
router specificity for, 384
Token Ring Protocol and OSI models compared, 17
Proxy ARP, 193. See also ARP (Address Resolution Protocol)
PUs (physical units), 340

R

RARP (Reverse ARP), 211, 236-237
RAW 802.3 Ethernet frames, 512, 645
Rayleigh Backscattered Signals, 99
Re-transmission lost errors, 305-309
reactive problem analysis, 6-7. See also troubleshooting
Receive Congestion (RC) errors, 288, 299-300, 423
receiver-not-ready SNA frame, 183
reflectometers. See optical time domain reflectometers (OTDRs); time domain reflectometers (TDRs)
relative time, 39, 125, 645
remote collision errors, 561, 645
Remote Monitoring (RMON) tools, 69-71
Remove Ring Station MAC frame, 368
REMs (ring error monitors), 338, 350
repeaters
  defined, 645

described, 385-387
Ethernet network, 523-524
  described, 539
  purpose of, 318
  Thin Ethernet, maximum number of, 496-496
  troubleshooting, 409-410, 414-415
Ethernet, 548, 548-550
  flow guides, 456-458
replies, NCP format, 164-167, 170-171
Report Active Monitor Error MAC frame, 367
Report NAUN Change MAC frame, 368
Report Neighbor Notification Incomplete MAC frame, 367
Report New Active Monitor MAC frame, 368
Report Ring Station Address MAC frame, 368
Report Ring Station Attachments MAC frame, 368
Report Ring Station State MAC frame, 368
Report Soft Error MAC frame, 353, 367, 420
Report Transmit Forward MAC frame, 367
reports
  cable test, 102
  generating
    LANVision, 82
    Network General Sniffer Analyzer, 59
    Network General Sniffer Reporter, 64-65
    Network Strategies Auto-Baseliner, 55-57
Request Initialization MAC frame, 345-346
Request Ring Station Address MAC frame, 368
Request Ring Station State MAC frame, 368
request-being-processed packets. See delay packets, Novell
request-to-reply overlaps, 128-129, 130-131
requests, 154-155. See also file server replies; request-to-reply overlap; workstation requests

Response MAC frame, 368
response time. See also file server replies
  defined, 645
  industry benchmarks vs. static baseline, 123-124
  measuring
    network timing and, 37-38
    overview, 20-21
    techniques, 124-125
retransmissions, network
  detecting and correcting, 127-128
  packet incompatibilities causing, 46
  problems caused by, 126-127
  SPX protocol enabling, 162
  in TCP analysis, 209-210
  by TCP nodes using PAR protocol, 202
Reverse Address Resolution Protocol (RARP), 192-193
ring cable testers, 645
ring insertion process
  activation of, 342-343
  bandwidth saturation causing reattempted, 135
  defined, 646
  duplicate address verfication, 344
  faulty NICs and failed, 400-401
  in FDDI configurations, 330
  monitor check, 343-344
  neighbor notification, 344-345
  physical insertion, 343
  possible causes of repeated, file servers, 391
  request initialization, 345-346
  security rights and failed, 406
  testing, 107
ring management roles, 333, 341
ring overlap, ring delay prevention of, 336
ring parameter servers (RPS). See RPSs (ring parameter servers)
Ring Purge MAC frame, 336, 367
Ring Purge process
  defined, 646
  described, 336-337
  purpose of, 350

in TCP/IP networks, 205
ring recoveries
  hard errors causing, 354
  in protocol analysis, 353
  soft errors causing, 353
Ring Recovery Mode Set beacon, 425
Ring (RI) ports, 645
Ring Scanner, Microtest, 102-105
Ring Station Initialization frame, 366
ring stations (RSs). See also destination ring stations; DTR (Dedicated Token Ring); originating ring stations
  assignment of AM role to, 336-337
  beaconing, 350-351
  causing intermittent bridge problems, 411
  defined, 646
  failure symptoms and causes, 403
  Normal Repeat mode, 349
  priority
    Access Control field and, 348
    on FDDI networks, 331
  removal from ring in ring insertion failure, 345-346
  as SMs, 334
  in soft error conditions, 353
  troubleshooting, 403-405
  abnormal bandwidth consumption, 428-430
  flow guides, 444-447
RIP (Routing Information Protocol)
  in analysis sessions, 171
  described, 169
  OSPF protocol and, 231
  protocol analysis of, 234
  as routing protocol, 230
  in TCP/IP environments, 211
RISC architectures
  Domino InternetworkLAN/WAN analyzers, 75
  HP Network Advisor, 95, 97
  LAN(WAN)Pharaoh Scope, 76
  Token Ring switches, 327

RJ45 phone-type connectors, 374, 523
Round Trip Time (RTT). See RTT (Round Trip Time)
router protocols, 646
routers
  block sizes vs. throughput supported, 36
  defined, 646
  described, 384-385
  Ethernet network, described, 536-538
  operation of, 226-228
  purpose of, 318
  troubleshooting
    Ethernet, 553-556
    Ethernet flow guides, 590-595
    Token Ring, 409-410, 413-414
    Token Ring flow guides, 451-456
routing. See also source routing
  alternatives to source-routing bridging, 309-314
  in Banyan VINES protocol analysis, 220-221
  broadcasts in establishing specific, 145
  DLC.LAN and DLC.MGR for Token Ring networks, 365-366
  dynamic, defined, 635
  excessive, 136-138, 300-302
  excessive routing, 311-312
  hop count levels
    NetWare networks, 293-295
    reducing high, 301-302
  identifying incorrect, ICMP messages for, 207
  Kalpana EtherSwitch and, 277-279
  MAC and LLC in, 157
  of packets through Ethernet switches, 527-528
  protocol analysis methodologies, 147
  SNA, 240-241
  technology of, 226-228
routing algorithms, 226-227
routing information
  examining packets for, 153

Novell RIP, 169, 171
  in setting up and maintaining connections, 155
  in SNA protocol analysis, 183
  in troubleshooting, bridge failures, 411-412
routing loops. See looping
Routing Path feature, Sniffer Analyzer, 60
routing protocols
  key protocols used, 229-230
  overview, 225
  specific protocols, 230-241
  theories of operation compared, 228-230
routing updates
  NSLP, 234
  StreetTalk database, 222
  VRTP, 220, 235
RPL (Remote Program Load) protocol, 182, 387
RPSs (ring parameter servers), 337, 345-346, 646
RS232 line monitors, 102
RS232 standards, 92, 646
RTMP (Routing Table Maintenance Protocol), 215, 216-217, 238-239
RTT (Round Trip Time), adjustability of, 202
RUNIX (Remote UNIX) protocol, 211
runt frame errors. See short frame errors
RX-Net cable, 102

S

SAP (Service Advertising Protocol), 168-169, 171
Scope Communication, Inc., 109-113
Scope Data product, 111, 112
security rights, ring insertion failures and, 406
segment continue (SNA) packets, 183
segment switching, 524-525
segments
  avoiding cross connects of, 545

Index

data transfer in transparent bridging across, 534
Ethernet
  Thin Ethernet, 496
  wiring hubs and, 524-525
TCP
  in data transfer, 201
  defined, 201
  troubleshooting flow guides, 572-574
self-shorting feature, Token Ring, 318
Sequence Number (TCP) field, 203
Sequence Packet Exchange (SPX) protocol, 162-164
server message block (SMB). See SMB (server message block) protocol
Service Access Points (SAPs), 157, 514
Service Advertising Protocol (SAP), 168-169, 171
Service Type (IP) field, 196
Session Control Protocol (SCP), 186
session layer, 16, 178, 214
Session Service, NetBIOS, 180
SFP case study, 283-288
shielded Twisted pair (STP) cable
  defined, 646
  described, 370-371
  main ring and backup path pairs in, 318
shielding, cable, 103
short frame errors, 563, 646
shorted cables, 393
Signal Loss Error beacon, 425
signal reflections
  in cable problems, 98
  detecting using TDRs, 543
signals
  attenuation caused by cable faults, 543
  repeater regeneration of, 386
  UTP cable capacitance, 545
Simple Mail Transfer Protocol. See SMTP (Simple Mail Transfer Protocol)
Simple Network Management Protocol (SNMP), 647

Single Attached Station (SAS) configurations, 331
sizing communication links, 7-8, 25-26
slot time, 505-506
SMB (Server Message Block) protocol
  in Banyan VINES environments, 220
  DECnet, 186
  NetBIOS and, 179
  as protocol within SNA protocol suite, 182
  in TCP/IP environments, 212
SMs (standby monitors), 334, 647
SMTP (Simple Mail Transfer Protocol), 201, 211
SNA (IBM Systems Network Architecture)
  defined, 637
  items to analyze in protocol suite, 183-184
  LAN Manager and, 339-341
  NetBIOS theory, 178-181
  overview, 175
  protocol suite
    internal layers, 175-178
    items to analyze within, 183-184
    protocol types within, 181-183
  routing, 240-241
SNA OVERVIEW test suite, LANalyzer, 293
SNAP (Subnetwork Access Protocol)
  AppleTalk and, 215
  in Banyan VINES environments, 220
  DECnet, 187
  described, 158-159
  in Ethernet frame transfer, 516-517
  in TCP/IP environments, 211
Sniffer Analyzers, Network General, 57-65
Sniffer Reporter, Network General, 64-65
Sniffer Servers, Network General DSS, 62

SniffMaster Consoles, Network General DSS, 62
SNMP MIB (Management Information Based) agents, 509
SNMP (Simple Network Management Protocol), 509-510
sockets, IPX packet, 162
The Soda Company case study, 309-314
soft errors
  auto-recovery from, 353
  breakdown of Token Ring, 420-424
  defined, 647
  Fluke 670 LANmeter, 109
  NIC failures and, 399, 400
  node problems, as indication of, 299
  types of, 32-33
software. See also applications
  documenting network, 247
  maximizing performance of, 23-25
  network analysis
    Network General DSS, 62
    as protocol analyzer component, 54
  network shell, defined, 642
  operating systems, verifying interoperability of, 27
Source and Destination IP Address (IP) field, 197
Source and Destination Port (TCP) fields, 203
Source Quench ICMP messages, 207-208
source routing
  analysis of, LANPharaoh analyzers, 76
  defined, 647
  described, 379-381
  router support for, 384
  in troubleshooting bridge problems, 411-412
Source Service Access Points (SSAPs), 157
spanning tree algorithm (STA), 380, 534-535, 647
splice losses, 99, 115

SPP (Sequence Packet Protocol), 220
SPX (Sequence Packet Exchange) protocol, 162-164
SQE (Signal Quality Error) collision detection, 50, 499, 547
SR. See source routing
SSCPs (system services control points), 177, 340
Standby Monitor Present frame, 366
standby monitors. See SMs (standby monitors)
star topology. See physical star topology
Starting Delimiter field, 358-359
State Auto Credit Corporation case study, 295-304
static baselines, conditions causing changes to, 30
Station Management (SMT) protocol, 331
statistics. See also workload characterization
   LAN Manager collection of Token Ring, 339
   LAN Network Probe, 85
   operational
      for analyzing effects of migrations, 4-5
      physical layer packet, 33-34
      upper layer protocol packet, 34-35
   products for gathering
      Dolphin ESP analyzer, 91
      Fluke 670/2 LANmeters, 108-109
      Frame Scope 802 Analyzer, 110
      HP Network Advisor, 96
      IBM Network Manager, 67-69
      LANalyzer, 88-90, 291-292
      LANdecoder, 80
      LANVista analyzer, 94
      LANWatch Network Analyzer, 78
      Sniffer Analyzer, 60
   workload characteristics, 314
store and forward mode switching, 527-528
Streaming Signal/Claim Token MAC Frame beacon, 425
Streaming Signal/Not Claim Token MAC Frame beacon, 425
StreetTalk database, 222
stress tests of model network design, 285-288
Subnetwork Access Protocol. See SNAP (Subnetwork Access Protocol)
support personnel tables, 249-250
switching
   Ethernet, 527-530
   Token Ring, 324-325
symbol coding. See Differential Manchester Encoding
symptoms. See also troubleshooting flow guides
   of application inefficiency, 21
   defining, 268
   Ethernet gateway failure, 556-557
   of slow response time, 20
   Token Ring
      of abnormally high bandwidth utilization, 285
      file server, 406-407
      MAU and wiring hub failures, 396-398
      NIC failure, 399-401
      repeater failure, 414-415
      router failure, 413
synchronous bandwidth allocation, 330
system services control points (SSCPs), 177

T

T(ANY_TOKEN) timer, 13, 336, 355
T(ATTACH) Token Ring protocol timer, 343-344, 355
T(BEACON_TRANSMIT) timer, 356-357
T(CLAIM_TOKEN) protocol timer, 355
TCP resets, 209
TCP (Transmission Control Protocol), 211
TCP/IP (Transmission Control Protocol/Internet Protocol)
   defined, 648
   described, 201-204
   Ethernet router reliance on, 536
   history of, 190-192
   overview, 189-190
   protocol suite
      internal layers, 192-194
      items to analyze in, 205-210
      original layers, 191-192
      protocol types, 210-213
      routing information protocols, 236-237
TDR signal tests, 99
   in benchmarking cable quality, 99
   cable unable to carry packets but passing, 106
Telesniffer, Network General, 62. See also Network General Sniffer Analyzer
Telnet, 201, 211
10BASE2 standard. See Thin Ethernet 10BASE2 networks
10BASE5 standard. See Thick Ethernet 10BASE5 cable; Thick Ethernet 10BASE5 networks
10BASE-F standard. See Fiber Optic 10BASE-F networks
10BASE-T standard, 631. See also Twisted-pair 10BASE-T Ethernet networks
10Broad36 design, 11. See also Ethernet networks
terminations
   bad Token Ring cable, 393-394
   in Ethernet networks, improper, 542
terminators
   cable-specific for TDRs, 99
   of thin Ethernet cabling segments, 495
T(ESCAPE) timer, 357
test equipment, cable, 100-115
TFTP (Trivial File Transfer Protocol), 211
T(GOOD_TOKEN) timer, 356
Thick Ethernet 10BASE5 cable
   Microtest Pair Scanner, 102
   specifications, 520
   testing, 544
Thick Ethernet 10BASE5 networks

Index 671

cabling and layout specifications, 520
defined, 647
design and layout, 498-500
troubleshooting, repeaters, 548
Thin Ethernet 10BASE2 networks
cable testing, 544-545
cabling and layout specifications, 521
defined, 647
design and layout of, 495-498
troubleshooting, repeaters, 548
throughput, file. See also transfer rates
application tuning and, 44-45
block sizes vs. capbility of, 36
defined, 24, 39, 636, 647
existence of standards for, 6
measuring, 39-40
described, 131-132
techniques, 132-133
network timing and measuring file, 37-38
time domain reflectometers (TDRs). See also optical time domain reflectometers (OTDRs)
defined, 647
Fluke 670 LANmeter, 109
Microtest Pair Scanner, 101-102
Sniffer Analyzer cable tester as, 59
theory of, 98-99
in troubleshooting
capacitance problems, 545
Ethernet cabling, 542-546
repeater failures, 415
using, 99
Wire Scope 100/155 cable testers, 111-113
time frames, examining packets for, 153
Time to Live (IP) field, 197, 205-206
timers
determining generation of new tokens, 13
reset in Ring Purge process, 336
Token Ring protocol, defined, 648
timing, communication

importance in network optimization, 37-39
increasing throughput by modifying application, 44
protocol analyzers in examining, 6-7
time stamp analysis of, 73
timing sequences, troubleshooting abnormal, 418-419
T(NEIGHBOR_NOTIFICATION) timer, 357
T(NOTIFICATION_RESPONSE) timer, 349, 357
Token Access control mechanism, described, 13, 320
Token Claiming process
defined, 648
described, 346-347
on FDDI networks, 330-331
lack of MAC fram detection initiating, 344
token errors, 424
token frames, 320, 332, 348, 358-360, 648
Token Ring addressing schemes, 648
Token Ring cables
test equipment for
Bytex Ring Out Cable tester, 105-108
Fluke 670 LANmeter, 108-109
Frame Scope 802 Analyzer, 110
IBM Cable Tester, 113
Microtest Scanners, 100-105
Token Ring chipset Agent, 316
Token Ring Frame Copied error, 271
Token Ring networks. See also beaconing; fault domains
4Mps vs. 16Mps, 323-324
adding backbone rings to, 295-304
auto-recovery process, 351-353
balancing nodes on, 295-304
bandwidth utilization levels, 133, 134
defined, 648
described, 12-15
design and layout, 315-319

Differential Manchester Encoding, 331-332
documentation
IBM Token Ring planning forms, 254-258
MAU rack layouts, 252-253
patch panel layouts, 253-254
duplicate address prevented by, 121
errors, workload characterization of, 32-33
finite state machines, 354
frame types, 332-333
hard error counting, 354
high-speed upgrades from, 328-331
history of, 10-11, 315-316
MAC packets, workload characterization of, 33-34
management roles, 333-339
multiple ring, 337, 338, 381
protocol analysis of
IBM Network Manager software, 67-69
LANalyzer DEFAULT test suite, 291-292, 298
Network General's DSS, 62
TCP/IP, 205
rings
breaking 4Mbps, into smaller, 328
switching modules and logical, 325
soft error counting, 353
source-routing bridging, 309-314
switching products, 324-325
technology advances, 324-325
troubleshooting, 267-272, 431-491
Token Ring Protocol model, OSI model and, 17
Token Ring protocol timers, 354-355, 355-358, 648
tokens
detection of lost, 336
early release of, 323
generation of new, 13
normal rotation time of, 287
prioritizing, 325
ring delay and, 336
in Token Ring operation, 320
topologies

defined, 3, 648
duplicate addresses prevented by, 121
Ethernet, most common types of, 494
network analysis software for specific, 54
supported by
 FireBerd analyzers, 69
 Foundation Manager Series, 63
 IBM Network Manager, 69
 LAN Network Probe, 83
 LANPharaoh Scope, 75
 LANVista analyzers, 92
 LANWatch analyzer, 77
 Sniffer Analyzer, 58
TOS (Type of Service Routing), 231
Total Length (IP) field, 196
T(PHYSICAL_TRAILER) timer, 355
trace files, 79, 139-140
Trace and Performance, IBM Network Manager, 67-69
traces
 defined, 648
 Dolphin ESP analyzer, 91
 IBM Network Manager Trace and Performance, 67-69
 in multiprotocol analysis
  paging through, 151-152
  responses to requests, 154-155
 products for gathering, 89
 reading offline, OffNet Sniffer, 65
 TRACKOL test, LANalyzer, 307
traffic. See also bandwidth utilization
 analysis of
  Frame Scope 802 Analyzer, 109-111
  LANalyzer, 88-90
 baseline and levels of, 30
 capturing peak and off-peak, 297-298
 causes of high levels of
  broadcasting, 118-119
  network retransmissions, 126
 loading networks with
  Frame Scope 802 Analyzer, 110-111
  LAN Network Probe, 85

Sniffer Analyzer, 59
 troubleshooting performance problems, 429-430
 monitoring, Microtest Ring Scanner, 104
 separating bursty from chatty, 566
 in troubleshooting, bridges, 410
transaction services, SNA, 176
transactions
 burst mode, 168
 capturing, in network timing optimization, 38
 multiplicity of, in moving data between nodes, 150, 151
transceivers. See also MAUs (Multistation Access Units)
 collision monitoring by, 507
 in Ethernet architecture, 496, 497
 Ethernet coax connections to, 522
 failures mimicking bad cable, 543
 jabbering caused by, 563-564
 with LEDs aiding troubleshooting, 507
 troubleshooting, 547
transfer integrity, network. See fluency, network; frame fluency; packet fluency
transfer rates. See also throughput
 memory levels and, 43
 optimizing
  application tuning and, 44-45
  configuration parameters and, 24
 transfer time, interpacket time in examining, 39
transmission control layer, SNA, 176. See also transport layer
Transmission Control Protocol/Internet Protocol (TCP/IP), 648
transmissions, data. See also retransmissions, network
 absolute time of, 38
 CSMA/CD, 505-506
 Differential Manchester Encoding, 331-332
 Ethernet methodology, 508
 network keep-alive connection, 144-145
 retries after collisions, 12

speed of
 100Mbps Ethernet, 530-532
 802.3 standard, 10
 Ethernet, all types of, 520
 Token Ring networks, Token Access method, 13-14
Transmit Forward MAC frame, 367
transparent bridging, 534-535, 553-556
transport control field, 170, 221
transport layer, 16, 162-164, 214
T(RECEIVE_NOTIFICATION) timer, 357-358
T(RESPONSE) timer, 356
triggering
 described, 55
 products supporting
  Dolphin ESP analyzer, 91
  LANdecoder, 80
  LANWatch Network Analyzer, 78
  Sniffer Analyzer, 58
T(RING_PURGE) timer, 357
Triticom. See LANdecoder monitors; LANVision monitors
troubleshooting. See also fault isolation; optimization, network, techniques; protocol analysis; reactive problem analysis; troubleshooting flow guides
cabling
 difficulty of coaxial, 12
 by sections on Token Rings, 106
 TDRs and, 98-99
case studies, 267-314
documentation
 importance of network, 243
 maintenance and service logs, 247-249
Ethernet networks
 bridges/routers, 553-556
 cabling, 542-546
 gateways, 556-557
 network peripherals, 556
 NICs, 550-552
 protocol analysis in, 557-564
 repeaters, 548, 548-550
 transceivers/MAUs, 547
 workstations/file servers, 552-553

Index 673

gateway access problems, case study, 268-272
ICMP as tool for
ICMP Ping messages, 206
messages, 198
NetWare error messages, 279-283
optimizing vs., 3
Token Ring networks
802.5 communications, 417-426
advantage of cable design for, 12
bridges, 409-410, 410-412
cable problems, 392-396
fault domains and lobe areas, 389-392
file servers, 405-407
gateways, 409-410, 415-416
high-layer communications, 426-430
MAUs and wiring hubs, 396-398
network peripherals, 408-409
NICs, 398-402
protocol analysis in, 416
repeaters, 409-410, 414-415
ring stations, 402-405
routers, 409-410, 413-414
unable to auto-recover from hard errors, 352
troubleshooting flow guides
Ethernet network
bridges, 586-590
cabling, 575-576
file server, 614-621
gateway, 608-614
modem, 602-605
multiport repeaters, 576-578
network peripherals, 598-602
network problem entry, 570-572
NICs, 583-586
overview, 569
printer, 605-608
protocol analysis, 621-629
router, 590-595
segments, 572-574
thick/thin repeater, 595-597
wiring hubs, 576-578
workstations, 579-583

Token Ring network
bridge, 448-451
cable, 436-438
fault domain/lobe area, 434-435
file server, 475-482
gateway, 469-475
MAU and wiring hub, 438-440
modem, 463-466
network peripheral, 459-463
network problem entry, 432-433
NIC, 441-444
printer, 466-469
protocol analysis, 482-491
repeater, 456-458
ring station, 444-447
router, 451-456
TRT (Token Rotation Time)
described, 287, 291-292
on FDDI networks, 331
in troubleshooting, 426
T(SOFT_ERROR_REPORT) timer, 353, 356
T(TRANSMIT_PACING) timer, 356
Twisted-pair 10BASE-T Ethernet networks
defined, 648
design and layout, 500-503
full duplex operation, 528
troubleshooting, wiring hubs and repeaters, 548-500
wiring hubs, 524
Type (ICMP) field, 199
Type of Service Routing (TOS), 231

U

UDP Destination Port field, 200
UDP Source Port field, 200
UDP (User Datagram Protocol), 200-201, 208-209, 211
unshielded Twisted pair (UTP) cables
defined, 648
described, 370, 371
RJ45 connectors, 374
testing, 545-546
upper layer protocols

address categories, 152-153
characterization of communications on, 34-35
duplicate address conflicts, 121
Ethernet network management of, 509-510
protocols encapsulating, 157-159
troubleshooting problems in, Token Ring networks, 426-430
upper protocol layers
network error measurements, for optimization, 42-43
network transfer integrity measurements, for optimization, 40-42
statistics, 34-35
in TCP/IP analysis, 210
upstream direction, 321, 649
Urgent Pointer (TCP) field, 204
User Datagram Protocol. See UDP (User Datagram Protocol)
users
Application layer and, 16
listing, 249-250

V

vampire taps, cable faults caused by, 544
vendor tables, product, 249-250
verification
configuration changes, effects of, 28-29
of interoperabililty, 26-28
operation, response time measurements in, 21
Version (IP) field, 195
VFRP (VINES Fragmentation Protocol), 220
VICP (VINES Internet Control Protocol), 220
VINES. See Banyan VINES (Virtual Internetworking System)
VIP (VINES Internet Protocol), 220
VIPC (VINES Interprocess Communication Protocol), 220
VRTP (VINES Routing Update Protocol), 220, 235-236

W

WANPharaoh Scope, 75-77
WANs (wide area networks)
  analysis of, as component of optimization, 7-8
  effective throughput on, measuring, 131-133
  protocol analysis of
    DominoLAN Internetwork and WAN analyzers, 74-75
    FireBerd analyzers, 71
    Network General products, 63
    WANPharaoh Scope, 75-77
  response times, mininum standard, 123, 124
  Watch Dpg parameters, keep-alive transmissions and, 144
wide area networks. See WANs (wide area networks)
Window Size exceeded message, 210
Window Size (TCP) field, 204
Windows, Microsoft
  products compatible with
    DominoLAN Internetwork and WAN analyzers, 72-75
    Foundation Manager Series, 63-64
    LANalyzer, 88-90
    LANPharaoh, 76
    LANVision, 82
    LANVista analyzers, 94
    Scope Data product, 111, 112
Wire Scope 100/155 Cable Testers, 109-113
wiring closets
  defined, 649
  described, 317-318
  MAUs in, advantages of locating, 252, 317
  patch panel layouts in, 253, 317-318
wiring hubs. See also intelligent hubs
  defined, 637, 649
  documenting locations of, 247
Ethernet
  described, 523-526
  variety of connectors on, 523
  troubleshooting, 396-398
  Ethernet flow guides, 576-578
  flow guides, 438-440
workload characterization
  after product implementations, 47-48
  bandwidth utilization, composite, 31
  categories measured in baseline studies, 30-31
  defined, 649
  node-by-node utilization, 31
workstation requests
  in file search methodology, 146
  in file throughput measurements, 40
  interpacket time in examining, 38-39
  in request-to-reply overlaps, 128-129, 130
workstations. See also ring stations (RSs)
  comparing to entire network, 110
  configuring communication parameters, 46-47
  documentation of, 246-250
  high collision rates at specific, 560
  interprocessing time, network timing and measuring, 37-38
  logon sequences, negotiations with server, 144
  memory configuration, for optimization, 43-44
  response time, measuring, 20-21
  retransmissions requested by, 127
  routing methodologies enabling communications with, 147
  troubleshooting, Ethernet flow guides, 579-583
  troubleshooting Ethernet, 552-553

X

X.25 CCITT recommendations, 74, 649
Xerox, development of Ethernet by, 10

Z

ZIP (Zone Information Protocol), 215, 216